THE

Grounds and Rudiments

OF

LAW and EQUITY,

Alphabetically Digefted:

CONTAINING

A COLLECTION of RULES or MAXIMS, with the *Doctrine* upon them, illuftrated by various CASES extracted from the Books and Records, to evince that thefe *Principles* have been the Foundation upon which the Judges and Sages of the Law have built their *folemn* Refolutions and Determinations.

THE WHOLE

Defigned to reduce the Knowledge of the LAWS of *ENGLAND* to a more regular Science, and to form them into a proper *Digeft*, for the Service of the Nobility, Clergy, Gentlemen in the Commiffion of the Peace, and private Gentlemen, as well as the PROFESSORS and STUDENTS of the Law.

With Three TABLES.

First, Of the Rudiments and Grounds.
Second, Of the New Cases.
Third, Of Principal Matters.

The SECOND EDITION.

By a GENTLEMAN of the *Middle Temple*.

THE LAWBOOK EXCHANGE, LTD.
Clark, New Jersey

ISBN 978-1-58477-935-3

Lawbook Exchange edition 2009, 2021

The quality of this reprint is equivalent to the quality of the original work.

The Lawbook Exchange, Ltd.
33 Terminal Avenue
Clark, New Jersey 07066-1321

Please see our website for a selection of our other publications and fine facsimile reprints of classic works of legal history:
www.lawbookexchange.com

Library of Congress Cataloging-in-Publication Data

Gentleman of the Middle Temple.
The grounds and rudiments of law and equity, alphabetically digested : containing a collection of rules or maxims, with the doctrine upon them, illustrated by various cases extracted from the books and records, to evince that these principles have been the foundation upon which the judges and sages of the law have built their solemn resolutions and determinations. The whole designed to reduce the knowledge of the laws of England to a more regular science, and to form them into a proper digest for the service of the nobility, clergy, gentlemen in the commission of the peace, and private gentlemen, as well as the professors and students of the law. With three tables. First, of the rudiments and grounds. Second, of the new cases. Third, of principal matters / by a gentleman of Middle Temple.
p. cm.
Originally published: 2nd ed. London, T. Osborne, 1751.
ISBN-13: 978-1-58477-935-3 (cloth : alk. paper)
ISBN-10: 1-58477-935-7 (cloth : alk. paper)
1. Law--Great Britain. 2. Equity--Great Britain. 3. Legal maxims--Great Britain. I. Title.
KD660.G468 2008
349.42--dc22
2008040197

Printed in the United States of America on acid-free paper

THE
Grounds and Rudiments
OF
LAW and EQUITY,

Alphabetically Digested:

CONTAINING

A COLLECTION of RULES or MAXIMS, with the *Doctrine* upon them, illustrated by various CASES extracted from the Books and Records, to evince that these *Principles* have been the Foundation upon which the Judges and Sages of the Law have built their *solemn* Resolutions and Determinations.

THE WHOLE

Designed to reduce the Knowledge of the LAWS of *ENGLAND* to a more regular Science, and to form them into a proper *Digest*, for the Service of the Nobility, Clergy, Gentlemen in the Commission of the Peace, and private Gentlemen, as well as the PROFESSORS and STUDENTS of the Law.

With Three TABLES.

First, Of the Rudiments and Grounds.
Second, Of the New Cases.
Third, Of Principal Matters.

The SECOND EDITION.

By a GENTLEMAN of the *Middle Temple*.

LONDON:

Printed for T. OSBORNE, in *Gray's-Inn*. MDCCLI.

THE

PREFACE.

THE following Sheets are intended to demonſtrate and explain the Reaſons and Principal Grounds of the Law of *England*, and by giving a general View of the whole Body, properly to prepare the Student for a more particular Obſervation of its ſeveral Parts; *Ab univerſalibus ad ſingularia procedendum eſt.* A Work of this Kind has long been wanted as a neceſſary Introduction to the Study of the Law; for though Mr. *Wingate* and Mr. *Philips* have treated of the Maxims of the Law, they are by no Means, at this Time, fit to be put into the Hands of a young Student; the Firſt, tho' very Prolix, containing but a few Principles, and thoſe explained by many obſolete and intricate Caſes; and the other being too ſuperficial to be of any real Uſe. On the contrary, this Work comprehends every Principle or Maxim

Maxim of Law that is to be found in any of our Books, either of Law or Equity, and has fully explained them in a comprehenſive Stile, by the moſt Modern Inſtances that the Nature of each particular Maxim would admit, and by a *great Number of Caſes never before printed.*

A TABLE

A TABLE OF THE Grounds and Rudiments.

A.

B.

A Table of the Principles of Law.

C.

2

52. *Con-*

E.

A Table of the Principles of Law.

E.

114. *Equity*

A Table of the Principles of Law.

A Table of the Principles of Law.

160. *Frustra*

A Table of the Principles of Law.

179. *He*

A Table of the Principles of Law.

210. *In-*

A Table of the Principles of Law.

221. *Jura*

A Table of the Principles of Law.

A Table of the Principles of Law.

255. *Law*

A Table of the Principles of Law.

 290. *Mort*

A Table of the Principles of Law.

O:

334. *Omnis*

P.

A Table of the Principles of Law.

S.

T.

A Table of the Principles of Law.

V.

504. *Vigi-*

A Table of the Principles of Law.

A TABLE OF THE Names of the New Cafes.

g Chrifto-

A Table of the Names of the New Cafes.

Kirk-

A Table of the Names of the New Caſes.

Stan-

A Table of the Names of the New Cases.

I INTRO-

INTRODUCTION.

Of Law.

In general.

NATURE hath taught all people to chuſe governors, judges and leaders: and that they might not be at the deſpotic will of ſuch rulers, all people have enacted laws as a guide both to the governors and governed: and that even in countries where revelation never came, or *Ariſtotle*'s politics were ever heard of; and where neither *Lycurgus*, *Solon*, or other eminent or prudent lawgivers lived, having no other foundation or origin than meer neceſſity: and therefore law is juſtly defined to be the rule of government and obedience.

Its definition and origin.

CICERO defineth it to be a certain rule proceeding from the will of God, perſuading that which is juſt and good, and prohibiting that which is evil. The learned *Selden* ſays, all laws were originally from nature, and are equally antient; and nature being the ſame in all, all laws were originally the ſame. *Dugdale* ſaith, *Lex eſt ſanctio ſancta, jubens honeſta & prohibens contraria.* Sir *Walter Raleigh* thus delivers himſelf on this ſubject, *Lex eſt vitae regula, praecipiens quae ſunt ſequenda et quae fugienda.*

The ſorts.

ST. Germain, in his *Doctor and Student*, divides laws into theſe three, 1. The law of nature; 2. The law of God, and 3. The law of man. Whilſt Mr. Serjeant *Finch* determines them to two, 1. Native; 2. Poſitive. The firſt being the law of nature, the latter comprehending the other two, namely, the law of God revealed in the holy ſcriptures, and the law of man.

Native.

THE laws of nature or reaſon are ſuch as are implanted in us, being written in our hearts, diſtinguiſhing good and evil; and theſe are perpetual and unchangeable.

God's law.

THE law of God is a certain law given by revelation to reaſonable creatures; (as to the *Jews* by means of their prophet *Moſes*, or to us Chriſtians, by a greater than *Moſes*, the lord of life, Jeſus Chriſt) ſhewing the will of God, for attaining eternal happineſs.

Human law.

THE law of man is a law made by human authority, for the well governing and ordering of any people, and is made by ſuch as are lawfully authoriſed thereunto, and muſt be ſuited to the tempers, diſpoſitions and other circumſtances of the people; and can juſtly propoſe no other end than to make the people good, and to bring them to virtue; which being done, all the purpoſes of government are anſwered. And this law of man muſt be built upon the baſis of the former laws, elſe it is not properly a law, but an impoſition and abuſe, and is altogether uſeleſs and vain, and void of all force.

Human law grounded on the law of God.

ALL human laws to bind, muſt be grounded on the law of God, whether we underſtand it of the moral law, written on the tables of our hearts, or of that law of God, which he hath in his great mercy and love revealed unto mankind; which is what we more immediately mean here; as ſuch law is the direct and proper object of politic government, and is the juſt bounds and limits of all human power. And this law is always like itſelf, and of equal neceſſity; it is the image of that righteouſneſs and holineſs in which God created our firſt parents, and the model of that perfection unto which we ſhall attain in the kingdom of heaven. And every human law muſt needs be ſo far void, as it is either contrary to, or deviates from this eternal unerring rule; whilſt a law thus grounded, being conſonant to reaſon and revelation, as both are one and the ſame eternal law, differently imparted to men, *viz.* the one by the light of reaſon, the other by revelation, is of force and binding on men.

Human law grounded on the law of reaſon.

AND as all human laws muſt be founded on the law of God, ſo they muſt alſo be conſonant to the law of reaſon; for *Nihil quod eſt contra rationem eſt licitum*; for reaſon is the life of the law, as law without it is but a dead letter: when law is not founded on reaſon, it ceaſeth to be law; as where a law, though generally good, yet by the circumſtances of a particular caſe is ſevere, for the righteouſneſs of the law can do no wrong, and rather than a wrong ſhould be done under colour or pretence of law, equity ſhall interpoſe, (which equity is taken and admitted as part of our common or principal laws of this realm) as it is in *Plowden*, the words of the law are not the law, but the internal ſenſe: all laws have a body and ſoul, the letter is that body, and the true meaning the ſoul; *quia ratio legis eſt ani-*

ma legis; and the profit of the law is in its meaning rather than in the letter, and therefore it is that the ſenſe of the law ſometimes ſhall not be carried ſo far as the letter would go, whilſt at other times it ſhall be extended beyond the letter; and it is equity which thus amplifies or diminiſhes the letter of the law.

Equity, what it is, and its uſe.

ARiſtotle, the philoſopher, defineth it thus, *Aequitas eſt correctio legis generatim latae, qua parte deficit*, and according to *Perionius*, *Aequitas eſt correctio quaedam legi adhibita, quia ab ea abeſt aliquid propter generalem ſine exceptione comprehenſionem*; both which definitions agree and come to the ſame thing, and which correction of general words is much uſed in the laws of *England*, as may be ſeen by many caſes in the books, and particularly in *Eiſton*'s caſe in *Plow*. 462. and thus it is that *Hooker* ſaith, that the general rules of law are to be practiſed according to their right meaning; for according to ſtrictneſs of law, ſaith he juſtly, in contracts and dealings which daily paſs between man and man, things, by ſtrictneſs of law might be done, which equity and all honeſt meaning forbiddeth; and yet the law is not unjuſt or defective; neither is equity againſt it, but above it, binding mens conſciences to things which the law cannot reach unto; *as that is a certain rule, and ſo unable to conſider circumſtances*, this ſupplying the ſilence of the law, *and taking in thoſe circumſtances, and judging according to conſcience.*

The binding force of human laws.

AND of a Law, thus grounded and moderated, a learned author well ſaid, *eſt omnium divinarum et humanarum rerum regina, et imperium legis imperium dei eſt*; for as it is ſaid in *Doctor and Student*, whatſoever is righteous in the law of man is righteous in the law of God, and laws of man not contrary to the law of God and reaſon, muſt be obſerved in the law of the ſoul: and he who deſpiſeth them deſpiſeth God; and he who reſiſteth them reſiſteth God; for the powers that are, are of God. See rule *Aequitas ſequitur legem.*

The common law, its grounds.

THE common law of *England* is grounded, 1. On the law of reaſon. 2. On the law of God. 3. General cuſtoms. 4. Maxims. 5. Particular cuſtoms; and 6. Statutes.

On the law of reaſon.

THE firſt of theſe, namely, the law of reaſon, is the power of the ſoul, diſcerning between good and evil, and this is obſerved in this, as in all other realms, of neceſſity; nay the law itſelf is nothing but reaſon; but then we muſt underſtand this with my Lord *Coke*, of an artificial perfection of reaſon, gotten by long ſtudy, obſervation and experience, for *nemo naſcitur artifex*, and not of the reaſon of every common, uninformed mind; for *neminem oportet eſſe ſapientiorem legibus*; much leſs may men ſet

up

up for adepts in law, and cavil with her principles, who are unlearned therein.

On the law of God.

THE ſecond ground of the law of *England,* is the law of God, revealed in holy writ, and this is the head and maſter-piece of all the reſt; whereof as St. *Auſtin* the father ſaid truly, *omnium legum eſt inanis cenſura, niſi divinae legis imaginem gerat.*

On general cuſtoms.

THE third foundation whereon the *Engliſh* laws are raiſed are certain general cuſtoms, of old time uſed throughout all the realm, and are ſuch as have been accepted and approved by both kings and people; and becauſe theſe are neither againſt the law of God nor the law of reaſon; but have been always or immemorially taken to be good and neceſſary for our commonwealth; they have from ſuch acceptance and uſe obtained the force and authority of law; and are what is properly called the common law, to the preſervation and obſervance whereof our ſovereigns ſwear at their coronations. And what is and what is not *common law,* is only determinable by the king's judges or parliament, and not by a jury or the country, neither by the king himſelf; for as my lord *Coke* told king *James,* that though he was the head of the law, yet his majeſty was not to be preſumed conuſant of the niceties of law, neither could of himſelf meerly, and without the means of his judges in his courts of *Weſtminſter-hall,* or of his lords in parliament, determine upon the properties, much leſs upon the lives of his ſubjects; nay the king by his warrant or royal command may not, though his judges and magiſtrates may, for good cauſe, impriſon the perſons of his majeſty's ſubjects; for that if wrong were done to ſuch ſubjects thereby, they could have no remedy againſt his majeſty, as they might againſt a fellow ſubject. *Rex ſub nullo niſi tantum ſub deo et lege,* ſays *Bracton,* and that the king can do no wrong, is a maxim known to the meaneſt; and therefore if wrong is done, it is not the king that did it, but his majeſty was deceived in ſuch act, and it was not properly his. And the ſame reaſon, as my lord *Hobart* ſaith juſtly, that ſupplies the king's ignorance in matters of fact, will alſo excuſe his want of knowledge even of the law in the niceties of it; for though we agree with the reverend and learned *Forteſcue* and the lord *Coke,* that it be the office of kings and princes to make themſelves acquainted with the general rules and notions of thoſe laws by which they are to govern, yet it cannot be expected, becauſe it is impoſſible they ſhould ſtudy it ſo cloſely as to know all the niceties and turns of it, as the lord *Coke* himſelf allows; for they have greater and much more important concernments; for he, ſaith my lord *Hobart,* ſpeaking of the king, ſtudies a greater art, *ſc. arcana regni,* the art of government, which is *ars artium,* and contains all other arts, as the commonwealth includes, and comprehends in it all private ſocieties. The end of kings, as of all other governors, in their very conſtitution, is the well governing of the people, and their ſtrength is in the hearts of their ſubjects; protection and allegiance are reciprocal ties.

2 *On*

On principles or maxims.

THE fourth ground of the law of *England* ſtands on divers principles or maxims, which have been always, or time out of mind, taken for law in this realm, and theſe are ſo high in authority, as they may not be queſtioned, but all men are bound to allow them without diſpute, as will fully appear hereafter.

On particular cuſtoms.

THE fifth ground of the laws of *England* ſtands on divers particular cuſtoms uſed in divers counties, towns, cities and lordſhips in this realm: and theſe cuſtoms, becauſe they are not againſt the law of reaſon, nor the law of God, though they are againſt the general cuſtoms or maxims above mentioned, yet are allowed and ſtand for law, in thoſe particular places where they are uſed: but then ſuch particular cuſtoms muſt be immemorial and reaſonable: and if any queſtion ariſeth whether there be ſuch cuſtom? it ſhall receive its deciſion from the jury or twelve men, and not from the judges; except the ſame be of record in the ſame court. Yet of the fitneſs or reaſonableneſs of any particular cuſtom the king's juſtices in his courts of record in *Weſtminſter-hall*, are, as I conceive, the only judges under parliament.

On acts of parliament.

ACTS of parliament are the ſixth ground of the common law: and theſe are laws, as is known to all, made by authority of parliament, that is to ſay, king, lords and commons, and are made to ſupply the defects of the law, and to puniſh wicked and reward good men. And theſe ſix are the only grounds that *St. German* remembers to have met with of the laws of *England*. But as theſe, as all the fixt rules of government, have an unavoidable mixture of ſeverity in particular caſes, equity or good conſcience is, in many of thoſe caſes, allowed to interpoſe; and therefore I ſubmit it, it may not be improper to ſee what that is, as conſidered by the lawyers.

Equity, what.

EQUITY, of which God is the efficient cauſe, is a right wiſeneſs which conſidereth all the circumſtances of the matter, and is tempered with the ſweetneſs of mercy. And as *ſummum jus ſumma eſt injuria*, as it cannot conſider circumſtances; and as this takes in all the circumſtances of the caſe, and judges upon the whole matter, according to good conſcience; this ſhews both the uſe and excellency of equity above any preſcribed law. The nature whereof is, as *Bracton*, *lib.* 1. *cap.* 3. ſaith, to amplify, enlarge, and add to the letter of the law (as is *Finch's law*, 6. *b.*) according to the equitable circumſtances of the caſe. And equity is ſo extenſive and various, that every particular caſe in equity may be truly ſaid to ſtand upon its own

particular

particular circumſtances; and therefore, under favour, I apprehend precedents not of that great uſe in equity as ſome would contend; but that equity thereby may poſſibly be made too much a ſcience for good conſcience.

Again equity is that, which is commonly called equal, juſt and good, and is a mitigation or moderation of the common law, in ſome circumſtances either of the matter, perſon or time; and often it diſpenſeth with the law itſelf. It miniſtreth a fit proportion ſuitable to circumſtances, and in a word is the correction or amendment of a good law, which by reaſon of its generality is defective in ſome particulars.

And again this is in oppoſition to, or rather for remedy againſt, the *ſummum jus*, which is moſt exact and preciſe law, and ſometimes repugnant to equity, which *ſummum jus* the civilians ſay is ſo full of rigour, as to be almoſt unjuſt, and that law in the higheſt degree is wrong in the higheſt degree. Yet with deference I apprehend, this ought not to be generally imputed to our laws; as they are moſt certainly the beſt ſet of human laws extant, having been, as my Lord *Coke* moſt wiſely obſerves, by ſo many ſucceſſions of ages fined and refined by an infinite number of grave and learned men, and by long experience grown to ſuch a perfection for the government of this realm, as to be the very perfection of reaſon; yet as theſe muſt be confeſſed to be general, and not capable of variation according to circumſtances, for if they were, they would be no longer a certain rule for the government of the people in general; therefore it is, that the wiſdom of our conſtitution hath provided that there ſhould be one ſuperintendant power to give relief in private caſes, where either for particular reaſons and circumſtances the public laws ought not to take place, or where the ſame are ſilent, or have not appointed remedy adequate to the caſe; for *aequum et bonum eſt lex legum*, and this authority it is which is called equity; as it meddleth only with matters of conſcience.

Of what equity holdeth cognizance in its abſolute power.

THE matters, of which equity holdeth cognizance in its abſolute power, are ſuch as are not remediable at law, and of them the ſorts may be ſaid to be as infinite almoſt, as the different affairs converſant in life: many of which may be ſeen in *Doct. & Stud.* my lord *Elſmere*'s obſervations, and ſcattered through the other books.

Where no relief either at law or in equity.

YET there are many other caſes in which there is no relief to be had either at law, or in equity itſelf, but the ſame is left to the conſcience of the party, as a greater inconvenience would from thence follow to the people in general; to avoid which the law muſt of neceſſity, and as the leſſer of two evils, ſuffer a miſchief to one or a few men, rather than a general inconvenience: yet in ſuch caſe the party is bound in conſcience to redreſs it, if he will avoid offending againſt conſcience, as much as if he really were compellable thereto by either law or equity; as if a man wage his law in an action of debt brought againſt him upon a juſt debt, here

 the

the plaintiff is deprived of all means of recovery, either at law or in equity, and yet the defendant is bound in confcience to pay him. Alfo if the grand jury, in an attaint, affirm a falfe verdict, given by the petit jury, there is no remedy but the confcience of the party. Alfo where there cannot be fufficient proof, there can be no remedy in chancery or equity, no more than at the common law. So in cafes where a man is not bound to difcover either at law or in equity, for that fuch difcovery would fubject him either to corporal punifhment or difgrace, if it turned out againft him; therefore the law, rather than it will compel him to difcover to fuch manifeft hurt of himfelf, or force him upon wilful and corrupt perjury, refers the matter for redrefs to his own confcience: and therefore the rule, *nullus recedat a cancellaria fine remedio*, doth not extend to thefe and the like cafes againft the law of confcience divine, but the offender ftandeth at the judgment of God only.

Of Maxims.

In general.

MAXIMS, rules, common grounds, *poſtulata*, or axioms, are the ſame. *Co. Lit.* 11. *a.*

A maxim is a propoſition to be of all men confeſſed and granted without proof, argument or diſcourſe. *Contra negantem principia non eſt diſputandum.* Co. Lit. 67. a.

A maxim, *i. e.* a ſure foundation, or ground of art, and a concluſion of reaſon, is ſo called, *quia maxima eſt ejus dignitas, et certiſſima authoritas, atque quod maxime omnibus probetur*; ſo ſure and uncontroulable as that it ought not to be queſtioned. *Co. Lit.* 10. *b.* 11. *a.*

Maxims are one of the grounds of the law of *England. Doct. & Stud. lib.* 1. *cap.* 8.

One may be excepted from the rigour of a maxim of the law, by another maxim of the law. *Doct. & Stud. lib.* 1. *cap.* 17.

Maxims may be taken for common law. *Doct. & Stud. lib.* 1. *cap.* 8. *lib.* 2. *cap.* 15.

How to be known.

THE maxims of the law may be known, partly by the law of reaſon, by the books, by records, and by ſeveral ſtatutes, wherein many of them are recited. *Doct. & Stud. lib.* 1. *cap.* 9.

Their antiquity, authority, excellence, and how favoured.

A Maxim is called a principle in law, *ſive principium, quod eſt quaſi primum caput*, from which many caſes have their original or beginning, which is ſo ſtrong that it ſuffereth no contradiction; and therefore it is ſaid in our books, that antient principles of the law ought not to be diſputed. *Contra negantem principia non eſt diſputandum.* Co. Lit. 343. a.

No reaſon need be aſſigned why they were firſt received for maxims; for it ſufficeth that they are not againſt the law of reaſon, nor the law of God, and that they have been always taken for law. And ſuch maxims are not only holden for law, but alſo other caſes like unto them, and all things that neceſſarily follow upon the ſame are to be reduced unto the like law, *&c. Doct. & Stud. lib.* 1. *cap.* 8. *lib.* 2. *cap.* 15.

Maxims are of the ſame weight in law as ſtatutes, and the general cuſtoms of the realm are their ſtrength and warrant. *Doct. & Stud. lib.* 1. *cap.* 8.

General rules are good and neceſſary to all people. *Doct. & Stud. lib.* 1. *cap.* 12.

Rules and maxims of law muſt be obſerved; and therefore though the rule be, *quod voluntas donatoris ſecundum formam in charta doni ſui manifeſte expreſſam de caetero obſervetur*, yet that will and intent muſt agree with the rules of law. *Co. Litt.* 20. *b.*

None may diſpute the antient principles of the law. *Co. Litt.* 11. *a.*

There is no diſputing of things manifeſtly true or falſe; for all argumentation is *a notioribus*. Hob. 163.

Maxims have been always taken for laws in this realm, ſo that it is not lawful for any that is learned to deny them; for every one of them is ſufficient authority to itſelf. *Doct. & Stud. lib.* 1. *c.* 8.

Where the words of a ſtatute create an eſtate of inheritance againſt a general rule of law, the law requireth that they be legally purſued. *Co. Litt.* 21. *b.*

Every proof ought to be by the higheſt, and moſt ſupreme cauſe, and nothing can be higher and more ſupreme, than the principles of law; and therefore they are to be allowed; for the very reaſon that they want not to be proved. 3 *Co.* 40. *a.*

Who to determine.

WHAT is a Maxim, and what not, ſhall always be determined by the judges, and not by 12 men. *Doct. & Stud. lib.* 1. *cap.* 8.

May be changed.

SOmetimes the old maxims of the law are changed by ſtatute, as there was ſometime a maxim and law of *England*, that no man ſhould have a writ of right but by ſpecial ſuit to the king, and for a fine to be made in chancery for it; which is now changed by *Magna Charta*, *cap.* 16. where it is *nulli negabimus, nulli vendemus rectum vel juſtitiam*, by which words *nulli negabimus*, a man ſhall have a writ of right of courſe in chancery without ſuing to the king for it; and by the words *nulli vendemus*, he ſhall have it without fine. *Doct. & Stud. lib.* 1. *cap.* 8.

PRINCIPLES OF Law and Equity.

1. *Acceſſorium non ducit ſed ſequitur principale.*

1. A Servant procures one to ſlay his maſter; this is not petit treaſon in the ſervant; being but felony in the principal. 40 *Aſſ. pl.* 25.

2. A parſon grants an annuity with a *nomine poenae*, his ſucceſſor ſhall be charged with the penalty due in the life of the predeceſſor, and not his executor. 7 *H.* 6. 19. *b.*

3. The profits of the office of a filacer ſhall not be put in execution upon a recognizance, ſtatute, or the like; becauſe the office itſelf, being an office of truſt, cannot. *Dy.* 7. *b.*

4. Tithes are not payable of oaks uſually top'd and lop'd; for the branches partake of the nature of the principal, for which no tithes are payable. *Fi. Law Engl.* 23, 24.

5. See *Cro. Eliz.* 477. *Co. Litt.* 152. *a.*

2. *Actori incumbit onus probandi.*

1. HE, who intends to avoid a deed of bargain and ſale by reaſon of non-inrolment within ſix months, muſt make good proof thereof. 4 *Co.* 70, 71. *b.*

2. When you will recover any thing from me, it is not enough for you to deſtroy my right, but you muſt prove yours better than mine; for *melior & tutior eſt conditio poſſidentis.* Hob. 103.

3. *Actus dei nemini facit injuriam.*

1. ONE is taken in execution and dies, the plaintiff may well reſort to a new execution; for the death of the defendant, which is the act of God, ſhall not turn to the prejudice of the plaintiff. 5 *Co.* 86. *b.* 87. *a. b.* *Cro. Eliz.* 555. S. C. *Stat.* 21 *Jac.* 1. *c.* 24.

2. See *Cro. Eliz.* 478. *Hob.* 40, 52, *&c.* 59. *Cro. Jac.* 694. 4 *Co.* 66. *a.* See next rule, caſe 1, 2.

3. See rule, *Equity to relieve where the matter lieth in compenſation.*

4. *Actus legis nulli facit injuriam.*

1. IF the ſon be lord, and the father tenant by certain rent, which is in arrear, the tenant dies, and the tenancy deſcends to the ſon, the rent is extinguiſhed by act in law, the tenure being all in the realty. So where the caſe was, that the father granted a rent-charge out of certain lands to his ſon in fee, the father dies, the rent is in arrear, and the land deſcends to the ſon, whereby the rent was extinguiſhed by act in law; the ſon brought debt againſt the executor of his father, for the arrearages incurred living the father: adjudged the action lay not; but for the arrears of an annuity *aliter*. 4 *Co*. 49. *a. for there the perſon only is bound, and it is not iſſuing out of the land.*

2. Recovery in debt on a bond againſt two, one was taken in execution, and ſuffered (wilfully by the gaoler) to eſcape; this ſhall not prejudice the plaintiff of his execution againſt the other: and yet the releaſe or diſcharge of one by the plaintiff ſhould diſcharge both; but at another day *Popham* was of a contrary opinion, and *Fenner* doubted; becauſe the voluntary eſcape had given the plaintiff remedy againſt the ſheriff by action for all the debt. And the caſe was after adjudged with *Popham*. *Mo*. 459. *The reaſon why the diſcharge of the one ſhall enure to both, is, becauſe otherwiſe the plaintiff might avoid his own diſcharge, by ſeeking his full remedy againſt the other defendant; which would be to ſuch defendant's wrong, who was intitled to contribution againſt his companion; and it was the plaintiff's own act to diſcharge one defendant, which act, according to another rule, ought to be conſtrued moſt ſtrongly againſt himſelf; and therefore to be extended to diſcharge both defendants. As to* Fenner's *doubt, it is clearly held by lord* Hobart, *fo*. 60. *that in ſuch caſe the plaintiff hath his choice to take the other defendant, or to get ſatisfaction from the ſheriff upon the eſcape; and ſure it would be hard in the preſent caſe to drive the plaintiff to his remedy againſt a gaoler,* &c. *who may be worth nothing; and to this purpoſe I remember to have met with a caſe where the plaintiff was not put over to his remedy againſt the gaoler,* &c. ideo quaere?

3. Debt *ſur judgment*, defendant pleaded he was taken *ſur ca.* and committed to the marſhal of this court, and had paid the money to him; on demurrer adjudged no plea: for the marſhal is not to receive the debt, but only to detain the defendant in priſon till he pay the plaintiff. But payment to the ſheriff *ſur fi. fa.* is a good plea; for he hath thereby an authority to levy the debt: but payment to the ſheriff *ſur ca' ſa'* is perhaps no plea for the reaſon aforeſaid. 2 *Lev*. 203.

4. See rules, *Nullum iniquum eſt in jure praeſumendum. Executio juris non habet injuriam.*

5. *Actus legitimi non recipiunt modum.*

1. THE acts of preſentation, inſtitution and induction, are all authorities given by law, and muſt be executed according to the form preſcribed by law, and cannot be modified; for *actus legitimi non recipiunt modum*; for the law gives the church, not the patron and ordinary, who are but ceremonious miniſters, and are appointed their manner and form, which they

they neither may exceed nor abridge. *Hob.* 153. *Co. Litt.* 344. *Hob.* 149. 2 *Jur. Eccl.* 373, *&c.*

2. So a man may aſſign a rent for dower, out of the dowable lands, without deed; but it muſt be for no leſs than for life. *Ibid.*

3. Nay, a jointure, which is but an imitation of dower, or a baſtard dower, cannot be made for the life of another. *Ibid.* 4 *Co.* 2. *b.* 3. *a.*

4. An eſtate, which by force of the *Stat.* 27 *H.* 8. *c.* 10. ſhall be in lieu and bar of a woman's dower, ought by the limitation of it to take effect immediately after the death of the huſband; and therefore no other eſtate, not expreſſed in the act, ſhall be taken, by the equity of the act, unleſs it hath the ſame commencement for the benefit of the wife as thoſe expreſſed purport; and therefore if the huſband make a feoffment in fee to the uſe of himſelf for life, and after to the uſe of *B.* for his life, and then to the wife for life for her jointure, this is not within the act, though *B.* die, living the huſband. So if the huſband make a feoffment in fee to *B.* for life, and then to the uſe of the wife for life, tho' *B.* dies, living the huſband, yet this is not good as a jointure within the Statute; for as they were out of the act at firſt, and as it was not certain that the wife's eſtate ſhould take place immediately on the death of the huſband, no ſubſequent event could bring them within the act, for *quod ab initio non valet tractu temporis non convaleſcet.* 4 *Co.* 2. *a. b.* So if lands are conveyed to the uſe of a feme before marriage for part of her jointure, and after marriage further lands are conveyed to her uſe in ſatisfaction of all her dower, and then the huſband dies, if the wife waive the lands conveyed to her after the marriage, ſhe ſhall have thoſe conveyed before marriage, and dower of the reſt; for lands conveyed to her in part of her jointure, or in part of ſatisfaction of dower, are no bar (for the incertainty) for any part of her dower. 4 *Co.* 3. *a.*

5. So if a debtor gives to his creditor a horſe or other thing in ſatisfaction of part of his debt, it ſhall be a bar for no part, for the ſame reaſon of incertainty. *Ibid.*

6. In caſe of quarentine, the wife muſt not depart from the houſe of her huſband upon his death, and return when ſhe pleaſes for the reſt of her days. *Hob.* 153.

7. If the king grants the office of *cuſtos rotulorum*, or chief juſtice, to two, it is void. *Ibid.* See 18 *E.* 4. 7.

8. The chief juſtice cannot grant the offices of his gift as chief juſtice, for leſs time than for life. *Ibid.*

9. If the king grants the cuſtody of the land of a lunatic, *abſque computo*, it is void. *Ibid.*

10. See rule, *Ceſſa regnare ſi non vis judicare.*

6. *Actus non facit reum niſi mens ſit rea.*

1. As to one *de non ſane memorie*, the law is, that he ſhall not loſe his life for felony or murder; becauſe the puniſhments are too grievous: (*ſcilicet*) for felony, 1. A man ſhall loſe his life; 2. In ſo odious a manner, *ſc.*, by hanging; for he ſhall be hanged between heaven and earth as unworthy of either. 3. He loſeth his blood, as to his anceſtry; for he is deemed the ſon of the earth, without anceſtor; and as to his poſterity, for his blood is corrupted, and he hath neither heir nor poſterity. 4. His lands. 5. His

 goods.

goods. 6. And in ſuch caſe the king ſhall have *annum, diem & vaſtum,* to the end his wife and children may be caſt out, his houſe eraſed, his trees rooted up, his meadows plowed, and all that he hath for comfort, delight, or ſupport, be caſt down and deſtroyed for his having feloniouſly offended againſt the law; and all this was, *ut poena ad paucos, metus ad omnes perveniat.* 4 Co. 124.

2. 1ſt, The puniſhment of a madman, who is deprived of his reaſon and underſtanding, may not be compared to any other puniſhment. 2ly, No felony or murder may be committed without a felonious intent and purpoſe; *et ideo dicta eſt felonia, quia fieri debet felleo animo*; but *furioſus non intelligit quid agit, et animo et ratione caret, et non multum diſtat a brutis,* and therefore cannot have a felonious intent. 4 *Co.* 124. *b.*

3. In criminal cauſes, as felony, *&c.* the act and wrong of a madman ſhall not be imputed to him; for in thoſe cauſes *actus non facit reum niſi mens ſit rea*; and he is *amens,* i. e. *ſine mente,* without his mind, or diſcretion; *et furioſus ſolo furore punitur,* a madman is only puniſhed by his madneſs; and ſo it is of an infant till fourteen, which in the law is the age of diſcretion. *Co. Lit.* 247. Yet he, who hath by his own vice, as the drunkard, who is *voluntarius daemon,* deprived himſelf of his underſtanding, what hurt or ill ſoever he doth he ſhall be accountable for, for his drunkenneſs aggravates it. *Co. Lit.* 246. *b.* 247. *a.*

4. A *non compos mentis* cannot commit petit treaſon, as a wife to ſlay her huſband, but they may in ſome caſes commit high treaſon, as it is for ſuch a one to ſlay, or even offer to ſlay the king; for the king *eſt caput et ſalus reipublicae, et a capite bona valetudo tranſit in omnes*; and therefore their perſons are ſo ſacred, that none ought to offer violence to them, but it is *crimen laeſae majeſtatis, et pereat unus ne pereant omnes.* 4 Co. 124. b.

7. *Ad ea quae frequentius accidunt jura adaptantur.*

ABators, intruders, feoffees of diſſeiſors, &c. *are out of the ſtat.* 37 H. 6. cap. 1. *becauſe the ſtatute is penal, and extends only to a diſſeiſin, which was the moſt common miſchief. See* Co. Lit. 238. a. b. 240. a. b. Doct. & Stud. lib. 1. cap. 8. cap. 17. Hob. 323. Co. Lit. *Continual claim and diſcontinuance,* &c.

8. *Admiralty not to hold plea of matters cognizable at law.*

General.

1. THE admiralty is a juriſdiction derived from the crown of *England,* and it is of two kinds. 1. *Juriſdictio voluntaria,* which is the power of the lord high admiral, as the king's general at ſea, over his fleet. 2. *Juriſdictio contentioſa,* which is the juriſdiction the judge of the admiralty hath *in foro contentioſo,* and this is confined, *by the laws of the realm,* to things done upon the high ſea only; but matters done on land, whether the ſame be here or beyond ſea, though the execution of it be in ſome meaſure upon the high ſea, and many more, belong not to the admiralty juriſdiction: and ſo the common and ſtatute laws confine and limit their juriſdiction to matters maritime, and that only to ſuch as are done on

the high ſeas. And this court is not founded upon the authority of the civil law, but hath both its power and juriſdiction by the law and cuſtom of the realm, in ſuch matters as are proper for its cognizance. *Ha. Hiſt. Law*, 34, 35, 36. And the civil law is allowed to be the rule of their proceedings, only ſo far as it is not contradicted by the laws of the land, or by the maritime laws, which have in ſome particular points prevailed here in derogation of the civil law, as by ſtat. 28 *H.* 8. *cap.* 15. *Ha. Hiſt. Law* 34, 35, 36.

2. If any of theſe inferior courts abuſe their authority, or exceed their delegation, *&c.* though the court of king's bench hath not power to hold plea of the matter libelled for; yet they may limit the juriſdiction, or grant prohibitions, or writs upon the ſtatutes of proviſions, according to the nature of the caſe. See *Godb.* 247.

3. The ſoil, upon which the ſea flows and reflows between high water and low water mark, may be parcel of a manor; yet reſolved when the ſea flows, and hath *plenitudinem maris*, the admiral ſhall have juriſdiction of things done upon the water, between the high water and low water mark. 5 *Co.* 107. *a.*

4. Reſolved, 1. That the court of admiralty hath no cognizance of things done beyond ſea. See *Stat.* 13 *R.* 2. *cap.* 5. They are only to meddle with matters done on the ſea, not with matters done within the realm. *Vide* 19 *H.* 6. 7. For things tranſitory done beyond the ſeas, are either triable in the king's court, or the party grieved may have his remedy before the juſtices where the fact was done beyond ſeas. 2. That the proceedings in the admiralty are according to the courſe of the civil law, and therefore not of record; and by conſequence the court of admiralty cannot aſſeſs and fine in ſuch caſe, as a court of record may do, *&c.* 12 *Co.* 104.

Particular caſes.

5. *Per Hale* chief baron *et tot cur':* Upon *Habeas corpus* to remove a priſoner in the admiralty, though the *Habeas corpus* be returnable the next term, the ſheriff or gaoler muſt not in the mean time ſuffer the priſoner to go at large, and if he does he is liable to an eſcape; for the writ impowers the gaoler only to bring him directly to the court, and if he gives him any liberty in the mean time, it is at his peril. *Hard.* 476.

6. On application for a prohibition to the court of admiralty to ſtay a ſuit there by mariners againſt two of the part-owners for wages, upon a ſuggeſtion that the contract was made on land, the court denied it; for the court of admiralty has ever been allowed to proceed for mariners wages: and though the plaintiffs have an employment in the ſhip as purſer, boatſwain, or the like, yet they are mariners, as well as others, and may ſue in the admiral's court for their wages: and that court having juriſdiction, are to proceed in their own way, though different from our law, as to the joining of all the plaintiffs or defendants; and if the proceedings be not according to their law, the remedy lieth there. *Note*; It was ſaid by one of the admiralty, that though the ſuit be againſt ſome of the owners, the courſe there is not to charge them with the whole, but according to their proportionable parts; *aliter* of the maſter, he cannot ſue in the admiralty; becauſe he contracts on the credit of the owners; but the mate and others may; for they contract with the maſter. *Salk.* 33.

7. On prohibition prayed to the admiralty: *Morice* was captain of a private man of war, wherein *Berkley* had an intereſt; and *Morice* took a merchant ſhip beyond the line, and *Berkley* ſued him in the admiralty for an account; *Morice* pleaded the ſtatute of limitations, 21 *Jac.* the cauſe of action appearing on the face of the libel more than ſeven years ſtanding before the ſuit commenced; and now *Morice* ſuggeſted, in order to gain a prohibition, that the court of the admiralty would not receive that plea: it was held that the plea ought to have been received; for that the ſtatute was pleadable there, and the refuſal was a good cauſe for a prohibition. The ſame, if they received it, and did not give ſentence thereupon as the common law requires: but a prohibition lies not before refuſal, becauſe the matter is triable there; and as to *Morice*'s abſence, the court ſaid that the abſence of the defendant was not material; for the act provided for the abſence of the plaintiff only; *et adjournat'*. Hard. 502.

8. Where a cauſe ariſeth at ſea it belongeth to the admiralty; but where at any port or land, it belongeth to the common law. *Hob.* 79, 213.

9. *Bourn* was impriſoned at *Dover* by the lord warden of the *Cinque ports*, becauſe he took an anchor and cable as a wreck, in the liberty of the rape of *Haſtings*, which the lord warden pretended to be within the *Cinque ports*, and to belong to him, having the juriſdiction of the admiralty there. *Bourn* was 23 weeks impriſoned there, whereupon an *Habeas corpus cum cauſa* was granted there; which the lord warden would not obey; wherefore now in open court, an *Alias habeas corpus* was prayed, with a penalty; his lordſhip pretending that this writ was not awardable to the *Cinque ports*, nor returnable by him, as the king's writ he pretended runs not there, &c. *Keeling*, the ſecondary in the crown, vouched a precedent 22 *E.* 1. in the exchequer, where proceſs out of that court for the king's debt was awarded to one of the *Cinque ports*; and becauſe they would not return the writ upon pretence of their privilege, that the king's writ did not run there, they were fined 100*l.* and 30 *H.* 6. that the king's writ in particular caſes may be granted to the lord warden of the *Cinque ports*. And *Mountagu* chief juſtice ſaid, the privilege of the *Cinque ports*, that the king's writ runs not there, is to be intended between party and party, but no ſuch privilege can be againſt the king: *And this writ is a prerogative writ, which concerneth the king's juſtice to be adminiſtred to his ſubjects; for the king ought to have an account why any of his ſubjects are impriſoned; and it is agreeable to all perſons and places; and no anſwer can ſatisfy it, but to return the cauſe, with* paratum habeo corpus, &c. and this writ hath been awarded out of this court to *Calis*, and all other places within the kingdom: *and to diſpute it is not to diſpute the juriſdiction, but the power of the king and his court, which is not to be diſputed:* and of this opinion were all the judges. And *Doderidge* ſaid, that he had often ſeen, that where an alderman, or any other officer, was diſplaced without cauſe, that a writ of reſtitution had been awarded hence to the *Cinque ports*, and that he remembered the caſe of one *Brierly* where it was ſo awarded; wherefore they all held, that an *Habeas corpus*, with a great penalty, ſhould be awarded at another day. *Cro. Jac.* 543, 544. *Vide* 692. *Salk.* Tit. *Admiralty, and fo.* 548.

9. *Aequitas*

9. *Aequitas ſequitur legem.*

General.

1. WHERE conſcience ſhall be ruled by law, is not only to be underſtood of the law of reaſon, and of the law of God, but alſo of the law of man, when not contrary to the law of God or the law of reaſon, but that it is ſuperadded to them, for the better ordering the commonwealth: for ſuch a law of man is always to be ſet as a rule in conſcience, ſo that it is not lawful for a man to turn from it; for ſuch a law of man hath not only the ſtrength of man's law, but alſo of the law of reaſon and the law of God, whereof it is derived; for laws made of man, who hath received of God power to make laws, are made of God; and therefore conſcience muſt be ordered by the law; and whether the law is to be forſaken for conſcience or not? is not to be underſtood of the law of reaſon or the law of God; for theſe two laws may never be departed from, neither is it to be underſtood of the law of man, made in particular caſes, and conſonant to the law of reaſon and the law of God; nor is it to be underſtood of a law made by man, commanding or prohibiting any thing to be done that is againſt the law of reaſon or the law of God: therefore after them who are learned in the laws of *England*, the ſaid queſtion, where laws are to be left for conſcience and where not, is to be underſtood in divers manners, and after divers rules: as, a man is bound to do to another, as he would be done unto, *&c. Doct. & Stud. lib.* 1. *cap.* 19. See *Weſt's precedents.*

2. In many caſes conſcience ſhall be ruled after the laws; as, the eldeſt ſon ſhall have his father's land by conſcience, as he ſhall in law. So in *Borough Engliſh* the youngeſt ſon ſhall enjoy. In gavelkind the ſons ſhall inherit together: and no other reaſon can be given why it ſhould be ſo in conſcience, but becauſe law is ſo. *Elſ. Obſ.* 78. *Doct. & Stud. lib.* 1. *cap.* 16.

Particular caſes.

3. An *Engliſh* bill for relief againſt the defendant for rent, the defendant being aſſignee of an aſſignee of a wine-licence leaſe made by the plaintiff, rendering 41 *l. per annum*, and it appeared that the defendant was a purchaſer of his intereſt in the leaſe for a valuable conſideration, and had no notice of the rent reſerved upon the original leaſe; and therefore the bill was diſmiſſed, becauſe it is a perſonal contract, which does not run with the licence; as in caſe of a leaſe of a fair, rendering rent, an action of debt does not lie againſt the aſſignee, and *aequitas ſequitur legem* in this caſe, eſpecially where the aſſignee is a purchaſer for a valuable conſideration without notice of the rent reſerved. *Hard.* 88.

4. A man ſeiſed of lands in fee, hath iſſue a daughter who is her father's heir apparent, the daughter takes huſband, and they have iſſue, the father dieth ſeiſed, and the huſband, as ſoon as he heareth of the death of the father, goeth towards the land to take poſſeſſion, and before he can get there his wife dieth, here the huſband ſhall not, even in conſcience, be tenant, *per le curteſy*, though he hath done every thing in his power to get poſſeſſion; and that becauſe he had not poſſeſſion in deed; and yet he ſhall be tenant by the courteſy of a rent, though his wife die before the day of

2 pay-

payment: ſo of an advowſon, though ſhe die before the avoidance. And in the firſt part of this caſe the huſband cannot be holpen by conſcience or in equity; for conſcience muſt always be grounded upon ſome law, and it cannot be grounded, in this caſe, upon the law of reaſon, nor upon the law of God; for it is not by theſe laws, that the huſband ſhall be tenant by the courteſy, but by the cuſtom of the realm; and therefore if ſuch cuſtom help him not, he cannot be aided by conſcience; for conſcience never reſiſteth the law of man, nor addeth to it, but where ſuch law of man is againſt reaſon or the law of God; in which caſe it cannot properly be called a law, but a corruption. *Doct. & Stud. lib.* 2. *cap.* 14, 15, 49, 50. *Cary's Rep.* 11.

5. Sir *Thomas Englefield*, the plaintiff's father, was ſeiſed of an eſtate for life in reverſion, on two eſtates, one in *Leiceſterſhire*, the other in *Wilts*, each of 1800*l. per annum* value, expectant upon the lives of two jointreſſes; remainder to his firſt and other ſons in tail; the remainder in like manner to his brother the defendant, and though he had theſe great expectances, yet he had little or nothing at preſent, and had been ſometime in priſon, and formerly was married, but had no children of that marriage, and was then ſixty years old, and intended never to marry: the *Wiltſhire* eſtate was ſold to Sir *Robert Howard*, whoſe lady was jointreſs of that part, and part of the purchaſe-money 2500*l.* was paid to the defendant for his intereſt therein, who agreed with Sir *Thomas* to pay him down in hand 600*l.* and 500*l.* a year for his life, to commence from the death of lady *Englefield* the other jointreſs, whoſe eſtate the defendant had bought in; (for without her the plaintiff's father having barely an eſtate for life, expectant on her death, could not make a good tenant to the *Praecipe*) a common recovery was ſuffered, and fines levied, and the defendant in actual poſſeſſion: after Sir *Thomas* married a young lady, had iſſue the plaintiff, and brought his bill, ſuggeſting fraud and circumvention, but on ſolemn hearing, his bill was diſmiſſed. It was ſaid that tho' the diſmiſſion is not a bar, plaintiff claiming as remainder-man, yet as the father had not, the ſon cannot have relief, on pretence of fraud; the plaintiff was not then in being, and his eſtate imaginary, and of no conſideration in law, and was well deſtroyed by the recovery before he was born; that the agreement was by conſent of all friends, and this demand, after twenty years enjoyment, on pretence of fraud; whereas if there was any fraud, it was to the plaintiff's father, whoſe bill was diſmiſſed; and the plaintiff had no eſtate in law, not ſo much as a right; that there was never any thing more than a contingency limited to him, and that fully diſtroyed before he was born. And the caſe of *Roſcurrocke* and *Barton* was cited; and in this caſe, if Sir *Thomas* had ſeven ſons, they would all have ſeveral ſpringing equities. But a reconveyance and account was decreed. 1 *Vern.* 443 to 448. *Englefield* contra *Englefield. In this caſe Sir* Thomas *could have no pretence to be relieved againſt his own agreement, made in full ſenſe of his intereſt, for good conſideration, and the general benefit of the family, as the ſame was to the liking of all, and for ſecuring the credit of the name and family, had Sir* Thomas *ſtill kept in the ſame mind not to marry; but as he afterwards did marry, and had iſſue the plaintiff, the reaſons of that agreement ceaſed, and contrary reaſons aroſe from the birth of the plaintiff, in his favour, againſt that agreement; and on the preſent circumſtances of the caſe, Sir* Thomas *muſt be conſidered as* particeps criminis,

minis, *or an actor in the fraud on the plaintiff, who must be understood to be in contemplation on the original settlement of the estate; which was for the preservation of the honour and dignity of the name.*

6. See 1 *Vern.* 14, 164, 294, 295. 2 *Rep. Chan.* 78. 1 *Chan. Ca.* 57, 83, 84, 238, 284. 2 *Chan. Ca.* 64. 3 *Chan. Ca.* 91, 126. *Gilb.* 83, 102, 136. *Prec. Chan.* 233. *Max. Eq.* 16.

7. See rules, *Equality is equity. Equity proper place to relieve legatees. Est boni judicis ampliare jurisdictionem. Trust of a term governed by the same rules in equity, as the limitation of the legal estate is at law.*

10. *Aequum et bonum est lex legum.*

1. THE true meaning of the statute 31 *H.* 8. of monasteries, *&c. W.* 2. 1 *Eliz.* to restrain ecclesiastics from wasting their possessions, and 1 & 2 *Ph. & Ma. cap.* 8. are to be favourably expounded, and according to natural equity, for the honour and service of God, religion and truth, without respect to legal ceremonies. 5 *Co.* 14. *a. b.* 11 *Co.* 66. *Magdalen Col. Hob.* 220. *Ann Needler* versus *Bishop of Winton.*

2. See rule, *It is the office of a temporal judge to advance laws made for religion according to their end*, &c.

11. *Agreements and contracts to be on good consideration, or mutual recompence.*

General, and rules.

1. ONE is not bound by his assumption or promise, unless it be on good consideration of another thing. 17 *E.* 4. 4. *b.*

2. A use may not be raised *sans* good consideration: and such consideration ought to be some cause or occasion meritorious, amounting to mutual recompence, in deed or in law. 21 *H.* 7. 18. *b. Dyer* 336. *b.*

3. A writ of annuity shall be maintained by a parson against a vicar, upon an ordinance of the ordinary, if there be *quid pro quo.* Fitzh. Nat. Brev. 152. G.

* 4. He, who will have the benefit of a mutual agreement, must shew that he has performed his part. See case *Duchess of Hamilton* and *Duke of Hamilton* before the house of lords, 28 *March* 1727.

* 5. Contracts are to be adjudged according to the law of the place where they were made. See case *York Buildings Company* and *Meers* before the house of lords, 23 *Nov.* 1728.

* 6. Where one person has trifled or shewed a backwardness in performing his part of the agreement, equity will not decree a specific performance in his favour, especially if circumstances are altered. See case before the house of lords *Hayes* and *Caryl*, 26 *Jan.* 1702.

* 7. One, who enters into articles in violation of a trust, shall never take benefit by the same articles. See case before the house of lords *Dale* and *Lynch*, 17 *August* 1715.

* 8. Equity will not carry unreasonable agreements into execution. See cases before the house of lords, * *Brain* and *Wooley*, 9 *Feb.* 1721. * *Carol* and *Chamberlyn*, 14 *July* 1721. * *Tap* and *Stanhope*, 24 *Mar.* 1720.

* 9. Nor where a perſon of weak underſtanding is drawn into it. See ſaid caſe *Carol* and *Chamberlyn.*

* 10. Nor where the method of obtaining them was not ſtrictly regular, though the ſame were in part executed. See *Rochford* and *Nugent's* caſe before the houſe of lords, 22 *May* 1724. and *Fitzgerald* and *Euſtace* 1733.

* 11. In agreements the ties muſt be reciprocal. *S. C.*

* 12. Decreed, that where the articles were not obtained with the ſtricteſt fairneſs, the conveyance made in purſuance of ſuch articles ſhall be ſet aſide: and the purchaſe only to ſtand as a ſecurity for the conſideration-money. See caſe before the houſe of lords *White* and *Leighborn*, 28 *Feb.* 1722.

* 13. An agreement made with an infant not binding, becauſe *ex parte*, and remedies not mutual. See caſe *Conway* and *Shrimpton*, 19 *Jan.* 1710. before the houſe of lords.

* 14. Agreements made in a tavern by ſurprize, not binding. *S. C.*

* 15. A contract for ſtock in the public funds, *&c.* at an unreaſonable price, ſet aſide. See caſe *Thompſon* and *Harcourt* before the houſe of lords, 13 *Feb.* 1721.

* 16. To be ſet aſide where an undue advantage has been taken of the weakneſs of another's underſtanding, or circumſtances; as being in priſon, or the like. See caſe before the houſe of lords *Moody* and *Stewart*, 28 *Feb.* 1728.

Particular caſes.

* 17. The father on his marriage had articled to ſettle his whole eſtate on that marriage, but neglected ſo to do; when the eldeſt ſon of that marriage attained his full age, the father without giving him notice of the articles, and with threats to allow him nothing unleſs he complied, and on promiſe to make an abſolute ſettlement on him in caſe he would comply, prevailed on him to join in making a ſettlement on the younger children, and thereby to give the father a power to make a jointure on another wife; the father afterwards gives bond to make ſuch jointure, and marries. This bond was ſet aſide, as againſt the heir, and the firſt articles eſtabliſhed: and the ſecond wife put to ſeek ſatisfaction of her bond out of the perſonal eſtate. See caſe *Ivers* and *Ivers* before the houſe of lords, 1734-5.

* 18. The father makes his ſon of the firſt marriage agree to a proviſion for the father's ſecond wife and their children, in his, the ſon's, own wrong, and who was, at the time of the agreement, ignorant of his right, and threatened by his father to be kept at home bare, and without any allowance, if he refuſed, but if he complied he was to be allowed 260 *l.* a year for his maintenance, *&c.* the ſon was relieved, and the agreement ſet aſide. See caſe before the houſe of lords *Scrope & ux'* verſus *Offley*, 24 *May* 1735.

12. *Alienatio, licet prohibeatur, conſenſu tamen omnium in quorum favorem prohibita eſt, poteſt fieri.*

THE licences of lords immediate and mediate to grant ſhall enure to two intents, *viz.* to a diſpenſation both of the ſtatute of *Quia emptores terrar'*, and of the ſtatute of *Mortmain*; becauſe their deeds ſhall be taken

taken moſt ſtrongly againſt themſelves; *Et quilibet poteſt renunciare juri pro ſe introducto.* Co. Lit. 99. a. See here of *Non obſtantes, &c.* and 4 *Co. Bozoun's* caſe.

13. *Alligari non debuit, quod probatum non relevat.*

1. THE defendant confeſſed that in a paſſion he had burnt his marriage articles: but it appearing he had produced them at a commiſſion ſince the time he pretended to have burnt them, he was committed to the *Fleet*; and though he after made oath, that he had them not, and could not produce them; and though it was inſiſted that notwithſtanding the burning them was a great miſdemeanor, yet a man was not to ſuffer perpetual impriſonment, becauſe he could not do what was impoſſible; yet he could not be diſcharged till he conſented to admit the articles were to the effect in the bill. 2 *Vern.* 561.

2. See 1 *Chan. Ca.* 11, 45, 56, 77. 1 *Vern.* 207.

3. See rules, *Nothing ſhall be a ground to direct a new trial to avoid a judgment at law, that would not be a ground for a bill of review to reverſe a decree. In odium ſpoliatoris omnia praeſumuntur. Iniquity bars equity. He, who hath done iniquity, ſhall not have equity.*

14. *Almanack, part of the law of the land.*

THE almanack is part of the law of the land, of which the court muſt take judicial notice. 6 *Mod.* 41. 1 *Salk.* 181. *S. C.*

15. *All the term in law but one day.*

1. WHEN a deed is ſhewed forth to the court, the ſame ſhall remain in court all that term, in cuſtody of the *Cuſtos brevium:* but at the end of the term, if the deed be not denied, then the law adjudgeth the deed in the cuſtody of the party to whom it belongeth; for a man's evidences are as it were the ſinews of his land; but if the deed be denied, then the deed, in judgment of law, remaineth in court until the plea is determined. *Co. Lit.* 231. *b.* 5 *Co.* 74. *b.* *Fitzh. Nat. Brev.* 244.

2. It ſhall be intended by preſumption in law, that a deed inrolled any part of the term was inrolled the firſt day of the ſame term; *ſtabit praeſumptio donec probetur in contrarium*; and therefore the plaintiff having in the principal caſe confeſſed the inrolment to be after the ſix months, the preſumption vaniſhes, and becomes of no force. See 4 *Co.* 71. *b.*

3. All the term is but as one day in law, and therefore a deed produced to the court ſhall remain in court all that term wherein it was ſhewn; but when the term is over, it ſhall go to the party who ſhewed it. And then it being in cuſtody of the adverſe party, another term, and not in court, the defendant cannot have *oyer* of it. 5 *Co.* 74. *b.*

16. *Apices juris non ſunt jura.*

1. THE law of *England* reſpecteth the effect and ſubſtance of the matter, and not every nicety or form of circumſtance. *Qui haeret in litera haeret in cortice, et apices juris non ſunt jura.* Co. Lit. 283. a. b.

2. Seeing that in conveyances, limitations of remainders are uſual *and common aſſurances*, it is dangerous by conceits, or nice diſtinctions, to bring them in queſtion. *Co. Lit.* 299. *a.*

3. It was ſaid by *Coke*, lord chief juſtice, and affirmed by the other judges, that then of late ſuch nice and ſtrained conſtructions had been made on letters patent, as to deſtroy the force and effect of them, ſo that many good letters patent were drawn in queſtion, *to the diſhonour of the crown, diſinheriſon of the ſubject, and againſt the true reaſon and antient rule of law, as his lordſhip ſaid appears through the books: and* talis certitudo, *ſays his lordſhip*, certitudinem confundit, *ſuch nice and captious pretences of certainty confound true and legal certainty. Et maledicta expoſitio eſt quae corrumpit et confundit textum.* And it was adjudged, that where the queen granted a manor to *B.* and his heirs, in the premiſſes of the letters patent, to have and to hold the ſaid manor to *B.* and his aſſigns, leaving out *heirs* in the *habendum*, that the fee of the manor paſſed by the premiſſes, and the *habendum* was void; for the premiſſes were ſufficiently certain to paſs the fee, and the omiſſion in the *habendum* ſhould not deſtroy or overturn that which was certain by the premiſſes; for her majeſty's intention appears to paſs the fee by the premiſſes, and her grant ought to be taken *ſecundum intentionem reginae, et non in deceptione reginae:* and when a literal and ſtrict conſtruction is made to make the king's grant void, *contra intentionem regis*, it ſounds in deceit of the king, and it is a great indignity to him *propter apices juris*, to make his charter under his *great ſeal*, of ſuch things as he might lawfully grant, to be of no effect. *Quia apices juris non ſunt jura.* 8 Co. 56. b. 57. a. Vide *tout le caſe.*

4. See rules, *Equity will not aid new inventions*, &c. *Law hath always ſuppreſſed new and ſubtile inventions*, &c. *He who takes ſecurity by a penalty*, &c. *Ca.* 1.

17. *Ars naturam imitatur.*

VIDE rule, *Lex ſpectat naturae ordinem.*

18. *Benedicta eſt expoſitio quando res redimitur a deſtructione.*

1. WHEN the lord of a manor, having many antient copyholds in the ſame vill, grants the inheritance of all of them to another, the grantee may hold courts for his cuſtomary tenants, and accept ſurrenders for the uſe of others, and make admittances and grants; for though it be no manor in law, for want of freeholders, yet as to the copyholders, the feoffee or grantee hath ſuch a manor, that he may hold courts for theſe purpoſes. 4 *Co.* 26. *b.*

2. Every manor, which consists of freeholders and copyholders, comprehends, in effect, two different courts, *viz.* One commonly called the court baron, *scil.* the court of the freeholders, who are suitors and judges; the other of the copyholders or copyhold tenants, whereof the lord, or his steward of the manor, is judge: and for this reason, when the lord grants over the inheritance of his copyholds, the grantee may hold such court for the copyhold tenants only, as his grantor before held, *&c.* for *benedicta est expositio quando res redimitur a destructione.* 4 Co. 26. b. Co. Lit. 58. a.

3. Though the lord, by his own act, may not at common law make of one manor divers manors, consisting of demesns and freeholds, yet he may make a customary manor, consisting of copyholds for the purposes aforesaid. 4 *Co.* 26. *b.*

19. *Beneficium non datur nisi propter officium.*

1. A Spiritual office draws with it a right to have the possessions belonging to such office; as in the case of an abbot or parson, *&c.* *Plowd. Com.* 500. *a. b.*

2. If the head and members of a college will receive a charity, with a yoke tied to it by the founder, they must bear it; for the charity may not be severed from the yoke; if they will have the one they must submit to the other. *Skin.* 491. *For as the office carries with it the benefice, so taking the benefice is an undertaking to perform the office in such manner and under the modes prescribed by the founder, who as master of his own charity may give it what form he pleases, so he give it legal shape; and sure it must be very indecent for him who thinks fit to take the benefit, to cavil at the terms the founder has thought fit to annex; since he might have left it if he had not liked it.*

3. Though the pope, before his usurped power taken away, made many appropriations *de facto* to nuns, yet he could not *de jure* so do; for a woman cannot be a pastor by the law of God, 1 *Cor.* 14, 34. 1 *Tim.* 2. 11, 12. and *Dyer*, in *Grindon's case*, says well, that it was a thing abominable, and I [lord *Hobart*] say more, that it was against the law of the realm. *Nay, whilst the law of the realm suffered it, and so tacitly admitted it might be done, and that by law, and so part of the law of the realm, yet admitting (for argument sake what I cannot grant) that it was then law, such law was void, as being unrighteous and against the law of God.* For it is, *as my lord* Hobart *continues*, of the essence of a pastor to be *didacticus* to teach the people, and also to be *hospitalis*, as is the statute of *Carlisle*, and to do alms and other works of charity in the places where the churches were founded; and it is, *and always was*, against the law of the realm; for *beneficium non datur nisi propter officium*, and it is no reply that the cure may be served by a curate for them; for the question is not how they can make a curate, but how they themselves are capable: and therefore as in 5 *E.* 3. 4. *Bro. Pat.* 108. 9 *E.* 4. 6. and 4 & 5 *Ph. & Ma.* *Dyer* 150. if an office of learning be given to a man utterly insufficient, it is utterly void, *&c.* *Hob.* 148, 149. *Our clergy from this rule, and particularly from this case, might take a lesson, that they are required to reside, to instruct the people, to be hospitable, and charitable, and that in their several parishes, and they ought to be studious to perform these offices, as the question*

2

ſtion may as well be put to them now, as heretofore to nuns, how they themſelves are capable? and not how they may make curates, which indeed of itſelf is a queſtion might puzzle a vicar.

4. See 3 *Lev.* 83.

20. *Benigne faciendae ſunt interpretationes, ut res magis valeat quam pereat.*

1. A Special verdict in ejectment; the declaration was of ſeveral meſuages in the ſeveral pariſhes of St. *Michael*, St. *James*, St. *Peter* and St. *Paul*, that part of the premiſſes lay in St. *Peter*'s and St. *Paul*'s; but there was no pariſh called St. *Peter*'s nor St. *Paul*'s. It was held clearly that the copulative (*et*) ſhould be referred to that which is real and had an exiſtence, *ut res magis valeat*, not to make St. *Peter*'s one pariſh and St. *Paul*'s another, but both one; and the words *ſeveral pariſhes* are ſupplied by the other pariſhes aforementioned; ſo that if there be any ſuch pariſh in being, as that of St. *Peter* and St. *Paul*, the copulative ſhall refer to that. As in 6 *E.* 3. *Praecipe* of ten acres in *A. B.* and *C.* there the lands muſt lie in every one of the vills; but if the *Praecipe* were *de manerio et de decem acris* in *A. B.* and *C.* there it would be well enough, though the manor lay elſewhere, provided the ten acres lay within the vills named, for then the laſt words are ſatisfied by the ten acres. And judgment *niſi*, *&c.* was given accordingly. *Hard.* 336.

2. See 2 *Bulſt.* 282. *Co. Lit.* 213, 301. *b.*

21. *Benignior ſenſus in verbis generalibus ſeu dubiis eſt praeferendus.*

Rules.

1. THE office of the judges is, on conſideration of all the words, to collect the true ſcope and intention of the ſpeaker, *&c.* 4 *Co.* 19. *b.*

2. *Senſus verborum ex cauſa dicendi accipiendus eſt. Et ſermones ſemper accipiendi ſunt ſecundum ſubjectam materiam.* 4 Co. 13. b. 14. a.

3. It is an excellent point of learning in actions for ſlander, to obſerve the occaſion of the words being ſpoken. 4 *Co.* 14. *a.*

4. The words ought to have convenient certainty. 4 *Co.* 15. *a.* 16. *a.* 18. *a. b.*

5. *Sermo relatus ad perſonam, intelligi debet de conditione perſonae.* 4 Co. 16. a.

6. Actions are not maintainable for brabling words. 4 *Co.* 18. *a.*

Caſes.

1. The plaintiff recited in his count, that whereas he was a juſtice of peace, ſurveyor of the duchy of *Lancaſter*, and had ſeveral other offices, the defendant ſaid of him, *Mr.* Stanhope *hath but one manor, and that he hath gotten by ſwearing and forſwearing:* adjudged words not actionable. 1ſt, Becauſe they were too general, and words, to charge any in an action

tion in which damages are to be recovered, ought to have convenient certainty. 2dly, The defendant did not charge the plaintiff with swearing and forswearing; for he might recover or obtain a manor by swearing and forswearing, and yet he neither be procuring nor assenting to it: and words which maintain an action ought directly to be applied to the plaintiff, and not by collection or inference; for damages ought to be given in regard of the hurt which he hath by the scandal. If one charge another that he hath forsworn himself, this is not actionable; 1st, Because it might be in common conversation, *et benignior sententia in verbis generalibus seu dubiis est praeferenda*. 2dly, It is usually a word of passion and choler; as if one says to another that he is a villain, a rogue, or a varlet, *vel similia*, these will not maintain an action; for *boni judicis est lites dirimere*; but if one say to another that he was perjured or forsworn in such a court, it is actionable; for by such words it appears that he had forsworn himself in a judicial proceeding. And *Wray* lord chief justice said, that the judges had resolved, that actions for scandal should not be maintained by any strained construction or argument, nor any favour be extended for their support, *&c.* 4 *Co.* 15. *a. b.* See 4 *Co.* cases *Actiones de scandalis, ou actions pur slander* throughout.

2. Action for these words, *Thou* (praefatam Johannam innuendo) *art* Mutcombe's *hackney, thou art a thieving whore, and a pockey whore,* (*innuendo* that the said *Joan* had the *French* pox) *and I will prove thee a pockey whore.* Moved in arrest of judgment, that the words were not actionable. First, *Thou art* Mutcombe's *hackney*, and the second, *Thou art a thievish whore*, is not an accusation of felony; for she may be thievish in that which is not felony; and for the last, the *innuendo* cannot make the words to be intended the *French* pox, when it is not shewn by any other circumstances, *&c.* Judgment for the defendant. *Cro. Ja.* 514.

3. *Action sur le case.* Whereas he was the son and heir of *John and Anne Elborow*, which *Anne* was daughter of *John Travel*, and had land by descent from them of 200 *l. per annum*; defendant envying his estate, speaking of the plaintiff and *Katherine* his wife, said, shall *Elborow*'s wife sit above my wife? he is but a bastard. *Quorum praetextu* he was much scandalized in his estate, and inforced to great expences to defend his title. Moved in arrest, that the words were not actionable; because he doth not shew that there was any speech about his estate, or that he was about selling or leasing out the lands, or that these words were spoken to scandalize his title. And that though the plaintiff said he was scandalized in his estate, and that the words were spoken maliciously, that was only the clerk's drawing and inserting; for it doth not appear that he had any temporal loss thereby; and therefore not actionable. As in *Anne Davis*'s case, 4 *Co.* 17. But all the court, besides *Doderidge*, held them to be scandalous, and adjudged for the plaintiff. *Cro. Ja.* 642, 643.

4. Vide 4 *Co.* 17. *a. b.* 18. *a.* *Cro. Ja.* 240, 241, 673, 674.

22. *Boni judicis eſt lites dirimere, et expedit reipublicae ut ſit finis litium, propter communem omnium utilitatem.*

1. THomas *Williams*, Eſq; brought his action *ſur le caſe* againſt *Henry Jones* clerk, and declared that the ſaid *Jones* being vicar of *Alderbury in com. Salop.* ought and was bound by himſelf, or other chaplain, to celebrate divine ſervice at *Woolaſton*, at his chapel of St. *John*, within the ſite and precinct of his manor of *Woolaſton* aforeſaid, within the pariſh of *Alderbury* aforeſaid, antiently erected, every *Sunday* and holiday throughout the year, before noon of each of the ſaid days, and to adminiſter the ſacraments to the ſaid *Thomas*, *et hominibus, tenentibus et ſervientibus ſuis, infra praecinctum ejuſdem manerii inhabitantibus, et commorantibus, &c.* on motion in arreſt of judgment it was reſolved, that the action lay not, but the remedy was in the court *Chriſtian*; but if it had been a private chapel only for *Williams* and his ſervants and family, within the ſaid manor, an action had lain on the preſcription for the lord; for in ſuch caſe he only ſhould have had it; but as it was public no action lay, for if the lord ſhould be allowed this remedy, every one of his tenants might have the ſame, and ſo there might be infinite actions for one and the ſame default. *Et boni judicis eſt, &c.* and yet they ſhall not be *ſans* remedy; for they may ſue in the ſpiritual court, *&c.* 5 *Co.* 72. *b.* 73. *a.* Vide 2 *Ju. Eccl.* 496. *et q.*

2. One ſhall not have an action for a nuſance in the highway, for it is common, and no reaſon that one perſon ſhould have an action, for by the ſame reaſon that one ſhould, every one ſhould; and then the party might be puniſhed an hundred times for one cauſe: but if any particular perſon hath a more particular damage than another, for ſuch particular injury he may have his particular action: but ſuch public injuries are remedial in the turns, leets, *&c.* 4 *Co.* 73. *a.*

3. If a man be diſturbed of a common way which the law giveth him, he ſhall have an action on the caſe, and recover damages; for when ever the law giveth any thing, it giveth alſo a remedy for the ſame; *quando lex aliquid alicui concedit, concedere videtur et id ſine quo res ipſa eſſe non poteſt*, but a difference is to be taken between a private way and a common one; for if one be diſturbed to go in the latter, yet he ſhall have no action, for the preventing multiplicity of ſuits; for if one might, all men might, and yet this caſe is not without remedy, but that is by preſentment in the leet or torn: but if one hath a particular damage, as that he and his horſe fell into a ditch made athwart the public way, he ſhall have an action for this ſpecial hurt and loſs. *Co. Lit.* 56. *a.*

4. True it is, that for a nuſance in the highway, without ſpecial damage, none ſhall have a private action; for it is not *damnum privatum, ſed damnum commune*; and therefore ought only to be puniſhed and reformed at the ſuit of the king; for a public nuſance ſhall not be reformed at the ſuit of a private perſon; for the damage is not private but public; and therefore the king, who is head of the commonwealth, ſhall have his remedy. 9 *Co.* 113. *a.*

5. In copyhold caſes, if the lord will not hold a court, the tenant hath no remedy to compel him to admit him, but in chancery; as is 4 *Co.* 28.

Weſtwick's caſe, 32 *H.* 6. 3. *Lit. fo.* 3. for it would be infinite if every copyholder, upon pretence of refuſal, might have an action. *Cro. Ja.* 368, 369.

6. See *Lit. chap. Frankalmoigne* 30. *b.* 27 *H.* 8. 27. *a.* 22 *H.* 6. 46. 1 *Ro.* 108. *Mo.* 842. 2 *Cro.* 491. 5 *Co.* 101. 2 *Ju. Eccl.* 495.

7. See rule, *Benignior ſenſus in verbis generalibus ſeu dubiis eſt praeferendus*, caſes 1, 2, 3.

23. *Bonum neceſſarium extra terminos neceſſitatis non eſt bonum.*

1. VIDE *Hob.* 144. *Mo.* 902. and 1 *Ro.* 464.

2. *Vide* rule, *Natura appetit perfectum.*

24. *Caveat emptor.*

1. *Caveat emptor qui ignorare non debuit quod jus alienum emit.* Hob. 99.

2. If a man buy lands whereunto another hath title, which the buyer knoweth not, yet ignorance ſhall not excuſe him. *Doct. & Stud. lib.* 2. *cap.* 47.

3. See rule, *Ignorantia facti excuſat.*

25. *Cauſa ſpiritualis committi poteſt principi laico.*

1. REſolved, that proxies, being in their original nature duties payable for viſitation, were grantable to the king, and the king became capable of ſuch grants when the duty was converted into a ſum of money certain, in nature of a penſion, or annuity; for by the antient law of the realm, the king hath power to viſit, reform and correct all abuſes and enormities in the church, and the ſtatute of *H.* 8. but remitted the antient juriſdiction to the crown, which the pope had uſurped. Proxy is but a profit of juriſdiction; and *Cauſa ſpiritualis committi poteſt principi laico.* Da. 4. a.

2. So he hath power to diſpence with the eccleſiaſtical laws, *&c. Hob. Colt* and *Glover*'s caſe. 14 *H.* 8. 7. *Palm.* 470. *Mo.* 755, 756. *Hob.* 147. *Davis* 72. *b.* 73. *a.* 5 *Co. De Jure Regis Eccl.* 9. 16. *b. Hawk. Pl. Cro. Praemunire, ſect.* 6. *Fitzh. Nat. Bre.* 22. *a.* 27 *E.* 3. 85. *a.* 6 *H.* 7. 14. *a. Co. Lit.* 44. *a.* 1 *Ju. Eccl.* 13. *Moor* and *Moor*'s caſe in chancery. The king may diſpence with the canons, but a metropolitan cannot, *no nor convocation convocated.* See alſo 5 *Co. De Jure Regis Eccl.* 17, 26, 28, 51. *Da.* 76, 77. *Mo.* 542. *Cro. Eliz.* 527, 542, 601. *Palm.* 25, 26, 27. *Da.* 91, 92. *Hob.* 81, 82. *Cro. Ja.* 335. *Cro. Ca.* 47, 68, 199, 356. *Dy.* 294. *Ha. Anal.* 19. *Salk.* 294. The Biſhop of St. *David*'s caſe. *Fareſt.* 56, 117. S. C. *Gilb.* 181. 2 *Pe. Will.* 119.

3. *Vide* rule, *Omnes reges dicuntur cleri.*

26. *Cessante causa cessat* { *Effectus,* *Causatum.*

1. THE king granted an office to one at will, and 10*l.* fee during life, *pro officio illo*, now if the king put him from his office, the fee shall cease. 5 *E.* 4. 8. *b.*

2. It is no principal challenge to a juror, that he hath married the party's mother, if she be dead without issue; for the cause of favour is removed. 14 *H.* 7. 2.

3. If after the lord had the wardship of the body and land, the lord released to the infant his right in the seigniory, or the seigniory descended to the infant, he would be out of ward, both for the body and land; for he was in ward in respect he was not able to do those services which he ought to have done to his lord, and which now are extinct; and *cessante causâ cessat causatum.* Co. Lit. 76. a.

4. If I make a lease of my lands, excepting all trees, which grow out of any wood, but upon the lands, by this exception the soil is not excepted, *as would be if they grew in a wood or grove,* but sufficient nourishment out of it is reserved, to preserve the vegetative life of the trees, without which they must perish: but if the lessor fell them, or with leave of the lessee rid them up, and eradicate them, there the lessee shall have the soil; for *cessante causa cessat effectus.* 11 Co. 49. b.

5. The church and religious houses, after that procurations were reduced to a sum certain, paid them to ordinaries, tho' visitation ceased, so that the rule *Cessante causâ, &c.* doth not hold in such cases. *Da.* 3. *a.*

6. Vide *Co. Lit.* 70. *b.* 248. *a.* 4 *Co.* *Lutterel's* case. *Davis* 1. *b.* *Hob.*

27. *Cessa regnare si non vis judicare.*

1. THE estates and persons of ideots and lunatics are, by law, intrusted to the king; (4 *Co.* 127.) if therefore the king should grant to one who intrudeth upon the possession of an ideot or lunatic, or takes their persons unlawfully, that he would not meddle with them, but let them do their pleasure, these grants were void; for to defend the subject is an act of justice, and office of a king which he cannot put off: *cessa regnare si non vis judicare.* And in these things the king is never supposed by law ill affected, but abused and deceived; for *eadem praesumitur mens regis, quae est juris.* So 7 *H.* 4. 42. the earl of *Kent's* case, if the king being but guardian grants the land in fee, the grant is void. So resolved 7 *Co.* 36. That the king cannot give away a penal law. So if the king having a lapse, should grant to an intruder that he would not present to the church, or if one should usurp upon the king's lapse, and the king should grant to the usurper, that he would not remove his clerk; the grant would be void. For this were a breach of that trust which the law reposed in the king. *Hob.* 155. *The prince's contentment ought to be the happiness of the subject, and the subject's welfare the security of the prince: having from this firmness of union, mentem sanam in corpore sano.*

2. See

2. See rules, *Actus legitimi non recipiunt modum*, cafe 6. *Admiralty not to hold plea of matters cognizable at law.*

28. *Chancery only controulable by parliament.*

JUdgments given in chancery are not to be controuled or reverfed in any other court, than the high court of parliament, which is the chiefeft of all other courts in this realm. 2 *West's Prec.* 177. *a.*

29. *Chancery not tied to the rules of the common law.*

THE abfolute power of chancery is not tied to the rules of the common law, but thereby matters may be examined *omnibus viis et modis quibus rei veritas melius sciri poterit*, and adjudged *fecundum allegata et probata*, and not by jury of twelve men, as at common law; but by examination of witneffes, as in the courts of the civil law. *Smith de Repub. Angl. lib.* 1. *cap.* 12. Neither is fuch precife form of pleading ufed in chancery as at law, nor may advantage be taken for mifpleading, or want of form, fo as the fubftance of the matter be fufficiently difclofed in confcience. *Diverf. Cur'* 106. 9 *E.* 4. 15. 24 *E.* 3. 45. 14 *E.* 4. 7. 37 *H.* 6. 43. 29 *Aff.* 13.

30. *Chancery not to be oufted of its jurifdiction.*

1. ONE may not fue in the chancery of *Chefter*, for a thing which in intereft concerns the chancellor there; for that he may not be his own judge; therefore in this cafe the party ought to fue in the chancery of *England*, for otherwife there fhould be a failure of right. *Ro. Abr.* 374.

2. In chancery, between Sir *John Egerton* and *The earl of Darby*, *Chamberlain of Chefter, and others*, for a farm in that county, Refolved, by the lord chancellor, the chief juftice of *England*, the mafter of the rolls, *Doderidge* and *Wynche*, juftices, 1ft, That the chamberlain of *Chefter* being fole judge of equity, cannot decree any thing wherein himfelf is party; for he cannot be judge *in propria caufa*; but where he is party the fuit fhall be heard in chancery, *coram domino rege*. 2dly, If the defendant dwelt out of the county palatine, he, who hath caufe to complain in equity, may alfo complain here in chancery; for in refpect that proceedings in chancery do bind the perfon only, if the perfon be out of the jurifdiction, the chamberlain of *Chefter* cannot relieve the party; and therefore *ne curia domini regis deficeret in juftitia exhibenda*, the fuit fhall be here in chancery, elfe the fubject fhould have good right and no remedy, which fhould be inconvenient: and this purfues the reafon of the common law, *&c.* although an action will lie in *Wales*, yet where he, who hath caufe of action, cannot have juftice there, he fhall fue in the king's bench; for where the particular courts cannot do juftice to the parties, they fhall fue in the king's general courts at *Weftminfter*, &c. In all cafes where it appears to the court, that thofe, who have liberty to take cognizance, do fail of right, as in matters of foreign plea, *&c.* the matter fhall be determined in the general courts of *Weftminfter*. 3dly, The king cannot grant commiffion to determine any matter of equity, but it ought to be determined in chancery, which

hath had, time out of mind, jurisdiction of those matters, and that by the law, *&c.* On consideration of the certificate of lord *Dyer & al'*, justices in queen *Elizabeth*'s time, concerning the jurisdiction of the county palatine of *Chester*, it was resolved, that for things transitory, though within the county palatine, the plaintiff may alledge them to be done in any place within *England*, and the defendant may not plead to the jurisdiction of the court, that they were done within the county palatine. 12 *Co.* 110. See *Dyer* 202, 716.

3. The bill was to be relieved against the grant of an annuity or rent-charge of 300*l. per annum*, charged upon his lands in *Ireland*, setting forth, that the same was obtained from the late lord *Arglasse* here in *London*, by a fraudulent practice by the defendant, who pleaded to the jurisdiction of the court, the lands being in *Ireland.* Plea over-ruled, and the defendant ordered to pay costs for endeavouring to oust the court of its jurisdiction. 1 *Vern.* 75, 76, 77, 135.

4. The bill was for relief concerning a trust of certain lands in *Ireland*; the defendant appeared and answered, without objecting to the jurisdiction of the court. But lord chancellor objected, this court could not hold plea of lands in *Ireland*, and lord *Arglasse* and *Muschampe*, *Pitt*, and *Arnold*'s cases were cited by counsel for the plaintiff; but lord chancellor over-ruled them because of the fraudulent bargains in lord *Arglasse*'s case made in *England:* and there could be no failure of justice in the present case; for they might have a *subpoena* out of this court returnable in the chancery of *Ireland*, as in cases between masters and apprentices in *London*; he had known *subpoenas* out of this court returnable in the mayor's court in *London* for persons who lived out of the jurisdiction; but, at the importunity of the plaintiff's counsel, gave them a week's time to search precedents: and after Sir *John Holt*, counsel *pro quer'*, cited the case of *Lake* and *Lord Ranelagh*, 8 Co. 1. in lord *Coventry*'s time, *Archer* and *Preston*, soon after the restoration, and the case of lord *Thomond* and *Spencer*, for precedents in this court, for decrees made concerning lands in *Ireland.* The defendant's counsel cited Sir *William Petytt*'s case, and the case of *The countess of Laucharte* versus *Obrian*, 24 *Car.* 2. the case of *Smith* and *Wheeler*, *&c.* After long debate, the judges concurred with his lordship, that the court had jurisdiction, and that judges in *England* were expositors of the *Irish* laws. The case of *Barnwel* and *Rochford*, a trial was directed touching a feoffment of lands in *Ireland.* Lord chancellor cited Sir *William Tirringham*'s case, decreed issue at law and changed the *Venue* to the county of *Salop.* 1 *Vern.* 405, 406. *Ro. Abr.* 597. 2 *Rep. Chan.* 188. 1 *Vern.* 167, 168.

31. *Charity to pursue the intent of the founder.*

1. A Decree of the commissioners of charitable uses was reversed for varying from the intent of the founder or donor. 2 *Mod. Ca.* 64, 65.

2. On exceptions to a decree of commissioners, the chancellor must decree according to equity, and the true intent and meaning of the donors and founders. *Du. Ch. Uses* 127.

3. A man devised 50*l. per annum*, for a lecture in polemical or casuistical divinity, so as the reader was a bachelor or doctor in divinity, and fifty years of age, and would read five lectures every term, and at the end

of each term deliver fair copies thereof to be kept in the univerſity; and in default of ſuch lecturer, he gave the ſaid 50*l. per annum* to ——— college in *Oxon.* Now the univerſity of *Cambridge*, with the conſent of the heir at law, would have mitigated the rigour of the qualification, *viz.* That a man of forty, and three lectures each term, and to deliver copies once a year. But the lord chancellor held them to the letter of the charity, and ſaid that the heir had no power to alter the diſpoſition made by his anceſtor. 1 *Vern.* 55, 56.

4. Lord *Rich*, founder of the hoſpital, among other rules, directs no leaſes ſhould be made for longer than 21 years, and the old rent to be reſerved, and no more, and that the fine ſhould not exceed two years value. The farm of *B.* part of the hoſpital lands, had been leaſed accordingly at 18*l. per annum*, and ſome corn rent, but the price of proviſion increaſing, the hoſpital (40.) made a leaſe, reſerving the old rent, but took a deed of covenant from the leſſee to pay an additional rent of 32*l. per annum*, over and above the reſerved rent. In (59.) the hoſpital, at the recommendation of lord *Warwick*, made a leaſe to *Atwood* ſenior, for 21 years, at the old rent of 18*l. per annum*, and by deed of covenant the leſſee covenanted to pay 32*l. per annum*, additional rent, and the hoſpital covenanted from time to time to renew, till the term was made up ſixty years, and in (79.) made a new leaſe accordingly; in (82.) the leaſe was renewed at the old rent, and an indorſement on the back of the deed of covenant of (59.) that, during the term of the laſt leaſe, the leſſee would pay additional rent. Sir *John Freacke* who had purchaſed of *Atwood*, brought a bill to have his leaſe renewed, purſuant to the covenant in (59.) and upon hearing, his bill was diſmiſſed; the covenant to renew till the term made up ſixty years, was contrary to the rule of the founder; whereupon Sir *John* refuſed to pay the additional rent, but was decreed to pay it, being on a different foundation; the additional rent being on account of the price of proviſions being dearer, and the further leaſes were in conſideration of the money to be laid out in the improvement of the premiſſes, that Sir *John* paying the ſame might enjoy for the remainder of the 21 years. 1 *Vern.* 410, 411, 422.

5. The caſe was, Dr. *Radcliffe*, the late phyſician, by will deviſed 300*l. per annum* to two perſons to be choſen by the archbiſhop of *Canterbury* and certain other truſtees out of *Univerſity* college in *Oxon*, which ſum he directed to be paid them for ten years for their maintainance, five years whereof they were to ſpend in *England*, in the ſtudy of phyſic, and the other five abroad; the defendant was one ſo choſen, and ſtudied here according to the direction of the will, and for that time received his ſalary; but after he did not go abroad on account of his ill ſtate of health, and thereupon *anno* 1730 he reſigned to the truſtees, who accepted his reſignation, and choſe another in his room *anno* 1735; the preſent information was exhibited againſt the defendant that he might account for five years ſalary, by him thus received. Mr. *Fazakerly* for the defendant argued, that in a late caſe, which came before the houſe of lords upon an appeal, their lordſhips were of opinion that the word *maintenance* included education, and therefore though that word was uſed in the preſent will, education muſt be intended by it as implied; he alſo argued that when the defendant had ſpent half his time in his education here in *England*, and was prevented by

 ill

ill health from going abroad, and thereupon had reſigned, and his reſignation accepted, and another choſen in his room, he ſubmitted it, that the preſent bill muſt be thought an unreaſonable one. My lord chancellor was of that opinion, and ſaid the name of the caſe cited was *Gandy* and *Anſtis*, ſo diſmiſſed the information. 2 *Ju. Eccl.* 157, 158.

6. The intention or will of founders or donors ſhall bind the king though not named, as appears *in ſtatuto Templorum, anno* 17 *E.* 2. where it is ſaid *ita ſemper quod pia et celeberrima voluntas donatorum in omnibus teneatur et expleatur, ut perpetuo ſanctiſſime perſeveret.* And the act *de donis* is notable to this purpoſe, for there it appears that it was both neceſſary and profitable that the will of the donor ſhould be obſerved; the words of which act to the preſent purpoſe are, *propter quod dominus rex perpendens quod neceſſarium et utile eſt, &c. apponere remedium* (and what was that remedy?) *ſtatuit quod voluntas donatoris in charta doni ſui manifeſte expreſſa de caetero obſervetur*, which binds the king himſelf, as in lord *Berkley*'s caſe, where it is ſaid, that men ought to obſerve the intent or will of others, and that to break them is very bad, &c. 11 *Co.* 72. *b.* 73. *a.*

7. See 8 *Co.* 131. *b.* *Skin.* 491. 1 *Vern.* 42.

32. *Children are de ſanguine patris et matris, ſed pater et mater non ſunt de ſanguine puerorum.*

VIDE rule, *Pater et mater et puer ſunt una caro.*

33. *Clerici non ponantur in officio.*

General.

1. HOLY church ſhall enjoy her liberties in quietneſs. *Stat.* 14 *E.* 3. *cap.* 1.

2. A prieſt not to be arreſted doing divine ſervice. *Stat.* 50 *E.* 3. 5. 1 *R.* 2. 15.

3. The common law, to the intent that eccleſiaſtical perſons might the better diſcharge their duty in celebration of divine ſervice, and not be entangled with temporal buſineſs, hath provided, that if any of them be choſen to any temporal office, he may have his writ *de clerico infra ſacros ordines conſtituto non eligendo in officium, &c.* and thereof be diſcharged. *Co. Lit.* 96.

4. If a man, who holds certain lands or tenements, by reaſon of his ſaid lands or tenements be elected into the office of bailiff, beadle, or reeve, or other like office, if he be a clerk, or within ſacred orders, he ought not to be elected to ſuch office; and if he be notwithſtanding ſo elected, &c. he may have a writ to diſcharge him, in the form in *Fitzh. Nat. Brev.* 175. (*B.*) and in the *Regiſter.*

Particular caſes.

5. Dr. *Lee* having lands within the level, was made an expenditor by the commiſſioners of ſewers; whereupon he prayed his writ of privilege in this court, and it was granted him; for the *Regiſter* is *vir militans Deo*

non

non implicetur ſecularibus negotiis; and the antient law is *quod clerici non ponantur in officio.* 1 Vent. 105. Dr. *Lee*'s caſe, 1 Mod. 282. S. C.

6. A writ of privilege was prayed to be excuſed from the office of expenditor; 1ſt, becauſe being an eccleſiaſtical perſon he ought not to be put in ſuch office; 2dly, for that all the lands he had in the level, are in leaſe for 99 years. Writ granted by *Rainsford* and *Moreton*, they only being in court. *Moreton* for the firſt cauſe, and *Rainsford* for the ſecond. 1 *Lev.* 303.

7. *Raymond* prayed a *Mandamus* to exempt him as archdeacon from being expenditor to commiſſioners of ſewers, being a ſecular office, and inferior to his degree; on 2 *Inſt.* 3. *&c.* court granted it *niſi.* 2 *Keb.* 693.

8. *Cur:* The clergy are liable to all public charges impoſed by act of parliament; as the principal caſe was for not ſending his cart and horſes to the repairs of the highways, *ſur le ſtat. ch.* 2. 1 Vent. 273.

34. *Colleges and other like bodies not to alien but* ſub modo *the allowance of the law.*

General.

1. STAT. 1 *Eliz.* was made for the benefit of ſucceſſors, that their poſſeſſions might not be charged or impoveriſhed; wherefore all ſuch grants as are againſt the ſucceſſor, are void. *Cro. Ca.* 49.

2. Stat. 1 *Eliz.* was always conſtrued to redreſs the miſchiefs which were at law, upon grants confirmed by deans and chapters, to the prejudice of ſucceſſors. 5 *Co.* 2, 3. 8 *Co.* 49. *Cro. Ca.* 50, 51.

3. At a parliament holden *Mich.* 43 & 44 *Eliz.* for conſideration of a bill for confirmation of conveyances made by ſubjects to the queen, and of letters patent from the queen to ſubjects, reſolved by the judges, aſſiſtants to the lords of parliament of the upper houſe, That leaſes made to the queen, by colleges, deans and chapters, wardens of hoſpitals, or others having ſpiritual or eccleſiaſtical livings, againſt the proviſion of the act 13 *Eliz. cap.* 10. are reſtrained thereby, as well as leaſes made to other perſons. 1ſt, Becauſe they are diſabled by the act to make any leaſe, gift, grant, *&c.* but only in the form by the ſtatute preſcribed; and if they cannot make eſtates, the queen can take none from them, *&c.* 2dly, The ſtatute 1 *Eliz.* which reſtrains biſhops from making eſtates, hath a ſpecial proviſion that they may make them to the queen, which proves that had not ſuch proviſion been made for the queen, as the act diſables biſhops to make eſtates, the queen might not take eſtates from them, contrary to the proviſion of the ſaid act. But no ſuch proviſion is in the ſaid act of 13 *Eliz.* 3dly, In divers caſes the queen is bound by act of parliament, though not named, nor bound by expreſs words; and therefore in all ſtatutes made to ſuppreſs tort, or to take away fraud, or to prevent the decay of religion, the king is bound though not named; for religion, juſtice and truth, are the ſupporters of the crown and diadems of kings, and therefore it is agreed 35 *H.* 6. 60. that the king ſhall be bound by the ſtatute *W.* 2. 1 *Eliz.* *&c.* *Summa ratio eſt quae pro religione facit.* 5 Co. 14. a. b.

* 4. By ſtatute 18 *Eliz.* all leaſes made by colleges, in which one third of the rent is not reſerved in corn, are declared void. And the corn ſo re-

ſerved

ferved is ordered to be applied to the ufe of the college, on pain of deprivation of the head or governor, and all others confenting to any mifapplication. See cafe *The Bifhop of Ely* verfus *Bently*, D. D. 6 *May* 1732, before the houfe of lords.

5. All innovations within the mifchief of the acts againft the impoverifhing of fucceffors, dilapidations, and decay of fpiritual livings, and hofpitality, *&c.* are by favourable conftruction taken to be within the laws provided againft fuch abufes. 5 *Co.* 14.

6. In the principal cafe the lords of parliament, being informed that divers deans and chapters, colleges, *&c.* had made leafes to the queen, as pretending the queen was not bound by the faid act 13 *Eliz.* caufed a claufe to be added in the firft branch of the act of confirmation, that it fhould not extend to make any leafe, grant, *&c.* good to the queen by any ecclefiaftical perfons, *&c.* who had not power by the laws and ftatutes of the realm to make it, which is more than was in the act of confirmation 18 *Eliz.* which was made to manifeft the matter to the laity; for it was held by the judges that the general words of the act 18 *Eliz.* hath not enabled fuch ecclefiaftical perfons to make leafes, or eftates to the queen, which by the faid act 13 *Eliz.* were upon good and important confiderations difabled. 5 *Co.* 15. *a. b.*

Particular cafes.

7. It was adjudged between the dean and chapter, and bifhop of *Hereford* and *Ballard*, that the grant of a next avoidance of a benefice by the dean and chapter was within the purview of the ftatute againft their alienations. So if they grant a rent-charge out of their poffeffions, it is within the equity, *&c.* 5 *Co.* 15. *a.*

8. Where an archdeacon makes a leafe for three lives according to the acts, and the leffee leafes for 100 years, and the archdeacon, bifhop and dean and chapter confirm it, yet it fhall not bind the fucceffor. So where the parfon of *Wefton* demifed his rectory to *Hodges*, then parfon of the fame rectory for 50 years, who affigned to *Throkmorton*, the bifhop confirms, living the leffor, and good: in which laft cafe it was refolved, that forafmuch as the faid leafe was before the ftatute 13 *Eliz.* and fo not reftrained by it, the confirmation made after the act to perfect the leafe, was not within the purview or intention of it, *&c.* 5 *Co.* 15. *a.*

9. A grant of the officialty of an archdeacon or commiffary to a bifhop to two, where they were only grantable to one for life, and being granted in reverfion, is void by the ftatute againft fucceffors, for the ftatutes reftrain all grants againft the fucceffor, befides grants of neceffity, and leafes for three lives or 21 years, where the antient rent is referved; and all other grants, as well of offices as other things not warranted by the ftatutes are made void againft the fucceffors. Vide 10 *Co.* 60. 5 *Co.* 14. and cafe between *Vaughan* and *Crompton*, 14 *Ja.* where it was adjudged, that a grant in reverfion of the office of *Regifter* of *Hereford*, was void, *&c. Cro. Ca.* 259, 49, 50. The office of parkerfhip and ftewardfhip, and other offices which are of neceffary ufe to bifhops, are allowed to be grantable, though they are new offices and new fees, if reafonable; and of the neceffity of them, and of the reafonablenefs of the fees, that court fhall judge. *Cro. Ca.* 48, 49, 50.

K 10. The

10. The offices of the officialty of an archdeaconry and of commiſſary of a biſhop, are grantable by ſtatutes 1 *Eliz.* and 13 *Eliz.* becauſe, as was pretended, not parcel of the poſſeſſions of the biſhopric or archdeaconry; ſo as they could not have any profit by them, and ſo not reſtrained by the ſtatutes. Reſolved they were within the words and intent of the ſtatutes. *Cro. Ca.* 258, 259.

11. Vide *Cro. Eliz.* 18. 11 *Co.* 66. *Magdalen College*'s caſe. *Hob.* 220. *Anne Needler*'s caſe.

35. *Communis error facit quaſi jus.*

ACcording to *Hanke*, 11 *H.* 4. 37. *Papa omnia poteſt*, and *Hill*, there 77. acknowledgeth him *haut et grand ſovereigne*, from whom all eccleſiaſtics have their power. And *Thirning* there calls him *Apoſtle*; from whence it followeth by conſequence, though upon a falſe ground, that his eccleſiaſtical acts muſt be allowed lawful, as upon the clearing the king's ſupremacy, when the clouds of ignorance were diſperſed, the conſequence of his power was as clearly declared, 25 *H.* 8. *cap.* 21. *ſect.* 2. and yet the crown always kept a poſſeſſion of it's natural power of diſpenſations *in ſpiritualibus*, 11 *H.* 4. 60. to retain a benefice with a biſhopric, and 11 *H.* 7. 12. double benefices; and ſo it came to this that *communis error facit quaſi jus*; when it aroſe from the error and ſufferance of ſtate and of courts of juſtice both; for *res judicata pro veritate habetur*, though it be not ſo indeed. *Hob.* 147. 2 *R.* 3. 7.

36. *Conditions extinct in part, all extinct.*

1. WHERE a condition diſpenſed in part, extinguiſhes wholly, as being odious in law. The caſe of revocation is clean contrary. *Hob.* 313.

2. See 3 *Ch. Ca.* 67, 70, 86, 88.

37. *Condition none may take advantage of, but who is either party or privy to it.*

IF a man give lands of his own meer motion to *H.H.* and to his heirs by indenture, upon condition that he ſhall yearly, at a certain day, pay to *J.S.* out of the ſame lands a certain rent, and if he do not, that then it ſhall be lawful for *J.S.* to enter, *&c.* if the rent in this caſe be not paid, yet may not *J.S.* enter, for there is an antient maxim in the law, that no man ſhall take advantage of a condition, but he that is party or privy to the condition, and this man is not party nor privy; wherefore he ſhall not have advantage of it. And though the feoffee intended, if the rent was not paid, that the ſtranger ſhould enter, yet as that is againſt law, the intent is void, but the feoffor himſelf may re-enter; for when the feoffment was made upon condition that the feoffee would pay a rent to a ſtranger, therein was concluded, that if the rent was not paid the feoffor might enter; for the words imply ſo much though it be not expreſſed; and when the feoffor went further, and ſaid that if the ſtranger was not paid he

 ſhould

ſhould enter, theſe words were void in law, and ſo the effect of the deed ſtood upon the firſt words; wherefore the feoffor may re-enter in law and conſcience, but *J. S.* in neither. *Doct. & Stud. lib.* 2. *cap.* 20.

38. *Condition to avoid a freehold cannot be pleaded without deed.*

THough the rule be, that a condition to avoid a freehold cannot be pleaded without deed, yet of a chattel it is otherwiſe. *Doct. & Stud. lib.* 1. *cap.* 8.

39. *Conditions which go to the defeazance of eſtates are to be taken ſtrictly.*

VIDE rules, *Tranſit tenementum cum onere. Limitations in reſtraint of marriage,* &c.

40. *Conditions precedent muſt be literally performed, not ſo of ſubſequent conditions, where the court can make compenſation.*

ROGERS married his niece to the plaintiff's father, and having lands to the value of 1500*l. per ann.* deviſed them to the defendant and others, to pay debts, and after for the uſe of the plaintiff and his heirs male; and declared his will, that the plaintiff ſhould have no benefit, unleſs Sir *F. Popham*, the plaintiff's father, ſhould ſettle on the plaintiff two thirds of his eſtate, ſettled on the ſaid father on his marriage, and on default thereof deviſed the ſame to his ſaid truſtees diſcharged of the ſaid truſt; the father, to give his ſon title, makes a ſettlement with power of revocation; the truſtees brought their bill againſt Sir *Francis* to compel him to make a ſettlement according to *Rogers*'s will; he anſwered he had made a ſettlement, but if it was not ſufficient, he was ready to make ſuch an one as the court ſhould direct; but before any thing done, Sir *Francis* died, leaving a will whereby he revoked all former ſettlements, and deviſed all his eſtate to the plaintiff, his ſon, firſt to pay debts, then to the plaintiff for life, then to his firſt, ſecond, third, and ſo on to his tenth ſon in tail, *&c.* which whole eſtate was alledged to be 6000 *l. per annum*, and the debts not above 30000 *l.* the plaintiff brought this bill to diſcover what debts the truſtees had paid, and to have an account, and be let into the benefit of the deviſe: it was ſaid the truſt was executed by the ſtatute, the words being *In truſt for the uſe and benefit of the plaintiff*, and therefore he might ſeek his remedy at law, which was true, but ſtill he was proper here in this court. (*Fry* and *Porter*'s caſe cited, and 1 *Salk.* 236.) *Lord chancellor:* This is no truſt, but an eſtate veſted at law, and well executed by the ſtatute of *Uſes*; it is a condition ſubſequent; precedent conditions muſt be literally performed, and this court will not veſt an eſtate where by reaſon of a condition precedent it will not veſt at law: but of conditions ſubſequent, which

are

are to deveft an eftate, it is otherwife; and there is a difference where the court can compenfate in damages for non-performance, where it is juft and equitable to relieve, but where it cannot give damages, there it will not relieve. If the fubftance of a condition is performed, though not the precife words, it is fufficient: but if the quantity of the eftate fhould fall fhort, that might make a new cafe, and referred to a mafter that point, and alfo to take account, *&c.* 1 *Vern.* 79. *&c.* and 167. *Vide poft.* rule, *Law favours juftice and truth*, &c. cafe, 22.

41. *Confcience muft always be grounded upon fome law.*

1. VIDE *Doct. & Stud. lib.* 2. *cap.* 14, 15. *cap.* 49. *cap.* 50. *Ca. Rep.* 11.

2. See rule, *Aequitas fequitur legem*, cafe 4.

42. *Confcience never refifteth the law of man, nor addeth to it, but where fuch law of man is againft reafon, or the law of God.*

1. VIDE *Doct. & Stud. lib.* 2. *cap.* 14. *cap.* 15. *cap.* 49. *cap.* 50. *Cary's Rep.* 11.

2. See rule, *Aequitas fequitur legem.*

43. *Confenfus eft voluntas multorum, ad quos res pertinet, fimul juncta.*

DEAN and chapter are not confined to their chapter-houfe, but may affemble and do their acts elfewhere; and therefore it is held 21 *E.* 4. 26. that where a deed bears date *in domo capitulari*, averment might be, that this deed was delivered elfewhere, to which intent in 27 *Aff.* 23. the cafe of the *Prior alien*, yet they ought to affemble in fome certain place, and that the major part be there prefent when they give their confent to any common acts; alfo the confent of the major part of the chapter ought to be given at the fame time, *fimul & femel*, and not fcatteringly and at feveral days; for it is not a confent, or not properly fo if not *fimul*; for *Confenfus eft voluntas multorum, ad quos res pertinet, fimul juncta*, and therefore *fi confentiant ut finguli & non collegialiter, cum actus per communem confenfum debeat expediri, non valet*, *&c.* Dav. 48. a. b.

44. *Confenfus non concubitus facit matrimonium, et confentire non poffunt ante annos nubiles.*

1. RESolved, that an infant within the age of confent fhall be in ward; for that the marriage is incompleat; for that to every marriage there ought to be confent; for *confenfus non concubitus facit matrimonium, et confentire non poffunt ante annos nubiles.* 6 Co. 22. a. b.

2. In

2. In the caſe of *M.* who was ſued in the court Chriſtian for marrying his wife's ſiſter's daughter, a prohibition was awarded, becauſe ſuch marriage is not forbid by the *Levitical* law. *Mo.* 907.

45. *Conſtructio legis non facit injuriam.*

1. WHEN the conſtruction of an act is left to the law, the law, which abhorreth injury and wrong, will never ſo conſtrue it, as it ſhall work a wrong. *Co. Lit.* 42. *a.*

2. *Legis conſtructio non facit injuriam*, and therefore if tenant for life maketh a leaſe for life generally, this ſhall be taken, by conſtruction of law, an eſtate for his own life who made the leaſe; for if it ſhould be a leaſe for the life of the leſſee, that would be a wrong to him in the reverſion. And ſo it is if tenant in tail make a leaſe for life generally, the law ſhall conſtrue this to be ſuch a leaſe as he may lawfully make, and that is for term of his own life; for if it ſhould be for the leſſee's life it would be a diſcontinuance, and conſequently the eſtate which ſhould paſs, by conſtruction of law, would work a wrong. *Co. Lit.* 183. *a. b.* 42. *a.* Yet if in the premiſſes lands are letten or a rent granted, the general intendment is, that an eſtate for life paſſeth, but if the *habendum* limit the ſame for years, or at will, this qualifies the general intendment of the premiſſes, and the reaſon of it is this maxim, *Quaelibet conceſſio fortiſſimè contra donatorem interpretanda eſt*, which is to be ſo underſtood that no wrong be done thereby. *Co. Lit.* 183. *a. Therefore on the maxim, that every man's deed is to be taken moſt ſtrongly againſt him, it is that the grantor ſhall have as large an eſtate as the other could lawfully grant. And the other maxim is to be ſo conſtrued, that it be without prejudice to another*, &c.

3. It is a general rule, whenever the words of a deed, or of the parties without deed, may have a double intendment, and one ſtands with law and right, and the other is wrongful and againſt the law, the intendment that ſtandeth with law ſhall be taken. *Co. Lit.* 42. *a. b.* 183. *a. b.*

4. To ſhut up this point, it hath been adjudged, that where tenant in tail made a leaſe to another for life generally, and after releaſed to the leſſee and his heirs, though between the tenant in tail and his leſſee a fee-ſimple paſſed, yet after the death of the leſſor, the entry of the iſſue in tail was lawful, which could not be if it had been a leaſe for life of the leſſee, for then by the releaſe it had been a diſcontinuance executed. *Co. Lit.* 42. *b.*

46. *Conſtructions to be according to what was the beginning.*

1. IF a ſervant leave his maſter's ſervice, and after kill his maſter, upon a malice that he bore him whilſt he was his ſervant, this is petit treaſon. 33 *Aſſ. pl.* 7.

2. The king being ſeiſed of the manor of *Beverly* in *Yorkſhire* in fee *in jure coronae*, a ſtranger erected a ſhop on a vacant plot of the manor, and took the profit of it without paying any rent to the crown; and after the queen granted the manor in fee to the earl of *Leiceſter*, who never either entered or took any rent for it: after the occupier of the ſhop died in poſſeſſion, and his ſon entered: this is no deſcent to toll the patentee's entry;

L for

for by his firſt erecting of the ſhop he could gain nothing againſt the king. *Dy*. 266. *b*.

47. *Conſtructions to be according to what was the cauſe.*

1. A Man makes me ſwear to bring him money to ſuch a place, or elſe he will kill me; I bring it him accordingly; this is felony in him. 44 *E*. 3. 14. *b*.

2. So if he makes me ſwear to ſurrender my eſtate unto him, and I do ſo afterwards; this is a diſſeiſin to me. 14 *Aſſ. pl.* 19 *Hil.* 15 *E*. 3.

3. So if one is impriſoned to make an obligation of a future day at another place, which he being at large accordingly doth; yet he ſhall avoid it by dureſs. 6 *R*. 2. 8 *H*. 6. 38 *H*. 6. 13.

4. Outlawry of treſpaſs is no forfeiture of lands, as outlawry of felony is, for though the not appearing be the cauſe of outlawry in both, yet the force of the outlawries ſhall be eſteemed according to the heinouſneſs of the offence, which is the principal cauſe and foundation of the proceſs. 3 *E*. 3. 84.

5. A man and feme ſole have a villain, and intermarry, and the villain purchaſeth lands, they cannot have the land by intireties, but by moieties jointly or in common, as they had the villain. *Fi. Law Engl.* 10.

48. *Conſtructions to be* ſecundum aequalitatem rationis.

1. THIS equality of reaſon in an eſpecial manner ſhineth and ſheweth forth itſelf in the conſtruction of ſtatutes; in extending things there provided, to miſchiefs in equal degree, whereof there are many pregnant examples; and alſo in the guiding the grounds and maxims of things which newly ariſe, by the rule of the common law. *Fi. Ley* 6. *b*. 15. *a*.

2. At common law uſes were nothing, but now being become as inheritances, they are eſteemed as other inheritances; ſo as there ſhall be a *poſſeſſio fratris* of an uſe. And the uſe of the land in *borough Engliſh* ſhall deſcend to the youngeſt ſon. 5 *E*. 4. 7. But it ſhall not extend to collaterals, as tenancy by the curteſy, dower, deſcent to toll entry, *&c*. 4 *Co*. 22.

3. A recognizance is acknowledged by the anceſtor, or judgment is obtained againſt him in an action of debt, and he dies ſeiſed of two acres, one whereof is held in *Borough Engliſh*; or if he hath iſſue two daughters who make partition, or if he die *ſans* iſſue, ſo as part of his land deſcend to the heir on the part of the father, and part to the heir on the part of the mother, in all theſe caſes, if one only be charged, he ſhall have contribution againſt the others; for they are *in aequali jure*. 3 Co. 12. b.

4. Two, four or more ſeverally ſeiſed of lands join in recognizance, all their lands ſhall be equally extended. 3 *Co*. 13.

49. *Conſtructions to be with equity and moderation, therefore to moderate the rigour of law.*

1. THE words of the law are not the law, but the juſt meaning thereof is it; *ratio legis eſt anima legis*, and ſometimes the ſenſe is to

 be

be taken larger than the letter of the law, and ſometimes it may not be extended ſo far as the letter, and equity is the judge thereof, which enlargeth or diminiſheth the letter according to what is equal in the caſe: this method of correcting the letter of the law is often neceſſary, and frequently uſed. As when an act of parliament is made, that whoever doth ſuch an act ſhall be a felon, and as ſuch ſhall die; yet if a man *non ſane memorie*, or an infant of tender age, who hath not diſcretion, do the act, they ſhall not be deemed felons, or put to death. So if an act was made that all, who receive, or give meat or drink, or other aſſiſtance or ſuccour, to one doing ſuch an act, ſhall be acceſſories to his act, and be put to death, if he was conuſant of the fact; yet if one doing this act come to his own wife, who, though ſhe know the matter, receives, and gives him meat and drink, ſhe ſhall not be acceſſory or guilty of felony; for in the generality of the ſaid words of the law, men of *non ſane memorie*, infants, femes covert, were not included in the intent: ſo equity corrects the generality of the law in theſe caſes, and abridges the words, *&c.* *Plow. Com.* 465. *a.* *&c.*

2. It is no treſpaſs for a man moderately to correct his apprentice. 21 *E.* 4. 53.

3. Nor to take and carry away another man's wife againſt the huſband's conſent, if it be to a lawful intent; as to ſue a divorce againſt her huſband; or to have the peace againſt him before a juſtice of peace. 21 *H.* 7. 13.

Conſuetudo. See *Cuſtom.*

50. *Conſuetudo eſt altera lex.*

CUSTOM is the ſoul and life of copyhold eſtates, for either without cuſtom, or if the copyholder break the cuſtom, he is at the will of the lord; yet obſerving the ſame, he is as well intitled to his eſtate according to the cuſtom, as he who hath a freehold at law; for *Conſuetudo eſt altera lex.* 4 Co. 21, 23.

51. *Conſuetudo eſt optima interpres legum.*

THE judges of the law conſtrue the grants of the king beneficially for his honour, and the benefit of the ſubject; and not ſtrictly or literally to the ſubverſion of ſuch grants. 6 *Co.* 5. Sir *John Mollins*'s caſe.

52. *Conſuetudo ex certa cauſa rationabili uſitata privat communem legem.*

1. CUSTOM in intendment of law is ſuch an uſage, that hath obtained *vim legis*, and is in truth a binding law to ſuch particular place, perſon and things which it concerns: and ſuch cuſtom may not be granted or eſtabliſhed by grant of the crown, 49 *E.* 3. 3. *a.* nor even by act of parliament, but is *jus non ſcriptum*, and made by the people of ſuch a place only, where the cuſtom runs, for where the people have found any act or thing to be good and beneficial, and apt and agreeable to their nature

ture and difpofition, they have ufed and practiced the fame immemorially, and fo, by frequent iteration and multiplication of fuch act, cuftom cometh, and being ufed time out of mind, obtaineth the force of a law. And fo the rule 44 *E.* 3. 19. is true, that no law fhall bind the people, but fuch as is made by their confent, for confent may be expreffed as well *facto* as *verbo*, and that which is expreffed *facto* is ftronger, and that which is expreffed by many acts, and continual acts of the fame kind is cuftom; and fo briefly cuftom is a reafonable act iterated, multiplied and continued *per le people de temps dont memorie ne cont.* And this is the definition of a cuftom which hath the force of law. And every cuftom is not unreafonable which is contrary to any particular rule or maxim of pofitive law; for *Confuetudo ex certa caufa ufitata privat com. legem*, as the cuftom of *gavelkind* and *borough Englifh* are againft the maxims of defcent of inheritance: fo the cuftom of *Kent*, The father to the bough the fon to the plough, *&c.* and every cuftom which may be hurtful to the intereft of a private perfon, is not therefore void, *&c.* *Da.* 32. *a. b.*

2. *Confuetudo ex certa caufa rationabili ufitata privat communem legem, quia confuetudo contra rationem introducta potius ufurpatio quam confuetudo appellari debet. Confuetudo praefcripta et legitima vincit legem.* Co. Lit. 113. a.

3. Cuftom ought to be certain; for *incerta pro nullis habentur.* Da. 33. a.

4. It ought to be certain, reafonable, and ufed with continuance. *Da.* 33. *a. b.*

5. Cuftom is fometimes admitted to derogate from the common law; for *confuetudo bona de caufa ufitata et approbata privat communem legem.* Calthorpe's *Readings of Copyholds, fo.* 20. *Da.* 33. a.

6. By cuftom a man may devife that his executors may fell the tenements he hath in fee-fimple, for a certain fum to diftribute for his foul; here the executors may fell to whom they pleafe, and ouft the heir; for a cuftom ufed upon a certain reafonable caufe, depriveth the common law. *Lit. fect.* 169. *Confuetudo fine veritate eft vetuftas erroris. Continuance without truth is the antiquity of Error.* In *Littleton*'s time a man could not devife his lands but by cuftom; but now he may do it generally by ftatutes 32 *H.* 8. *cap.* 2. 34 *H.* 8. *cap.* 5. *&c.*

7. See 4 *Co. Copyhold Cafes.* *Calthorpe's Readings*, &c.

53. *Confuetudo femel reprobata non poteft amplius induci.*

General.

1. CUSTOM ought to have continuance *fans* interruption for time immemorial; for if it hath been difcontinued within the time of memory, the cuftom is gone. *Da.* 33. *b.*

2. When a man hath a lawful eafement by prefcription, another cuftom immemorial may not take it away. 9 *Co.* 58.

Particular cafes.

3. As if a copyhold is leafed by the lord for life or years, according to the courfe of the common law, it fhall never after be demifed as a copyhold according to the cuftom; for as continuance maketh a cuftom, fo difcontinuance deftroyeth it. *Nihil tam conveniens eft naturali aequitati, quam unumquodque diffolvi eo ligamine quo ligatum eft.* Da. 33. a. b.

4. Though a *Modus* for tithes had been varied by subsequent composition for sixty years, and had been once paid in kind, yet that did not destroy the *Modus.* 2 *Ju. Eccl.* 122. See the case at large 1 *Ju. Eccl.* 449, *&c.*

54. *Consuetudo vincit communem legem.*

CUSTOM and immemorial usage may create and consolidate inheritances; for *consuetudo vincit communem legem.* 4 Co. 21. a.

55. *Contingency may not depend upon a contingency.*

1. IN the case at bar the demise made to *Thomas* depended upon a contingency precedent, and upon a meer uncertainty, so that until that happened, the interest or term intended to be demised is not certain, nor the land bound by it. And as *Thomas* died before it was reduced to any certainty, the lease could never take effect, or vest in his executors or administrators, for the reasons given in arguing the cause. It was also objected against the demise to *Thomas*, that if he had been alive, yet it could never have vested in him; for he died before *Ralph* or *William*, and they survived *Elizabeth*, and by the express condition precedent, *Ralph* might not take unless *Elizabeth* died within the term, and *William* could not take unless *Ralph* died *infra terminum praedict'*, which is as much as to say, that if *Ralph* died before *Elizabeth*; for the term is for 80 years, if she should so long live, and *Thomas* might not take unless *William* died in the life of *Elizabeth*, sc. *infra terminum praedict'*, and *William* and *Ralph* also survived *Elizabeth*, so that both contingencies failing, *viz.* the death of *Ralph*, and the death of *William*, in the life of *Elizabeth*, the demise to *Thomas* could never commence; and the demises to *Ralph* and *William* are both void, yet the limitation precedent, (*viz.* the death of *Ralph* and *William* in the life-time of *Elizabeth*,) as to the lease to *Thomas*, is not void; for that his interest might depend upon both contingencies, and so was the intention of the parties, which was affirmed *per totam curiam*; and lord chief justice *Popham*, put this case, If *A.* demise to *B.* for 30 years, after the death of *C.* if *C.* die within 10 years next coming; if *C.* survive the 10 years, the term shall never take effect. So in the principal case his lordship said, the lease to *Thomas* could not commence, unless *William* died before *Elizabeth*; but he survived her, therefore the lease to *Thomas* could never commence. And his lordship further said, the lease to *Thomas* was void for another reason, namely, that it might not commence upon a contingency which depended upon another contingency; as here the demise to *Thomas* depended upon the contingency annexed to the demise made to *William*, and the lease to *William* depended upon the contingency annexed to the demise to *Ralph*; and to this purpose he cited 12 *Ass. pl.* 5. *A.* leased to *B. sur condition*, that if *A.* paid to *B.* 10*l.* within such a certain time, that he should re-enter, and if he did not pay before the day, and *B.* paid him 10*l.* at a day after, that he should have fee: they neither pay the money, and after both days *A.* enters, and *B.* ousts him, *A.* brings assise and took nothing by his writ. 1 *Co.* 153. *The Rector of* Chedington's *case, ove tout le case.*

2. *Nicholas Searle* devised to his niece *Mary Bryant* and the heirs male of her body, upon condition, and provided she intermarry with, and have

iſſue male by one ſurnamed *Searle*; and in default of both conditions, he deviſed to *Elizabeth Bryant* in the ſame manner, and in default thereof he deviſed to *George Searle* for 60 years, if he ſo long lived; remainder to the heirs male of the body of the ſaid *George*, and their iſſue male for ever. It was adjudged, 1ſt, That the deviſe to *Mary* was a good deviſe of an eſtate-tail, and ſo was the eſtate to *Elizabeth*, but it is an eſpecial intail, it is to her and to the heirs male of her body, begotten by a *Searle*, which is a middle intail, not the higheſt nor the loweſt; for it might have been to her and the heirs of her body, begotten by *George Searle*, which had been more particular, yet this is a good eſtate-tail within the ſtatute *de donis*; for it is within the reaſon of the ſtatute. 2dly, The words *upon condition, &c.* though they are expreſs words of condition, ſhall be taken to be a limitation. So it is held 1 *Ven.* 199, 202, and chief juſtice *Holt* ſaid, he ſaw no reaſon why they might not be ſo conſtrued in a deed, though the law had not been carried ſo far. And ſo the ſenſe is, if ſhe have no iſſue by a *Searle*, upon her death, the eſtate ſhall remain over. 3dly, That the eſtate-tail of *Mary* and *Elizabeth*, or either of them, doth not ceaſe by marrying with one who is not a *Searle*, for the remainder over is in default of both conditions, and in the mean time it is limited to her, and the heirs male of her body, and ſhe may ſurvive the firſt huſband, and marry a *Searle*, and ſo there is a poſſibility as long as ſhe lives. If the eſtate had been to *Mary* and the heirs male of her body, by a *Searle* to be begotten, provided and upon condition if ſhe do marry any but a *Searle*, that then it ſhall remain, and be to *George Searle* and his heirs. *A common recovery ſuffered before marriage would not have bar'd the eſtate-tail and remainders; and though ſhe after married with another, it ſhould not have avoided the recovery.* And the court took a difference between a collateral condition and a condition that runs with the land. If the donor reſerve a rent with a condition to re-enter, a recovery will not bar it; otherwiſe it is, if it be to re-enter for non-payment of a ſum in groſs. *Salk.* 570.

3. Vide 2 *Co.* 72. 2 *Cro.* 461. *Perk. Par.* 745. 3 *Ch. Ca.* 29, 50. 1 *Mod.* 108, 111. 1 *Co. Rector of* Chedington's *caſe throughout.*

56. *Contracts are to be taken according to the intent of the parties, expreſſed by their own words.*

1. ALL contracts are to be taken according to the intent of the parties expreſſed by their own words, and if there be any doubt in the ſenſe of the words, ſuch interpretation muſt be made as is moſt ſtrong againſt the grantor or obligor, that he may not by obſcure wording of the contract find means to evade and elude it. *Gilb.* 249.

See rules, *Law regards the intention of the parties. Equity is to execute the intent of the parties. In things of election the party is to ſhew that he hath made it.*

57. *Contra negantem principia non eſt diſputandum.*

SEE rule, *Principia probant et non probantur.*

58. *Copy-*

58. *Copyhold muſt be immemorial.*

1. IF a copyhold be leaſed by the lord for life or years according to the courſe of the common law, it ſhall never after be demiſed again according to the cuſtom; for *Conſuetudo ſemel reprobata non poteſt amplius induci*; for as continuance makes a cuſtom, ſo diſcontinuance deſtroys it. *Nihil tam conveniens eſt naturali aequitati, quam unumquodque diſſolvi eo ligamine quo ligatum eſt.* Da. 33. b.

2. See 4 *Co. Of Copyholds*, Calthorp's *Readings of Copyholds.*

59. *Copyholder derives his eſtate from cuſtom, and not out of the eſtate of the lord.*

1. A Copyholder doth not derive his eſtate out of the eſtate or intereſt of the lord only; for then the copyhold eſtate ſhould ceaſe, when the eſtate of the lord determined. But it was reſolved, that the life and ſoul of a copyhold is the cuſtom of the manor; and when the grant *or admittance* is made by any one having a lawful eſtate or intereſt, the copyholder is in by the cuſtom, without any regard to the eſtate or perſon of the grantor, &c. 4 *Co.* 23. *b.* 24. *a.*

2. Where the lord of a manor, wherein are many copyholders for life, marries, and after a copyholder dies, and the lord after his coverture grants the lands again according to the cuſtom of the manor for life, and dies, the wife ſhall not avoid this grant in a writ of dower. 4 *Co.* 24. *a.*

3. So if feoffee of a manor *ſur* condition, make a voluntary grant of copyhold eſtate according to the cuſtom, and after the condition is broken, and the feoffor re-enters, yet the grant by copy ſhall ſtand. 4 *Co.* 24. *a.* Vide *Dy.* 342.

60. *Copyholder is in by him who ſurrendered, and not by the Lord.*

1. WHEN a copyholder ſurrenders to the uſe of another, and the lord admits him, now he, who is ſo admitted, is in by him who made the ſurrender, &c. for the lord is nothing but an inſtrument to make the admittance, and he, who is admitted, ſhall not be ſubject the charge or incumbrance of the lord, &c. 4 *Co.* 27. *b.*

2. When the lord hath made his admittance according to the effect of the ſurrender, nothing remains in him but the reverſion of the eſtate. 4 *Co.* 29. *b.*

3. When the tenant of a copyhold ſurrenders the land to the lord to the uſe of another, the lord by the cuſtom (which makes the law in ſuch caſe) hath but a cuſtomary power to make admittances *ſecundum formam et effectum ſurſum-redditionis*, and though the lord ſhould grant the lands to another, that would be a thing without warrant; for he ought to do it according to the ſurrender, and he who is admitted ſhall be in by him who made the ſurrender, and not by the lord; for if the lord, after ſuch ſurrender,

der, grant to *Cestuy que use* and a stranger, it shall all enure to *Cestuy que use*. So if he admitted *Cestuy que use* upon condition, the condition is void. 4 *Co.* 28. *b.*

4. When a copyholder surrenders into the hands of the lord to the use of *M.* and *K.* without limitation of any estate, they shall have but an estate for life; for as well estates as descents shall be directed by the rules of the common law, as a necessary consequence upon the custom, unless there be a special custom (which always hath been observed) within the manor, that these words *sibi et suis*, or *sibi et assignatis*, or the like, might create an estate of inheritance: and the estates in these cases are limited upon the surrender, and are always annexed to the estate of him to whose use the surrender is made. And always the surrender to the lord is general, without limitation of any estate: the lord is but an instrument in this case, and when he hath admitted according to the effect of the surrender, nothing remains in him but the reversion. 4 *Co.* 29. *a. b.*

5. The lord is bound in conscience to hold a court to admit. 4 *Co.* *Dy.* 264. *a.*

61. *Corpus humanum non recipit aestimationem.*

IF a *Ca. Sa.* be executed, that is in law sufficient for the whole debt; for *Corpus humanum non recipit aestimationem*, so that if you take it at all, you must take it for the whole debt. *Hob.* 59. According to *Bract. Minima poena corporalis est major qualibet pecuniaria.* And *Rush.* saith, *Mortuus homo non est homo, and a prisoner is a dead man: perdit domum, familiam, vicinos, patriam*; and therefore the last named author well calls imprisonment a civil death.

62. *Cuilibet in sua arte perito est credendum.*

1. SEE *Co. Lit.* 125.

2. *Vide* rule, *Quod quisquis norit in hoc se exerceat, sicut ad quaestionem facti non respondent judices, ita ad quaestionem juris non respondent juratores.*

63. *Cui licet quod majus, non debet quod minus est non licere.*

1. REsolved, that where the custom of the manor was, that copyhold lands might be granted in fee-simple, that a grant to one and the heirs of his body is within the custom; for be it a fee-simple conditional, or estate-tail, it is within the custom: so he might grant for life or years by like custom; for an estate in fee-simple comprehends all. 4 *Co.* 23. *a.* 30. *a.*

2. See 5 *Co. De jure regis Eccl.* 6. *b.* 7. *a.*

64. *Cujus est dare, illius est disponere.*

1. A Creditor agrees with his debtor to take less than his debt, so he be paid by such a day, the debtor fails of payment, and brings his bill, suggesting some equitable excuses for not making precise payment;

 and

and that he tendered within two or three days, but the defendant refufed, and fued at law for the whole. Demurrer, for that the bill contained no equity, and that the plaintiff having failed, he was not bound to take lefs; and demurrer allowed. 1 *Vern.* 211.

2. Lord keeper in this cafe faid, he was fully fatisfied it was not originally a mortgage, but an abfolute purchafe, but his lordfhip believed *Sabine* might complain he had fold his eftate too cheap, and that thereon *Barrel* might declare if he would pay his money within a year, and 100*l.* for his pains, he fhould have his eftate again; and cited Sir *Anthony Cage*'s cafe, of a claufe to repurchafe, and faid that where there was a claufe to repurchafe, that the time limited ought to be precifely obferved. And as to ferjeant *Barrel*'s agreement, it was but reafonable for his trouble; for that the eftate was more valuable, as having gone through a lawyer's hands, who underftood the title, and that might be a means to encourage purchafors. So difmiffed the bill. 1 *Vern.* 268, 269. Note; *To make it a mortgage, were cited the cafes* Cole *and* Martin, *and* Beale *and* Collins.

3. A college is the founder's creature, and he may give it what fhape he pleafes, fo it be a legal one. *Skin.* 502.

4. The founder's will is his reafon, in difpofing and ordering his own, and we may not take this power from him, becaufe we think it unreafonable. *Skin.* 481.

5. Every man is mafter of his own charity, to appoint and qualify it as he pleafes. *Skin.* 481.

6. The authority of the founder to vifit, is an authority by the common law, &c. and whereof the courts of law will judicially take notice, but that of a vifitor conftituted, is not fo, but derivative and limited. *Skin.* 497.

7. The court intends that the vifitor will do right. *Skin.* 454.

8. A vifitor by appointment has no greater authority or power, than the founder giveth him, he is the founder's creature, and receives his being, power and authority, from him, and he may not exceed the power given him; *Qui poteft dare poteft difponere.* Skin. 454.

9. Charities founded and endowed by private perfons, are fubject to the private government of thofe who erect them; and therefore if there be no vifitor appointed by the founder, in all fuch cafes of eleemofynary corporations, the law doth appoint the founder and his heirs to be vifitors; they are patrons, and are not to be guided by the common known laws and rules of the kingdom; but fuch corporations are to be governed by the particular laws and conftitutions affigned them by the founder. *Skin.* 483.

10. *Vifitation* is a facred truft, and if it be invaded, a prohibition lieth; and this is the privilege of every founder, upon the general rule of reafon, *Cujus eft dare,* &c. and this is mentioned in the cafe of *Phillips* and *Bury*, *Show. Parl. Ca.* 51. 4 *Mod.* 112. and *Stillingfleet*'s cafe, 413, &c. *Gilb.* 178 *to* 183.

11. Vide *Gilb.* 165, 182. *Show. Parl. Ca.* 51. *Skin.* 497, 454. *Fitz. Nat. Brev.* 42. *A. B. C. D.* *Skin.* 474, 646, 479, 485, 489, 492, 493, 495, 498. 8 *Aff.* 29, 30. 1 *Mod.* 12, 82, 84. 3 *Lev.* 2, 1. 3 *Mod.* 295. 4 *Mod.* 106. 5 *Mod.* 404, 452, 236, 238, 240, 241. 1 *Show.* 74. 1 *Keb.* 166. 1 *Vern.* 456, 457. 1 *Pe. Will.* 326. 2 *Ju. Eccl.* 188, &c. 196, &c.

65. *Cujus eſt diviſio, alterius eſt electio.*

1. WHERE parceners agree that the eldeſt ſiſter ſhall make partition of the tenements, ſhe is to chuſe laſt after all the others. *Lit. ch. Parceners, ſect.* 245. *Brac. lib.* 2. 77. *Fleta, lib.* 5. *cap.* 9. *Brit. cap.* 72. gives the preference, as does *Lit. ſect.* 244. (where partition is by an indifferent perſon) to the eldeſt ſiſter, yet this deſcendeth not to her heir, as are theſe books, and *Co. Lit.* 166. *b.* But where the eldeſt ſiſter is not an actor in the partition, it not only deſcends, but ſhall go to her huſband who is tenant by the curteſy, or to her aſſignee; for the rule of law is *Cujus eſt diviſio, alterius eſt electio*; for the reaſon of the law is, for the avoiding of partiality, *Ipſae etenim leges cupiunt ut jure regantur*, which might apparently follow, if the eldeſt might both divide and chuſe. *Co. Lit.* 167. *a. b.*

2. *Thomas Wilſon* brought prohibition againſt the biſhop of *Carliſle*, and ſaid that there was within his pariſh of *Grayſtock* this cuſtom for tithing of wool, that if an inhabitant have five fleeces or above, that after ſheering and binding up of the ſaid five fleeces *abſque fraude et dolo, fideliter ſolvet rectori poſt monitionem, &c. apud oſtium domus manſionalis ejuſdem inhabitantis infra parochiam praedict', decimam partem inde abſque aliquibus viſu vel tactu novem partium ejuſdem lanae reſid' per rectorem habendum vel ſcrutandum in plenam, &c.* and that the parſons have accepted it; and then lays, that the biſhop of *Carliſle* pretending himſelf parſon or commendatory, *&c.* the biſhop pleads himſelf parſon, *&c.* and demurred in law to the cuſtom. And it was adjudged for the biſhop; for the ſubſtance of the preſcription is laid, that the very true tenth is and ought to be paid, without fraud, which is not preſcriptable; for it is common right; then the ſole point preſcriptable is, that this is without view or touch of the nine parts, which in effect is repugnant to the other; for when you have laid truth in the former part, you lay the way to fraud in the latter; for it is againſt common reaſon, that any man ſhould judge or divide for himſelf, and then take choice of his own diviſion, againſt the rule of partition. *Lit.* For the truth of the tenth depends upon the proportion it holds with the nine parts; and therefore for the pariſhioner, who is in the nature of an adverſary, to ſet out a part for the tenth, which he only affirms to be juſt, is to give him power to tithe as he liſts: and it's a weak anſwer to ſay, that if it be not a juſt tenth, he may refuſe it, and ſue for his due; for firſt he hath no means to know or be aſſured whether it be true or not; ſo his ſuit may be cauſeleſs, ſure he may be, it will be fruitleſs: but the law was provided not to engender but prevent ſuits; and therefore provideth that things be done by indifferent means and perſons, that there be no ſuſpicion of indirect dealing. If a man be judge in his own caſe, and judge amiſs, a writ of error would redreſs it: ſo if a biſhop diſturb or would not admit the clerk, he might be compelled; yet the law provides better, that is, that you have your right; and therefore that your means be ſuch as is likely to produce it. You may challenge the array or polls, you ſhall remove the *Venire facias* to another officer, as the coroner, where the ſheriff is ſuſpected in law, by a proviſional challenge afore, to avoid delay, which is a kind of injury. *Hob.* 107, 108.

Custom. See *Consuetudo.*

66. *Customary inheritances, such as copyholds, shall not have any collateral qualities which do not concern descents.*

1. WHERE the custom is, that copyholder may grant in fee, he may grant any lesser estate; for fee-simple includes all. 4 *Co.* 23. *a.*

2. A man shall not be tenant by the curtesy, *sans* special custom. 4 *Co.* 22. *b.*

3. A wife shall not be endowed of a copyhold but where there is a special custom; but where she is so dowable, she shall have all incidents thereto. 4 *Co.* 30. *b.*

4. See 4 *Co. Copyhold cases*, and *Calthorpe's Readings.*

67. *Custom cannot be grounded upon fraud.*

1. THE *East-India* company sued their factor for an account of 12000*l.* in gold he carried hence into *India*; he on his account demanded (according to the usual custom) allowance for so much paid for custom to the king of *India*; it was insisted that he did not pay it: so on the question, whether the factor or the merchant should have the benefit of the custom? it was referred to two merchants, they certified that by the course of merchants the factor should retain; for that if the principal freight, by his non-payment had been lost, he must have answered it to the employer; and so run the hazard wholly. And in this case, the factor by the law in *East India*, had it been discovered that he had concealed the gold, and not entered it in the custom-books, would have lost his life as a felon. Two other merchants certified the employer was to have the benefit of the non-payment of the customs. And upon these certificates it was decreed, that the factor should have the benefit of the customs; for it was a duty to be paid, and the employer could make no title to it against him that was in possession; and he that hath possession hath right against all but him that hath the very right. 1 *Chan. Ca.* 25.

2. The factor had stolen the customs of certain goods, of which a bill was to have account, and to discover whether he had paid the said customs or not? The defendant by answer insisted, he was not bound to answer that part of the bill; for that the plaintiff, who was the employer, was not intitled to these customs, nor any advantage thereof whether they were paid or not. On exception, the master certified the answer sufficient. On exceptions to the report, the case above (*Smith* and *Oxenden*) was cited, but it was insisted for the plaintiff, this case was not like that; for that was of custom stolen from a foreign king, and this was of custom stolen from our own king; and that it would be of evil consequence, and an encouragement to evil factors, if the court should give an opinion for them in a matter of fraud, as this was. And whereas it was insisted by the defendant's counsel, that it was the course of merchants, that factors should have the benefit

benefit of cuſtoms themſelves, and not the principals; becauſe the penalty would fall on the factor if diſcovered: it was declared that could not be called a cuſtom, being grounded upon fraud; and therefore the court ordered that the defendant ſhould anſwer whether he paid the cuſtom or not. 1 *Chan. Ca.* 30. Vide *Smith* againſt *Oxenden*, 1 *Chan. Ca.* 25. *Antiquity joined with verity is to be reverenced, but without verity it is only oldneſs of error. That only is truly currant which is antiently true; therefore what is founded in error, no uſage can ſupport.*

3. The defendant employed the plaintiff as his factor beyond ſea, and brought an action of account againſt him, and had judgment *quod computet*; the plaintiff brought his bill here to have an allowance upon account for what he had ſaved without paying the cuſtom for thoſe goods (which could not be allowed before the auditor, as was ſaid); and an allowance was decreed againſt the employer; and ſo referred to a maſter to take the account. 1 *Chan. Ca.* 76. Note; *This caſe is founded upon the rule of equity, that he ſhall have ſatisfaction who would have ſuſtained the loſs,* i. e. *where he is not* particeps criminis, *but if he be criminal himſelf, it is otherwiſe; for one ſhall not take advantage of his own wrong.*

4. *Hix*, a tinner in *Cornwall*, articled with *Papilion* to ſell and deliver to him ſixteen tons of tin, free from all cuſtoms and duties; part of the price was paid, and the reſt ſecured to be paid; after the tin was ſeiſed, for that the coinage had not been paid, which by the cuſtom of the *Stannaries* is a forfeiture, in caſe the tin be ſold before coinage paid or ſecured: and becauſe the forfeiture was by *Hix*, *Papilion* ſued him to be relieved, he having covenanted to deliver it cuſtom free. Lord chancellor diſmiſſed the bill, ſaying, I will break this trade between the tinners and the merchants: for by this trade the king is couzened, and the coinage duty ſeldom anſwered. 1 *Chan. Ca.* 256.

5. The plaintiff made *Willet* his factor to ſell linens for him; he took them up at the cuſtom-houſe, &c. and ſold them to the defendants *Wingfield* and *Bowater* for 115*l.* and before payment died indebted by ſpecialty more than his aſſets would extend to pay, and (*int' al'*) by covenant, on his marriage, to leave his wife, if ſhe ſurvived him, 3000*l.* his widow adminiſtred, and inſiſted the 115*l.* in the hands of *Wingfield* and *Bowater*, was liable not only in equity to reimburſe her what was due to *Willet* as factor, but ſhould come into the aſſets, and be liable to her articles and the debts by ſpecialty. Decreed the money to be paid the plaintiff, diſcounting thereout what was due to *Willet* as factor, and that with coſts, as having made an ill defence to ſatisfy her articles out of the plaintiff's eſtate; a factor is in nature of a truſtee, and though he has right at law, yet he is in equity but a truſtee. 2 *Ven.* 638.

6. Where a factor ſmuggles foreign cuſtoms, and yet ſets them down to his maſter, as paid *ſur* account; chancery would not relieve, for that the factor ventured his life. But *North*, lord keeper, ſaid he was not ſatisfied of it, for that he ventured his maſter's goods, as well as his own life. *Skin.* 149. *And quaere whether this is not wrong, as it is an argument for foreigners to do the ſame by us; for by a parity of reaſon, that our traders may do it to other foreign governments, others may do it to us.*

7. In this caſe, a difference was taken by my lord chancellor, that if an executor, or truſtee of money, place it out in the funds or on other ſecurity,

 whereby

whereby he gains confiderably, he fhall have the whole benefit to himfelf, in refpect of the hazard he run of being a confiderable lofer thereby, which he muft have born. But if fuch truftee or executor were an infolvent perfon at the time of placing out fuch truft-money, there the *Ceftuy que truft* fhall have the whole benefit gained thereby, as he only could have born the lofs thereof, if any had happened; the truftee or executor, by reafon of his infolvency, being incapable thereof, and confequently running no hazard at all. *Prec. Chan.* 505.

68. *Debile fundamentum fallit opus.*

1. IF a fpiritual corporation, to which a church is appropriate, be diffolved, the church becomes difappropriate. 3 *E.* 3. 74.

2. A lord confirms the eftate of the diffeifor (of lands in antient demefne) to hold free, yet after it is recovered by the diffeifee, it fhall be antient demefne again; for the eftate, upon which the confirmation enured, is defeated. 49 *E.* 3. 8.

3. When the eftate, whereunto a warranty is annexed, is defeated, the warranty is alfo defeated. *Lit.* cap. *Warranty.*

69. *Decreta conciliorum non ligabant reges noftros.*

1. WHatfoever the pope did in this kingdom was of no force, but *coram non judice.* Hob. 146.

2. *Decreta conciliorum non ligabant reges noftros.* Mo. 906.

3. *Mo.* 542, 755, 756. 5 *Co. de Ju. Regis Eccle.* 1, 2, 5, 10, 13, 14, 15, 23, 28, 40. 4 *Inft.* 342, 343. *Co. Lit.* 44, 99. 5 *Co.* 51. 11 *Co.* 49. 22 *Aff. pl.* 5. *Da.* 4, 51, 52, 71, 72, 76, 88. *Hob.* 143, 147, 81, 82. *Pal.* 463, 470, 477. *Fitz. Nat. Brev.* 22. *Cro. Eliz.* 527, 542, 601. *Cro. Jac.* 37, 335, 517. *Cro. Ca.* 47, 68, 199. *Ha. Annal.* 18, 19, 23, 24.

4. *Vide* rules, *De una praefumptione ad aliam tranfivit Romanus pontifex. Rex eft mixta perfona, &c. Rex eft monarcha et imperator, &c. Omnes reges dicuntur clerici. Caufa fpiritualis committi poteft principi laico.*

70. *De non apparentibus et non exiftentibus eadem eft ratio.*

1. LORD *Hobart*, Prudence is *Quod dubitas ne feceris. De non apparentibus et non exiftentibus eadem eft ratio.* Hob. 295.

2. The matter of an indictment ought to be full, exprefs, and certain; and not to be maintained or fupported by argument or implication, *&c.* 4 *Co.* 44. *b.*

3. The indictment being *Veredictum, id eft dictum veritatis,* and matter of record, ought to import all the truth which is neceffary by law; for *De non apparentibus, &c.* 4 Co. 47. a. 48. a.

71. *Descent tolls an entry.*

General.

1. AS descent is the worthiest means to come to lands, so hath the heir more privilege than any that by other order or means come to lands, *&c.* In antient time if the disseisor had been in long possession, the disseisee could not have entered upon him, nor upon his feoffee, if he had been a year and a day in quiet possession: but now the law is changed in both cases; only the dying seised being an act in law, doth hold at this day, and this was the law before the conquest: and one reason of this antient law may be, says lord *Coke*, that the heir cannot suddenly, by intendment of law, know the true state of his title: and for that many advantages follow the possession and tenant, the law taketh away the entry of him, who would not enter upon the ancestor, who is presumed to know his title, and driveth him to his action against the heir that may be ignorant thereof. To a descent to toll an entry dying seised is necessary; and it must be of such tenements as are corporeal and lie in livery, and not of inheritances incorporeal which lie in grant, as advowsons, rents, commons in gross, and such like; for descents of such do not put him, who hath right, to an action; and the reason of the difference is, for that houses serve for the habitation of them; and lands are to be manured for the sustenance. The like law is of an abatement, or intrusion, and of their feoffees or donees, *&c.* *Co. Lit.* 237. *b.*

2. Descents which toll entries are in two manners, (to wit) where the descent is in fee, or in fee-tail: descents in fee which toll entries, are as if a man, seised of certain lands or tenements, is disseised by one who hath issue and dieth seised, so that the lands descend to such issue by course of law, and not by his own act, wherefore his entry is taken away, and he is put to his writ of entry, *&c.* to recover. *Lit. sect.* 385. Descents in tail, which take away entries, are as if a man be disseised, and the disseisor giveth the land to another in tail, and the tenant in tail hath issue and dieth seised, and the issue enter, in this case also the entry of the disseisee is taken away, and he is put to his writ of entry *sur* disseisin against the issue of the tenant in tail. *Lit. sect.* 386.

3. At common law if the disseisor, abator or intruder, had died seised soon after the wrong done, the disseisee and his heirs had been barred of their entry, without any time limited by law; but now by the stat. 37 *H.* 6. 1. except such disseisor, *&c.* had been in peaceable possession of such manor, *&c.* whereof he died seised, for five years next after such disseisin, *&c. sans* entry or continual claim, *&c.* the entry is not taken away, *&c.* but after five years the disseisee must make such continual claim; and it is said, says lord *Coke*, that abators and intruders are out of the statute, because the statute being penal only extends to disseisees, which was the most common mischief, *et ad ea quae frequentius accidunt jura adaptantur.* Also the feoffee of the disseisor is out of the statute and remains at common law, and whether the disseisin be with or without force, the law is the same; for this statute is to be taken favourably, for advancement of the antient right, (*as is, as I conceive, every other statute*). Bodies politic and their successors are within this statute, *&c.* *Co. Lit.* 238. *a. b.* *Vide etiam* 240. *a.*

4. A difference is to be taken between a right for which the law giveth remedy by action, and a title for which the law giveth no ſuch remedy, but by entry only; as where the feoffee upon condition, as in *Lit. ſect.* 391. hath a right to the land, his entry is taken away, becauſe he may recover by action; but where he hath no remedy by action, his title of entry cannot be taken away, becauſe he hath no remedy by action: therefore, if his entry ſhould be taken away, he would be for ever barred. So is the law in caſe of *Mortmain*; ſo where a woman hath a title to enter *Cauſa matrimonii praelocuti*, no deſcent ſhall toll the entry; ſo it is of a deviſee; ſo of the king's patentee dying before entry; and the reaſon of this difference is, becauſe there is but a title, and no remedy by action in theſe caſes, *&c. Co. Lit.* 240. *a. b.*

5. The general rule is, that it is not lawful for any man to enter upon a deſcent, yet the reaſonableneſs of the law excepteth from this rule or ground, an infant who hath right, and hath ſuffered ſuch deſcent, and him alſo who hath made continual claim, and ſuffereth them to enter notwithſtanding, *&c. Doct. & Stud. lib.* 1. *cap.* 17. *etiam cap.* 8.

6. If he in reverſion diſſeiſe his tenant for life, and die ſeiſed, this is a deſcent to take away the entry of tenant for life, but this is not ſufficient to toll the entry of a ſtranger; becauſe as to him it is but the eſtate for life ſtill, and but a fictitious and not a deſcendable eſtate. *Hob.* 323. *Co. Lit.* 238. *a.*

Particular caſes.

7. In a writ of right between *Plat* demandant and *Holford* tenant, the defendant pleaded that he was within age, and in by deſcent, and prayed that the parol might demur till his full age; whereunto the demandant replied that he was ſeiſed until the tenant diſſeiſed him, and traverſed the deſcent; and day was given to the tenant to adviſe what he would do. *Hob.* 266.

8. Tenant in tail having agreed to ſell, and received part of the conſideration money, was decreed to ſell, but ſtood out to a contempt, and died. A bill was brought to revive againſt the iſſue in tail, but was diſmiſſed; for though the tenant in tail had power, and might have barred the iſſue, yet as he did not execute that power, he is not concluded; for tenant in tail did not do the neceſſary acts, (to wit) levy fines or ſuffer any recoveries for the barring the iſſue. *Prec. Chan.* 278.

9. The heir is not to be diſinherited but upon a neceſſary implication. 1 *Vern.* 323, 376.

10. See *Lit.* 95. *Co. Lit.* 241, 242, 243, 245, 246, 247, 248, 249, 250, 253, 289, 298, 328, 336, 337, 338, 353, 362, 364, 388. See alſo *Continual claim and diſcontinuance*, and *Stat.* 32 *H.* 8. *cap.* 13. See rule, *Law favours juſtice and truth*, &c.

72. *Deſignatio unius perſonae eſt excluſio alterius; et expreſſum facit ceſſare tacitum.*

1. THE law ſhall never ſeek out a perſon where the parties themſelves have appointed one; as if the condition on a mortgage be to pay the mortgagee or his heirs the money, and he die before the day, it muſt not

not be paid to his executors, but to the heir; but if the condition was to him, his heirs or executors, there the mortgagor is left to his election. *Co. Lit.* 210. *a.*

2. If a man makes a feoffment in fee *sur* condition, that the feoffee ſhall pay the feoffor, his heirs or aſſigns, 20*l.* at ſuch a day; and before the day the feoffor makes his executors and dies, the feoffee may pay the ſame either to the heir or the executors; for they are his aſſignees in law to this intent. But if a man make a feoffment in fee *ſur* condition, that if the feoffor pay to the feoffee, his heirs or aſſigns, 20*l.* before ſuch a feaſt, and before the feaſt the feoffee maketh his executors, and dieth, the feoffor ought to pay the money to the heir and not to the executors, for the executors in ſuch caſe are no aſſigns in law; and the reaſon of the difference is, becauſe in the firſt caſe the law muſt of neceſſity find out aſſigns, and there cannot be any aſſignee in deed, for the feoffor had but a bare condition, and no eſtate in the land which he could aſſign over; but in the other caſe the feoffee hath an eſtate in the land, which he may aſſign over; and where there may be aſſigns in deed, the law ſhall never ſeek out or appoint any aſſigns in law; and though the feoffee made no aſſignment of the eſtate, yet the executors cannot be aſſignees, becauſe aſſignees were only intended by the condition to be aſſignees of the eſtate: but if the condition be to pay the money to the feoffee, his heirs or aſſigns, and the feoffee make a feoffment over, it is in the election of the feoffor to pay the money to the firſt feoffee, or to the ſecond feoffee, and ſo if the firſt feoffee dieth, the feoffor may pay the money either to the heir of the firſt feoffee, or to the ſecond feoffee; for the law will not force the feoffor to take knowledge of the ſecond feoffment, nor of the validity thereof, whether the ſame be effectual or not, but at his pleaſure; and the firſt feoffee and his heirs are expreſly named in the condition. *Co. Lit.* 210.

3. If a feoffment be made on condition, that if the feoffee pay to the feoffor at ſuch a certain time 20*l.* then the feoffee ſhall have the land to him and his heirs; but if he fail at the day, that then it ſhall be lawful for the feoffor or his heirs to re-enter, *&c.* and afterwards, before the day appointed, the feoffee ſells the land to another, and makes a feoffment; if the ſecond feoffee tender the money at the day to the feoffor, who refuſeth, *&c.* the ſecond feoffee hath an eſtate in the land, clear of the condition; and that becauſe the ſecond feoffee hath an intereſt in the condition for the ſafeguard of his tenancy; or if the firſt feoffee after ſuch ſale tender the money, *&c.* this ſhall be good enough for the ſafeguard of the eſtate of the ſecond feoffee, becauſe the firſt feoffee was privy to the condition; and ſo the tender of either of them two is good, *&c. Lit. ſect.* 336. And in all good dealing the firſt feoffee ought to pay the money, and ſave the eſtate of his feoffee. *Co. Lit.* 208. *a.*

4. See the rule, *Expreſſum facit ceſſare tacitum.*

73. *De una praeſumptione ad aliam tranſivit Romanus pontifex.*

AFTER the biſhop of *Rome* had taken upon him to be the ſpiritual prince or monarch of the whole world, he attempted to give laws to all nations, as a mark of his ſovereignty; but well knowing *quod ubi non eſt*

2 *condendi*

condendi authoritas, ibi non eſt parendi neceſſitas, he offered his laws with caution; and therefore at firſt he cauſed certain rules for the government of the clergy only, and which he called decrees, and not laws or ſtatutes: which being received by his obedient clergy, he then attempted to draw the laity to obedience thereto: and firſt he propounded certain rules or ordinances for faſting days, to be obſerved by the laity as well as clergy, which he called by the moderate name of *Rogations*, and not laws or ſtatutes: but when he found laymen, out of their blind zeal, took in theſe ordinances of abſtinence, then this impoſtor went further, and carried on his incroachments, making ſtill more and further reſcripts and orders, to bind not only his obſequious clergy, but alſo the laity; as well ſovereign princes as their people, and that not only in ſpirituals, but in matters concerning their civil and temporal eſtates and rights; ſo monſtrous were the impoſitions of this uſurper; for *De una praeſumptione, &c. See* Da. 69. b. 70, 71, *&c.* 1 Ju. Eccl. *The courſe of the popes uſurpation*, &c. *and the oppoſition the ſame met with*, &c.

74. *Deus ſolus haeredem facere poteſt, non homo.*

IN caſe of deſcents of inheritances, the law reſpecteth primogeniture, birth-right, proximity, and the intire blood; but it gives no regard to the worthineſs or ſufficiency of the heir; and therefore the law caſts inheritances upon ideots, infants, *&c.* as well as upon men of diſcretion: the law reſpecteth not the dignity of the perſon in caſe of deſcent of an inheritance; for *Primogeniture* has a prerogative given it by the law of God, and *therefore is* ſo preferred in our law, and is moſt worthy. *Dav.* 35. *b.* 36. *a.* See *Bract.* 62. *Co. Lit.* &c.

75. *Diſcovery draws with it relief.*

1. A Perſon, who had furniſhed neceſſary tackling for a ſhip, which was afterwards ſold, prays a diſcovery of the perſonal eſtate of one of the part-owners, who was dead, and to have relief againſt his executors and the ſurviving part-owners. Lord chief baron *Gilbert* ſaid, that the chief diſtinction upon the rule, that diſcovery ſhould draw with it relief, ſeemed to be that where a diſcovery is prayed, and a liquidated debt admitted by the anſwer, the court might then proceed to give relief; but where the debt was unliquidated, being uncertain, and ſounding in damages, it was proper for a jury to aſcertain it; there being nothing for a court of equity to found a determination on. That though this caſe was within the mercantile law, yet being admitted by the anſwer, that the charge was for tackling, *&c.* a court of equity muſt grant them redreſs, as a court of admiralty would, (*viz.*) upon the bottom of the ſhip, and that it would be very hard to ſend them back again, there to obtain relief; and that all the part-owners ought to make ſatisfaction, having received the profit of the voyage, which the ſhip was enabled to perform by the plaintiff's furniſhing the tackle, *&c.* Baron *Hale* ſaid, In the preſent caſe, the proceedings in this court were very proper, and they might go on; for in the court of admiralty ſeamens wages are recoverable, and they are likewiſe chargeable upon the bottom of the ſhip, and yet chancery retains bills for them.

And Sir *John Trevor*, late maſter of the rolls, uſed to ſay, That a court of equity had a concurrent juriſdiction with them. *Gilb.* 227, 228. *Barn.* 278, 279.

2. See rule, *In things of election the party is to ſhew that he hath made it.* Diviſion, *either at law or in equity*, ca. 7.

76. *Dies dominicus non eſt juridicus.*

1. THE *Sabbath* day is no day for law cauſes. Upon a fine levied with proclamations according to the ſtatute 4 *H.* 7. *cap.* 24. if any of the proclamations be made on the lord's day, all the proclamations are erroneous; for the juſtices may not ſit on that day; but it is a day excepted from ſuch buſineſs by the common law, for the ſolemnity of it; to the intent that all people may apply themſelves to prayer and ſerving of God. *Fi. Law Engl.* 7.

2. No plea ſhall be holden *Quindena Paſchae*, becauſe it is always the *Sabbath*; but it ſhall be *Craſtimo quindenae Paſchae.* Fitzh. Nat. Brev. 17. (F.)

3. If a writ of *Sci. Fa.* out of the common pleas bear teſte upon a *Sunday*, it is error; becauſe that it is not *Dies juridicus in banco. Dy.* 168.

4. No ſale on a *Sunday* ſhall be ſaid a ſale in market overt, to alter the property. 12 *E.* 4. 8.

5. But on a *Sunday* a conſtable may ſerve a warrant to find ſureties for good behaviour. *Sty.* 250. See *Stat.* 29 *Car.* 2. *cap.* 7. *ſect.* 6.

77. *Deficiente uno non poteſt eſſe haeres.*

IT is the blood which is between every heir and his anceſtor, that makes him heir; for without blood he may not inherit; and therefore he, who hath the full and intire blood, ſhall inherit before another, who hath but part of the blood of the anceſtor; for *ordine naturae totum praefertur unicuique parti.* And therefore *Bracton* ſaith, *Quod propter jus ſanguinis duplicatum, tam ex parte patris, quam ex parte matris, dicitur haeres propinquior ſoror, quam frater de alia uxore.* And *Britton* ſaith, That right of blood in this caſe, makes the female to forecloſe the male. The heir ought to have in him two bloods, the blood of the father and the blood of the mother; theſe bloods commix'd in him by lawful marriage, conſtitutes and makes him heir; ſo that none may be heir to any unleſs he hath in him both the bloods of him to whom he maketh himſelf heir; and therefore the heir of the half blood ſhall not inherit, becauſe he wants one of the bloods which ſhould make him heir, &c. *Deficiente uno non poteſt eſſe haeres.* And upon this reaſon, according to *Britton cap.* 5. If a man be attaint of felony by judgment, his heirs begotten after are forecloſed all ſucceſſion, as well of the part of the mother as of the father; as they born afterwards had not two bloods inheritable in them; becauſe at the time of their generation, the blood of the father was corrupted; for *ex leproſo parente leproſus generatur filius*; and when the father is attainted of felony, his inheritable blood is corrupt; and ſo his ſon hath but an half blood; that is, the blood of the mother uncorrupt; and therefore having but one blood, he may not inherit even to her, &c. 3 *Co.* 41. *a. b.*

78. *Dispensatio est mali prohibiti provida relaxatio, utilitate seu necessitate pensata.*

1. *DIspensatio est relaxatio juris*, and permits that to be done, which the law before had prohibited or forbidden. 21 *H*. 8. 6. *a*. *Dav*. 69. *a*.

2. Dispensations, say the canonists, *Non debent trahi ad communem legem*. Da. 81. a.

3. *Dispensatio est provida relaxatio mali prohibiti, utilitate vel necessitate pensata*. Pal. 476.

4. The intention ought to be regarded, and not the precise words, in the king's grants. *Pal*. 476. 9 *Co*. The earl of *Salop*'s case. A dispensation takes away and prevents the offence, whilst a pardon only takes away the punishment. *Palm*. 476.

5. It is safe and good policy in the king's licences to *Mortmain*, to have *non obstantes* of the statutes of *Mortmain*, and not only of the statute of *Quia emptores terrarum*; but it appeareth by *Littleton*, that there needeth not any *non obstante* of the statutes of *Mortmain*, for the king shall not be intended to be misconusant of the law. And when he licenceth in *Mortmain*, he need not make any *non obstante*; for it is apparent to be granted in *Mortmain*, and the king is the head of the law; and therefore *praesumitur rex habere omnia jura, &c. in scrinio pectoris sui*, for maintaining his grants to be good according to law. *Co. Lit*. 99. *a*.

6. *As to dispensations for pluralities, unless in cases of absolute necessity, they must needs be allowed to be odious both to God and all good men; and therefore by no means intitled to have any favour, extended to their support, but on the contrary, as my lord* Gilbert *wisely and piously says, No construction can be too liberal to make parsons reside*, &c. Dispensatio est vulnus quod vulnerat jus commune. And all abuses shall be removed, as said a certain canonist, *si duo tantum verba*, (viz.) *non obstante*, *non impedirent*, were removed. *Da*. 69. *Vide et nota tout le case avec les citations*. It is said a bishop shall be but *unius uxoris vir*, that is according to the exposition of the canonists, that he shall have but one cure; for as they hold by *commendams*, *bigamia contrahitur in ecclesia*; and so it was a primitive bishop said when another benefice was offered him in *commendam*, *absit ut cum sponsa habeam concubinam*. Da. 75. *Which shews what were the sentiments of the primitive christians in this matter*. And it is to be observed *Marsil. Pat*. pronounced a curse against the court of *Rome*, where they were invented, for introducing them: and indeed they have been of most dangerous consequence to all the commonwealths in *Christendom*, as may be collected from my lord *Coke* in his 7 *Rep*. 36. and *Dav*. 69. and other the best authorities. For as saith the canonists, *Commenda est materia odiosa et restringibilis*. Pal. 460. 1 Ju. Eccl. the evils of dispensation.

79. *Distinguenda*

79. *Diſtinguenda ſunt tempora.*

THE ſtatute 23 *H.* 8. was made for the taking away ſuch ſuperſtitious uſes, as praying for ſouls ſuppoſed to be in purgatory, and ſuch like; not to ſuppreſs the erecting of grammar ſchools, and maintenance of the poor, *&c.* Before the making this ſtatute divers ſup rſtitions and errors in the chriſtian religion, which had a pretence and ſemblance to charity and devotion, were diſcovered by the light of God's word, and theſe only, and not good and pious uſes, were intended to be tolled by the ſtatute; for no time was ever ſo barbarous as to take away education and ſcience, or ſupporting the poor, *&c.* but by this and all other the ſtatutes, ſuch uſes are intended to be maintained, *&c. Diſtinguenda ſunt tempora.* 1 Co. *Porter's* caſe.

80. *Doloſus verſatur in univerſalibus.*

19 *E.* 3. Where the king grants a licence to appropriate an advowſon generally, without any recital, this ſhall not extend to appropriate an advowſon held *in capite*, becauſe the grant is general, *Et doloſus verſatur in univerſalibus.* Mo. 321. *See* next rule.

81. *Dona clandeſtina ſunt ſemper ſuſpicioſa.*

1. IN an information againſt *Twyne*, *in Camera ſtellat'*, for contriving and publiſhing a fraudulent gift of goods; the caſe was upon the ſtat. 13 *Eliz. cap.* 5. and was this, *Pierce* was indebted to *Twyne* in 400*l.* and alſo to *C.* in 200*l. C.* brought debt againſt *Pierce*, and pending the writ, *Pierce* being poſſeſſed of goods to the value of 300*l.* ſecretly made a general gift, by deed, of all his goods and chattels, real and perſonal whatſoever to *Twyne*, in ſatisfaction of his debt, but ſtill *Pierce* continued in the poſſeſſion of the ſaid goods, and ſome he ſold, and the ſheep he ſheared and marked with his own mark. *C.* had judgment againſt *Pierce*, and a *Fi. Fa.* to the ſheriff, who coming to make execution on the ſaid goods, ſeveral perſons with force, by *Twyne's* command, reſiſted the ſheriff, claiming them to be *Twyne's* goods, by virtue of the ſaid gift, made on good and lawful conſideration. Reſolved, The gift fraudulent and within the ſtatute. In this caſe it was reſolved, 1ſt, That the gift had the ſigns and marks of fraud. 2dly, Becauſe the gift is general *ſans* exception of his apparel or other neceſſaries, for it is commonly ſaid *Quod doloſus verſatur in generalibus.* 3dly, The donor continued in poſſeſſion, and uſed the goods as owner, and traded with others therewith, and deceived and defrauded ſuch perſons as he dealt with. 4thly, It was made in ſecret, *Et dona clandeſtina ſunt ſemper ſuſpicioſa.* 5thly, It was done pending the writ. 6thly, There was a truſt between the parties, for the donor continued the poſſeſſion, and uſed the goods as his own proper goods; and fraud is always apparelled and clad with truſt, and truſt is the cover of fraud. 7thly, The deed ſaid that the gift was made honeſtly, truly and *bona fide*; *Et clauſulae inconſuetae ſemper inducunt ſuſpicionem.* 2. It was reſolved, though there was ſuch debt due to *Twyne*, and ſo a good conſideration of the gift, yet it was not

not within the proviſo of the ſaid act; for though it be a good conſideration, yet it was not *bona fide*; for no gift ſhall be ſaid *bona fide* within the ſaid proviſo, that is accompanied or coupled with any truſt; for the proviſo ſays, good conſideration and *bona fide*; ſo that good conſideration will not do, if it be not alſo *bona fide*. And therefore when a gift is in ſatisfaction of a debt, it muſt be, 1ſt, In a public manner, for ſecrecy is a badge of fraud. 2dly, The goods ought to be appraiſed to the true value, and the deed to expreſs in particular, that it is in ſatisfaction of a true debt. 3dly, Preſently after the gift the donee ought to take poſſeſſion; for continuance of poſſeſſion in the donor is a mark of truſt, and every truſt is out of the ſaid proviſo; for a truſt between the donor and donee is in truth a fraud to other creditors, for thereby they are defeated of their juſt debts. A good conſideration within the proviſo, is a valuable one, and a gift made *bona fide*, is without any truſt either expreſſed or implied; ſo that ſuch gifts muſt be both on good conſideration and *bona fide*: all ſtatutes made againſt fraud, are to be conſtrued liberally, and expounded beneficially to ſuppreſs fraud, &c. *Twyne* was convicted of fraud, and he and all the others of riot. 3 *Co.* 80. Twyne's *caſe*.

2. If leſſee for years aſſign his term by fraud to defeat an execution, and the aſſignee aſſigneth *bona fide*, in the hands of the ſecond aſſignee, it is not liable to the execution. If a man who hath goods to the value of 30*l.* be indebted to one in 20*l.* and to another in 10*l.* and the debtor aſſigns to him to whom he owes 10*l.* all his ſaid goods worth 30*l.* with intent, that for the reſt above the 10*l.* he ſhould be favourable to him, it is void, as it is fraudulent. But *Foſter* ſaid it ſhould not be void for the whole, but only for the ſurpluſage, as *Twyne*'s caſe. *Quaere* ſaith *Godb.* 161.

3. Inſtances of concealment are evidences of fraud. *Barn.* 4.

82. *Donatio principis intelligitur ſine praejudicio tertii.*

1. THE prerogative of the king ſhall do no wrong to a ſubject. *Da.* 75. *a.*

2. Though the king may diſpenſe with a ſtatute prohibiting a matter indifferent to be done, yet he cannot change the common law by his patent. 37 *H.* 8. *Bro. Pat.* 100. 6 *H.* 7. 4. *Dav.* 75. *b.*

3. Though the grant of the crown be *ex gratia ſpeciali, certa ſcientia, et mero motu*, yet this ſhall not extend the grant beyond the intention and meaning expreſſed in ſuch grant, &c. neither may the crown make a grant by *non obſtante* againſt the common law. So the king may not grant a protection in a *Quare impedit* or aſſize with a *non obſtante* of any law to the contrary, for the miſchief that might follow to the plaintiff, &c. 4 *Co.* Bozoun's *caſe*.

4. The king may not diſpenſe with the common law with a *non obſtante*. Dav. 75. b.

5. The king may not grant to a man to be his own judge. *Da.* 75. *a.*

6. The king may not grant a *commendam* to the prejudice of a lay patron. *Da. Le caſe de commenda.*

7. The king may not diſpenſe with any to do a nuſance in the highway. *Dav.* 75. *a.*

8. The king may not grant that if a man treſpaſs upon me, I ſhall not have an action againſt him. *Dav.* 75. *a.*

83. *Dower favoured.*

General.

1. UPON a poſſeſſion in law, a woman ſhall be endowed; and yet no man ſhall be tenant *per le curteſy* of lands, without his wife have poſſeſſion in deed. *Doct. & Stud. lib.* 2. *cap.* 15.

2. And where a woman is dowable by act or rule in law, equity ſhall not bar her to claim her dower. *Cro. Car.* 190, 191.

3. A woman ſhall be endowed of the beſt of her huſband's poſſeſſions. As if the huſband held of *J. S.* by 3*d.* who held over of another by 20*d.* and *J. S.* releaſe to the huſband, ſo that he now holds by 20 *d.* the wife being endowed, ſhall hold only by the third part of the 3*d.* and not by the third part of the 20*d.* *Fitzh. Dower* 131.

Particular caſes.

4. *J. S.* ſeiſed in fee, bargains and ſells to the huſband for 120*l.* in conſideration that he demiſe to him and his wife for their lives, rendering a pepper corn rent, and with condition that if he paid the money at the end of 20 years, the bargain and ſale ſhould be void; he redemiſeth accordingly, and dies: the wife brings dower. Though *Croke* and *Jones*, to whom it ſtood referred out of chancery, conceived it againſt equity, and the agreement of the huſband at the time of the purchaſe, that ſhe ſhould have it againſt the leſſee; for it was intended that they ſhould have it immediately redemiſed to them, as ſoon as they parted with it; and it is but in the nature of a mortgage. And upon a mortgage, if the lands be redeemed, the wife of the mortgagee ſhall not have dower. And if a huſband take a fine *ſur cognizance de droit come ceo*, and renders *arrere*, although it was once the husband's, the wife ſhall not have dower; for it is in him, and out of him *quaſi uno flatu*, and by one and the ſame act: yet in this caſe the judges conceived, that by the law ſhe was to have dower; for by the bargain and ſale the land was veſted in the huſband, and thereby his wife intitled to dower; and when he redemiſed it upon the former agreement, yet the leſſees are to receive it ſubject to this title of dower; and it was his folly that he did not join another with the bargainee, as is the antient courſe in mortgages. And when ſhe is dowable by the act or rule of law, a court of equity ſhall not bar her to claim her dower, for it is againſt the rule of law; and where no fraud or covin is, a court of equity will not relieve. Upon a conference with other juſtices at *Serjeants-Inn* upon this queſtion, who were of the ſame judgment, *Jones* and *Croke* juſtices certified their opinion to the court of chancery, that the wife of the bargainee was to have dower, and that a court of equity ought not to preclude her thereof. *Cro. Ca.* 190, 191. *Show. Parl. Ca.* 72. S. C. *cited.*

5. If the lands of *J. S.* are ſequeſtred for a perſonal duty, and he marries and dies, though the lands were ſequeſtred before marriage, yet the wife's right of dower will attach upon them; for this ſequeſtration ſhall not ſo far bind or cover them, as to hinder the wife of her dower. 1 *Vern.* 118.

6. If

6. If a man devise certain lands, money, goods, *&c.* in lieu and satisfaction of dower, the wife cannot have both: but she may waive the devise and claim dower, or take the devise in lieu of dower, at her election. 2 *Chan. Ca.* 24. See 1 *Chan. Ca.* 181. 1 *Vent.* 340. 4 *Co.* 1. Vernon's *case.*

7. But if the husband deviseth lands to his wife during her widowhood, without naming any consideration, she shall have both; because a will imports a consideration, and may not be averred to be in bar; for there may be no averment *dehors* the will, *&c.* 4 *Co.* 1. Vernon's *case.* *Co. Lit.* 36. *Mo. pl.* 103. *Cro. Eliz.* 128. 3 *Co.* 27. *Dy.* 220.

8. *L.* left legacies out of his personal estate to his wife, and devised her part of his real estate during her widowhood, and gave the residue to trustees for 21 years, for the payment of debts and legacies; the remainder of his whole estate he devised to the plaintiff, who was his godson, and of his name, but a remote relation, for life, *&c.* though this was not declared in lieu of dower, yet in equity it ought to be so taken; for from the giving away the rest of his estate to other uses, it might be collected and intended from the will, that the testator so intended; and a collateral satisfaction may be a good bar to dower in equity, though not pleadable at law: and decreed that she must either take her dower and waive the devise, or take the devise and waive her dower. This decree was after reversed by lord keeper *Wright.* 2 *Vern.* 365.

9. See *Fi. Law* 126, 127, 128. *Lit.* 7. 9 *E.* 4. 47. *and* 2 *H.* 7. 6. *Sav.* 57. 1 *E.* 6. 12. (17.) *Fitz. Abr.* 306. *a.* 309. *b.* *Reg.* 170. *a.* *Bulst.* 173. *Noy* 108. 2 *Leon.* 10. *Eq. Abr.* 208. *Lit. chap.* Dower. *Co. Lit.* *Palm.* 18, 78. *Ridl. View*, &c. 80, 81. 1 *Chan. Rep.* 254. *Perk.* 349. 1 *Co.* 123. 4 *Co.* 1. Vernon's *case.* *Doct. & Stud. lib.* 2. *cap.* 22. *Dy.* 11. 2 *Vern.* 436, 404. *Gilb.* 229. *Prec. Chan.* 351.

10. See rule, *Quod ab initio non valet, &c.*

84. *Eadem mens praesumitur regis quae est juris, et quae esse debet, praesertim in dubiis.*

A Lapse is an act and office of trust reposed by law in the ordinary, metropolitan, and lastly in the king (who is *certum et stabilimentum justitiae*); the end of which trust is to provide the church of a rector, in default of the patron; yet as for him and to his behoof; and therefore as he cannot transfer his trust to another, so he cannot devest the thing wherewith he is trusted to any other purpose; and therefore though the king or bishop may suffer the church to stand void, (which yet is *culpa*) yet they cannot bind themselves, that they will not fill the church; for that were *injuria et malum in se*; and therefore shall be judged in law, in deceit of the king; for *eadem mens, &c.* The estates and persons of ideots and lunatics are by law intrusted to the king; if therefore the king should grant to one who intrudeth upon the possession of an ideot or lunatic, or takes their persons unlawfully, that he would not meddle with them, but suffer them to do their pleasure, such grants were void, *&c.* *Hob.* 154, 155.

85. *Ecclesia Ecclesiae decimas solvere non debet.*

PRohibition, and surmiseth that he was parson, and the defendant was vicar of the same church, and sued him in court Christian for tithes, upon an endowment that the vicar should have the tithes of all the lands within the parish; and alledgeth, that he pleaded there, that he is parson *impersonee* there; and that the lands, whereof tithes are demanded, are parcel of his glebe; and that they of the spiritual court would not allow of his plea; and held a prohibition lay upon this surmise; for *Ecclesia decimas solvere ecclesiae non debet.* And *Tanfield* said, this matter was lately in question between *Young* and the parson of *Boxley*, and adjudged no tithes should be paid of glebe lands. But *Popham* said, if the vicar be endowed to have all the small tithes within the parish, and the parson make a lease of his glebe land, the lessee shall pay the small tithes arising therefrom to the vicar, and the gross tithes thereof to the lessor; which was agreed *per Curiam.* Cro. Eliz. 479.

86. *Ecclesia est infra aetatem, et in custodia domini regis.*

MIchaelmas 23 E. 1. *Inter adjudicata coram rege,* Hunt' f. 83. *in thesaur' scaccar' sic adjudicatur, Quod ecclesia est infra aetatem, et in custodia domini regis, qui tenetur jura et haereditates ejusdem manutenere et defendere.* 11 Co. 49. a. b. 33 E. 3. 5 Co. 13. b.

87. *Ecclesiastical courts may not hold plea of matters determinable at law or in equity.*

General.

1. FLETA, *Leges autem anglicanas, licet non scriptas, leges appellari non absurdum.* And lord *Hale*, that they have their power by long immemorial use, and no account can be given of the original or beginning of the common law: there are no monuments, much less any clear and certain accounts of the original foundation of the *English* kingdom or state; by whom, and when planted: and therefore, saith his lordship, we cannot possibly know the original of the laws thereof; but this we know, as it is in *Doct. & Stud.* and indeed runs through all the books, they are grounded on, 1. The law of reason. 2. The law of God. 3. General custom or immemorial usage. 4. Principles or maxims, which have been always taken for law, and may not be denied, *&c.* 5. Particular customs, and 6. Acts of parliament or statutes. And those things which come in abridgment of the common law are not to be favoured in construction, as are the books, and particularly lord *Hobart.* Chancery is a fundamental court as antient as the kingdom. *Hob.* 63. It is a court of state. 1 *Chan. Ca.* 124. It is to judge according to conscience. *Ell. Obs.* 46 *to* 56. It is the refuge of the poor. *Ell. Obs.* 115. And can do no wrong. 2 *Chan. Ca.* 217. The equity of chancery shall controul the courts of law, and also *a multo fortiori*, the ecclesiastical courts. 1 *Chan. Ca.* 201. Whereas the ecclesiastical laws and courts are only derived from the indulgence of the

 crown,

crown, and the acceptance of the people, 1 *Ju. Eccl.* 168, 169. and *Jura ecclesiastica sunt limitata.* *Co. Lit.* 96. *a.* *Salk.* 553. And are such as are allowed by, and must not be against the common law or statutes, or usages of the realm, *&c.* *Co. Lit.* 344. *a.* *Ha. Hist. Law* 53. 2 *Inst.* 488. *Hard.* 63. *Dav.* *Doct. & Stud.* These inferior and subordinate laws were not from the pope, neither from councils, or any his or their authority; but were extracted from antient canons, *&c.* *Pal.* 458. 5 *Co.* *De Ju. Regis Eccl.* 9. *a.* And may be corrected, explained or abrogated by the civil power. 5 *Co.* *De Ju. Regis Eccl.* 32, 33. *Keil.* 181. They are of no inherent force. *Poph.* 156, 157. *Da.* 72. *Doct. & Stud. lib.* 2. *cap.* 26. *Vau.* 329. *Seld. of Tithes, cap.* 14. *fo.* 412, 413, 414. *Ha. Hist. Law* 27, *&c.* But under the superintendancy, and subject to the controul of the temporal courts, as well chancery as other. And all ordinaries, and others having ecclesiastical jurisdiction, are subordinate officers to the king and his courts at *Westminster*, for the better execution of justice, *&c.* *Co. Lit.* 344. *a.* *Doct. & Stud. lib.* 2. *cap.* 10, 20, 25, 28, 29. 1 *Vent.* 291, 313, 319. *Show.* 158. *Gilb.* 208. 1 *Pe. Will.* 12. *Hob.* 155, 294. *Fitzh. Abr. Excom.* 21. 5 *Co. De Ju. Regis Eccl.* 15. *b.* 22. *b.* 23. *b.* 27. *a.* *Co. Lit.* 134. *a.* *Hob.* 290. 2 *Inst.* 637. 3 *Inst.* 145, 146, 147, 148, 149, 150. 2 *Mod.* 257. *Stat.* 31 *E.* 3. *cap.* 4. 3 *H.* 5. *cap.* 5. 21 *H.* 8. *cap.* 5. 26 *H.* 8. *cap.* 15. *Co. Pl. fo.* 116. *Rast. Pl.* 603. 1 *Cro.* 262. 2 *Keb.* 301. *Pal.* 318. *Comb.* 448, 449. 4 *Inst.* 336. 12 *Co.* 72. 2 *Inst.* 94, 647, 653, 657. *Mo.* 781. *Ha. Hist. Law* 41. 1 *Ju. Eccl.* 200 *to* 233, 252, 340, *to the end.*

Particular cases.

1. In cases of chattels, debts, lay-fees. *Ro. Abr. Praemunire, fo.* 311, *ca.* 2. *Hob.* 84. *Ro. Abr.* 301, *ca.* 11. 308, *ca.* 20. *Yelv.* 39, 129. *Fitz. Nat. Brev.* 40. *L.* *Dy.* 151.

2. Though *in ordine ad spiritualia.* Hob. 121.

3. Where boundaries of parishes, *&c.* *Ro. Abr.* 291.

4. Where the matter hath already received a determination at law. *Fitz. Nat. Brev.* 42. *C. D. E.* *Ro. Abr. Prohibition* 294. *ca.* 15. 312. *ca.* 1. 319, *O.* 3 *Inst.* 122. 1 *Co.* 139.

5. Where suit pending both at law and in the spiritual court at the same time for the same matter. *Fitz. Nat. Brev.* 43. *G. H. J.*

6. Where the party is sued in the ecclesiastical court for acts done in the temporal courts. *Fitz. Nat. Brev.* 42. *F.* 12 *Co.* 43. *Ro. Abr. Prohibition, fo.* 303. *ca.* 3. *R. ca.* 7.

7. Where the only remedy is in equity. *Ro. Abr. Prohibition* (*Q.*) *ca.* 1. *Hard.* 96. *Hob.* 365. 2 *Ro.* 285. *Gilb.* 208. 1 *Ju. Eccl.* 534.

8. Where suits at the same time both in equity and the ecclesiastical court. 2 *Chan. Ca.* 85. *Skin.* 287.

9. Where the ecclesiastical courts have not jurisdiction of the whole matter, or cannot give equal relief, *&c.* *Ro. Abr. Prohibition, ca.* 5. *Pre. Chan.* 137, 546, 547. *Gilb.* 1, 2, 26, 140, 152. 1 *Vent.* 40, 53. 2 *Vern.* 211, 493.

10. Where these petit courts hold plea of matters only cognizable in any inferior temporal court, or other court. *Ro. Abr. Prohibition* 311. *ca.* 2. 313. *ca.* 3. 4. 5. 317. (*H.*) *ca.* 4. *Hob.* 15, 16. *Ro. Abr. Prohibition,*

fo. 318.

fo. 318. *ca.* 6. *Hob.* 246. *Gilb.* 181. *Show. Parl. Ca.* 51. 4 *Mod.* 112.

88. *Eodem modo quo factum est dissolvitur.*

1. AN obligation or other matter in writing cannot be discharged by any agreement by word. 19 *E.* 4. 1. *b.*

2. All the court held, that of a donative, beginning only by the foundation and erection of the donor, he hath the sole visitation and correction, and the ordinary nothing to do therewith; and as he comes in by him, so he may restore or resign to him, *&c.* for *Eodem modo quo factum,* &c. *Cro. Jac.* 63. *Yelv.* 60. *Mo.* 765. *S. C.*

3. One makes a voluntary settlement on another, who agrees afterwards to deliver the same up without consideration, this agreement shall bind in equity; for that a voluntary settlement may be surrendered voluntarily. *Pre. Chan.* 69.

4. Vide *Cro. Ja.* 516. 2 *Ro.* 97. *H.* 5 *H.* 7. 33. 4 *H.* 7. 7. *b.*

89. *Eodem modo quo quid constituitur* } *dissolvitur,* *eodem modo* } *destruitur.*

1. SAID in the principal case, the feme had lost the name of countess by taking of another husband; for thereby all the names or additions she had before are lost; and therefore the writ, which was in the name of countess, shall abate for that reason. 6 *Co.* 53. *b.*

2. *Note*; A difference between a baroness and a countess by marriage and descent. If a baroness, *&c.* by marriage, marry again under nobility, she hath lost her name of dignity; for, in such case *si mulier nobilis nupserit ignobili, desinit esse nobilis*; but where she is noble by birth or descent, whomsoever she marries, she still remains noble; for birth-right *est character indelibilis*: but what is got by marriage, by marriage may also be lost; for *eodem modo quo quid constituitur dissolvitur.* 6 Co. 53. b.

3. See 1 *Ro.* 461. 4 *Co.* 118. *b.*

4. See *The last rule.*

90. *Eo ligamine quo ligatum est dissolvitur.*

1. SEE *Cro. Ja.* 517. *Da.* 33. *b.*

2. See *The two last rules.*

91. *Equity. Equality is equity.*

General.

1. BRacton, lib. 1. cap. 3. *Aequitas est rerum convenientia, quae paribus in causis paria jura desiderat, et omnia bene coaequiparat, et dicitur aequitas, quasi aequalitas,* whose nature is, as *Finch* saith in his law, *fo.* 20. to amplify, enlarge and add to the letter of the law.

2. *Aequitas*

2. *Aequitas eſt verborum legis directio efficiens, cum una res ſolummodo legis cavetur verbis, ut omnis alia in aequali genere eiſdem caveatur verbis*, and this definition ſeems to accord with *Bracton*'s definition, *Aequitas eſt rerum convenientia, &c.* Plow. Com. 467. a.

3. There are two ſorts of *Leges conſcientiae*; the one is *Lex conſcientiae politicae*, by which the chancellor ordereth matters; in which law of conſcience there is reſpect had unto the laws, cuſtoms and ſtatutes of this commonwealth; and the other is, *Lex conſcientiae divinae*, for which there is no compulſive relief in this world, but the offender ſtandeth at the judgment of God only: and this in time paſt was ſaid to be examinable between the offender and the confeſſor. *Elſ. Obſ.* 48.

4. *Note*; In antient time, where the matter was againſt reaſon, and the party had no remedy at law, the uſe was to ſue for remedy in parliament, and the parliaments were holden on courſe twice every year; but now, ſaith lord *Elſmere*, ſuits are in chancery, and the parliaments are not ſo often holden. Vide *Rot. Parl.* and *Bro. Parl.* 33. *Elſ. Obſ.* 47.

5. Equity judgeth *ſecundum aequum et bonum.* Hob. 225.

6. Equity delights in equality. 1 *Pe. Will.* 9.

7. Proportion is the moſt equal and juſt law, and moſt conſonant to reaſon. *Hard.* 209.

Particular caſes.

1. In the caſe of *Carpenter* and *Carpenter*, cited in the principal caſe, the huſband on marriage had given bond to ſettle particular lands to the uſe of himſelf for life; the remainder to the wife for life; the remainder to the iſſue of that marriage in tail: the huſband having after ſold part of theſe very lands; the lord chancellor on rehearing reverſed part of the decree, ſaying the jointreſs and iſſue were equal purchaſers, and that the loſs muſt be born in proportion: and ſo in any caſe where the jointreſs and iſſue claim by the ſame ſettlement, if there be a prior incumbrance, the jointreſs muſt contribute, and bear her proportion, and not lay the whole burthen on the heir. 1 *Vern.* 440.

2. *Harris* having a conſiderable perſonal eſtate, and four children, made his will in writing, and gave ſeveral legacies to each of his children, and gave his ready money, plate and houſhold ſtuff to his wife, upon truſt and confidence, that ſhe would not diſpoſe thereof, but for the benefit of her children. She makes her will, calling herſelf her huſband's executrix and reſiduary legatee, and gave ſeveral legacies to ſome of her children, and only 5*s.* to the plaintiff and her children, and deviſed all the reſt of her eſtate to her ſon *Bartholomew.* The bill was brought for a diſtributory part; the bequeſt being a void one, and a breach of truſt; after long debate, and ſeveral precedents, the lord chancellor decreed an equal diſtribution. 1 *Vern.* 66, *&c.*

3. The bill ſets forth, that the plaintiff's wife's father was a citizen of *London*, and that he had not advanced her in his life-time, and demanded her cuſtomary part, and prayed an account. The points inſiſted on were, that the father had given her 400*l.* which was ſaid could not be an advancement, as it was not given her as a marriage portion, but long after marriage, and without any agreement that it ſhould be for a portion, and was a free gift, and a great part at chriſtenings and lyings-in. The other ſide inſiſted, this

this 400*l.* ought to be thrown into hotchpot, if the plaintiff will come in for his wife's cuſtomary part or ſhare. But this was denied, and ſaid this was as the caſe of an heireſs having lands in frank-marriage, which muſt be caſt into hotchpot, but not lands conveyed to her by her father or other anceſtor: and it was further ſaid, that the father was a great *Chymiſt*, and had given receipts to the value of 500*l.* to the defendant, who had married the plaintiff's wife's ſiſter, and therefore it was inſiſted that they ought to be accounted for, as part of the father's perſonal eſtate; and to incline the court to think they were of ſuch value, the plaintiff offered to give ſo much for them. But Mr. Solicitor and Mr. *Keck*, (after lord commiſſioner of the great ſeal) ſaid it would be a ſcandal to the city of *London* to make ſuch receipts and trifles part of a citizen's eſtate. Lord chancellor: I will not ſo far countenance theſe receipts, (which are only pieces of quackery, to cheat the people), as to put any value upon them in chancery; for ought I know, a receipt to make mince-pies, or catch rats, may be as valuable. The plaintiff not conſenting to caſt into hotchpot the 400*l.* his bill was diſmiſſed. 1 *Vern.* 61, *&c.*

4. *Hole*, *Harriſon* and *S.* were bound with another in a recognizance to the chamberlain of *London*; the plaintiff *Harriſon* was ſued thereupon, and paid the whole money, and now ſued *Hole*, who was bound with him, for contribution. *Hole*, *Harriſon* and *S.* being all bound, the principal was dead inſolvent, and *S.* was run away. The queſtion was, in what proportion the contribution ſhould be, (*viz.*) a third or a moiety? Decreed a moiety; for *S.* is inſolvent. 1 *Chan. Ca.* 246. *Nelſ.* 15 *and* 203. *S. C.* Vide 1 *Vern.* 70, 297, 404, 440.

5. Where there is a ſpecific legacy, the legatee muſt have his ſpecific legacy intire, though the other legacies fall ſhort; but where there are ſeveral money legacies, as 100*l.* to one, 50*l.* to another, *&c.* though the deviſor directs the 100*l.* to be paid firſt, yet if the others fall ſhort, the legatee of the 100*l.* muſt abate in proprotion. 1 *Vern.* 31.

6. Sir *George Crooke*, having three daughters only, by his will directs that his lands ſhall deſcend and come amongſt his daughters, in ſuch ſhares and proportions as his wife by deed in writing ſhould direct. She makes an unequal diſtribution, giving little to the plaintiff, who brought her bill, inſiſting that the giving the wife ſuch power, was only to keep her children in obedience. And the plaintiff, having behaved herſelf dutifully, ought to have an equal ſhare. The defendant pleaded the will, and that the wife having ſuch a power had by deed appointed ſo much to one daughter and ſo much to another, and though the deed was with power of revocation, yet it was never revoked. As to the power of revocation, it was only an authority in the wife, and that being once executed, ſhe could not reſerve ſuch power to herſelf. And whether the wife might, or not, make ſuch unequal diſtribution, the court would not now determine on the plea, but ordered it ſhould ſtand for an anſwer, with liberty to except; but declared the circumſtances muſt be very ſtrong, as bribery or corruption, to take away the power given to the wife by the expreſs words of the will. For the plaintiff was cited the caſe of *Cragrave* and *Perroſt*, where a man having two daughters, one by a former, the other by his preſent wife, gives his eſtate to his wife, to diſtribute between his two daughters, as his wife ſhould think fit, and ſhe gave 1000*l.* to her own daughter, and 100*l.* to the other,

 and

and there the court decreed an equal diſtribution. On the other ſide was cited *Swetnam* and *Woolaſton*, where an eſtate was given to a man to diſtribute among his nephews and nieces, ſo as he ſhould think fit: a bill being brought by one of the nieces, who had nothing appointed her, was diſmiſſed. In the principal caſe, at another time, the court ordered to be attended with precedents. 1 *Vern.* 355, 356 *and* 414, 415. Note; *Though no decree appears in this caſe, yet the court ſeemed inclined to ſupport the execution of the power.*

7. A man borrows money on mortgage, and after takes more on bond of the ſame perſon, he ſhall not redeem without paying the bond too, tho' there was no mention that the mortgage ſhould ſtand a ſecurity for the bond debt. So if there are two mortgages, and one is defective, he muſt redeem both or neither. The ſame if an heir come to redeem where there is both mortgage and bond, he ſhall not redeem without paying the bond, ſo he be bound in the bond. 1 *Vern.* 244, 245. See 1 *Ch. Ca.* 97. 2 *Ch. Ca.* 164. *Nelſ.* 389. *Gilb.* 105. *Prec. Ch.* 18, 19, 89, 407.

8. Vide 1 *Vern.* 39, 40, 41, 45, 47, 63, 68, 69, 107, 34, 167, 94, 90, 96, 453, 460, 482, 162, 164, 297, 404, 427, 456. 2 *Vern.* 103, 225, 64, 463. 1 *Vern.* 464, 336, 476, 478, 334, 472, 477. 1 *Chan. Ca.* 135, *&c.* 256, 257, 262, 267, 279, 280, 135, 148, 223, 238, 240, 243, 248. *Nelſ.* 15, 203, *S. C.* *Max. Eq. Fi. Ley* 20. 1 *Chan. Ca.* 138, 139, 164, 171, 174, 295. *Wiſeman's Civil Law* 18, 19. *Hard.* 209. *Salk.* 426. *Gilb.* 227.

9. See rules, *Equity favours younger children.* *Diſcovery draws with it relief.*

92. *Equity cannot change things, nor make them act contrary to their eſſential natures and properties.*

A Court of equity can no more let a man in, to defeat an eſtate upon a power of revocation, without a due execution of the power, than the common law could let a man in, to defeat an eſtate upon condition, without performance of the condition; or than a court of equity can let a man in, to defeat a voluntary conveyance, without a power of revocation; for it is all but a condition which muſt be performed, or no advantage taken of it; and a court of equity may do great things, but they cannot alter things, or make them operate contrary to their eſſential natures and properties. 3 *Chan. Ca.* 67. See *The laſt rule.*

93. *Equity favours aſſent to legacies.*

1. SEE 1 *Vern.* 330. 1 *Chan. Ca.* 269.

2. See rule, *Equity favours ſeiſin.*

94. *Equity favours attornment.*

1. SEE 1 *Chan. Ca.* 269. 1 *Vern.* 330. 2 *Co.* 68.

2. See rule, *Equity favours ſeiſin.*

95. *Equity favours livery.*

1. SEE 1 *Vern.* 330.
2. See rule, *Equity favours ſeiſin.*

96. *Equity favours ſeiſin.*

1. A Rent-ſeck is granted. Equity will decree ſeiſin, and the rent to be paid to the grantee. 1 *Ro.* 378.

2. Where there is no remedy at law, as in the principal caſe, equity will grant one; but where there is one, equity will not grant a further one, though that at law be not available: as where an annuity was granted out of a rectory, the glebe was but 40*s.* *per annum*, and the tithes not being liable to diſtreſs, there was no remedy: equity decreed the whole rectory to be liable to the annuity. 1 *Chan. Ca.* 79.

3. An annuity was deviſed by will, and by the ſame will lands were deviſed to an half brother of the deviſee of the annuity, this being a rent-ſeck without ſeiſin, and no power of diſtreſs, and the deviſee of the land having promiſed to pay it; the court decreed the deviſee of the land to give ſeiſin of the rent to the deviſee of the annuity. 1 *Chan. Ca.* 147.

4. The plaintiff, lord of the manor of *Finchley*, pretending himſelf lord, and ſeiſed of rents of the defendants as tenants of the freehold; a trial was directed, and found for the plaintiff; and decreed the tenure and ſeiſin be admitted without further trial. Lord keeper: Tenants uſe their landlords badly now. 1 *Chan. Ca.* 269. Note; *Attornment, ſeiſin, aſſent to legacies,* &c. are favoured in equity.

5. See 1 *Chan. Ca.* 185, 269, 273. 1 *Vern.* 330. 1 *Ro.* 375. *Mo.* 805.

97. *Equity favours republication of wills.*

1. REvocations are favoured for the benefit of the heir. 2 *Mod. Ca.* 71, 77.

2. Yet a revocation is not to be intended, no more than the diſinheriſon of the heir. *Idem* 73.

3. The making a codicil, and annexing it to the will, is no republication of the will. *Prec. Chan.* 441. 2 *Vern.* 722, *&c.*

4. See 1 *Vern.* 330. 2 *Vern.* 722. *Hard.* 374. 1 *Ven.* 341. 2 *Mod.* 313. 3 *Rep. Chan.* 155 *to* 161. *Prec. Chan.* 439. *Barn.* 191, 192, 229.

98. *Equity favours younger children.*

1. LANDS were deviſed to the feme for life, after to be ſold by the executor, for younger childrens portions. The executor dies, the feme dies; the younger children prefer their bill againſt the heir; who demurs, becauſe but an authority in the executor, who is dead. Demurrer over-ruled. 1 *Chan. Ca.* 35.

2. A conveyance, purporting a feoffment, may operate as a covenant to ſtand ſeiſed, though generally a defect in a voluntary conveyance ſhall not be ſupplied and made good here: yet if a man voluntarily make a ſettlement, as a proviſion for his children, and for their maintenance, ſuch voluntary conveyance ſhall be ſupplied and made good here. 1 *Vern.* 40. See *Ca.* 36.

3. One by will made proviſion for his younger children out of a copyhold eſtate, but the ſurrender was only into the hands of one of the cuſtomary tenants; yet decreed for the younger children; ſo the defect was well ſupplied againſt the heir at law; there being many precedents in this court of the like nature. 1 *Vern.* 132, 133.

4. One having power, by deed or will in writing, to charge lands with 500*l.* deviſes the ſame to younger children, but the will was not ſealed, yet decreed good againſt a tenant in tail under the ſettlement. 1 *Chan. Ca.* 263.

5. So where one having ſuch power, ſends inſtructions for a conveyance to charge them with younger childrens portions. 1 *Chan. Ca.* 264.

* 6. A defect in the ſurrender of a copyhold to the uſe of a laſt will was ſupplied; eſpecially being for the benefit of the deviſor's children. *See* caſe before the houſe of lords, *Lloyd* verſus *Barton*, 18 *Feb.* 1715.

7. Wife being *priviment enſient* at her huſband's death, the child could not be provided for by law, but the court ordered the child to have ſufficient allowance. *Tot.* 157.

8. Tenant in tail, with remainder in fee, levies a fine, and ſettles his eſtate on truſtees. In the firſt place to pay his eldeſt ſon 100*l.* *per annum*, and then to make proviſion of 100*l.* a-piece for his younger children, to be raiſed and paid according to their ſeniority, and maintenance in the mean time. Lord chancellor decreed, that whereas at the time of the ſettlement the party was a widower and had eight children, and declared he never intended to marry again; yet in regard he afterwards married a ſecond wife and had many children by her, that the children by her were equally intitled with the children by the firſt. And that whereas the deed directed the proviſion to be raiſed and paid according to their ſeniority, that yet, in caſe of deficiency, they ſhould be paid in average. That ſome of the younger children dying in the life of their father, their adminiſtrators ſhould not have benefit of this proviſion, (*caſe* 320.) but the ſame ſhould ceaſe. But in caſe any of the daughters had been married in the life of the father, and died, the huſbands, as their adminiſtrators, ſhould have had their portions: and no certain time being appointed, but the ſame being left indifferent, it doth not naturally attach till the death of the father. And whereas the eldeſt ſon had purchaſed in a ſtatute, which was an incumbance on the eſtate, he ſhould be allowed no more than he paid, (ſee *Caſe* 48, 330, 445, 465.) and that the eſtate muſt be looked upon as liable, in the firſt place, to ſatisfy this incumbrance, and then to raiſe 100*l.* *per annum* and arrears, and the ſurplus for raiſing the proviſion for younger children, but that their maintenance ſhould go on in the mean time. 1 *Vern.* 335, 336.

9. One deviſes a copyhold eſtate to his grandſon; and *Sommers*, lord chancellor, decreed it good, and that equity ought to ſupply a ſurrender in this as well as in caſe of a ſon; the grandfather being bound to provide for him: but the houſe of lords reverſed this decree; as equity ought not

not to ſupply ſuch defect in disfavour of the heir at law, unleſs it was in favour of a ſon or daughter; and not then neither, if it was to diſinherit the eldeſt ſon. But it was not material that ſuch ſon was provided for before, nor how far; for the father only is beſt judge whether he hath fully advanced his child, or not. *Salk.* 187.

* 10. The executor waſtes the fund for younger childrens fortunes; this is a *Devaſtavit* in him, for which he ſhall account. But the younger children have no remedy over, out of the real eſtate; as there was a ſufficient perſonalty, or might have been, had it not been for the executor's wilful neglect. See caſe *Morgan* and *Morgan*, before the houſe of lords, 21 *April* 1736. *It would be hard to make the corruption or neglect of the executor work to the hurt of the heir, who is an innocent party.* See *Salk.* 155. 1 *Vern.* 336. *Prec. Chan.* 397, 439, 585.

11. *A.* being long in poſſeſſion of a mortgage in fee, deviſed it to his daughters *B.* and *C.* and their heirs, and died. *B.* marries, and dies. And on the queſtion, whether the ſhare of *B.* ſhould be deemed a real or perſonal eſtate, and ſo whether it ſhould deſcend to her heir, or to her huſband as adminiſtrator? Decreed to the heir. So if a man ſo ſeiſed, deviſeth to his ſon and his heirs, and that they ſhall go as an inheritance; ſurely the heir, if this mortgage be paid off, ſhall receive the money, and not the executor; for he had a governing power, and may diſpoſe of it as an inheritance ſo long as it may continue ſo: and the money, when paid off, ſhall go as he intended the land; but note, this is, when it is in his own family, and when his intent appears plainly by the words of the will; for though it cannot abſolutely paſs a fee, yet as much as can ſhall paſs. And ſo it is in all caſes where a man has children, *&c.* *Gilb.* 2. 3.

12. A bill was brought for raiſing the wife's portion out of a reverſionary term, expectant on her father's death. The caſe was, that *Thomas Maidwell*, the father of the plaintiff's wife, upon his marriage, ſettled to the uſe of himſelf for life; remainder to truſtees for 500 years; remainder to the heirs male of his body by his intended wife; and if he ſhould happen to die without iſſue male of his body by his wife, and there ſhould be one or more daughters of their two bodies, *which ſhould be unmarried, or not provided for at the time of his death*; ſuch daughter, if but one, ſhould have 2000*l.* and 30*l. per annum*, iſſuing out of the profits, till the portion ſhould become due; which was to be paid at eighteen or day of marriage: and a power for truſtees to raiſe it by ſale or mortgage of the term, or perception of profits. There was but one daughter, and no ſon of this marriage. The wife died, the daughter above 21, and married to the plaintiff. The queſtion was, Whether the truſtees could raiſe her portion in the life of her father? And on great conſideration, it was held by *Cowper*, lord chancellor, 1ſt, That though a term is limited in remainder, to commence after the death of the father, yet if the truſt is to raiſe a portion, payable at the age of eighteen, or marriage, the daughter may compel a ſale of the term. 2dly, So it is if the truſt of a term for raiſing daughters portions be limited to take effect, in caſe the father dies without iſſue male by his wife, and the wife dies without iſſue male, leaving a daughter, in ſuch caſe the term is ſaleable in the life of the father; that ſo far it had been carried already, but he doubted whether he could have gone ſo far in caſe the matter was *res integra*; but that the reaſoning, upon which it had been founded, was, that

2 by

by the death of the mother, the poſſibility of the iſſue male was extinct; that all that was contingent in the caſe has happened: it is become impoſſible that there ſhould be iſſue male; and as to the father's death, that is not contingent, for all men muſt die; and it is now the ſame thing to ſay, when the father ſhall die without iſſue male by his wife, or to ſay when the father ſhall die; and if this caſe had gone no further, it had been no more than the father is tenant for life; the remainder to truſtees for 500 years, for raiſing daughters portions, payable at the age of eighteen, or marriage: and now all contingencies being happened, and out of the caſe, it ſhould ſeem within the reaſon of the firſt reſolution. That the caſe of *Graves* and *Mattiſon*, 2 *Jo.* 201. comes fully up to this reſolution: Sir *Edward Graves* made a ſettlement to the uſe of himſelf for life; remainder to the uſe of his firſt ſon in tail male; the remainder to truſtees for 40 years; remainder to himſelf in fee. The term is declared to be in truſt, in caſe it ſhould happen that Sir *Edward* ſhould die without iſſue male of his body, then the truſtees ſhould raiſe 5000*l.* for daughters portions, payable at the age of 21 or marriage, with a proviſion for maintenance in the mean time; the wife died, leaving two daughters and no iſſue male. And by *Pemberton*, *Dolben* and *Raymond*, it was reſolved, That the right to the portion was veſted, by the mother's death without iſſue male, in the life of the father; for otherwiſe the father might live ſo long, that the portions might be of little ſervice. Thus far the court has gone for convenience, that young women might have their portions when they moſt wanted them. But in the principal caſe, the daughter, who is the ſubject of the proviſion, muſt be a daughter unmarried, or unprovided for at the time of the father's death, which is a contingency not yet happened; and therefore it comes not within the reaſon of either of the rules. As to the 30*l.* *per annum* for maintenance, he held, that muſt be intended in caſe the father dies without iſſue male, leaving a daughter under the age of eighteen, or not married; becauſe otherwiſe this abſurdity muſt follow, that the daughter muſt be paid maintenance-money in the life of the father, and that out of the profits of a term that is not to commence till after his death. That this caſe was too ſtrong for the court to attempt to get over, and to do it would create great confuſion; and it would be to no purpoſe for any one to make deeds, if the argument of convenience or inconvenience ſhould prevail to over-rule them. Bill diſmiſſed. *Salk.* 159, 160.

13. Vide 1 *Vern.* 324, 334, 337, 462, 476. 2 *Ven.* 365. *Prec. Ch.* 5, 6. 3 *Chan. Ca.* 13. 1 *Chan. Ca.* 265. 3 *Rep. Chan.* 190.

99. *Equity has a concurrent juriſdiction with the admiralty.*

1. SEE rules, *Admiralty not to hold plea of matters cognizable at law. Diſcovery draws with it relief.*

2. See *Salk.* 33. 2 *Ven.* 181. 1 *Ven.* 146, 343. 1 *Lev.* 60. *Raym.* 3. 3 *Mod.* 244. 6 *Mod.* 24, 25, 100, 422. *Stat.* 4 & 5 *Annæ*, *cap.* 16. *ſect.* 18, 19, 20. 1 *Vern.* 21. *Gilb.* 227, 228.

100. *Equity has a concurrent jurisdiction with the ecclesiastical courts.*

General.

1. CHancery will restrain the jurisdiction of inferior courts, as are all spiritual courts. 1 *Chan. Ca.* 203.

2. Chancery hath an original jurisdiction, or at least a concurrent one with the spiritual courts. *Gilb.* 1. 1 *Ju. Eccl.* 151, 152.

3. Lord keeper declared, that the judges of the ecclesiastical courts were as subject to the equity of chancery, as judgments in the common law courts. *Nelſ.* 434. 1 *Chan. Ca.* 201. *Gilb.* 208. 1 *Ju. Eccl.* 152.

4. If chancery see the exercise of the jurisdiction of a surrogate be to an infant's prejudice, *&c.* it is incumbent on chancery to interfere, and take care the infant be not prejudiced, *&c.* 1 *Ju. Eccl.* 530. *ca.* 8.

Particular cases.

5. The bill bas against an administrator *& al'*, for distribution according to the *Stat.* 22 *Car.* 2. which statute the defendant pleaded, and that thereby the ordinary is made the judge to distribute, and is appointed to take security; and therefore the plaintiff ought to sue there, and not here. Lord chancellor over-ruled the plea. 2 *Chan. Ca.* 95.

6. An infant legatee sueth in a court ecclesiastical, and pending the suit, sueth in chancery: the former suit depending being pleaded, the plea was disallowed; for there is no such security for the infant's advantage as here: and possibly not for interest, if placed out, and for bringing in account here, *&c.* 2 *Chan. Ca.* 85.

7. The probate of wills did not belong to the spiritual court by the ecclesiastical laws, but came to them by custom and usage: and it is but of late, as *Fairfax* said in *Fitz. Abr.* 148. that they had the probate thereof; and still by usage they are to be proved in *Courts Baron* where such custom prevails. And in this *Fineux* and all the justices agreed 11 *H.* 7. 12. (9 *Rep.* 38.) when the will is proved in the ecclesiastical court, the court has executed its authority (see 2 *Ju. Eccl. fo.* 106. *Havers*'s case); but the executors are to sue in the temporal courts to get in the estate of the deceased. So that the several distinctions in our law, touching this jurisdiction, will fall under five heads. 1st, That the spiritual court is the only court now, that has authority to receive the probate of wills, (of personal estates) and to give a sanction to them; because the jurisdiction of the county court (*where they were originally proved*) is lost by non-usage, and since *Magna Charta ca.* 18. the king's courts did not intermeddle. But here must be excepted all courts baron that have such usage for probate of wills. 2dly, The seal of the ecclesiastical courts authenticates the will; and as in *Raym.* 406, 407. the seal of the ordinary in such case regularly cannot be contradicted; because if there be no way in the temporal courts to prove the will relating to chattels, it must go on in the spiritual court, and the determintaition there must be final; and therefore in such case, if they shew a probate under the hand of the ordinary, the temporal courts cannot receive evidence that the will was forged, or that the testator was *non compos*, or that another person was executor:

but they may receive evidence, that the ſeal was forged, or the will repealed, or that there were *bona notabilia*, becauſe that is not in contradiction to the real ſeal of the court, but admits and avoids it. *Lev.* 235, 236. *Vau.* 207. 1 *Show.* 293. And ſince the eccleſiaſtical courts have the probate of wills now, the temporal courts cannot prohibit them in their inquiries, Whether the teſtator was *non compos*, or not? Or whether revoked, or not? Becauſe theſe are neceſſary for authenticating the will. *Hard.* 131, 313. *But theſe courts and their magiſtrates, judges and officers are to take with them*, 3dly, That if a temporal matter be pleaded in bar of an eccleſiaſtical demand, though they may proceed in the eccleſiaſtical court, yet it muſt be according to the temporal law, or elſe the temporal courts will hinder them. *Show.* 158, 173. 1 *Ven.* 291. 3 *Mod.* 283. If the ſpiritual court admit a will, but will not give the probate to the executor, becauſe he cannot give ſecurity for a juſt adminiſtration, a *Mandamus* lieth; for though they are to determine whether or no there be a will or not? Yet if there be a will, the executor has a temporal right, and they cannot put any terms upon him, but what are mentioned in the will; and therefore if they will not grant the probate, where they admit there is an executor, the court will grant a *Mandamus*. 4thly, If a man gives lands to be ſold for payment of debts, and diſpoſes of the money to ſeveral perſons; that cannot be ſued for in the eccleſiaſtical court, but only in a court of equity; becauſe there is not a legacy meerly of goods and chattels, but it ariſes originally out of lands and tenements, and they have a teſtamentary juriſdiction touching chattels only. *Hob.* 2 *Ro.* 285. 5thly, Courts of equity can hold plea concerning a legacy, and likewiſe concerning the deviſe of a *reſiduum*, which is but a legacy. They may in notorious caſes declare a legatee who has obtained a legacy by fraud, to be truſtee for another: and as to the deviſe of a *reſiduum*, nothing can be more clear, for ſince the caſe of *Foſter* and *Munt*, 1 *Vern.* 473. where-ever an executor hath had a ſpecific legacy, he has been looked upon as a truſtee of the *reſiduum* for the relations, in a courſe of diſtribution; and no body ever attacked theſe decrees in favour of the relations, (ſee 2 *Vern.* 648.) upon this head of argument, that they were contrary to the eccleſiaſtical juriſdiction. *Gilb.* 203. Marriot's *caſe*.

8. Nobody ever thought that declaring a truſt in any of theſe caſes mentioned above in *Marriot*'s caſe, was an infringment upon the eccleſiaſtical juriſdiction. *Gilb.* 209.

9. See 1 *Vern.* 26, 93, 90, 27, 134. 1 *Ju. Eccl.* 530. 2 *Ju. Eccl.* 106, *&c.*

10. See rule, *Diſcovery draws with it relief.*

101. *Equity is to enforce the execution of agreements.*

1. EQUITY will compel the performance of agreements in ſpecie, as it looks upon articles for a purchaſe of land, equal to a conveyance; for if the purchaſer dieth before any conveyance is executed, and deviſeth theſe lands, they ſhall paſs in equity. 1 *Chan. Ca.* 39. Vide 1 *Vern.* 201, 217, 48. 2 *Vent.* 353. Yet it muſt be fair. 2 *Chan. Ca.* 17. 1 *Vern.* 227, 167, 271.

2. It

2. It was ſaid in the principal caſe, that it had been held by ſome, that even a bargain and ſale inrolled by *Ceſtuy que truſt* of an eſtate-tail, ſhall bind the iſſue, in regard that ſuch a truſt is not within the ſtatute *De donis.* And it was reſolved in the principal caſe, that a common recovery, or a fine by *Ceſtuy que truſt*, ſhould have the ſame effect and avail in equity, and bind the truſt in the ſame manner, as the ſame would have bound the eſtate in law, in caſe he had had the legal eſtate in him. 1 *Vern.* 440.

3. Equity will not relieve againſt the terms of an agreement, though it may ſeem in nature of a penalty. *Prec. Chan.* 102.

4. Neither will equity eſtabliſh an agreement, where founded in fraud. *Prec. Chan.* 538. *Vide* 574. For *aequum et bonum eſt lex legum; and the office of equity is to ſuppreſs fraud.*

5. *A.* makes a voluntary ſettlement on *B.* who after agrees to deliver it up without conſideration, yet this agreement ſhall bind in equity; for a voluntary ſettlement may be ſurrendered voluntarily. *Prec. Chan.* 69.

6. A huſband had made a proviſion for his wife, and agreed that her fortune, which was in truſtees hands, ſhould be laid out in the purchaſe of lands: this agreement, though after marriage, was not to be conſidered as voluntary, ſo as to be ſet aſide in favour of a creditor of the huſband, for on a bill by the huſband, the court would not have decreed for him, without a ſettlement, and the creditor can be in no better or other condition than the huſband himſelf would have been in. *Prec. Chan.* 22.

7. Sealing, not neceſſary to bring agreements out of the ſtatute. *Prec. Chan.* 16, 560.

8. The agreement is by parol only, yet the defendant confeſſing it by his anſwer, without inſiſting on the benefit of the ſtatute, equity will decree execution; becauſe there is no danger of perjury. *Prec. Chan.* 208, 374. 2 *Chan. Ca.* 136, 143, 164. *Nelſ.* 343. *Gilb.* 437.

9. Agreement, though not in writing, being executed on one part, and enjoyment had under it; equity will not deſtroy it. *Prec. Chan.* 519. *Vide* 533.

10. A ſettlement was made by the huſband on his wife for a jointure, the huſband covenanted that the lands were worth 800*l.* a year, and that if the ſame were ſhort, his other eſtate ſhould be liable to ſupply the defect. After, all the other eſtate of the huſband, not in the jointure, was mortgaged, and afterwards he acknowledged a judgment to the plaintiff, who was his taylor, and had been bound with him in ſeveral bonds. The judgment was defeazanced on payment of 550*l.* The huſband makes his will, and deviſeth all his lands for the payment of his debts. The plaintiff brought the bill to have the truſt performed and to be paid. The defendant, ſon of this marriage, in his anſwer confeſſeth the deviſe for payment, but ſets forth the indenture, covenant and mortgage; and inſiſted they were prior, and ought to be firſt paid; and cited a caſe where a man covenanted to make a jointure of 500*l.* a year, mentioning no lands, and there the lands were bound even againſt a purchaſer. Mr. *Keck* admitted that to be ſo. But where particular lands are ſettled, and the huſband covenants they are of ſuch value, it binds the perſon only: but this caſe indeed was ſtronger, for he had made his other lands liable to the defect of the jointure in value. Mr. *Keck* alſo admitted, that where lands are generally deviſed for payment of debts, there all ſorts of ſecurities, whether ſtatutes, judgments, bonds or ſimple

 contracts,

contracts, ſhall be paid in average. But then there is this difference, that if the deviſee and truſtee to pay debts, be alſo executor, then the lands ſo deviſed becomes legal aſſets, and the debts muſt be paid according to their precedency or ſuperiority at common law. And ſo it was reſolved in the caſe of *Hixine* and *Mortley*, which was agreed to be law on all ſides; and this caſe being ſo, it was agreed that the lands ſhould be ſold according to the truſt in the will, for payment of debts. And that the plaintiff be let in for ſatisfaction of his judgment, which had ſlept 40 years. 1 *Vern.* 63, *&c.*

11. See *Salk.* ſub tit. *Chancery*, *Duke Hamilton* and *Lord Mohun*'s caſe, 2 *Vern.* 201, 202, 423. 1 *Chan. Ca.* 84, 68, 172, 236, 238, 243, 274, 212. *Nelſ.* 67, 68, 72, 128, 138, 164, 144, 167, 170, 119, *&c.* *Gilb.* 71. *Prec. Chan.* 89, 102. *Nelſ.* 180, 183, 190, 201, 224, 230, 231, 235, 254, 261, 262, 326, 343, 374. *Gilb.* 11, 13, 14, 15, 108, 109. *Vue le Livre* 141, 143, 160, 188. Contra *Prec. Chan.* 175, 186. *Gilb.* 152. 2 *Vern.* 386, 498, 671, 752. 1 *Vern.* 53, 326. 1 *Rep. Ch.* 4, 164. 1 *Chan. Ca.* 250. *Prec. Ch.* 456, 497, 239. *Gilb.* 160, 167. 2 *Vern.* 379. *Prec. Ch.* 16, 17, 19, 20, 25, 26, 29, 30, 69, 70, 538, 560, 575. *Gilb.* 64. 1 *Pe. Will.* 61, 104, 105, 106. *Prec. Chan.* 462. *Eq. Abr.* 218. 2 *Vern.* 373. 1 *Chan. Ca.* 39, 173, 208. 2 *Chan. Ca.* 63, 78. *Vern.* 13. 1 *Chan. Ca.* 49. 2 *Vent.* 350. 1 *Chan. Ca.* 236.

102. *Equity has a power, upon circumſtances, to relieve againſt penalties, judgments and executions, and to abate, moderate, and ſometimes diſcharge damages and coſts.*

1. THE mortgagee had obtained judgment in ejectment, and entered on the premiſſes, and thereby prevented the creditors, who had ſubſequent ſecurities, from entring; and ſuffered the mortgagor to take the profits. And now the other creditors coming to redeem, it was ordered that the mortgagee ſhould be charged with all the profits he had or might have received from the time of his entry. 1 *Vern.* 270.

2. If the leſſor will avoid the leaſe for non-payment of rent at the day, equity will relieve againſt ſuch forfeiture. *Car.* 45.

3. The plaintiff, tenant for life by copy *durante viduitate*, felled trees, which was preſented and found by the homage; and ſo a forfeiture. A bill was brought for relief againſt the forfeiture, offering, if it appeared it was ſo, to make ſatisfaction. Iſſue directed to find whether the primary intention in felling the timber was to do waſte; declaring in caſe of wilful forfeiture, this court would not relieve. 1 *Chan. Ca.* 96. ſee 95. Admiſſion by the lord, diſpenſeth with a former forfeiture. The father committed a forfeiture, the lord nevertheleſs ſeiſed an heriot upon his death, and yet would avoid the heir's eſtate for that forfeiture, which he could not, becauſe the taking of an heriot alloweth a dying ſeiſed. *Tot.* 107. Yet where the father commits a forfeiture, and dieth, and the ſon is admitted as heir by deſcent, it was decreed that this purgeth not the forfeiture; becauſe the father dying ſeiſed of no eſtate, the ſon can be admitted to none. *Tot.* 107. *Ideo quaere.*

103. *Equity is a creature of chancery, and as ſuch to be governed as conſcience directs by that court.*

THough the lord keeper was not poſitive in the main point, yet he ſaid as to the agreement by the father, whether to be avoided by the ſon, now defendant, that in caſe the land had been intailed *de facto*, and agreed, no agreement could bind the iſſue without fine or recovery, or other legal bar: yet he ſaid the agreement to intail was not an intail, and though it raiſed an equity againſt him that made it, yet that equity is a creature of this court, to be governed as conſcience directs by this court; and ſaid that the ſtatute *De donis* was an ambitious act in favour of lords againſt the king, and for that vouched the lord *Elſmere*; but before he ſaid this, there were ſome propoſals of agreement. And at length the caſe was compoſed. 1 *Chan. Ca.* 236.

104. *Equity is part of the law of* England.

1. EQUITY is part of the law of the land. 1 *Chan. Ca.* 141. 2. *Plow. Com.* Eaſton's *caſe*, *Elſ. Obſ.* *Bract. lib.* 1. *cap.* 3. *Finch's Law* and *Weſt's Prec.* *Doct.* & *Stud.* See *next rule*.

105. *Equity is to moderate the rigour of the law.*

1. EQUITY is that which is called equal and good, and ſometimes equal and juſt, and mitigates or moderates the law written in ſome circumſtances; and as law is that which maketh all things ſtreight, ſo equity is that which diſpenſeth with many points of the law, meaſuring out to every man that that is his. It is a reaſonable meaſure, containing in itſelf a fit proportion, ſuitable to the perſons, matters, places, times and other circumſtances. And it differeth from law, as law is a determinate ſentence: but equity is a certain proportion and allay on good and juſt occaſions, ſetting aſide the common rules of law, and is therefore ſometimes called a ruled kind of juſtice, allayed with the ſweetneſs of mercy. Sometimes plain dealing is called equity, which is oppoſite to the dealing of man by nice points of law, &c. 2 *Weſt's Prec.* 174. *b.* 175. *b.* 176. *a.*

2. Equity is two fold, 1ſt, Written, and 2dly, Not written. 1ſt, Written where the caſe in all points is anſwerable to the law without any different circumſtances requiring any change or alteration of the law. 2dly, Unwritten where particular facts fall out which have no certain line or ſquare ſet out for them in the law already made; ſo that they muſt be decided according to their circumſtances, yet as near as may be to the principles of law. And herein is the greateſt uſe of equity; and therefore it is moſt fitly called an unwritten equity, not becauſe the judges thereof are at liberty to define and determine of it, without regard to the law written; but becauſe it taketh a juſt liberty not to bind itſelf to the general rules of the law, but to determine according to the particular circumſtances of the caſe. 2 *Weſt's Prec.* 175. *a.*

3. Strict

3. Strict law is ſevere and not to be moved, it taketh order for things once for all: and its grounds and principles are univerſal, from which it will not turn; whereas equity particularly and carefully examineth the cauſes, times, perſons and matters, with all and every of their differences, together with all the other circumſtances, and on all theſe gathered together, frameth an abſolute and perfect deciſion. *St. Germain* to the like effect ſaith, equity is a righteouſneſs tempered with mercy, which conſidereth all the particular circumſtances of the deed. *Doct. & Stud. lib.* 1. *cap.* 16. 2 *Weſt's Prec.* 175, 176.

4. It is diſcretionary in equity, whether to interpoſe, or not, where there is no remedy at law; as in caſes of voluntary conveyances and the like. *Prec. Chan.* 84. *Yet I conceive where there would be a failure of juſtice, equity, by the rules of conſcience, which are the guides of equity, is bound to interpoſe and ſupply the defects of the law, as are the books, unleſs in particular caſes where equity is forbid on account of ſome general inconvenience.*

5. God is the efficient cauſe of equity. And the law of nature, the law of nations, and good manners, are the material cauſes thereof; the formal cauſe thereof, is the ſquaring the circumſtances of facts with the rules of law. And the final cauſe is to keep an equality amongſt men. 2 *Weſt's Prec.* 175. *a. b.*

6. And there is a difference between equity and clemency; equity being always firmly tied to the will of the law, whither ſoever it inclineth, whether to clemency or ſeverity; but clemency is only proper for the prince, or thoſe magiſtrates that have the like power of adminiſtration of juſtice as princes have. 2 *Weſt's Prec.* 175. *b.*

7. See 3 *Chan. Ca.* 73, 134. *Prec. Chan.* 46, 47, 233, 236. *Nelſ.* 417.

106. *Equity looks upon that as done which ought to be done.*

*1. ALL agreements are to be conſidered as performed, which are made on valuable conſiderations; and they are alſo to be conſidered as done at the time when, according to the tenor thereof, they ought to have been performed; and they are alſo deemed to have the ſame conſequences; in regard that the perſon, or any other claiming authority under him, ought not to benefit by his own laches or default, nor thoſe for whoſe profit ſuch contract was made to ſuffer thereby. See caſe *Frederick* verſus *Frederick*, before the houſe of lords, 4 *May* 1731. And therefore

2. If a purchaſer dieth before any conveyance of the purchaſed lands executed, having deviſed the ſame, they ſhall paſs in equity; for equity looks upon articles for a purchaſe equal to a conveyance. 1 *Chan. Ca.* 93.

3. So a bill was brought to compel the performance of a parol agreement for a leaſe of an houſe, in confidence of which agreement the plaintiff had laid out a conſiderable ſum of money. The defendant pleaded the ſtatute of frauds, and his plea was allowed. But the lord keeper was of opinion, if the bill had charged it was part of the agreement, that the agreement ſhould have been put into writing, that would have altered the caſe, and poſſibly have required an anſwer. 1 *Vern.* 151.

* 4. Tenant for life with power to make leaſes for 21 years, ſo the ſame be in poſſeſſion, and at the beſt improved rent, makes a leaſe, and a year after

after gives a note to another of his tenants under his hand, that he will renew his and the other tenants leafe fo often as he fhall be required. Decreed to renew at the old rent for 21 years, if he fhall fo long live: this decree was pronounced by the court of exchequer in *Ireland* 21 *Feb.* 1736. * and affirmed by the houfe of lords here 7 *April* 1738. See alfo *Obara* and *Oneil*, 12 *Feb.* 1717, both cafes before the houfe of lords.

* 5. Yet a written agreement being unreafonable, equity would not carry it into execution, but decreed it to be delivered to the party for whofe benefit it was defigned, that he might make the moft of it at law. *See* cafe before the houfe of lords, *Squire* and *Baker*, 27 *Feb.* 1726, alfo * *White* and *Leighbourn*'s cafe, 28 *Feb.* 1722. * *Green* and *Green*, 25 *Jan.* 1710. * *Thompfon* and *Harcourt*, 13 *Feb.* 1721. * *Moody* and *Stewart*, 28 *Feb.* 1728. all before the houfe of lords.

6. *And where an equal agreement cannot, by reafon of any fubfequent act of parliament or the like, be performed in the whole; yet the fame fhall be executed in fuch part as is lawful, as was the cafe of* * Doctor Betfworth, & al' of Doctors Commons *againft* The Dean and Chapter of St. Paul'*s*, *before the houfe of lords*, 2 May 1728, *alfo cafe* * Bridge *and* Hitchcock, *before the houfe of lords*, 24 June 1716.

* 7. And in matters executory, as in cafe of articles directing a conveyance, where the words of the articles are either improper or informal, equity will direct a conveyance, not according to fuch improper or informal expreffions, but in a proper and legal way, fo at leaft as to anfwer the intent of the parties. *A fortiori* in the cafe of a will. *See* cafe before the houfe of lords, * The earl of *Stafford* and *Hobart*, *Anno* 1709. And equity will carry marriage articles into ftrict execution. *See* cafe before the houfe of lords, 5 *Feb.* 1719, *Trevor* and *Trevor*, and alfo cafe * *Martin* and *Martin*, 6 *March* 1726, and *Gleg* and *Gleg*, 14 *May* 1728. * ——— and *Stanley*, 5 *March* 1714. * *Weft* and *Erifey*, *Feb.* 1727. * *Vernon* and *Vernon*, 23 *March* 1731-2. * *Onefby* and *Dodfwel*, 21 *Jan.* 1702. * *Pocklington* and *Sir Compton Donfvile*, *Feb.* 1729. * *Blake* and *Blake*, *May* 1729. * *Newgent* and *Newgent*, 6 *Feb.* 1737.

8. See rules, *Equality is equity. Equity favours younger children. Equity is to execute the intent of the parties. Equity rectifies miftakes. Equity is to enforce the execution of agreements.*

9. See alfo 2 *Chan. Ca.* 91. 2 *Vern.* 295, 296. *Gilb.* 165.

107. *Equity may carry the debt beyond the penalty on circumftances.*

General.

1. WHERE fecurity is taken by penalty, the penalty cannot be exceeded, nor fo much taken if compenfation may be without it. 1 *Ch. Ca.* 24.

2. On a bond to perform covenants, the party fhall recover no more than he is really damnified, and fhould recover on a trial at law. 1 *Rep. Chan.* 197, *&c.*

3. No relief beyond the penalty of a recognizance for the performance of covenants. 1 *Rep. Chan.* 94, 95.

Particular cases.

4. Lord *Belmont*, *anno* 1647, being under great oppreſſions from the then uſurped powers, and going abroad, lent 600*l.* to *G.* on a recognizance of 1000*l.* which he took in the name of the defendant *Buſh*, and intended as a proviſion for his infant daughter then but two years old. *B.* at the ſame time executed a declaration of truſt, and covenanted that the now plaintiff the infant ſhould enjoy. Lord *Belmont* died in *Perſia*, *anno* 1654, *G.* ſells his eſtate, and *B.* acknowledges ſatisfaction; and in 1657, and not ſooner, the plaintiff had knowledge of this truſt and the breach of it, and then brought her bill for relief. The defendant by his anſwer, inſiſts that he was but 18 when he executed the declaration, and the declaration, tho' made for the infant, was indeed to protect the father's eſtate, and that he never had the cuſtody of the recognizance, nor any conſideration for acknowledging ſatisfaction, but the lord *Belmont*'s widow delivered up the ſame, and believes received the money due on the ſame, and whereupon he acknowledged ſatisfaction, and believes he had ſome warrant for ſo doing, but that the ſame was burnt in the fire of *London*. And further, that after all this time of 30 years he ought not to be charged with this pretended breach of truſt: and his counſel inſiſted further, that the plaintiff ought to prove ſome fraud in the truſtee, or that he received the money to his own uſe. Lord chancellor: It lies on the defendant, who ought to diſcharge himſelf. There is no doubt but an infant may be a truſtee, and the breach was after he was of age; and therefore decreed him to pay principal, with damages not exceeding 1000*l.* being the penalty; and cited *Hob.* where *Ceſtuy que truſt*, in an action on the caſe againſt his truſtee, ſhall recover for breach of truſt in damages. 1 *Vern.* 342, *&c.*

5. *Anno* 1638. thoſe under whom the plaintiff claims a debt of 1300*l.* acknowledged a judgment for 2000*l.* but the penalty was defeazanced on payment of principal and intereſt. The defendant for 10 or 12 years kept the plaintiff out of his debt by fencing with prior incumbrances, which in truth, were ſatisfied, and by a pretended intail, which on trial at law were found againſt him. The plaintiff had exhibited a former bill, and only prayed the defendant might come to account, what, if any thing, was due to him on thoſe prior incumbrances, and that the plaintiff might be ſatisfied his debt; but did not pray further, as he might, that if the defendant ſhould be found to have received more than his due, that he might pay the overplus to the plaintiff. Upon the account it was found that the defendant was over paid 400*l.* and the plaintiff's now bill was for this money towards his debt, and to be ſatisfied his principal, intereſt and coſts. The defendant pleaded the former bill and proceedings, and that after account here, the plaintiff had proceeded at law, and revived his judgment by *Sci' Fa'*, and taken execution by *Elegit*, and that thereupon the defendant had brought the whole penalty of the bond into the common pleas, and inſiſted that equity ought not to charge him beyond the penalty. The plea was allowed. Yet equity does ſometimes carry on the debt beyond the penalty. As where the party had been delayed by the injunction of this court; but then it has always been againſt the plaintiff, and never known the plaintiff hath charged the defendant further than he could at law. The plea was principally allowed, becauſe the plaintiff had, after account, ſurceaſed his pro-

profecution in this court, and proceeded at law; and therefore having elected to proceed at law, he fhould not now refort back to equity. 1 *Vern.* 349, 350. *Show. Parl. Ca.* 15, 16.

6. The cafe was upon an appeal to the houfe of lords for relief againft a decree in chancery. The appellant *Elizabeth* had executed a bond of 140*l.* penalty, conditioned for the payment of 72*l.* 20 *April* 1676. And by means of feveral promiffes and delays in payment, and privileges and other occafions intervening, this bond was not fued till lately, when *Solvitur ad diem* was pleaded, and after iffue joined and notice of trial, upon fome difcovery of defect of evidence to prove the bond, it was moved to alter the plea, which being denied, a bill was brought in chancery, on fuggeftion that the appellant had never executed the bond, or that it was gained by fraud, and was without confideration. The refpondent on the other hand preferred a bill for difcovery of fuch bond, *&c.* and on hearing it was decreed, That the appellant fhould not be relieved only againft the penalty; and referred to a mafter to compute the principal and intereft due thereon, and to tax cofts for the refpondent both at law and in equity; and that what the mafter fhall find due, be paid as the mafter fhould appoint; who computed the principal and intereft at 154*l.* and cofts at 67*l.* and appointed payment 20 *October* following. On hearing of the appeal, two *quaeries* were made. 1ft, Whether, as there had been fome difference concerning the proof of the bond, the court fhould have decreed without directing an iffue at law to try the validity of the bond. But it was held that, as the bond was not denied in pleading at law, chancery had done right, as they could not well have directed any other iffue than the parties themfelves had joined in at law; and though it was pretended that the attorney had fo pleaded without authority, yet the court paid no great regard to that pretence, becaufe of the remedy over, againft the attorney, if the fact was really as pretended. Another queftion was, Whether equity could juftly award more than the penalty? That the order being to fave againft the penalty, no more ought to have been awarded or decreed. But it was faid, that notwithftanding that, when the fame was referred to a mafter, to tax principal and intereft, the order bound the party to pay both, though it fhould amount to more than the penalty; and the meaning of the firft part was only to relieve againft the penalty, in cafe the money due for principal and intereft came to lefs than the penal fum. And efpecially as there were crofs caufes, and as this cafe was circumftanced, and after fuch delay, and fuch pleadings in the king's bench. And as to the cofts it was held no caufe for appeal, nor in truth, was it ever known to be a caufe, if the merits were againft the appellant; and fo the decree was affirmed throughout. *Show. Parl. Ca.* 15, 16.

7. See *Cary* 1, 2. 1 *Chan. Ca.* 23, 24, 226. 2 *Chan. Ca.* 184, 185, 225. 1 *Vern.* 34, 40. *Salk.* 154. 2 *Rep. Chan.* 88. *Eq. Abr.* 92.

8. See rules, *He who hath done iniquity fhall not have equity. He who takes fecurity by a penalty, ought not to have more, nor indeed fo much, if compenfation for the damages may be made without it,* ca. 2. *Equity to relieve where the matter lieth in compenfation.*

108. *Equity*

108. *Equity not to relieve, where there is relief, or may be good defence, at law.*

1. WHERE there is no remedy at law, equity will grant one; but where there is one, equity will not grant a further remedy, though that at law be not available. 1 *Chan.* 79, 147, 269.

2. Where no fraud or covin is, a court of Equity will not relieve, *Cro. Ca.* 190, 191.

3. Confcience never refifteth the law of man, nor addeth thereto, but where fuch human law is contrary to the law of reafon or of God; in which cafe it cannot properly be called a law, but corruption. *Doct. & Stud. lib.* 2. *cap.* 15.

4. The chancery in its abfolute power holdeth fuit by *fubpoena* only of fuch matters, as are not remediable by the common law. *Per Prifot cap. Juf. in com. Banco,* 37 *H.* 6. 14. and by *Jenney Apprentic.* 39 *E.* 6. 26. *Confcience* 6. *Elf. Obf.* 46.

5. The chancellor holdeth plea but of matters not remedial by the common law; and that he muft judge according to truth, and not upon the default of the party, as the common law doth. *Elf. Obf.* 47.

6. Matters of freehold are not properly determinable in equity, though they have been there determined. (*Q.*) Matters properly determinable at law are not properly relievable in Equity. *Hard.* 51.

7. Vide 1 *Vern.* 71, 119. *Syd.* 109.

8. See alfo rule, *Equity favours feifin.*

109. *Equity proper interpreter of ftatutes.*

1. LORD chancellor faid a court of equity was as proper a judge or interpreter of an act of parliament, as a judge at law. 1 *Chan. Ca.* 55, 56, but the chancellor cannot add to a ftatute, 228.

2. All ftatutes made againft fraud are to be conftrued liberally, and expounded beneficially to fupprefs fraud. 3 *Co. Twyne's* cafe.

3. See 1 *Chan. Ca.* 205, 228. *Co. Lit.* 272. *a. b.* 290. *a.* 360. *a.* 365. *b.* 366. *a.* 381. *b.*

4. See alfo rule, *Statutes to be conftrued in equity.*

110. *Equity proper place to relieve legatees.*

1. *A.* Bequeaths a legacy, and makes baron and feme his executors, and dies. The baron after makes his will, and makes the feme and his fon executors, and dies. The legatee of *A.* brings a bill againft the feme and her fon, fetting forth the cafe *ut fupra*; and chargeth that the eftate of *A.* liable to the payment of the legacy, is all come to the hands of the feme and her fon. The fon demurred, for that the feme who was the furviving executor of *A.* was only liable to his legacy; and the fon being executor of one of *A.*'s executors who died firft, leaving an executor of *A.* furviving, was not privy in law. Yet inafmuch as it was charged that the fon had gotten the eftate of *A.* the demurrer was over-ruled; the court declaring that

tho

the eſtate of *A.* in whoſeſoever hands, ought to be liable to his legacies. 1 *Chan. Ca.* 57.

2. See rule, *Equity has a concurrent juriſdiction with the eccleſiaſtical courts.*

111. *Equity is to execute the intent of the parties.*

1. THE miſtake in the name in a conveyance, being heir male, holpen, and lands to paſs according to the intent of the parties. *Tot.* 228.

2. A mortgagee in fee enters for a forfeiture, and enjoys ſeven years, and then abſolutely ſells to *J. S.* *Curia:* The eſtate ſhall not be looked upon as a mortgage in the hands of *J. S.* ſo as to make it a part of his perſonal eſtate; but it ſhall be for the benefit of the heir. 1 *Vern.* 271.

3. Lady *Wentworth* having iſſue by her former huſband Sir *John Wentworth* two ſons, (*viz.*) *T.* and *J.* ſettled the lands in queſtion on herſelf for life; remainder to *John* her ſaid ſecond ſon and his heirs, he paying to the lady *K.* her daughter, 1500*l.* within ſix months after the death of the elder brother, in caſe he died without iſſue, and if he did not pay the 1500*l.* that then the lands ſhould go to the lady *K.* and her heirs. *T.* is dead *ſans* iſſue, and the lands deſcended to *J.* an infant, and the land not being worth 1500*l.* he would not redeem. Now lady *K.* being dead without iſſue, the queſtion was between the earl of *Winchelſea*, adminiſtrator of his ſaid daughter lady *K.* and the lady *Elizabeth*, ſiſter and heir of the lady *K.* The lord chancellor, aſſiſted by chief juſtice *Bedingfield* and chief baron *Atkins*, diſmiſſed the plaintiff's bill, declaring it was not a bare ſecurity for money, but a ſettlement with a plain limitation over on default of payment, and the intention of the party appears, *&c.* and to make the eſtate a redeemable eſtate, would be to deſtroy the known difference in the law books, between a limitation over and a condition. 1 *Vern.* 402, *&c.*

4. In all caſes a court of equity is to conſider what was the real intent of the teſtator. And they cannot declare a truſt according to their own fancy, nor according to what the teſtator ſhould have willed; for then they, and not the teſtator, make the will. But they may, according to the real intention of the teſtator, declare a truſt upon ſuch will, though not contained in the will itſelf: which is in theſe three caſes; 1ſt, In the caſe of a fraud upon a legatee. 2dly, Where the words imply a truſt for the relations. 3dly, In caſe of a legatee's promiſing the teſtator to ſtand as a truſtee for another. *Gilb.* 209.

5. Vide 1 *Vern.* 110, *&c.* 201, *&c.* 138, 159, 222, 267, 457, 298. 2 *Vern.* 201, 71, 77, 244, 245, 363, 432, 433. 1 *Chan. Ca.* 68, 174. 3 *Chan. Ca.* 13, 19, 86.

6. *Vide etiam* rules, *Equity rectifies miſtakes and ſupplies defects. Equity looks upon that as done which ought to be done*, ca. 2. *That ſhall have the benefit which hath or would have ſuſtained the loſs.*

112. *Equity rectifies miſtakes and ſupplies defects.*

General.

1. MISTAKES of a name of a corporation holpen in equity. *Tot.* 228.

2. The miſtake of a name in a conveyance, being heir male, holpen, *&c.* *Tot.* 228.

3. The miſtake of the clerk amended by the record. *Tot.* 228.

4. The word *heir*, left out of the clauſe of a reſervation, ſupplied in equity. *Tot.* 229.

Particular caſes.

5. The plaintiff makes a leaſe of lands to the defendant, meaning that all woods growing thereupon ſhould be excepted, ſaving for neceſſary botes; but by miſtake of the clerk, by putting in *hereafter excepted*, where there was no exception afterwards, whereupon the defendant cut down wood, but was ordered to be ſtay'd. *Tot.* 228, 229.

6. The plaintiff became ſurety for the defendant to *B.* in 100*l.* bond, and the defendant giving a counter-bond to ſave the plaintiff harmleſs of a bond of 200*l.* whereby, by means of this miſtake, the counter-bond was void in law, yet relieved here. *Tot.* 229.

7. Miſpriſion in a counter-bond rectified. *Tot.* 229.

8. So concerning the miſtaking of a power, made good here. So where miſrecited. *Tot.* 229.

9. A leaſe made by dean and chapter, miſreciting the name of their corporation, holpen in chancery. *Max. Eq.* 55. *margin.* See *Tot.* 228.

10. The plaintiff had a bond *in Quadraginta libris* to pay 200*l.* which ſhould have been *Quadringentis.* The defendant was ſued in chancery as heir and executor of the obligor, the obligor having bound himſelf and his heirs. Plaintiff had relief, *&c.* 2 *Chan. Ca.* 225.

11. Vide 1 *Chan. Ca.* 267. *Tot.* 131. 1 *Rep. Chan.* 162. 2 *Ro.* 434.

113. *Equity regards ſubſtance, not ceremony.*

1. LANDS were deviſed to the feme for life, after to be ſold by an executor for younger childrens portions; the executor dies; the feme dies; the younger children bring their bill againſt the heir, who demurred, becauſe but an authority in the executor, which is dead with him; but the demurrer was over-ruled. 1 *Chan. Ca.* 35.

2. A man, after marriage, voluntarily gave bond to ſettle a jointure, and did it, and the bond was delivered up; after his death the jointure being evicted, it was decreed ſhe ſhould recover her dower; and what that fell ſhort of the jointure ſhe ſhould, being adminiſtratrix, retain out of the perſonal eſtate. 1 *Vern.* 427.

3. The teſtator ſeiſed in tail of freehold lands, and in fee of copyhold, deviſed the copyhold to the defendant, who was intitled to the remainder of the freehold, and the freehold he deviſed to the plaintiff. The defendant, apprehending there had been a recovery by the teſtator, agreed, without any conſideration, with the plaintiff, that each ſhould enjoy according to the

 will;

will; but after finding there had been no recovery, he brought his action to recover the freehold lands; and the plaintiff his bill to establish the agreement, which was decreed accordingly. 1 *Chan. Ca.* 84.

4. Devise was of lands to the plaintiff and his heirs male, but the testator declared his will to be, that the plaintiff should have no benefit of this devise, unless the plaintiff's father should settle on the plaintiff two full thirds of his estate settled on the said father on his marriage. The father devised all his estate to the plaintiff his son. First for payment of his debts; then to the plaintiff for his life; remainder to his first and other sons in tail. Though by the will he was only tenant for life; whereas by the condition he was to have either fee or fee tail, it being in case of a will. Yet the court conceived it well enough, and answered the testator's intent better, than if the condition had been literally performed; and declared that if the substance of the condition was performed, that should serve the turn. 1 *Vern.* 79.

5. The marriage was to be with the consent of the father under a penalty or forfeiture of the fortune. The father was in treaty for her marriage, and the jointure agreed on, and directions given to draw the writing accordingly. But before assurances were settled, the young couple married without the father's knowledge. Decreed a marriage with his consent; as there was an express assent both before and after the consummation, and the case thus circumstanced, as hath been mentioned, and no disagreement or alteration of the father's good liking in the mean time. 1 *Rep. Chan.* 1. See 1 *Mod.* 310.

* 6. A lease is a sufficient authority to possess by, though the formalities of law are wanting; so that if it happen to be evicted, yet the tenant shall be allowed for what he hath laid out for lasting improvements and melioration of the estate. *See* case before the house of lords, *Hamilton* and *Lady Cardross.* 8 *April* 1712. Vide *Gilb.* 48.

Even judges in the finding of verdicts often more respect the substance than the circumstance; and therefore where the case concerneth the life of man, which is more favoured than any thing in the world, the judges regard the substance and not the circumstance. 9 *Co.* 112. *a.* 113. *and the whole case.*

7. *Max. Eq.* 53, *&c.* 1 *Chan. Ca.* 39, 150, 290, 260, 264, 265. 1 *Vern.* 83, 84, 85, 138, 159, 170, 176, *&c.* 17, 217, 201, 48. 2 *Vent.* 353. 1 *Chan. Ca.* 7, 132, 173, 208, 49. 2 *Chan. Ca.* 63, 49, 78. *Car.* 24. 2 *Rep. Chan.* 216, 218. 1 *Vern.* 13. 2 *Vent.* 350. 2 *Rep. Chan.* 212. *Hard.* 204. 1 *Rep. Chan.* 168, 283. 1 *Chan. Ca.* 176, 246, 10, 13. 1 *Rep. Chan.* 185. 2 *Chan. Ca.* 29, 30, 87, *&c. S. C.* 1 *Vern.* 79. 1 *Mod.* 310. 2 *Rep. Chan.* 24, 366. 1 *Chan. Ca.* 22, 138. 1 *Mod.* 300, 310. 2 *Rep. Chan.* 24, 366. 1 *Vern.* 20. 2 *Rep. Chan.* 23. 2 *Chan. Ca.* 95. 2 *Rep.* 26. 2 *Chan. Ca.* 109. 1 *Salk.* 231. 2 *Vent.* 352, 356. 1 *Vern.* 20, 83. 1 *Mod.* 306, 308. 1 *Vern.* 406.

8. See rule, *Limitations in restraint of marriage*, &c.

114. *Equity is to prevent multiplicity of ſuits, or circuity of actions.*

1. THE bill was for a perpetual injunction to ſtay the defendant from bringing any more ejectments to try his title at law, ſuggeſting that the plaintiff had five verdicts, and that it was an unreaſonable vexation, *&c.* and therefore to put the plaintiff's title in perpetual peace was the bill. Lord keeper was of opinion, that to give this court an original juriſdiction, there ought to be a fraud or truſt, or ſome accident to fall out in the caſe, or elſe to prevent ſome general inconvenience; as between the lord of a manor and the tenants to ſettle their ſeveral rights, if in caſe the right between the lord and the ſeveral tenants was to be ſettled by ſeparate actions, the difficulty upon the lord would be inſupportable by reaſon of the multiplicity of ſuits at law: the like in ſettling buttings and boundaries, *&c.* therefore this court will interpoſe, and direct an iſſue to be tried, which when tried, and the conſcience of the court thereby informed and ſatisfied, this court will then put the whole in peace by a perpetual injunction. But this caſe his lordſhip thought was in its nature new, and did not fall under the general notion of a bill of peace; being only between *A.* and *B.* and one man is able to contend with another. He ſaid he was very well ſatisfied of the vexatiouſneſs of the defendant in this caſe; but then he ſaid the law was clear in this point, and coſts would attend the event of ſuch trial. And if this caſe was a grievance in the law, it was proper for another juriſdiction, *viz.* in parliament, eſpecially ſince parliaments are ſo frequent; ſo that it would be a piece of arrogance in him to take upon him the reformation of the law, though it needed it. *Gilb.* 2. See 1 *Vern.* 22, 266, 308. *Parl. Ca.* 17. 1 *Chan. Ca.* 2, 121, 123.

2. A bill was brought againſt an executor, to diſcover aſſets, and for ſatisfaction; it was ſaid for the defendant, that the plaintiff ought not to have relief here; for that he had a proper remedy at law. But the court being poſſeſſed of the cauſe, and the ſame being as proper for this court as at law, it was decreed, to avoid circuity of actions, that the defendant ſhould account and make the plaintiff ſatisfaction. 2 *Rep. Chan.* 37.

3. A guardian places his ward for education, and orders his correſpondent to pay to a third perſon, from time to time, ſuch money as ſhould be demanded of him, for the uſe of the ward; in purſuance whereof ſeveral ſums were paid to her, and for her uſe, and receipts taken from her as by order of the guardian. After the ward, being juſt come of age, came to the correſpondent, and deſired two ſeveral ſums, which were paid her, and receipts taken as by order of the guardian. After the ward and guardian ſettled accounts, and exchanged releaſes, but theſe two ſums were not brought to account. And now, after the guardian's death, it was decreed the ward ſhould pay the correſpondent; for it was her proper debt, and ſhe was releaſed from her guardian; and though the credit was at firſt given to the guardian, yet the money being paid to her, and not by her paid to the guardian, the correſpondent had a fair claim againſt her, even to avoid circuity of ſuits. *Parl. Ca.* 17, 18.

4. See 1 *Vern.* 22, 122, 266, 443, 498, 308. 1 *Chan. Ca.* 311. 2 *Chan. Ca.* 225. *Hard.* 115. *Gilb.* 227. *Barn. Lord* and *Lady Vane*'s caſe. *Expedit reipub' ut ſit finis litium propter communem omnium utilitatem.*

5. See alſo rules, *Aequitas ſequitur legem*, ca. 5. *Diſcovery draws with it relief. Equity will never decree a ſuit where it may decree a remedy.*

115. *Equity to relieve where there is no remedy at law.*

1. A Copyholder can have no aſſiſe of common againſt his lord, but is to be relieved in equity. *Tot.* 108.

2. Equity will compel the lord of a manor to admit the tenant. If the lord will not hold a court, equity will compel him; for an action will not lie againſt the lord, and there is no remedy but in chancery. *Cro. Ja.* 368. 2 *Bulſt.* 336. *S. C.*

3. So if an erroneous judgment be given in a copyhold court, in a *formedon* or the like, a bill may be brought in equity to reverſe it. 1 *Ro.* 373. *Lane* 98.

4. If the lord will exact arbitrary fines, equity will reſtrain him. *Dy.* 164. 1 *Rep. Chan.* 34, 96. 2 *Rep. Chan.* 134. For without this remedy in equity the lord might exact a fine to the value of the eſtate, and ſo the tenant loſe his eſtate. *Max. Eq.* 24, 25.

5. A bill was brought for 3*l.* for a rent of 5*s. per annum*, arrear for 12 years, and alſo for the future rent, the plaintiff ſuggeſted that the deeds by which the rent was created, were loſt; there was a proof of a conſtant payment of it till the laſt 12 years. And the maſter of the rolls decreed the defendant to pay the arrears and growing rent; becauſe he ſaid it was uncertain what kind of rent it was, and ſo no remedy at law: and here the perſon is made liable for the rent, which, for ought appeared, he was not at law. 1 *Chan. Ca.* 120.

6. The defendant's teſtator gave the plaintiff 1000*l.* payable at 21, the bill ſuggeſted the defendant waſted the eſtate, and prayed he might give ſecurity to pay the legacy when due. So decreed. 1 *Chan. Ca.* 121.

7. A rent or penſion was of 1*l.* 14*s. per annum*, granted by *H.* 6. to *Eaton* college, iſſuing out of lands. *Riggs*, executor of the tertenant brought this bill to be revlieved for the arrears of this rent in his teſtatrix's life-time. The bill ſuggeſted, that the college knew not the land out of which &c. and ſo could not diſtrain. *Beauchamp* was the preſent tertenant, and though the perſon of the tertenant was not chargeable with the rent at law, but only the lands by diſtreſs; yet forasmuch as the teſtatrix held the land, and did not pay the rent, it was ſaid that thereby the perſonal eſtate of the teſtatrix was augmented. And ſo the maſter of the rolls decreed the executor to pay the arrears as far as he had effects of the teſtatrix's eſtate. 1 *Chan. Ca.* 121.

8 See 1 *Chan. Ca.* 78, 79, 144, 147, 146, 184, 198, 256, 257, 262, 267, 279, 280, 135, 148, 223, 238, 240, 243, 248, 193, 195. 2 *Chan. Ca.* 68, 188. *Nelſ.* 242. *Doct. & Stud.* 85, 155. *Cary* 11. 1 *Vern.* 119. *Mar. Rep.* 159. *Nelſ.* 378. 2 *Rep. Chan.* 387. 1 *Vern.* 367. *S. C. Show. Parl. Ca.* 67. 1 *Vern.* 309, 359. *Max. Eq.* 25. *Lat.* 24, 146. 1 *Ch. Ca.* 98, 286. 1 *Vern.* 455. 1 *Chan. Ca.* 271. 2 *Chan. Ca.* 84.

9. *Vide* rule, *Equity will prevent or redreſs wrongs and miſchiefs.*

116. *Equity will never decree a ſuit where it may decree a remedy.*

1. THOUGH the plaintiff hath had diſcovery here, which was inſiſted was the end of his ſuit, and ſo his bill to be diſmiſſed. *Curia:* as to diſmiſſion to law, becauſe the plaintiff hath had diſcovery here, when the court can determine the matter, it ſhall not be an hand-maid to other courts, nor beget a ſuit to be ended elſewhere. 2 *Chan. Ca.* 200.

2. See 2 *Vern.* 429, 438, 458 *or* 498. 2 *Chan. Ca.* 201.

3. See rule, *Equity to prevent multiplicity of ſuits.*

117. *Equity will not relieve where no fraud or covin.*

1. EQUITY will not eſtabliſh an agreement founded in fraud. *Prec. Chan.* 538, 574.

2. Where a woman is dowable by act or rule in law, equity will not bar her to claim her dower. *Cro. Ca.* 190, 191.

3. Fraud is always apparelled and clad with truſt, and truſt is the cover of fraud. 3 *Co. Twyne's* caſe.

4. Secrecy is a badge of fraud. *Ibid.* Vide 1 *Cro.* 138.

118. *Equity will not aid new inventions in derogation of the common law, and tending to introduce perjury, forgery or fraud.*

1. IT is in no man's power to create new natures in law, according to new inventions, except they may ſtand with *Jus commune*, which is *Natura univerſa, &c.* Hob. 154.

2. See *Gilb.* 63.

3. See rules, *The judges and ſages of the law have always ſuppreſſed new and ſubtile inventions in derogation of the common law. Periculoſum eſt res novas et inuſitatas inducere. Ratio eſt radius divini luminis.*

119. *Equity will prevent or redreſs wrongs and miſchiefs.*

General.

1. THE Lord keeper was of opinion, that to give this court juriſdiction, there ought to be a fraud or truſt, or ſome accident to follow in the caſe, or elſe ſome general inconvenience to be prevented. *Gilb.* 2.

2. In all caſes where the matter lieth in compenſation, whether the condition be precedent or ſubſequent, equity will relieve. 1 *Vern.* 83, 167, 223, 270, *&c.* 456. 2 *Vern.* 222, 561.

3. No advantage ſhall be taken of the penalty or forfeiture, where a compenſation may be made. *Max. Eq.* 44, 45.

4. Where a man has satisfied the obligation without taking an acquittance, or having any other evidence thereof, so as he is without remedy at common law, yet he may be holpen by *subpoena*, as he may in many other cases where conscience serveth for him. *Doct. & Stud. lib.* 1. *cap.* 12.

5. Equity hath jurisdiction to quiet men in their possession. *Per Coke.* 3 *Bulst.* 34. *Lit. Rep.* 166. *S. C.* 1 *Ro.* 190. 1 *Vern.* 156.

6. Tenant, after possibility of issue extinct, so tenant for life, though by express grant dispunishable of waste, shall be restrained from pulling down of houses, or defacing of a seat. 2 *Chan. Ca.* 32. *Jointress tenant for life. Nels.* 190, 220, 221. Tenant for life ordered to repair the destruction he had made, though dispunishable. *Prec. Chan.* 455. An injunction was granted to stay waste in favour of an infant *in ventre sa mere.* Prec. Chan. 50. Barn. 274. *Tenant per le curtesy* injoined from committing waste. *Hard.* 96. So of a jointress. *Max. Eq.* 30. *margin.* Waste done by one who held by covenant, therefore not punishable by law, yet holpen here. *Tot.* 285. So in felling timber. So in ploughing antient pasture. So of antient Meadow. *Max. Eq.* 30. *margin.*

Particular cases.

7. If there be lessee for life; remainder for life; reversion or remainder in fee; lessee in possession does waste, though he is not punishable at law, yet he shall be restrained in chancery; for it is a particular mischief. 1 *Ro.* 377.

8. *Note* a difference where the tenant is dispunishable by the nature of his estate, or express grant, as also to the kind of waste; for the first shall be restrained generally, whilst the other shall only be restrained from the destruction of houses, *&c.* 1 *Rep. Chan.* 242. 1 *Vern.* 23. *Salk.* 161. 2 *Chan. Ca.* 23. *Max. Eq.* 30. *margin.*

9. Goods were devised to the defendant for life, and after his death to the plaintiff, by whom a bill was brought to compel the defendant to give security for delivery to the plaintiff after defendant's death, or the value thereof, and decreed. 1 *Rep. Chan.* 110.

10. The defendant's testator gave the plaintiff 1000 *l.* payable at 21. The bill suggested that the defendant wasted the estate, and prayed he might give security to pay the legacy when due, and so decreed. 1 *Chan. Ca.* 121.

11. An apprentice, after he is out of his time, may have a bill to oblige his master to sue the covenants of his indenture in a certain time; else the master might stay his action as long as he pleased, and till the plaintiff's witnesses were all dead. 1 *Chan. Ca.* 70.

12. It being alledged in the bill, that the defendant, a surviving partner, carrying on a distinct trade for himself, with the persons who were debtors to the joint trade, to oblige such debtors, forbore to call in the debts: ordered on motion, that an able attorney be appointed to sue for and recover the debts; unless the defendant would give security to answer the moiety of the outstanding debts. 1 *Vern.* 118.

13. The wife being *priviment enseint* at the death of he husband, the child *in ventre sa mere* could not be provided for by the law, yet this court ordered that the child should have sufficient allowance. *Tot.* 157.

14. An officer within the ſtatute 5 *E.* 6. (as I take is a ſurrogate) makes a defeazance of his office, rendering thereout 90 *l. per annum*, and exhibits a bill to have an account. The defendant pleads the deputation void by the ſtatute; and ought to have no account, it being in effect a farm within the ſtatute. *Curia:* After long debate the plea was allowed. 2 *Chan. Ca.* 42. See 48. 2 *Inſt.* 148.

This ſtatute is provided againſt the ſelling of offices, and extendeth as well to offices eccleſiaſtical, as to temporal offices concerning the adminiſtration of juſtice. See 1 *Ju. Eccl.* 233.

15. How the eccleſiaſtical courts are in many caſes compelled to do their duty, and reſtrained in their encroachments on temporal juriſdiction, and the prerogative of the crown, and rights of the ſubject. See 1 *Ju. Eccl.* tit. *Mandamus*, *Prohibition*, *Praemunire*, &c.

16. See 1 *Chan. Ca.* 1, 2, 3, 15, 16, 46, 47, 48, 224. 2 *Vern.* 186. 1 *Vern.* 23, 32, 61, 73, 198, 190, 415, 416. 1 *Chan. Ca.* 55, 56, 3, 47, 152, 270. *Gilb.* 23, 208. 2 *Chan. Ca.* 225. *Nelſ.* 236. 2 *Chan. Ca.* 67, 76, 165. 1 *Chan. Ca.* 75, 80. 2 *Chan. Ca.* 42, 48. *Car.* 65. 1 *Vern.* 190. 1 *Ro.* 383. 1 *Vern.* 105, 185, 308, 312. 1 *Rep. Chan.* 41. 1 *Vern.* 456, 469. 2 *Vern.* 426.

17. See rules, *Equity favours younger children. Equity to execute the intent of the parties. Eccleſiaſtical courts may not hold plea of matters determinable at law or in equity. Admiralty not to hold plea of matters cognizable at law. Equity hath a concurrent juriſdiction with the admiralty. Equity hath a concurrent juriſdiction with the eccleſiaſtical courts.*

120. *Equity relieves againſt accidents.*

1. Accidents are proper objects of relief. 2 *Chan. Ca.* 30.

2. Obligee in a bond loſeth it by accident, equity will relieve. *Lat.* 24. Though the bond voluntary. 1 *Chan. Ca.* 77.

3. An executor under a revoked will, without notice of the revocation, pays legacies, and after the revocation is proved, he ſhall be allowed thoſe legacies. 1 *Chan. Ca.* 126.

4. The truſtee for an infant receiveth 40*l.* of the truſt-money, and is robbed by his ſervant of 200*l.* whereof the 40*l.* was part, he ſhall be allowed it; for he was only to keep it as his own. 2 *Chan. Ca.* 2.

5. A bond was entered into before the wars, conditioned to pay 40*l. per annum* for 12 years, out of the profits of an office, which was taken away by the uſurpation. The obligor being ſued on the bond, and the office revived, he exhibited his bill to be relieved againſt the bond. The obligee inſiſted that the office continued ſome part of the 12 years, and being now revived, the obligor ought to pay the 40*l. per annum* for the 12 years or be diſmiſſed; for the obligee having the law with him, ought not to be hurt in equity, without ſatisfaction according to the condition. It was decreed the obligor ſhould pay the 40*l. per annum*, for ſo many years as the office continued, and thereupon the bond to be delivered up. 1 *Chan. Ca.* 72. See 83, 84.

6. The cauſe being heard about 1664, and one point being, that the heir of the obligor having paid a debt of his anceſtor's upon bond, might be reimburſed by the executor of the obligor, who had perſonal aſſets, the heir

heir having been forced by ſuit to pay the debt. Decreed for the heir. Upon exceptions taken to a report in this cauſe, which came on before Mr. baron *Atkins*, 29 *June* 1668, there was this point. Whereas *A.* alone was bound to the teſtator, the executor delivered up the bond, and took another to himſelf for the ſame debt, whereby, as was alledged by the counſel for the executor, the ſecurity was bettered; and whether this in equity ſhould be charged as aſſets in the executor's hands, he having delivered up the old bond, was the queſtion? Againſt him it was inſiſted, that taking the new bond had altered the property of the debt, ſo that if the executor died inteſtate, his adminiſtrator would have the debt: whereas had it reſted on the old bond, the adminiſtrator *de bonis non* of the firſt teſtator ſhould have it, ſubject to the firſt teſtator's debts. It was admitted, that at law this charged the executor as a converſion and receipt of ſo much of the eſtate. But it was inſiſted, that in equity he having taken the ſame perſon and another bound, and offering to aſſign the bond to the heir, it ought not to charge him: eſpecially when the heir is plaintiff in equity, as here. And it was ruled, that the executor ſhould not be charged with the money by altering the ſecurity, but that he ſhould aſſign it to the heir. 1 *Chan. Ca.* 74. For it is not equity that the executor ſhould ſuffer for his care in taking a new bond with further ſecurity; and the debt was loſt not by his default, but through accident only, againſt which equity relieves.

7. See 1 *Chan. Ca.* 72, 83, 84, 126, 191, 78. 2 *Chan. Ca.* 16, 207, 208. 1 *Vern.* 60, 460. *Max. Eq.* 29, 8.

8. *Vide* rule, *Equity will prevent or redreſs wrongs and miſchiefs.*

121. *Equity requires that a gift which defeats other, ſhall be made upon as high and good conſideration as the things are, which are to be defeated thereby.*

1. IF a man be indebted to five ſeveral perſons in the ſeveral ſums of 20*l.* and hath goods to the value of 20*l.* and makes a gift to one of them of all his goods, in ſatisfaction of his debt, but there is a truſt between them that the donee ſhall deal favourably with him in regard of his poverty, or to permit him, or ſome other for him, to uſe the good, for his benefit, and is content to be paid when the donor ſhall be able: this ſhall not be ſaid to be *bona fide* within the ſtatute 13 *Eliz. cap.* 5. for to be *bona fide* it ought to be in a public manner made, before the neighbours, and not in ſecret; for ſecrecy is a badge of fraud. Alſo the goods ought to be fairly appraiſed, and the continuance of poſſeſſion in the grantor is another mark of fraud, *&c.* and the words *good conſideration* and *bona fide* do not extend to every gift made *bona fide*; and therefore there are two ſorts of gifts or good conſideration, (*ſcil'*) Conſideration of nature or blood, and valuable conſideration. As to the firſt, in the caſe put before, if he ſo indebted, in conſideration of natural affection, give all his goods to his ſon or couſin; as the others would loſe their debts, *&c.* which are things of value, the intention of the act was that the conſideration in ſuch caſe ſhould be valuable; for equity requires, that a gift which defeats another ſhould be made upon as high and good conſideration as the things are which are to be defeated by it. 3 *Co.* 81, *&c.*

2. See *Plow. Com.* 50. *b.* 351. *a.*

122. *Equity to relieve against fraud.*

General.

1. FOR force, fraud and accident, equity relieves. 1 *Chan. Ca.* 72. Fraud is a thing odious. 3 *Chan. Ca.* 85. It is the mother of wrangle, contention and intricacy. *Co. Lit.* 3. *b.* It comprehends all manner of unfair means to cheat another. *Nelf.* 439. It is not to be prefumed, but muft be proved; and fo none is to be convicted of fraud where the evidence is doubtful. 3 *Chan. Ca.* 85, 114. It is neither prefumed by common or civil law. *Nelf.* 185. A man is not to be prefumed guilty of fraud on his death bed. *Nelf.* 16. *Prec. Chan.* 303, 304. Fraud properly relievable in equity. 1 *Chan. Ca.* 291. Fraud or covin vitiates fuch acts as in their own nature or fimply are lawful; equity will relieve in cafes of fraud where the defendant fuppreffed a marriage fettlement. Decreed againft him, that the plaintiff fhould enjoy. 1 *Chan. Ca.* 270. 3 *Chan. Ca.* 122. *Nelf.* 185. Where he, who has right, tells the purchafer that the vendor has a good eftate, when he knew not the contrary at the time. 2 *Chan. Ca.* 108, 128. Where the hufband accounted with his wife's guardian before marriage. 2 *Chan. Ca.* 159, 160. Where one is prevailed with by falfe fuggeftions. 3 *Chan. Ca.* 74, 87, 61, 94, 103, 104. *Prec. Chan.* 3, 4. Where concealment. 3 *Chan. Ca.* 104, 105. Where there is furprize attended with fraud and circumvention. *Chan. Ca.* 114, 115, 56, 59, 74, 75, 80. *Nelf.* 431. Where the reverfion is fraudulently conveyed to him who had the term, to hinder younger children from having their fhares by merger of the term. *Nelf.* 220. Where young heirs are brought into unequal bargains. 1 *Chan. Ca.* 276. 2 *Chan. Ca.* 120, 121, 137. *Nelf.* 295, 296. *Prec. Chan.* 150, 218. Where fraud is ufed to draw in purchafers. 2 *Chan. Ca.* 108, 128. * 3 *Chan. Ca.* 85. *Nelf.* 394. Equity will never give countenance to demands of an unfair nature, as in the particular cafe it was for attending at auctions as a puff to enhance the price of goods; nor fuffer them to be fet up againft juft and fair demands. In an account, a crofs bill for fuch purpofe difmiffed with cofts. *See* cafe before the houfe of lords, * *Walker* and *Gafcoigne*, 6 *March* 1726. When advantage is taken, either in value, or confideration of the ignorance or diftrefs of the vendor, fet afide, and purchafe deed only to ftand a fecurity for what was really and *bona fide* paid. *See* the cafes * *Gold* verfus *Morgan*, 24 *March* 1730, and * *Furgafon* and *Maitland*, 25 *March* 1731, both before the houfe of lords.

Particular cafes.

2. Truftee in fraud fettles the truft-eftate on his own daughter in marriage, fet afide. *Nelf.* 470.

3. A copyholder having furrendered to the ufe of himfelf and his wife and their daughters, then mortgages. This mortgage not allowed to defeat the fettlement; for as it was a copyhold, the mortgagee might eafily have known the hufband's eftate. *Prec. Chan.* 1. *But if it had been a real eftate, I conceive it had been otherwife.*

4. A man of an eftate employs a fcrivener to procure him 1000*l.* of fome gentleman, declaring he will not have it of a mechanic. The fcri-

vener treated with a vintner, and receives and pays his client 300*l.* of the money, and takes 300*l.* to himſelf, and the reſt, being 400*l.* was delivered in wines not worth more than 150*l.* the gentleman gave recognizance, which being ſued, he brought the preſent bill. And decreed a perpetual injunction againſt the recognizance on the plaintiff's payment of the 300*l.* and intereſt. *Prec. Chan.* 81.

5. The bill was to be relieved againſt a purchaſe made by the defendants from the plaintiff's father, ſuggeſting he had been circumvented and impoſed upon by the defendants, who inſiſted on their purchaſe; and ſhew, that firſt, there were articles, and then conveyances and a fine. And the father, ſeeing the plaintiff uneaſy thereat, took a releaſe from him of all his right. Notwithſtanding all this, the lord keeper ſet the purchaſe aſide, it appearing art was uſed by the defendant, he pretending to help the father to a wife with a great fortune, he being almoſt in his dotage, and that to qualify himſelf for the lady, it was neceſſary that he ſhould convert his land into money, though it was proved he was ſenſible, and abſolute owner, and might have ſold or given his eſtate away, and that after it was done he ſaid that if it was then to do, he would do it. 1 *Vern.* 205, 206.

6. An uncle on the marriage of his niece gives 1200*l.* and the father takes bond from the ſon-in-law for 200*l.* if the daughter dies *ſans* iſſue, living the huſband, the daughter after died without iſſue. On the bond being ſued, the huſband brings the preſent bill, and is relieved; the bond being in nature of a marriage-brocage bond. *Prec. Chan.* 267.

7. *Lukener* brings an action againſt *Montagu* for lying with his wife; pending the ſuit, *Montagu* conveys in truſt to pay debts in the ſchedule annexed, and ſuch as he ſhould appoint in ſuch a time. *Lukener* recovers 5000*l.* and brought the preſent bill to be relieved againſt this deed as fraudulent. *Curia:* The deed is not fraudulent either at law or in equity, for the debts named in the deed; for the plaintiff was no creditor then; and though it was made to prefer his real creditors, before this debt when it ſhould come to be ſuch, yet this was a debt only founded in malefeazance or tort; and therefore it was conſcience in him to prefer the others before it. But the plaintiff may have an intereſt in the ſurplus, after the debts provided for by the deed, in which thoſe appointed in ten days are included. *Prec. Chan.* 106.

8. The huſband coming home, found the plaintiff naked, going to bed to his wife; and thereupon the plaintiff gave him a note for 500*l.* and after gave judgment, and laſt of all ſurrendered a copyhold by way of mortgage as a ſecurity. On a bill to be relieved againſt the ſecurity, alledging a contrivance, and that he was drunk, and that he was threatned. Lord chancellor: There is no proof of a plot, or that he was ſo diſordered or frightened, for he continued of the ſame mind in cool blood, at giving ſeveral ſecurities, and joined in the report, that it was for a bargain of graſs: if a jury had given damages, equity could not have relieved: and why here? where he has ſettled them againſt himſelf; it ſhews he thought them reaſonable. Let the bill be diſmiſſed, but without coſts, the defendant having bragged of his bargain. But his lordſhip ſaid he would relieve againſt the penalties. *Prec. Chan.* 266.

9. *Thomas*, earl of *Ardglaſs*, for 300*l. anno* 1675, granted a rent-charge of 300*l. per annum* out of his eſtate of 1000*l. per annum*, to hold to the

2 defen-

defendant and his heirs for ever, to commence from the firſt *Michaelmas* or *Lady-day* after the grantor's death without iſſue male, with a proviſo to be void if he ſhould have iſſue male, which ſhould attain 21; after the grantor makes a ſettlement of his eſtate, for 300*l.* to the uſe of himſelf for life; remainder in tail to all his iſſue male; remainder in tail to the plaintiff his uncle, which was according to a former ſettlement made by the anceſtor of his family, and which the grantor on his marriage had barred: and then the plaintiff, and earl *Thomas* brought their bill to be relieved againſt this grant: after the bill brought, the defendant got a releaſe from earl *Thomas* the grantor; and the now earl's bill was, that earl *Thomas* being dead, to ſet aſide the grant and releaſe on payment of 300 *l.* and intereſt. On the rehearing many caſes were cited where unreaſonable bargains made with young heirs had been ſet aſide here. And when this bargain was made, the earl was very young, had left his lady, and lived in riot and debauchery, and that the conſideration was but one year's purchaſe, and that the contingency of the earl's dying without iſſue, was an artifice of the defendant's, the earl being diſabled, as appeared in proof, to get children, and that ſo the defendant had been informed by the earl's ſurgeon, and therefore the contingency ought not to be looked upon but as it was in the defendant's eye, who was his companion in his debaucheries. And it appeared he was ſolicitous to draw the earl into like bargains with other people; and as to the releaſe, that it was obtained without conſideration, and that after the ſaid ſettlement made on the plaintiff. Lord keeper declared he was fully ſatisfied in the decree before made, which was for a reconveyance or releaſe on payment, and perpetual injunction. And ſaid, if he was to die preſently he would make it. About a year after there was another bill, and the caſe was, *George Pitt*, Eſq; had got a like grant of 300*l.* *per annum*, from the ſame lord by *Muſchamp*, defendant in the former cauſe, his agency, and the decree was to reconvey or releaſe on like payment of principal and intereſt, and alſo a perpetual injunction. *Fraus eſt celare fraudem.* *Pitt* pretended ignorance, that he did not know the earl, and that he did not make the bargain himſelf; but that was by reaſon of a conſciouſneſs he had that he ſhould be examined to it. 1 *Vern.* 237, *&c.* *Vere Eſſex* earl of *Ardglaſſe* plaintiff, *Henry Muſchamp* defendant, and earl *Ardglaſs* againſt *Pitt.*

10. The father tenant for life draws his ſon, being in diſtreſs, in to ſuffer a recovery; the ſon was relieved by ſetting the recovery aſide. *Barn.* 433.

11. On treaty of marriage between the plaintiff and her huſband, her father would not conſent, becauſe the huſband was indebted 200*l.* to *B.* on bond, in which he and his mother were bound; to remove which objection, the mother and her younger ſon gave a freſh bond to *B.* and the former bond was cancelled, but the huſband after gave his brother a counter-bond, and paid the intereſt during his life; and it was in proof that the now widow the preſent plaintiff, being in love, contrived this way to ſatisfy her father, and that the marriage might take effect. But now being ſued by the brother on the counter-bond as adminiſtratrix to her huſband, ſhe brought her bill to be relieved. Lord chancellor: This is a plain fraud, and contrivance, by which the father was drawn in, and his lordſhip declared, if the huſband had been plaintiff he ſhould have been relieved; and therefore decreed the bond to be delivered up. 1 *Vern.* 348.

12. There

12. There is no doubt but an infant may be a truftee, and accountable for a breach of truft committed after he attains his full age, as was the principal cafe. 1 *Vern.* 342, *&c. Jevon* and *Bufh. See the cafe at full under rule, Equity may carry the debt beyond the penalty on circumftances,* cafe 4.

* 13. Though there be no direct proof, that a man is *non compos* or delirious, yet if the deed was executed *in extremis,* it cannot be fuppofed that he had a mind adequate to the bufinefs he was about, and that he might more eafily be impofed upon, efpecially the provifion in the deed being fomething extraordinary. See cafe *Fane* and *The duke of Devonfhire,* before the lords, 16 *Jan.* 1718.

* 14. A leafe obtained from one *non compos* fet afide. See cafe *Val. Quin,* Efq; and *Langley Clerk,* on an appeal from the exchequer in *Ireland,* and heard before the houfe of lords, 21 *April* 1736.

* 15. An agreement was between a mother and her fon, and was relieved againft; for that the deeds executed between them were for the mother to refign her jointure and accept an annuity; fhe being at the time haraffed and uneafy. See cafe before the houfe of lords *Archer* and *Archer,* 2 *March* 1718. Alfo cafe * *Clarke* and *More,* 26 *Nov.* 1718. See alfo lord *Dyer*'s readings upon the ftatute of wills, 4.

* 16. Advantage taken of the vendor's unhappy circumftances, being in gaol, and exceeding poor, by drawing him into an unequal agreement for the fale of his eftate, fet afide, and the eftate made a fecurity only for the money really and *bona fide* advanced, with intereft: and this, though the purchafer was really to run great hazard, and to be at great expence and trouble, in many forefeen and unavoidable law fuits about the premiffes, and alfo was at the hazard of lofing the advance-money, and expences in the future, to be laid out by him, being in all likelihood never able to reimburfe himfelf in cafe he fhould fail of fuccefs in the litigations, and difappointed of the eftate. See cafe before the houfe of lords * *Gordon* and *Crawford,* 17 *April* 1730. See alfo * *Gold* and *Morgan,* 24 *March* 1730. *Furgafon* and *Maitland,* 17 *March* 1731.

17. The defendant had drawn in the plaintiff, being a young man, and purchafed of him his eftate at a great under-value, the title being defective and the tenant evicted; there being a covenant for quiet enjoyment and other fecurities entered into by the plaintiff, the bill was for relief againft actions on thefe covenants. And for the defendant it was faid, that he ought to have the value of the lands evicted. *Curia:* The defendant, who was a lawyer, and ought to have underftood a title, purchafed at great under-value, and the title being defective and the land evicted, it is unreafonable he fhould make any advantage of this *catching bargain*; and therefore decreed him his purchafe-money without intereft, only deducting mefne profits. 1 *Vern.* 320. *Zouche* verfus *Swaine.*

* 18. The eftate not anfwering in value to the particulars to be allowed for. See cafe *Sir William Barker, Bart.* verfus *Damer,* before the houfe of lords. 7 *April* 1731. Note; *This was in favour of the heir under a marriage agreement.*

* 19. Eight days after the wife came of age, and two days before her marriage, fhe was drawn in to execute a releafe without her hufband's privity;

vity; the treaty of marriage being public, the releaſe was ſet aſide. See caſe *Norton* and *Heron*, before the houſe of lords, 21 *April* 1732.

20. Where there is a parol agreement made for a leaſe, and the leſſee enters and builds, this court will eſtabliſh it on the foot of fraud in the leſſor, notwithſtanding the ſtatute of frauds, *&c.* becauſe contracts executed in part, are not always within the ſtatute, though executory contracts are. 2 *Mod. Ca.* 35. *Savage* and *Foſter.*

21. The mother, at the requeſt of her brother, who being ill, and not having time to ſurrender a copyhold to the uſe of his will, gave bond to her ſon, for whom the brother intended the ſaid copyhold, to ſurrender to him, where in fact ſhe was heir. Decreed ſhe was a truſtee for her ſon. 2 *Mod. Ca.* 62, 63. 1 *Vern.* 296.

22. One having made his wife executrix, the ſon perſuaded her to prevail with his father to make a new will, and to name him executor, promiſing to be a truſtee for his mother: this truſt was decreed. 2 *Mod. Ca.* 62, 63. 1 *Vern.* 296.

23. See 1 *Rep. Chan.* 10, 132, 146, 188. 2 *Rep. Chan.* 266, 396. 3 *Rep. Chan.* 74, 75. *Co. Lit.* 4. *a.* 3 *Co.* 80. *Stat.* 13 *Eliz. cap.* 5. 27 *Eliz. cap.* 4. 29 *Car.* 2. *Elſ. Obſ.* 107, 108. *Mar. Rep.* 183. 1 *Ch. Ca.* 99, 217, 225, 133, 154, 276, 74, 75, 83, 118, 150, 256, 292, 27, 30, 37. 2 *Chan. Ca.* 2, 16, 17, 103, 144, 186, 240, 249, 120, 137. 3 *Chan. Ca.* 64, 91, 122. *Nel.* 209, 295, 298, 322, 287. 1 *Vern.* 19, 20, 32, 71, 75, 86, 131, 135, 167, 271, 277, 141, 145, 218, 227, 285, 370, 294, 320, 186, 474, 408, 409, 411, 412, 431, 451, 452, 277. 2 *Vern.* 14, 27, 33, 77, 107, 445, 465, 467, 468, 469, 475, 348, 480, 483, 484, 230, 488, 145. *Prec. Chan.* 13, 14, 17, 18, 132, 76, 165, 218, 233, 157, 522. *Gilb.* 122, 148, 169, 221, 222, 259. 1 *Lev.* 197. *Lutw.* 484. 3 *Lev.* 118. *Salk.* 344. 4 *Mod.* 406, 410. 5 *Mod.* 4. *all S.C.* 5 *Mod.* 175. 2 *Vent.* 175, 359. 1 *Danv.* 28. 1 *Show.* 35. 3 *Mod.* 239. 5 *Mod.* 13, 14. 1 *Vent.* 489. *Lutw.* 130. 3 *Keb.* 672. 5 *Mod.* 351. * *See* caſes before the houſe of lords, * *Murray* and *Charters*, 28 *March* 1734. * *Auſten* and *Flack*, 20 *Feb.* 1733, and * *Sherret*'s caſe, 14 *April* 1735.

123. *Equity to relieve where the matter lieth in compenſation.*

General to, and rules.

1. IT is laid down as a rule, that in all caſes where the matter lieth in compenſation, let the condition be precedent or ſubſequent. equity will relieve. 1 *Vern.* 83, 167, 223, 270, *&c.* 456. 2 *Vern.* 222, 561. *Salk.* 156. *Max. Eq.* 44, *&c.* It is alſo a general rule, that a nude agreement is not good either in law or equity. *Contra*, if the conſideration be only unequal. 1 *Chan. Ca.* 42.

2. If a man be bound in a penalty to pay money at a day and place by obligation, and intending to pay it, is robbed by the way; or hath intreated by word ſome further reſpite at the hands of the obligee, or cometh ſhort of the ſame by any misfortune, and ſo failing of the payment, doth neverthelefs provide and tender the money in a ſhort time after; in theſe and many

other ſuch like caſes the chancery will compel the obligee to take his principal with ſome reaſonable conſideration of his damages (*quantum expediat*); for if this was not ſo, men would do that by covenant which they do now by bond. *Cary* 1. The like favour is extended againſt ſuch as would take advantage, upon any ſtrict condition, for undoing the eſtate of another in lands upon a ſmall or trifling default. *Cary* 1. So if two be jointly and ſeverally bound to pay money, and the obligee will give longer day, or other favour to the one, and then will ſue the other for the debt, he ſo ſued may ſue in chancery. 9 *E*. 4. 41. *Cary* 1. Where an obligee is ſurety and ſued alone, by the cuſtom of *London*, he ſhall make the reſt contribute. So where the ſurety pays a debt and has no counter-bond, by the ſame cuſtom he ſhall maintain an action againſt the principal. 1 *Vern*. 456. Wherever the court can give compenſation, it can relieve. *Salk*. 156.

Particular caſes.

3. One deviſes lands to his younger ſon, called *Styles*, and by his will declares that in caſe his ſaid ſon be in any wiſe hindered or prevented from enjoying thoſe lands, then in lieu he gave him all thoſe lands called *Barabar*. The plaintiff charges that he was heir of the deviſor, but that neither he nor the deviſor were intitled to more than a moiety of *Styles*, and that the defendant *J. N.* a ſtranger, was intitled to the other moiety, and had evicted the deviſee; and ſets forth, that *Barabar* was of much greater value than *Styles*, and that it was not his fault that the deviſee did not enjoy, and charged a combination between the defendants, and prays relief as to the over-value of *Barabar*. *Cur'*: This being a condition that lay in compenſation, the plaintiff ought to be relieved, and decreed the deviſee ſhould have a compenſation for the land evicted, ſet out in *Barabar*. 1 *Vern*. 270, 271.

4. A creditor agrees with his debtor to take leſs than his debt, ſo it ſhould be paid preciſely at ſuch a day. The debtor fails of payment, and brings this bill, ſuggeſting ſome equitable excuſes for not making preciſe payment, and that he tendered the money within a day or two, and that the defendant refuſed, and ſued for the whole at law. Demurrer, becauſe the bill contained no equity, and that the plaintiff having made failure, the defendant was not bound to take leſs. Lord keeper allowed the demurrer, and ſaid *Cujus eſt dare ejus eſt diſponere*. 1 Vern. 210.

5. On review, the error aſſigned was, that the defendant's wife's father having given portions to his daughters, in caſe they ſhould releaſe to his heir their right to certain lands. One of the daughters happened to die before ſhe had releaſed, and therefore the heir refuſed to pay the portions, which was 2000*l*. to each daughter, and the lands to be releaſed were not worth 500*l*. the performance of the condition was prevented by the act of God. The defendant demurred, and inſiſted, that this was a condition precedent, and not being performed there could be no relief; and cited *Fry* and *Porter*'s caſe, and the words here are, *If his daughters ſhould releaſe, then he appointed ſuch and ſuch portions*. Mr. ſerjeant *Maynard* made a difference between a condition on giving a portion, and a portion given on condition; for in the former caſe the portion does never ariſe unleſs the condition be performed. Lord keeper inclined to over-rule the demurrer. Agreed the cauſe to be heard *de integro*. 1 Vern. 223.

6. The

6. The truſtees of the eſtate of *Thomas Wentworth*, an infant, having raiſed 3000*l.* out of the real eſtate of their infant, which was then in hand, they laid it out in lands which lay commodious to the infant's eſtate, and took the conveyance in their own names, in truſt for him, in caſe when he became of age he ſhould accept the ſame at the price; and this was done with the conſent of the grandmother, who was the infant's guardian. The infant died under age; and the queſtion was, Whether the heir of the infant ſhould have the eſtate, or whether it ſhould be looked upon as a ſecurity for the money, and go to the adminiſtrator of the infant? Decreed, the truſtees ſhould pay the 3000*l.* to the adminiſtrator with intereſt only according to what they had made by the profits of the purchaſed lands. 1 *Vern.* 403, *&c.* 435, *&c.*

7. *Straton*, a freeman of *London*, having a ſon and daughter, deviſed two thirds of his legatory part to his daughter, but if ſhe married without the conſent of her mother, her brother was to have 500*l.* of what was ſo given to the daughter. She married *ſans* conſent of her mother. *Per curiam:* This is not to be taken *in terrorem* only; but on her marriage without conſent, the bequeſt is a good bequeſt over, and an intereſt veſted in the brother, who in this caſe may be looked on as a perſon the teſtator conſidered, and had in his thoughts as well as the daughter, as to proviſion, and was, according to the difference taken by lord chief juſtice *Hale*, in the caſe for *Henry Bellaſiſe*, and in the caſe *Davis* and *Hatton*, 2 *Vern.* 357.

8. A father left his daughters 20000*l.* each at 21 or marriage, which ſhould firſt happen, ſo as the marriage was with the conſent of the mother and truſtees, and after they ſhould be reſpectively 16, and if they either married before that age or without conſent, then ſuch daughter to have only 10000*l.* And directed the ſurplus of his perſonal eſtate ſhould be veſted in lands and ſettled on his daughters and their iſſue, with croſs remainders; in the father's life-time a treaty of marriage was in hand between the plaintiff and his lady, but before agreement the father died, and the plaintiff married his ſaid lady before 16, but with conſent. *Quaere*, Whether ſhe ſhould have 20000*l.* or only 10000*l.* The duke of *Southampton*'s caſe was cited, where relief was given in like caſe; and the court decreed the 20000*l.* to the plaintiff, *&c.* 2 *Vern.* 223, 224.

9. *Pritty*, by will gave 3000*l.* to his daughter at 21 or marriage, and put her in the care of *Scriven*. There was a proviſo if ſhe married without *Scriven*'s conſent, her legacy which was 3000*l.* was to ceaſe, and to be but 500*l.* and made the defendant, his ſon, executor and reſiduary legatee. She married without conſent, yet the court decreed her the whole 3000*l.* with intereſt from her marriage; and principally becauſe it was not deviſed over, but to fall into the ſurplus. 2 *Vern.* 294.

10. *H.* deviſed lands to *J.S.* and his heirs, on condition to pay 20000*l.* to the heir at law, *viz.* 1000*l.* a year for the firſt 16 years, and 2000*l.* *per annum* till the whole ſhould be paid; and the heir entered for non-payment of one of the 1000*l.* *per annum*, and *J.S.* brought his bill; and it was objected that the condition reſtores the heir, and that chancery ought not to aid in diſinheriſon of him: but it was reſolved by *Cowper*, lord chancellor, 1ſt, That the entry of the heir in the preſent caſe, was only to enforce the payment of his principal, as where a mortgagee enters; and

that the court can give him intereſt for the ſame from the time it became payable; and that whereſoever the court can give ſatisfaction or compenſation for the breach of a condition, they can relieve. 2dly, That for every 1000 *l.* from the time it became payable, the legatee or heir ſhould have intereſt; becauſe both the ſum and time were certain and paſt. 3dly, That there is to be no deduction of any taxes; becauſe it is not to iſſue or ariſe from the lands, but is given as a ſum in groſs, ſecured by entry on the land for non-payment. *Salk.* 156.

11. See 1 *Vern.* 19, 20, 32, 68, 79, 167, *S.C.* 456, 260, 319. 2 *Vern.* 452. 1 *Chan. Ca.* 138, 183, 142, 189, 95, 96, 89, 226, 122, 40, 58, 141, 142, 108, 22. 2 *Rep. Chan.* 23, 24, 95, 26. 1 *Mod.* 300, 306, 308. 2 *Chan. Ca.* 23, 95, 198. *Salk.* 231. 1 *Rep. Chan.* 1, 22. 1 *Mod.* 310. 2 *Rep. Chan.* 366, 391. 2 *Vent.* 356, 352. 1 *Chan. Ca.* 110, 184. 1 *Sid.* 442. 2 *Chan. Ca.* 219, 241. 1 *Chan. Ca.* 170, 24, 226, 184, 189. 3 *Chan. Ca.* 135. *Nelſ.* 47. *Prec. Chan.* 533. 1 *Vern.* 223, 207. *Nelſ.* 98, 145, 234, 236, 183, 244, 261. *Skin.* 285. *Gilb.* 26, 27. *Prec. Chan.* 348. 2 *Pe. Will.* 626. *Doct. & Stud.* *Cary's Rep.* *Tot.* *Bacon's Abr.* *Ca. Eq.*

124. *Equity will relieve againſt one's own act according to circumſtances.*

1. BY ſtatute 11 *H.* 7. *inter al'* it is enacted, if any woman, who hath lands of the gift of her huſband, or any the anceſtors of the huſband, ſuffer any recovery againſt her by covin, ſuch recovery ſhall be void, and it ſhall be lawful for him, who ſhould have the land after the woman, to enter, and to hold as in his firſt right, *&c.* *Doct. & Stud. lib.* 1. *cap.* 31.

2. If two men have a wood jointly, and one ſell it, and keepeth the money to himſelf, his companion hath no remedy at law, for that when they took the wood jointly they put each other in truſt, and were content to occupy together; therefore the law ſuffers them to order the profits thereof according to the truſt that each put in the other. And yet he who took all the profits is bound in conſcience to render half to his fellow; for as the law giveth him a right only to half the land, ſo it giveth him a right only in conſcience to half the profits; and yet it cannot be ſaid that the law is againſt conſcience; for the law willeth not that one ſhall take all the profits, but leaveth it to their conſcience. *Elſ. Obſ.* 78. See *Doct. & Stud. lib.* 1. *cap.* 19.

3. By a marriage agreement the intended wife was to have more than her father, mother, and two ſiſters, and the father was greatly indebted. The court would not decree the agreement, but left the plaintiff to law. 2 *Chan. Ca.* 17.

4. See *Nelſ.* 46. 1 *Chan. Ca.* 16. 1 *Vern.* 348. *Prec. Chan.* 538, 574.

125. *Equity to ſupply defects.*

1. *J. S.* being ſeiſed of lands in *Dorſetſhire*, *Somerſetſhire* and *Devonſhire*, thoſe in *Dorſetſhire* being of equal value with both the others. And having two nephews, one the ſon of his ſiſter *Henley*, the other of his ſiſter *Lee*, to prevent diſputes he executed a conveyance, and ſettled all to the uſe of himſelf for life; the remainder to his ſon, if he ſhould happen to have any intail. And then appointed the lands in *Dorſetſhire* to his nephew *Henley*, and in the other counties to his other nephew, and in numbering them up, a farm of 60*l.* *per annum*, was omitted, but in the limitation to *Henley* came theſe words, *And all other my lands and tenements, whereof no uſe is already limited, the ſame ſhall be unto the uſe of my nephew* Henley, *&c.* by which words, *Henley*'s counſel would have it paſs to him; to which it was anſwered by the counſel on *Lee*'s part, that it could not paſs by the general words; for though there is that omiſſion when he diſtributed the land, yet in the limitation to himſelf for life, remainder in tail, there mention is made of it, ſo it is not within the general words, *Whereof no uſe has been already limited*; for an uſe hath been limited to himſelf for life. And *Lee*'s counſel inſiſted he ought to have it, becauſe the ſcrivener ſwore it was intended him, and ſo was his inſtructions, and it was purely the omiſſion of the clerk. But the chancellor would decree for neither, but left the land in queſtion to deſcend equally between the two nephews. 1 *Vern.* 37, 38.

2. A conveyance, purporting a feoffment, may operate as a covenant to ſtand ſeiſed; though generally a defect in a voluntary conveyance ſhall not be ſupplied and made good here, yet if a man voluntarily make a ſettlement, as a proviſion for his children, and for their maintenance, ſuch voluntary conveyance ſhall be ſupplied and made good here. 1 *Vern.* 40.

3. A man by will made a proviſion for his younger children out of copyhold lands, but the ſurrender was made into the hands of one cuſtomary tenant only, and ſo defective. Yet decreed for the younger children, and ſo the defect well ſupplied againſt the heir at law; there being many precedents in the court of chancery. 1 *Vern.* 132, 133.

4. A feme covert agrees to ſell her inheritance, ſo ſhe might have 200*l.* ſecured to her. The lands were ſold, and the money veſted in truſtees. A creditor of the huſband brings the preſent bill to ſubject the money to the payment of his debt and charge; the wife promiſed it ſhould be chargeable. *Per Curiam:* This money ſhall not be liable to the payment of any of the huſband's debts, nor ſhall any promiſe by the wife for that purpoſe, ſubſequent to the original agreement, be obliging on that behalf. 2 *Vern.* 64, 65.

5. Where a feme covenants, by agreement with her huſband, to ſurrender or levy a fine, though the huſband die before it be done, yet this court will compel her to make good the agreement. 2 *Vern.* 61.

6. The plaintiff lent 50*l.* to the defendant's uncle, and took a warrant of attorney to confeſs judgment in ejectment for three cloſes upon a feigned demiſe for 20 years. *Court:* It is a defective ſecurity, and amounts to an agreement in equity to charge the lands, and decreed accordingly againſt the heir. 2 *Vern.* 151.

7. A devise of a personalty for life to the wife, though not said to be in lieu of dower. Yet lord *Sommers* held it ought in equity to be so taken, *&c. For collateral satisfaction may be a good bar to dower.* 2 Vern. 365.

8. Where the words *Shall stand and be seised,* left out of a conveyance made in pursuance of marriage articles, were supplied against the heir, and the plaintiff decreed to enjoy, as though the words had been in. 1 *Rep. Chan.* 162.

9. Resolved, That a recovery of *Cestuy que trust* shall bar, and transfer the trust as it should an estate at law, if it were upon consideration. 1 *Ch. Ca.* 49. See 68, 213. 2 *Vent.* 350. 2 *Chan. Ca.* 64, 71, 78. 1 *Vern.* 14.

10. See 1 *Chan. Ca.* 10, 35, 23, 39, 70, 87, 173, 208, 236, 263, 264. 2 *Chan. Ca.* 63, 68, 71, 78, 29, 30, 87. *Car.* 24. 1 *Vern.* 13. 2 *Vern.* 69, 163, *&c. Tot.* 131. 1 *Rep. Chan.* 168, 183, 185, 283. 3 *Chan. Ca.* 86. 2 *Rep. Chan.* 68, 216, 212, 218, 432.

11. *Vide* rule, *Marriage the highest consideration in law.*

126. *Equity will not vest an estate, where by reason of a condition precedent it will not vest at law; but of conditions subsequent, which are to devest an estate, it is otherwise.*

VIDE rules, *Conditions precedent must be literally performed; not so of subsequent ones where the court can make compensation. Equity to relieve where the matter lieth in compensation.*

127. *Estate of testator, in whosesoever hands, ought to be liable to his legacies.*

SEE rule, *Equity proper place to relieve legatees.* 1 Chan. Ca. 57.

128. *Est boni judicis ampliare jurisdictionem.*

General.

1. THE judges and sages of the law, for matters in law, are called, and indeed to all intents of law such they are, *Consilium regis.* Co. Lit. 304. a. b. Hob. 163. And they in his courts, by his immediate authority, have power derived down to them from the king, to keep all inferior jurisdictions within their several limits, and to enforce them to do their several offices where they are negligent therein. And so it is that they suspend the proceedings of the ecclesiastical courts by prohibition, *&c.* and, if cause be, can send their writs mandatory, commanding these inferior courts to discharge their office to their suitors, as are *Ha. Anal.* 20. and almost infinite other authorities. And the temporal judges are by no means bound by the rules of the civil or ecclesiastical laws, but are at full liberty to follow the course of their own law and courts, where the others differ from them. 1 *Pe. Will.* 12. *And therefore it is with the highest regard, and the utmost deference to their*

2 *lordships,*

lordships, the temporal judges, I speak it from the authority of my lord Coke, *they are always to have an eye that the ecclesiastical jurisdiction usurp not upon the temporal.* 2 Inst. 615. *And to preserve the laws of the realm in their full force and authority, and to suppress and punish all invasions thereon, as the same are the preservers of the prerogative royal, and the rights and liberties of the people; for* major haereditas venit unicuique nostrum a jure legibus quam a parentibus. *And therefore they are to see that none of the inferior courts extend their power beyond their due and limited bounds, to the derogation of the temporal laws and courts; and not only so, but they may extend temporal jurisdiction, so as to come at, as far as is possibly consistent with reason and justice, the several cases in judgment before them; for it is the office* Boni judicis ampliare jurisdictionem, *where the circumstances of the case so require.*

Particular cases.

2. On motion for a discharge of the defendant's wife, who was taken upon an attachment for want of appearance, the case appeared to be thus, the defendant's wife being a widow and having a considerable fortune, on the defendant's application to her by way of marriage, proposed the settling her own fortune upon herself separately, wherewith he was not to intermeddle; and accordingly before marriage, a settlement was made and executed, and the marriage took effect. Some time after the husband being very much indebted was arrested, and the creditors proceeding to execution and to seise his goods, to prevent which, the wife gave a note, that if they would discharge the action, which was for 2000*l.* she would pay the debt out of her own estate; and accordingly the action was discharged; but she after refused to make good her agreement; so the bill was to enforce execution, and was against the husband and wife, and a *subpoena* was taken out against both, and actually served upon the wife at her house, but the husband could not be found; after which neither the husband nor wife appearing, an attachment was sealed against both, and the wife taken, and now she moved to be discharged, on several affidavits that her husband was actually gone to *Holland* before the filing of the bill; and so process against her without her husband was irregular, and that she ought to be discharged; and it was said that at law there could be no proceeding against the wife without her husband, and that equity followed the law in this particular. On the other side was said, that the wife in this case was not to be considered as a feme covert; that she having an estate settled on her before marriage, for her separate use, this made her a feme sole, and a separate person from her husband, and so her agreement binding on her; that they had done all they could to bring in the husband; that they had made him a party to the bill, taken out a *subpoena* against him and his wife, and for not appearing they have taken out attachments likewise against both; that if they could not in this case proceed against the wife, the justice of the court would be eluded, and it would be easy for any man to settle his estate upon his wife, and then get out of the way, and so bid defiance to his creditors. And Sir *Joseph Jekyll* (after master of the rolls) said, it was the saying of a very great man, *Est boni judicis ampliare jurisdictionem*, and he thought to extend the arm of justice further than usual, when otherwise there would be a failure of justice, was the duty of every court; that in some cases a

woman

woman may ſue without her huſband; and that nothing was more common than for a wife in this court, even to ſue her own huſband; and ſurely in this caſe the plaintiff ought not to loſe the benefit of the wife's agreement, by her ſending her huſband abroad; and cited the caſe *Duboiſe* and *Dowle* to this purpoſe. But the lord keeper ſeemed to be of opinion, that the proceſs in this cauſe without the huſband was irregular, and that they ought to ſtay till the huſband returned, when they might renew the proceſs againſt both. To which it was anſwered, Suppoſe the huſband ſhould never return, muſt they then be totally deprived of the benefit of this agreement? On which my lord ſaid, he would aſk the maſter of the rolls's opinion, and be governed by that; and after the maſter of the rolls coming into court, was clear of opinion, that the proceſs in this caſe without the huſband was regular; that the huſband was joined in the ſuit only for conformity, and ſaid a woman by her marriage did not loſe her diſcretion or underſtanding, but rather improved it by her huſband's teaching, and cited *Moore* and *Huſſey*, *Hob.* 93. where ſeveral caſes are cited wherein a feme covert without her huſband ſhall be chargeable, and ſaid the practice of this court had been conſtantly ſo; on which the defendant prayed time till the firſt day of next term, to put in her anſwer, and on her entering her appearance with the regiſter, and paying the coſts of the motion it was granted, and ſhe was diſcharged out of cuſtody.

Note; In this caſe *Howe* moved, that the defendant ought not to be heard to move for her diſcharge, becauſe ſhe not having appeared by her clerk in court, was not at all in court, but a perfect ſtranger, and ſo could not regularly make an application by her counſel, till ſhe had brought herſelf into court, by directing her clerk to enter an appearance for her; but of this no notice was taken, either by the court or counſel on the other ſide. *Gilb.* 83, 84. *Prec. Chan.* 328. *S. C.* Vide *Compleat Attorney* 326, 328.

3. *Vide* rule, *It is the office of temporal judges to advance laws made for religion, according to their end, though the words are ſhort and imperfect.*

129. *Eſt quiddam perfectius in rebus licitis.*

General.

1. SO St. *Paul*, 1 Cor. x. 23. *All things are lawful, but all things are not expedient.* And this is finely ſpoken by *Tully*, *Eſt aliquod quod non oportet, etiamſi licet; quicquid vero non licet, certe non oportet.* Hob. 159.

2. A jointreſs reſtrained from committing waſte. *Nelſ.* 190. The ſame of tenant for life, and ordered to repair the deſtruction he had made; tho' he was diſpuniſhable of waſte. *Nelſ.* 220, 221. *Prec. Chan.* 454. Tenant after poſſibility of iſſue extinct, and tenant for life, though by expreſs grant diſpuniſhable of waſte, or by truſt, ſhall be reſtrained from pulling down of houſes or defacing a ſeat. 2 *Chan. Ca.* 32. *Gilb.* 127. *Salk. S.C.* A bill was preferred in favour of an infant *en ventre ſa mere*, to reſtrain waſte, and decreed, and an injunction was granted *inde.* *Prec. Chan.* 50. See *Barn.* 274. A patron may reſtrain an incumbent from waſte, *&c.* *Barn.* 399, 400.

Particular cases.

3. See *Mildmay's* case, *Coke, lib.* 1. 177. a leaſe for 1000 years was diſallowed, though a power was reſerved to limit any eſtate for years, for any reaſonable conſideration, as to him ſhould be thought good, yet the land was his own before. 4 *E.* 2. *F. Waſt.* 11. A leaſe of an houſe and land, *et quod poſſit commodum ſuum inde facere meliori modo, quo ſibi viderit expedire, ſine contradictione aliqua*, yet he may not pull down the houſe; for there is nothing more contrary to liberty than licentiouſneſs, nor to diſcretion than fooliſhneſs. *In maxima potentia minima licentia.* Hob. 159.

* 4. Though he was by expreſs words diſpuniſhable of waſte, yet injoined from cutting down timber, &c. which is either ornamental or a ſhelter to the family ſeat. *Packer* and *Lord Bolingbroke & al'* in *Canc'.* 15 *March* and 29 *April* 1726, and after affirmed in the houſe of lords, *March* 1728. See alſo caſe * *Lord Blaney* and *Mahon* before the houſe of lords, 27 *March* 1723.

* 5. A leaſe was with a penalty of 100*l.* for every acre ploughed or dug up. Leſſee digs for gravel, and raiſes much more than the penalty, and ſubmits in his anſwer to pay the penalty; but inſiſts on payment thereof he is not to be injoined from digging for the future; yet injoined from digging any more for the remainder of the term. See caſe *Chriſt's hoſpital* and *Pugh*, before the houſe of lords, 20 *March* 1727.

130. *Eventus varios res nova ſemper habet.*

SEE the rule, *Periculoſum eſt res novas et inuſitatas inducere.*

131. *Every iſſue ought to conſiſt of an affirmative and a negative.*

11 *Co.* 10. *b.*

132. *Every man's deed or covenant is to be taken moſt ſtrongly againſt himſelf.*

General.

1. ALL contracts are to be taken according to the intent of the parties: and if there be any doubt, ſuch interpretation muſt be made as is moſt ſtrong againſt the grantor or obligor, that he may not, by dark obſcure and uncertain wording of the contract, find away to evade it. * *Gilb.* 249, &c. Every unequal agreement is not fraudulent. See caſe before the houſe of lords, * *Lord Thomond* and *Hamilton, anno* 1733. Contracts are to be adjudged according to the law of the place where the ſame were made. See caſe before the houſe of lords, * *York Buildings Company* and *Meers*, 23 *November* 1728. Equity will not carry unequal agreements into execution. See caſe *Brain* and *Wooley*, before the houſe of lords, 9 *Feb.* 1721,

And * *Stop* and *Stanhope*, 24 *March* 1720. * *Thompson* and *Harcourt*, 13 *Feb.* 1721, and * *Squire* and *Baker*, 27 *Feb.* 1726, all before the houſe of lords. Nor where a perſon of weak underſtanding is drawn into it. See caſe * *Carol* and *Chamberlain*, before the houſe of lords, 14 *July* 1721, alſo * *White* and *Leighbourn*, 28 *Feb.* 1722. Nor where the method of obtaining them is not ſtrictly regular, though the ſame is in part executed. See caſe before the houſe of lords, * *Rochford* and *Nugent*, 22 *May* 1724. See alſo * *Fitzgerald* and *Uſtace*, *anno* 1733, for in agreements the ties ought to be reciprocral, *ibidem.* * An agreement to make a leaſe is a good leaſe in equity; and a confirmation of ſuch leaſe by him in remainder is good; ſee caſe before the houſe of lords, *Lord Cater* and *Neagle*, 1 *March* 1717. *Dedi et conceſſi* may amount to a grant, a feoffment, a gift, a leaſe, a releaſe, a confirmation, a ſurrender, and it is in the election of the party to uſe it to which of theſe purpoſes he pleaſeth. *Co. Lit.* 301. *b.* If a warranty be made to one, his heirs and aſſigns, by expreſs words, the aſſignee ſhall take the benefit, and have a *warrantia cartae*. *Fitz. Na. Bre.* 135. 9 *E.* 2. *Garr. del Chartres* 30. 36 *E.* 3. Tit. *Garr.* 1. 4 *H.* 8. *Dy.* 1. 5 *Co.* 16. *b.* When divers do a treſpaſs, the ſame is joint or ſeveral, at the will of him to whom the wrong is done, yet if he releaſe to one of them, all are diſcharged; becauſe his own deed ſhall be taken moſt ſtrongly againſt himſelf; and if two men are jointly and ſeverally bound in a bond, if the obligee releaſe one, both are diſcharged. *Co. Lit.* 232. *a.*

Particular caſes.

* 2. Covenants and agreements are to be conſidered moſt ſtrongly againſt the party; as tenant for life, with power to make leaſes for 21 years, ſo the ſame be in poſſeſſion and at the beſt improved rent, makes a leaſe, and a year after gives a note to another tenant under his hand, that he will renew his and the other's leaſe, ſo often as he ſhall be required: Decreed to renew at the old rent for 21 years, if he ſhall ſo long live. This decree was pronounced in the exchequer in *Ireland*, 21 *Feb.* 1736. and affirmed by the lords here. 17 *Feb.* 1738.

3. Baron and feme termors of an houſe in *Fleetſtreet*, called *The three Conies*, for a long term of years. The huſband alone makes a leaſe for part of the term, in theſe words, *The houſe or tenement in* Fleetſtreet, *called* The three Conies, *with all the chambers, cellars and ſhops*, &c. *excepting and reſerving to the huſband by name, the ſhops* propter proprium & ſolum uſum et occupationem. The baron died within the term, and the wife enters as to the ſhops upon the tenant, and is re-ouſted, and brings ejectment, and the defendant pleads *non ejecit.* On motion for judgment for the plaintiff to recover his term in the ſhops, it ſeemed to *Weſton*, that ſhe ought to have it; for that the exception and reſervation trenched upon all the leaſe, and the ſhops were not leaſed. *Sed Dyer contra:* For that it appears by the expreſs words before, that the ſhops were leaſed generally; and this reſervation or exception, is but ſpecial and temporary, (*viz.*) during the occupation and uſe of the leſſor himſelf, according to 3 *H.* 6. 53. where the trees were not expreſly excepted out of the leaſe, *ſed quod bene liceret* to the leſſor *ſuccidere, dare et vendere arbores, &c.* *Item nota ſupra*, the exception and reſervation is made to the huſband leſſor by name only, without ſaying to his executors or aſſigns, *&c.* *Item nota*, the exception of

 the

the ſhops, is of all the ſhops, which is contrary to the leaſe itſelf; and therefore is a void exception. *Et ſic fuit opinio aliorum juſtitiariorum tandem.* Dy. 264. b.

4. Tenant in fee makes a leaſe of lands to *B.* to have and to hold to *B.* for life, without mentioning for whoſe life, it ſhall be taken to be for the life of the leſſee; for it ſhall be taken moſt ſtrongly againſt the leſſor. *Co. Lit.* 42. *a.*

* 5. Covenant to grant a new leaſe at the end of the term, under the ſame rents and covenants; the new leaſe ſhall be likewiſe with covenants to renew, *&c.* See caſe before the houſe of lords, *Bridge* and *Hitchcock*, 24 *June* 1716.

* 6. The earl of *Godolphin* agrees with builders before the act made for the building of *Blenheim* houſe at the expence of the crown; and recites that he made ſuch agreement at the inſtance and deſire of the duke of *Marlborough*; the duke is bound by ſuch agreement, and as well liable to pay for the work done after the ſtatute as before. See caſe *Ducheſs of Marlborough* and *Strong*, before the houſe of lords, 8 *May* 1721.

7. In covenant the plaintiff declared, that the defendant and *J. S. convenerunt pro ſe et quolibet eorum*, that they or either of them would load ſuch a ſhip, and pay for the freight, *&c.* The defendant pleaded in abatement, that other covenantors were in full life, and not named, and prayed judgment of the writ: and it was agreed by all, that *obligamus nos et utrumque noſtrum* in a bond is joint and ſeveral. *Sed per Holt* chief juſtice, there is a diverſity between *A.* and *B. conveniunt et quilibet eorum convenit*, and *A.* and *B. conveniunt pro ſe et quolibet eorum*; for in this firſt *quilibet eorum convenit* expreſly ſevers the lien, but *pro quolibet eorum* ſeems to go to the thing to be done, that is, that they both or either of them would do it. *Sed reliqui juſtic' contra*, and judgment was, that the defendant ſhould anſwer over. *Salk.* 393.

8. If one grant a rent-charge to another out of his lands, the grantee hath two remedies; either by way of diſtreſs or writ of annuity; for the grantor having granted it, he hath charged his perſon, and having granted it out of his lands, he hath charged his lands alſo; and having thus granted two remedies, it muſt be in the election of the grantee, who is to have the advantage of theſe remedies, which he will have. *Gilb.* 250.

9. In the caſe *Hill* and *Grange*, (*Plow.* 172.) if a man make a leaſe for years, and reſerve a rent payable at *Michaelmas* and *Lady-day*; and there is a condition, if the rent be behind, and unpaid at the ſaid feaſts, and ten days after, that the leſſor may re-enter, the conſtruction of ſuch leaſe has been, that the rent is due at the day, ſo that the leſſee may diſtrain for it, though to ſave the condition the leſſee may tender it at the laſt of the ten days, becauſe thoſe are days of grace given by the condition, that he may ſave his eſtate by the tender. *Gilb.* 250.

10. The caſe was (1 *Vent.* 58.) that the condition of a bond was, that the obligor ſhould bring the ſon and daughter of *J. S.* at their full age, to give ſuch releaſe as a third perſon ſhall require; the defendant pleads that the ſon is alive, and under age, whereto the plaintiff demurs, and the demurrer is allowed; for the force of the bond is not ſuſpended till they are both of age; becauſe it is to be taken not conjunctively, but reſpectively and disjunctively; for the obligor undertakes, that the daughter ſhall releaſe

at her full age as well as the son; and if she does not the condition is broken. *Gilb.* 250.

11. There is a resolution in the case *Sayer* and *Gleane*, (1 *Lev.* 54, 55.) in debt on an obligation, that if a ship put to sea, and either the goods or the obligor come safe, he should pay such a sum, over and above the use allowed by the statute; the defendant pleaded that the obligor died before he returned; and it was objected, that the defendant had an election to pay at which of the contingencies he would; and therefore the executors of the obligor were excused, because their testator never returned safe; but it was resolved that the law supplies the words, *which should first happen*, and no prejudice to the executors of the obligor; because it was the sense of such contract, that payment should arise on either of the contingencies. *Gilb.* 250.

12. See *Gilb.* 48. 1 *Pe. Will.* 9. 1 *Vern.* 21, 22, 28, 48, 141. 2 *Lev.* 9. 1 *Mod.* 175. 1 *Vent.* 137. 1 *Vern.* 167, 449. 1 *Chan. Ca.* 119, 120, 196, 197, 210. 2 *Chan. Ca.* 211, 212. 4 *Co.* 26, 27. *Co. Lit.* 99. *a.* 237. *Hob.* 168, 169, 170, &c. *Poph.* 182. 2 *Bulst.* 258. *Skin.* 60. *Sid.* 48. 3 *Cro.* 26. *Saund.* 284. 2 *Lev.* 80. 3 *Lev.* 283. *Lat.* 233. 1 *Inst.* 112. *b.* 1 *Leon.* 276, 279. 4 *Leon.* 27. *Rol. Abr.* 15. *Dy.* 318. *Co. Lit.* 183. *a.* 1 *Co.* 154. *a. b.* *Farest.* 158. *Dy.* 97.

13. *Vide* rules, *Constructio legis non facit injuriam. Quaelibet concessio fortissime contra donatorem interpretanda est. Contracts are to be taken according to the intent of the parties, expressed by their own words. In things of elections, the party is to shew that he hath made it. Expressio eorum, quae tacite insunt, nihil operatur, &c.*

133. *Every man is to recover by his own strength, and not by the weakness of his adversary's pretensions.*

1. IN *Quare Impedit*, if any thing in the count be traversed, it must be such part as, if true, is inconsistent with the defendent's title, and if false or found against the plaintiff, doth absolutely destroy his title. Nay, if the traverse leaves no title in the plaintiff, it is good enough, whatsoever becomes of the defendant's. *Show. Parl. Ca.* 221.

2. In the case of *The bishop of Worcester* and *Jervis*, in *Vau.* 53. it is said, That the king ought to maintain his own, and not to question the defendant's title; he cannot desert that which he hath alledged for himself, and fall upon the defendant's title: if the right be not his, he has no cause to complain of the defendant, though another hath right. *Every man is to recover by his own strength, and not by the weakness of the defendant's pretensions.* Parl. Ca. 221.

* 3. *He, who recovers, must recover on the strength of his own, and not on the weakness of his adversary's title.* And it is sufficient to the defendant that the plaintiff hath no title appearing. See case before the house of lords, *Burgh of Perth* and *Presbytery* there, 5 *March* 1729-30.

134. *Every one ought sic uti suo ut alienum non laedat.*

General.

1. IN an house, four things are to be desired, *Habitatio hominis, delectatio inhabitantis, necessitas luminis, et salubritas aeris.* And for all or any of these being interrupted, an action lieth, and damages shall be recovered; but for prospect, which is only a matter of delight, and not of necessity, no action lieth; and yet it is a great commendation to an house if it have a long and large prospect, *unde dicitur, Laudaturque domus, longos quae prospicit agros;* but the law does not give actions for such matters of delight. And *Solomon* says, *Eccl.* xi. 7. *Dulce lumen est, et delectabile oculis videre solem. Et olim* (*ut Plutarch*) *rex Aethiopum interrogatus quid optimum? Respondebat lucem, &c.* And if stopping of wholesome air be a good cause of action, *a fortiori* the corruption of the air, as was the case at bar, must needs be a good cause and foundation for an action; for the rule is, *Probibetur ne quis faciat in suo, quod nocere possit alieno. Et sic utere tuo ut alienum non laedas.* 9 Co. 58. *Aldred*'s case.

Particular cases.

2. *Aldred* brought case against *Benton*, for that the plaintiff being seised of an house and land, the defendant, having a little orchard contiguous, interrupted his lights by an erection, *&c.* and rendered the air unwholesome by building of an hog-sty and keeping hogs, *&c.* and on *non culp.* pleaded, he was found guilty of both, and damages assessed; and on motion in arrest of judgment, that the action lay not, for that the erection of the hog-sty was necessary for the sustentation of man, and one ought not to have so delicate a nose as not to endure the savour of hogs; for *Lex non favet delicatorum votis.* Yet it was resolved the action lay; for in an house, four things are desireable, *ut supra.* 9 Co. 57. *Aldred*'s case.

3. *Thomas Bland* brought case against *Mosley*, and declared that *James Bland* was seised, *&c.* and that he and all those, *&c.* time whereof, *&c.* have had and used to have for them and their tenants, *&c.* on the *West* part of the said house seven windows to a piece of ground adjacent, which piece of ground time whereof, *&c.* was without any building. By means of which windows the said *James* and all those, *&c.* are used time whereof, *&c.* for them and there tenants to have several wholesome and necessary easements and commodities by reason of open air and light, *&c.* and that the said *James* demised to the plaintiff; and that the defendant mischievously intending to deprive him, *et obscurare mesuagium praedictum horrida tenebritate, &c.* had erected a new building upon the said piece of land, *&c.* so close that the said lights were stopt, by which the plaintiff lost his easements, *&c. et maxima pars mesuagii praedicti horrida tenebritate obscurata fuit, &c.* the defendant pleaded in bar *quod infra praedictam civitatem Ebor. talis habetur, et a toto tempore cujus, &c. habebatur consuetudo,* (*viz.*) *quod siquis habuerit fenestras ad visum per easdem versus terram vicini sui, vicinus ille visum illar' fenest' obstruere super terram illam solebat et posset, sicut melius viderit sibi expedire,* by force of which custom he justified the stopping of the windows; upon which the plaintiff demurred in law. And adjudged the bar was insufficient for two causes, 1st, When a man hath a

 law-

lawful easement by prescription, another custom immemorial may not take it away, for the one custom is as antient as the other. As if one man has a way over the lands of another by custom, the other may not prescribe to stop the said way; for in both this and the principal case the prescription or custom might have lawful commencement. 9 *Co.* 58. *a. b.*

4. *Wray*, chief justice: For stopping as well of the wholesome air as of light, an action lieth, and damages shall be recovered for them, for both are necessary; for it is said *vescitur aura aetheria:* and the words *horrida tenebritate*, &c. are significant and imply the benefit of light. But he said that for prospect, which is only matter of delight and not necessary, no action lieth. 9 *Co.* 58. *b.*

5. Levying a brick-kiln or a lime-kiln, is good and profitable, yet if erected so near an house, that when it burns, the flames of it so enter the house that it cannot be inhabited, an action lieth. So if one hath a water-course near his house for his necessary uses, if a glover levy a lime-pit for calves-skins and sheep-skins, so near this water-course, that the corruption of the lime-pit corrupts it so that the tenants go away, case lieth; as was adjudged 13 *H.* 7. 26. *b.* and this standeth well with the rule, *Probibetur ne quis faciat in suo, quod nocere possit alieno*, &c. 9 Co. 59. a.

6. *Vide* lord *Coke's Entries*, tit. *Nusance*, *fo.* 406. *b.* He, who hath a several piscary in a water, shall have case against one for erecting a dye-house, *per quod proficuum piscariae suae praedict' totaliter amisit*, &c. so in the principal case for erecting the swine-sty, &c. 9 *Co.* 59. *a.*

7. Vide *Cro. Ca.* 510. 1 *Rol.* 88, (40.) 5 *Co.* 57, &c.

135. *Every rightful fee-simple is either by purchase or descent.*

General.

1. EVERY man, who hath a rightful fee-simple, hath it either by purchase or descent. But one may be in of a wrongful estate by disseisin, intrusion, abatement, usurpation, &c. *Co. Lit.* 2. *a.*

2. Every man who hath a lawful estate in fee-simple, hath it either by descent or purchase. *Co. Lit.* 13. *b.* 14. *a.*

Particular to

Purchase.

3. Purchase is when one cometh to lands by conveyance or title. And disseisins, abatements, intrusions, usurpations and such like estates gained by wrong, are not said in the law to be purchases, but oppressions and injuries. *Co. Lit.* 3. *b.*

4. A purchase is always intended by title, and most properly by some kind of conveyance, either for money or some other consideration, or freely of gift, for that is in law also a purchase. *Co. Lit.* 18. *a. b.*

Descent.

5. A descent, because it cometh meerly by act in law, is not said to be a purchase. *Co. Lit.* 18. *a. b.*

6. Descent in legal understanding is taken when land, *&c.* after the death of the ancestor, is cast, by course of law, upon the heir; and this is the noblest and worthiest means whereby lands are derived from one to another; because it is wrought and vested by the act of law, and right of blood, to the worthiest and next of blood and kindred of the ancestor; and therefore it hath not in the common law altogether the same signification that it hath in the civil law; for the civilians call him *Haeredem, qui ex testamento succedit in universum jus testatoris*; but, by the common law he is only *heir*, who succeedeth by right of blood. And this agreeth well with the etymology of the word *heir*, to whom the lands descend; for *haeres dicitur ab haerendo, quia qui haeres est haeret, hoc est, proximus est sanguine illi cujus est haeres*; so as he that is *haeres, sanguinis est haeres, et herus haereditatis.* Now as descent is the worthiest means to come to lands, *&c.* so hath the heir more privileges than any that by other order or means come to lands, *&c.* *Co. Lit.* 237. *a. b.*

136. *Exceptio probat regulam.*

* 1. By lord chancellor: The exception is to be construed as the general clause, out of which the exception is taken. *Exceptio probat regulam de rebus non exceptis.* And if an exception shall have that effect to explain the general clause out of which the exception is taken, it is reasonable that the general clause should have this effect to explain the exception likewise. *Wingfield* versus *Newton*, *in Canc.* 6 *Feb.* 1729.

2. Vide *Co. Lit.* 9. *a. b.* 2 *Roll* 99.

137. *Exceptio unius est exclusio alterius.*

* LORD chancellor: As the specialty debts amount to more than the legacy in question, and as the personal estate has been exhausted in the payment of them, the plaintiff must be intitled to stand in the place of such specialty creditors, and so to receive a satisfaction out of the real estate. His lordship also said, that legacies are acts of bounty, and the natural fund for the payment of them is the personal estate only. His lordship also said children are considered in this court, as being in some degree creditors by nature. *Corefield* and *Lingen*, *in Canc.* before lord chancellor, 3 *March* 1739.

138. *Ex diuturnitate temporis omnia praesumuntur solemniter esse acta.*

1. IF all the witnesses to a charter of feoffment be dead, the violent presumption, which standeth for a proof, is continual and quiet possession; for *Ex diuturnitate temporis, &c.* also the deed may receive credit

per

per collationem sigillorum, scripturae, &c. et super fidem cartarum mortuis testibus erit ad patriam de necessitate recurrendum. Co. Lit. 6. b.

2. See 2 *Ju. Eccl.* 464, 465, 466, 467, 480, 483.

3. See also rule, *Omnia praesumuntur solemniter esse acta.*

139. *Executio juris non habet injuriam.*

1. IT was resolved, that forasmuch as in the case at bar a *Capias* was awarded against the countess of *Rutland*, by the court of common pleas, that the sheriff, or his officer by his warrant, might without any offence execute it; for they are not to dispute the authority of the court, but to execute the warrants to them directed, whereto they are sworn; and though it appeared in the *Capias*, that she was a countess, against whom, by the law in such case, no *Capias* lay, *et ignorantia juris non excusat*, and principally sheriffs and other ministers of law and justice, as was objected; yet forasmuch as in some cases, as in cases of contempt, *&c. Capias* lies against them; therefore it was resolved, that the sheriff and his ministers ought not to examine the judicial acts of the court, but to execute the writ: wherewith agreeth the opinion, 36 *H.* 8. *Dy. fo.* 60. If a *Capias* or *Exigent* come to the sheriff against a duke, earl, *&c.* in case where it doth not really lie against them, yet he ought to serve the writ, and not to dispute the validity thereof. But the truth of the case of the countess of *Rutland* was, that the serjeant who had the warrant to arrest the countess on the said *Ca. Sa.* being apprehensive that she would be rescued by her servants and dependants, *&c.* whereby the sheriff might be charged, the serjeant at mace advised *S.* the plaintiff in the suit, to enter a feigned action for 1000*l.* before the sheriffs of *London*, according to the custom there, whereupon they would first arrest the countess, and by force thereof bring her to the *Compter*, and then take her body in execution upon the *Ca. Sa.* Hereupon the serjeant, with many more, came to the countess in her coach in *Cheapside*, and shewing her the mace, and touching her body with it, said we arrest you, Madam, at the suit of *S.* which were all the words they said to her, but compelled her coachman to drive her ladyship to the *Compter* in *Woodstreet*, at the door of which, the sheriff came, and brought the countess to his house, where she remained seven or eight hours, till she actually paid the debt. It was resolved, that the sheriff, or any other by his authority, who arrested another person, ought, upon the arrest, to shew at whose suit, out of what court, for what cause, and when the process is returnable; to the intent, if it be for any execution, he might satisfy it, and free his body from the arrest, if he so pleased; and if it came upon mean process, either to agree with the party, or put in bail, and know when he was to appear. And as this case was circumstanced, it was resolved, that the said general arrest could not be said to be by force of the *Ca. Sa.* and that the arrest of the said countess by the said serjeant at mace of their own heads, and without other warrant, was against law, and the said countess falsly imprisoned. And so in summons in real actions, *&c.* Vide 3 *E.* 3. 48. 43 *E.* 3. 32. 50 *E.* 3. 16, *&c.* And a severe sentence was given against *S.* the serjeant, and other their confederates. And the entry of such feigned actions in *London* were all utterly condemned by the whole court; for by colour of law and justice, they, by such feigned means, acted against

both law and juſtice, and ſo made law and juſtice the author and cauſe of tort and injuſtice. *Vide Stat.* 5 *H.* 4. *c.* 8. in the preamble. 6 *Co.* 52. The counteſs of *Rutland's* caſe.

2. Held if a man bring an action on a falſe ſurmiſe, in a proper court, the defendant cannot bring an action againſt him and charge him with it as a fault directly and *ex diametro*, as if the ſuit itſelf were a wrongful act; for *Executio juris non habet injuriam.* The law is good, but the abuſe of it is the fault. *Hob.* 266.

3. If one be impriſoned upon a formal ſuit, though there was no good cauſe of action, yet if he give bond for his releaſe, he ſhall not avoid it by dureſs; for it was by law, though the plaintiff untruly procured it. *Hob.* 266, 267.

4. But if you charge me with a crime in a court which is no way capable of the cauſe, I may have an action, and lay that very complaint to be the ſlander; *aliter*, if in a proper court. *Hob.* 266, 267.

5. Now to the principal caſe, if one ſue me in a proper court, yet if his ſuit be utterly without ground of truth, and that certainly known to himſelf, I may have caſe againſt him for the undue vexation and damage he hath put me unto by his ill practice, though the ſuit itſelf be legal, and I cannot complain of it, as it is a ſuit; and therefore, 16 *E.* 3. *Fitzh. Deceipt* 35. A cognizee of a ſtatute ſued execution againſt his deed of defeazance, whereupon the cognizor had deceit. *Hob.* 267.

6. If a man ſue me, and pending that ſuit, commence another againſt me, to this I have a plea in abatement which proves the latter ſuit unjuſt, and vexatious: But if he diſcontinue the former, he may bring a new action. *Hob.* 267.

7. Likewiſe I may have caſe againſt him, who ſues me againſt his own releaſe, or after the money duly paid; yea, though it be upon a ſingle obligation. *Hob.* 267.

8. So where one bargains and ſells his land at common law, and refuſeth to make aſſurance, and conveys it to another with notice, the firſt bargainee may have an action upon the caſe, or deceit, as well as a *ſubpoena.* *Hob.* 267.

9. But two cautions are to be obſerved to maintain actions in theſe caſes. 1ſt, That the new action muſt not be brought before the firſt determined; becauſe it cannot ſooner appear that the firſt was unjuſt; which is the reaſon given by the judges, 2 *R.* 3. And that is the reaſon that a writ of conſpiracy lieth not till the plaintiff be lawfully acquitted. 2dly, The other rule is, that there muſt not only be a thing done amiſs, but alſo a damage already fallen upon the party, or elſe inevitable. *Hob.* 267.

10. And therefore 19 *H.* 6. 44. if a man forge a bond in my name, I can have no action upon the caſe yet, but when I am ſued I may, for the wrong and damage, though I may avoid it by plea. But if it were a recognizance or fine, I may have deceit preſently, before execution; for *Quae incontinenti, vel certo fiunt, ineſſe videntur.* 43 *E.* 3. 20. Diſceit againſt one who procured a *formedon* by colluſion. *Hob.* 267.

11. *Hob.* 320. *Doct. & Stud. lib.* 2. *cap.* 47.

12. *Vide* rule, *Eſt quiddam perfectius in rebus licitis. Ignorantia facti excuſat. Liberty the greateſt jewel.*

140. *Executor, where rightful, there can be no executor de ſon tort.*

1. THE plaintiff being the widow of *A.* ſued the defendant, who was his executor, for ſatisfaction for ſeveral debts of the teſtator's, which ſhe, having poſſeſſed herſelf of his eſtate, had paid; the executor having gotten all the eſtate out of her hands. It was much controverted, whether ſhe ſhould be holpen herein? For though executor of his own wrong ſhall be allowed all payments made to any but himſelf, yet ſhe was not executor of her own wrong; for where there is a rightful executor, as here, there can be no executor *de ſon tort.* Yet it reſembled that caſe; and the court doubting much what to do in this caſe, decreed, by conſent of counſel, that ſhe ſhould be allowed for all payments which ſhe had made and were incumbent on the executor to pay, according to the courſe of law: but that if ſhe had made any payments out of the order and rule that the law left the executor liable to, ſuch payments ſhe ſhould not be allowed for, if they were to the prejudice of the executor. 1 *Chan. Ca.* 33.

2. As to charging one as executor *de ſon tort* in the courts of common law; Lord chancellor ſaid, The manner is not to charge them, that they were executors of their own wrong, for that was held once to be bad, but they muſt be charged as executors *teſtamenti et ult' voluntatis*; neither is there any way to charge executors *de ſon tort* in the eccleſiaſtical court, but the remedy is for the adminiſtrator *de bonis non,* to commence a ſuit in equity upon the foot of a breach of truſt and fraud, and as to an appeal being a proper remedy, his lordſhip ſaid, that in my lord *Holt*'s time an executor was ſued in the eccleſiaſtical court for an account by a perſon who was neither creditor nor legatee; and it was objected thereunto, that an appeal was the proper remedy; but the court there ſaid he had been called into a juriſdiction which had not proper cognizance of the matter; wherefore they granted a prohibition; the reſt of the court were of the ſame opinion with my lord in the particular caſe, and accordingly the rule was made abſolute. 2 *Ju. Eccl.* 79, 80. caſe *Tucker* and *Towel.*

141. *Ex facto jus oritur.*

1. A Woman was removed by two juſtices from *O.* to *C.* thence by two juſtices to *B.* and ſhe voluntarily returned to *O.* and there bears a baſtard child. *Note*; It was not ſaid in the firſt order that the two were juſtices. *Holt,* chief juſtice, It ſhould be ſaid that they were juſtices and (*Quor. unus*) though the *Quorum* is often omitted; for it is a ſpecial authority out of ſeſſions. It is ſaid ſhe came to ſettle contrary to law, but they ſhould ſtate the fact, not the law; for *Ex facto jus oritur.* If there be any fraud in conveying a woman to bear a child in any pariſh, yet the child may be ſent with its mother, to the place of her laſt ſettlement. The caſe was referred to the judges of the aſſiſe. *Comb.* 285, 286.

2. A decree ought to be grounded on fact, *Ex facto jus oritur*, else by the clerk's course the defendant should be barred of review in all cases; for the plaintiff in a bill of review cannot alledge fact contrary to what is stated in the decree to be proved, *&c.* 2 *Chan. Ca.* 162.

142. *Ex malis moribus bonae leges natae sunt.*

1. IF we look into our own history we shall find, if the laws of provision and *praemunire* had not been made, these realms had lost the name of imperial, and of kingdoms too, and had been long ago made tributary provinces to the bishop of *Rome*; or rather part of St. *Peter*'s patrimony in demesne; our kings had had their scepters wrested out of their hands, their crowns spurned from their heads, their necks trode upon, and made lacquies or footmen to the bishop of *Rome*, as some emperors and *French* kings have been; our prelates been made his chaplains and clerks, our nobility his vassals and servants, our commons his slaves and villains, if these acts of manumission had not freed them, *&c.* *Dav.* 85. *a. b.* 86, 87. *b.* 88. *a. b. to the end.*

It was a great blasphemy when the devil said, I will ascend and be like the highest; but it is still greater blasphemy to personate God, and bring him in, saying, I will descend and be like the prince of darkness: and what is it better, to make the cause of religion to descend to the cruel and execrable actions of murdering princes, butchering people, and subverting of states and governments? Surely this is to bring down the Holy Ghost, instead of the likeness of a dove, in the shape of a vulture, and to hang out of the bark of a Christian church, a flag of pirates and assassins. *Ira hominis non implet justitiam dei.*

2. See 1 *Ju. Eccl. Divisions, The course of ecclesiastical usurpations; the opposition the same have met with throughout, and the several statutes provided against such encroachments.*

143. *Ex nuda submissione non oritur actio.*

General.

1. STAT. 9 & 10 *W.* 3. *cap.* 15. *sect.* 1. after 11 *May* 1698. all merchants and others, desiring to end any controversy (for which there is no remedy but by personal action or suit in equity) by arbitration, may agree that their submission of the suit to the award or umpirage of any persons, shall be made a rule of any of his majesty's courts of record, which the parties shall chuse, and may insert such their agreement in their submission, or the condition of the bond or promise, and on producing an affidavit of such agreement, and upon reading and filing of such affidavit in the court so chosen, the same may be entered of record in such court, and a rule of court shall be thereupon made, that the parties shall submit to, and finally be concluded by such arbitration or umpirage; and in case of disobedience thereunto, the party neglecting or refusing shall be subject to all the penalties of contemning a rule of court, and process shall issue accordingly; which shall not be stopt or delayed by any order, *&c.* of any other court either of law or equity, unless it appear on oath, that the arbitrators and umpires misbehaved themselves, and that such award was corruptly

corruptly or unduly procured. *Sect.* 2. Any arbitration or umpirage procured by corruption or undue means, ſhall be void and ſet aſide by any court of law or equity, ſo as ſuch corruption or undue practice be complained of in the court where the rule is made for ſuch arbitration, before the laſt day of the next term after ſuch arbitration made and publiſhed to the parties. *Cay's Abr. Stat.* tit. *Arbitration.* See rule, *Quae non valent ſingula, juncta juvant.* Caſe *Giffard* and *Vaux.*

2. *Vinyor* brought debt againſt *Wylde* upon a bond of 20*l.* of arbitration, in which caſe three points were reſolved. 1ſt, That though *Wylde* was bound in an obligation, *to ſtand to, abide, obſerve,* &c. *the rule,* &c. *arbitrament,* &c. yet he might countermand it; for a man may not by his own deed raiſe ſuch an authority, power or warrant not countermandable: as if I make a letter of attorney to make livery, or ſue an action in my name, or aſſign auditors to take an account, or make a factor, or ſubmit myſelf to an arbitrament, though they are by expreſs words irrevocable, yet they may be revoked. So if I make my laſt will and teſtament irrevocable, yet I may revoke it; for neither my act nor words can alter the law, and make that irrevocable which in its own nature is revocable; whether it be by bond or otherwiſe that the ſubmiſſion is made, the authority of the arbitrator may, be revoked or countermanded: but then in the one caſe he forfeits his bond, though in the other he loſeth nothing; for *ex nuda ſubmiſſione non oritur actio.* 2dly, It is not material to the plaintiff to aver, that the arbitrator had notice of the countermand; for it is implied in the words *revocavit et abrogavit omnem authoritatem, &c.* for *ſans* notice it is no revocation or abrogation of the authority; and therefore if there was not notice, the defendant might join iſſue, *Quod non revocavit, &c.* and if there was no notice, it ſhall be found for the defendant, *&c.* 3dly, It was reſolved, that by this countermand or revocation of the power of the arbitrator, the obligee may take advantage of the obligation; for two cauſes, 1ſt, Becauſe the obligor hath broken the words of the condition, which are, *that he ſhould ſtand to and abide,* &c. *the rule, order,* &c. and when he countermands the authority of the arbitrator, *he doth not ſtand to and abide,* &c. which were put into the condition with intent that no countermand ſhould be, but that it ſhould be finiſhed by the arbitrator, and that his power ſhould endure till he had made an award. And when the award made, then are theſe words to compel the parties to perform the ſame, *viz. obſerve, perform, fulfil, and keep the rule, order,* &c. 2dly, The other reaſon is, that the obligor, by his own act, hath made the condition of his bond, which was made to ſave him from the penalty thereof, impoſſible to be performed by him. 8 *Co.* 80. *Vinyor*'s caſe.

Particular caſes.

3. The bill was for relief againſt an award ſubmitted to by parties, and bonds for performance; the court would neither eſtabliſh or affirm, nor overturn the award; unleſs circumvention, fraud or corruption; *aliter* if it had been by order of the court. 3 *Rep. Chan.* 89. *Vide* 82.

4. One of the parties to an award having made a ſubmiſſion in court, purſuant to the late act of parliament, dies before the money paid. No *Sci. Fa.* can iſſue againſt the heir or executor, to enforce payment; for the award, though eſtabliſhed by the court, is not in nature of a judgment

or

or decree to be profecuted, but of a contempt which dies with the perfon. So held all the judges, they being confulted in this matter, as a matter concerning all the courts. *Prec. Chan.* 223.

5. On a bill of review to reverfe a decree which confirmed an award, the party had not affented, tho' the fubmiffion was by order of chancery, and the folicitor affented and attended by counfel and himfelf, yet as the party's affent did not appear, though the decree was figned and inrolled, the court reverfed it. 1 *Rep. Chan.* 195.

6. An award was by private fubmiffion without order of court, and crofs bills were, one to eftablifh it, and the other to be relieved againft it. Both bills difmiffed and fent to law. 2 *Rep. Chan.* 34, *et ante* 30. 1 *Vol.* 86, 141, *&c.* 3 *Vol.* 20. *Eq. Abr.* 80.

7. A voluntary award decreed, being affented unto, and in part executed. 3 *Rep. Chan.* 304.

8. An award was, that one party fubmitting fhould have fuch lands, not mentioning his heirs. Yet this award having been long made, and three of the four arbitrators (the fourth being dead) having certified their meaning to be, that he fhould have the inheritance to him and his heirs; Decreed accordingly. 1 *Rep. Chan.* 85.

9. The court would not fet afide the award on account of any hardfhips therein, becaufe the arbitrators were judges of the parties own chufing, and the plaintiff had notice, and might have been heard, had he pleafed. So the bill was difmiffed with cofts. 2 *Mod. Ca.* 63, 64.

10. A bill was to have the benefit of an award. The defendant demurred, for that he ought to feek remedy at law. Demurrer over-ruled. 2 *Rep. Chan.* 30, 39.

11. If one party performs an award, equity may compel the other thereto. But if a perpetuity be awarded, it is againft the courfe of chancery, and void. But the defendant is not bound to difcover any thing to fubject himfelf to the penalty of the bond, being under litigation at law. 1 *Rep. Chan.* 142.

12. Vide 1 *Rep. Chan.* 85, 86, 141, *&c.* 3 *Rep. Chan.* 10. *Eq. Abr.* 80. *Max. Eq.* 53 *to* 60. 2 *Rep. Chan.* 24, 366. *Eq. Abr.* 39, 41. 2 *Rep. Chan.* 28, 304, *&c.* 68, 69. 3 *Rep. Chan.* 17. 1 *Chan. Ca.* 40. 1 *Rep. Chan.* 195. 1 *Chan. Ca.* 86. *Salk.* 70. 1 *Rol. Abr.* 268. *Mar.* 111. *Sty.* 351. 3 *Lev.* 17. 2 *Mod.* 227. 1 *Vern.* 259. 3 *Rep. Chan.* 76. 1 *Rep. Chan.* 198.

144. *Ex paucis dictis intendere plurima poffis.*

SEE *Lit. fect.* 384. and *Co. Lit.* 237. *a.*

145. *Expedit reipublicae ut fit finis litium, propter communem omnium utilitatem.*

1. IF a man be difturbed of a common or way, or a ditch be made overthwart it, that he cannot pafs, yet he fhall not have an action of the cafe; and this the law provideth to prevent multiplicity of fuits; for if any one man might have an action, the confequence would be, all men

 might.

might. Yet the law for this nusance hath provided an apt remedy, (*viz.*) presentment in the leet or torn, unless where a man hath a particular damage; as if he and his horse fall into the ditch, whereby he receiveth hurt and loss; for this special damage, which is not common to others, he may have an action upon his case; as was resolved by the court of king's bench, 27 *H.* 8. in which case it was said, that it had been adjudged in that court between *Westbury* and *Powell*, that where the inhabitants of *Southwark* had, by custom, a watering place for their cattle, which was stopt up by *Powel*, that in that case, any inhabitant of *Southwark* might have an action; for otherwise they should be without remedy; because such a nusance is not presentable in the leet or torn. *Note* the diversity, says lord *Coke*, because it is not a common nusance to all the king's subjects; and what is not so to all, is not presentable in the leet or torn. *Co. Lit.* 56. *a.* 9 *Co.* 113. *a.*

2. A copyholder having right to common may have his action of the case against a stranger, for putting his cattle to depasture there; for he might take them for damage fesant, as is held 24 *E.* 3. 42. 46 *E.* 3. 23. 15 *H.* 7. 2 and 12. which proves it to be a wrong, and damage done to him, &c. and it is no answer to say, then every other commoner might have his action too for the same cause; and so actions for small offences be multiplied, as in *Williams*'s case, 5 *Co.* 72. of a common chapel or church, an action lieth not for non-performance of divine service; nor for a common nusance in the highway, &c. 2. If the commoner hath freehold in his common, and the lord, or any other, will depasture, &c. he may have assise. And by consequence, in the case at bar, the commoner having but common at will by copy, shall have case, &c. 9 *Co.* 112. *b.* 113. *a. b. Vue le case et note bien plus excellent matter.*

3. Public nusances shall only be punished and reformed at the suit of the king; for they may not be reformed at the suit of any private person; for the damages are not private but public. But *privatum damnum sive nocumentum* shall be reformed by action of any private person grieved. But *commune nocumentum* at the suit of the king, who is the head of all the commonwealth. But trespass done to several commoners is *privatum*, and not *commune nocumentum*; and so adjudged in 27 *Ass. pl.* 6. Presentment was in the leet, that *J. N.* had inclosed such lands, which ought to be in common for all the inhabitants of the vill, &c. *ad commune nocumentum inhabitantium villae praedict'*, and this presentment was adjudged void; for it is a private and particular tort to the particular inhabitants of this particular vill, and no public or common nusance, &c. 9 *Co.* 113. *a. b.*

4. Vide 5 *Co.* 101. 2 *Cro.* 491. *Syd.* 34. 2 *Ju. Eccl.* 493, 494, 495.

5. *Vide* rule, *Equity will prevent multiplicity of suits.*

146. *Expressio eorum quae tacite insunt nihil operatur.*

General.

1. THOUGH the law says, that when a man grants lands he grants the underwoods inclusively; and so when he grants his house he grants all the several rooms in it; yet in 33 & 34 *Eliz. B. R. inter Kenisham* and *Redding*, the queen leased the parsonage of *Greenwich*, with all

2 the

the woods and underwoods exprefly thereunto belonging (*exceptis omnibus groffis arboribus, bofcis et maëremiis*); the opinion of the court was, That the exception, as to underwoods, was void. But they held, that the exception was only to be extended to great woods. So in the cafe 9 *Eliz.* *Dy.* 264. which proves that the rule, *Expreffio eorum quae tacite infunt nihil operatur*, is to be underftood, having refpect to itfelf only, and not having relation to other claufes. *Hob.* 170.

Particular cafes.

2. One having but one clofe in *D.* demifeth all his lands in *D.* (excepting that one clofe) the exception is void, *&c.* *Hob.* 170.

3. If *A.* grants 20*s.* rent in his manor, (*viz.*) by the hands of one fo much, and of another fo much; and the tenants affigned are but at will, the whole manor is charged; for the (*viz.*) being of no effect, cannot fruftrate the premiffes, which are fufficient of themfelves. *Hob.* 172.

4. If a man hath lands in an hamlet, and other lands in another part of the town; if he grant his land in that town, (*fcil.*) in the hamlet, no more will pafs. But if he grant all his lands in the whole town, (*viz.*) in the hamlet, all the lands will pafs, and the (*viz.*) is void. *Hob.* 173.

5. By a grant of trees by him in fee-fimple, they are abfolutely paffed from him and his heirs, and vefted in the grantee, and go to his executors or adminiftrators, being in underftanding of law divided as chattels from the freehold; and the grantee hath power incident to, and implied in the grant to fell them when he will, without any other fpecial licence, *&c.* *Hob.* 173.

6. A devife of the profits of the inheritance gives power to fell, *&c.* 1 *Chan. Ca.* 240.

7. If the king in his grant recites, that another holds the manor of *D.* for his life, and granteth the fame manor to *B.* for his life; in this cafe the law implieth, that the fecond grant fhall take effect or commence from and after the determination of the firft. 8 *Co.* 56. *b.*

8. A copyholder devifeth to *J. S.* for 20 years after the death of his wife, to raife portions for younger children; here as the devife is to a ftranger, in the mean time it fhall defcend to the heir. But had the devife been to the heir, then an eftate would have arifen to the wife by implication. 1 *Vern.* 22.

9. One feifed of a copyhold furrenders to the ufe of his will, by which he faith, my debts and legacies being firft deducted, I devife all my eftate, both real and perfonal, to *J. S.* Lord chancellor: This fhall amount to a devife to fell for payment of his debts. 1 *Vern.* 45.

10. Where there is an exprefs eftate limited, no implication ought to be admitted to controul it. *Expreffum facit ceffare tacitum.* *Bamfield* and *Popham*'s cafe, 1 *Pe. Will.* 56.

11. Refolved, There being an exprefs eftate given to *Popham* for life, the remainder to his firft and every other fon, *&c.* the words [*if* Popham *fhould die without iffue male*] fhould not enlarge the eftate; in regard thefe amounted only to make an eftate-tail by implication, and words of implication will never deftroy what was before expreffed. 1 *Pe. Will.* 55.

12. Vide *Pal.* 437. 1 *Pe. Will.* 79, 84. *Doct. & Stud. lib.* 2. *cap.* 20. *Cro. Eliz.* 702. *Dy.* 77. 5 *Mod.* 29. *Mo.* 26, 29. *Yelv.* 94. *Hard.* 4. *Pal.*

Pal. 508. *Saund.* 284. *Prec. Chan.* 39, 44, 181. 1 *Chan. Ca.* 32, 249. *Nelf.* 195, *S. C.* *Hob.* 170. *Barn.* 304.

13. See rules, *Defignatio unius perfonae eft exclufio alterius. Expreffum facit ceffare tacitum. Condition none may take advantage of, but who is either party or privy to it. Every man's deed or covenant to be taken moft ftrongly againft himfelf.*

147. *Expreffum facit ceffare tacitum.*

IF the condition of a mortgage be, that if the feoffor pay to the feoffee, or his heirs, fuch a fum at fuch a day, *&c.* there, after the death of the feoffee, where he dieth before the day, payment ought to be made to the heir. *Lit. fect.* 339. So he cannot pay the money to the executor; for, as *Lit.* faith in this cafe, the payment ought to be to the heir, *Et hoc cafu, defignatio unius perfonae eft exclufio alterius. Et expreffum facit ceffare tacitum.* And the law fhall never feek out a perfon, when the parties themfelves have appointed one, *&c.* *Co. Lit.* 210. *a.*

148. *Favendum eft ecclefiae quam parfonae.*

1. THE king's temporal courts by his immediate authority have power derived from him, to fufpend the proceedings of the ecclefiaftical courts by prohibition, *&c.* if caufe. *Ha. Anal.* 20. 1 *Ju. Eccl.* tit. *Prohibition*, alfo tit. *Praemunire* and *Mandamus. Where it appears clearly, that thefe ecclefiaftical courts are but petit fubordinate courts, fubject to the controul of the king's fuperior temporal courts; and that the judges, minifters, and officers thereof, for any neglect of their duty, may be enforced thereunto by the king's courts at* Weftminfter; *and in cafe of their exceeding their ftinted power and jurifdiction may be feverely punifhed by the fame temporal authority. And that for this clear reafon, for that the authority indulged to the church is but by allowance of the temporal power, which hath referved to its felf the fuperintendancy of this indulged jurifdiction, and neceffarily of reforming their Errors, and correcting and punifhing their faults, as by many ftatutes, and adjudged cafes reported in the books, and by many records may appear.*

2. The temporal courts muft always have an eye that the ecclefiaftical jurifdiction ufurp not upon the temporal. 2 *Inft.* 615. *I conceive it is the duty of the temporal judges to preferve the laws of the realm in their full force,* et ampliare jurifdictionem, *and to fuppref s and punifh all and every ufurpations upon its authority, whether it be by depreciating thereof or raifing any other to its derogation and diminution. And particularly if any ecclefiaftical judges or minifters, or any their officers, or others of their party fhall ever be found, either by writing, fpeaking or acting, thus bafely bufying themfelves, to the hurt of the temporal law, which is the foul of the prerogative and of the rights and liberties of the fubject, both fpiritual and temporal; they will, according to antient ufage and the old common law and conftitution of our country, and the office of our temporal magiftrates, be deemed and punifhed, as their demerits by fuch laws fhall demand.*

3. The judges of the common law do not look upon themfelves, *as indeed they are not*, bound by the rules of the civil law; but at liberty to

follow their own where the two laws differ. 1 *Pe. Will.* 12. *But the ecclesiastical judges are strictly to follow the rules of the common law, where there is such mixture or variance, which sufficiently demonstrates their inferiority and dependance to and on the superior temporal laws and courts, and how much it is the duty of ecclesiastical judges to know the laws of the realm in all such cases.*

4. It is the office of judges to advance all laws made for religion, according to their real end, though the words be short and imperfect. *Hob.* 157. 2 *Inst.* 615, 616. And when any thing is used to the displeasure of God, it hurts as well the soul as the body: and temporal rulers have not only the cure of the bodies but also of the souls of the people, and shall answer for them if they perish by their default. *Doct. & Stud. lib.* 1. *cap.* 32. *Merito summa habetur ratio quae pro religione facit.* Hob. 295.

5. Vide 4 *Co. Digbye's* case. 5 *Co.* 14. *b.* 11 *Co.* 70. *b.* *Jenk.* 162, 166, 233. 2 *Chan. Ca.* 18. *Salk.* 294. *Carth.* 484. *Bishop of St. David's* case. 1 *Ro.* 452. 1 *Ju. Eccl.* 322, 323, *&c.*

6. See rule, *Summa est ratio quae pro religione facit.*

149. *Fee-simple cannot depend upon a fee-simple.*

1. A Man cannot have a more large or greater estate of inheritance than fee-simple. *Lit. sect.* 11. And this extends as well to fee-simple conditional and qualified, as to pure and absolute. And he, who hath a fee-simple conditional or qualified, hath as ample and great an estate as he who hath an absolute fee. And from this estate in fee-simple, estates-tail and all other particular estates are derived: and because a man cannot have a more ample or greater estate; therefore two fee-simples absolute cannot be of one and the self same land. If the king make a gift in tail, and the donee is attainted of treason, the king hath not two fee-simples, *viz.* the antient reversion in fee, and another fee determinable upon the dying *sans* issue of tenant in tail, but they are complicated and conjoined together. So it is if such tenant in tail convey to the king, his heirs and successors, the king hath but one fee united in him. And yet in several persons, by act in law, a reversion may be in fee-simple, determinable in another by a matter *ex post facto*; as if a gift in tail be to a villain, and the lord enters, he hath a fee-simple qualified, and the donor a reversion in fee; but if the lord infeoff the donor, now both fee-simples are united, and he hath only one fee in him: but one fee cannot depend upon another, by grant of the party. *Co. Lit.* 18. *a.*

2. Two fee-simples, which may stand in several persons distinct, when they meet in one person cannot do so, but the great and absolute fee doth swallow up the base and limited fee. *Hob.* 323.

3. A limitation of an inheritance after an absolute fee-simple, is not a good limitation; because that would be to make a perpetuity, which the law will not admit: but if it be upon a contingent fee-simple, it is otherwise. 2 *Chan. Ca.* 19.

4. In an ejectment on a special verdict, the case was, A man having three sons, *John*, *Edward* and *William*, and lands in three several vills, *viz.* *A. B.* and *C.* deviseth the lands in *A.* to his son *John*, the lands in *B.* to *Edward* his son, the lands in *C.* to *William* his son; and that if any of them

died, the other surviving should be his heir. *John* the eldest had issue *J.* and dies; the question was, Whether the lands in *A.* shall go to *Edward* and *William* the younger sons, or to the heir of the eldest? *Fleming*, chief justice said, that he conceived it might vest in the two younger sons by way of remainder: and these words, *that every one shall be heir to the other*, tantamounts and implies that every one shall have it after the other; for although the freehold of the eldest son shall be drowned by the descent of the fee; yet it was not so drowned, but that by his death the surviving sons should have it for their lives, by this limitation, and the intent of the will; whereof such construction is to be as made to uphold it if possible it may be. But all the justices, besides *Fleming*, were of opinion, in regard nothing but a freehold passed by the devise, the reversion in fee descending upon the eldest son, had drowned the estate; and that his death afterwards, could not revive and revest the remainder in *William* and *Edward*. *Cro. Jac.* 260, 261.

5. See 3 *Chan. Ca.* 19, 29, 31, 32. *Mod.* 115. *Rol. Abr.* 612. 1 *Ro. Rep.* 337. 1 *Lev.* 11, 12. 2 *Lev.* 59. 2 *Saund.* 386.

150. *Felix qui potuit rerum cognoscere causas.*

THEN we are truly said to know any thing, when we know the true cause thereof: *tunc unumquodque scire dicimur, cum primam causam scire putamus: scire autem proprie est rem ratione et per causam cognoscere.* Co. Lit. 183. b.

151. *Felony, the punishment annexed to it was, ut poena ad paucos, metus ad omnes, perveniat.*

THE punishment of felony is grievous, 1. To lose his life; 2. In so odious a manner, as to be hanged by the neck between heaven and earth as unworthy of both; 3. To lose his blood, as well to his ancestry; for he is reckoned the son of the earth without any ancestor; as well as to his posterity, for his blood is corrupt, and he hath neither heir nor posterity; 4. His lands; 5. His goods; and in such case the king hath *annum, diem et vastum*, to the intent that his wife and children may be cast out, his houses and buildings laid waste, his trees rooted up by the roots, his meadows ploughed, and all things that he hath for his comfort, delight or sustenance, be wasted and destroyed, because he hath so feloniously offended against the law; and all this was, *ut poena ad paucos, metus ad omnes, perveniat*, &c. 4 Co. 124. b.

152. *Feme covert under obedience of her husband, cui ipsa in vitâ suâ contradicere non potuit. Non est sui juris, sed sub potestate viri.*

General.

1. THE law of nature hath put a feme covert under the obedience of her husband, and hath submitted her will to his, which the law followeth, *cui ipsa in vitâ suâ contradicere non potuit*, and therefore

will

will not bind her by her act joining with her husband; because they are judged his acts and not hers: so she wants free will. 7 *E.* 4. The wife *Cestuy que use*, she and her husband sold the land, she received the money, and they both required the feoffee to make the estate to the vendee; and yet she after her husband's death was relieved against the feoffee, and might also against the vendee if he were privy to the use. *Note*; This was in equity, which judgeth *secundum aequum et bonum.* Hob. 225.

2. The law of *England*, for necessity's sake, of commerce and the like, by a law of policy, makes bold with this law of nature in an especial kind, and therefore allows a fine levied by the husband and wife, because she is examined of her free will judicially by an authentic person, trusted by the law and the king's writ, and so she is taken in a sort as a sole woman, as also when she comes in by receipt; but this being but a fiction of law must not be extended beyond that, that the law hath granted as a privilege. Nay more, if a feme covert levy a fine as if she were sole, this shall bind her for the reason before given; that she shall not be received to say she was covert, tho' her husband shall; and he may enter and restore the land to himself and his wife both. 17 *E.* 3. 52. 7 *H.* 4. 23. 7 *Co.* 8. The countess of *Bedford*'s case, *Hob.* 225.

As to her person.

3. The husband has a right to the custody of his wife, and may confine her, but not imprison her, much less put her *dum compos mentis* in a mad-house: and if he should, she may apply to the spiritual court for a divorce *propter saevitiam:* but the feme cannot bring an *homine replegiando* against her husband; for the nature and proceedings in a writ *de homine replegiando* are such, as cannot be maintained by a woman against her husband. *Gilb.* 149. *Prec. Chan.* 492.

* 4. An information was moved for against *Newton & al'*, for putting a feme covert into a mad-house without cause, and a rule to shew cause was made: it appeared, upon a former motion, this court had granted an *habeas corpus* to take her out of another mad-house, in which she had been confined, and sometime after the above mentioned rule was made absolute; for as the court was pleased to declare, it would be of very dangerous consequence to let such a matter pass without taking notice of it in a pretty severe manner. It was urged against the feme, that she had been taken in an adulterous correspondence, for which the husband might justly confine her in his own or in another's house; and the counsel against her said they could see no reason, why not, in a mad-house. The court admitted the husband might confine his wife, but declared they would by no means allow such things as these. *B. R.* 2 *Geo.* 2. *The king* and *Newton & al'.*

Her acts.

5. Regularly she cannot sue without her husband. *Greenwood of courts* 13. *Yelv.* 210. *Though in equity she may not only sue without him, by her next friend, but may even sue her own husband.*

6. Her answer is none without him, 2 *Chan. Ca.* 173. *Unless where he is made a party for conformity's sake, or she hath a separate estate.*

7. No decree can be against her without him. 2 *Chan. Ca.* 173.

8. She

8. She may fue in her truftees names. 2 *Chan. Ca.* 102. *Prec. Chan.* 376. *But fuch fuit may not be without her confent.*

9. Having a feparate eftate, fhe may fue without her hufband, or may fue him. *Gilb.* 83, 84, 152. *Prec. Chan.* 275, 329.

10. If a feme covert confent in court, though no party to the fuit, yet fhe is bound. 2 *Chan. Ca.* 101.

11. So fhe is barred by a fine being examined. *Gilb.* 18, 19. *See before General cafes* 1, 2.

12. She is not to be examined againft her hufband. *Co. Lit.* 6. Though in a matter where fhe was only concerned as executrix. 2 *Chan. Ca.* 39. Yet a wife was examined to difcover her hufband's deceit. *Tot.* 158. So in *Criminal cafes.*

Her feparate eftate.

13. Money given to the wife for her maintenance, becaufe her hufband is an unthrift; the hufband pretends the money to be his, but ordered to be at her difpofing. *Tot.* 158.

14. A feme covert having a feparate eftate, on her hufband's being arrefted, to procure his enlargement, promifed payment and was bound; cafe *Dubois* and *Dowle* was cited. The court refolved, that a bill having been filed againft her and her hufband, and a *fubpoena* ferved on her, was good, and procefs of contempt againft her was well; for her hufband was only party for conformity fake, and cited *Moore* and *Huffey*, *Hob.* 95. where feveral cafes are cited, wherein the wife is chargeable without the hufband; and fo on her praying time, and entering her appearance with the regifter, fhe was difcharged, paying coft of the motion. *Note*; Mr. *Howe* moved, that fhe not being in court ought not to be heard, being an utter ftranger, but no notice was taken of that. *Prec. Chan.* 328. *Gilb.* 83, 84. *S. C.*

* 15. The wife having a feparate allowance, and living apart, may make a gift of what fhe faves as a feme fole. See the cafe before the houfe of lords, *Gage* and *Leicefter*, 6 *Dec.* 1715. See 1 *Chan. Ca.* 82, 118. *Pre. Chan.* 44, 121. 2 *Chan. Ca.* 182.

* 16. The cafe was, that the plaintiff's wife had by cruel treatment been forced to leave her hufband, and carry away with her two young children, which, by her labour, and affiftance of friends, fhe maintained, without any help from the plaintiff. They lived 30 years, or thereabouts, feparate. One of the faid children, being a fon, and grown up and fettled in the world, became poffeffed of fome perfonal eftate, and particularly of two feveral bonds of 100*l.* each, one on the *Eaft India Company*, and the other on one *Ledger*; the fon being thus poffeffed made his laft will and teftament in writing, and thereby devifed *Ledger*'s bond to his father, the now plaintiff, and gave the faid *Eaft-India* bond to his mother, *to her own ufe, and fo as his father fhould have nothing to do with it*, and made his mother fole executrix and refiduary legatee, and died. The executrix proved the will, and delivered faid *Ledger*'s bond to the plaintiff, who releafed her as executrix as aforefaid; after the executrix growing old, infirm, and paft her labour, offered the faid *Eaft-India* bond to the defendant, (with whom and in whofe family fhe had lived as a fervant, all or the greateft part of the time fhe was parted from her faid hufband) and defired he would take the fame to maintain her for her life, which the defendant refufed:

2 where-

whereupon ſhe applied herſelf to ſeveral others for the ſame purpoſe, but ſuch application proving fruitleſs, ſhe addreſſed herſelf again to the defendant, who after ſome difficulty, in conſideration of her long and faithful ſervice, and long continuance in his family, was prevailed with to come to ſuch agreement with her, but the ſame was only by parol and not reduced into writing; yet in execution thereof, the defendant told and ſtrictly charged his wife, and only ſon, in caſe of his the defendant's death, before them and the ſaid executrix, to keep and maintain her as long as ſhe ſhould live, on the conſideration aforeſaid, which they both promiſed to do. And the executrix, in execution of her part of the ſaid agreement, deſired the defendant to go with her to the *Eaſt-India* houſe, which he doing, ſhe received all the dividends and intereſt due on the ſaid *Eaſt-India* bond, and then cancelled the ſame, and directed a new one to be made in the defendant's name, and which was accordingly done. The ſaid executrix dying in a year's time, or thereabouts, the plaintiff brought the preſent bill againſt the defendant, and charged his ſaid late wife with having eloped from him, and carrying this bond away with her, and which he charged to be his property. The defendant by his anſwer inſiſted, that ſhe did not elope, but was ſo forced from her ſaid huſband, the plaintiff, as aforeſaid. That ſhe was an honeſt, ſober and induſtrious woman. That ſhe had maintained herſelf and her children as aforeſaid. That ſhe lived with the defendant, and in his family, the greateſt part of the time ſhe was from the plaintiff; that ſhe always behaved herſelf in every regard well; and that to the plaintiff's knowledge, who came ſeveral times to ſee her at the defendant's houſe. The anſwer further ſet forth the bond in queſtion, ſo to have been the plaintiff's ſon's, and ſo deviſed to the mother, and after veſted in the defendant as aforeſaid, with all the circumſtances mentioned. On reading the proofs, the anſwer was well ſupported; and particularly it appeared from the evidence of the ſcrivener, who drew the will, that it was the true intention of the teſtator, that the ſaid *Eaſt-India* bond ſhould be to the ſeparate uſe of the mother, free from all controul and interpoſition of the plaintiff. Bill diſmiſſed. The court declaring that the meaning of the teſtator was plain, that this bond ſhould be for the ſeparate uſe of his mother, and that he did but his duty therein; and that the agreement having been ſo executed as aforeſaid on both ſides, was of ſuch ſort as ought to be eſtabliſhed in a court of equity. *Relfe* and *Budder*, *in Scac'*, *Hil.* 11 *Geo.*

Their ſeparation.

17. Where agreements have been made for pin-money, or ſeparate maintenance, if the wife refuſe to live with her huſband, without good reaſon, this court refuſes to aſſiſt in the recovery, and in ſuch caſes have ſtopt it. *Barn.* 136. See *the whole caſe.*

18. Neither willfulneſs of the wife, nor pretence of kindneſs of the huſband, nor his deſire of cohabitation, ſhall avail any thing to ſtay payment of alimony. 1 *Chan. Ca.* 251.

19. No alimony without ſeparation, except *pro expenſis litis.* 1 *Chan. Ca.* 251.

20. The wife was ordered to return to her huſband, and further to try his uſage, the court declaring, on complaint, they would hear her with favour. 1 *Chan. Ca.* 251. 1 *Vern.* 53.

21. Alimony to ceaſe on their coming together again. *Nelſ.* 154.

22. If any real danger, the wife may reſort to the decree. *Nelſ.* 154. *Prec. Chan.* 240. 1 *Vern.* 326.

Agreements between them.

* 23. Covenant that the wife ſhall diſpoſe of her perſonal eſtate, does not extend to what ſhall come to her after marriage. See caſe before the houſe of lords, *Pilkington* and *Cuthberton*, 11 *May* 1711.

* 24. Wife not bound by agreement, being under age. See caſe *Lucy* and *More*, before the houſe of lords, *anno* 1730.

* 25. Agreements between them though informal, and out of regular method, to be executed according to the intention of the parties. See caſe *Halfpenny* verſus *Lady Lawley*, before the houſe of lords, 10 *February* 1734.

153. *Fictio cedit veritati.*

1. FIction is never admitted where truth may work. As *Ceſtuy que uſe* and his feoffee join in a feoffment, it ſhall be the feoffment of the feoffee. *Hob.* 311.

2. If a man ſeiſed of three acres holden in chief, makes a feoffment of all to the uſe of ſuch perſon, and of ſuch eſtate as he ſhall give or diſpoſe by his will; and he after by his will gives and deviſes all his lands to *J. S.* and his heirs; this ſhall carry but two parts of the lands in point of the deviſe. *Hob.* 160.

3. See laſt rule, alſo *Hob.* 225. 12 *Co.* 42. *Mo.* 765. *Yelv.* *Cro.* 1 *Ro. Rep.* 462.

154. *Fictio juris eſt ubi non eſt veritas.*

SEE the laſt rule and reference.

155. *Filiatio non poteſt probari.*

RULE *Semper praeſumitur pro legitimatione puerorum.*

156. *Flumina et portus publica ſunt, ideoque jus piſcandi omnibus commune eſt in portu fluminibuſque.*

General.

1. THough this rule, which is a rule of the civil law, be thus, and ſo found in *Bracton*, yet by the common law of *England*, a man may have a proper and ſeveral intereſt as well in the water or river as the piſcary; and therefore the water may be granted. 11 *R.* 2. *Plow. Com.* 154. *a.* If one grant to another *aquam ſuam*, the piſcary in it paſſeth; becauſe it is included in the word *Aqua*. And in *Nat. Brev.* 123. A *quod permittat* lieth *de libera piſcariâ*; alſo it lieth in grant and tenure; and by

a grant thereof the soil passeth; it is demandable by a *praecipe, &c. Da.* 55. *b.* 57. *b.*

2. One may have a freehold in a piscary. *Fitzh. Ass.* 422. And it is a freehold of itself, and need not be appendant. *Fitzh. Ass.* 427. 12 *H.* 3. *Ass. De libero tenemento, scil.* of a piscary and recovered; also a man may make a bailiff of his piscary; and by *Linwood* 101. *Proventu fluminum decimae solvi debent*; yet *Pisces non offerebantur in templo.* Tho. Aquin. 1, 2, *q.* 102. Da. 56. a.

The sorts, and to whom belong.

3. There are two kinds of rivers, *viz.* navigable and not navigable. Every navigable river, so far as the sea ebbs and flows, is *flumen regale*, and the fishery a royal one, and belongs to the king by his prerogative; but in every other river not navigable, and in the fishery there, the tertenants *ex utraque parte aquae* have interest of common right. *Da.* 56. *a.* 57. *a. b.* 58. *a. Vue le case.*

Where and wherefore the king hath interest therein.

4. The reason wherefore the king hath interest in such navigable rivers, so high as the sea ebbs and flows, is because such rivers partake of the nature of the sea, and is a branch thereof before it flows. 22 *Ass. pl.* 93. 8 *E.* 2. *Fitzh. Coron.* 399. And the sea is only under the dominion of the king; as is said 6 *R.* 2. *Fitzh. Pro.* 46. *la mer est del ligeance del roy, come de son corone d'Engleterre.* It is his proper inheritance, and therefore he shall have the lands gained from the sea. *Dy.* 15 *Eliz.* 226. *b.* 22 *Ass. pl.* 93. Also the king shall have grand possessions of the sea, *balaenas et sturgiones, &c.* which are *pisces regales*; and no subject may have these without special grant of the crown. *Praero. Regis, cap.* 11. *Stan.* 37, 38. *Bract. lib.* 3. *cap.* 3. 39 *E.* 3. 35. *a.* The king shall have wild swans, as *volatilia regalia*, upon the sea and its arms. See the case of swans, 7 *Co.* So wreck is a royal perquisite. See 5 *Co.* 107. Sir *Henry Constable*'s case. And upon this reason, before the *Stat.* 18 *E.* 3. no person might go beyond sea without special licence of the king, but there it is enacted that the sea shall be open for all merchants, and all ports and havens, which are *ostia et januae regni*, belong to the king, he being *custos totius regni*; and *Fitzh. Nat. Brev.* 113. *a.* the king is bound to save and defend his realm, as well against the sea as enemies; and that the king hath as great prerogative and interest in the branches of the sea and navigable rivers, as far as the sea ebbs and flows in them, as he hath in the high sea, is manifest from many authorities and records. *Da.* 56. *a. b.* 57. *a. b.*

How may pass and be demanded, &c. *in the case of a subject.*

5. *Vide ante* General. *Co. Lit.* 5.

In the case of the king.

6. A royal piscary, or any part thereof, may not pass by the grant of the land adjoining, or by a general grant of all piscaries; for it is a royal piscary not belonging or appurtaining to lands, but is a piscary in gross, and parcel of the inheritance of the crown; and general words in the king's grants shall not pass such a special royalty as belongs to the crown by prerogative;

rogative; as Mines Royal, Amerciaments Royal, Eſcheats Royal, do not paſs by the general word of all Mines, Amerciaments and Eſcheats; and to this intent are many caſes directly in point in the caſe of Mines. *Plow. Com.* 333. *b.* 334. *a.* and 9 & 10 *Eliz.* 268, 269. The grant of the king ſhall paſs nothing by implication. 2 *H.* 7. 13, *&c.* *Da.* 57. *b.*

7. See *Bract. lib.* 2. *cap.* 12. *Co. Lit.*

157. *Fortunam faciunt judicem.*

1. PArtition among parceners by lot, is, as if there be four parceners, and after partition of the land is made, every part of the land by itſelf is written on a ſcrol, and is covered in a ball of wax, ſo as none may ſee the ſcrol, and then the four balls of wax are put into an hat, to be kept in the hands of an indifferent perſon, and then the eldeſt daughter ſhall firſt put her hand into the hat and draw out her ball or lot, and then the ſecond, and ſo on to the laſt, and each to take the lot that ſhe hath drawn; in which caſe they ought each to ſtand to her chance and allotment. *Lit. ſect.* 246. Of this partition by lot antient authors write, that in that caſe coparceners *fortunam faciunt judicem.* Of this ſort of diviſion you may read in Holy Scripture, where it is ſaid *Dedi vobis poſſeſſionem, quam dividetis ſorte.* See *Numb. chap.* xxvi. *ver.* 54, 55. and *chap.* xxxiii. *ver.* 54. *Co. Lit.* 167.

2. Vide *Fleta, lib.* 5. *cap.* 9. *Bract. lib.* 2. 75. *Brit. cap.* 72.

158. *Fraus eſt celare fraudem.*

General.

1. ASſignment of goods, aſſigned where the aſſignor remained in poſſeſſion, to be deemed fraudulent *quoad* the landlord and creditors, and ſo *Prec. Chan.* 233. See 3 *Co.* 80.

2. *Dona clandeſtina ſunt ſemper ſuſpicioſa.* 3 Co. 81. a. Prec. Chan. 286. Gilb. 220.

Particular caſes.

* 3. The caſe was, A man brings an action, obtains judgment, and ſues out execution againſt the goods of the defendant, to defeat which, an aſſignment of the goods is ſet up to be made to one to whom the defendant was *bona fide* indebted, to pay him and other creditors. Upon the whole it appeared to his lordſhip, that the aſſignment was executed *pendente lite* at common law, and that the goods remained in the aſſignors hands or poſſeſſion; and therefore his lordſhip was of opinion that the aſſignment was fraudulent as to the plaintiff, and ſhould not defeat his execution, or his judgment obtained for his debt. Before lord chancellor *King*, about *Trin.* 1732. This decree, as I conceive, ſeems well ſupported by the whole of the arguments in *Twine*'s caſe, 3 *Co.* 80, *&c.*

4. There being an old intail deed which the elder brother knew not of, he makes a ſettlement on his marriage which the younger brother ingroſſed, he having privately the intail deed by him; the wife dies, and the huſband marries again, being ſtill ignorant of the intail, and the younger brother

2 alſo

alfo ingroffed the fecond fettlement, ftill keeping the intail deed fecret. The brothers differing, the elder treats of a marriage for his nephew *Raw*, and propofed to fettle his eftate on that marriage, but died *fans* iffue before the marriage took effect, having firft by his will given his eftate to his wife for life, then to *Raw* and his heirs, who after married purfuant to that treaty, and fettles upon the iffue of that marriage. The younger brother brings ejectment, and evicts the widow jointrefs; whereupon fhe and *Raw et ux'* brought there bill, and fhe was relieved, and had a perpetual injunction, but not *Raw*; becaufe the younger brother was privy to her fettlement, and confeffed he did not difcover the intail, out of fear his brother would have barred him; but it did not appear that he was cognizant of *Raw*'s match, who was but a voluntary devifee. *Prec. Chan.* 35, 36. *Raw et ux' Potte* verfus *Potte*.

* 5. Fraud in getting a releafe from his daughter a few days after fhe came of age, and but a few days before her marriage, and without the privity of the hufband, fet afide. See cafe * *Norton* and *Heron*, 21 *April* 1732, before the houfe of lords. So an agreement obtained by fraud and furprize, fet afide. See cafe *Archer* and *Archer*, before the houfe of lords, 2 *March* 1718.

* 6. Releafe of equity of redemption obtained by furprize or mifreprefentation, fet afide. See cafe *Kirkway* and *Blake*, before the houfe of lords, 23 *May* 1721.

7. *Vide* feveral rules *antea*, *Where equity to relieve*, and *poftea*, *Wherever there is fuppreffio veri*, &c.

159. *Fraus eft odiofa, et non praefumenda.*

Eft odiofa.

1. ALL ftatutes made againft fraud fhall be conftrued liberally, and expounded beneficially to fupprefs fraud. 3 *Co.* 82.

2. The common law fo abhors fraud and covin, that all acts, as well judicial as others, though of themfelves juft and lawful, yet being mixt with fraud and deceit, are, in judgment of law, tortious and unlawful: *Quod alias bonum et juftum eft, fi per vim vel fraudem petatur, malum et injuftum efficitur.* 3 Co. 78. a.

3. If a feme, who hath good right to dower, caufe *J. S.* to differfe the tertenant, and then recovers dower againft *J. S.* fhe fhall not be tenant in dower, though fhe hath fo recovered; becaufe fhe is privy to an unlawful act which fhould be the means of her eftate. 18 *H.* 8. 5.

Non praefumenda.

4. Fraud is not to be conceived unlefs it be expreffed. In the principal cafe, the father purchafed copyhold lands to him and his wife, and to *Ralph* their fon and his heirs, and two years after became an inn-keeper, and received the profits of the land until 4 *Auguft* 4 *Car.* he became debtor by bond to *J. B.* and others, and committed divers acts of bankrupcy, and was adjudged a bankrupt, &c. after the father and mother dying, the fon entered, &c. Held by *Bramfton*, *Jones* and *Crooke*, againft *Berkley*, that he was no bankrupt, as being an inn-keeper; for he does not get his living

by buying and ſelling, *&c.* all agreed a copyhold was within the ſtatutes of bankrupts; but the other three judges againſt *Berkley*, held that being purchaſed before he was a tradeſman, and ſo long before he became debtor, it is not within the ſtatute, *&c.* for *fraus eſt odioſa, et non praeſumenda.* Cro. Ca. 549, *&c.*

5. The earl of *Lincoln* purchaſed in lady *Gorge*'s name, ſhe being his daughter; and after kept courts and made leaſes in his own name, and always took the profits, and after ſold to Sir *Sidney Mountague*; and lady *Gorge* never queſtioned the matter in the life of her father; yet held, unleſs ſome fraud diſcovered, it is not within the Stat. 27 *Eliz.* although there be many badges of fraud. *Cro. Ca.* 550, 551.

6. See *Mar.* 34, 35, *&c.* 3 *Chan. Ca.* 85. 3 *Mod.* 328. *Jo.* 437.

7. See alſo rules, *Equity to relieve againſt fraud. Fraus eſt celare fraudem.*

160. *Fruſtra expectatur eventus, cujus effectus nullus ſequitur.*

EXcommunication under the pope's bull is of no ſort of effect or force whatſoever, to diſable any perſon here in theſe realms. And, as their lordſhips, the judges, were pleaſed to declare, whoever ſhould plead ſuch excommunication, or otherwiſe dare or preſume to uſe the ſame, muſt be in a hard caſe, ſhould the crown duly reſent the affront. And their lordſhips further reſolved, that no cauſe whatſoever ariſing within theſe realms, nay, though the ſame ſhould be ſpiritual, can be determined at *Rome*, *quia fruſtra expectatur eventus, cujus effectus nullus ſequitur.* 5 Co. De Ju. Regis Eccl. 15. b. 1 Ju. Eccl. *tit.* The Pope an Uſurper, *&c.*

161. *Fruſtra fit per plura, quod fieri poteſt per pauciora.*

1. THE difference taken by *Mowbray* was, when a layman gives lands to a vicar, and when he is endowed by the ordinary of the parſon's land, *&c.* in the firſt of which caſes the ordinary hath not power to diſſolve the vicarage, as to the land; but otherwiſe it is in the other. *Vide* 20 *E.* 3. *Annuity* 32. 16 *E.* 3. *Annuity* 24. and *Bre.* 152. *J.* And therefore in regard the ordinary might have diſſolved it, *&c.* (See *Plow. Com.* 497.) That which the ordinary of the dioceſe might do, the pope might have done, who had ſupreme juriſdiction over all ordinaries; *ideo fruſtra fit per plura, quod fieri poteſt per pauciora, &c.* Cro. Jac. 516, 517.

2. See rule, *In praeſentia majoris ceſſat potentia minoris.*

162. *Furioſus ſolo furore punitur.*

1. VIDE *Co. Lit.* 247.

2. See alſo rule, *Actus non facit reum niſi mens ſit rea.*

163. *Generalia praecedunt, ſpecialia ſequuntur.*

1. IN a writ and in the plaint the general ſhall be put in demand before the ſpecial, as land before meadow, paſture, wood, *&c.* and wood before alders, willows, *&c.* *Regiſter fo.* 2. Note; *This is the courſe of the Regiſter.*

2. See *Co. Lit.* and the *Entries, &c.*

164. *General words cannot be applied to particulars.*

DEclared by lord keeper, That general words not particula ly applied, ought not to ſhake a decree, for if they did there would be no end of ſuits. 1 *Chan.* 218.

165. *Grant cannot be made but to him, who is party to the deed, except it be by way of remainder.*

IF a man of meer motion give lands by indenture to *H.* and to his heirs, upon condition that he ſhall yearly, at a certain day, pay *S.* out of the ſame lands a certain rent; and if he do not, that then it ſhall be lawful for the ſaid *S.* to enter, *&c.* tho' the rent be not paid, yet may not *S.* enter; for he was no party to the deed, ſo can take no advantage of the condition; and it cannot work by way of remainder of the reverſion, though every deed is to be taken moſt ſtrongly againſt the grantor, and the taking it ſo would be an attornment in itſelf, yet the intent muſt be according to law, and here that cannot be; for *S.* is no party to the deed; and therefore it cannot be taken by way of grant of the reverſion, becauſe of the above rule, that no grant can be made but to him who is party, except by way of remainder. *Doct. & Stud. lib.* 2. *cap.* 20.

166. *Haeres eſt eadem perſona cum anteceſſore.*

1. BEtween *Oates* and *Frith*, the caſe was, That the father being ſeiſed in fee, he and his ſon and heir apparent by their indenture leaſed lands to the defendant for years, to begin after the death of the father, rendering rent unto the ſon. The father died, the leſſee entered, and for rent in arrear the ſon diſtrained, the leſſee brought treſpaſs, and had judgment; for the reſervation was held void; for though the ſon proved heir, it bettered not the caſe by event, but the reſervation muſt have been to the heir or heirs of the leſſor by that name; for that is the only word of privity in law requiſite in reſervation of rents and conditions; for the heir is, in repreſentation, in point of taking by inheritance, *eadem perſona cum anteceſſore*; and though in ſuch caſe the rent could never be demanded by the father, yet the heir ſhall take it from the father as inherent and riſing from the root of the reverſion, which was his father's, and which he takes by deſcent from the father. So the rent itſelf, which was in the father, though not to be demanded, becauſe not yet due, yet it was ſo his, that he might have releaſed and diſcharged it, by the word *rent*, though not by the word *action*;

it

it not being in his time a matter in action. So note a difference, *says his lordship*, between this case, where rent is reserved upon a lease of the ancestor to the heir first, and where the ancestor grants an annuity or makes a warranty for a like charge against his heirs, first omitting himself, all such grants are utterly void; for no man can charge his heir but as part of himself, and therefore beginning with himself; and such charges stand naked and have nothing that was first in the father, and comes from him to them, whereunto they may cleave as a rent to a reversion in the former case. *Hob.* 130, 131.

2. Vide *Co. Lit.* 47, 99, 143, 192, 197, 213, 214. 11 *Co.* 10, 12, 18. 12 *Co.* 36. *Plow. Com.* 71. *Dy.* 45, 180, 361. 2 *Leon.* 214. *Mod.* 362, 575. *Yelv.* 168. 1 *An.* 23.

3. See also, *Nemo est haeres viventis.*

167. *Heir favoured.*

What.

1. *HAeres*, in the legal understanding of the common law, implieth that he is *ex justis nuptiis procreatus*; for *haeres legitimus est quem nuptiae demonstrant*, and is he to whom lands, tenements and hereditaments, by the act of God, and right of blood do descend of some estate of inheritance. *Co. Lit.* 7. b. 237. *b.*

The sorts.

2. There are two sorts of heirs, *Haeres natus, et Haeres factus.* Gilb. 129. Prec. Chan. 3.

General.

3. The heir who comes in by descent, hath more privilege than any that by other order or means come to lands, &c. *See several instances,* Co. Lit. 237. b.

To whom preferred.

To the wife.

4. Lands were settled upon marriage on trustees, &c. and that if the wife survived she should have the profits of the leases, as the same were then let. The husband made leases and advanced the rent. Decreed the improved rent to the heir. 2 *Mod. Ca.* 32, 33.

5. Devise to the wife until the son attain 21, his death at 13 determines her interest in favour of the heir; but if deficiency to pay debts, &c. *aliter.* *Gilb.* 36, 76. *Abr. Eq.* 195. *Co. Lit.* 295. *b.*

6. The profits of lands are devised to the wife for life, then to be sold for the payment of 100*l.* to the heir at law, and 150*l.* to another; no more shall be sold than to pay these legacies, so that all the land shall not be sold, and the residue of the money go to the wife, neither be distributed according to the statute. *Prec. Chan.* 62.

7. The husband devised the lands in question to his wife for life; the son exhibits a bill, pretending the devise to the wife void; because 25 *Eliz.* the lands were intailed on his great grandfather, to whom he was heir intail; and to discover the deed intail. The wife had the writings in her hands,

hands, and ſhe is ordered to bring in all writings; and it fell out the deed of intail was amongſt the reſt. The heir by motion *ex parte*, gets the writings out of court, and on motion after was ordered to bring them in again, and they are now in court. At hearing Mr. *Keck* (after lord commiſſioner of the great ſeal) prays the heir may not make the court an inſtrument to help him to the deed, but that the defendant may be in the ſame condition ſhe was before the writings were brought in by her, in obedience to the court; for though the deviſe was voluntary, and not in purſuance of articles on marriage, yet unleſs the heir would confirm her eſtate, he ought not to be aſſiſted by the court; for there is a conſideration (*to wit*) to provide for his wife; and ſo it had been if the father in like manner had deviſed to younger children, for the conſideration is good in law (wife) to raiſe an uſe at common law; he affirmed there were precedents for him, and the rather becauſe the father had power to dock or bar the intail. Lord chancellor: I will never help againſt a purchaſer, but here it is a bounty in this caſe; and in ſuch caſe, the heir having a good title ſhall be aided; and decreed the deeds to the plaintiff. 2 *Chan. Ca.* 4. Vide poſt. *Jointure favoured.*

* 8. One conveyeth all his lands in truſt to pay debts and legacies, and then by will deviſeth all his perſonal eſtate to his wife, yet the perſonal eſtate ſhall come in aid of the real. See caſe *French* and *Chicheſter*, before the houſe of lords, *Feb.* 1707.

To adminiſtrators.

9. The heir is preferred to the adminiſtrator, and ſhall inforce him to preſerve the inheritance from ſale, by paying debts out of the perſonal eſtate, though the lands were deviſed to pay debts. 1 *Chan. Ca.* 281.

To executors.

10. The cauſe being heard about 1664, and one point being that the heir of the obligor, who had paid a debt of his anceſtor upon bond, might be reimburſed his money by the executor of the obligor, who had perſonal aſſets, the heir being forced, by ſuit, to pay the debt. Decreed, the executor ſhould reimburſe him as far as there were perſonal aſſets come to his hands. 1 *Chan. Ca.* 74. Vide poſtea, *In doubtful caſes. Money to be reckoned as land.* Vide poſt. *Ca.* 23, 24.

To a purchaſer.

11. Tenant in tail having agreed to ſell, and received part of the conſideration money, is decreed to ſell; but ſtanding out and dying in contempt, the bill was to revive againſt the iſſue in tail, but diſmiſſed; for though tenant in tail had power, and might have barred his iſſue, yet as he did not execute that power, the iſſue is not concluded; for the tenant in tail did not do the acts, (*to wit*) levy a fine or ſuffer a recovery for barring the iſſue. *Prec. Chan.* 278.

The ſeverals wherein he is favoured.

Not to be diſinherited.

12. He is not to be diſinherited but by a neceſſary implication. 1 *Vern.* 323, 376.

13. Nor without expreſs words. 2 *Vern. Hutton* and *Simpſon*'s caſe.

14. All deviſes by implication to diſinherit him, muſt be neceſſary. *Gilb.* 115, 138.

15. The heir diſinherited is to be helped if by any conſtruction he may. *Gilb.* 31, 41.

In doubtful caſes.

16. In doubtful caſes the heir is to be preferred before the executor. 1 *Chan. Ca.* 7. 98. *Margin.* 2 *Chan. Ca.* 49, 115, 152, 156. 2 *Vent.* 359. 1 *Salk.* 154. 1 *Vern.* 167, 204, 271. 2 *Mod. Ca.* 71.

Money to be reckoned as land for him.

17. Lands deviſed to be ſold to pay debts and legacies is not reckoned money for executors or reſiduary legatees againſt the heir. 1 *Chan. Ca.* 14, 98, 280, 281.

18. Money to be laid out in land, is for him to be reckoned as land. 1 *Chan. Ca.* 14.

The perſonal eſtates to be firſt liable.

19. Declared by the lord chancellor, that not only the heir, in caſe he be charged with the debts of the anceſtor; but a deviſee of the lands ſhall be unburthened too of a debt lying on the land, by the perſonal eſtate in the hands of an executor or adminiſtrator, and ſo ſhall a deviſee of a mortgage, &c. 2 *Chan. Ca.* 84, 85.

20. Perſonal eſtate ſhall pay mortgages in favour of the heir; *aliter* of a deviſee. 1 *Chan. Ca.* 271. 2 *Chan. Ca.* 197. *Gilb.* 129. *Vide* next foregoing caſe, and *Quaere.*

21. *Haeres factus* of the whole ſhall have aid of the perſonal eſtate; but deviſee of a particular eſtate only, ſhall not. *Prec. Chan.* 3. *Quaere ſur ceo, this being ſaid by* Rawlinſon *only,* Maynard *and* Kecke *ſaying nothing to it.*

22. As hath been ſaid, the heir is intitled to aid out of the perſonal eſtate to diſcharge mortgages; yet having ſold the inheritance, he has loſt that aid; for the equity which he had thereto was in conſideration, and for the ſake of the inheritance deſcended upon him, that it might be clear to the family: ſo bill diſmiſſed. *Prec. Chan.* 207.

* 23. One by will makes both his real and perſonal eſtates liable to pay his debts. Decreed the heir ſhould pay the debts by ſuch a time, or in default the real eſtate to be ſold; but liberty was given the heir to proſecute for remedy over, out of the perſonal eſtate. See caſe before the houſe of lords, *Sydolphe* and *Langbourn*, 23 *Feb.* 1705.

24. The reſidue of the perſonal eſtate is deviſed to the executors, yet it ſhall be firſt liable to pay debts, though the lands were deviſed to be ſold for that purpoſe. *Gilb.* 72, 129. *Aliter*, if a ſpecific legacy be to the executor, or the reſiduum given to another. *Gilb.* 72, 73, 129.

Defects not to be ſupplied againſt him.

25. A defective ſettlement is not to be ſupplied againſt the heir in favour of a baſtard, though the father and mother after intermarried. *Gilb.* 139.

26. Voluntary conveyances defective ſhall not be made good againſt him. 1 *Chan. Ca.* 244.

27. One deviſeth his copyhold eſtate to his grandſon, and decreed the will good, and that equity ought to ſupply a ſurrender, but the houſe of lords reverſed the decree, and held equity ought not to ſupply ſuch a defect in disfavour of the heir at law, unleſs in favour of a ſon or daughter, and not then neither, if to diſinherit the eldeſt ſon, *&c. Salk.* 187. Tit. *Copyhold, Kettle* and *Townſend*'s caſe.

28. A copyholder by deed conveyed to his baſtard daughter, who was admitted, but there was no ſurrender; the court would not ſupply the want of a ſurrender againſt the heir in favour of the baſtard, for ſhe was to be conſidered here as a meer ſtranger, being *nullius filia:* and though the father might be bound to provide for her, yet this court was not to make good a voluntary defective conveyance for a ſtranger, *&c. Prec. Chan.* 475. And yet where a freeman of *London* gives bond and judgment for his executors, *&c.* to pay 500*l.* for baſtards and their mother, his teſtamentary part was liable. *Prec. Chan.* 17, 18. Vide ante, *To whom preferred. To the wife.* Ca. 6, 7.

Reſulting truſts for him.

29. *H.* had three ſons, *A. B.* and *C.* and deviſed his lands to *B.* his ſecond ſon, after the death of his wife; to hold to him and his heirs, and then to his own right heirs. *H.* died and *B.* entered, and died *ſans* iſſue, living the eldeſt ſon. *Et per cur':* The ſecond ſon had only an eſtate tail, and the eldeſt ſon ſhall take by deſcent and not by the will; and ſo the deviſe over is void in point of limitation; for his intent was, that the lands ſhould deſcend from himſelf, and not from his ſon *B.* If the deviſe over had been to a ſtranger, it had been void, and *B.* had taken a fee, but here it is only an eſtate-tail. And the word *heirs* can import no more than iſſue; for *B.* could not die without heirs, living heirs of the father. *Salk.* 233. 1 *Pe. Will.* 23. *Nottingham* and *Jennings*'s caſe. See *Cro. Jac.* 416. *Cro. Ca.* 58 and 238. and *quaere* the laſt.

* 30. Deviſe to *A.* upon ſpecial truſt and confidence, that he ſhould pay all the teſtator's juſt debts, this is a reſulting truſt after debts paid for the heir. See caſe * *Kirrick* and *Blake,* 11 *March* 1727. See alſo * *Errington* and *Carrick,* 15 *May* 1728, and *Tirwith* and *Trotman,* 11 *May* 1714, all before the houſe of lords.

Legacies to ſink into the real eſtate for his benefit.

31. See *Prec. Chan.* 196, 213, 216. 2 *Vern.* 617. and *Gilb.* 11. *all S. C.*

Real eſtate not to be twice charged.

32. Lands deviſed to truſtees to raiſe money for ſeveral purpoſes, and they raiſe it out of the profits, the land is thereby diſcharged, and they muſt have reſort to the truſtees. *Prec. Chan.* 143.

In ſuits.

33. He is not bound by a decree againſt his anceſtor in tail, to bar the intail. *Gilb.* 164, 165. 1 *Chan. Ca.* 220. *Prec. Chan.* 278.

34. He

34. He is not to be prejudiced in not bringing a bill in time; for his laches ſhall not prejudice him as another perſon's. *Prec. Chan.* 541.

35. See 1 *Chan. Ca.* 176, 178, 98, 74. 2 *Chan. Ca.* 197. 3 *Chan. Ca.* 131. 2 *Mod. Ca.* 170, 171, 185, 186, 187, 188, 189, 190, 197. 1 *Chan. Ca.* 297. 2 *Chan. Ca.* 5, 59, 197. *Prec. Chan.* 439, 452, 381, 54, *&c.* 1 *Rep. Chan.* 18. 2 *Vern.* 99, 215, 420. 1 *Rol. Abr.* 317, *&c.* 2 *Vent.* 359. *Salk.* 154.

36. See rules, *Every rightful fee-ſimple one hath either by purchaſe or deſcent. Equity favours younger children. Perſonal eſtate to go in eaſe of the real. In teſtamentis ratio tacita non debet conſiderari, &c. Deſcent tolls entry.*

168. *Heir in fee-ſimple muſt be he, who hath ſanguinem duplicatum.*

1. DEſcent, *deſcenſus*, cometh of the *Latin deſcendo*, and legally ſignifieth when lands do by right of blood fall unto any after the death of his anceſtor; or deſcent is a means whereby one doth derive to himſelf title to any lands, as heir to ſome of his anceſtors, *&c. Co. Lit.* 13. *b.*

2. None ſhall have lands by deſcent as heir to any man, unleſs he be his heir of the whole blood. *Lit. ſect.* 6.

3. No man can be heir to a fee-ſimple by the common law, but he who hath *ſanguinem duplicatum*, the whole blood, that is, both of the father and of the mother, ſo as the half blood is no blood inheritable by deſcent; becauſe he, who is but of the half blood, cannot be a complete heir, for that he hath not the whole and complete blood; and the law in deſcents in fee-ſimple doth reſpect that which is complete and perfect. And this maxim doth not only hold where lands are claimed or demanded by one as heir, but alſo in caſe of appeal of death; for if one brother be ſlain, the other of the half blood ſhall not have an appeal (albeit he ſhall recover nothing therein, either in the realty or the perſonalty) becauſe in the eye of the law, he is not heir to him; alſo this rule extends to a warranty. *Co. Lit.* 14. *a.*

4. See *Lit. ſect.* 737. 3 *Co.* 4.

5. See rule, *Deficiente uno non poteſt eſſe haeres.*

169. *Heir not to be charged but as part of his anceſtor.*

1. SEE *Hob.* 130, 131.

2. See Rule, *Haeres eſt eadem perſona cum anteceſſore. Nemo eſt haeres viventis.*

170. *Heir to inherit any land, muſt be of the blood of the firſt purchaſer.*

IT is an old and true maxim in law, that none ſhall inherit any land as heir, but only the blood of the firſt purchaſer; for *refert a quo fiat perquiſitum.* As for example, *Robert Coke* taketh the daughter of *Knightley* to to wife, and purchaseth lands to him and to his heirs, and by *Knightley* hath issue *Edward*, none of the blood of the *Knightleys*, though they be of the blood of *Edward*, shall inherit, albeit he had no kindred but them; because they were not of the blood of the first purchaser, *viz.* of *Robert Coke*. *Co. Lit.* 12. *a.*

171. *Heir not bound where the ancestor is not.*

1. *FLETA, Nota, Quod haeres non tenetur in angliâ ad debita antecessoris reddenda, nisi per antecessorem ad hoc fuit obligatus, praeterquam debita regis tantum*; *a fortiori* in case of a warranty, which is in the realty. *Co. Lit.* 386. *a.*

2. It is a maxim of the law, that the heir shall never be bound by an express warranty, but where the ancestor was bound by the same warranty; for if the ancestor were not bound, it cannot descend upon the heir. *Co. Lit.* 386. *a.*

3. But a warranty in law may bind the heir, though it never bound the ancestor. *Co. Lit.* 386. *a.*

172. *He, who can sell an estate in fee, must have an estate in fee.*

1. SEE rule, *Nemo plus juris ad alium transferre potest quam ipse habet.* 2. See also *Salk.* 240. 4 *Co.* 24. *b.* *Doct. & Stud. lib.* 1. *cap.* 8. 2 *Mod. Ca.* 40, 42. *Vau.* 181. 2 *Rep. Chan.* 237.

173. *He, who claims by descent in fee-simple, must make himself heir to him, who was last seised.*

FATHER, uncle and son; the son purchaseth land and dieth *sans* issue; the uncle is his heir, and may enter, and if he doth enter and dieth without issue, the father shall have the land as heir to the uncle. *Lit. sect.* 3. But if the uncle doth not enter, then the father may not inherit, because of the maxim, that a man who claimeth as heir in fee-simple to any man by descent, must make himself heir to him who was last seised of the actual freehold and inheritance; and if the uncle in this case do not enter, he has but a freehold in law, and no actual freehold, but the last seised of the actual freehold was the son, to whom the father cannot make himself heir. *Note*; The uncle in this case is heir, but not absolute heir, for if after the descent to him the father hath issue, such issue shall enter upon the uncle: so where one hath issue a son and a daughter, an after born son shall inherit to the first brother, *&c.* *Co. Lit.* 11. *b.*

174. *He, who derives an eſtate from another, muſt take it upon thoſe terms upon which it is conveyed.*

1. SEE 3 *Chan. Ca.* 132.
2. See rule, *Cujus eſt dare, ejus eſt diſponere.*

175. *He, who hath done iniquity, ſhall not have equity.*

General.

1. THIS rule is to be extended only to the wrong done by him to the party againſt whom he ſeeks equity. 1 *Chan. Ca.* 134, 293. For another rule is, *He, who would have equity, muſt do equity to the ſame perſon from whom he ſeeks it.* See *Francis's Maxims in Equity*, and *Abr. Eq.* and the other books.

Particular caſes.

2. If the leſſor will avoid the leaſe for non-payment of rent at the day, equity will relieve againſt the forfeiture. But if the leaſe were gained by fraud, or granted upon a falſe ſuggeſtion, equity will not in ſuch caſe relieve the leſſee; for that were to relieve fraud in chancery. *Car.* 45.

3. Plaintiff for only 90*l.* lent took a bond for 800*l.* from the defendant when he was drunk, and had judgment upon it; the defendant in right of his wife was intitled to certain lands, which were in others in truſt for her; a bill was brought to have thoſe lands ſubjected to ſatisfaction. But the court would not relieve, not even for the money the plaintiff had really lent, but diſmiſſed his bill. 1 *Chan. Ca.* 202. *But had the defendant in this caſe come into equity to be relieved againſt the judgment for fraud, he ſhould have been obliged to pay the money really lent.* See rule, *Equity to relieve againſt fraud*; *for he, who would have equity, muſt do it.*

4. The bill was to be relieved for a debt owing by bond from Sir *J. S.* to whom the lady the defendant was executrix, which debt and bond the plaintiff, in his anſwer to a former bill, had ſworn was fully ſatisfied to him; but that was to avoid a ſequeſtration of the debt, as was alledged. And the maſter of the rolls, though that anſwer was ſet forth in the defendant's anſwer in this cauſe, would not ſuffer the anſwer to be read againſt the plaintiff, but decreed the defendant to ſatisfy the debt. 1 *Chan. Ca.* 154. *For though the rule be, That he who hath committed iniquity (as here in the falſe anſwer) ſhall not have equity; yet it ſeems, that is to be underſtood when the iniquity is done to the defendant himſelf,* &c. Max. Eq. 5, 6, 45, *&c.*

5. See 1 *Chan. Ca.* 156, 202, 209, 226, 250, 293. 2 *Chan. Ca.* 15, 17. 1 *Vern.* 452.

6. See alſo rules, *Equity will redreſs or prevent wrongs and miſchiefs; will relieve againſt fraud; and where the matter lieth in compenſation.*

176. *He who hath not offended may not be punished.*

1. VIDE 4 *Co.* *Actiones de scandalis ou actiones pur slander.* Lord *Cromwell's* case, *Yelv.* 47.

2. See also rules, *Usury odious in law.* *Nemo debet bis puniri pro uno delicto.*

177. *He, who takes security by a penalty, ought not to have more, nor indeed so much, if compensation for the damages may be made without it.*

1. *ANNO* 1642, Sir *Nicholas Crispe* and four more became bound to the defendant's testator in 1600*l.* for the payment of 1000*l.* and interest at six months end. The interest was duly paid till 1644. *Michaelmas* 1662, the defendant got judgment against Sir *Nicholas* and one other of the obligors for 1600*l.* (being the penalty,) afterwards there was paid by them, against whom the judgment was, and the other obligors, at several times, to above 1600*l.* and so the bill was to have the judgment vacated, and the bond delivered up, paying so much as would make up the penalty of the judgment, and interest for the same since the judgment. It was insisted *pro quer'*, that when judgment was had on the bond, it remained no longer a debt on bond, nor was interest due on the judgment, so as what was paid after must be taken as paid on the judgment; and if they had brought the 1600*l.* into court at law, (and offered to pay it before execution) the court at law would have accepted it; and therefore, being willing to make up what was paid already the full of the judgment, and damages since the judgment, ought to be relieved against the judgment. *Pro defendente* it was insisted, that there was more money due for interest on the bond, and that that was paid as well by those obligors, against whom there was no judgment, as by those against whom the judgment was; and what was paid by those against whom there was no judgment, their part of what was paid in by course of the court was to be taken as interest; there being more interest due on the bond than the money paid; and there is no equity in this case to hinder the defendant from recovering what he can at law, there being much more in conscience due; and if what is justly due be to be received by any course of law, no equity ought to hinder, so as he do not receive more than principal, interest and costs, which the defendant offers to take on account. It was replied by the plaintiff's counsel, that one satisfaction by any of the obligors shall be a discharge at law to the rest; and a release to one obligor is a discharge to all the rest. And when a man takes a security by a penalty, he sets up his rest there, and makes himself judge of what he would have, and ought not to have more. And after a long debate, where the case of *Whitchcot* and *Underhill* was cited, it was ordered, that the plaintiff do pay so much, with what was paid, as will make up the penalty of the judgment and damages at six *per cent.* for the penalty and costs here and at law, and thereupon the bond to be delivered up, and the judgment vacated; but with this proviso, that if 250*l.* paid in *November* 1662, were paid before the judgment, and the judgment entered after of that term, that that must be taken as paid for interest, because the defendant received

received it on the bond, the judgment then not being entered, which a maſter is to examine, and if he find it, to allow the ſame as paid on the bond for intereſt, and the maſter to take the account. 1 *Chan. Ca.* 23, 24. *So Note, ſaith the reporter, That a judgment on bond, on which there is more due than the penalty for principal and intereſt, is worſe ſecurity than the bond only; this ſeems, ſaith he, very hard and unreaſonable, and the equity hereof may well be queſtioned.*

2. *Davis*, employed as a maſter of a ſhip by the *Eaſt-India* company, covenanted with them, that he would pay a certain mulct for every cloth carried, &c. in the ſhip, and took the defendant's teſtator to be his mate, who made the ſame agreement, *mutatis mutandis*, with *Davis*, and gave a bond of 50*l.* for due performance of his part; but he, without *Davis's* knowledge, carried ſo many cloths as the mulct came to 70*l.* which the company deducted out of the maſter's wages, and the 50*l.* would not ſatisfy, and therefore he prayed relief, and a diſcovery of the teſtator's eſtate. Defendant demurred. 1. The relief for more than the penalty of the bond, is not proper in equity. 2. That part of the bill which ſtands for diſcovery of aſſets was ill; becauſe the charge in the bill was not poſitive, that aſſets, or any goods came to the defendant's hands; ruled in both points accordingly. 1 *Chan. Ca.* 226.

3. Vide 1 *Chan. Ca.* 77, 95, 96, 97. 1 *Vern.* 342. 1 *Rep. Chan.* 95. *Max. Eq.* 3. *Curſ. Canc.* 210.

4. See alſo rule, *Where the matter lieth in compenſation.*

178. *He, who will claim a benefit by part of a will, muſt abide by the whole will.*

1. SO pronounced by his honour the maſter of the rolls, at the rolls, 4 *July* 1737.

2. Vide *Prec. Chan.* 354.

179. *He who will have equity muſt do it.*

Exceptions to the rule.

1. OUT of this general rule are to be excepted, 1. Such conditions as are repugnant to the law of God, of reaſon, or the common law. 2. Such as are repugnant or contrary to the eſſence of the grant, &c. 3. Such as are only added *in terrorem*, in reſtraint of marriage, &c. 4. Where the condition becomes impoſſible by the act of God, &c. 5. Where there is a fraud or practice in him who claims benefit by the breach. 6. In all caſes which lie in compenſation, the time for the performance may be inlarged, though in the caſe of a condition precedent. 7. 'Tis alſo ſufficient if the intent of it be performed, though not ſtrictly in the words thereof. 1 *Chan. Ca.* 53. *margin.*

General.

2. The plaintiff mortgaged to the defendant, who afterwards advanced to the plaintiff more money on bond; the plaintiff brought his bill to redeem, the defendant inſiſted to be paid his bond debt as well as the money ſecured by the

the mortgage; and though there was no ſpecial agreement for the lands ſtanding ſecurity for the bond debt, yet the plaintiff was not allowed to redeem without paying that too. 1 *Vern.* 244. 3 *Salk.* 84. And in caſe the heir is bound in the bond, he muſt pay that debt, as well as the debt ſecured by the mortgage. 2 *Chan. Rep.* 164. 1 *Vern.* 245. So where there are two mortgages and one is defective, if the heir will redeem he muſt take both. 1 *Vern.* 245. 2 *Chan. Rep.* 23. *But he muſt be heir to his father, and take as ſuch.*

Particular caſes.

3. For where father tenant for life, remainder to his ſon in tail, mortgaged the lands, and the ſon after borrows money of the ſame mortgagee, on ſecurity of the ſame lands; he was not decreed to redeem his father's mortgage, becauſe he was a ſtranger to his father, as to his eſtate, whereof he is in by the donor, and *per formam doni*, and not by deſcent from or as heir to his father. See 2 *Chan. Ca.* 23.

4. If a mortgage be as a counter-ſecurity for entering into a bond of 4000*l.* and after the mortgagor prevails on the mortgagee to enter into a further bond for 2000*l.* though there be no agreement that the mortgage ſhould ſtand as a counter-ſecurity for entering into the laſt bond, yet the heir ſhall not redeem without paying that alſo. 2 *Chan. Ca.* 23. Neither ſhall the heir redeem without paying both. 2 *Chan. Ca.* 97.

5. Baron and feme mortgage the wife's land, the mortgage is forfeited, the huſband pays part, and after borrows as much more as he had paid. Decreed that the mortgagee having an eſtate in him by the forfeiture of the mortgage, he ſhall hold againſt the heir till the whole money is paid, principal, intereſt and coſts; and if the heir will not ſo pay, he ſhall be foreclosed. 1 *Vern.* 41.

6. On motion for an injunction to ſtay proceedings at law on a bond, upon an offer made to give judgment with a releaſe of errors, the lord keeper ſaid, That this was not ſo beneficial as might be thought; for that notwithſtanding the releaſe of errors, the plaintiff might bring a writ of error, and put the defendant to plead his releaſe, and ſo delay time as long as if no releaſe of errors had been; but the plaintiff's offering to be bound by an order of this court to bring no writ of error, an injunction was awarded. 1 *Vern.* 120.

7. A lunatic had made a mortgage before his lunacy for 50*l.* which his committee transferred, and took three or four hundred pounds more upon it; but the lord keeper decreed no more than the 50*l.* binding on the eſtate; for the committee had but an eſtate during pleaſure; and therefore could not make leaſes, incumber, build, or improve, without ſpecial order of the court. 1 *Vern.* 262, 263.

8. *Hill* having reverſed a decree obtained by *Notte*, (See 1 *Vern.* 167.) dies. A bill was brought, charging that the defendant was tenant in tail, and had covenanted for further aſſurance, and therefore it was prayed that he might be compelled to perform his covenant in ſpecie, and to levy a fine; but the court denied the plaintiff any relief; and the lord chancellor ſaid, that on hearing of *Notte*'s bill, he thought it an hard caſe, though he did not ſee ſufficient reaſon to ſet aſide the contract: but as to this bill his lordſhip ſaid, a contract that carried an equity, to have it decreed in ſpecie, ought

N n to

to be without all objection: and ſaid, that the purchaſing from heirs was grown too common, and therefore would not countenance it, and diſmiſſed the bill, and left the plaintiff to his action at law on the covenant. 1 *Vern.* 271, 272. 2 *Chan. Ca.* 120. *S. C.*

Note; In this caſe the lord chancellor ſaid, by the civil law, a bargain of double value ſhall be avoided, and wiſhed it were ſo in *England.* 2 *Chan. Ca.* 121. See 136, *like caſe.*

9. See 1 *Chan. Ca.* 53, 87, 202, 261. 2 *Chan. Ca.* 136, 212. 1 *Vern.* 29, 141, 294, 467. 2 *Rep. Chan.* 247, 98, 360.

10. See alſo rules, *Equity to relieve againſt fraud. He, who hath done iniquity, ſhall not have equity.*

180. *He, who would redeem, muſt make a title to the equity of redemption.*

THE plaintiff claimed as heir general to redeem. The defendant by his anſwer ſet forth a deed of intail, intitling another to the equity of redemption. The plaintiff prayed he might redeem at his peril, but was not admitted, unleſs he could make it out that the eſtate-tail was docked. 1 *Vern.* 182.

181. *Humanum eſt errare.*

SEE 1 *Ju. Eccl.* 368.

182. *Id certum eſt quod certum reddi poteſt.*

General.

1. INcertainty is the mother of contention. *Co. Lit.* 9. *a.*

2. Certainty engenders repoſe, and incertainty contention. *Plow. Com.* 25. *a.*

3. Many things uncertain of themſelves, being reduced to certainty, by ſuch means as either the law appoints, or the party himſelf aſſigneth, may take effect. *Hob.* 174.

4. It ought to be a conſtant and perpetual certainty, or elſe it is ill. *Comb.* 44.

5. In ſome caſes there may be certainty in incertainty. *Co. Lit.* 96.

Particular caſes.

6. As one may hold of his lord to ſheer all the ſheep depaſturing within the lord's manor, and this is certain enough, albeit the lord hath ſometimes a greater and other times a leſſer number there; and yet this incertainty, being referred to the manor, which is certain, the lord may diſtrain for this incertainty. *Co. Lit.* 96.

7. It is a maxim in law, that no diſtreſs can be taken for any ſervices that are not put into certainty, nor can be reduced to any certainty. *Co. Lit.* 96. *a.*

8. Upon

8. Upon an avowry, damages cannot be recovered, for that which neither hath certainty, nor can be reduced to any certainty; for *oportet quod certa res deducatur in judicium.* Co. Lit. 96. a.

9. Debt upon a bond, conditioned for the performance of the arbitrament of *J.S.* ſo as the ſame be delivered on 28 *February* following, at the ſhop of *John Rolfe*, ſcrivener in *Cornhill*; the defendant pleaded *Nul tiel arbitrament.* The plaintiff ſhews the arbitrament 27 *February*, and what, and that it was delivered at the ſhop of *John Rolfe*, ſcrivener in *Cornhill*, and ſhews the breach; whereupon the defendant demurred. One cauſe aſſigned by *Grimſton* was, for that the ſubmiſſion is 19 *January*, and the arbitrament the 27 *February*, and it is not ſaid to be delivered at the ſaid ſhop, nor to the above named *John Rolfe*, and a plea ſhall be taken ſtrongly againſt him who pleadeth it. *Sed non allocatur*; for it ſhall not be intended another perſon nor another ſhop, unleſs the contrary had been ſhewn. 2dly, Becauſe the arbitrament was uncertain, to pay the charges in ſuch a ſuit. *Sed non allocatur*; for they are certain enough, when the attorney has made a bill of charges; wherefore it was adjudged for the plaintiff. *Cro. Ca.* 383.

10. An award was, that one party ſhould pay the other 10 *l.* and the coſts of a ſuit now depending in an inferior court, and then to give mutual releaſes. *Per Cur'*: To pay ſuch coſts as the maſter ſhall tax, is good; for *id certum eſt quod certum reddi poteſt*; but this is uncertain and carries it further than has hitherto been allowed. *Adjournatur.* Salk. 75. *Tamen quaere, whether the coſts in this caſe are not as certain by reference, as in the caſe next preceding, or to pay ſuch coſts as the maſter may tax.*

11. *Gilb.* 48, 61. *Pal.* 32, *&c.* 264, 277, 318. *Yelv.* 112. 4 *Co.* 15. *a. b.* 1 *Co.* 176, 177. *Hob.* 313. *Co. Lit.* 6. *a.* 231. *a.* *Cro. Eliz.* 10. 5 *Co.* 6. *a.* *Plow. Com.* 523. *b.* 2 *Vent.* 242. 4 *Co.* 34. 6 *Co.* 6. *a.* 8 *Co.* 56.

183. *Id poſſumus quod de jure poſſumus.*

ID poſſumus quod de jure poſſumus, therefore where 9 *E.* 6. an office was given to one, *if he were able to exerciſe it*, theſe words were deemed idle; for the law ſaith, that he ſhall not have it, if he be not able to exerciſe it. *Lane* 116.

184. *If the ſubſtance of a condition is performed, it is ſufficient.*

VIDE rules, *Equity to relieve where the matter lieth in compenſation. Condition precedent muſt be literally performed*, &c. *Equity will not veſt an eſtate, where by reaſon of a condition precedent it will not veſt at law. He who will have equity muſt do it.*

185. *Igno-*

185. *Ignorance of one's right not to prejudice his right.*

1. THE mother, after the death of her husband, had released her dower to her son, under a false pretence that her late husband had left her 3500*l.* in lieu of dower. On the plaintiff's marrying with the son this release was produced, and shewn to the plaintiff and her relations, and in confidence thereof the marriage took effect, and a settlement was made and the portion paid. On the question, Whether the mother, who had recovered dower at law, should be concluded by this release, and obliged to part with her dower, to make good the plaintiff the daughter's settlement? the court decreed for the plaintiff; tho' it was insisted the release was gained by practice of the son, after the death of the father, and such false pretence, whereas the 3500*l.* devised to the mother was not meant or intended to be in lieu of dower, and the son, who had surprized her in the release, had also defrauded her of the 3500*l.* 2 *Vern.* 131, *&c.*

2. Vide 1 *Vern.* 19, 32, 206. 2 *Chan. Ca.* 108.

3. See rules, *Wherever there is suppressio veri, &c. Equity to relieve against fraud. In odium spoliatoris omnia, &c.*

186. *Ignorantia facti excusat.*

General.

1. IGnorance of the deed, which may be called the ignorance of the truth of the deed, may excuse in many cases. *Doct. & Stud. lib.* 2. *cap.* 46.

Particular cases.

2. If a man buy an horse in a market overt of one, who had no property to him, not knowing but that he had right, he hath good right and title to the horse; and the ignorance shall excuse him; also if a man retains another's servant, not knowing he is retained with him, ignorance excuseth him; the law is the same of him who retaineth another's ward. If homage be due, and the tenant after the homage due maketh a feoffment, and the lord ignorant of the feoffment distrain for the homage, ignorance excuseth him. Also if a man be bound in an obligation to repair the houses of the obligee by such a time, as often as need shall require, and after there is need of repairs, but the obligor knows it not, there his ignorance shall not excuse him; for he having bound himself must take knowledge at his peril; but had the condition been, that he should repair such houses as the obligee should assign, and after he doth assign certain houses to be repaired, but the obligor knows not of it, ignorance shall excuse him; for he bound himself to no repairs certain, but such as the party shall assign, and if he assign none, the other is bound to none, and therefore since he, who should make the assignment, is privy to the deed, he is bound to give notice of his own assignment; yet had the assignment been to a stranger, he must have taken knowledge at his peril, *&c. Doct. & Stud. lib.* 2. *cap.* 47.

3. But if a man buy lands whereto another hath title, but the buyer knoweth it not, yet that ignorance doth not excuse him, no more than of

goods. Alſo if a ſervant come with his maſter's horſe to a town, that, by cuſtom, may attach goods for debt, and upon a plaint againſt the ſervant, an officer of the town, by information of the party, attacheth the maſter's horſe, thinking it was the ſervant's; ignorance excuſeth not; for when a man will do an act, as to enter into land, ſeiſe goods, take diſtreſs, or ſuch other, he muſt by the law at his peril ſee that what he doth be lawful. So if a ſheriff by replevin deliver other beaſts than were diſtrained, though the party that diſtrained ſhew him that they were the ſame, yet an action of treſpaſs lieth againſt him, and ignorance ſhall not excuſe, for he ſhall be compelled by law, as all officers commonly are, to execute the king's writ at his peril, according to the tenor of it, and to ſee that the act he doth be lawfully done, *&c. Doct. & Stud. lib.* 2. *cap.* 47. *Dy.* 25, 29.

4. See rules, *Caveat emptor. Executio juris non habet injuriam.*

187. *Ignorantia juris non excuſat.*

General.

1. *IGnorantia juris non excuſat.* Skin. 491. Ignorance of the law excuſeth no man, not that all men know the law; but becauſe it is an excuſe every man would plead, and none can tell how to confute him; therefore of neceſſity, for the general good, all men are preſumed conuſant of the law; though of the fact he may be ſometimes ignorant, and that ignorance be his ſufficient excuſe.

2. Ignorance of the law, though it be invincible, doth not excuſe but in few caſes; for every man is bound at his peril to take knowledge what the law of the realm is, as well ſtatute as common. *Doct. & Stud. lib.* 2. *cap.* 47.

Particular caſes.

3. If a penal ſtatute be made, and it is enacted that the ſtatute ſhall be proclaimed by ſuch a day in every ſhire, which is not done before the day, after the day a man offends againſt the ſtatute, he ſhall run in the penalty if there be no further words in the ſtatute to help him; and the reaſon is, becauſe there is no ſtatute made in this realm but by the aſſent of the lords and commons, who repreſent the ſtate of the whole nation; and every ſtatute there made is of as ſtrong effect in law, as if all the commons were there preſent in proper perſon at the making thereof; ſo the law preſumeth there needeth no proclamation, when it is made by their authority; and though it be enacted, that it ſhould be proclaimed, that is but of favour and not of neceſſity; and therefore not to be taken that the intent of the legiſlature was that it ſhould be void if not proclaimed; and that any ſhould be diſcharged by the law by ignorance, there are but few caſes, as it might in ſome caſes be applied to infants, *&c. Doct. & Stud. lib.* 2. *cap.* 46.

4. Reſolved, Foraſmuch as in the caſe at bar, a *ca' ſa'* was awarded againſt the counteſs of *Rutland* by the court of common pleas, that the ſheriff, or his officer by his warrant, might, without any offence, execute it; for they are not to diſpute the authority of the court, but to execute the writs to them directed, whereto they are ſworn; and though it appear in the *capias* that ſhe was a counteſs, againſt whom, by law, no *capias* lieth, *et ignorantia juris non excuſat*, eſpecially ſheriffs and other miniſters of law and juſtice, as was objected; yet foraſmuch as in ſome caſes of contempt, *&c.*

a *capias* lies againſt them; therefore it was reſolved, that the ſheriff and his miniſters could not examine the judicial acts of the court, but were to execute the writs; wherewith agrees the opinion 36 *H.* 8. *Dy.* 60. If a *capias* or *exigent* come to a ſheriff againſt a duke, earl, *&c.* where it doth not lie againſt them, the officer ought to ſerve the writ, and not to diſpute the validity of it. 6 *Co.* 54. *a.*

5. Vide 1 *Co.* 175. *Mildmay*'s caſe. *Hob.* 223. *Comb.* 269.

6. See rules, *Executio juris non habet injuriam. Ignorantia facti excuſat. Caveat emptor. Ignorance of one's right not to prejudice his right.*

188. *Imperſonalitas non concludit nec ligat.*

VIDE rule, *Simplicitas eſt legibus amica, &c.*

189. *Impotentia excuſat legem.*

1. RESolved on a ſpecial verdict, That a parſon ought to reſide on his rectory, upon the parſonage houſe, and not in another, though within the ſame pariſh; for the ſtatute doth not only intend for ſerving the cure and hoſpitality, but alſo for the maintenance of the houſe for habitation of the parſon, and that not only for himſelf but for his ſucceſſors, that they alſo might maintain hoſpitality there; yet lawful impriſonment without covin, or want of a parſonage houſe, are good excuſes for non-reſidence; for *impotentia excuſat legem*, and theſe caſes are excepted out of the act by conſtruction of law: ſickneſs alſo *ſans* fraud, as was held in *Scac' Trin.* 39 *Eliz.* is alſo a good excuſe, if the patient removed by advice of his phyſician *bona fide*, for better air and the recovery of his health. See 6 *Co.* 21.

2. See *Mo.* 540, 448. *Gilb.* 230. 2 *Ju. Eccl.* 401, 402.

3. See alſo rules, *No conſtruction can be too liberal to make parſons reſide and take care of their pariſhes. Quando duo jura concurrant, &c.*

190. *In aequali jure melior eſt conditio poſſidentis.*

DRURY brought error upon a judgment given in *B. R.* in a *Quare impedit* brought by the queen, where the caſe was, A counteſs being a widow, retained two chaplains, and then a third, who purchaſed a diſpenſation to have two benefices with cure, and was advanced to two, whereof the firſt was above 8*l.* a year; and if he was lawfully qualified within the ſtatute 21 *H.* 8. *cap.* 13. was the queſtion in *C. B.* for if it was a lawful qualification, then the firſt benefice was not void by acceptance of the ſecond, and by conſequence no ſuch title to preſent by lapſe devolved to the queen: and it did not appear by the pleadings, that the firſt two chaplains were alive at the time the third was advanced, but only that the two firſt were alive at the time the third was retained: whereupon the great queſtion aroſe in *B. R.* It had been adjudged in *C. B.* that a title to preſent by lapſe was devolved to the queen, and judgment given accordingly. And after many arguments at the bar and bench on error in *B. R.* the former judgment was affirmed, in which two points were reſolved; 1ſt, When the counteſs retained two chaplains, they are capable of difpenfation according to the act 21 *H.* 8. whereby it is provided, That every countefs, being a widow, may have two chaplains, whereof every one may purchafe licence or difpenfation; and when fhe hath retained two the ftatute is executed; for fhe cannot have more capable of difpenfation, and the retainer of the third may not deveft the capacity of difpenfation which was vefted by their retainer in the firft two. And though the countefs might, at common law, have as many chaplains as fhe pleafed, yet fhe may not have more than two capable of difpenfation by the ftatute, and reafon requireth that he who hath ferved longeft fhould be firft preferred; *qui prior eft tempore potior eft jure.* Vide *Dy.* 312. By the opinion of *Catlin*, *Saunders* and *Dyer*, if a lord, who is allowed but three chaplains, retains fix at one and the fame time, and all are preferred, thofe firft promoted are warranted by the ftatute, and yet the retainer was not according to the ftatute; but *in aequali jure melior eft conditio poffidentis.* 2dly, Refolved, that when the firft two were retained according to the ftatute, and fo the ftatute executed, the retainer of the third, though good at law, yet was void to give him capacity to purchafe difpenfation within the ftatute; and therefore, though the other two were dead before the third's advancement, yet as they were alive at his retainer, *which retainer was at the common law, and not by the ftatute*; therefore he ought to have had a new retainer after the deaths of the other two, and before his advancement; for *quod ab initio non valet, in tractu temporis non convalefcet.* As if the fon and heir apparent of a baron retain a chaplain, and his father dies, and the chaplain purchafeth difpenfation, this retainer, though by letters under hand and feal, will not ferve him; becaufe they were not good at firft; and if a baron retains two chaplains according to the ftatute, and they purchafe difpenfations, and are advanced according to the ftatute, now if the lord difcharge either of them from his fervice, he may not retain another during his life; for by fuch means he might advance chaplains *fans* number, and fo the ftatute be defrauded; for the ftatute limits three only to have the benefit of the ftatute, as was adjudged in *C. B. Pafch.* 28 *Eliz. Rot.* 1130. in a *quare impedit*, between the queen and the bifhop of *Gloucefter*, and *Edward Savacre*, and affirmed on error in *B. R.* and it was faid *this ftatute fhould be taken ftrongly againft pluralities*; and therefore it was held, that if a baron, who by the ftatute might retain three chaplains, be made warden of the *Cinque ports*, who might have a chaplain in refpect of his office, yet he fhould have but three. So if a baron having three, be made an earl, he fhall have but five in all, *et fic de caeteris.* 4 Co. 89. *Drury*'s cafe. See alfo *Acton*'s cafe, 5 *Co.* 89. *Mo.* 277, 561, 562, 678. *Cro. Eliz.* 839. *Dy.* 312. *Plow.* 88. *An.* 200. *Hob.* 103, 199.

191. *Incerta pro nullis habentur.*

1. A Grant of all his trees and woods upon *Black-acre*, as reafonably may be fpared, is a void grant unlefs referred to a third perfon what might be fpared. *Dy.* 91.

2. Upon two feveral writs for the fame matter againft the fame perfon, returnable at the fame time, both fhall abate. *Manfel*'s cafe.

3. The lord chancellor ſaid, he took it for a rule, that whereſoever there is a demand in law or equity, there muſt be a certainty of the thing demanded to be adjudged or decreed. 1 *Chan. Ca.* 309. See *Dav.* 33.

4. See alſo rules, *Salus populi eſt ſuprema lex. Id certum eſt, quod certum reddi poteſt. Law favours juſtice and truth,* &c.

192. *In chancery every particular caſe ſtands on its own bottom, or on its own particular circumſtances, which is not ſo at law.*

1. THE common law relieves not particular caſes againſt the general rule, but in chancery every particular caſe ſtands on its own particular circumſtances; and though in general the law will not relieve, yet equity doth, ſo as the example introduce not a general miſchief. 2 *Chan. Ca.* 93. Vide *The introduction to theſe ſheets, equity what, of what it holdeth cognizance, and where no relief either at law or in equity.*

2. Equity in every caſe is governable by the circumſtances. 3 *Chan. Ca.* 45.

3. There is no doubt but there may be good ground, in ſome caſes in equity, to ſet aſide that which is good at law. 3 *Chan. Ca.* 73.

193. *Incidents may not be ſevered.*

1. ONE grants to another eſtovers to be burnt in ſuch an houſe, they ſhall go with the houſe, by whatever title holden; for the one is inſeparably incident to the other. *Fi. Ley* 5. *a.*

2. Lord and tenant by fealty and homage, the lord releaſes his fealty, this is void; for fealty is incident to homage. 7 *E.* 4. 11.

3. An office of ſkill and diligence, or an annuity *pro conſilio impendendo,* may not be forfeited by attainder for treaſon. *Fi. Ley* 5. *a. b.*

4. Leaſe of a manor, except the ſervices; the exception is void, for it is parcel of the thing demiſed. *Dy.* 97.

5. See 31 *E.* 3. *Aſſ.* 44. *Bro. Abr. Incident* 34. *Co. Lit.* 93, 251. *Plow. Com.* 500. *Hob.* 181, 215, 216. *Skin.* 491.

194. *Incivile eſt, niſi totâ ſententiâ perſpectâ, de aliqua parte judicare.*

1. IN the ſame ſentence it is vain to imagine one part before another; for though words can be neither ſpoken nor written at once, yet the mind of the author comprehends them at once, which gives *vitam et modum* to the ſentence. *Hob.* 171. But in grants of particulars ſufficiently once aſcertained, another miſtaking will not fruſtrate, though it be falſe. *Hob.* 171. But a thing certain may be diminiſhed tho' not wholly made void, as was *Ognel*'s caſe, 4 *Co. Hob.* 171. See *Cro. Eliz.* 255. 2 *Co.* 23. *b.* 51. *a.* 55. *a.*

2. *Liberum maritagium* are ſuch words of art, and ſo neceſſarily required, as they cannot be expreſſed by words equivalent, or amounting to

as much; as if a man gives lands to a man with his daughter *in connubio ſoluto ab omni ſervitio*, &c. yet there paſſeth in this caſe but an eſtate for life, for ſeeing that theſe words *in liberum maritagium* create an eſtate of inheritance againſt the general rule of law, the law requireth that they ſhould be legally purſued. *Co. Lit.* 21. *b.*

3. If divers parcels of lands be contained in a deed, and ſeiſin is delivered of one parcel according to the deed, all the parcels paſs; though he ſaith not (in name of all, &c.) becauſe the deed contains all. So if there be divers feoffees, and livery of ſeiſin be only to one. If a man make a charter in fee, and deliver ſeiſin for life *ſecundum formam chartae*, the whole fee paſſeth; for it ſhall be taken moſt ſtrongly againſt the feoffor, &c. *Co. Lit.* 48. *a.*

4. See 2 *Co.* 55. *b.* *Cro. Eliz.* 255. *Cro. Ca.* 155. *Cro. Eliz.* 131. *Cro. Jac.* 175. 3 *Lev.* 339. 2 *Vent.* 142. 1 *Mod.* 27. 6 *Mod.* 66. *Salk.* 346. *Skin.* 531, 543, 544, 545. *Dal.* 5, 30, 57, 79. 2 *Ro. Abr.* 65. *Co. Lit.* 6. *a.* 299. *a.*

5. *Vide* rules, *Conſtructions to be ſecundum aequalitatem rationis. To be with equity and moderation*, &c. *Quae non valent ſingula, juncta juvant.*

195. *In conſimili caſu conſimile debet eſſe remedium.*

VIDE rule, *Ubi eadem ratio, ibi idem jus*, and *Hard.* 65.

196. *In fictione juris ſemper aequitas exiſtit.*

1. IF one diſſeiſe me, and cut the trees, graſs, or other emblements growing upon the lands, and after I re-enter, I ſhall have an action of treſpaſs againſt him *vi et armis*, for the trees, graſs and emblements, &c. for after my re-entry, the law, as to the diſſeiſor and his ſervants, ſuppoſeth the freehold all along to have continued in me; but if my diſſeiſor maketh a feoffment in fee, gift in tail, leaſe for life or years, &c. and after I re-enter, I ſhall not have treſpaſs *vi et armis* againſt them, who come in by title, for the fiction of law, that the freehold continued in me always, hath not relation to make one, who came in by title, to be a wrong doer *vi et armis*; for *in fictione juris ſemper aequitas exiſtit*, but in ſuch caſe I ſhall recover all the meſne profits againſt my diſſeiſor in the ſame manner, as a diſſeiſee ſhould have recovered in an aſſiſe at common law, before the ſtatute of *Glouceſter*, *cap.* 1. damages only againſt the diſſeiſor. Alſo it is to be preſumed that the feoffee gave a conſideration to the diſſeiſor, and that is the reaſon he ſhall be charged with all, &c. 11 *Co.* 51. *a. b.*

2. Diſſeiſor is diſſeiſed, and the firſt diſſeiſee re-enters, he ſhall not have an action of treſpaſs againſt the ſecond diſſeiſor; becauſe that the fiction of law, as to the actions, extendeth only to the firſt diſſeiſor; and if I might puniſh here the ſecond diſſeiſor, he would be twice charged, &c. 11 *Co.* 51. *b.*

3. See rules, *Equality is equity. Nemo debet bis puniri*, &c.

197. *Infinitum in jure reprobatur.*

VIDE rule, *Law favours justice and truth*, &c. Hob. 159.

198. *Inheritances may lineally descend, but not ascend.*

1. THERE is father, uncle and son, the son purchaseth lands in fee-simple, and dies *sans* issue, living his father; the uncle, and not the father, shall have the lands as heir to the son, yet the father is nearer of blood; because it is a maxim in the law, that inheritances may lineally descend but not ascend, *&c. Lit. sect.* 3.

2. Only lineal ascent in the right line is prohibited, and not in the collateral. *Quaelibet haereditas naturaliter quidem ad haeredes haereditabiliter descendet, nunquam quidem naturaliter ascendit. Descendit itaque jus quasi ponderosum quod cadens deorsum recta linea vel transversali, et nunquam reascendit ea via qua descendit post mortem antecessorum, a latere tamen ascendit alicui propter defectum haeredum inferius provenientium*; so as the lineal ascent is prohibited by law, and not the collateral; and in the prohibiting the lineal ascent, the common law is assisted with the law of the twelve tables. *Co. Lit.* 11. *a.*

199. *Iniquity bars equity.*

1. THE defendant by a trick got the deed into his hands, and burnt or cancelled it. The court said, where deeds are suppressed, *omnia praesumuntur*, and would not direct a trial at law, which had not been denied, had not the defendant been guilty of fraud. 1 *Chan. Ca.* 293.

2. The plaintiff having made false pretences of love to the defendant, and debauched her, and got her with child, gave a bond of 500*l.* conditioned for payment of 50*l.* no place was appointed where to be paid; wherefore he brought his bill, and offered to bring the 50*l.* into court, but the court would not grant an injunction. 2 *Chan. Ca.* 15.

3. The plaintiff and defendant having married two daughters of *J. S.* on his decease there were some loose papers concerning some accounts between the plaintiff and the father, put together in a bundle and sealed up by two persons then present, and delivered to the defendant to be safely kept, he being told they were matters of concern; and there being now an account decreed of the estate of *J. S.* which was to be equally distributed between the plaintiff and defendant, the defendant demanded, as due from the plaintiff to his father's estate, for diet, *&c.* 2300*l.* but it appeared on proof, that the defendant had altered the bundle, and displaced the papers, and that it could not be known what papers had been taken out; and the master having reported that the defendant had suppressed the evidences; the court therefore disallowed the defendant's whole demand against the plaintiff, though he swore he had produced all, and though they appeared to be half-yearly accounts relating to one another, and not one missing, but the account carried down to within a little time of the testator's death; and though the lord chancellor declared himself satisfied, that all the

papers were produced, yet for the reaſons aforeſaid he wholly diſallowed the demand. 1 *Vern.* 452.

4. The bill was to call the defendant, the plaintiff's ſteward, to an account; the defendant, by way of plea, inſiſted the plaintiff ought not to be relieved in this court. 1ſt, For that ſhe had brought a bill here before, and alſo ſued at law for the ſame matter, and on election choſe to have the bill diſmiſſed, and not having ſucceſs at law would now reſort back to equity. 2dly, For that ſhe had in a violent manner ſeiſed the defendant's writings and evidences, and even impriſoned his perſon: and *detinue* of charters is a good plea in account at law, and ought to be ſo here; and that though the plaintiff might alledge the trunk reſtored, yet that ought not to excuſe; for ſuch violent ſeiſure is evidence of the plaintiff's deſign to take from the defendant ſome material papers, and when ſhe had got them it is to be preſumed ſhe took them, and it is not to be expected that the defendant ſhould prove what papers the plaintiff took. *Cur':* As to the firſt objection, diſmiſſion on election is not peremptory, no more than a nonſuit at law; and as to the ſecond, though ſuch proceedings are not to be approved or countenanced, yet they cannot amount to a forfeiture of the right, which the plaintiff hath to call her ſteward to an account; and tho' *detinue* be a good plea at law in bar of account, yet it is not good to ſay the plaintiff did once ſeiſe his papers or writings, but it is the detinue of them which makes the plea good; and as to the impriſonment, the defendant hath his remedy by action; but a man may ſurely juſtify detaining his ſervant who was taking away his goods; the court therefore ordered, that whereas there was a conſiderable ſum of money in the trunk, that the money as well as the writings ſhould be reſtored; for though the defendant might be greatly in the plaintiff's debt, yet ſhe was not to levy her own debt after that manner, and ordered the defendant to anſwer. 2 *Vern.* 32, 33.

5. See 1 *Chan. Ca.* 96, 154, 209, 250. 2 *Chan. Ca.* 15, 102. 1 *Vern.* 53. *S. C. Max. Eq.* 6. *Margin.* 2 *Vern.* 426.

6. See alſo rules, *He, who hath done iniquity, ſhall not have equity. He, who will have equity, muſt do it. In odium ſpoliatoris, &c. Wherever there is ſuppreſſio veri, &c.*

200. *Injuria non praeſumitur.*

1. IT ſhall rather be intended he cometh to the deed by lawful, than wrongful means, *Lit. ſect.* 377. except ſome proof, *&c. contra.*

2. *Omnia praeſumuntur legitima facta, donec probetur in contrarium. Injuria non praeſumitur.* Co. Lit. 232. b.

3. *Quaere de dubiis, quia per rationes pervenitur ad legitimam rationem.* Lit. ſect. 377.

4. See rule, *Fraus non eſt praeſumenda.*

201. *In majore ſumma continetur minor.*

1. VIDE 5 *Co.* 114. *Wade's* caſe.

2. See alſo the rule, *Omne majus continet in ſe minus.*

202. *In maxima potentia minima licentia.*

1. THerefore tenant after poſſibility of iſſue extinct, and tenant for life, though by expreſs grant diſpuniſhable of waſte, *&c.* ſhall be reſtrained from pulling down of houſes or defacing a ſeat. 2 *Chan. Ca.* 32. *Gilb.* 127. *Salk.* *S. C.* So of a jointreſs. *Nelſ.* 190. So of tenant for life. *Nelſ.* 220, 221.

2. A bill was preferred in favour of an infant *in ventre ſa mere*, to reſtrain waſte, and decreed, and an injunction granted. *Prec. Chan.* 50. *Barn.* 274. And waſte and deſtruction being of this ſort committed, was decreed to be repaired by the party, though diſpuniſhable of waſte. *Prec. Chan.* 454. And ſuch muſt not ſuffer premiſſes to run out of repair. *Nelſ.* 190. *Mildmay*'s caſe. 1 *Co.* 175. *Hob.* 159. For there is nothing more contrary to liberty than licentiouſneſs, nor to diſcretion than fooliſhneſs. *In maxima potentiâ minima licentia.* Hob. 159. *Eſt quiddam perfectius in rebus licitis.* And St. *Paul* himſelf ſaith, *all things are lawful, but all things are not expedient.* See his firſt Epiſtle to the *Corinthians.*

3. See rule, *Eſt quiddam perfectius in rebus licitis.*

203. *In odium ſpoliatoris omnia praeſumuntur.*

General.

1. WHerever there is a *ſuppreſſio veri*, or *ſuggeſtio falſi*, the releaſe, *&c.* ſhall be void. 1 *Vern.* 19, 20.

Particular caſes.

2. Three daughters being equally intitled as co-heirs, the huſband of one fearing to be in law, and being made to believe he ſhould pay coſts, releaſed his ſhare to the other ſiſters, who were to bear the charge of the ſuit; his ſhare amounted to above 1000*l.* this releaſe was ſet aſide, and *Luxford*'s caſe cited, that miſapprehenſion of the party ſhall avoid his releaſe. 1 *Vern.* 32.

3. The bill was to be relieved againſt a purchaſe made by defendants from the plaintiff's father, ſuggeſting he had been circumvented and impoſed upon; the defendants inſiſted upon their purchaſe, and ſhew that firſt there were articles, and then conveyances purſuant thereto, and a fine; and that the father ſeeing the plaintiff uneaſy thereat, took a releaſe from him of all his right. Notwithſtanding all this, the lord keeper ſet the purchaſe aſide; it appearing art was uſed with him, *&c.* 1 *Vern.* 205.

4. The defendant took out execution in breach of an injunction of this court, and the bailiffs who ſerved it, having found a place in a wall made up again with bricks, wherein was hid 150*l.* took it away, and did great ſpoil in the plaintiff's goods; the order by the late chancellor was, that the defendant ſhould make ſatisfaction; and now this matter coming before the lord keeper, it was ſaid the plaintiff ought to ſeek his remedy againſt the officers, but the order was confirmed; for it would be an idle thing to put a thief to his oath to accuſe himſelf; for he, who has ſtolen, will not ſtick to forſwear it; and therefore *in odium ſpoliatoris*, the oath of the party

party ſhall be a good charge upon him, who hath done the wrong. 1 *Vern.* 207.

5. See 1 *Chan. Ca.* 96, 154, 293. *Hob.* 99. 1 *Vern.* 49, *&c.* 53, 19, 20, 32, 452, 467, 294. 2 *Vern.* 561, 308, 32, 129, 295. 2 *Pe. Will.* 680. 1 *Vern.* 53. *S. C.* *Fra. Max. Eq.* 6, 129. *Prec. Chan.* 7.

6. See alſo rules, *Iniquity bars equity. Wherever there is ſuppreſſio veri, &c. He, who will have equity, muſt do it. He, who hath committed iniquity, ſhall not have equity.*

204. *In odium ſpoliatoris, the oath of the party wronged ſhall be a good charge upon him who hath done the wrong.*

SEE laſt rule, caſe 4.

205. *In praeſentia majoris ceſſat potentia minoris.*

1. THE pope formerly, being conſidered as ſupreme ordinary over all other ordinaries, uſed to viſit, correct, diſpence, and tolerate within every dioceſe of this realm ſole, and he uſed to make appropriations *ſans* the biſhop. And theſe matters were then taken for good, or at leaſt ſuffered. And the biſhop, who was taken but for an inferior ordinary, never contradicted it: but it was uſed and accepted as good; for *in praeſentia majoris ceſſat potentia minoris*, and ſo appropriations made by the pope ſole *ſans* the ordinary, were taken as good. The caſe in *quare impedit* 29 *E.* 3. was cited, brought by the earl of *Sarum* againſt the prior of *Montague*, where the appropriation was pleaded, made by the apoſtle, with the aſſent of the king, without mentioning the ordinary, and was allowed good; and many caſes of like ſort were cited, and the pope uſed to make proviſions before the ſtatute 25 *E.* 3. reſtrained him; where the proviſor was in without any admiſſion, inſtitution or induction, for or by means of the biſhop, and ſo the pope's authority, being taken as abſolute, bound the biſhop as his inferior; and ſuch authority and juriſdiction as the pope uſed in this realm, was acknowledged by the parliament *anno* 25 *H.* 8. and other ſtatutes, to be in the king, ſo that he had that juriſdiction, and lawfully might uſe all ſuch as the pope was accuſtomed to uſe within this realm; and from that king the ſame authority deſcended to his ſon and other ſucceſſors to the crown. And he, *E.* 6. being ſupreme ordinary, might and did appropriate, *&c.* of his own authority and juriſdiction *ſans* the biſhop; and to ſuch effect in the principal caſe, he put theſe words in his charter, *authoritate noſtra regia ſuprema, &c.* Plow. Com. 498, *&c.* But it could not be *ſans* conſent of the patron, 498. *a.* *b.* 500. *a.*

2. All the judges declared the law to be, that a reſignation by the dean of *Wells* to the king, was good and effectual, as to the head of the church, as if it had been to the biſhop, and the deanary was void by it. *Plow. Com.* 498. *a.* For *in praeſentia majoris ceſſat potentia minoris.*

3. But an appropriation cannot be made without the conſent of the patron, becauſe the patron hath a temporal inheritance in the advowſon, that

is to ſay, a fee-ſimple, which the ordinary, nor in antient time the pope, could not take from him, nor alter without his conſent; but in appropriations the patron is a party, and the ordinary is the agent, and does all what he does, in this matter, in execution of what the patron hath ordained, and is all intended to be done at his requeſt, as the benefit is his. The king is ſupreme patron as king, and not in reſpect of the ſupreme juriſdiction which the realm, by the ſtatute, hath acknowledged in him, and which the pope exerciſed before, 499. *a. b.* 500. *a.* And the king by this prerogative may provide to a church and diſpence without juriſdiction, *&c.* 500. *a.* 503. *a.* and appropriate as ſupreme ordinary, by his eccleſiaſtical juriſdiction, 501. *a.* If the king found a church, hoſpital or free chapel donative, he may exempt the ſame from ordinary juriſdiction, and his chancellor ſhall viſit the ſame, nay, if he found the ſame, without any ſpecial exemption, the ordinary is not, but the king's chancellor is to viſit them; and as the king may create donatives ſo exempt, ſo he may by his charter licence any ſubject to found ſuch church or chapel, and to ordain that it ſhall be donative, and not preſentable, and to be viſited by the founder, and not by the ordinary. *Co. Lit.* 344. *a.* Nay if the meaneſt ſubject erect and endow a chapel, hoſpital, *&c.* he is the natural viſitor and not the ordinary; for the party comes not in by means of the ordinary, but by the appointment of the founder, *&c.* See *Gilb.* 181, 178 *to* 183. *Show. Parl. Ca.* 51. 4 *Mod.* 112. *Co. Lit.* 96. *Skin.* 484, 494. *Fitzh. Nat. Brev.* 42. (*A.*) (*B.*) *Pal.* 451. 13 *Co.* 11. *Elſ. Obſ.* 26. 1 *Pe. Will.* 326. 3 *Lev* 212. *Skin.* 502. *Fitz. Abr. Excom.* 9. 1 *Mod.* 12, 260. 2 *Mod.* 257. *S. C. Mo.* 755. *Ha. Anal.* 19. 1 *Ju. Eccl.* 5. *b.* 26. 2 *Ju. Eccl.* 182, 481, *&c.* 486 *to* 493.

206. *Intention being clear, all means, without which that cannot be attained, muſt be ſupplied by a court of juſtice.*

1. A Man is ſeiſed of divers manors, lands or tenements in fee, of ſocage tenure, and by his will in writing deviſeth all his ſaid manors, lands and tenements to his ſiſter and her heirs for ever, (except out of this general grant my manor of *R.* which I do appoint to pay my debts) and made two executors by name, and died, and one of them died, and the other took upon him the charge of the executorſhip, and ſold the manor to *R.* in fee for 300*l.* for the purpoſe aforeſaid; and, by the opinion of the court, he well might, and that by reaſon and circumſtances this was the intention of the teſtator, and not to leave the reverſion to the heir, but to truſt his executor with the ſale for the ſpeedy payment of his debts. *Dyer* 371. *b.*

2. See 1 *Chan. Ca.* 177. 2 *Leon.* 220.

207. *Intention being ſecret and not declared, it muſt give way to the legal intent.*

1. THE teſtator made two executors, and deviſeth to them *reſiduum bonor'*, *&c.* after the debts and legacies paid; one of them died, and his adminiſtrator ſued the ſurviving executor, to have a moiety of the ſurpluſage. The defendant inſiſted they were joint deviſees, and took the reſidue as legatees, and not as joint executors. Lord keeper decreed *pro quer'*, for in caſe of executors the teſtator intended an equal ſhare to his executors: and by chief juſtice *Roll*'s advice it was decreed, that where a deviſe was to two equally, notwithſtanding the word *equally*, the deviſees were jointenants, yet the intention prevents the ſurvivorſhip: the cauſe was diſputed, but to the diſſatisfaction of the bar decreed; for where the intention is ſecret and not declared, the ſecret intention muſt give way to the legal intent. 1 *Chan. Ca.* 238, 239.

2. The caſe was, The father ſeiſed in fee, mortgaged the lands, and alſo gave a ſtatute to pay, *&c.* and made his will, and deviſed 500*l.* to his daughter and died; the mortgagee took ſo much of the perſonal eſtate in execution on the ſtatute, that there was not ſufficient aſſets left to pay the legacy; decreed the daughter ſhould have relief againſt the heir, he being eaſed out of the perſonal eſtate, which was liable to her legacy. Lord chancellor: Where the heir is indebted by mortgage made by his father, or by other means as heir to his anceſtor, the perſonal eſtate in the hands of the executor ſhall be employed in eaſe of the heir; but if no aſſets to pay other creditors, or other end of the teſtator, or his legacies, the heir ſhall not turn his charge on the perſonal eſtate. In this caſe here was ſufficient to pay the debt by the mortgage, *&c.* and the legacy out of the perſonal eſtate, and when both can be ſatisfied, both ſhall be ſatisfied, and the contrivance to make the perſonal eſtate liable towards ſatisfaction of the mortgage (looks like a fraud) and ſhall not prejudice the legatee, but ſhe ſhall have recompence againſt or upon the mortgage, though originally not liable to her. And my lord cited ſeveral precedents decreed upon the ſame reaſon. 2 *Chan. Ca.* 4, 5.

3. Privacy in making a will, or looſe words to hide the teſtator's intent, or to keep the family quiet, *&c.* are not to be regarded, much leſs to be taken to amount to a revocation. 3 *Chan. Ca.* 81, 82, 88, 117, 127.

4. See rules, *Equity to execute the intent of the parties. Law regards the intent of the parties.*

208. *Intent without act not puniſhable.*

1. THE purpoſe or intent of a man without act, is not puniſhable by law; *ubi non eſt lex, ibi non eſt tranſgreſſio, quoad mundum.* 4 Co. 16.

God only can ſearch the heart, and know the thoughts of man; for the thoughts of man are deceitful above meaſure, much leſs can one man dive into the thoughts of another; for they are unſearchable and paſt finding out

out, nothing being more inconſtant and deceitful, ſo as they can only be gueſſed at by overt acts, and that with great incertainty, and therefore human laws can go no further than to judge of the intent by the act.

2. See rules, *Law regards the intent of the parties. Uſury odious in law. Equity is to execute the intent of the parties.*

209. *Intereſt reipublicae ne maleficia remaneant impunita.*

General.

1. PEreat unus ne pereant omnes. 4 Co. 124. b.

Particular caſes.

2. The defendant prayed that ſeveral notes or writings, appearing to be forged by the plaintiff in the defendant's name, might be torn or obliterated. The ſolicitor general ſaid that it could not be, but that they muſt be kept, that the king may proceed againſt the criminal. 1 *Vern.* 66.

3. On a *Certiorari* was returned a conviction upon 43 *Eliz. cap.* 7. ſetting forth, *Whereas complaint has been made unto us*, &c. *by Sir* R. B. *that the defendant in the night-time cut down divers lime-trees of the ſaid Sir* R. B. *&c.* the juſtices awarded that he ſhould pay ſo much for damages. The defendant was ſtiled Gent. in the order; and one objection was, that a Gentleman was not within the ſtatute, which ſpeaks of Vagabonds, and ſuch baſe people, and inflicts a baſe puniſhment, *viz.* whipping, which the law never intended for gentlemen. *Cur'*: Whether the defendant be a gentleman, or not, is not material; for if a man of quality will do a baſe or mean thing, there is no reaſon or juſtice why he ſhould be exempt from the puniſhment; the quality of the offender is rather an aggravation than a leſſening of the offence. *Salk.* 181, 182.

4. *Spencer*, biſhop of *Norwich*, and others, were puniſhed for receiving money, *&c.* from the *French* king, which drew them without the king's licence, to yield up caſtles and forts in *France* committed to their cuſtody. 3 *Inſt.* 144.

5. The ſpiritual court may puniſh a biſhop for any offence againſt the duty of his office, as a biſhop, and as it relates to that; for eccleſiaſtical perſons are ſubject to the canons; and as the clergy are under different rules and duties, it is reaſonable they ſhould be puniſhed in the eccleſiaſtical courts, and particularly if it be a matter not cognizable at law; and it is reaſonable and fit the clergy ſhould have a power to cleanſe their own body from ſcandalous members. *Cawdry*'s caſe, 5 *Co. De jure regis Eccl.* 6. See *Lator*'s caſe in *Dav.* 84. and biſhop of *St. David*'s caſe in *Salk.* 294. And as it is reaſonable and fit they ſhould thus do, it muſt be unpardonable if they do not uſe this power to ſo good a purpoſe, *&c.* 2 *Ju. Eccl.* 364, 365. See alſo 1 *Lev.* 238. and *Ruſhworth*'s caſe in 1 *Ju. Eccl.* 526. 2 *Ju. Eccl.* 323.

6. See *Jenk.* 162, 166. 5 *Co. De jure Eccl.* 27, 28. 4 *Inſt.* 329. 1 *Keb.* 39. *Hob.* 121. 5 *Co.* 74. *b.* 2 *Ju. Eccl.* 266, *&c.* 362 *to* 372.

210. *Intereſt reipublicae ſuprema hominum teſtamenta rata haberi.*

General to, and rules.

1. *ULtima voluntas eſt legitima diſpoſitio de eo, quod quis poſt mortem fieri velit.* Swyn. 18. Orph. Leg. ſect. 2. And a will hath relation to the teſtator's death, and not to the making; for till his death he is maſter of his own will. 2 *Ju. Eccl.* 35. *Omne teſtamentum morte conſummatum.* Co. Lit. 322. b. *Et ultima voluntas teſtatoris eſt perimplenda ſecundum veram intentionem ſuam, &c.* Co. Lit. 322. b.

2. It is againſt the rule of law to make a will void, if by any conſtruction it can be made good. 1 *Chan. Ca.* 178.

3. It is a rule that a general clauſe in a will is not to prejudice a particular deviſe. 1 *Rep. Chan.* 145.

4. *In teſtamentis ratio tacita non debet conſiderari, ſed verba ſolum ſpectari debent*; for *multa poſſunt movere mentem teſtatoris quae nos latent, ideo per divinationem mentis durum eſt a verbis recedere.* 2 Chan. Ca. 155.

5. The will is to be taken together as one intire ſcheme. 2 *Mod. Ca. Acherly* and *Vernon's* caſe, and *fo.* 77. *Nelſ.* 27.

6. No words are to be rejected that are capable of ſignification. 2 *Mod. Ca.* 157, *&c.* 1 *Chan. Ca.* 178. *Pop.* 131. *Gilb.* 11, 118, 133, 136, 209.

7. The teſtator's intent is to govern, and artificial reaſon not to be admitted, *ibid.* and 1 *Chan. Ca.* 79, 80, 178. *Sparrow* and *Shaw's* caſe, 2 *Ju. Eccl.* 44. caſe 9.

8. The heir is to be favoured in doubtful caſes. See rule, *Heir favoured in doubtful caſes.* 2 Ju. Eccl. 44, 45. caſes 8. 10.

Particular caſes.

9. A man ſeiſed of certain lands held in ſocage, had iſſue two daughters, *A.* and *B.* and deviſed all his lands to *A.* and her heirs, to pay unto *B.* a certain ſum of money at a certain day and place; the money was not paid. And it was adjudged, that theſe words, *To pay*, &c. did amount in a will to a condition, and the reaſon was, becauſe the land was deviſed to *A.* for that purpoſe, otherwiſe *B.* to whom the money was appointed to be paid, ſhould be remedileſs, *et intereſt reipublicae, &c.* and the leſſee of *B.* recovered the moiety of the land in ejectment. *Co. Lit.* 236. *b.*

10. A man deviſes ſeveral ſpecific legacies, and (*int' al'*) to his grandchildren, to be paid at 21 or marriage; and after deviſes *that all his legacies ſhall be paid in a year after his deceaſe. Cur':* The ſubſequent clauſe which ſeems to contradict the payment of the legacies to the grand-children, in point of time, muſt be ſo conſtrued that it be not repugnant to the former clauſe; and therefore the latter clauſe muſt relate only to the other ſpecific legacies given to the other legatees, and not to the grand-childrens legacies. 2 *Mod. Ca.* 154, 57, 58. See *Cro. Ca.* 293.

* 11. A man deviſes 100 *l.* a-piece to his two grand-daughters, remitting all due to him for their maintenance; education is included. See caſe *Anſtis,*

ſtis, Eſq; *Garter*, againſt *Gandy et ux'*, 27 *March* 1734-5, before the houſe of lords.

* 12. A defect in a ſurrender of a copyhold to the uſe of a laſt will, ſupplied, eſpecially where it is for the benefit of the deviſor's children. See caſe before the houſe of lords *Lloyd* verſus *Barton*, 18 *Feb.* 1715.

13. Equity will imply a truſt in a will where there is fraud. *Gilb.* 208, 209.

14. Wills to pious uſes are favoured. *Gilb.* 44. So in favour of teſtator's children. *Nelſ.* 159, 160.

15. It is a good will, tho' made in form of an indenture. 1 *Chan. Ca.* 248. *Nelſ.* 195. *S. C.* But a will is not good, *ſine animo diſponendi*, nor a teſtament *ſine animo teſtandi.* Swin. 19.

16. Words in a will tranſpoſed in ſupport of contingent remainders, where the deviſor ſo intended. 2 *Chan. Ca.* 10, 11.

17. The witneſſes to a will, even under the ſtatute of frauds, need not ſign all at the ſame time or place, or in one another's preſence. *Gilb.* 262, *&c.*

211. *In teſtamentis ratio tacita non debet conſiderari, ſed verba ſolum ſpectari debent; ideo per divinationem mentis durum eſt a verbis recedere.*

How to be conſtrued according to the intent of the teſtator.

General.

1. THE teſtator's intent is to govern, and artificial reaſon not to be admitted. 1 *Chan. Ca.* 79.

2. And it muſt not be made void if by any conſtruction of law, it can be made good. 1 *Chan. Ca.* 178.

3. *Voluntas donatoris eſt obſervanda.* Poph. 132.

Conſonant to the rules of law.

4. The intention of the teſtator is to be purſued in the conſtruction of wills, as far as may be conſiſtent with the rules of law. 2 *Ju. Eccl.* 45.

5. Foraſmuch as in teſtaments the principal point to be conſidered, is the intent of the teſtator, the words ought to be ſo conſtrued, and applied to perform it. Reaſon and the duty of the judges require that there be ſuch expoſition of the words made, that the intent of the teſtator and the law of the realm be obſerved. And this conſonant to law and good equity. *Plow. Com.* 523. *b.*

6. A remainder cannot be limited to depend upon a fee-ſimple. A man may diſpoſe at his will and pleaſure, *ſo as it be according to the rules of law.* Cro. Eliz. 525, 526. *But one may not deviſe againſt the rules of law.* Ibid.

7. *J. T.* deviſed all his lands and goods, after his debts and legacies paid, to *R. Toby* and *Mary* his children, equally to be divided between them. Reſolved, 1ſt, That only an eſtate for life paſſed; for though the deviſe

 of

of the lands and goods are coupled together, and it is a devife of the goods for ever; yet for the lands, there being no words to pafs an inheritance, only an eftate for life paffeth; and tho' it was objected that the devife of the lands was after his debts and legacies paid; fo that this is limited after he hath made an end of difpofing; and was made to his children, of which his heir was one; fo as that he intended to give as much to one as to another; yet the court held only an eftate for life paffed. *Popham* faid it may be doubted if any land did pafs, in cafe he had a term for years in land, and fo the devife of lands fupplied, and that only the term fhall pafs. 2dly, They all conceived it was a joint eftate, and that they fhould not take in common, for he doth not appoint a divifion to be made; but *Fenner* faid, that 2 *Eliz.* between *Hyde* and *Southcoat*, it was adjudged that a devife of lands to be equally divided was a tenancy in common, but here it is to two to be equally divided, and it is not certain that a divifion fhall be made. *Cro. Eliz.* 330. *ideo quaere.* Vide 3 *Co.* 39. *b.*

To be collected from the will itfelf.

8. The intent of the teftator is to be collected out of the written words, and nothing is to be admitted, in the conftruction which is in any wife contrary to the words; neither are words to be rejected which may be reduced to any legal conftruction; yet if any words are contrary to law or infenfible fuch words muft be rejected. 1 *Chan. Ca.* 79, 80, 178.

To be taken together.

9. The will is to be taken together as one intire fcheme. 2 *Mod. Ca.* 68 *to* 80. *Nelf.* 27.

10. A general claufe in a will is not to prejudice a particular devife. 1 *Rep. Chan.* 145.

Words to be tranfpofed.

11. One feifed in fee of lands, devifeth to another and his heirs; and after in the laft part of his will devifeth a rent to another of 40*s.* out of the lands, with a claufe of diftrefs; this is a good devife of the rent to one, and of the land to another; and yet the land was firft devifed. For it is the office of the court, fo to place the words fpoken at one time, as that one part may ftand with the other; and that the devife of the rent fhall precede the devife of the land, and fo all repugnancy be avoided. So where one devifed a leafe for years to his fon during all the term, but yet that his wife fhould have it during her life: this was a good devife to the wife of the term, for fo long as fhe fhould live, and yet at firft he gave all to the fon; but the court is fo to expound the words, that the intent of the teftator may be obferved; and that was, that the wife fhould firft have the term during her life, the fon after. And fo the words of gift to the fon, which were firft, fhall be laft placed in the fenfe: and the words for the wife, which were fubfequent, fhall precede in conftruction. *Plow. Com.* 523. *a.*

Where

Where ambiguous.

12. *Walmesley:* It is a good way, when the words in a will are ambiguous, so as the intent may not be collected, to expound the will according to the law, and so there shall not be any prejudice. *Cro. Eliz.* 743.

13. Without words of condition, the judges have expounded the will to make a condition, where the intent of the testator was such. *Plow. Com.* 523. *b.*

14. If a man hath lands in fee, and other lands for years, and deviseth all his lands and tenements, the fee-simple lands pass only, and not the lease for years: and if a man hath a lease for years and no fee-simple lands, and deviseth all his lands and tenements, the lease for years passeth; for otherwise the will should be merely void. *Cro. Ca.* 293.

15. See last rule, case 10.

Where uncertain.

General.

16. A will must be construed according to the intent of the devisor, where a certain intent may be collected; but where it is uncertain, it is void. And the intent of the devisor ought to be collected from plain words, and not from words which ingender confusion; and if it may not be collected by the words it is void. *Cro. Eliz.* 743.

Particular.

17. A devise to two and *haeredibus,* so to *melioribus hominibus* in *D.* is void, for the incertainty; for it cannot be known whom he intended to be the best men. *Cro. Eliz.* 743.

18. One infeoffed his two sons to the use of himself for life, and after to the use of them and their heirs, *ad ultimam voluntatem suam perimplendam*; and after devised to *Sharpe* in fee. *Gaudy* held that *Sharpe* should take nothing; for an use cannot be limited upon an use: but the words *ad performand' ultimam voluntatem* are void; and to that opinion *Clench* agreed, but *Fenner* doubted; wherefore it was adjourned. *Cro. Eliz.* 382, 383.

What a good devise by implication.

19. One deviseth all his goods to his wife, and after her decease, that his son and heir should have the house; though there be no devise by express words made to the wife, but by implication only, as the heir may not have it during the life of the wife, she shall have it for life, according to the intent of the devisor. *Plow. Com.* 522. *a. b.*

The heir to be favoured.

20. The words in a will being ambiguous, and capable of a construction in favour of the heir, is to be so construed. 2 *Ju. Eccl.* 44.

21. Agreed by all the judges, that the words in a will, which disinherit the heir at common law, ought to have an apparent intent, and not to be ambiguous and doubtful; and that the intent ought to be collected out of

 the

the words of the will; and not from any foreign intendment or averment. *Cro. Ca.* 369.

22. The devisor supposing he had power to dispose of the inheritance, deviseth the same, and ordereth incumbrances to be discharged thereout; afterwards it turning out that the estate could not pass according to the devisor's intention, it shall not, though in favour of the heir, be construed he intended to saddle his other estate with these incumbrances. 2 *Ju. Eccl.* 45.

23. *Ejectione firmae*, special verdict found, wherein the case was, *Bishop* being seised of divers lands called *Hayes* lands, extending into two vills *Cokefield* and *Cromefield*, devised all his lands in *Cokefield*, called *Hayes* lands, to *J.* his youngest son, and his heirs; and after, in another part of his will, he willeth, that if his son *J.* dieth without issue, that his wife should have *Hayes* lands, and dieth; *J.* also dieth without issue. And whether the feme shall have *Hayes* lands in *Cromefield*, or only that in *Cokefield*, was the question? And it was resolved by the whole court, that she should only have that which was in *Cokefield*; because there was no more devised to the youngest. But *Popham* said, if the devise had been to the eldest son, and that if he died *sans* issue, that his wife should have *Hayes* lands; there peradventure she should have all, because the eldest son had all; the one part by devise, the other by descent; and she should have all which he had; wherefore it was adjudged accordingly. *Cro. Eliz.* 674.

24. See rule, *Ultima voluntas testatoris est perimplenda secundum veram intentionem suam.*

25. See also 1 *Chan. Ca.* 60, 166. *Mo.* 145. 2 *Chan. Ca.* 155. 3 *Chan. Ca.* 81, 87, 88. 3 *Chan. Ca.* 117, 127. 10 *H.* 8. 9. 1 *Inst.* 9. 1 *Mod.* 57. 3 *Lev.* 71, 304. 1 *Jo.* 137. *Lat.* 34. 9. 2 *Lev.* 15, 104. 1 *Mod.* 189. *Salk.* 228, 237, 231, 347. *Yelv.* 73. 2 *Leon.* 147, 221. 3 *Leon.* 78. *Plow.* 28, 344. 2 *Mod. Ca.* 57, 58, 77. *Poph.* 131, 132, 144. *Gilb.* 11, 118, 131, 136, 209. 1 *Chan. Ca.* 309. *And.* 29. 3 *Lev.* 180, 181, 373. 3 *Mod.* 290. 2 *Lev.* 56, 156. 3 *Cro.* 52. 1 *Cro.* 356. *Lat.* 40. 2 *Chan. Ca.* 10, 11, 155. *Nelf.* 27, 159, 160, 354, 403, 433. 3 *Cro.* 359, 679. 2 *Vern.* 545. 2 *Sid.* 126, 136, 149, 151. 2 *Mod.* 9, 292. 1 *Vern.* 250. *Hob.* 65. 1 *Leon.* 251, 254. *Co. Lit.* 111. *a.* *Ow.* 141. *Fitzh. Nat. Brev.* 198. *b.* 3 *Cro.* 128, 387. 2 *Vent.* 368. 1 *Mod.* 272, 308. 1 *Vern.* 30, 199, 208, 246, 302, 332, 381, 431, 468, 470, 512, 522, 538, 546, 553, 573, 620, 638, 653, 666, 667, 686, 740. *Skin.* 147, 182. *Ben.* 35, 204. 2 *Mod. Ca.* 39, 93, 154. *Hob.* 18. 3 *Co.* 20. *b.*

212. *In things of election the party is to shew that he hath made it.*

Election.

Of estate.

1. THREE tenements were devised to the wife in lieu of dower; and after the husband sells one tenement; the feme may take the remainder or dower, but not both; neither shall she have satisfaction for the tenement

nement ſold; for ſhe muſt take the will as it ſtood at the death of the teſtator. 2 *Chan. Ca.* 24.

Of time of payment.

2. This was an action on the caſe on a promiſſory note, whereby the defendant promiſes to pay the plaintiff 23*l.* at the day of marriage of the defendant, or the day of his death; the plaintiff avers the defendant married *Lucy Greave*, whereby the action accrued; the defendant demurred generally; the plaintiff joins. It was objected, that there being two days of payment mentioned (to wit) the day of marriage, and the day of death; and the defendant being to do the firſt act, that is to pay the money; that he, according to the caſe of Sir *Rowland Hayward*, 2 *Co.* 35. has his election on which of the times he will make the payment. Lord chief baron *Gilbert:* I think in this caſe the defendant has no election, but muſt pay the money on his marriage; for Sir *Rowland*'s caſe, *and all caſes upon bonds and promiſſes*, turn upon this general rule, *That all contracts are to be taken according to the intent of the parties, expreſſed by their own words; and if there be any doubt in the ſenſe of theſe words, ſuch interpretation muſt be made as is moſt ſtrong againſt the grantor or obligor, that he may not, by his own obſcure wording of the contract, find means to evade and elude it.* Therefore if a man grants a rent of 20*l.* or a robe to one and his heirs, the grantor ſhall have the election; for he is the firſt agent, by the delivery of the one, or the payment of the other, *viz.* he having, by his contract, undertaken to do the one act or the other, he has ſtill left it in his election to chuſe which he will do; but if a man grants a rent-charge to another out of his lands, it is but one act to be done, and the grantee hath two remedies, either by way of diſtreſs, or by writ of annuity; for the grantor having granted it out of his lands, he hath charged his lands alſo; and having thus granted two remedies, it muſt be in the election of the grantee, who is to have the benefit of theſe remedies, which he will have. So in the caſe of *Hill* and *Grange*, *Plow.* 172. If a man make a leaſe for years, and reſerves a rent payable at *Michaelmas* and *Lady-day*, and there is a condition, that if the rent reſerved be behind and unpaid at the ſaid feaſts, and ten days after, that then the leſſor ſhall re-enter; the conſtruction of ſuch leaſe hath been made, that the rent is due at the day, and the leſſor may diſtrain for it; but to ſave the condition the leſſee may tender at the laſt of the ten days; becauſe thoſe are days of grace, given by the condition, that the leſſee may ſave his eſtate by the tender; and therefore if he tender at the laſt of the ten days, it is ſufficient; and this is likewiſe the day for the leſſor to demand the rent, in order to have advantage of the condition broken. In the caſe *Boſvil* and *Coats*, (1 *Vent.* 58.) the condition of the bond was, that the obligor ſhould bring the ſon and daughter of *J. S.* at their full age, to give ſuch releaſes as a third perſon ſhould require; the defendant pleads the ſon alive and under age, to which the plaintiff demurs; and the demurrer allowed; for the force of the condition is not ſuſpended till they are both of age; becauſe it is not to be taken conjunctively but reſpectively and disjunctively; for the obligor undertakes that the daughter ſhall releaſe at her full age as well as the ſon, and if ſhe doth not, the condition is broken. And ſo univerſally, when any perſon undertakes to pay money on two ſeveral contingencies, the natural ſenſe of ſuch contract is,

 that

that he muſt pay it at either of the ſaid contingencies, for the putting of it in, that he ſhall pay it at the one or the other, is for the benefit of the obligee or promiſſee, that he may have his money at any of the contingencies happening; and this is the genuine ſignification of thoſe words, and likewiſe that which is ſtrongeſt againſt the obligor or promiſſor; for if he would have the payment ſuſpended by both the contingencies, the promiſſor or obligor muſt take care, in expreſs words, to limit the payment after the happening of both contingencies. And there is an expreſs reſolution in the caſe of *Sayer* and *Gleane*, (1 *Lev.* 54, 55.) in debt on an obligation, that if a ſhip put to ſea, and either the goods or the obligor come ſafe, he ſhould pay ſuch a ſum, over and above the uſe allowed by the ſtatute; the defendant pleaded, that the obligor died before he returned. And it was objected, that the defendant had an election to pay at which of the contingencies he would; and that therefore the executors of the obligor were excuſed, becauſe their teſtator never returned ſafe. But it was reſolved, that the law ſupplies the words, *which ſhould firſt happen*, and no prejudice to the executors of the obligor, becauſe it was the ſenſe of ſuch contract, that payment ſhould ariſe on either of the contingencies; but it is much ſtronger in this caſe; becauſe the promiſe is to pay at the day of marriage, or day of death; now if the payment were not to be made at the day of marriage, that part of the promiſe were vain and idle, and to no purpoſe; for ſince 'tis certain all muſt die, the putting into the contract *the day of marriage*, would be altogether inſignificant, ſince, according to the defendant's expoſition, the payment could not be made on the day of marriage of the defendant, but muſt wait till the time of his death; and therefore judgment muſt be for the plaintiff. *Gilb.* 249, 250, 251.

Of remedies, and how to proceed, and where general.

3. The plaintiff ſhall not be put to election before an anſwer put in. 1 *Vern.* 103.

4. A plaintiff here may elect either generally to proceed here or at law; or ſpecially to proceed for part here, and the other part at law; but the court will judge of the reaſonableneſs of ſuch election. *Gilb.* 183.

Either in one court of equity or another.

5. The bill was brought here, and a plea to it allowed; the plaintiff declines it, and brings a new bill in the exchequer for the ſame matter; the plaintiff was ordered to elect in which court he would proceed; and if he elect to proceed *in Scac'* his bill here is to be diſmiſſed; if in this court, then an injunction is to be awarded to ſtay his proceedings *in Scac'*, *niſi cauſa*. 2 Rep. Chan. 2.

Either at law or in equity.

6. Where the plaintiff has a remedy to obtain the poſſeſſion of goods by trover, yet if thoſe goods were only by way of ſecurity, and conſequently there is a matter of account, the plaintiff is proper in taking his remedy here. *Barn.* 30. The ſame is where a pledge is of goods, or where there is a mortgage, the party is at liberty to take his remedy here, if he thinks proper. *Barn.* 39.

7. By the antient courfe of the court, a perfon might bring his action at law againft the reprefentative of the deceafed, and alfo his bill here for a difcovery of affets. Though now his lordfhip faid it was eftablifhed, that if the party proceeds in equity, it muft be both for difcovery and relief, and not to proceed both at law and in equity. *So that the antient courfe is altered, and fure with great reafon, as equity on a difcovery may relieve and prevent a double vexation and expence; for difcovery could only be in equity, and this means prevents the party the trouble of feeking relief at law on difcovery made here.* And where the party hath proceeded in both courts, feveral orders have been made, driving him to his election; and it is a general rule, that a perfon fhall not be allowed to proceed both at law and in equity for one and the fame demand at the fame time. But his lordfhip alfo declared, that where the court fees that the reprefentative is confeffing judgments, that is a reafon, that the court will not require the party to make his election, *&c.* And his lordfhip obferved the prefent cafe was, that the original bill was filed 31 *October*, and the anfwer came in 27 *November* following; and in the beginning of *Michaelmas* term a judgment was confeffed to *Murray* for 4000*l.* and that the adminiftration was in fome meafure granted to the defendant by leave of this court. The plaintiff had entered a caveat againft it, though the fame was after withdrawn. His lordfhip thought it the proper order, that the plaintiff fhould make a fpecial election, to proceed at law to recover judgment, and here for a difcovery, and an account of affets, but that he fhould not be at liberty to take out execution without leave of this court, and fo his lordfhip was pleafed to order. *Barn.* 278, 279.

8. See *Plow. Com.* 501. *b.* 2 *Chan. Ca.* 200. 1 *Chan. Rep.* 44, 52, 55. 2 *Rep. Chan.* 9, 21. 2 *Chan. Ca.* 87, *&c.* 1 *Vern.* 105, 298, 471. *Barn.* 391.

9. See alfo rule, *Every man's deed or covenant to be taken moft ftrongly againft himfelf.*

213. *Jointenancy odious in equity.*

General.

1. THE advantage of furvivorfhip is againft equity. 1 *Chan. Ca.* 58. 1 *Vern.* 361. 1 *Rep. Chan.* 261. 1 *Vern.* 271. 2 *Chan. Ca.* 64, 65. 1 *Vern.* 425.

2. Yet a truft may furvive, as is the following cafe.

Particular cafes.

3. Upon a bill in the exchequer, the cafe was, the father of the defendant *Rowel* gave inftructions for his will to be put in writing, that his meffuages and lands fhould be fold by *Howe* and another, for payment of his debts and legacies, and made other executors, and died, without making any other publication of his will. One of the truftees for fale died before any fale, and now the furvivor and the heir were compelled to fell, becaufe the lands were tied with a truft which will furvive in equity. *Hard.* 204. *Lit. fect.* 169. *Co. Lit.* 112. *b.* 113. *a.* *Dy.* 371. 1 *Chan. Ca. Margin* 295.

4. One having devifed the furplus of his eftate, after debts paid, to *A.* and *B.* *B.* dies. It was adjudged in the delegates, and decreed by lord *North*, and now confirmed by the lord chancellor, that it was a joint devife, and fhould furvive to *A.* And his lordfhip's opinion was further, that if *A.* and *B.* had been executors, and *A.* had poffeffed a moiety of the goods, and died, it would have been all one. And the cafe of *Cox* and *Quaintock*, was cited, where there were two joint executors, and one died, adjudged his executor or adminiftrator fhould not have an account againft the furvivor. 1 *Vern.* 482. But *Note*; The cafe *Cox* and *Quaintock* (which fee 1 *Chan. Ca.* 238. *Finch C. B.* 176.) was decreed to the diffatisfaction of the bar; for where the intention is fecret and not declared, the fecret intent muft give way to the legal intent. And if an adminiftrator, then an adminiftrator *de bonis non* muft have it.

5. Three perfons being jointly interefted in the truft of a term for years; one of them mortgaged his third part, and the queftion was, Whether the jointenancy was fevered? And it was determined to be a fettled point in chancery, that if *H.* makes his will, and devifes his lands to one in fee, and after mortgages it to another in fee, this is not a total revocation, but the equity of redemption fhall pafs by this devife. But *Cowper* lord chancellor held, that jointenancy is odious in equity; and that as to the cafe of the will, it might be for the benefit of the mortgagor, that his will fhould not be revoked; but that it is to the difadvantage of the mortgagor that the jointenancy fhould continue; becaufe if it happen he fhould die firft, all his intereft goes from his reprefentatives to the furvivor, unlefs it fhall be conftrued a feverance. *Salk.* 158.

6. Two perfons having jointly ftock'd a farm and occupied as jointenants, the bill was to be relieved againft furvivorfhip, one being dead; and though it was actually proved in the caufe, that the deceafed was informed what the confequence of the law was in cafe he fhould die, and that he thereupon replied he was content the ftock fhould furvive; yet the lord keeper was clear of opinion that the plaintiff ought to be relieved; and faid, if the farm had been jointly taken by them, and proved a good bargain, there the furvivor fhould have had the benefit of it: but as to a ftock employed in way of trade, that fhould in no cafe furvive; the cuftom of merchants as to bills of exchange, is now extended to inland bills; and the cuftom of merchants is extended to all traders to exclude furvivorfhip; and though it is common for traders in articles of copartnerfhip to provide againft furvivorfhip, yet that is more than is neceffary; and he faid, he took the diftinction to be, where two become jointenants or jointly interefted in a thing by way of gift or the like, there the fame fhall be fubject to the confequences of law; but as to a joint undertaking, as in the way of trade or the like, it is otherwife. And decreed for the plaintiff accordingly. 1 *Vern.* 217.

7. *Thomas Goodwin* being poffeffed of feveral leafehold houfes for feveral terms for years, makes his will, and thereby devifes the fame to *Anne* his wife for her life; and after her death he gives and devifes the fame to *Alice Buinian* and her three fons, to be equally amongft them; it was decreed they took as tenants in common, though there was no mention of any divifion to be made, or equally to be divided between them; accordingly the plaintiff, who was adminiftrator of *Alice Buinian*, and had brought

this bill for an account of the profits, had a decree for an account of the fourth part of the rents and profits for the time to come. *Gilb.* 146, 147.

8. See 1 *Vern.* 32, 35, 353, 482. *Cro. Eliz.* 743. 2 *Vern.* 63, 385, 557. *Dy.* 371. *Co. Lit.* 112, 113. *Prec. Chan.* 491, 163, 164, 167, 168. *Skin.* 182. 1 *Pe. Will.* 96, 28, *&c.* 2 *Show.* 91. *Cro. Ca.* 57. *Cro. Jac.* 416. *Prec. Chan.* 332. 1 *Pe. Will.* 14, 21. *Barn.* 396. *Doct. & Stud. lib.* 2. *cap.* 25. *Prec. Chan.* 120, 121, 124, 332. *Elʃ. Obʃ.* 77. *Barn.* 423.

214. *Jointure favoured in equity.*

As to value.

* 1. MArriage articles recite that the lands covenanted to be ſettled, were 500 *l.* a year; though there was no expreſs covenant that they were ſo, yet decreed the deficiency to be made up. See caſe before the houſe of lords, *Glegg* and *Glegg*, 14 *May* 1728.

2. This bill was to have a jointure which was defective in value made good, the huſband having covenanted that the lands were of 400 *l. per ann.* value, whereas in truth they were but 350 *l.* decreed the covenant ſhould be performed in ſpecie according to the value then, and not as they are now; lands being every where fallen. But if the covenant had been 400 *l. per annum*, and ſhould ſo continue, then they ſhould have been made up to the preſent time; it was ſaid for the defendant, that this value was only in the firſt articles, and not in the ſettlement, where there is no covenant as to the value; and that the plaintiff ought not to revert back from the ſettlement to the articles, as the ſettlement was executed in lieu of them; and though the plaintiff was an infant then, and ſo it was not her deed, yet her father accepted it for her. *Sed non allocatur.* 1 Vern. 217. Prec. Chan. 369. Abr. Eq. 221. caſe 8.

Jointreſs not to diſcover or part with writings.

3. The plaintiff, heir at law, brought this his bill for the deeds and writings, which he alledged concerned his eſtate. The defendant inſiſted ſhe had a jointure of part, ſo ought not to diſcover or part with the writings until her jointure was confirmed. *Cur'*: Confirm her jointure, or you ſhall not ſee the deeds. 1 *Vern.* 479. 2 *Vern.* 701.

Title evicted.

4. A term may be ſet aſide to let a jointreſs into her jointure; *aliter* of a dowreſs. *Prec. Chan.* 65, 97.

5. If *J.S.* gives a voluntary bond after marriage to make a jointure on his wife, and does it accordingly, whereupon ſhe gives up the bond; the huſband dies, and the wife is evicted, the jointure ſhall be made good out of the perſonal eſtate, there being no creditors; for the delivering up of the bond by a feme covert could no way bind her. 1 *Vern.* 427.

Agreements to be performed in ſpecie in favour of a jointreſs.

6. *J. S.* before marriage articles to ſettle a jointure, and the marriage is after in confidence thereof had, but the huſband dies before the ſettlement made; execution of the articles decreed. 2 *Vent.* 343.

7. *A.* in consideration of a marriage portion, articles to settle a jointure, but dies before the portion paid, or any settlement made; the wife administers, and so intitles herself to the money, and brings her bill against the heir to have the jointure. She shall have no relief, for she ought not to have both. But the reporter puts a *quaere*, she being intitled to these several demands in distinct capacities, and debts may hereafter appear to exhaust the assets; and in case the husband had actually received the portion, she would have had it as his administratrix. 1 *Vern.* 463.

8. *A.* on his first marriage, settles to the use of himself for life; remainder to his first and other sons in tail; the wife dies without issue. *A.* on his second marriage, in consideration of a portion paid, agrees to settle part of these lands, as a jointure, on such second wife; the court will set aside the first settlement as fraudulent against the jointress, who is a purchaser for a valuable consideration. 1 *Chan. Ca.* 100. See *Show.* 350.

Resulting trust for her.

9. If a feme joins with her husband in a fine and mortgage of her jointure lands, there results a trust for her when the mortgage is paid, to have the lands. 2 *Chan. Ca.* 161. So she may redeem, and if she pays more than a third of the principal, her executor may hold till reimbursed.

10. So if a jointure is made of lands in mortgage, she may redeem, and her executor shall hold over till repaid with interest. 2 *Vent.* 343.

Construction for her.

11. *A.* being seised in fee, by indenture, in consideration of marriage of his son, covenanted to levy a fine to certain uses, but none was levied; after he made his will, reciting this deed in his will, and deviseth and confirmeth all estates given and granted to his son in marriage according to the said deed. Resolved, The will had reference to the deed, and passed the lands and estates as were intended to be conveyed by the deed and fine, &c. *Show.* 350. *Salk.* tit. *Devise.* Vide *Cro. Eliz.* 68. *Cro. Jac.* 148.

12. See 2 *Chan. Ca.* 98. *Prec. Chan.* 65, 97, 369. *Nels.* 388.

13. See also rules, *Law regards the intent of the parties*, &c. *Equity to execute the intent*, &c. *Heir favoured.*

215. *Ipsae etenim leges cupiunt ut jure regantur.*

1. Forasmuch as the chancery bridleth the rigour of the common law, by giving actions and exceptions for remedies where by law none were, according to equity and conscience, to maintain *aequum et bonum*, the common people term the chancery the court of conscience, yet herein conscience is so regarded, that law be not neglected; for they must join hands in the moderation of extremity; *ipsae etenim leges cupiunt ut jure regantur, id est, ut levi, facili ac benigna interpretatione temperentur, vereque dicitur nullus recedat a cancellariâ sine remedio.* 4 H. 7. 4. 2 West's Prec. 176. b.

2. See *Co. Lit.* 166. *b.* 167. *a. b. Hob.* 107.

3. See also rule, *Cujus est divisio alterius est electio*, case 1.

216. *It*

216. *It is the office of temporal judges to advance laws made for religion, according to their end, though the words be ſhort and imperfect.*

General.

1. THE king's temporal courts have power derived from the crown, to ſuſpend the proceedings of the eccleſiaſtical courts by prohibition, premunire, *&c.* if cauſe. *Ha. Anal.* 20.

2. And they muſt always have an eye that the eccleſiaſtical juriſdiction uſurp not upon the temporal. 2 *Inſt.* 615.

3. And the temporal judges are not bound by the rules of the civil law, but are at liberty to follow their own rules, where the two laws differ. 1. *Pe. Will.* 12.

4. And it is their office to advance all ſuch laws as are made for religion, according to their end, though the words be ſhort and imperfect. *Hob.* 157. See *Magdalen College*'s caſe, 11 *Co.* 66. and 2 *Inſt.* 615, 616.

5. For when any thing is uſed to the diſpleaſure of God, it hurteth not only the body but the ſoul. And temporal rulers have not only the cure of the body but alſo of the ſoul, and ſhall anſwer for them if they periſh in their default. *Doct. & Stud. lib.* 1. *cap.* 32.

6. The judges and ſages of the law, for matters in law, are called *Concilium regis.* Co. Lit. 304. a. b. Hob. 163. And the lord chancellor is keeper of the king's conſcience, and controuls both courts of law and the eccleſiaſtical courts. 1 *Chan. Ca.* 203. *Gilb.* 1. 1 *Ju. Eccl.* 526.

7. If the eccleſiaſtical judges act contrary to law, may not this court (*B. R.*) oblige them to act according to, or to purſue the law? Is there any difference between granting a prohibition to ſtop them going wrong, and a *Mandamus* to guide them right? 1 *Pe. Will.* 47. The eccleſiaſtical judges are in conſcience bound to know the temporal laws. *Doct. & Stud. lib.* 1. *cap.* 20. *lib.* 2. *cap.* 25. 1 *Pe. Will.* 12.

Particular caſes.

8. If one be impriſoned by eccleſiaſtical authority, on complaint to the temporal courts, that he is impriſoned without cauſe, the temporal courts will ſend to have the body, and to be certified of the cauſe, which if the eccleſiaſtical courts do not, the temporal courts do and ought to deliver him; for where the temporal judges ſee not a juſt cauſe of the party's impriſonment by the eccleſiaſtical courts, the temporal judges (as being bound by oath) are to deliver him. 2 *Inſt.* 615, 616. 4 *Inſt.* 329.

9. Where this court (chancery) ſees reaſon to think there will be a miſapplication of the inteſtate's eſtate, and an abuſe and waſting to the prejudice of an infant by a limited adminiſtrator, who is only a truſtee for the infant, this court is to take care that the infant be not prejudiced, *&c.* 2 *Ju. Eccl.* 108. See *The whole caſe much excellent matter.*

The king bound by ſuch laws.

10. In ſeveral caſes the king is bound by acts of parliament, though not named in them nor bound by expreſs words; as in all ſtatutes made to ſuppreſs wrong, to take away fraud, or to prevent the decay of religion; for religion, juſtice and truth are the ſupporters of the crowns and diadems of kings. And therefore it was agreed 35 *H.* 6. 60. that the king ſhall be bound by the ſtatute *W.* 2. *cap.* 5. which was provided againſt tortious uſurpations, though he be not named in the ſtatute. So in lord *Berkley*'s caſe, *Plow.* it is adjudged if a gift in tail be made to the king, he may not alien to defraud him in reverſion, or his iſſue, but he is bound by the ſtatute *de donis*, and the act 1 *Eliz.* to reſtrain eccleſiaſtics from waſting their poſſeſſions, which were given to maintain the ſervice of God, ſhall bind the crown, unleſs ſpecial proviſion had been made by the ſame act to the contrary. *Et ſumma eſt ratio quae pro religione facit.* 5 Co. 14. a. b. The king being head of the commonwealth, may not be an inſtrument to defeat the proviſion of an act of parliament made *pro bono publico.* 15. b.

11. It was unanimouſly reſolved by the judges, That the act 13 *Eliz.* extended to reſtrain the maſter and fellows from conveying their poſſeſſions to the queen, tho' ſhe is not named expreſly in the ſame act; for the general letter of the act extends to her; and if ſhe ſhould be exempted, it ought to be by conſtruction of law, which cannot be for the reaſons in the ſaid act, *viz.* the queen, lords and commons, have adjudged, as appears in the preamble, long leaſes made by colleges, *&c.* are againſt reaſon; *a fortiori* eſtates in fee-ſimple, *&c.* and the law, which is the perfection of reaſon, may not expound acts of parliament againſt reaſon. 2. The law hath adjudged theſe cauſes of dilapidations, to be to the decay of all ſpiritual livings, to the decay of hoſpitality, and the utter impoveriſhing of ſucceſſors, upon all which muſt enſue fearful and dangerous conſequences, *viz.* the decay of true religion, and the ſpiritual worſhip of God, *&c.* great ignorance of religion, and decay of chriſtian profeſſion; for none will apply himſelf, or his ſons, or thoſe committed to his charge, to the ſtudy of divinity for nothing; and therefore it was unanimouſly reſolved, that the ſtatute which provides for the maintenance of religion, the advancement of ſound learning, and the relief of the poor, ſhall be extended generally according to the words, and ſhall bind the crown; and particularly this act 13 *Eliz.* which ſo provides. And out of theſe colleges, deans and chapters, *&c.* the church is as well furniſhed with grave and learned divines, for the inſtruction of the people in the true religion, as the commonwealth with learned men for better adminiſtration of juſtice, as well temporal as eccleſiaſtical, which (true religion and juſtice) are the main pillars which ſupport the crown and king; and therefore of all others the king who is *perſona mixta, medicus regni, pater patriae, et ſponſus regni,* who *per annulum* is eſpouſed to the realm at his coronation, ſhall not be exempt out of this act by conſtruction of law; as it would be againſt reaſon, cauſe dilapidations, to the decay of ſpiritual livings, of hoſpitality, and to the utter impoveriſhing of ſucceſſors; and by conſequence draw on a decay of religion and juſtice; and therefore true it is, *quod ſumma ratio eſt quae pro religione facit, and* Weſt. 1. *ult. Summa charitas eſt facere juſtitiam ſingulis, et omni tempore quando neceſſe fuerit,* which is to be underſtood, that the law will never preſume that any one

Uu will

will do any thing againſt religion or any religious duties, *&c.* ſo in the caſe at bar the law ſhall never make any conſtruction againſt the maintenance of religion, advancement of learning, and maintenance of the poor, as the *Stat.* 1 *&* 2 *Ph. & Ma. cap.* 8. made for theſe ends, ought to be favourably expounded to bind the crown, *&c.* 11 *Co.* 70. *a. b.* 71. *a. b.* The king is the fountain of juſtice and common right, he is God's vicegerent, and as ſuch can do no wrong. *Rex hoc non poteſt facere, quod non poteſt injuſte agere.* Where a neceſſary and profitable remedy is provided by any act, and for the ſuppreſſion of tort, it ſhall bind the king, as *Stat.* 13 *E.* 4. and *Stat. De donis, &c.* 11 *Co. Magdalen College*'s caſe; *vue tout le caſe.*

12. See *Hob.* 147, 157. *Jenk.* 162, 166, 233. 4 *Co.* 124. 4 *Inſt.* 329. 2 *Inſt.* 615, 616. 2 *Chan. Ca.* 18. 1 *Ro.* 452. 1 *Ju. Eccl.* 158, 160, *&c.* 327, 352, 353, 369, 429, *&c.*

217. *Judicandum eſt legibus non exemplis.*

1. *IT muſt needs be, that examples not founded in law can never be lawful; ſo this rule needs no comment; for though* communis error facit quaſi jus, *yet it is but* quaſi, *and when the miſts of error are diſſipated, the meer appearances or ſhadows of law alſo vaniſh.*

2. See *Vaugh.* 27. *Hob.*

3. See alſo rule, *Communis error facit quaſi jus.*

218. *Judges in* England *are expoſitors of the* Iriſh *laws.*

SEE rule, *Chancery not to be ouſted of its juriſdiction.*

219. *Judges have always ſuppreſſed new and ſubtile inventions in derogation of the common law.*

General.

1. THE wiſdom of the judges and ſages of the law hath always ſuppreſſed new and ſubtile inventions in derogation of the common law; and therefore the judges ſay in one book, We will not change the law which always hath been uſed; and in another, It is better that it be turned to a default, than the law ſhould be changed, or any innovation made. *Co. Lit.* 282. *b.*

Particular caſes.

2. Caſe upon the cuſtom of merchants, and declared that the defendant *per notam ſive billam ſecundum conſuetudinem* promiſed to pay ſixty guineas to the plaintiff, if the plaintiff ſhould be married within two months, and avers that he was married, *&c.* The defendant demurs. The court inclined againſt the cuſtom; this not being by way of negotiation, but a note to pay money upon a meer contingency, which by this artifice they would make equal with a bond, and not ſet forth any conſideration; and they

ſaid it is the duty of the judges to ſuppreſs new inventions. *Comb.* 227, 228. See *Gilb.* 249, *&c.*

3. See rule, *In things of election the party is to ſhew that he hath made it. Div. of time of payment.*

220. *Judicium ſemper pro veritate accipitur.*

JUdgment, *Judicium, quaſi juris dictum,* the very voice of law and right, therefore *Judicium ſemper pro veritate accipitur.* The antient words of judgment are very ſignificant, *conſideratum eſt*; becauſe the judgment is always given by the court upon due conſideration had of the record before them, *&c. Co. Lit.* 39. Some judgments are final, and ſome not. *Ibid.*

221. *Jura eccleſiaſtica ſunt limitata.*

General to the common law.

1. THE common law is the moſt antient and fundamental law of the land. And

Eccleſiaſtical laws, from whence.

2. The privileges of the church derive themſelves only from the indulgence and favour of princes, and had no foundation in the antient common law; and though the privileges of the church are confirmed by divers acts of parliament, yet that hinders not, but that there was an antient common law in which they, *the ſpiritual or eccleſiaſtical laws,* had no bottom; ſo that the law of holy church had bounds ſet to it. *Hard.* 63. *And theſe pompous, bigg, ſwelling names, are little, if any thing more, than mere empty ſounds, conjured up by thoſe who have made it their intereſt, to awe the ignorant, and wanton in the fruits of falſhood and deceit.*

3. Theſe laws and courts derive their exiſtence from the favour of princes, and acceptance of countries, for the gracing of eccleſiaſtical perſons ſet over the church, by and under ſuch princes, *and temporal governors*; and in ſuch countries where they were ſo allowed; and particularly in theſe kingdoms, they owe their juriſdiction to the favour and condeſcenſion of our ſovereigns and the reception of the people, and not to any inherent authority in the church, or prelates or other ſubordinate governors thereof. 1 *Ju. Eccl.* 168, 169. *Jura eccleſiaſtica ſunt limitata,* 169. The eccleſiaſtical juriſdiction is limited to certain ſpiritual and particular caſes. And the courts in which theſe cauſes are heard, are called *Fora eccleſiaſtica.* Co. Lit. 96. a. *And as this juriſdiction flows from this beginning, the pretence of its being of divine original, can only grow from one of theſe two cauſes, namely, either groſs and willful ignorance, or ſet purpoſe to deceive.*

How

How restrained.

Particular means.

By prohibition.

4. A prohibition lies to the ecclesiastical court, for denying a copy of the libel; for *jura ecclesiastica sunt limitata*, and the party, *in common honesty*, ought to know whether the matter be within their jurisdiction, and how he is to answer? 1 *Ro.* 337. So it is where these courts take undue means to enforce their sentences. *Ro. Abr.* 302. So where they pay not a due regard to the king's pardon. See 1 *Ju. Eccl.* 342 *to* 349, inclusive. So where they act oppressively. 1 *Ju. Eccl.* 349 *to* 351, inclusive. So where they either cannot administer right, want jurisdiction, or exceed their jurisdiction. 1 *Ju. Eccl.* 351 *to* 359. For other particular cases, when and where these courts are restrainable by the temporal courts, and where they may be, and how punished, &c. see 1 *Ju. Eccl.* 425, *to the end, and the second Volume throughout.* And as for the particular method of proceeding in the prohibition, see 1 *Ju. Eccl.* 363 *to* 392, inclusive.

By praemunire.

5. For what this offence is, the heinousness of it, from what cause it first grew, and by what laws, and how punishable, and the method of proceeding in it, see 1 *Ju. Eccl.* tit. *The pope an usurper*; *The course of ecclesiastical usurpation*; *The oppositions the same have met with*, and *Praemunire* throughout.

6. *And as these courts are thus to be restrained or injoined in many cases, so it may not be improper to add here, that they also may be commanded and inforced to their duty, in cases where they refuse to do justice to their suitors*; *and that, by* Mandamus *from the king's temporal courts.* See 2 *Inst.* 615, 616. 4 *Inst.* 329. 1 *Pe. Will.* 47. *Gilb.* 208. *Skin.* 101, 176. 1 *Vent.* 5. *Fitzh. Nat. Brev.* 44. (*H.*) 5 *Co. De Ju. Regis Eccl.* 23. *b.* 14 *H.* 4. 14. 2 *Inst.* 623. 3 *Ass. pl.* 19. 1 *Sid.* 403. *Doct. & Stud. lib.* 2. *cap.* 32. *Salk.* 553, 468. 3 *Mod.* 335. 1 *Ju. Eccl.* 351, *cap.* 4. 430. *ca.* 2, 3, 4. 431. *ca.* 4, 5. 2 *Ju. Eccl.* 96, &c. 98, &c. 72, *Justice* and *Jones*'s case, 278. *The King* and *Wheeler*'s case, 196. *The King* and *Walker*'s case, 288. *Speak* and *Born*'s case, 304. *Pritchard*'s case, also the next case, 305. *Comberbach*'s case, 323. *The King* and *The Bishop of Litchfield and Coventry.*

222. *Jura naturae sunt immutabilia.*

What and how to be considered.

1. THE law of nature may be considered in two manners. 1st, General. 2dly, Special. 1st, General, when referred to all creatures, reasonable and unreasonable; for unreasonable creatures live under a rule given them by nature, necessary to them. 2dly, When specially considered, which is also the law of reason, it belongs only to reasonable beings,

ings, namely, Man created to the image of God; and this law is binding on all, and is always good and righteous, ftirring and inclining a man to good, and abhorring evil, and is written in the heart what is to be done and what avoided; and this is unchangeable; and therefore againft this law, prefcription, ftatute nor cuftom may not prevail; and if any are brought againft it, they are void. *Doct. & Stud. lib.* 1. *cap.* 2.

Particular cafes.

2. By the law, regularly femes covert, infants, ideots and lunatics, cannot grant *in pais*; yet if any of them levy a fine, as in *Mary Portington's* cafe, 10 *Co.* 42. it binds them alfo for the ufes thereupon declared by the deed, as being a part of the operation of the fine. But note the reafon, fays lord *Hobart*, which is not becaufe the law binds fuch perfons; for therein *jura naturae funt immutabilia* ftill; but clean contrary, becaufe the law finds them perfons not difabled, nor admits the averment of fuch difablement; becaufe it is certified by invincible and indifputable credit of the judge, that they were perfect and able perfons; and fo here is a law of policy, that doth not cancel the law of nature, but only bounds it in point of form and circumftance, it being better to admit a mifchief in particular, even againft the law of nature, than an inconvenience in general; and it is not the law of nature to admit any improbable furmife againft authentic record or evidence. *Hob.* 224.

3. A benefice with cure could never have been appropriated to women, in truth, though the pope *de facto* made many; for a woman cannot be a paftor by the law of God. 1 *Cor.* xiv. 34. 1 *Tim.* ii. 11, 12. *Dyer* in *Grendon's* cafe fays well that it was abominable, and I (lord *Hobart*) fay more, that it was againft the law of the realm; for *beneficium non datur nifi propter officium*; and thefe are not capable; and the bufinefs is to make the patron and his fucceffors perpetual parfons, which here fhould be a priorefs and her fucceffors, which fails; for *jura naturae funt immutabilia.* Hob. 148.

4. Where the fault of a *commendam* is in its conftitution, as in the principal cafe, and fo not warranted by the laws of *commendams*, but is againft the very nature of them, it makes it none at all; and fo it can bear no execution; for *jura naturae funt immutabilia*; and if you change its effential form it may be fome other thing, but it is not now the fame that it was; *omnis forma, per quam quaeque res in propriâ fpecie conftituitur, perfectio quaedam eft: perfectum eft cui nihil deeft fecundum fuae perfectionis vel naturae modum*; and to fhew that a good execution will not profit where the conftitution is defective, fee *Mildmay's* cafe, *Coke lib.* 1. 175. and lord *Paget's* cafe, 1 *Co.* 154. *Vernon's* cafe, *lib.* 4, 2. fo *Trin.* 12 *Ja. Rot.* 3264. *Hob.* 151.

223. *Jurare in propria causa est saepenumero, hoc seculo, praecipitium diaboli ad destruendas miserorum animas ad infernum.*

General.

1. A Party interested may not be a witness. *Co. Lit.* 6. *b.* 7. *a.*

Particular cases.

2. In an information upon the statute of *Usury*, the party to the usurious contract shall not be admitted a witness against the usury; for, in effect, he should be *testis in propriâ causâ*, and should avoid his own bond, *&c.* and assurance, and discharge himself; and though he commonly raises up an informer to exhibit the information, yet, *in rei veritate*, he is the party, *&c.* *Co. Lit.* 6. *b.*

3. A wife cannot be produced either for or against her husband, *quia sunt duae animae in una carne.* Co. Lit. 6. b.

4. See rule, *None may be judge in his own cause.*

224. *Jus accrescendi inter mercatores locum non habet.*

1. WHERE there are two joint-merchants, the wares, merchandizes, debts or duties that they have as such, shall not survive, but go to the executors of the deceased; and this *per legem mercatoriam*, which is part of the law of the realm, for the advancement and continuance of commerce and trade, which is *pro bono publico*; for the rule is, that *jus accrescendi inter mercatores pro beneficio commercii locum non habet.* Co. Lit. 182. a.

2. See *Comb.* 474.

3. See also rule, *Jointenancy odious.*

225. *Justice to be preferred to charity.*

General.

1. *SUmma charitas est facere justitiam, &c.* 11 Co. 70. b.

2. Justice is preferable to charity. 1 *Chan. Ca.* 137.

Particular cases.

3. And therefore debts are to be paid before legacies. 1 *Chan. Ca.* 137.

4. A copyholder surrenders to the use of a grammar school, the lord is compellable to admit the tenant, because it is not prejudicial to him, as he has but one tenant, after whose death, his fine is due as it was before, and the use of the land is only to the corporation; *aliter*, had the surrender been to the corporation; for then the lord would have been hurt in his services; the same if the custom of the manor be to devise to one only, and to have an heriot after his death, the tenant may not surrender to two, though to a charitable use, because the lord is delayed of his heriot. *Du. Ch. Uses* 140, 142.

5. The plaintiff's bill was to have ſatisfaction of a debt owing to him from *Anthony Dean* deceaſed, who by his will had deviſed all his lands to the defendant *P.* and to the heirs of his body; with remainder over to others: and in another part of his will, reciting that he owed the plaintiff *P.* money on account, he therefore deviſed to him all his perſonal eſtate, and made him executor, willing him to pay his debts. Upon reading of the will, though the clauſe for payment of debts ſeemed to relate to the perſonal eſtate only, and though the lands were deviſed to the defendant in tail with remainders over, and it was objected that the tenant in tail could not be a truſtee; yet the court decreed both real and perſonal eſtate to be ſold for payment of the teſtator's debts. 1 *Vern.* 411. Note; *This decree was affirmed in parliament on appeal.*

6. Vide 1 *Chan. Ca.* 135, *&c.* 1 *Vern.* 260. 2 *Ju. Eccl.*

226. *King can do no wrong.*

1. IF lands before the ſtatute *De donis* had been given to the king, and to the heirs of his body, he could not before iſſue had have aliened in fee, but only to have barred his iſſue, as a common perſon might, and not to have barred the reverſion, for that ſhould have been a wrong, in caſe of a ſubject, and the king's prerogative cannot alter his caſe, nor make his eſtate greater than the donor gave him; and it is a maxim in law, that the king can do no wrong. *Co. Lit.* 19. *b.*

2. The reaſon why the king ſhall not be exempt by the conſtruction of law out of the general words of acts made for religion and charity, and to ſuppreſs wrong, is, becauſe he is the fountain of all juſtice and common right; and being the lieutenant of God, he can do no wrong. *Solum rex hoc non poteſt facere, quod non poteſt injuſte agere*; and with this agrees *Alton Wood*'s caſe, 1 *Co.* 44, *&c.* Lord *Berkley*'s caſe, in *Plow. &c.* 11 *Co. Magdalen College*'s caſe, 5 *Co.* 14. *a. b.* *Anne Needler* and *The Biſhop of Wincheſter*'s caſe, in *Hob.* 220.

3. See rule, *It is the office of temporal judges to advance laws made for religion*, &c.

Rex eſt { *Perſona mixta cum ſacerdote.*
Monarcha, &c.

Rex { *Non poteſt fallere nec falli,*
quod injuſtum facere non poteſt.

227. *King can neither grant, take or command, but by matter of record.*

1. THE king's excellency is ſo high in the law, that no freehold may be given to him, or derived from him, but by matter of record. *Doct. & Stud. lib.* 1. *cap.* 8.

2. The king's grants are not good but by letters patent and ſpecial words of grant; and nothing of inheritances paſſeth from him without the word *Heirs*; and if he be deceived, his grant is void. But of titles by writ to parlia-

parliament *aliter*; see case * *The Duke of Athol* and *The Earl of Derby*, before the house of lords 1737.

3 Vide 1 *Vern*. 277.

228. *King, head of the law, and fountain of justice.*

1. THE king is *stabilimentum justitiae*. Hob. 154.

2. The king is the fountain of justice and common right, and God's vicegerent, and, as such, can do no wrong, as in *Alton Wood*'s case, *supra*. Stat. *de donis*, Stat. *de Monasteriis, Collegiis, &c.* and *Anne Needler*'s case in *Hob. &c.* see also *Plow. Com. Grendon*'s case.

3. *Vide* rules, *King may not be supposed ignorant of law. Dispensatio est mali prohibiti, &c.* ca. 45.

229. *King is always of full age.*

1. SEE *Stat.* 7 *E.* 6. *cap.* 3.

2. See rule, *Rex est monarcha & imperator in regno suo.*

230. *King may not be supposed ignorant of the law.*

THE king may not be taken to be ignorant of the law; because he is head of the law: and therefore when he, in the particular case, granted the advowson to the dean and chapter, and the grant is *ex certa scientia, &c.* (though the dean and chapter had no licence to purchase in *Mortmain*) yet it is to be understood, the king would have them to have it, notwithstanding the statute of *Mortmain*; and therefore by the words, *ex certa scientia*, it is to be presumed he took cognizance; and so the grant itself countervails a grant, and clause of *non obstante, &c.* Plow. 502. a. b. And yet my lord *Coke*, with great bravery and a true spirit of liberty, told king *James*, on *Bancroft*'s idle complaint against prohibitions, *&c.* that his majesty could not in his own person adjudge in any case, either criminal, or betwixt party and party, concerning inheritance, chattels or goods, *&c.* but that the same ought to be determined in some court of justice, according to the laws and customs of the realm; and that it is the court that gives the judgment; and that though the king sat in parliament with his lords, and was supreme judge over all, yet the reversals, *&c.* there were by the king, *with the assent of the lords*; and so though his majesty might sit in the star-chamber also, yet this was to consult with the justices upon such questions as should be proposed to them, and not *in judicio*; and that tho' his majesty might also sit in his bench, yet it's the court that gives the judgment, that being always *per curiam*; and that the judges are sworn to execute justice according to law; and therefore his majesty could not take any cause out of any of his courts, and pronounce judgment himself upon it; and that no king since the conquest had assumed these matters to himself, but that they were solely determined by the courts of justice. And further, that though God had endowed his majesty with excellent science, and great endowments of nature, yet his majesty was not learned in the laws of his realm of *England*; and causes which concerned the lives, inheritances, goods or fortunes of his subjects, were not to be decided by natural reason, but by the artificial reaſon and judgment of the law, which required great ſtudy and experience to attain, and was the meaſure of the ſubjects right, and the protection of his majeſty in ſafety and peace; and that though his majeſty *non debet eſſe ſub homine*, yet he was *ſub deo et lege*. And my lord *Hobart* ſaith, that the ſame reaſon that ſupplies the king's ignorance of matters in fact, will alſo excuſe his want of knowledge even of the laws in the ſubtilties of it; for he ſtudies a greater art, *ſcil. arcanum regni*, the art of government, which is *ars artium*, and contains all arts, as the commonwealth includes all private ſocieties.

Tu regere imperio populos Romane memento,
Hae tibi erunt artes, paciſque imponere morem.

Hob. 224.

231. *King not bound by acts of parliament, unleſs expreſly named.*

SEE rule, *Rex eſt mixta perſona cum ſacerdote.*

232. *King, the power of him and his court is not to be diſputed.*

SEE rule, *Admiralty not to hold plea of matters cognizable at law, throughout, and particularly* Bourn's *caſe.*

233. *Lands are holden mediately or immediately of the crown.*

1. ALL lands and tenements in *England*, in the hands of ſubjects, are holden mediately or immediately of the king; for in the law of *England*, we have not properly *allodium*, that is, any ſubjects lands that are not holden; unleſs you will take *allodium* for *ex ſolido*, as it is often taken in domes-day book; and tenants in fee are there called *alodarii* or *aloarii*, and he is called a tenant, becauſe he holdeth of ſome ſuperior lord, by ſome ſervice; therefore the king, in this ſenſe, cannot be ſaid to be a tenant, becauſe he hath no ſuperior but God Almighty; the poſſeſſions of the king are called *ſacra patrimonia*, and *dominica coronae regis*; but though a ſubject hath not properly *directum*, yet he hath *utile dominium*. Co. Lit. 1. a. b.

2. All advowſons are held mediately or immediately of the crown, and therefore it is that regularly the king muſt aſſent to every appropriation; for he might be hurt by this marriage, *as the books call it*; for if the advowſon is held of him immediately, then he hath a poſſibility to have ſome advantage of the tenure, by wardſhip, relief or the like, which is taken away by this conjunction; for it is never to be expected the patronage ſhould return to lay-hands, *&c.* and if it be held immediately of a ſubject, yet it is held medi-

ately of the crown; for all the lands in the realm are held immediately or mediately of the crown; and neceſſarily the lands wherein the church, *&c.* ſtands, were held of the crown, and the patronage by poſſibility might eſcheat, or otherwiſe might come to the crown; and if not, yet the crown might have benefit by the lapſe, *et nullum tempus occurrit regi*, and every advantage which the king might otherwiſe have had is loſt by the appropriation. *Plow. Com.* 498. *a.* 499. *a.* 500. *a.*

3. Concerning the tenure of lands it is to be underſtood, that all lands are holden of the crown, either mediately or immediately, and that the eſcheat appertaineth to the immediate lord and not to the mediate; and the reaſon why all lands are holden of the crown, either immediately or by meſne lords, is this, that the conqueror having gotten all the lands of the realm into his own hands in demeſn, taking from every man all eſtate, tenure, property, and liberty of the ſame, except religious and church lands, and the lands in *Kent.* As he gave the ſame again out of his own hands, he ſtill reſerved rents, knights and other ſervices, and retributions to him and to his heirs; and this reſervation is that which is called the tenure of lands, in which reſervation he had four inſtitutions exceeding politic, and ſuitable to the ſtate of a conqueror. 1. Marriage. 2. Knight-ſervice. 3. Homage and fealty. 4. *Primer ſeiſin*, to paſs other tenures neceſſary to his eſtate. *Bac. Uſe of the Law* 30, *&c.*

234. *Lands may lineally deſcend, but not aſcend.*

1. ONLY lineal aſcenſion in the right line is prohibited and not collateral. *Co. Lit.* 11. *a.*

2. In prohibiting the lineal aſcent, the common law is aſſiſted with the law of the twelve tables. *Numb. cap.* 27. See *Brit. cap.* 119. *Fleta, lib.* 6. *cap.* 1.

3. See rules, *Pater et mater et puer ſunt una caro, and the references there. Inheritances may lineally deſcend, but not aſcend.*

235. *Lands ſhall not be inalienable.*

SEE 1 *Pe. Will.* 106.

236. *Law and equity both ſhall prevail againſt equity only.*

General.

1. IT is generally true, that the law and equity together ſhall prevail againſt equity only; but then it is with this diſtinction, that the equity that goes along with the law, is of the ſame nature and as ſtrong as the other equity. *Gilb.* 15.

Particular caſes.

2. A judgment creditor brought a bill againſt a prior conuſee of a ſtatute, who had extended the lands to diſcover what was due on the ſtatute, and on payment to have it ſet aſide. The defendant pleaded that after he had extended the land, he came to an account with the cognizor, who, in

2 con-

consideration of what was due to the plaintiff, made an absolute conveyance of part of the land, and that he was a purchaser without notice, for a valuable consideration. Plea allowed. 1 *Chan. Ca.* 36.

3. So where a like bill was by a judgment creditor, to discover lands subject, *&c.* not knowing the place, nor who tenant, *&c.* 2 *Chan. Ca.* 47.

4. So of a bill to discover bankrupt's estate; defendant may plead being purchaser *sans* notice. 2 *Chan. Ca.* 135, 136. 1 *Vern.* 27. *S. C.* For the rule is, that a purchaser for valuable consideration shall not be bound to discover to his own hurt. 2 *Chan. Ca.* 73. see 1 *Chan. Ca.* 36. Where a purchaser is not bound to take notice of the other's title or demand, though by matter of record, though he is of a decree bound to take notice. 2 *Chan. Ca.* 48. And the notice must be plainly denied. 1 *Chan. Ca.* 34, 161, 156, 252.

5. If the purchaser buys in an eign incumbrance without notice of the mesne, he shall protect his purchase, with the eign incumbrance bought in. 1 *Vern.* 49. *Salk.* 155, 120, 129, 34, 371. 1 *Chan. Ca.* 36. Though he bought in the eign after he had notice. 2 *Vent.* 339. 3 *Chan. Ca.* 132. 1 *Vern.* 52. 2 *Chan. Ca.* 208. Notice before conveyance executed, good. 1 *Chan. Ca.* 31. *Gilb.* 91. Notice to one who purchaseth for another, good. 1 *Chan. Ca.* 38. *Nelf.* 367, 378. Exception on recital, good notice. 1 *Chan. Ca.* 291. Notice to counsel, is notice to the client. 3 *Chan. Ca.* 110. *Gilb.* 8. But though there be a trust in the title, yet if the purchaser purchased *sans* advice of counsel, and knew not of it, he shall be relieved. 3 *Chan. Ca.* 110, 123. But if the counsel did not go through the business, such notice is not good. *Gilb.* 8. Presumed notice, as matters of record. 1 *Chan. Ca.* 37, 144, 231. Payment of rent by tenant, subsequent to the agreement between the lord and dowress, implies notice to the tenant. 1 *Chan. Ca.* 247. The heir is presumed from counter-parts to have notice. 1 *Chan. Ca.* 260. A jointress is presumed to have notice, having covenants against leases, *&c.* 1 *Chan. Ca.* 260. One need not take notice of such, if not party. 1 *Chan. Ca.* 167. See *Barn.* 82, 221, 236, 359, 367.

6. A voluntary conveyance shall be binding against the party and his heirs; because a volunteer has equal equity with either of them; and having the law shall prevail; but where there is only an agreement, or covenant for such voluntary conveyance, it shall not be executed against the heir who has equal equity with a volunteer. *Max. Eq.* 53. *margin.* See 1 *Vern.* 17, 191, 218. 1 *Chan. Ca.* 243.

7. A purchaser came into a man's study and took and put in his pocket a statute, which would have fallen upon his estate; though he thus unfairly gained the advantage, yet the court would not take it from him. 1 *Vern.* 52.

8. The plaintiff claimed under an old intail, and complained that the defendant had gotten and concealed the settlement and evidences, and prayed a discovery, and to have them delivered up. The defendant pleaded that for 6870*l.* really paid, he was a purchaser, and demanded if he should be bound to discover further, *&c.* Plea allowed. 1 *Chan. Ca.* 68.

9. If an executor or trustee compound debts or mortgages, and buy them in for less than is due upon them, he shall not take the benefit of it himself, but other creditors and legatees shall have the benefit; and for want of

of them the advantage ſhall go to the party intitled to the ſurplus; but if one act for himſelf, and being not in the circumſtances of a truſtee or executor buy in a mortgage for leſs than is due, or for leſs than it is worth, he ſhall be allowed all that is due upon the mortgage; for he ſtands in the place of him who aſſigned, *viz.* the mortgagee, who might have given it to him *gratis*; and what is due muſt be the meaſure of the court's allowance, and not what he gave; for that might have been more than it is worth, as well as leſs; and ſince he runs the hazard, if loſs happeneth, he ought to have the benefit in caſe it turn to advantage. *Salk.* 155.

10. See *Gilb.* 13, 14, 15. *Prec. Chan.* 89, 158, 407, 419, 494, 511. 1 *Chan. Ca.* 97. 2 *Vern.* 691, 698. *Gilb.* 151. 1 *Rep. Chan.* 69, 171. 3 *Rep. Chan.* 62. 1 *Chan. Ca.* 162. 2 *Rep. Chan.* 142. 1 *Chan. Ca.* 201, 119. 2 *Vent.* 338, 343, 377. 1 *Chan. Ca.* 162. *S. C.* 1 *Vern.* 47, 49, 107. 1 *Chan. Ca.* 168. 2 *Chan. Ca.* 98. 1 *Vern.* 41. *S. C.* *Hard.* 318. 1 *Chan. Ca.* 243. 2 *Chan. Ca.* 4. 1 *Vern.* 480. 2 *Chan. Ca.* 133. 1 *Rep. Chan.* 173. 1 *Chan. Ca.* 156. 1 *Vern.* 100, 464, 365. 2 *Rep. Chan.* 265. *Salk.* 416. 1 *Chan. Ca.* 100. 1 *Vern.* 440. 1 *Chan. Ca.* 170, 103. 1 *Rep. Chan.* 275. *S. C.* 1 *Chan. Ca.* 22. 1 *Vern.* 69, 196, 293.

237. *Law driveth no man to ſhew what by intendment he doth not know.*

1. ONE pleaded he was choſen knight of the ſhire by a majority, and good without ſhewing the certain number; for the election might be by voice or hands or otherwiſe; ſo that the number could not be eaſily known. *Fi. Ley* 12. *b.* 13. *a.*

2. One is bound in a bond to ſerve *J. S. in omnibus mandatis ejus licitis*: it is a good plea to ſay he ſerved him lawfully, without ſhewing in what ſervice, or on what commandment; for no ſervant can remember all his ſervices. 10 *H.* 4. 15.

3. One may aver covin generally, without ſhewing in what manner; for covin is a ſecret thing contrived privately between two or three, to the prejudice of another. 4 *E.* 6. 46.

4. See 4 *Co.* *Lutterel*'s caſe, 7 *H.* 4. 8.

238. *Law favours juſtice and truth, but abhors falſhood, variance, contrariety, folly, negligence, delay, unneceſſary circumſtances, circuity of actions and matters of vexation, infiniteneſs and uncertainty.*

Favours juſtice and truth.

1. *EXecutio juris non habet injuriam*, the law is good, the abuſe thereof is the fault. *Hob.* 266.

2. Statutes to ſuppreſs tort, or toll fraud, bind the king, though not named; for juſtice and truth are the ſupporters of his diadem. 5 *Co.* 14.

3. The

3. The king may not determine the office of a ſheriff or any part of it, without making a new ſheriff for the execution and adminiſtration of juſtice. 4 *Co.* 33.

4. Entries of feigned actions in *London*, were utterly condemned by the whole court; for that by colour of law and juſtice, they by ſuch means acted againſt both, and made law and juſtice the author and cauſe of tort and injuſtice. 4 *Co. Counteſs of* Rutland's *caſe*.

5. If one grants a rent-charge to another out of his lands, the grantee hath two remedies, by way of diſtreſs, or writ of annuity; for the grantor having granted it, he hath charged his perſon; and having granted it out of his lands, he hath charged his lands alſo; and having thus granted two remedies, it muſt be in the election of the grantee, who is to have the advantage of theſe remedies, which he will have. *Gilb.* 250.

Abhors falſhood.

6. If a man brings debt for two payments at two days, whereof one is not yet come, and that appears of the plaintiff's own ſhewing, he thereby abated his own writ. 9 *H.* 7. 3.

7. Upon a reverſion granted to two men, or of two acres, or for forty years, or for life; with remainder over, and the tenant attorn to one, or for one acre, or for part of a year, or to the grantee for life only, yet ſuch attornment is good for all; but if the tenant had notice of the true grant, then the attornment is void for all; for that the law abhors falſhood. 2 *Co.* 68.

8. See rule, *Conſtructio legis non facit injuriam.*

Variance.

9. If the writ vary from the bond, or other ſpecialty, in name, ſurname, or the like, in debt or annuity; or the count vary from the writ, as in debt for 20*l.* and declare only for 10*l.* both ſhall abate. 11 *E.* 4. 2. 8 *E.* 4. 2.

10. See 4 *Aſſ. pl.* 2. 7 *H.* 6. 22. 32 *H.* 6. 3. *Fi. Law Engliſh* 50, *&c.*

Contrariety.

11. A bond is made *ſolvendum nunquam*, this *ſolvendum* is void, and the bond inſtantly due. 21 *E.* 3. 46.

12. A leaſe of a manor, except the ſervices, the exception is void; for it is parcel of the thing demiſed. *Dy.* 97.

13. See 4 *E.* 4. 29. 21 *H.* 7. 11. *b.* 2 & 3 *Ph. & Ma.* 153.

Folly.

14. Waſte did not lie at common law againſt leſſee for life or years, becauſe it was the leſſor's folly to make ſuch a leaſe and not reſtrain his leſſee by covenant, condition or otherwiſe, that he ſhould not do waſte. 5 *Co.* 13. *b.* 4 *Co.* 16. *b.*

15. Baron and feme, in right of the wife, have title and right to enter into tenements which another hath in fee or in tail, and ſuch tenant dieth ſeiſed, in ſuch caſe, after the death of the huſband, the wife may enter upon the iſſue in by deſcent; for that the deſcent is avoided during the coverture;

verture; but where ſuch title is given to a feme ſole, and ſhe takes huſband, who ſuffers a deſcent, ſhe may not enter, for it was her folly to take ſuch an huſband, as would not enter in time, *&c.* *Lit.* 95.

16. See 4 *Co.* 62. *b.*

Negligence.

17. A recovery in a writ of right bars all, though their right be never ſo good, who put not in their claim in a year and a day; for *vigilantibus et non dormientibus jura ſubveniunt.* 5 E. 3. 222. See *Hob.* 347. *Where this rule goes not to the king.*

Delay.

18. He who pleadeth a record in delay (as to prove the plaintiff excommunicated) muſt have it ready to ſhew; otherwiſe it is if he plead it in bar. 3 *H.* 6. 15. *b.*

19. In dilatory pleas both defendants ought to join. 12 *H.* 7. 3.

20. A plea in bar which goes in delay, muſt be good to every common intent. 8 *H.* 7. 9.

Unneceſſary circumſtances.

21. One who is in court ready to join the defendant, may do it *ſans* proceſs, as vouchee, the plaintiff's leſſor being prayed in aid, when the defendant in replevin avoweth upon him, or the meſne when the lord *Paramount* avoweth againſt him, but joinder in aid cannot be by attorney *ſans* proceſs. 2 *H.* 6. 1. *b.*

22. Covenant is with the leſſee to make a new leaſe on ſurrender of the preſent one, and after the leſſor makes a leaſe for a further term to a ſtranger, here the covenant is broken, though the leſſee hath not ſurrendered, which according to the words was to be firſt done, for that it would be to no purpoſe as the other hath diſabled himſelf, either to take the ſurrender or make a new leaſe. 5 *Co.* 21.

23. Vide 4 *E.* 3. 170. 1 *H.* 6. 4. *b.*

24. See alſo rule, *Conditions precedent muſt be literally performed, not ſo of ſubſequent conditions, where the court can make compenſation.*

Circuity of actions.

25. See rules, *Equity to prevent multiplicity of ſuits. Boni judicis eſt lites dirimere, &c.*

26. See alſo *Manſel's* caſe, 6 *Co.* 31. 22 *H.* 6. 46. *Salk.* 550. 2 *Inſt.* 491. 1 *Vent.* 3, 120, 265. *Lit. lib.* 2. *cap. Frankalmoigne* 30. *b.* 27 *H.* 8. 27. *a.* 5 *Co.* 72, 73. *Sid.* 34, 35. *Cro. Jac.* 368. 2 *Ro.* 108. *Mo.* 842. 5 *Co.* 17, 18. *Co. Lit.* 385. *a.*

Infiniteneſs.

27. An act explanatory (as 32 *H.* 8. *cap.* 36. which explains 4 *H.* 7. *cap.* 24. of fines) ſhall not be conſtrued againſt the letter; for at that rate there would want a new act to make an explanation of ſuch expoſition, and ſo *in infinitum.* 3 *Co.* 31, *and* 87.

 Uncertainty

Uncertainty.

28. Uncertainty is the mother of contention and confuſion. *Co. Lit.* 9. *a.* *Vue le liver.*

29. See alſo the rule, *Id certum eſt quod, &c.*

239. *Law favoureth life, liberty and dower.*

General.

1. IN *favorem libertatis*, it is commonly ſaid, that three things are favoured in law, life, liberty and dower. *Co. Lit.* 124. *b.*

Life.

2. *Vide* rules, *Actus non facit reum niſi mens ſit rea. Equity regards ſubſtance not ceremony.*

Liberty.

3. *Impius et crudelis judicandus eſt, qui libertati non favet. Angliae jura in omni caſu libertati dant favorem.* Fort. cap. 42. Vide poſt. *Liberty the greateſt jewel.*

Dower.

4. Vide ante, *Dower favoured.*

240. *Law favours the public quiet.*

1. SO common recoveries are favoured, as they are become common aſſurances. 3 *Co.* 3, 6. 2 *Co.* 74.

2. Whether a recovery be a bar to an eſtate tail, or not, may not be diſputed; becauſe a great part of the inheritances of the realm depend upon it. *Manſel's* caſe, ſee 1 *Co.* 154, 175. *Et jura naturae ſunt immutabilia.*

241. *Law is the perfection of reaſon.*

1. AS lord *Coke* couragiouſly and wiſely anſwered to king *James* the firſt, cauſes which concerned the life, inheritance, goods and fortunes of his ſubjects, are not decided by natural reaſon, but by the artificial reaſon and judgment of law, which requires long ſtudy and experience before a man can obtain the cognizance of it, and that the law was the golden mete-wand and meaſure to try the cauſe of the ſubjects, and which protected his majeſty in ſafety and peace, &c. ſee 12 *Co.* 59, 60. *This his lordſhip ſaid, as hath been before obſerved, amongſt much more excellent matter well worth reading and obſerving, in anſwer to* Bancroft's *groundleſs complaint,* Michaelmas 5 Ja. *on* Sunday, 10 November. See *The Introduction to Ju. Eccl. fo.* 44 *to the end.*

2. *Inter cuncta leges, et percunctabere doctos.* Co. Lit. 232. b.

3. Law is the inheritance of the people; kings govern by it, and cannot govern without it. *Kitch.* 2. *b.* 4. *a.*

4. The

4. The law is the perfection of reafon, and fo cannot fuffer any thing that is inconvenient, but rather a mifchief. *Co. Lit.* 97. *b.*

5. *Quod eft ex jure, id eft juftum; quod ab injuriâ proficitur injuftum; quid autem fit jus, et fi quo confiftat injuria legis eft definire.*

242. *Law more refpecteth a leffer eftate by right, than a larger eftate by wrong.*

1. TEnant in fee makes a leafe of lands to *B.* to have and to hold to *B.* for term of life, without mentioning for whofe life, it fhall be for the life of the leffee; for it fhall be taken moft ftrongly againft the leffor; and an eftate for one's own life is higher than for the life of another. But if tenant in tail makes fuch leafe, it fhall be taken to be for the life of the leffor; for the law more refpecteth a leffer eftate by right than a larger eftate by wrong; as if tenant for life in remainder diffeife the particular tenant for life, now he hath a fee-fimple; but if the tenant for life die, now is his wrongful eftate in fee, by judgment in law changed to rightful eftate for life. *Co. Lit.* 42. *a. b.*

2. See *Co. Lit.* 19. *a. b.*

243. *Law not to be altered.*

By act in païs.

1. IF I make my laft will and teftament irrevocable, which in its own nature is revocable; yet I may revoke it; for neither my act nor my words can alter the law, and make that irrevocable which in its nature is revocable. 8 *Co. Vinyor's* cafe.

By act of parliament.

2. Sometimes the old maxims of the law are changed by ftatute. *Doct. & Stud. lib.* 1. *cap.* 8. *So of the other common laws.*

Rule.

3. *Leges Angliae fine parliamento mutari non poffunt.* 2 Inft. 619.

244. *Law prefers the public good to a private.*

1. IF tenant in dower fow the land, and die before the corn is ripe or cut, it belongeth to her executors, and not to him in reverfion; otherwife it is of grafs and fruits. *Doct. & Stud. lib.* 1. *cap.* 20. *The common good requireth the lands fhould be fown with corn for man's fuftenance.*

2. In time of war a man may juftify making bulwarks in another man's foil without licence, or raifing a houfe, for the fafety of the neighbourhood. *Dy.* 36. *b.*

3. A fheriff may break open the doors of one's houfe to take a felon, but not to ferve a *capias* for a trefpafs; for that is a particular cafe, and not for the common weal. *Fi. Law Eng.* 39.

4. Fifhermen may juftify bringing their nets to the adjoining land to dry; for fuch fifhery is for the public good. A millftone lifted up to be

 picked,

picked, &c. cannot be diſtrained, becauſe it remains parcel of the mill, which is for the commonwealth. 14 *H.* 8. 25.

5. Things brought into an inn, or into a fair or market to be ſold, or cloths in a taylor's ſhop, or a horſe at a ſmith's to be ſhod, are not diſtrainable. 22 *E.* 4. 49. *b.*

6. See rule, *Rex eſt mixta perſona cum ſacerdote.*

245. *Law regards the intent of the parties.*

1. RESolved that every contract executory imports in it an *aſſumpſit*; for when one agrees to pay money, or to deliver any thing, he thereby aſſumes or promiſſes to pay or deliver it; and therefore when one ſells any thing to another, and agrees to deliver it at a certain day, and the other in conſideration thereof agrees to pay ſo much money at ſuch a day; in theſe caſes both parties might have debt or caſe; for the mutual executory agreement of both parties imports reciprocal actions; with which agrees *Plow. Com.* 128. And in ſome caſes it would be inconvenient if debt lay only, and not caſe; as in *Redmayne* and *Peck*'s caſe, *Dy.* 133. they agreed together, that for a certain conſideration *Redmayne* ſhould deliver to *Peck* 20 quarters of barley yearly during his life, and for not delivering them one year, adjudged the action well lay, otherwiſe it would be miſchievous to *Peck*, who ſhould be drove to his action of debt, which he himſelf could never have, but his executors or adminiſtrators; becauſe debt lieth not in theſe caſes, but after the laſt day incurred. So if a ſum of money be given in marriage to be paid at ſeveral days, caſe lies for non-payment at the firſt day; but debt not till the laſt. 4 *Co.* 94. *a. b.* See *Cro. Car.* 241.

2. But this intention of the parties muſt be governed by the rules of law; and therefore where there is *debitum in praeſenti, quamvis ſit ſolvendum in futuro*, yet becauſe the right of action is in him, the releaſe of all actions is a diſcharge of the debt itſelf, and ſo may an executor before probate releaſe, and yet he can have no action before; * and ſome ſay that the ordinary may releaſe, though he can have no action; but if a man by deed covenant to build a houſe or make an eſtate, &c. and before covenant broken, the covenantee releaſeth to him all actions, ſuits and quarrels, this doth not diſcharge the covenant itſelf, becauſe at the time of the releaſe *nil fuit debitum*, and there was no cauſe of action in being; but in that caſe a releaſe of all covenants is a good diſcharge of the covenant before it be broken. *Co. Lit.* 292. *b.*

3. *In many caſes the intention of the party is void to all intents, if it be not grounded according to law.* Doct. & Stud. lib. 2. cap. 20. *Vide antea* rule, *Condition none may take advantage of, but who is either party or privy to it.*

4. So if one man make a leaſe to another for life, and after, of his meer motion, confirm it for life, to remain after his death to another and his heirs; in this caſe, that remainder is void in law and conſcience; for by law there can no remainder depend upon an eſtate, but that the ſame eſtate beginneth at the ſame time with the remainder, and in this caſe the eſtate began before, and the confirmation enlarged not his eſtate, nor gave him any new eſtate, &c. *Doct. & Stud. lib.* 2. *cap.* 20.

* See 8 *Co.* 135. And *quaere* if the ordinary may releaſe.

5. The purpofe or intention of a man without act, is not punifhable by law. 4 *Co.* 16. *b.*

6. Lands devifed to the heirs of *J.S.* now living, it was held that the eldeft fon of *J. S.* fhould take, though in ftrictnefs of fpeech he was not heir during the life of his father; but heir apparent only, as in *Burchet* and *Durdant's* cafe, cited in *Prec. Chan.* 57. *So note the difference, where by will, which is favourably taken, and where the intention of the devifor is to be purfued, and when by deed, which is to be taken ftrictly.*

7. See the rule, *Intent without act not punifhable.*

8. See alfo 4 *Co.* 16. *Dy.* 113. *Cro. Ca.* 241. *Cro. Ja.* 505. *Co. Lit.* 214. *b.* 313. *a.* 217. *b.* 183, 301. *b.* 302. *a.* 307. *Lit. fect.* 352. *Hob.* 160.

246. *Law rejecteth all fractions or divifions in a day.*

1. ON the queftion, From what time a leafe fhall commence, from the day of the date or the delivery? Three points were refolved. 1. That it fhall be from the day of the delivery, and not of the date; for the delivery only makes it of force, and not the words *This indenture* and the like. 2. That whereas the faid indenture was delivered at four in the afternoon of 20 *June*, the leafe fhall end the 19th; *for the law in its computation rejects all divifions of a day, for the incertainty, which is the mother of wrangle.* 3. That the day of the delivery of the leafe fhall be taken inclufive, and be part of the time, where it is limited to commence from the making; but if it were *a die confectionis*, or *a die datus*, there the day of the date is excluded; where the words of the ftatute 27 *H.* 8. *cap.* 16. of inrolments are (within fix months of the date of the fame writings indented) the fix months muft be accounted from the date, if dated, and not from the delivery, but if not dated, then from the delivery. The day of the date and from the date are the fame; for, in judgment of law, the date includes all the day of the date. 5 *Co.* 1. *a. b.*

2. See *Co. Lit.* 46. *b.* 2 *Cro.* 647. 3 *Lev.* 438.

3. See rules, *All the term but one day in law. Dies dominicus non eft juridicus. Diftinguenda funt tempora. Every man's deed or covenant to be taken moft ftrongly againft himfelf.*

247. *Law requireth order and decency, and principally refpecteth the fubftance.*

General.

1. *ORDER is the ftrength and beauty of fociety.* Ratio eft anima legis.

Particular cafes.

Order.

2. An abbot, prior, or other man of religion, in doing of homage, fhall not fay, Sir I become your man, but Sir I do you homage; for he hath profeffed himfelf to be only God's man. *Lit.*

3. The tenant ought to seek the lord to do him homage if he be within *England*; for this service is personal as well of the lord's side as of the tenant's, for the law requireth order and decency; and therefore *Bracton* saith, *adire debet* (he who is to do homage) *domino suo, ubicunque inventus fuerit in regno, vel alibi, si possit commode adire, &c.* and the same law is for fealty. *Co. Lit.* 104. *b.* 105. *a.*

Decency.

4. A feme sole, when she doth homage, shall not say, I become your woman; for it would be wrong she should be any man's woman but her husband's when she shall be married. *Lit.*

5. So a woman shall not be quartered for treason, for the decency of her sex, but only drawn and hanged. *Fi. Ley* 14. *b.*

6. See *Co. Lit.* 97, 105. 8 *H.* 6. 23. *b. lib. intrat.* 47 *E.* 11.

7. See rule, *Negatio destruit negationem, &c.*

248. *Law respecteth the excellency of some persons.*

AS the king, queen, noblemen, *&c.* and giveth them singular privileges above others. *Fi. Ley* 7. *b.* see the same *Eng. fo.* 26.

249. *Law respecteth the ties of nature.*

1. AFfection for the provision of the heirs male which one may beget, brotherly love, *&c.* are good considerations to raise an use, though long acquaintance and intimacy are not. *Fi. Ley* 7. *b.*

2. A man may infeoff his son and heir pending a *praecipe quod reddat* against him, and is not in danger *de artic' super Chart. cap.* 11. for a son is bound to assist his father when he is able. 6 *E.* 3. 274. So one brother may maintain another. 32 *H.* 6. 2. *b.*

3. Brothers or cousins may not wage battle in a writ of right. *Fi. Ley* 7. *b.*

4. A statute, that all such as succour or give meat or drink, or other aid, to such an one who hath committed such or such an offence, knowing of it, shall be accessary to the offence, is not to be extended to a wife who receives or gives meat or drink to her husband, *&c. Fi. Ley* 7. *b. Plow. Com.* 465.

250. *Law respecteth time.*

In time of peace or war.

1. THE law more countenanceth things done in time of peace than in time of war. *Fi. Ley* 10. *a.*

2. Disseisin and descent *sur ceo* in time of war, will not toll an entry. *Lit.* 97.

3. Usurpation in time of war doth not put a rightful patron out of possession, *&c.* 7 *E.* 3. *Fitzh. Presentment* 2. *Fitzh. Nat. Brev.* 31.

Day

Day or night.

4. Rent payable at a day certain, he hath all the day till night to pay it; but if it be a great ſum of money, he ought to take ſo long before ſun ſet, that the money may be counted; for the other is not bound to tell it in the night. *Fi. Ley* 10. *a.*

5. A man may not diſtrain in the night for rent in arrear. 11 *H.* 7. 5. but he may for damage feaſant, for the neceſſity. 11 *H.* 7. 5.

Sunday.

6. See rule, *Dies dominicus non eſt juridicus.*

251. *Law tendereth the weakneſs and imperfection of men.*

1. A dying ſeiſed of the diſſeiſor is no deſcent to toll the entry of the diſſeiſee, being all the time within age, covert baron, in priſon, or out of the realm. *Lit.* 385, *&c.*

2. Where a leaſe is to baron and feme, the ſurvivor ſhall not be charged for waſte during the coverture. 2 *H.* 4. 3.

3. An infant tenant in tail, ſuffered a recovery by his guardian, it ſhall bind him; becauſe he may have remedy againſt his guardian by action on the caſe; *aliter* if by attorney, for that is void; becauſe he hath not any remedy over againſt him. *Godb.* 161.

252. *Law to bind all muſt be aſſented to by all.*

General.

1. THE rule 44 *E.* 3. 19. is, that no law ſhall bind the people but ſuch as is made with their conſent. *Da.* 33.

How to aſſent.

2. And conſent may be as well by deed as by word, and that which is expreſſed *facto* is ſtronger, and that which is expreſſed by many and continual acts of the ſame kind, is cuſtom, and ſo briefly cuſtom is a reaſonable act, iterated, multiplied and continued by the people *de temps d'ont memorie ne court.* Da. 33.

To the canons.

General to, and rules.

3. Canons do not bind here but as they are received and allowed, but when ſo allowed, they are as parcel of our laws, as in *Cawdrie*'s caſe, 5 *Co.* Dr. *Huſſey*'s caſe, 7 *H.* 8. *Keil. Pal.* 469.

4. No canon eccleſiaſtical can be made or executed without the royal aſſent. *Vau.* 229.

5. Eccleſiaſtical decretals of their own authority bind not here. *Doct. & Stud. lib.* 2. *cap.* 26.

6. Canons, though ordained by the king's royal licence, and after affirmed by his royal authority, bind not the laity. 12 *Co.* 72. 2 *Inst.* 94, 647. 653, 657. *Ro. Abr.* 454. *Mo.* 782. Becaufe the laity are not reprefented in convocation, and therefore their confents not given, and a man can no more be under the obligation thereof than any other law, without his confent expreffed or implied, which is not in regard to the canon law. *Salk.* 673. 20 *H.* 6. 13. *Bro. Abr. Ordinary.* 2 *Ro. Abr.* 226. 2 *Cro.* 670. 2 *Brow.* 38. *Cro. Ca.* 588. *Palm.* 379.

7. The clergy are bound by canons *in re ecclefiaftica*, becaufe they are parties. 12 *Co.* 72. But they are not bound thereby in temporal matters. 12 *Co.* 72. *Mo.* 755.

8. The canons of 1603, do not bind the laity. 2 *Ju. Eccl.* 308. *Vue le mefme liver, fo.* 332, 333, 334.

9. Canons bind only ecclefiaftical perfons, and not the laity; becaufe they are made only by the clergy in convocation, and laymen are not bound, becaufe fuch canons have not the affent of the commons and the temporal lords. *Gilb.* 160.

As to particular perfons.

1. Chancellors. See 2 *Ju. Eccl.* 272, *&c.*
2. Surrogates. *Ibid.* 275, *&c.*
3. Proctors. *Ibid.* 276, *&c.*
4. Regifters. *Ibid.* 278, *&c.*
5. Apparitors. *Ibid.* 284, *&c.*
6. Parifh Clerks. *Ibid.* 286, *&c.*
7. Sextons. *Ibid.* 304, *&c.*
8. Church-wardens, Sides-men, *&c.* *Ibid.* 305, *&c.*
9. School-mafters of the eftablifhed church.

10. The chief queftion was, Whether a fchool-mafter might be profecuted in the ecclefiaftical court, for not bringing his fcholars to church, contrary to the 79 canon, *anno* 1603? And it was the opinion of *Treby* chief juftice, and *Powel* juftice, and the court, that the fchool-mafter being a layman, was not bound by that canon. 1 *Pe. Will.* 32.

11. The lord chief juftice faid, he did not think *Rufhworth*'s being a clergyman, made the cafe any ways different from what it would have been if he had been a layman; for he could not think that the canons in 1603, made in convocation and confirmed by the crown, without being confirmed in parliament, *bound even the clergy in any matter but* in re ecclefiaftica; for if this were otherwife, as his lordfhip obferved, there would be this confequence, That if a clergyman were head of a college, he might be bound in matters relating to him in that capacity; and fo in any other temporal right. 2 *Ju. Eccl.* 329, 330.

12. No ecclefiaftical law or canon can reftrain one of the liberty the law gives him to teach fchool, *&c.* for the common law or cuftom of the realm cannot be abrogated but by act of parliament. See 1 *Ju. Eccl.* 162, *&c.* And therefore no canon can do it; for they are but of flender force in comparifon of an act of parliament; nay even a parfon himfelf exercifing the employment of a fchool-mafter, (*other than in the fchool of a cathedral church*) head of a college, minifter of an impropriation, donative or

free chapel or other exemption, is clearly discharged of all canonical obedience, as no parties to the passing of those particular laws. 2 *Ju. Eccl.* 317, 318, *&c.*

10. Dissenting school-masters. *Ibid.* 333, *&c.*
11. Midwives, *&c.* *Ibid.* 334, 452.

13. References, *Noy.* 123. *Bishop of St. David's* case in *Salk.* and *Farest.* 1 *Pe. Will.* 29, 30, 31. *Cro. Jac.* 532. *Cro. Ca.* 551, 670. *Ro. Ab.* 287. *Hard.* 378. *Carth.* 118. *Salk.* 672. 1 *Ju. Eccl.* 90, 127, 165, 321, 336, 353. 2 *Ju. Eccl.* 272, *&c.* 321, 322, 323, 329, 333, 364, 366, 334. See *also the Introduction to Ju. Eccl. fo.* 2.

14. See rule, *Consuetudo ex certa causa rationabili usitata privat communem legem*, ca. 1.

253. *Law will admit no proof against that which the law presumeth.*

1. IF tenant in tail discontinue the tail, and dieth leaving issue, and the uncle of the issue release to the discontinuee with warranty, *&c.* and dieth without issue, this is a collateral warranty to the issue in tail, because the warranty descendeth upon the issue in tail, who cannot convey himself to the intail by means of his uncle. *Lit. sect.* 709. The reason is, because the law presumeth that the uncle would not unnaturally disinherit his lawful heir of what came to him by other means than the uncle's, but that he would leave him greater advancement. *Nemo praesumitur alienam posteritatem suae praetulisse*; and in this case they will admit no proof against that which the law presumeth. *Co. Lit.* 373. *a.*

2. And so it is of all other collateral warranties; for no man is presumed to do a thing against nature. *Ibid.*

3. So if rent be behind for 20 years, and the lord make an acquittance, for the last rent due, all the rest is presumed to be paid: and the law shall admit no proof against the presumption. *Co. Lit.* 373. *a.*

4. So if a man be within the four seas, and his wife hath a child, the law presumeth it the husband's child; against which the law will admit no proof. *Co. Lit.* 373. *a.*

5. If one innocent be accused of felony, and flieth for the same, though he judicially acquitteth himself of the felony, he shall, notwithstanding his innocence, forfeit all his goods and chattels, debts and duties, for his flight, for as to the forfeiture the law will admit no proof against the presumption in law grounded upon his flight; and so in many other cases; yet the rule is, *quod stabitur praesumptio donec probetur in contrarium*, but it hath many exceptions. *Co. Lit.* 373. *a. b.* *See much of this learning through the whole chapter of Warranty*, &c. *what the law was in lord* Coke's *time.*

6. See 28 *E.* 3. 14. 29 *E.* 3. 36. 11 *H.* 4. 55. 37 *H.* 6. 19. *Dy.* 271. 3 *Co.* 65. *b.* *Mo.* 88, 426, 643. *An.* 14. *Ro. Abr.* 95. 3 *Leon.* 258. 1 *Keb.* 95, 113. 2 *Keb.* 346. *Comb.* 59.

254. *Law will not drive a man to allow what he is endeavouring to defeat.*

IN an *Assise* for the mastership of a chapel against *J. S.* the plaintiff need not name *J. S.* master, because he is to disprove *J. S.*'s interest. 10 *H.* 7. 9.

255. *Law will rather endure a particular mischief than a general inconvenience.*

General.

1. THE general grounds of the law of *England* heed more what is good for many, than what is good for one single person only. *Doct. & Stud. lib.* 1. *cap.* 12, 18.

2. *Nihil quod est inconveniens est licitum*, and the law, that is the perfection of reason, cannot suffer any thing inconvenient. It is better, saith the law, to suffer a mischief that is particular to one, than an inconvenience that may prejudice many. *Co. Lit.* 97. *a. b.*

3. Every custom that may be hurtful to the interest of a private person, is not therefore void. *Da.* 32. *For if it be for the general good, it is still to be observed; as the law prefers a general good to a private interest.*

4. There are presumptions of law so violent, as though they be false, a man shall not be allowed to aver against them.

Particular cases.

5. As in a *praecipe* the tenant pleaded himself villain to *J. S.* and that he hath nothing but his villainage; the demandant had no reply, though it was false, but his writ must needs abate till, statute 37 *E.* 3. admitted the counter plea. *Mansel*'s case and 16 *H.* 7. So in replevin, if upon avowry the tenant disclaims he shall have judgment though it be false; for the law believes that these parties will not do themselves wrong in so high a degree. *Hob.* 297.

6. Also the law presumeth violently, that a layman cannot be absolutely discharged of tithes; and therefore will not allow a prescription of such discharge, holding it more reasonable that some one man should suffer a mischief to lose such a privilege, being so improbable and of so dangerous consequence, than, for his particular, to admit a spoil of the church, and decay of religion; according to the rule *Omne magnum exemplum aliquid habet ex iniquo, quod publica utilitate compensatur*, and though you shall be allowed your discharge by grant, when it appeareth; yet when it appears not, *stabitur praesumptio.* Hob. 297.

7. See *Doct. & Stud. lib.* 2. *cap.* 50, 51. *Hob.* 224. 4 *Co.* 124. *Wiseman's Civil Law* 46. *Co. Lit.* 552. *b.*

8. See also rules, *Actus non facit reum nisi mens sit rea*, ca. 9. *Law will admit no proof against that which the law presumeth. Aequitas sequitur legem. Res inter alios acta, &c.*

256. *Law will rather ſuffer things againſt the principles of Law, than that a man ſhall be without a remedy.*

1. ON procefs to avoid an outlawry one ſhall not be diſabled by another outlawry. 7 *H.* 4. 40.

2. If the lord diſtrain tortiouſly, and the beaſts return to the tenant, yet he may have his replevin; for that he could not have treſpaſs againſt his lord. 33 *E.* 3. *Fitzh. Replevin* 44. *Fitzh. Nat. Brev.* 69. *b.*

3. One after judgment gone againſt him for the king, may plead a charter of pardon, or the like done meſne between the verdict and the judgment; and that becauſe he cannot have an *audita querela*, otherwiſe of a common perſon. 11 *H.* 7. 10.

257. *Law will not ſuffer wrong.*

General.

1. THE law was provided not to engender, but prevent ſuits; and therefore provides that things be done by indifferent means and perſons; that there be no ſuſpicion of indifferent dealing. *Hob.* 107. *Vue tout le caſe.*

Particular caſes.

2. *Quod eſt jure, id eſt juſtum, quod ab injuria proficitur injuſtum; quid autem ſit jus, et in quo conſiſtat injuria, legis eſt definire.*

3. Every man is bound to make recompence for ſuch hurt as his beaſts ſhall do in the corn or graſs, *&c.* of his neighbour, though he knew not of it. *Doct. & Stud. lib.* 1. *cap.* 9.

4. Men outlawed or excommunicated may bring actions as executors; ſo a villain ſhall againſt his lord, for they are to recover *en auter droit.* 21 H. 6. 30. b.

5. If an alienation be made in *Mortmain*, or a fine levied of a reverſion of lands held *in capite ſans* licence, the tenant is not compellable to attorn. 17 *E.* 3. 7. 45 *E.* 3. 6. See *Two laſt rules.*

258. *Legacies to be paid out of the perſonal eſtate.*

General.

1. THough the real eſtate be charged with the payment of legacies, as being either deviſed or conveyed to truſtees for payment of legacies, yet the perſonal eſtate ſhall be firſt applied, as in caſe of debts. 1 *Chan. Ca.* 297. But where in a particular deviſe or other expreſs proviſion, *aliter. Prec. Chan.* 451. 2 *Vern.* 718.

Particular caſes.

2. The teſtator ſeiſed in fee entered into a ſtatute, and deviſed a legacy of 500*l.* the cognizee took all the perſonal eſtate in execution; ſo that there was nothing left to pay the legacy; equity decreed the real eſtate to ſtand charged with the legacy. 2 *Chan. Ca.* 4. And yet the land was not

charged with the legacy originally; but as there was sufficient of the personal estate to pay the legacy, had it been so applied, instead of being applied to satisfy the statute, in ease of the heir's lands; so far as the real estate is eased by this application of the personal estate, the real estate shall be liable to the legacy. 2 *Chan. Ca.* 117.

3. *N.* seised in fee, and indebted by bonds, by his will gives legacies to his children, (for whom he had otherwise provided before) and devises his lands to his eldest son in tail, whom he also made executor: now the legatees brought bill to come against the real estate, in the place of the bond creditors, and to be paid out of the lands, as the bond creditors would: and the court seemed to admit, if the lands had descended, the legatees might have been relieved in this manner, but since the testator had devised them, it was resolved they ought to be exempted; for it was as much the testator's intention, that the devisee should have this land, as the others the legacies; and a specific legacy is never broke into in order to make good a pecuniary one: also this case is out of the statute against fraudulent devises; because the debts are paid, and the children being otherwise provided for, are not in the nature of creditors. *Nota*; This case was upon an appeal from a decree of the master of the rolls, who held the real estate should be so charged, that both the debts and legacies should be paid. *Hern* versus *Merick*, *Salk.* 416.

4. *A.* bequeaths a legacy and makes baron and feme executors, and dies, and the baron makes his will, and the feme and his son executors, and dies. A legatee of *A.* exhibits a bill against the feme and her son, and chargeth that the estate of *A.* liable to the legacy, is come all to the hands of the feme and her son. The son demurred, for that the feme was the surviving executor of *A.* and only liable, and the son being executor of one of *A.*'s executors, who died first, leaving an executor of *A.* to survive, was not privy in law, nor accountable for the estate of *A.* which though it be so in point of law, yet inasmuch as it was charged that the son had gotten the estate of *A.* the demurrer was over-ruled: the court resolving that the estate of *A.* in whosesoever hands, ought to be liable to his legacies. 1 *Ch. Ca.* 57.

5. See 1 *Rep. Chan.* 134, 288. 2 *Rep. Chan.* 2. 1 *Chan. Ca.* 257, 258.

6. See also rule, *Personal estate to go in ease of the real.*

259. *Legal reason est summa ratio.*

1. THE law is the perfection of reason. *Co. Lit.* 97.

2. Law is the fountain of justice and common right. 11 *Co.* 72.

3. As the law is the perfection of reason, so reason is the life of the law; nay the common law itself is nothing but reason, which is to be understood of an artificial perfection of reason gotten by long study, observation and experience, and not of every man's natural reason; for *nemo nascitur artifex.* This *Legal reason est summa ratio*; and therefore if all the reason that is dispersed into so many several heads were united into one, yet could he not make such a law, as the law of *England*; because by many successions of ages it hath been fined and refined by an infinite number of grave and learned men, and by long experience grown to such a perfection for the government of this realm, as the old rule may be justly verified

 of

of it. *Neminem oportet esse sapientiorem legibus*, which is the perfection of reason. *Co. Lit.* 97. *b.* See 11 *Co.* 10. *b.*

260. *Leges Angliae sine parliamento mutari non possunt.*

General.

1. WHAT the law doth warrant in case of prohibitions, to keep every jurisdiction within its true bounds and limits, cannot be altered but by act of parliament. *Quia leges Angliae sine parliamento mutari non possunt.* 2 Inst. 619.

Particular cases.

2. When the clergy were most importunate to have the canon to make infants legitimate, which were born before espousals, marriage following; as the church looked upon such as lawful issue; it was rejected in the parliament of *Merton*; *omnes comites et barones una voce responderunt, nolumus leges Angliae mutari, quae hucusque usitatae sunt.* Kelw. 7 *H.* 8. 181. b. Da. 70. b. 1 Ju. Eccl. 63.

3. See 2 *Inst.* 602. 1 *Ju. Eccl.* The opposition which ecclesiastical usurpations have met with.

4. Vide etiam ante *Law not to be altered.*

261. *Leges posteriores priores contrarias abrogant.*

General.

1. *THIS rule must be understood only to extend to such prior laws, as are by these subsequent laws intended to be abrogated or taken away, or where the former law is repugnant to the new one*; for it was resolved that the statute 23 *H.* 8. *cap.* 10. did not extend to take away the good and charitable uses in the case at bar, namely, *The maintaining a grammar school and poor people*, &c. 1 Co. 25. b. *vue tout le case.*

Particular cases.

2. *Allen Clerk* devised certain lands in *London* to the master, fellows and scholars of *Trinity College Cambridge*, and their successors for ever, for finding certain grammar schools for poor scholars: and on question, Whether this was a good devise, notwithstanding the statute of lands *ad manum mortuam non ponend'*, or any other law, act or statute? It was held good by the statute 1 & 2 *Ph. & Ma.* and that the said statute *Ph. & Ma.* ought to be favourably expounded. *Dy.* 255.

3. It was moved in arrest of judgment, that an information lieth not against baron and feme, for the recusancy of the wife, to recover 20*l.* a month; for the statute 7 *Jac. cap.* 6. appoints that if a feme covert be convict, she shall be committed to prison; and if the husband redeem her out of prison, he shall pay 10*l. per mensem*; so that the statute, being *lex posterior*, abrogateth the former law, that the husband shall not be charged with the recusancy of the wife, but only at 10*l.* the month; and not with that neither but to redeem her out of prison. *Sed non allocatur*; for this statute doth not alter any of the former laws, but prescribes that a feme co-

vert

vert recusant being convicted, if she, after three months, do not conform herself, she shall be committed to prison, unless the husband will pay 10*l.* for every month she shall be out of prison and not conformed. *Cro. Jac.* 529.

4. See *Cro. Jac.* 121. 4 *Salk.* 182, 353, 369, 378, 383, 450. 4 *Mod.* 50. *Fitz-G.* 124.

5. See rules, *Leges Angliae sine parliamento mutari non possunt. Law not to be altered.*

262. *Length of time no objection to redemption in case of a mortgage.*

1. THE bill was to redeem a mortgage. The defendant demurred, for of the plaintiff's own shewing the mortgage was 60 years old; demurrer over-ruled; because it was charged in the bill, that the mortgagor agreed the mortgagee should enter and hold till satisfied; which is in the nature of a *Welsh* mortgage; and in such case length of time is no objection. 1 *Vern.* 418.

2. See 1 *Vern.* 395, 477.

263. *The lesser estate merges in the greater.*

General and what.

1. ESTATE in lands are properly said to be merged or confounded, when the lesser estate meets with the greater, in the same person, and in the same right; as *terminus et feodum non possunt constare simul in unâ eademque personâ*, and the pregnant reason of this is put in the case of *Bracebridge*, *Plow. Com.* 319. *b.* because that a term is a time finite, and the finite, of necessity, ought to be merged and confounded in the infinite. *Da.* 4. *b.* *Note* the diversity between merger and extinguishment. *Ibid.*

Terms and inheritances.

General to them.

2. The term and inheritance being in the same hand, the term is merged. *Prec. Chan.* 252.

3. A term may merge in the inheritance by both being in the same person. 3 *Chan. Ca.* 15, 31. 2 *Mod. Ca.* 124. *Whitchurch* and *Whitchurch.*

Particular cases.

4. A lease is to *A.* and his assigns, *habendum* to him during his life and the lives of *B.* and *C.* adjudged this limitation good; for where it was objected, that where one hath two estates in him, the greater shall merge the less, and that an estate for one's own life, is much higher than one for the life of another; and that therefore this estate for his own life and the lives of the other, may not stand together; whereto it was answered and resolved, that the lessee had but one estate which hath this limitation, *scil.* during his life and the lives of two others, and he hath but one freehold; and therefore there can be no merger of estate; but he hath an estate

of freehold to continue during theſe three lives, and the longeſt liver of them. 5 *Co.* 13. *a.*

* 5. One intails his eſtate on an eldeſt ſon, chargeable with a fortune to a younger, and in caſe of the younger's death without iſſue, ſuch fortune to deſcend as an eſtate-tail; both after deſcend upon the ſame perſon, this is not a merger of the fortune, but remains a debt upon the real eſtate, for the benefit of the creditors. See caſe *Irwine* and *Sir Alexander Cumming, Bart.* before the houſe of lords, 4 *May* 1733.

Copyhold and inheritance.

6. A copyholder in tail takes a conveyance in fee, the copyhold is merged. 1 *Vern.* 458.

7. A copyholder in tail, remainder in fee, purchaſed the freehold from the lord. Lord chancellor declared, That the purchaſe of the freehold attached the other eſtate, being but an eſtate at will, and that the copyhold was merged; and that a purchaſer from the copyholder, who ſo bought in the inheritance, ſhould hold againſt the iſſue in tail. 1 *Vern.* 393.

8. *Ejectione firmae.* The caſe was, *Lettice Knowles*, copyholder for life, ſurrenders in conſideration of 20*l.* to the uſe of *Dorothy Whiſtler*; the lord accepts of the ſurrender, and grants to *Dorothy* for life, and ſhe is admitted, and dies; *Lettice* now claims as her former eſtate, and let to the defendant, and the lord enters and let to the plaintiff; upon this verdict; for the defendant, it was argued that when a copyholder for life ſurrenders to the uſe of another who is admitted, the firſt copyholder hath *quaſi* a poſſibility, or the remainder of an eſtate; that if he ſurvive him to whoſe uſe the ſurrender is made, that he ſhall have it again. But agreed that if a copyholder for life ſurrenders his eſtate, to the intent that the lord ſhould grant to whomſoever he pleaſed, then his eſtate was drowned, but not here; and for that the book 9 *Eliz. Dy.* 264. was cited; but all the court conceived ſhe may not have it again, but that her eſtate is merely determined by the ſurrender, and that to that purpoſe there is no difference, to ſurrender all her eſtate to the uſe of one, and to ſurrender generally; and the book above warrants no ſuch difference; for if a tenant for life ſurrender to the uſe of another, and the lord grant it, he is merely in by the lord, and not by the copyholder who ſurrendered; but if a copyholder in fee ſurrender to the uſe of another for life, who is admitted, he is in *quaſi* by the copyholder, and who on his death ſhall have it again, but not here; whereupon it was adjudged for the plaintiff. *Note*; This judgment was impeached by writ of error, and the matter in law aſſigned for error, and by all the juſtices in *C. B.* and barons of the exchequer, the judgment was affirmed. *Cro. Ca.* 204, 205. See 4 *Co.* 27. *b.* 28. *b.* 29. *b.* 5 *Co.* 20. *Co. Lit.* 41. *Plow. Com.* 555.

9. Vide 2 *Rep. Chan.* 174. 2 *Leon.* 114. *Mo.* 371. *b.* 376. *b.* 2 *An.* 22, 29, 43. 2 *Cro.* 56, 57, 202. 1 *Ro.* 439.

264. *Lex citius tolerare vult privatum damnum, quam publicum malum.*

RULES, *Res inter alios acta, &c. One not to be prejudiced by the act of a third perſon. Law will rather endure a particular miſchief than a general inconvenience.*

265. *Lex neceſſitatis eſt lex temporis, ſcil. inſtantis.*

AND therefore it is well ſaid, *neceſſitas legum vincula irridet*, but this is when you may perceive the caſe brought to extream neceſſity, *&c.* the law permits you not to kill him who aſſails you when you draw near your laſt refuge, becauſe you foreſee you ſhall be driven to it, but you muſt forbear till that neceſſity be at its full period; for till then it may be otherwiſe prevented or remedied. *Hob.* 159.

266. *Lex nil facit fruſtra.*

1. WHERE I ſuffer an injury joined with a loſs, the law ſhall give me a remedy and recompence according to my certain and uncertain loſs; yea, and ſometimes where the thing is not in being but utterly extinguiſhed. *Hob.* 43. And touching the uncertainty if a man grant an advowſon with warranty, and the tenant in a writ of right of advowſon vouch, he ſhall have, if he loſe, recompence in value of land, or other certain profit, and yet the advowſon of itſelf is utterly of an uncertain value. So of a liberty *bona et catalla felonum, &c.* Hob. 43.

2. See *Jenk.* 256. *Co. Lit.* 197. *b.*

267. *Lex non cogit ad impoſſibilia.*

1. IT was reſolved, that the leſſee for years in the caſe at bar, claiming under letters patent from the queen, ought to ſhew the letters patent made to the leſſee for life; for it is a maxim in the law, that he who is party or privy in eſtate or intereſt, or he who juſtifies in right of him who is party or privy pleading a deed; though he ſo privy claims but parcel of the original eſtate, yet he ought to ſhew the original deed to the court; and the reaſon why deeds ſo pleaded ſhall be ſhewed to the court is, that to every deed two things are neceſſary. 1. That it be good in law, and this is called the legal part; becauſe the judgment of it belongeth to the judges of the law; the other concerns matter in fact, *viz.* if it be ſealed and delivered as a deed, and this is triable *per pais*; and therefore every deed ought to prove itſelf, and to be proved by others; as to the proving itſelf, it is in two manners, 1ſt, As to the words, *whether good in law*, which the court is to judge of. 2dly, If it is not raſed or interlined in points or places material; and hereof the judges antiently judged on view, *&c.* 7 *E.* 3. 57. 25 *E.* 3. 41. 41 *E.* 3. 10. *&c.* But of late the judges have ſuffered it to be tried by the jury, *&c.* 3dly, That it might appear to the court and parties, whether it was upon condition, limitation, or with power of revocation, *&c.* if the deed be poll, or it want a counter-

counter-part of the indenture, the other party may take advantage of any of these matters. And with this agrees *Lit. cap. Condition, fo.* 90, 91. 40 *Aſſ.* 34. And theſe are the reaſons of law, that deeds pleaded in court ſhall be produced and ſhewn to the court; by which it appears how dangerous it is, to ſuffer any, who in pleading ought to ſhew the deed itſelf to the court, upon the general iſſue, to prove it in evidence by witneſſes to the jury, or to prove it by copy; for that the viciouſneſs, raſing or interlineation, or other defects in theſe caſes do not appear to the court; or the deed might be upon condition, limitation, or with clauſe of revocation; and by this means truth and juſtice, and the true reaſon of the common law ſhould be ſubverted; but yet in great and notorious extremities, as by the malancholy accident of fire, wherewith his evidences were burnt, there it appearing to the judges, they may, in favour of him who ſuſtained ſo great loſs by fire, ſuffer him to prove his deed by witneſſes in evidence to the jury; leſt calamity ſhould be added to calamity, 28 *Aſſ. pl.* 3. but in the 12 *Aſſ. pl.* 16. the judges would not ſuffer a deed to be given in evidence which was not ſhewn before to the jury. *Vide* 26 *Aſſ. pl.* 2. the like 10 *Co.* 92. *a. b.*

2. But the copy of a record may be ſhewn and given in evidence before the jury; for records are of ſo high a nature, and of ſo great credit in law, that they can be no otherwiſe proved than by themſelves, and no raſure or interlineation ſhall be preſumed in them; and therefore a copy of a record, being teſtified to be true, is permitted to be given in evidence; but the ſure way is to exemplify it under the great ſeal, or at leaſt under the ſeal of the court. 10 *Co.* 92. *b.* 93. *a.*

3. And in the caſe of caſualty by fire, there ought to be very great circumſpection and diſcretion in the judges; for notwithſtanding ſuch caſualty, he in pleading ought to ſhew the deed itſelf to the court, elſe the plea ſhall be inſufficient, and judgment be given againſt him; for the law will rather ſuffer a miſchief in a private caſe, than an inconvenience, which would, by breaking a rule of law, be introduced to the public. 10 *Co.* 93. *a.*

4. And the deed ought not only to prove itſelf, but to be proved by others, that is to ſay, by witneſſes, that it was ſealed and delivered; elſe though the fabric and compoſition of the deed be lawful, it is but defective without the other. 10 *Co.* 93, *&c.*

5. Reſolved, if one plead ſeiſin of a copyholder in fee, and claims under him; he ought to ſhew of whoſe grant, as he ought to ſhew of any other particular eſtate; and though it was ſaid it may be ſo antient that it may not be ſhewn who was the firſt grantee, yet it was held ſufficient to ſhew the admittance of the laſt heir, which is in the nature of a grant, and may be pleaded by way of grant. *Cro. Jac.* 103.

6. A leſſee for years not to alien *ſans* licence, obtains a licence to alien part; the leſſor grants the reverſion; the leſſee attorned and then aliened; the grantee enters; the leſſee brings treſpaſs; the grantee juſtifies by reaſon of the condition; the leſſee ſhews his licence. *Cur'*: The plea is good enough without ſhewing it; becauſe of its nature it could not be without writing, and there did not any intereſt paſs thereby, but a reſtraint only ſet at liberty; and it is a thing executed, and his aſſignee peradventure hath it, for the fortifying his eſtate; and though the alienation was after attornment and grant of the reverſion, *&c.* yet it is good enough. *Cro. Jac.* 102, 103.

2 7. The

7. The cafe was, A feme fole made a leafe for life, and the leffee did wafte, and the hufband releafed, and delivered the deed to an indifferent hand, to be delivered to the defendant upon certain conditions to be performed; the defendant performs them, the hufband gets the releafe and keeps it from the leffee, and baron and feme bring wafte; the leffee on this fpecial matter may plead the releafe without fhewing it. *Vide* 10 *E.* 3. 40. So if baron and feme are impleaded in an action real, where the default of the wife is the default of both, if the demandant take the feme of the tenant from him, this fhall not turn the tenant to a default. So in dower, detinue of charters, *&c.* by the demandant, is a good plea. 20 *H.* 7. 5. So of tenant by ftatute merchant or ftaple, *&c.* he is not to fhew the deed; for he came in by procefs of law againft the will of him who hath the deed; and hath not means of coming at it; otherwife of a leafe for life or years, *&c.* for there he came in by the leffor, and might have taken covenant or other fecurity for peaceable enjoyment, *&c.* 5 *Co.* 75. *a.*

8. Trefpafs for tithes taken; the defendant juftifies as fervant, and doth not fay *hic in curia prolat'*; and for this caufe the plaintiff demurred in law generally; and judgment for the plaintiff; and now error is brought and affigned, for that he being but a fervant, the letters patent from the queen do not belong unto him, and therefore his plea was good without fhewing of them: but all the juftices and barons conceived, in regard he derives his authority from the patentee, and not by act in law, but by his command, he ought to fhew the letters patent, as well as he who claims by affignment under the patent; but he who claims under an act in law, for that he had no means to make the patentee fhew it, may juftify without fhewing it. Wherefore judgment was affirmed. *Cro. Jac.* 317.

9. See 5 *Co.* 76. *a. b.* *Cro. Ca.* 209, 442. *Cro. Jac.* 137, 669. *Cro. Eliz.* 9, 22, 67, 188, 249, 656, 697. *Cro. Jac.* 515, 645, 652, 716. 1 *Sid.* 82, 146, 293. 1 *Vent.* 46, 165, 242, 255. 3 *Lev.* 104, 137, 238. 2 *Lev.* 95. 1 *Mod.* 18, 206, 262. 3 *Mod.* 147. 6 *Mod.* 194. *Salk.* 125, 467, 536. 2 *Lev.* 2. 1 *Vern.* 45. *Skin.* 113. *Lutw.* 379, 405, 410. *Saund.* 320. 1 *Lev.* 44, 93. 2 *Lev.* 95. 3 *Lev.* 104, 137. 1 *Mod.* 104, 264, 265. 2 *Mod.* 201. 3 *Mod.* 191. 3 *Keb.* 273. *Raym.* 282. 1 *Vent.* 257. *Co. Lit.* 197. *b.* 231. *b.* *Hob.* 96.

10. See rules, *Lex fpectat naturae ordinem.* *All the term in law but one day,* ca. 6.

268. *Lex plus laudatur quando ratione probatur.*

LES *arguments et les reafons del' ley, &c. ratio eft anima legis*; for then are we faid to know the law, when we apprehend the reafon of the law, that is, when we bring the reafon of the law to our own reafon, that we perfectly underftand it as our own; and then, and never before, we have fuch an excellent and infeparable property and ownerfhip therein as we can neither lofe it, nor any man take it from us, and will direct us (the learning of the law is fo chained together) in many other cafes; but if by your ftudy and induftry you make not the reafon of the law your own, it is not poffible for you long to retain it in your memory; and well doth our author couple argument and reafon together, *quia argumenta ignota et obfcura ad*

lucem

lucem rationis proferunt et reddunt splendida; and therefore *argumentari et ratiocinari* are many times taken for one, *&c.* *Co. Lit.* 394. *b.* 395. *a.*

269. *Lex spectat naturae ordinem.*

1. IF the tenant hold of his lord by a rose, or by a bushel of roses, payable at the feast of St. *John* the baptist, if the tenant dieth in winter, the lord cannot distrain for his relief until the time that roses by the course of the year may have their growth, *&c.* and so of the like. *Lit. sect.* 129. *Lex spectat naturae ordinem. Lex non cogit ad impossibilia.* The argument *ab impossibili* is forcible in law, *impossibile est quod naturae rei repugnat.* And *Littleton* puts a difference between corn and roses; for corn will last; and therefore the tenant must deliver it presently before the time of growth; and so of saffron and the like; but roses or other flowers that are *fructus fugaces*, cannot be kept, and therefore are not to be delivered till the time of growing; neither is the tenant driven by law, artificially to preserve roses; for the law, in these cases, respecteth nature and the course of the year, *et ars naturam imitatur.* Co. Lit. 92. a.

2. See *Co. Lit.* 197. *b.*

3. See also rule, *Lex non cogit ad impossibilia.*

270. *Liberty the greatest jewel.*

General.

1. THE common law holdeth the body the greatest pain and highest coertion; for as our blessed Saviour saith, the body is of more worth than raiment, *&c.* and in *Job*, *pellis pro pelle*, all a man hath he will give for his life, but touch his flesh or his bones, *&c.* and imprisonment toucheth both. *In salva et arcta custodia.* Hob. 61.

Particular cases.

2. Of all executions, that of the body in law is esteemed the best, as also in the law of nature it is the best, and most forcible, and therefore 7 *H.* 6. 6. by the opinion of *Cotismore*, if two executors have judgment, and one prays a *capias*, and the other *fi. fa.* the *capias* shall be awarded as best for the testator; and the common law gave not that execution, as being too hard and heavy, but only in the case of wilful wrong, *vi et armis*, for which none was thought too hard, *&c.* *Hob.* 61.

3. And therefore barons were not subject to it, but on great contempts, nor yet since the statute 25 *E.* 3. though not specially exempted. *Hob.* 61.

4. Though in trespass *vi et armis*, at common law, against a baron a *capias* lieth not, nor after by the equity of the common law upon the statute, because the estate of a baron is intended sufficient; yet 11 *H.* 4. 15. *in homine replegiando*, against lady *Spencer*, a peeress of the realm, *viz.* a baroness born, it was granted; because it was an high injury to the person whom she eloined. *Hob.* 61.

5. See rules, *Ignorantia facti excusat. Executio juris non habet injuriam.*

271. *Licet consuetudo sit magnae authoritatis, nunquam tamen praejudicat manifestae veritati.*

1. THE plaintiff brings an action in *London*, for that the defendant called the plaintiff's wife a whore, and the defendant removed it by *habeas corpus* in *B. R.* and it was moved for a *procedendo* to remand it; for that the action was maintainable in *London* for these words, but not at common law; but the motion was denied *per totam curiam*; for such custom to maintain actions for such brabling words is against law, *licet consuetudo sit magnae authoritatis*, &c. 4 Co. 18. a.

2. A prohibition was moved for to stay proceedings in the consistory court of *London*; for that it appeared on the face of the libel, they had no jurisdiction; this being a libel which chargeth the defendant with calling the plaintiff's wife whore in *London*, but as it was after sentence, *Fortescue*, justice, said, a prohibition did not lie upon the face of the libel, without affidavit of the custom that an action lies there; for as the judge said, we are not obliged to take notice of their customs; and said he remembered two or three cases to this purpose. Prohibition denied, because moved the last day of term. 2 *Ju. Eccl.* 218.

3. This was upon a rule to shew cause why a prohibition should not be granted to the consistory court of the bishop of *London*. Mr. *Strange* said that the foundation on which the rule was obtained, was, that it was for calling a woman whore, and that the words appeared in the libel to be spoken in *London*; but he submitted it, the words did not appear to be spoken there; for they are laid to be spoken in the parish of St. *Giles Cripplegate*, *London*, *or in some other place in the neighbourhood thereof*, *or near thereto adjoining*; and in such case, where there is not sufficient certainty appearing on the libel, usually the party makes affidavit that the words were spoken in *London* and not elsewhere; and he further observed the charge was only for saying the other had a barstard, without directly calling her whore; and in these cases the court expects the word *whore* should be particularly expressed. Lord chief justice thought there was sufficient ground to believe the words were spoken in *London*; and that he thought them sufficient of themselves, &c. Rule made absolute for so much of the words as were spoken in *London*. 2 *Ju. Eccl.* 218, 219.

4. See 6 *Co.* 6. *a. b.* 1 *Vent.* 343. *Pal.* 379. *Salk.* 547, 548. 2 *Ro. Abr.* 296. *Lutw.* 1039, 1042.

272. *Limitations, in restraint of marriage, over to another, makes them good; else such restraints are only* in terrorem.

General to, and rules.

1. AS to the question, Where *in terrorem* and where not? Where to work a forfeiture, there should be a devise over, else it is to be taken only *in terrorem*; otherwise strangers executors might run away with great part of a man's estate from his children. That the distinction where

 a devise

a devife over, and where not, has been taken in all cafes, and was certainly a very good one, and though lawyers know it would be no forfeiture, yet the parties did not; and therefore it would be fome terror to them: but thefe reftrictions could hold no longer than the parties come of age, after which they would be intitled to their fortunes, and might bring a bill for recovery; that thefe claufes in reftraint of marriage have never been taken favourably. *Prec. Chan.* 562. *Note*; In this cafe were cited *Fry* and *Porter*'s cafe, 1 *Vent.* 300. 1 *Chan. Ca.* 122. Sir *And. Bellafis*'s cafe, 346. *Lloyd* and *Hughe*'s cafe, and *Lord Salisbury*'s cafe, *&c.*

Particular cafes.

* 2. *Cambel* devifed 6000*l.* to his grand-daughter *Catherine Burton*, to be paid on the day of her marriage, with intereft from the teftator's death, in cafe fhe married with the confent of *Samuel Burton*, Efq; her father; but if fhe married without fuch confent, or died before marriage, then the teftator limited this 6000*l.* to all the children of his the teftator's brothers and fifters, to be equally divided amongft them; then the teftator died, and the faid *Catherine* being then about 19 years old, the father, by friends, moved a match for her with lord *Netterville*; but after, *Burton* weighing his own circumftances, and his inability to make good the propofals by his friends made to lord *Netterville*, entered into fchemes to accomplifh the match without entering into ftrict fettlement or agreement; and to that end gave the lord and lady frequent opportunities of coming together, and at length finding their affections engaged, went one day out in his chariot on purpofe, as was proved in the caufe, to give the young couple an opportunity of being privately married, and which accordingly took effect the laft day of *February* 1731; after *Burton* taking advantage of the marriage being thus had, and under pretence that the lord and lady had not obtained his confent, prevailed upon his lordfhip in full form to make a confiderable fettlement on his lady by her late maiden name, and to be married again with full appearance of his the faid *Burton*'s confent, as being party to the faid fettlement, and confenting to the faid marriage; but the parties to whom the 6000*l.* was given over, brought their bill, infifting the marriage in *February* 1731, was without *Burton*'s confent. But it was decreed by the lord chancellor in *Ireland*, that the lord and lady *Netterville* were well intitled to the faid fortune, to be applied as by the articles was agreed. And on appeal the decree was affirmed by the lords here, *April* 1737.

* 3. *I leave and bequeath to my Daughter* Anne 2000l. *to be paid her on the day of marriage, or at the age of* 21 *years, which fhall firft happen; and in cafe my faid daughter* Anne *fhall marry with the confent and approbation of* Robert Oliver, *Efq;* Berkley Taylor, *Efq;* John Croker, *Efq; and my faid fon* John, *or any two of them; I further leave and bequeath to my faid daughter* Anne, *the additional fum of* 2000*l. more,* **otherwife not.** *Anne* coming of age, writ to *Oliver* to know what fortune fhe was intitled unto, who fent her counfel's opinion, that fhe was intitled to the additional 2000*l.* whether fhe fhould marry with or without confent; *the fame not being given over.* After her brother *John*, difliking the match he faw her carrying forward, declared fuch diflike to her and warned her, that if fhe proceeded in it, fhe would forfeit the additional 2000*l.* and on their referring themfelves to another counfel, who was a relation of the family,

he was in opinion with the brother; however, the lady thought proper to proceed in this amour, and ſo the marriage took place. And on a bill by the huſband and wife, the court of exchequer in *Ireland* decreed it a forfeiture, *Holmes et ux'* verſus *Lyſaght*; and 24 *May* 1733, an appeal was to the lords here, but it ended by compromiſe. *Had* 4000l. *been given to her, but on condition if ſhe married without ſuch conſent, that then* 2000l. *of it ſhould be gone and loſt to her; in ſuch caſe, it not being given over, on her having ſolicited the conſent neceſſary, though ſhe had not obtained it, as I take it, the firſt opinion had been right; as it was not in ſuch caſe given over; but the preſent caſe is plainly of a condition precedent, to be performed on her part; ſhe was firſt to marry, and that with ſuch conſent, to make her title to the additional* 2000l. *and thoſe were the terms on which ſhe was to have it,* **and not otherwiſe.** *Had ſhe never married, this additional ſum could never have been raiſed; and her marrying, but that without conſent, was falling principally ſhort of the terms annexed; and that too in the very point armed againſt, and ſo makes a total breach of that condition.*

* 4. Admiral *Grayden* by his laſt will and teſtament gave 1000*l.* to his daughter *Mary* to be paid at 21 or day of marriage, which ſhould firſt happen, provided ſhe married with the conſent of his executors *Mary Grayden* the teſtator's mother, *Mary Grayden* his wife, and *Jeremiah Grayden* his brother; and in caſe ſhe died before ſuch age or marriage as aforeſaid, then he gave and bequeathed the ſaid 1000*l.* to his two younger ſons *Benjamin* and *Gregory Grayden*; and the ſurplus of his perſonal eſtate he deviſed in truſt for his wife and children, to be divided amongſt them as if he had died inteſtate. All the executors died before the daughter attained her age of 21 or marriage. *Mary* the mother made her will *anno* 1733, in the beginning of which ſhe gave her ſaid daughter *Mary* certain ſpecific legacies, and towards the end thereof ſhe gave the ſurplus of her perſonal eſtate to be diſtributed among her three younger children, and about the middle of the will was the following clauſe, *And my will is, that if my daughter marries before her age of* 21, *without the conſent of my executor under his hand and ſeal firſt had and obtained, if living, then ſhe ſhall not be intitled to any part of ſuch legacies as I have given her, and in ſuch caſe my will is, that the ſame ſhall go to my two younger ſons* Benjamin *and* Gregory Grayden; and afterwards towards the end of the ſaid will, ſhe made *John* her eldeſt ſon her executor. The ſame year the teſtatrix died, and *John* renounced the executorſhip, and thereupon adminiſtration with the will annexed was granted to *Tinwel.* Soon after this, *Robert* the ſon of Sir *Henry Hicks* commenced an amour with the ſaid *Mary* the daughter, who then lived in the houſe of *Tinwel* the adminiſtrator, who acquainted Sir *Henry* therewith; and on Sir *Henry*'s diſapprobation thereof, *Tinwel* acquainted *Robert* the ſon therewith; notwithſtanding which, *Robert* proſecuted his addreſſes, and particularly on *Tinwel*'s further application to *Robert* about the month of *July* 1736, and deſiring him to deſiſt and think no more of that matter, he declared to *Tinwel* in the preſence of two other perſons, that he was actually and really married to the lady, and that on the 16 *Jan.* 1735; and on being aſked who was the clergyman or parſon who married him, he refuſed to tell, ſaying it muſt be kept a ſecret from his father; after this he took the lady away, he cohabited with her, he acknowledged himſelf to be her huſband and owned her for his wife, they viſited as huſband and wife, ſhe was called

called by his name, ſhe had her arms with his engraven on a piece of plate, and whilſt they thus lived together as huſband and wife he had a child by her, the child was regiſtred as the child of *Robert* and *Mary Hicks* in the pariſh of St. *Giles*, and that by Mr. *Hicks*'s own direction. When the young lady, *anno* 1737, came of age, this bill was preferred by her brothers *Benjamin* and *Gregory*, againſt Mr. *Hicks* and their ſiſter, by the name of *Mary Hicks*, and againſt *Tinwel* claiming the benefit of her forfeiture of what ſhe had otherwiſe been intitled unto under the wills of her father and mother. Mr. *Hicks* put in four different anſwers, and in every one of them he denied his marriage. *Mary* anſwered alſo, but demurred to that part of the plaintiffs bill which required her to anſwer whether ſhe was married to Mr. *Hicks* or not, as they did alſo to the inquiry whether ſhe had not a child by him; and brought her croſs bill by the name of *Mary Grayden* againſt the plaintiffs in the original cauſe, and againſt *Tinwel*, praying the benefit of what was bequeathed her by the ſaid two wills. Mr. *Chute* for the plaintiffs in the original cauſe, for authority, cited *Rogers* and *Pain*, before lord *King*, 14 *May* 1720, and that of *Hichocks* and *Hickocks*, determined by his now lordſhip *July* 1737, alſo *Garbot* and *Hilton*, laſt week at the rolls. Mr. *Browne* on the other ſide cited the caſe of *Peyton* and *Bury*, at the rolls, [2 *Pe. Will.* 626.] 6 *May* 1731, and that of *Fountain* and *Harp*, alſo at the rolls, 13 *March* 1730. His lordſhip ſaid, he had not ſeen a cauſe attended with ſuch extraordinary circumſtances, and that it was a melancholy thing ſo little regard ſhould be paid to the injunctions of parents and the common rules of decency; however, it was not his office to determine upon the moral characters, but upon the legal and equitable rights of the parties; and that the queſtions are, 1ſt, Whether the lady is married or not? 2dly, And if ſhe is, what are the conſequences ariſing from thence, in reſpect to the portions given her by the wills of her father and mother? And as to the firſt of theſe, his lordſhip held that if ſhe was married, it would be doing the lady a great injury to think otherwiſe, and that the evidence of it is ſo ſtrong that any jury would credit it; but his lordſhip ſaid it would be another queſtion if this matter aroſe in a collateral cauſe, and between other parties; but between themſelves, his lordſhip declared his opinion, that it is ſufficiently proved, and that had it been at all doubtful, he ſhould have directed an iſſue, but in the preſent caſe he thought it not proper. 1ſt, Becauſe it is clear *Hicks* and ſhe cohabited together as huſband and wife. 2dly, She had a child by him; and obſerved, there's no proof offered on the part of the defendant in the original cauſe, to make this matter in the leaſt doubtful. And the proofs for the plaintiffs are extremely ſtrong. 1ſt, It is agreed on all hands that here was a courtſhip in order to a marriage, and that carried on in *Tinwel*'s houſe, and that he very prudently acquainted Sir *Henry Hicks* therewith, and though Sir *Henry* diſapproved thereof, yet the ſon would and did continue his addreſſes, and in *July* 1736 declared he was married 16 *January* 1735; this declaration he made in the preſence of two other people. And to the queſtion, Who it was that married them? he refuſed to anſwer, ſaying it muſt be kept a ſecret from his father; after all this, he took the lady away, lived with her, acknowledged her to be his wife, they viſited together as ſuch, ſhe is called by his name, a piece of plate is engraven with both their arms; and what is more material than all the reſt, ſhe has a child

child by him, and that regiſtred by *Hicks's* order as the child of *Robert* and *Mary Hicks* in the pariſh of St. *Giles.* This his lordſhip looked upon as ſuch an evidence of a marriage as muſt convince any jury; and ſaid that many verdicts in favour of marriage had been on ſuch ſort of evidence, eſpecially where Inheritance is not concerned, nor other parties prejudiced. As to the conſequences ariſing from this marriage, 1ſt, With regard to the will of the father, his lordſhip obſerved, it firſt related to 1000*l.* particularly given to this lady. 2dly, To a ſhare in the ſurplus not before particularly diſpoſed of. As to the clauſe of forfeiture his lordſhip ſaid, that no ways relates to the ſhare in the ſurplus; for which reaſons ſhe muſt clearly be intitled to that; and the clauſe of forfeiture, in this will, meerly relates to the 1000*l.* and is to this effect; *It is given to her, to be paid at* 21, *or day of marriage, which ſhall firſt happen.* **Provided ſhe marries with the conſent of the three executors, and if ſhe does not, then it is given over.** All the executors died before ſhe attained her age of 21, or married; wherefore his lordſhip held the conſent of no other perſon was neceſſary; his lordſhip alſo obſerved the condition to be a ſubſequent one, and ſaid it is the general rule of law, *that if ſuch a condition become impoſſible the party is excuſed. On this foundation it is, that the caſes have been in this court,* cited by the defendant's counſel, *that where a legacy is given upon a ſubſequent condition, that the party marry with the conſent of his executors, and he appoints two, if one dies the party is at liberty to marry without the conſent of the other*; nor can it be ſaid at all, that the conſent of *Tinwel* was neceſſary, who was adminiſtrator *de bonis non* of the father. What remains, relates to the will of the mother, and hereon two queſtions ariſe; one concerning the ſpecific legacies given to the daughter; the other concerning the ſhare in the ſurplus; and as to both theſe, his lordſhip's opinion was, that her intereſt in both was forfeited. The condition is inſerted about the middle of the will, and is *My will is, that if my daughter marries before ſhe attains her age of* 21, *without the conſent of my executor under his hand and ſeal firſt had and obtained, if living, then ſhe ſhall not be intitled to any part of ſuch legacies* **as I have given her.** And this condition, his lordſhip held, related to all the legacies given her, as well to a ſhare in the ſurplus as to the ſpecific legacies. *A teſtator is conſidered as having the whole of the will in his thoughts at the ſame time, though he cannot ſpeak the whole of his mind at once.* And his lordſhip further ſaid, had indeed the condition immediately followed the bequeſt of the ſpecific legacies, there might have been more colour for the objection; but as it was at a great diſtance from the firſt as well as the laſt, it ought in reaſon to extend to all; and his lordſhip ſaid further, that the only doubt ariſes from this expreſſion in the conditional clauſe, namely, *the legacies which I have given her*; but the whole of the legacies are to be conſidered as given at the ſame time. But it has been objected, that the marriage in the preſent caſe is not a breach of this condition; becauſe *John* who was appointed executor renounced, and adminiſtration with the will annexed was granted to *Tinwel*; but his lordſhip was, notwithſtanding this, of opinion, that the conſent of *John* the ſon was neceſſary; for as his lordſhip obſerved, the word *executor* is deſcriptive of the perſon, and lands have often been given to perſons under that name. It is a perſonal power given to him who was appointed executor; the words are, *if he be living,* which ſhews that he himſelf was perſonally conſidered.

 For

For thefe reafons his lordfhip's opinion was, the plaintiffs in the original caufe were intitled to all the benefit, under the will of the mother, which their fifter would have had, provided fhe had married with the confent of her eldeft brother; but *Hicks* hath been the occafion of the whole of the original caufe, and as he hath denied his marriage by his anfwer, his lordfhip thought fit, and accordingly directed that he fhould pay the cofts of this fuit. Decreed *accordant*. *Grayden* and *Hicks*, in *Canc'* before lord chancellor, 7 *December* 1739.

5. See 1 *Chan. Ca.* 22, 53, 122, 138, 140, 141, 142. *Gilb.* 26. *Nelf.* 98, *&c.* 145, 234, 236, 183, 244, 261. 2 *Chan. Ca.* 1, 23, 95. 1 *Vern.* 20, 300. *Skin.* 285, *&c.* *Prec. Chan.* 348, 226. 2 *Pe. Will.* 626.

273. *Linea recta femper praefertur tranfverfali.*

What.

1. 1ft, LINEAL defcent is conveyed downwards in the right line, as from the grandfather to the father, from the father to the fon, *&c.* 2dly, Collateral is from the fide of the lineal, as grandfather's brother, father's brother. *Co. Lit.* 10.

Who to inherit.

2. The father's brother and his pofterity fhall inherit before the grandfather's brother and his pofterity; *et fic de caeteris*; for *propinquior excludit propinquum, et propinquus remotum, et remotus remotiorem.* Co. Lit. 10. b.

3. He is neareft who is fo *jure repraefentationis* as to defcents; for legally he is neareft, and he reprefents the perfon of his anceftor, who would have been the neareft had he been alive, and therefore ftands in his ftead to inherit. See *Co. Lit.* 10. *b.*

4. Therefore if a man purchafe lands in fee-fimple, and die *fans* iffue, his next coufin collateral of the whole blood, how far fo ever from him in degree, may inherit, and have the land as heir to him. *Lit. fect.* 2. But this extends not to heirs in tail. *Co. Lit.* 10. *a.*

274. *Major haereditas venit unicuique noftrum a jure legibus, quam a parentibus.*

SEE rule, *Eft boni judicis ampliare jurifdictionem.*

275. *Majus dignum trahit ad fe minus.*

1. AN adulterer takes away another man's wife, and puts her in new clothes, the hufband may carry away with his wife the clothes. 11 *H.* 4. 31.

2. A box fealed up with deeds goes to the heir together with the deeds, and not to the executor. 10 *Eliz.* 323.

3. A bafe mine, wherein is contained gold, fhall go to the king, for the worthinefs of the gold. 10 *Eliz.* 323.

4. The

4. The body of a man is more worthy than the land; therefore land ſhall enſue the nature of the perſon. 3 *Eliz.* 238.

5. If three jointenants be diſſeiſed, and they arraign an aſſiſe, and one of them releaſeth to the diſſeiſor all actions perſonal, this ſhall bar him, but it ſhall not bar the other plaintiffs; for, in regard to them, the realty ſhall be preferred; *et omne majus trahit ad ſe minus dignum*; and in a writ of ward brought by two, the releaſe of the one ſhall not grieve the other, but ſhall inure to his benefit; for he ſhall recover the whole, and hold his companion out. *Co. Lit.* 285. *a.* See 1 *Show.* 21.

276. *Majus dignum praecedat.*

General.

1. THE intire thing muſt be demanded in a *praecipe* before the moiety, part or parts. *Regiſter.*

2. And that which is of greater dignity before that of leſs. *Regiſter* 88.

Particular caſes.

3. As an houſe before land, a caſtle before a meſſuage or a manor, arable land before meadow, paſture, wood, or any other ſoil; and that this is the courſe of the *Regiſter*, ſee *the ſame.*

4. So in replevin, a ſuit is for two chattels, one living, the other dead; the live chattel ſhall be firſt demanded. *Regiſter* 88. *b.*

5. Where two have the preſentment to a church, one to have two turns the other the third, if he who hath the third turn be plaintiff in a *quare impedit*, he ſhall not begin firſt with his own turn, but with the other's two turns. *Dy.* 299. *b.*

277. *Majus dignum continet in ſe minus.*

VIDE rules, *Neceſſity creates equity. Acceſſorium ſequitur principale.*

278. *Mala grammatica non vitiat chartam.*

THE law, that principally reſpecteth ſubſtance, muſt judge according to the intention of the parties, and not according to grammatical conſtruction; for *mala grammatica non vitiat chartam.* Co. Lit. 146. b.

279. *Maledicta expoſitio eſt quae corrumpit textum.*

General.

1. WORDS ſuperfluous, vain and idle, which deſtroy the deſign, are to be rejected and laid aſide. *Et maledicta expoſitio eſt quae corrumpit textum.* 4 Co. 35. a. *Vide poſt.* caſe 5. 6.

So the king's grant, general.

2. See 4 *Co.* 34 *et* 35, *&c. ſupra*, being *Bozoun*'s caſe.

3. It was ſaid by *Coke* chief juſtice, and affirmed by the other juſtices, that of late ſuch nice and ſtrict conſtructions had been made of ſome letters patent, as to ſubvert the force and effect of them, and many good ones had been drawn in queſtion, to the diſhonour of the king, diſinheriſon of the ſubject, and againſt the true reaſon and antient rule of law. *Et talis certitudo certitudinem confundit.* Such nice and captious pretence of certainty confounds true and legal certainty; *Et maledicta expoſitio eſt quae corrumpit et confundit textum.* 8 Co. 56. b.

4. The grants of kings are ſo to be conſtrued as ſhall be beneficial for his honour and the relief of the ſubject, and not to be ſtrict or literal in ſubverſion of ſuch grants. 6 *Co.* 6. *a.*

Particular caſes.

5. In the principal caſe it was reſolved, that the king was not deceived in his grant; for he had recited the eſtate of the tenant for life, and that he was alive; ſo as the king knew very well he could not grant in poſſeſſion that which another had for his life; but it ought to take effect as it may by law; and the caſe of lord *Chandos*, 6 *Co.* 55. was reſolved a ſtronger caſe; for there the king miſtook the law, thinking that by the ſurrender of the letters patent the eſtate-tail was extinct, and that he thereupon was ſeiſed in fee, and ſo granted the manor in poſſeſſion, and yet the reverſion paſſed without any word of reverſion; for the grant ought to take effect as by law it may: but in the caſe at bar the king miſtook nothing, nor did he take upon him to grant what he had not power to grant, neither was he deceived in any part of his grant. And *when the king's charter may be taken to two intents good; in many caſes it ſhall be ſo underſtood as is moſt beneficial for the king; but if they may be taken to one intent good, and to another intent void; then for the honour of the king, and the benefit of the ſubject, it ſhall be ſo taken that the king's grant may take effect, for it was not the king's deſign to make a void grant.* 8 Co. 56. a.

6. King *Richard* II. granted to the abbot of *Waltham*, that he nor his ſucceſſors ſhould not be *collectores decimarum, &c. conceſſ. regi per clerum Angliae, nec alicujus inde parcellae:* in this caſe if the grant ſhould be taken literally, *per clerum Angliae*, i. e. *per totum clerum Angliae*, the grant is void; for all the clergy of *England* never convened in or came to one convocation, but each province had a ſeparate convocation; and therefore the grant of the king ſhall not be taken in ſuch a ſenſe as to make them void, but in ſuch a ſenſe as may make them ſtand in law, *&c.* and this is a ſtronger caſe than the caſe at bar; for there the letter of the grant well ſtandeth with the intention of the king, *&c.* but in the caſe of the grant to the abbot of *Waltham*, the letter of the grant and the intention of the king vary, and there the letter gives way to the intention of the king, *&c.* 8 *Co.* 56. *a. b.*

7. It was reſolved in the caſe of the king's auditor, where the queen grants a manor to *B.* and his heirs, in the premiſſes of the letters patent, to have and to hold to him and his aſſigns, omitting heirs in the *habendum*, yet the fee paſſeth by the premiſſes, and the *habendum* is void; for the premiſſes were ſufficiently certain to paſs the fee-ſimple, and the omiſſion in the *habendum* ſhall not vitiate what was certain by the premiſſes; for the queen's intent appeared by the premiſſes to paſs the fee-ſimple; *and her grant ought to be taken ſecundum intentionem regis, et non in deceptionem regis;* which would

be a great indignity to the king to make his grant under the great ſeal, of things which he might lawfully grant, to be void and of none effect, *quia apices juris non ſunt jura*, &c. 8 Co. 56. b. 57. a.

8. See rule, *Apices juris non ſunt jura*.

280. *Malum quo communius eo pejus.*

THE intention of the ſtatute to ſuppreſs ſuperſtitious uſes, was to prohibit all ſuch ſuperſtitious uſes as were public in churches, for the general miſchief which might grow from them; for *malum quo communius eo pejus*, and not to forbid private prayers in their chambers or like private places; which cannot be attended with ſuch ill conſequences, and to ſo dangerous examples. 4 *Co.* 109. *b.* *The antiquity and frequency or prevalency of a miſchief greatly aggravates it.* See rule, *Communis error facit quaſi jus.*

281. *Marriage the higheſt conſideration in law.*

General.

1. THAT marriage is the very higheſt conſideration in the law, ſee 2 *Mod. Ca.* 17.

2. A ſettlement on marriage is not to be ſet aſide, there being no fraud or incapacity in the huſband; but general that he was weak. It is not neceſſary that he ſhould be a learned or an ingenious man. 2 *Mod. Ca.*

Particular caſes.

3. Marriage contracts made in all countries, are to be obſerved in all; and therefore a contract made in *France* was enforced here. *Prec. Chan.* 208.

4. Marriage even without a portion paid, is a ſufficient conſideration to give the grantee greater equity than the heir. 1 *Vern.* 17.

5. The plaintiff, the duke of *Norfolk*, married Sir *Henry Wood*'s daughter, and now comes as adminiſtrator of his ſaid late wife, by this bill, for an account of the perſonal eſtate of his ſaid late wife, (to wit) the profits of her real eſtate received by the truſtees in her life-time. The caſe ariſes upon the conſtruction of a deed of ſettlement and will of the ſaid Sir *Henry*, wherein (*int' al'*) it was recited that a marriage was intended between the plaintiff and the daughter of the ſaid Sir *Henry*, and then comes a clauſe, in caſe the daughter ſhould live to attain the age of 16, and ſhould refuſe to marry the plaintiff, then the plaintiff ſhould have 20000*l.* out of his perſonal eſtate; and after comes another clauſe, that if it ſhould happen that the ſaid intended marriage ſhould not be till after his daughter was 16, then he ſettles his real and perſonal eſtate upon the duke the plaintiff and his wife, for their lives, &c. The marriage takes effect, the lady under 16, and ſhe dies before 17 without iſſue; account decreed. 1 *Vern.* 339.

6. Articles, covenant, or even a bare promiſe before marriage to ſettle a jointure, ſhall be executed in equity againſt the heir. 1 *Vern.* 17.

7. So where the huſband covenanted that the lands ſettled in jointure, were of ſuch a value. 1 *Vern.* 217.

8. So where the father offered 1500*l.* with his daughter. 1 *Vern.* 201.

9. So where a brother promises that, if the wife's fortune made so much, he would leave his brother, the husband, his estate, and he after married himself, and settled the same on his wife, *&c.* yet the agreement was decreed; the marriage taking place upon the expectation of the performance of this promise. 2 *Vent.* 353.

10. A man makes an agreement with the mother of the wife, previous to the marriage, and after the marriage had, comes to a new agreement; the first agreement being more beneficial to the issue of the marriage, was decreed to be performed. *Nels.* 91, *&c.*

11. A man makes a settlement in consideration the wife had parted with her former settlement made after the marriage, but in consideration of a marriage fortune secured, but no proof of any previous agreement, yet the court presumed it, so not merely voluntary, but good against creditors. *Prec. Chan.* 101.

12. The husband was to make a settlement on the wife, and in consideration thereof to receive the fortune; the wife dies *sans* issue before the settlement made; the husband shall not have the fortune, for the settlement was a condition precedent. *Gilb.* 188.

There are many cases in the books to shew that agreements made in derogation of the marriage contract are to be set aside, whether by way of marriage-brocage or secret trust or conveyance, in fraud of the marriage agreement, *&c.* and also that agreements of a third person have been enforced, where it has been the consideration of, and real occasion of the marriage.

Of what things marriage is a suspension.

* 13. When a power was given to a woman, at the time unmarried, to dispose by will; and she afterwards married. Decreed, that the marriage is a suspension of her power, but if she survives her husband the power revives. See case before the house of lords 9 *Feb.* 1727, *Rich* and ——. See 1 *Chan. Ca.* 117. *Prec. Chan.* 41, 237, *&c.* 408. 2 *Cro.* 170, 571. 1 *Sid.* 58. 5 *Co.* 70. *b.* *Mo.* 855. *Lit.* 32. *Hob.* 216. 1 *Cro.* 373. 8 *Co.* 136. *Co. Lit.* 264. *b.* 343. *b.* *Dy.* 140. *Yelv.* 156. *Ro.* 935. 2 *Cro.* 222. *Salk.* tit. *Extinguishment.*

What a good evidence of marriage, cohabitation, &c.

14. See case *supra Grayden* and *Hicks*, *sub* tit. *Limitations, in restraint*, &c.

Church books.

15. * Entry of a marriage in a church book, no evidence of that marriage, unless the identity of the persons be sufficiently proved; or the same be strengthened by proof of cohabitation, or allowance, or confession of the parties. See case in the house of lords *Draycot* and *Talbot*, 28 *Jan.* 1718.

16. References, 1 *Rep. Chan.* 216. 1 *Vern.* 406, 427. 2 *Chan. Ca.* 29, 30, 87, *&c.* 1 *Rep. Chan.* 275. *S. C.*

282. *Matter of higher nature determines that of more base or inferior nature.*

1. IF an offence which is murder at law, be made high treafon, no appeal lies of it; fo that the leffer offence, namely the murder, is gone, and the offence is now to be confidered high treafon, whereof no appeal lieth. *Dy.* 50.

2. Where one hath a liberty by prefcription, and takes a grant from the king by patent, this determines the prefcription; for matter in writing determines matter in deed. 21 *H.* 7. 5. *So, as I take it, if one indebted to another on fimple contract, gives fpecialty for the fame debt, the fimple contract is gone, or if articles on marriage or the like, are reduced into a formal fettlement, the articles,* &c. *are no more to be confidered in law; though on circumftances of fraud or practice, a court of equity poffibly may refort back to the articles, and confider the original agreement, and how far the fettlement is purfuant.*

283. *Melior et tutior eft conditio poffidentis.*

1. *MELIOR eft conditio poffidentis ubi neuter jus habet.* Jenk. 118.

2. It is regularly true in law, that if upon the whole record it appear that the plaintiff had no caufe of action, and efpecially if that appear of his own fhewing, that the court fhall never give judgment for him, however the defendant has mifbehaved himfelf in pleading; for *melior eft conditio poffidentis*; and the defendant is fafe if the affailant mifs him; for *vana eft fine viribus ira. Rigway*'s cafe, 3 *Co.* 52. and *Barton*'s cafe, 5 *Co.* 69.

3. See *Hob.* 103, 199.

284. *Meliorem conditionem ecclefiae facere poteft praelatus, deteriorem nequaquam.*

General.

1. DIlapidations and diminutions of ecclefiaftical livings are torts, and are *quodammodo* punifhable at law; for the mafter, dean, *&c.* for dilapidations and wafte, or diminution of the revenues of their houfes, *&c.* might be deprived, as appears by 35 *E.* and 29 *E.* 3. 16. 2 *H.* 4. 3. 11 *H.* 6. 20 *H.* 6. 46. 9 *E.* 4. 34. *Godb.* 259. 1 *Ro.* 335. 2 *Bulft.* 158.

2. Lord *Coke* faith, Wherever *Littleton* putteth his cafe of an abbot or prior, the fame law is of a bifhop, dean, archdeacon, prebendary, parfon, vicar, and the like. And another thing his lordfhip obferved was, that an abbot or prior cannot difclaim, *&c.* for regularly it is true, *quod meliorem conditionem ecclefiae fuae facere poteft praelatus, deteriorem nequaquam*; and again, *ecclefiae fuae conditionem meliorem facere poffunt fine confenfu, deteriorem non poffunt fine confenfu*; therefore none of thefe may difclaim; becaufe they alone cannot deveft any fee which is vefted in their houfe or church; for the wifdom of the law would never truft one fole perfon with the difpofition of the inheritance of his houfe or church: but an abbot or prior hath his convent,

convent, the biſhop his chapter, the parſon and vicar their patron and ordinary, *&c.* *ſans* whoſe aſſent they could not paſs any inheritance. *Co. Lit.* 102. *b.* 103. *a.*

3. Remedy by prohibition is againſt any pulling down the houſe, *&c.* or other waſte againſt the incumbent. *Mo.* 917.

Particular caſes.

4. If the parſon of a church will do waſte to the inheritance of his church, for his own private gain, in felling trees; the patron may have a prohibition againſt him; for the parſon is ſeiſed as in right of his church, and his glebe is the dower of his church, for thereof it was endowed; and ſo ſpeak many antient records. 11 *Co.* 49. *a.*

5. 2 *H.* 4. 3. *b.* if the biſhop or archdeacon abate, and fell all the trees, he ſhall be depoſed as a dilapidator. 29 *E.* 3. 16. *accordant. Vide* 27 *Aſſ. pl.* 10. 20 *H.* 6. 46. 10 *E.* 4. 19. And the treatiſe intitled *Ne rectores proſternant arbores in coemeterio*, which is but a declaration of the common law, in theſe words, *Prohibemus ne eccleſiarum rectores arbores in coemeterio creſcentes praeſumant proſternere indiſcrete, niſi cum cancellus eccleſiae neceſſaria indiget refectione, &c.* and this is generally true, *meliorem conditionem eccleſiae facere poteſt praelatus, deteriorem nequaquam.* 11 Co. 49. b.

6. The plaintiff, patron, brought a bill, ſetting forth that the defendant parſon had committed waſte, and therefore prayed an injunction to reſtrain future waſte, and an affidavit was made of the waſte done. The lord chancellor ſaid he was fully ſatisfied that the injunction ought to be granted, and ſaid it appeared 11 *Co.* 49. that the patron may have a prohibition in the courts of law, in a caſe of this nature. So if a prebendary commits waſte in his prebend. The biſhop of *Durham* committed waſte, whereupon redreſs was by writ out of chancery, that neither he nor his ſervants commit waſte in the premiſſes. And his lordſhip ſaid, that the reſolution of the parliament was agreeable to the reaſon of the caſe before mentioned, namely, that as in the former caſes where private perſons are patrons, the remedy for them is by prohibition; ſo in caſe of biſhopricks where the king is patron, there ought to be the like remedy. 3 *Ro. Abr.* 85. There are three or four inſtances wherein prohibitions have been granted in the caſe of waſte committed by eccleſiaſtical perſons. A prohibition was the ordinary remedy for waſte at common law, and on that ground it is that injunctions of that kind are granted in this caſe; for theſe reaſons his lordſhip ſaid, the patron may have an injunction, *&c.* and ordered accordingly. *Barn.* 399, 400. *Eccleſiaſticks and their miniſters and officers are compelled to their duty by* Mandamus *from the temporal courts, as well as by church cenſures; and they are reſtrained from committing oppreſſion and wrong, not only by the cenſures of their own courts, but alſo by prohibition and* praemunire *from the temporal courts, which have full authority to deal out to them a juſt proportion of puniſhment for ſuch oppreſſion and wrong.*

7. See 2 *Bulſt.* 279. 2 *Ro.* 335. 2 *Ro. Abr.* 813. *Mo.* 917. 1 *Ro.* 199, 252. 3 *Bulſt.* 116, 119, 158. 1 *Show.* 353. *Het.* 30. *Far.* 127. *Show. Par. Ca.* 62. 1 *Vent.* 307, 316, 323. 1 *Keb.* 354. 2 *Ju. Eccl. fo.* 357 *to* 362, 415, *&c.* pretty fully of this doctrine, and *Watſon* biſhop of *St. David*'s caſe taken upon an excommunication. in *Salk.* and alſo in *Fareſt.* and in 2 *Ju. Eccl.* 365, *&c.* *S. C.*

285. *Mens teſtatoris in teſtamentis ſpectanda eſt.*

General.

1. IT is agreeable to law and juſtice, and to true piety, to ſee that the will of the dead be performed; and though the law has aſcertained how eſtates ſhall go where there is no will; yet where there is one, and that diſpoſes otherwiſe than the law would, in ſuch caſe the law will compel a performance. *Show. Parl. Ca.* 196.

2. ——*Legum ſervanda fides; ſuprema voluntas*
Quod mandat, fierique jubet, parere neceſſe eſt.

3. In wills the intention of the party is to be regarded; for the ſtatute 21 *H.* 8. leaves the teſtator at liberty to expreſs his mind as he pleaſeth; but of conveyances which are at common law it is otherwiſe; for they are tied up to ſet forms and ſet words. 7 *Co.* 40.

4. It is only the intention of the party, which both makes and revokes a will. 1 *Ro. Abr.* 615. *Mo.* 429. *Cro. Ca.* 23. *Sid.* 90. 1 *Keb.* 357. *Show. Parl. Ca.* The earl of *Lincoln*'s caſe, and *Seymore* and *Noſworthy*'s caſe, in *Hard.* 374.

5. *In teſtamentis ratio tacita non debet conſiderari, ſed verba ſolum conſiderari debent. Multa poſſunt movere mentem teſtatoris, quae nos latent; ideo per divinationem mentis durum eſt a verbis recedere.* 2 Chan. Ca. 155.

6. Wills are to be conſtrued according to the intent of the teſtator, 1 *Chan. Ca.* 79, 80. 2 *Chan. Ca.* 11. *Pop.* 131. *Nelſ.* 159, 160. *Gilb.* 11, 118, 133, 209. *Nelſ.* 354, 433. *Plow. Com.* 523. *b.* if conſiſtent with the rules of law. * See caſe before the houſe of lords *Sparrow* and *Shawe*, 15 *April* 1729.

7. The will of the deviſor, expreſſed by his teſtament, ſhall be performed according to his intent, *ſecundum veram intentionem ſuam.* Co. Lit. 322. b.

Particular caſes.

* 8. The caſe was, The deviſor being ſeiſed in fee deviſed to his wife for life, and 500*l.* more to her to be raiſed by ſale of timber, coals, or any part of the eſtate, at her election, and in caſe ſhe died before it was raiſed, then ſhe had power, by deed or will, to appoint to raiſe it in like manner; but if the truſtees, or thoſe for whom they ſhould ſtand ſeiſed, and particularly the deviſor's two ſiſters, who were the next takers, ſhould raiſe the ſame, then the power to ceaſe. And, after the deceaſe of his wife, he deviſes to his ſaid truſtees and the ſurvivor, without the words, *their heirs, or the heirs of the ſurvivor,* ſubject as aforeſaid, in truſt for his ſiſters *A. L.* and *D. E.* equally betwixt them during their natural lives, without committing of waſte; and if either of his ſiſters die leaving iſſue or iſſues, then for ſuch iſſue or iſſues of the mother's ſhare, or elſe in truſt for the ſurvivor or ſurvivors of them and their reſpective iſſue or iſſues; but if it ſhall happen that both my ſaid ſiſters die without iſſue as aforeſaid, and their iſſue or iſſues to die without iſſue or iſſues lawfully to be begotten; then the truſtees to ſtand and be intruſted for *ſeveral others over* in remainder. One of the ſiſters dies without iſſue, and the other enters, and levies a fine and ſuffers a recovery, to make herſelf miſtreſs of the fee, and

well, for ſhe had an eſtate-tail. See caſe * *Sparrow* and *Shaw* before the houſe of lords 17 *March* 1729-30. See alſo caſe * *Davies* and *Gibbs*, 17 *March* in the ſame year. Alſo the earl of *Tankerville* and *Gray*, 14 *March* 1728, all before the houſe of lords; and alſo caſe * *Coleſon* and *Coleſon*, at the rolls 20 *July* 1739.

How to be conſtrued.

General.

9. All the words of a will muſt ſtand together. *Nelſ.* 27. 1 *Chan. Ca.* 309. And it muſt not be made void, if by any conſtruction of law it can be made good. 1 *Chan. Ca.* 178. *Nelſ.* 403.

Who may take.

10. *Lord chancellor:* Without queſtion one may take as heir male of the body of a perſon deceaſed, who is no heir general of the ſame perſon; 1ſt, Becauſe the intent of the teſtator is manifeſt and appears at firſt view, who was the perſon meant to take thereby. 2dly, The diſtinction between taking by purchaſe and taking by deſcent, where the words are the ſame, though it be mentioned in books of good authority, yet it ſeems to have no good foundation of reaſon or of law to ſupport it; and if it ſhould prevail in all caſes, it would overthrow another rule of law, as certain and as well eſtabliſhed, which is, that a perſon may take by purchaſe, if he be ſufficiently deſcribed, though he has neither addition of chriſtian or ſurname given him; nay though his chriſtian name be falſe or miſtaken; as appears by ſeveral caſes in *Co. Lit.* 3. *a.* and if ſo, certainly ſuch diſcription of the perſon, as has all the marks and characters whereby he may be known, and is defective in none, muſt be ſufficient to intitle him under that diſcription. *Gilb.* 133.

Where the reſidue undiſpoſed.

11. The reſidue undiſpoſed of is to be diſtributed according to the ſtatute, there being legacies to the executors; for the preſumption is, by giving them legacies, he intended them no more than what he had ſo expreſly given them in his will. *Gilb.* 74, 75, 126, 184, 200, 208, 209. 1 *Vern.* 473. 2 *Vern.* 648. *Prec. Chan.* 82, 92, 94. *Nelſ.* 177, 178, 351, 352. *Prec. Chan.* 231, 263, 264, 324. 1 *Pe. Will.* 7, 8, 9. 2 *Ju. Eccl.* 48. *ca.* 6. *and fo.* 50. *ca.* 9.

As to averments dehors.

12. If a man deviſe lands to his wife for life generally, it may not be averred to be for her jointure, and in ſatisfaction of her dower, and that for two reaſons. 1ſt, Becauſe *a deviſe imports a conſideration in itſelf,* and therefore as *a deviſe may not be averred to be to the uſe of any other than the deviſee, unleſs it be expreſſed in the will, no more may a deviſe be averred to be for a jointure or in lieu of dower, unleſs it be expreſſed in the will; but ſhall be taken for a benevolence.* 2dly, All the will concerning lands *per le ſtat.* 32 & 34 *H.* 8. ought to be in writing, and no averment ought to be taken out of the will, but what may be collected from the words contained in the will. 4 *Co.* 4. *a.* See ſtat. of *Frauds*, and *Selwin*

and *Brown*'s caſe in 2 *Ju. Eccl.* 50. where this doctrine ſeems now to be fully ſettled.

13. References, *Jenk. Margin* 277. 2 *Chan. Ca.* 10, 11, 155. *Mo.* 145. 1 *Co.* 176. 2 *Co.* 76, 4 *Co.* 3, 4, 71. 5 *Co.* 26, 68. 7 *Co.* 40. 8 *Co.* 155. 1 *Mod.* 117. *Salk.* 232, 235. 1 *Lutw.* 735, 791. *Ro. Ab.* 579, 413, 414. 2 *Bro. Abr.* 2, 676, 750, 779, 790. 2 *Leon.* 70. *Mo.* 222, 356, 592. *Godb.* 131, 432. *Jenk.* 115. 1 *Vern.* 20, 30, 37, 38, 254. 2 *Vern.* 98, 100, 252, 337, 339, 517, 539, 559, 647, 648, 738. *Nelſ.* 312, 313, 403.

286. *Minima poena corporalis eſt major qualibet pecuniaria.*

SEE rules, *Corpus humanum non recipit aeſtimationem. Equity regards ſubſtance*, &c.

287. *Miſpleading ſhall not prejudice in chancery.*

General.

1. THE courſe of the chancery is the law of the chancery. 1 *Chan. Ca.* 106, 92.

2. Chancery is not unbounded, but limited by precedents and the practice of former times, and it is dangerous to extend its authority further. 3 *Ch. Ca.* 95, 136.

Rules and their reaſons.

3. Where there is right and equity, forms of that court and orders ſhall not hinder to examine. 2 *Chan. Ca.* 251.

4. In chancery a man ſhall not be prejudiced for miſpleading or want of form, *&c.* *Elſ. Obſ.* 30.

5. *Note*; The chancellor ſaid that a man ſhall not be prejudiced by miſpleading or for default of form; but according to the verity of the matter; and the chancellor muſt judge *ſecundum conſcientiam, et non ſecundum allegata.* Elſ. Obſ. 69.

6. Miſpleading or default of form ſhall not be prejudicial in the chancery. *Elſ. Obſ.* 69.

7. In pleading, a default in form ſhall not, in any caſe, be prejudicial in the chancery; for it cannot be called a court of conſcience, if the act of the clerk in pleading ſhould cauſe the party to loſe his ſuit and his expences. *Elſ. Obſ.* 67.

8. In chancery it is not neceſſary or requiſite that the bill be all certain, according to the ſolemnity of the common law, for it is but a petition. *Elſ. Obſ.* 68.

9. Chancery is always open; it is the refuge of the poor; it correcteth the rigour of the law (yet the acts thereof ſhall do no prejudice); it hath an admiral juriſdiction, and hath, at leaſt, a concurrent juriſdiction with the eccleſiaſtical courts. *Elſ. Obſ.* 2 *Chan. Ca.* 217. *Nelſ.* 438. *Gilb.* 1.

10. It hath juriſdiction of infants, ideots, lunatics, in caſes of femes covert, of truſts, matters of fraud, accidents, forfeitures and penalties, to relieve againſt the ſeverities of law, and to give relief where none at law, and is only controulable in parliament, *&c.* See before *ſub* tit. *Chancery*, &c.

the

the ſeveral diviſions. Elſ. Obſ. 2 *Chan. Ca.* 217. 3 *Chan. Ca.* 136. *Gilb.* 1, 2, 172, *&c.* 119, 120. 1 *Chan. Ca.* 201. *Nelſ.* 438. 1 *Vern.* 176. *Hard.* 23, 120.

288. *Modus et conventio vincunt legem.*

Particular caſes.

1. TO every tenant for life, the law, as incident to his eſtate, without proviſion of the party, giveth him three kinds of eſtovers, *i. e.* 1ſt, Houſe-boot, which is two-fold, *viz. Eſtoverium aedificandi, et ardendi.* 2dly, Plough-boot, *i. e. Eſtoverium arandi.* And 3dly and laſtly, Hay-boot, *i. e. Eſtoverium claudendi.* And theſe eſtovers muſt be reaſonable, *eſtoveria rationabilia*; and theſe the leſſee may take upon the land without aſſignment, unleſs reſtrained by ſpecial covenant; for *Modus et conventio vincunt legem.* Co. Lit. 41. b.

Where relieved againſt.

2. The plaintiff put his ſon clerk to the teſtator of the defendant when he lay ill of the ſickneſs whereof he died, and gave 120*l.* and articles were had, wherein it was provided, that in caſe the maſter ſhould die within a year, that then 60*l.* of the money ſhould be returned; the maſter never recovered, but died in three weeks. The court, notwithſtanding the parties had provided againſt accidents, for a certain ſum to be returned in caſe the maſter died, and that *Modus et conventio vincunt legem*, decreed 100 guineas to be paid back to the plaintiff the father. 1 *Vern.* 460.

3. An apothecary takes an apprentice with a ſum of money, and puts him away, for miſdemeanors, after he had lived ſome time with him. The court decreed the maſter to refund 30*l.* of the money; and the rather becauſe the indentures were not inrolled, ſo as the matter was not properly cognizable before the chamberlain of *London.* 2 *Vern.* 64.

4. References, *Co. Lit.* 19. *a.* 12 *Co.* 72. *Hob.* 160. 1 *Chan. Ca.* 84, 85, 110.

289. *Moneta eſt juſtum medium et menſura rerum commutabilium.*

General, to its uſe, and what it is.

1. EVERY commonwealth ought to have a certain ſtandard of money; for none can be without contract, and no contracts without equality; and that cannot be without money; for though at firſt exchange was in uſe, yet that was found very inconvenient, and in many caſes impoſſible, through the difficulty of dividing of many things, and other like obſtacles; and therefore money was invented, as well for the convenience of commerce as for the reducing contracts to equality. *Moneta eſt juſtum medium et menſura rerum commutabilium; nam per medium monetae fit omnium rerum, quae in mundo ſunt, conveniens et juſta aeſtimatio.* And to this intent it was that *Keble* ſaid 12 *H.* 7. 23. *b.* That every thing might be valued by money, by which words is to be underſtood, money coined; and the great advantage of

having a certain ſtandard of money and of meaſures is well ſhewn by *Budelius* in theſe verſes,

Una fides, pondus, menſura, moneta ſit una,
Et ſtatus illaeſus totius orbis erit.

Dav. 19. a.

Wherefore ſo called.

2. *Moneta dicitur a monendo; quia impreſſione nos moneat cujus ſit moneta. Cujus imago et ſuperſcriptio eſt haec.* Dav. 19. b. Hob. 43.

How made and what neceſſary thereto.

3. Three things are neceſſary to the making of lawful money. 1. Authority of the prince. 2. The print. 3. And the value. Though there are ſix things or circumſtances which ought to concur for the making lawful or currant money. 1. Weight. 2. Fineneſs. 3. Impreſſion. 4. Denomination. 5. Authority of the prince. 6. Proclamation, &c. *Dav.* 19. *b.* 20. *a.* See *Next diviſion.*

From whence it receives its value, &c. *from the king.*

General.

4. The king only can coin or make money within his dominions, and no one elſe without his licence, and if any preſume to do it, it is treaſon at common law; as appears by ſtat. 25 *E.* 3. *cap.* 2. which is but a declaration of the common law; and by *Glanvil, Britton* and *Bracton*, before this ſtatute, *Stamford fo.* 2 *et* 3. and in the caſe of mines, *Plow. Com.* 316. *a.* this matter is moſt clear, and there it is ſaid that the king ſhall have all gold and ſilver mines; becauſe if the ſubject was allowed them, yet by law he could not coin them, or ſet value upon them; for that belongs only to the crown; and that only is the thing which makes it currant. *Da.* 19. *a. b.*

Particular.

5. And that the king by his prerogative might ſet a price or valuation upon all coins, appears from this extraordinary caſe 21 *E.* 3. 60. *b.* In the time of the conqueror the abbot of *St. Edmonds Bury* complained to the king in parliament, that whereas he was exempt from the juriſdiction of the ordinary by ſeveral antient charters, that the biſhop of *Norwich* had viſited his houſe againſt thoſe charters of exemption; wherefore it was granted and ordained in parliament, that if for the time to come the biſhop of *Norwich*, or any of his ſucceſſors, ſhould go againſt the exemption aforeſaid, they ſhould pay to the king or his heirs, 30 *Talentes* or *Beſauntes*. After this, *viz.* in the time of *E.* 3. the biſhop of *Norwich* viſited the houſe again, againſt the ordinance aforeſaid; and this contempt being found in *B. R.* a *ſci. fa.* iſſued againſt the biſhop, to ſhew wherefore he ſhould not pay the king the 30 *Talentes* or *Beſauntes*; and upon an inſufficient plea pleaded by the biſhop, the court awarded that the king ſhould recover the *Talentes* or *Beſauntes*, and that the taking ſhould be interpreted by the king himſelf; for theſe *Talentes* or *Beſauntes* being uncertain in their value, as *Budeus* ſaith, *Quod talenta ſunt varia, et pondera ſunt potius quam numiſmata,*

ta, the king hath the power of ſetting a certain value upon them, according to the rule, *Monetae aeſtimationem dat, qui cudendi poteſtatem habet*; and in this point the common laws of *England* agree well with the rules of the civil law, *Jus cudendae monetae ad ſolum principem, hoc eſt, imperatorem de jure pertinet. Monetandi jus principum oſſibus inhaeret. Jus monetae comprehenditur in regalibus, quae nunquam a regio ſceptro abdicantur.* And yet by antient charters this prerogative hath been communicated to ſome ſubjects, as the archbiſhop of *Canterbury*, the archbiſhop of *York*, and the biſhop of *Durham*, the dean of St. *Martin's le Grand*, &c. Da. 20. a. b.

He may make it of what matters, in what form, he may eſtabliſh the ſtandard or change it in ſubſtance or impreſſion, or inhanſe, debaſe, or decry it, &c. *at his royal will.*

6. As the king by his prerogative may make money of what matter and in what form he pleaſeth, and eſtabliſh the ſtandard of it, ſo he may change it in ſubſtance and impreſſion, and inhanſe or debaſe the value of it, or utterly decry it to meer bullion; and this is *Moneta deſenſa et prohibita*, &c. and that the king hath exerciſed this authority, appears from many notorious changes of money, made in the reigns of ſeveral kings ſince the conqueſt, which changes were made by the kings without parliament, though there have been many acts of parliament for the ordering of exchange, and prohibiting the exportation of money made and ordained by the king, and the importation of foreign and falſe money, &c. *Da.* 20. *b.* 21. *a.* &c.

He may make foreign coin currant.

7. As *Spaniſh* ſilver, &c. made currant by the king's proclamation, is lawful money of *England*; ſo *French* crowns were lawful money by proclamation. And ſo the king, by his abſolute prerogative, may make any foreign coin currant, and lawful money of *England* at his pleaſure. 5 *Co.* 114. *b.*

290. *Mortgage may not be redeemed when the mortgagee cannot compel payment of the mortgage money, for that the remedy ought to be reciprocal.*

1. THIS *rule carries its reaſon with it.*

2. References, 1 *Chan. Ca.* 1, 2, 63. 1 *Rep. Chan.* 122, 123. 2 *Rep. Chan.* 58, 159, 247. 1 *Vern.* 7, 8, 192, 215, 268. 2 *Vern.* 84, 288.

291. *Multa tranſeunt cum univerſitate, quae per ſe non tranſeunt.*

1. IF a man, ſeiſed of lands as heir of the part of his mother, makes a feoffment in fee, reſerving rent to him and to his heirs, this rent ſhall go to the heirs of the part of the father; but if he makes a gift in tail, or a leaſe for life, reſerving a rent, the heir of the part of the mother ſhall have the reverſion; and the rent alſo, as incident thereunto, ſhall paſs with it;

but the heir of the part of the mother ſhall not take advantage of a condition annexed to the ſame; becauſe it is not incident to the reverſion, nor can paſs therewith. *Co. Lit.* 12. *b.*

2. If a man had been ſeiſed of a manor as heir of the part of the mother, and before the ſtatute of *Quia emptores terrar'* had made a feoffment in fee of parcel, to hold of him by rent and ſervice, altho' they be newly created, yet for that they are parcel of the manor, they ſhall with the reſt of the manor deſcend to the heir of the part of the mother, *Quia multa tranſeunt cum univerſitate, quae per ſe non tranſeunt.* Co. Lit. 12. b.

3. If a man hath a rent-ſeck of the part of his mother, and the tenant of the land grant a diſtreſs to him and his heirs, and the grantee dieth, the diſtreſs ſhall go with the rent to the heir of the part of the mother, as incident, *&c.* *Co. Lit.* 12. *b.* 13. *a.*

4. A man ſeiſed as heir of the part of his mother, makes a feoffment in fee to the uſe of him and his heirs, the uſe, being a thing in truſt and confidence, ſhall enſue the nature of the land, and deſcend to the heir of the part of the mother. *Co. Lit.* 13. *a.*

5. A man hath a ſeigniory as heir of the part of the mother, and a tenancy doth eſcheat, it ſhall go to the heir of the part of the mother. *Co. Lit.* 13. *a.*

6. If the heir of the part of the mother, of lands whereunto a warranty is annexed, is impleaded, and vouch, and judgment is given againſt him, and for him to recover in value, and dieth before execution, the heir of the part of the mother ſhall ſue execution to have in value againſt the vouchee; for *the effect ought to purſue the cauſe, and the recompence ſhall enſue the loſs.* Co. Lit. 13. a.

7. To every tenant for life, the law, as incident to his eſtate, without proviſion of the party, giveth three kinds of eſtovers, *&c.* and theſe the leſſee may take upon the land demiſed, without any aſſignment, *&c.* *Co. Lit.* 41. *b.*

8. The tenure in frankalmoigne is an incident to the inheritable blood of the grantor, and cannot be transferred nor forfeited to any other, no more than a founderſhip of an houſe of religion, *&c.* *Co. Lit.* 99. *a.*

9. A man ſeiſed of lands in fee, hath divers charters, deeds and evidences, and makes a feoffment in fee, either with or without warranty, only againſt him and his heirs, the purchaſer ſhall have all the charters, deeds and evidences, as incident to the land, *et ratione terrae*; to the end he may better defend the land himſelf, having no warranty, to recover in value; for the evidences are as it were the ſinews of the land, and the feoffor not being bound to warranty, hath no uſe of them, *&c.* *Co. Lit.* 6. *a.*

10. If a nobleman, knight, eſquire, *&c.* be buried in a church and have his coat-armour and pennons with his arms, and ſuch other enſigns of honour as belong to his degree or order ſet up in the church: or if a grave-ſtone or tomb be laid or made, *&c.* for a monument of him, here, though the freehold of the church be in the parſon, and that theſe are annexed to the freehold, yet cannot the parſon or any other take them or deface them, but he is ſubject to an action from the heir of him in whoſe honour and to whoſe memory they were ſet up; and ſome hold that the wife or executor, who firſt ſet them up, may have an action againſt any who deface them

them in their time. *Co. Lit.* 18. *b.* 3 *Inſt.* 202. 12 *Co.* 104, 105. *Mo.* 878. *Godb.* 200, 279. *Ro.* 57. *Lamb.* 496. *Noy* 104. *Sid.* 206. *Ro. Ab.* 625.

11. So a coat of arms placed in any window, or monument in the church or church-yard, cannot be beaten down or defaced, by the parſon, churchwarden, ordinary or any other; and if they be, the heir by deſcent, intereſted in the coat, may have an action upon the caſe; for the heir is inheritable to the arms as to an heir-loom. *Cro. Jac.* 366. *Salk.* 347.

12. References, *Dal.* 93. *Ro. Ab.* 827. 2 *Ro. Ab.* 791. *Co. Lit.* 27, 54. 1 *Co.* 87. *a.*

13. See rule, *Acceſſorium ſequitur principale.*

292. *Natura appetit perfectum.*

1. *COmmenda ſemeſtris* grew out of a natural equity, that in the time of the patron's reſpite given him to preſent, the church ſhould not be without a proviſional paſtor, which was a law of neceſſity, agreeable to the law of nature; and this might, upon the ſame reaſon, be continued with revenues, ſo long as this reſpite laſted. But after the lapſe juſtly incurred, the *commendam* is to ceaſe, for then the ordinary may collate; for *natura appetit perfectum, &c.* 18 E. 3. 21. and 1 H. 7. 21. The biſhop may ſequeſter if the king preſent not; and 12 *H.* 8. 8. by *Pollard*, the biſhop muſt ſee the cure ſerved if the parſon fail, at his own coſt. And *Linw. de jurejurando, cap. Preſbyt. verb. oblationis.* If a biſhop celebrate divine ſervice in any pariſh of his dioceſe, he may require the offerings of that day. And upon the ſame reaſon, if the executors being called by the ordinary, will not prove the will, the ordinary may commit adminiſtration till they do it. *Hob.* 144.

2. *Vide* rule, *Bonum neceſſarium extra terminos neceſſitatis non eſt bonum.*

293. *Neceſſitas facit illud licitum quod non eſt neceſſe ad alios.*

1. REferences, 1 *Ro.* 452, 474. *Mo.* 902. *Hob.* 144.

2. See alſo laſt rule.

294. *Neceſſitas legum vincula irridet.*

1. REference, *Hob.* 159.

2. See rules, *Natura appetit perfectum. Lex neceſſitatis eſt lex temporis.*

295. *Necessitas vincit legem.*

General.

1. *SAepenumero necessitas vincit communem legem, et quod necessarium est licitum est.*

Particular.

2. As if two jointenants are of lands, to them, and to the heirs of one of them; they may not join in a writ of right; but two jointenants, and to the heirs of one of them of an advowson, shall join in a writ of right of advowson; and the reason of the difference is, because in the first place they have several means and remedies, as is agreed in 46 *E.* 3. 21. but in the other case, if tenant for life do not join with him in fee, neither the one nor the other should have any remedy; and therefore in such case *necessitas vincit legem.* 5 Co. 40. b.

296. *Necessity creates equity.*

1. A Bill was to examine witnesses *in perpetuam rei memoriam,* to prove a *Modus decimandi.* The defendant demurred, for that the bill was to establish a custom against the church, and in prejudice of tithes, which are due *de communi jure.* Demurrer over-ruled. 1 *Vern.* 185.

2. The defendant pleaded he was a purchaser *bona fide,* for a valuable consideration, but there being several badges of fraud alledged in the bill, though the defendant had in his plea denied them, yet as he had not denied them by way of answer, that so the plaintiff might be at liberty to except, the plea was over-ruled. 1 *Vern.* 185.

3. After recovery or verdict at law, resolved on demurrer, that the party shall not be put to answer. 1 *Vern.* 176. *Stat.* 4 *H.* 4. *Hard.* 23, 120.

4. The motion was for a *supersedeas* to a writ *de cautione admittenda,* for that they had taken a writ to the sheriff without any affidavit filed, that the bishop refused to admit of caution, &c. and for that reason a *supersedeas* was awarded. And the lord keeper declared, that finding the court often troubled for writs *de cautione admittenda,* he thought the right of it was, that if there was a sentence for a man to pay money, or to do other matter in the spiritual court, he ought to perform that before he is admitted to his writ *de cautione admittenda*; for it is in vain to take security *parere mandatis ecclesiae,* whilst a man refuseth to obey the sentence. But the reporter puts a *quaere,* and supposeth a man to be excommunicated for not coming to church, or not receiving the sacrament, how can he do that till his caution is admitted, and he absolved? 1 *Vern.* 119.

5. Lands were settled on *Davies* and his wife for their lives; remainder to trustees to preserve contingent remainders; remainder to their first and every other son in tail male. The plaintiff and his wife had been 12 years married and no issue, and having contracted debts, the bill was, that they might be enabled to sell part to pay their debts. The defendant, the

 trustee,

truſtee, ſet forth the ſettlement, and confeſſed that the plaintiffs had been ſo long married, and had no iſſue, and believed they never would have any, and that they had contracted ſeveral debts, and ſubmitted to do as the court ſhould direct, being indemnified. And for the plaintiff it was ſaid, that in ſuch caſes, the court had decreed lands to be ſold: and cited the caſe of *Digby* and *Cornwallis*, and Sir *John Tufton*'s caſe, and ſaid neceſſity doth create a natural equity. Lord keeper could not tell how he could make ſuch decree, but at the plaintiff's importunity he gave time till *Michaelmas* to attend him with precedents. 1 *Vern.* 181, 182.

6. The defendant *R. S. anno* (81) made a mortgage of the lands in queſtion for 1000 years for 1000*l.* and intereſt, and confeſſed a judgment to another for 150*l.* and after on his marriage ſettled the ſame lands to the uſe of himſelf for life; remainder to truſtees for the life of the huſband to preſerve contingent remainders; remainder to the wife for life; remainder to the firſt and other ſons in tail; remainder to his own right heirs. The defendant having no iſſue articles to ſell the ſame lands to the plaintiff, who brings a bill, and therein ſets out theſe matters, and that the truſtees refuſed to join, and the mortgagee threatned to enter, and prayed ſpecific execution of the agreement, and that the truſtees might join in the conveyance; the huſband and wife by their anſwer ſet forth the ſettlement, that they had been married ſix years, and had no iſſue, confeſſed their contract with the plaintiff; and that they were ready to perform it; the truſtees alſo ſet out the ſettlement and ſubmitted to do as the court ſhould direct, being indemnified. For the plaintiff it was inſiſted, that the ſettlement being only of an equity of redemption, the mortgagee was not bound thereby, but might enter and alſo forecloſe, which would bind even the iſſue. And that the huſband and wife not being able to redeem, the ſale was neceſſary, alſo that the benefit of redemption would be loſt, as well to the huſband and wife as to the iſſue, if there ſhould be any. His honour decreed, the truſtees to join in the ſale and to be indemnified; the ſettlement being only of an equity of redemption, and the wife being in court and examined, whether ſhe freely conſented or not? 2 *Vern.* 303, 304.

7. The motion was for a mandatory writ to the chief juſtice of the king's bench, to command him to ſign a bill of exceptions in the caſe of lord *G. et al'*, who were convicted of a riot in *London*, and precedents were produced where a writ of this ſort had iſſued out of this court, to the judge of the ſheriffs court in *London.* Motion denied; for the precedent produced was to an inferior court; and he would not preſume but the chief juſtice of *England* would do what was juſt in the caſe, *&c.* and if they had wrong done them, they might right themſelves by actions on the caſe. And if the court had power to grant ſuch writ, it was diſcretionary, and not *de curſu.* 1 *Vern.* 175.

8. The bill was for a debt due to the plaintiff as executor; the defendant pleaded an outlawry of the plaintiff in bar, but the plea was over-ruled; the plaintiff ſuing *en auter droit.* 1 Vern. 184. *And ſo it is of others who are diſabled to bring actions in their own rights, yet* en auter droit *they may ſue or be ſued.*

9. The cuſtom of the manor was, that the copyholds had been uſually granted by copy in fee-ſimple, or for life, or for years. Held by *Fenner* and *Popham*, that an eſtate-tail might be of theſe cuſtomary lands; for that

an eſtate-tail might be wrought out of ſuch lands by equity of the ſtatute *de donis*; for otherwiſe there can be no eſtate-tail of copyhold lands; for by uſage it cannot be maintained, for that no ſuch eſtate was before this ſtatute; and this is within the time of limitation, after which a uſage cannot make a preſcription. *Poph.* 33, *&c.*

10. References, 1 *Vern.* 177, 330. 2 *Rep. Chan.* 144. *Skin.* 78. *Fi. Ley* 9. *b.* *Co. Lit.* 6. *b.*

297. *Negatio deſtruit negationem, et ambo faciunt affirmativum.*

TWO negatives make an affirmative in grammatical conſtruction; for *negatio deſtruit negationem, &c.* yet the law that principally regardeth ſubſtance, may judge otherwiſe according to the intention of the parties, and not according to grammatical conſtruction; for *mala grammatica non vitiat chartam.* Co. Lit. 146. b.

298. *Negative cannot be proved.*

General.

1. WItneſſes cannot teſtify a negative, but an affirmative. *Co. Lit.* 6. *b.*

What a good evidence, and the courſe.

2. When a trial is by witneſſes, regularly the affirmative ought to be proved by two or three witneſſes; as to prove a ſummons of the tenant, or the challange of a juror or the like, but when the trial is by the verdict of 12 men, there the judgment is not given upon witneſſes, or other kind of evidences, but upon the verdict, and upon ſuch evidence as is given to the jury, they give their verdict. *Co. Lit.* 6. *b.*

The ſorts of evidence.

3. *Bracton* ſaith there is *probatio duplex, viz. viva,* as by witneſſes *viva voce,* and *mortua* by deeds, writings and inſtruments. *Lib.* 5. *fo.* 400.

Preſumptions.

General to, and the ſorts.

4. Many times juries, together with other matters, are much induced by preſumptions, whereof are three ſorts, (*viz.*) violent, probable and light or temerary.

Particular caſes.

5. *Violenta praeſumptio* is many times *plena probatio*; as if one be run through the body with a ſword in an houſe, whereof he inſtantly dieth, and a man is ſeen to come out of that houſe with a bloody ſword, and no other man was at that time in the houſe. *Co. Lit.* 6. *b.*

6. In caſe of a charter of feoffment, if all the witneſſes to the deed be dead, as no man can keep his witneſſes alive, and time weareth out all men, then

then violent preſumption, which ſtandeth for a proof, is continual and quiet poſſeſſion; for *ex diuturnitate temporis omnia praeſumuntur ſolemniter eſſe acta*; alſo the deed may receive credit *per collationem ſigillorum, ſcripturae, &c. et ſuper fidem chartarum, mortuis teſtibus, erit ad patriam de neceſſitate recurrendum.* Co. Lit. 6. b.

7. The reaſon wherefore the warranty of the uncle, having no right to the land intailed, ſhould bar the iſſue, is becauſe the law preſumeth, that he would not unnaturally diſinherit his lawful heir, being of his own blood, of a right which he, the uncle, never had, but came to the nephew by another means, unleſs he would leave him greater advancement. *Nemo praeſumitur alienam poſteritatem ſuae praetuliſſe.* And in this caſe the law will admit no proof againſt that which the law preſumeth, and it is the ſame of all other collateral warranties; and that becauſe of the preſumption, that no man is to be preſumed to do any thing againſt nature. See *Co. Lit.* 373. *a.*

8. So if a rent be behind for 20 years, and the lord make acquittance for the laſt that is due, all the reſt are preſumed to be paid, and the law will admit no proof againſt it, *&c. Co. Lit.* 373. *a.*

9. See rules, *Ex diuturnitate temporis, &c. Nemo praeſumitur alienam poſteritatem, &c. Law will admit no proof againſt that which the law preſumeth.*

299. *Neminem oportet eſſe ſapientiorem legibus.*

General.

1. LAW, legal reaſon, or the reaſon of the law, *ſumma eſt ratio,* and particularly of the laws of this realm, as lord *Coke* juſtly ſaith, the old rule is verified, *neminem oportet eſſe ſapientiorem, &c.* for it is the very perfection of reaſon. See *Co. Lit.* 97. *b.*

Particular.

2. It was reſolved that foraſmuch as in the caſe at bar, a *ca. ſa.* was awarded againſt the counteſs by the court of common bench, that the ſheriff or his officer, by his warrant, might without any offence execute it; for they are not to diſpute the authority of the court, but to execute its writs directed to them; and *indeed* to this they are ſworn, *and therefore thereto bound by law and conſcience*; and though it appear in the caſe, that ſhe was a counteſs, againſt whom it lieth not, *et ignorantia juris non excuſat,* eſpecially ſheriffs, and other like miniſters of law and juſtice; yet as a *ca. ſa.* lieth in ſome caſes, as in caſes of contempt, *&c.* againſt them; therefore it was reſolved, that the ſheriff and his miniſters or officers ought not to examine the judicial acts of the court, but to execute the writ, as is *Dy.* 60. If a *capias* or *exigent* come to the ſheriff, againſt a duke, an earl, *&c.* where none lieth againſt them, yet they are to ſerve it, and not to argue or diſpute the validity of it. 6 *Co.* 54. *a.* See *Doct. & Stud.*

I 300. *Nemo*

300. *Nemo debet bis puniri pro uno delicto.*

General and rules.

1. ONE convicted of manslaughter being allowed his clergy, it is a good bar in an appeal of murder. 4 *Co.* 45. *b.*

2. And though the law gives an appeal, as a means to be justly revenged for the death of the husband, *&c.* yet it ought to be instantly pursued; and as it threatens death to the party, it ought to be in all points strictly pursued. *Yelv.* 205. *Ha. Ple. Cro.* 190, 247. *Tri. per Pais* 454. *Co. Lit.* 287. *Fitzh. Abr.* 258.

3. If one be convicted either by verdict or confession, upon an insufficient indictment, and no judgment is upon it given, he may after be indicted and arraigned; for that his life was never in jeopardy, and the law had not its end. 4 *Co.* 45. *a.* 47. *a.*

Particular cases.

4. It was resolved in the principal case, that if the count had been sufficient, then being convicted at the suit of the party, he should not after be impeached at the suit of the king; but the count was insufficient, and so he was discharged. 4 *Co.* 39. *b.* 40. *a.*

5. *Wetherel* brought an appeal of murder against *Darby*. The defendant pleaded *non cul'*, and was found guilty of *homicide*, and had his clergy; and after was indicted of murder, and was arraigned at the suit of the queen, and pleaded the former conviction, and appeal at the suit of the party. Adjudged a good bar. 4 *Co.* 40. *a.*

6. *Hudson* brought an appeal of maihem against *Lee*, and counted that the defendant the eighth day of *January*, *anno* 28 *Eliz.* feloniously maimed him in his left hand, *&c.* The defendant pleaded, that before the appeal brought, the plaintiff brought trespass in *C. B.* of assault, battery and wounding, against the defendant the same eighth day of *January*, *&c.* to which the defendant pleaded *non cul'*, and was found guilty, and damages assessed to 200 marks for the assault, battery and wounding, and 10*s.* costs, and judgment upon it given, and satisfaction acknowledged before the appeal brought, and avers that the battery and wounding in the action of trespass, and the said maim whereof the said appeal is now brought, were one and the same and not divers; and it was moved that this was no bar, for two reasons. 1st, Because the maihem is of an higher nature than the action of trespass; for in the appeal it is, that the defendant *felonice* him *maihemed*; and the rule of law is, *that recovery or bar in one action is a good bar in another, of either equal or of an inferior nature, but not in action of a higher nature; as recovery or bar in one assise is a good bar in another assise, but not in a* mordancestor, *nor is a recovery or bar in a* mordancestor *a good bar to a writ of right; nor is an action brought for goods carried away, any bar in an appeal of robbery, for the appeal of robbery is of an higher nature than the other.* And this was moved, admitting the appeal was brought for the same matter; but it was moved that the appeal was brought for the maim only, and therefore it is said felony, which may not be applied to trespass; and the action of trespass for the battery and wounding doth not concern the maim; and therefore it was agreed 22 *Ass. pl.* 82. That after

 the

the plaintiff in appeal had recovered for the maihem, he might have trefpafs for the battery, whereby it appears that the appeal meddles with the maihem only. But it was refolved *per totam Curiam*, That the bar was good; for in every cafe when the plaintiff for a tort or injury is only to recover damages, he fhall never be twice fatisfied for one and the fame matter or thing, *juxta illud*; *nemo debet bis puniri pro uno delicto, et Deus non agit bis in ipfum*; and in both thefe actions, of appeal and trefpafs, the plaintiff may recover only damages: and it appeared to the court, by the defendant's bar, which the plaintiff by his demurrer had confeffed, that he, in the very action of trefpafs which he had brought for the battery and wounding, had recovered damages for the maim; for this clear reafon, that wounding includes maihem and more. And the defendant hath averred that the wounding in the action of trefpafs and the maihem in the appeal were the fame; fo that though the appeal of maim is an higher action; yet forafmuch as in it he fhall only recover damages, and damages he hath actually recovered in the action of trefpafs; therefore refolved, that the bar, in the cafe at bar, was good. And *Wray* chief juftice, faid, That fo it was lately adjudged in the fame court, which record he had feen, and it agreed with the book 41 *Aff.* 16. and the book 2 *R.* 3. 14. is good law; for in the appeal of robbery the plaintiff fhall have judgment againft the defendant for his life, and not for damages. 4 *Co.* 43. *a. b.*

7. See rule, *Ufury odious in law.*

301. *Nemo eft haeres viventis.*

Heir.

Who is, how made, and from whence named.

1. HEIR, *haeres*, in the legal underftanding of the common law, implieth that he is *ex juftis nuptiis proceatus*; for *haeres legitimus eft, quem nuptiae demonftrant*, and is he to whom lands, tenements or hereditaments, by the act of God and right of blood do defcend, of fome eftate of inheritance; for *folus Deus haeredem facere poteft, non homo*; *dicuntur autem haereditas et haeres ab haerendo, quod eft arcte infidendo*; *nam qui haeres eft haeret*; *vel dicitur ab haerendo, quia haereditas fibi haeret, licet nonnulli haeredem dictum velint quod haeres fuit, hoc eft dominus terrarum, &c. quae ad eum perveniunt, &c.* Co. Lit. 7. b.

Rules.

2. One cannot be heir till after the death of his anceftor; in the mean time, he is called *haeres apparens*, heir apparent. *Co. Lit.* 8. *a.*

3. And this alfo is a pofitive rule, That a man cannot raife a fee-fimple to his own right heirs by the name of heirs, as a purchafe, neither by conveyance of lands, nor by ufe, nor by devife. Nay more, if a man devife lands to a perfon that is next heir, and his heirs, the devife is void, and it worketh by defcent, *&c. Hob.* 30, 31.

Particular cases.

4. *Francis Archer*, ſeiſed of lands in fee, held in ſocage, by his will in writing deviſed the ſame to *Robert Archer* the father, for his life, and after to the next heir male of *Robert*, and to the heirs male of the body of ſuch next heir male: *Robert* had iſſue *John*, *Francis* died, *Robert* infeoffed *Kent*, with warranty, upon which *John* entered; *Kent* re-entered, and after *John* died, &c. and *int' al'* it was agreed by *Anderſon*, *Walmſley*, *et al'* the court, that *Robert* had but an eſtate for life; for that he had an expreſs eſtate for life deviſed to him, and the remainder is limited to the next heir male of *Robert* in the ſingular number, and the right heir male of *Robert* may not enter for the forfeiture, in the life of *Robert*; for he cannot be heir ſo long as *Robert* lives, &c. 1 *Co.* 66. *b.* *Cro. Eliz.* 453. *S. C.*

5. References, *Co. Lit.* 99. *b.* 2 *Vern.* 249, 444, 616. *Gilb.* 7, 41, 116, 131, 138, &c. *Prec. Chan.* 3, 475. *Co. Lit.* 299. *b.* *Eq. Abr.* 197. 1 *Vern.* 282, 172, 14, 410, 411. *Nelſ.* 313, 128, 257. *Pre. Chan.* 53, 147. 1 *Vern.* 93, 407, 453, 460, 469. 2 *Vern.* 104, 188, 189, 341, 357. 3 *Mod.* 45. 1 *Vern.* 234, 282, 172, 419, 429, 471, 469. *Nelſ.* 282, 97, 166, 167, 138, 201, 380, 164, 272, 175, 176. *Prec. Chan.* 2, 381, 439, 452, 443, 461, 544. *Hob.* 31. 1 *Leon.* 70. 1 *Vent.* 334. 4 *Mod.* 255. *and caſe* Beaumont *and* Long, *Co. Lit.* 26. *b.* 164. Cowden *and* Clerk's *caſe in Hob.* 29. Pybus *and* Mitford, *Dy.* 171. *And* Shelley's *caſe*, 2 *Leon.* 23, 27. *Cro. Eliz.* 108. *Lit. ſect.* 30. *Cro. Ca.* 24. 1 *Mod.* 226. 2 *Mod.* 207. *Prec. Chan.* 463. *Co. Lit.* 3. *a.* *Year book* 9 *H.* 6. 23, 24. 11 *H.* 6. 12. 37 *H.* 8. *Bro.* tit. *De donis ſect.* 61. *Lit. ſect.* 352. *Prec. Chan.* 461, &c. 54, &c. 544, 57, 143, 162, 196, 207, 213, 267, 475, 278, 31, 32, 319, 87. *Nelſ.* 161, 267. 2 *Vern.* 617.

302. *Nemo plus juris ad alium transferre poteſt, quam ipſe habet.*

1. A Releaſe or confirmation, made by him who had no right at the time, is void, though a right come to him after; unleſs made with warranty, and then the warranty ſhall bar him to all right which may come to him after. *Doct. & Stud. lib.* 1. *cap.* 8.

2. The guardianſhip of an infant is not aſſignable over; being but a bare power or truſt. 2 *Mod. Ca.* 40, 42. *Vaugh.* 180. 2 *Rep. Chan.* 237.

3. Error on a judgment in *C. B.* in ejectment, wherein a ſpecial judgment was found to this effect; *H.* ſeiſed in fee, deviſeth to his wife for life, *and then to be at her diſpoſal to any of her children who ſhall be then living.* *H.* dies, leaving a ſon and a daughter and his wife; who then enters and married a ſecond huſband, and he and ſhe by leaſe and releaſe convey the lands to *A.* and his heirs, to the uſe of the wife for life, *ſans* impeachment of waſte; remainder to her daughter and the heirs of her body; remainder to the ſon and his heirs, with a power to revoke and limit new uſes: The firſt queſtion was, Whether the wife had an eſtate in fee, or only an eſtate for life, with power to diſpoſe of the inheritance? And the court

court held this to be only an eſtate for life, with a power to diſpoſe of the inheritance. *Et per Parker*, lord chief juſtice, The difference is, where a power is given with a particular limitation and deſcription of eſtate, and where generally: as to executors to ſell or give; for *he that can give or ſell an eſtate in fee, muſt have an eſtate in fee.* 2. The queſtion was, Whether this power could be conſtrued as a power appendant to the eſtate for life, ſo as by the deſtroying of that, it might be deſtroyed or extinguiſhed; or a collateral one? And *Powell* juſtice ſaid, this was not a power appendant or appurtenant, nor in the nature of an emolument to the eſtate, like a leaſe for life, with a power to make a leaſe for 21 years; for that effects the eſtate for life and is concurrent with it, and has its being and continuance, at leaſt for ſome part, out of it; but the power here ariſeth out of the eſtate, and has its effect upon another intereſt; ſo that the eſtate for life is perfect without it, and no ways altered or affected by the execution of it. *Et adjournatur*, and afterwards at another day, lord chief juſtice *Parker*, (*afterwards earl of* Macclesfield *and lord high chancellor*) delivered the opinion of the court, that this was only an eſtate for life, and that the diſpoſing power was a diſtinct gift; becauſe the eſtate given is expreſs and certain, and the power comes in by way of addition; and that this differs from the other caſes, which are general and indefinite, *viz.* a deviſe to *J.S.* and that he ſhall ſell, or a deviſe to *J. S.* to ſell, *&c.* in theſe caſes, becauſe the party is impowered to convey a fee, he is conſtrued to have one; he having no expreſs eſtate divided from the power; but here the power is a ſeparate gift diſtinguiſhed from the eſtate, and the eſtate given is a certain and expreſs eſtate. *Salk.* 239, 240.

4. References, 4 *Co.* 24. *b.* *Cart.* 232.

5. See rules, *He who can ſell or give an eſtate in fee muſt have an eſtate in fee. Quod per me non poſſum nec per alium.*

303. *Nemo poteſt habere duas militias, nec duas dignitates.*

1. A Cardinalſhip at *Rome* made a parſonage at *Durham* void. *Pal.* 459. A cardinalſhip makes void a biſhoprick in *England.* 4 *Inſt.* 357. A biſhop taking another biſhoprick, the firſt is void. *Palm.* 462, 464. *Vaugh.* 21. A parſon or dean taking a biſhoprick in *Ireland* makes the firſt church void; *nemo poteſt habere, &c.* for it is impoſſible a man ſhould be in two places at the ſame time, *&c.* *Pal.* 458, 459, 469. *Dav.* 21. A prebendary made a dean, the prebend void. 5 *E.* 2. *Breve* 800. *accordant.* *Pal.* 461. One having a benefice with cure to the value of 10*l.* or more, receives another, the firſt is void. *Stat.* 21 *H.* 8. *Dy.* 255, 237. *Vaugh.* 21. *Hob.* 166, 168. *Dy.* laſt caſe. Parſon made a biſhop, voids the parſonage. *Palm.* 345. 11 *H.* 4. 60 *and* 74. *Dy.* 159. 4 *H.* 4. 2. 32 *H.* 6. 5 *E.* 4. 19, 24. *Pal.* 346, 347, 348, 349. *Dy.* 347. 4 *Co.* 75 *and* 78. 6 *Co.* 29. *Dy.* 377. *Co. Ent.* 368. *Cro. Ca.* 357. *Caſe Archbiſhop Armagh* and *Attorney General*, 2 *Ju. Eccl.* 414.

2. See rule, *Clerici non ponantur in officio.*

304. *Nemo praesumitur alienam posteritatem suae praetulisse.*

SEE rules, *Negative cannot be proved. Presumption general to, and the sorts*, case 7.

305. *Nemo tenetur divinare.*

1. IT was resolved if the lord, in case of uncertain fines, assess a reasonable fine and require the copyholder to pay it, he is not bound to pay it presently; because he could not tell what fine the lord would assess; *et nemo tenetur divinare*; wherefore he could not provide a certain sum; and therefore he must have a convenient time to pay it, if the lord himself limit no certain time for it; but otherwise it is of fines certain. 4 *Co.* 23. *b.* 24. *a.* 27. *b.* 28. *a.*

2. And this rule may extend to the king himself, as to matter of fact, though he is not to be supposed ignorant of the law; for that he is the head of the law and fountain of justice. *Plow. Com.* 501. *b.* 502. *a. b.* 503. 11 *Co.* 11. *a. b.* 3 *Co.* 4. *b.* *Hob.* 224. *Introduction to Ju. Eccl. last part.*

3. See rules, *Ignorantia facti excusat. King not to be supposed ignorant of the law.*

306. *Nemo tenetur seipsum prodere.*

1. BILL *in Scacc'* to discover on what consideration a bond was given, which had been assigned *al roy* as a debt in aid. The court were of opinion that a man was not bound to discover the consideration of a bond, which implies in itself a consideration. And so baron *Atkins* said it had been ruled in chancery. *Hard.* 200, 201.

2. A bill was by the attorney general against the defendant, to discover his real and personal estate, and what secret and fraudulent gifts and deeds he had made and executed, he being outlawed, whereby all his goods and the profits of his real estate were forfeited. The defendant demurred, *quia nemo tenetur prodere seipsum*, and to discover his estate upon forfeiture; the demurrer was over-ruled, and the defendant ordered to answer; because the king is intitled by course of law, and the outlawry is in the nature of a gift *al roy*, or a judgment for him; and a common person in like case might have a bill for discovery to enable him to take out execution; *quod nota* says the serjeant. *Hard.* 22.

3. The bill was to discover goods imported contrary to the new act of navigation, for which the defendant ought to pay double customs. It was likewise alledged that the attorney general would not prosecute for the forfeiture, but the duties only. Defendant demurred, because a penalty ensued; the goods being forfeited by the act of tonnage and poundage; and after discovery had, the attorney general may relinquish his bill, and begin *de novo* for the penalty, and is not bound by the allegation of the bill. To this it was answered, That the attorney general waiving the forfeiture, might sue for the

the duty by bill of discovery; as in the case of tithes, where the plaintiff only requires single value: and that after the attorney general had informed upon the penal law, none else could; and the court inclined to this opinion. *Sed adjournatur. Hard.* 137. See *Gilb.* 187.

4. The bill was in the *English* exchequer, and charged that the plaintiff in *May* 1658 became incumbent of the church of *Bersted* in the county of *Kent*, and that the defendant *June* 1658 and 1659, by colour of an order of sequestration made by the committee in the county of *Southampton*, as they pretended, had seised divers tithes of several parishioners within the plaintiff's parish, and which tithes were due to the plaintiff. To discover the particulars and value, and to have them paid to the plaintiff was the end of the bill; whereto the defendant demurred, as a matter determinable at law, and a criminal matter; but the court put the defendant to answer, because it is matter of discovery: as in case where a man by colour of title enters into the house or lands, and possesses himself of the goods and profits. It may be impossible for the plaintiff to discover the particulars without such bill, nor is it a charge by way of trespass, but under a colour of title. So where a will is proved and administration revoked, such a bill is necessary and usual for the goods, and yet there was in strictness of law a trespass; so here. *Hard.* 182, 183.

5. *Spendelow*, the present parson, sues Sir *William Smith*, executor of *Smith* the last incumbent, for dilapidations, in the arches; there was, *int' al'*, a question about a lease for years, which was alledged to be taken by Sir *William* in his own name, but covinously in trust, and for the use of the said *Smith* the said late parson; and hereupon they would put Sir *William* to his oath, to answer concerning the covin; whereupon the court granted the prohibition *quoad* examining him upon oath concerning the covin; for though the original cause belong to their cognizance, yet the covin and fraud is criminal, and the avowing of it to be *bona fide* is punishable, both in the star-chamber, and by the penal law of fraudulent gifts, and therefore not to be extorted out of him by oath; also the exposition of the statute 13 *Eliz. cap.* 10. of dilapidations, and what shall be covin, or not within the law, rests not in them to judge, but in the courts of common law. *Hob.* 84.

6. In all sentences for divorce and separation only a *mensa et thoro*, there is to be a restraint inserted in the sentence, that the parties shall live chastely and continently, and that they will not, during each other's life, contract matrimony with any other person; and for the better observation of this last clause, the said sentence of divorce shall not be pronounced until the party or parties requiring the same have given good and sufficient caution and security into the court, that they will not any ways break or trespass the said restraint or prohibition. *Canon* 107. Yet the ecclesiastical court may not examine the party on oath, whether he or she hath contracted matrimony or not, *&c.* for *nemo tenetur seipsum prodere. Clifford* and *Huntley*'s case, *Ro. Abr. Prohibition* (*T.*) *case* 6. 2 *Ju. Eccl.* 31, 32.

7. Bill was for defendant to discover what estate he had or claimed in such premisses, and whether they were in mortgage, and whether there was any power of redemption. The defendant pleaded his being an absolute purchaser for valuable consideration, and that some years after a fine was levied to him of them, and that he had no notice of the plaintiff's title.

Plea allowed, though he did not ſhew at what time, or for what conſideration. And the chief baron ſaid, that ſo it had been held in *Sherley* and *Fagg*'s caſe, lately in chancery. *Hard. Day* verſus *Cornudel.*

8. The bill was to diſcover an antient deed of intail ſuppoſed to be in the defendant's hands, charging that he had peruſed it; and in diſcourſe had acknowledged it, *&c.* The defendant ſaith by plea, that he was a counſellor with *A. B.* and that on a reference between the parties, it was agreed that nothing that paſſed thus ſhould be made uſe of on either ſide, or be diſcloſed. The lord chancellor ordered that what the defendant knew only as a counſellor, or under ſuch contract of ſilence, he ſhould not be put to anſwer. 1 *Chan. Ca.* 277.

9. *Snelling* had a judgment againſt *Sidenham* of 1200 *l.* for payment of 500 *l.* *Squibb* purchaſed of *Sidenham* for a valuable conſideration without notice; *Snelling* ſues *Squibb* to diſcover lands ſubject, *&c.* that he might extend, he not knowing the place nor who tenants. *Squibb* pleaded his purchaſe for a valuable conſideration without notice. The lord chancellor allowed the plea, and ſaid that *Squibb* ought not to be compelled to diſcover what lands were liable. 2 *Chan. Ca.* 47, 48.

10. The aſſignee of a commiſſion of bankrupcy againſt *Portman* exhibited his bill againſt the defendant, to diſcover lands, *&c.* which were the bankrupt's at the time of breaking. *Hutchins* (afterwards lord commiſſioner of the great ſeal) for the defendant, pleaded that he was a purchaſer for a full and valuable conſideration, without notice of any act of bankrupcy, or that *Portman* was a bankrupt, or of any commiſſion, and refuſed to make diſcovery. And the plea was allowed by lord *North* lord keeper. 2 *Ch. Ca.* 136.

11. The plaintiff by his bill charged that on the mortgage made by *W.* to *A.* there was a truſt declared for the benefit of the plaintiff, but *A.* having ſince conveyed to the other defendant *D.* he refuſed to diſcover the truſt. The defendant *D.* by anſwer ſaid that on the ſaid mortgage there was no truſt declared for the benefit of the plaintiff, whereto the plaintiff replied. And the *quaere* at the hearing was, Whether the defendant *D.* ſhould be obliged to produce the deed or not? Lord keeper: I will not oblige him to produce it; by this method all purchaſers may be blown up. 2 *Vern.* 463. *Tamen quaere*, ſays *The Reporter.*

12. References, *Gilb.* 187. *Ro. Ab.* (*T.*) *Ca.* 1. 4. 5. 6. 65. 4 *Mod.* 306. *Hob.* 84. 2 *Keb.* 352. *Hard.* 172, 173, 137 *to* 147. *Co. Lit.* 247. *a. b.* *Regiſter* 228. *b.* *Fitzh. Nat. Brev.* 202. 4 *Co.* 123. *b.* *Hard.* 143, *Co. Lit.* 2. *b.* *Nelſ.* 135. 2 *Vern.* 414. 1 *Rep. Chan.* 40. 2 *Vol.* 221. *Gilb.* 101. *Mo.* 906. 4 *Leon. Ca.* 261. *Ray.* 88, 221. 1 *Vern.* 27, 95, 107, 110, 136, 204, 208, 399, 407, 484. 2 *Ju. Eccl.* 31.

13. See rule, *Purchaſer without notice*, &c.

307. *Nihil*

307. *Nihil in lege intolerabilius eſt eandem rem diverſo jure cenſeri.*

WHERE the courts are divided and hold different opinions, as in the principal caſe, for the honour of the law, and for the repoſe of the ſubject, in the appeaſing ſuch differences of opinions, *quia nihil in lege intolerabilius eſt eandem rem diverſo jure cenſeri*, the caſe was publickly argued before all the judges of *England*, *&c.* 4 *Co.* 93. *a.*

308. *Nihil magis juſtum eſt, quam quod neceſſarium eſt.*

1. IMpoſts or impoſitions are the third kind of duties payable for merchandize, and are ſometimes rated and aſſeſſed by parliament, and then they are in nature of ſubſidies; and ſometimes they are impoſed by prerogative royal, for ſupporting the neceſſary charges of the crown, and then *nihil magis juſtum eſt, quam quod neceſſarium eſt.* The impoſts upon wines in this realm was firſt aſſeſſed by parliament, and limited to be paid for a certain term of years, which being expired, is continued by prerogative. *Dav.* 12. *a.* *Vide etiam* 22. *b.*

2. See rules, *Natura appetit perfectum. Neceſſitas facit illud licitum, &c. Neceſſitas legum vincula irridet. Neceſſitas vincit legem. Neceſſity creates equity.*

309. *Nihil quod eſt contra rationem eſt licitum.*

1. REaſon is the life of the law, nay the common law itſelf is nothing but reaſon; which is to be underſtood of an artificial perfection of reaſon, gotten by long ſtudy, obſervation and experience, and not of every man's natural reaſon; for *nemo naſcitur artifex*, and this legal reaſon *eſt ſumma ratio*, *&c.* Co. Lit. 97. b. *See* Doct. & Stud.

2. See rules, *Law is the perfection of reaſon. Ratio eſt radius divini luminis.*

310. *Nihil quod eſt inconveniens eſt licitum.*

AN argument drawn from inconvenience is forcible in law, *nihil quod eſt inconveniens eſt licitum*, and the law which is the perfection of reaſon, cannot ſuffer any thing that is inconvenient. *Co. Lit.* 97. *a.* *Doct. & Stud.*

311. *Nihil tam conveniens eſt naturali aequitati, quam unumquodque diſſolvi eo ligamine quo ligatum eſt.*

1. CUſtom ought to have continuance *ſans* interruption of time, whereof, *&c.* for if it be diſcontinued within memory, the cuſtom is gone; as if a copyhold be leaſed by the lord of the manor for life or years, according to the cuſtom of the common law, it ſhall never more be demiſed

as

as a copyhold according to the cuſtom. 18 *H.* 8. *Dy.* 30. *b.* *Conſuetudo ſemel reprobata non poteſt amplius induci*; for as continuance maketh the cuſtom, ſo diſcontinuance may deſtroy it. *Nihil tam inconveniens eſt, &c.* Da. 33. b. *See* 2 Ju. Eccl. *and* quaere; *for there, tho' the* Modus *had been varied by ſubſequent compoſition for* 66 *years or more, and had been once actually paid in kind, yet that did not deſtroy it.* 2 Ju. Eccl. 122. *See* 1 Ju. Eccl. 449, *&c. The caſe at length, where his lordſhip lord chancellor obſerved, there was ſtrong evidence of the* Modus *or cuſtom; and therefore, though there had been a compoſition and ſuch variation,* &c. *yet all that ought not to toll the* Modus *ſo well proved and eſtabliſhed; for thus to reaſon, I ſubmit it, would be to give an incroaching prieſt advantage of his own wrong, againſt an honeſt abuſed pariſhioner, againſt all the rules of known honeſty and common juſtice; for all* Modus's, *as other cuſtoms and compoſitions, are to be preſumed founded either in immemorial and reaſonable uſage, or elſe in a well grounded compact and agreement; and if notwithſtanding ſuch uſage, or agreement had for good and valuable conſideration, a man ſhall be compelled to pay tithes, where he ought to be excuſed therefrom on payment of ſuch* Modus *or compoſition; and that meerly becauſe through weakneſs, or ignorance of his exemption from tithes in kind, he hath ſubmitted, under thoſe diſadvantages, to an alteration in payment, or to tithes in kind, would be to give the oppreſſor advantage of his own wrong and of his pariſhioners ignorance or weakneſs; whereas the rule is, that no man is to be hurt by his ignorance of his right. As to the caſe of the lord and copyholder, I ſubmit it, that caſe ſtands upon a very different reaſon, the lord there, with full knowledge of his privilege, agrees to deſtroy it: which is not the latter caſe by any means; therefore theſe caſes may well receive theſe different determinations. Beſides, as I conceive, theſe baſe tenures are not countenanced in law, as being too plain marks of ſlavery or ſervitude, in a free and trading nation; as the ſame tends to enervate the peoples induſtry, and reduce their courage, to the hurt both of the prince and the public weal.*

2. References, *Cro. Ja.* 5, 6. 2 *Ro.* 97. *Jenk.* 166.

312. *No conſtruction can be too liberal to make parſons reſide,* &c.

General.

Statute.

1. THE ſtatute 21 *H.* 8. is to be taken ſtrictly againſt pluralities. 4 *Co.* 90. *b.*

Canons.

2. No licence or diſpenſation for keeping more benefices with cure than one, ſhall be granted to any, but to ſuch as in the canon are for that purpoſe mentioned; wherein is provided, that ſuch pluraliſt be, by good and ſufficient caution, bound to make his *perſonal reſidence*, in each of his benefices, for ſome reaſonable time in every year, *&c.* as may be collected from *Canon* 41. and every beneficed man, licenced by the law of this realm, *upon urgent occaſion of his ſervice, not to reſide upon his benefice*,

 ſhall

ſhall cauſe his cure to be ſupplied by a curate that is a ſufficient and licenced preacher, if the worth of the benefice will bear it. But whoſoever hath two benefices, ſhall maintain a preacher licenced, in the benefice where he doth not reſide, except he preach himſelf at both of them uſually, as is the ſenſe of the 47th *Canon*. See 2 *Ju. Eccl.* 451. *And further by the canons of the church even thoſe excuſed reſidence, are by good and ſufficient caution, to be bound to reſidence* **perſonal**, *in each of their livings, for ſome reaſonable time in every year, ſo as they are not, in any caſe, to be altogether non-reſident, but only on* **urgent occaſions**; *much leſs are they for any whim or humour of their own to neglect their perſonal cure*; a multo fortiori *they are not to turn renegado's, and leave their people to wander, or be devoured of the deſtroyer. But here I am aware of an objection, namely, that theſe canons interfere with the ſtatute law of diſpenſations in this caſe. However that may be, is the buſineſs of non-reſidents, rather than mine, to conſider, who have their own conſciences to ſatisfy and quiet in this matter. But granting the canons, as being ſubſequent in time, to the ſtatute intended, as well as weaker in power, as being made by ſo much a meaner authority, as convocation is than the grand counſel aſſembled in parliament; and though it be true theſe canons have never been aſſented to, or received by the people, and therefore no lien upon them, nor perhaps upon the clergy themſelves* ſtricto jure; *as this may be conſidered as a temporal indulgence; yet I muſt ſo far give way to their authority over eccleſiaſtics, as to admit, that as theſe canons were made in public convocation by and with the aſſent and conſent of all the clergy, and confirmed,* **at their humble and earneſt intreaty,** *by the royal aſſent, they may be binding on the clergy themſelves, and that the rather for theſe reaſons, 1ſt, For that the good of the church requires reſidence, and therefore, in her ſenſe, no conſtruction can be too liberal to make parſons reſide.* Summa eſt ratio quae pro religione facit. *And by the antient canons* un home ne puiſſoit aver forſque une benefice, niſi en caſe de neceſſitie ou utilitie del' ecclifie. Et diſpenſatio eſt relaxatio juris, *admitting that to be done which the law had prohibited before. So* diſpenſatio eſt vulnus, quod vulnerat jus commune, *ſay the canoniſts*; *and as they alſo ſay,* commenda eſt materia odioſa et reſtringibilis; *and according to the opinion of a good and pious biſhop of old,* **a diſſenter from the moderns in ſome countries,** *this practice of pluralities and non-reſidence or abſence from their cure of ſouls in paſtors was looked upon, in the then old faſhioned ſenſe of the church, as a ſpiritual adultery.* Abſit, *ſays our good old man,* ut cum ſponſa habeam concubinam, &c. 2. *For that the common law requires it.* 1. *For the diſcharge of the cure, that the parſon being always on the ſpot, be always ready, when ever any of his ſpiritual offices call him.* 2. *For hoſpitality, alms-deeds,* &c. 3. *For keeping a good correſpondence with his pariſhioners,* &c. 4. *For maintenance of the parſonage houſe,* &c. *for himſelf and ſucceſſors.* 5. *For good example; the parſon being bound to preach in his life as well as doctrine, and for frequent viſitation and inſtruction of the ignorant and reprobate,* &c. 3. *For that example to his brethren the neighbouring clergy requires it,* &c. 4. *For that this is a duty he owes in common juſtice, as well as by the laws of holy church, to his patron whoſe inheritance the advowſon is, and alſo to his ſucceſſor, who both ſuffer in dilapidations. And* 5. *and laſtly,* inter al', *for that he hath in moſt ſacred manner, and by moſt ſolemn and repeated obligations bound himſelf thereto,* &c. &c. &c.

Particular cases.

3. *Michaelmas* 10 *H.* 6. *fo.* 8. *J. S.* brought debt against *John*, rector of *T.* in *C. B.* The defendant said, that he was, before the day of the writ purchased, demurrant and conversant at *B.* in the county of *N. Sed non allocatur*; for a parson shall be intended, by the law, resident upon his benefice, for the cure of souls which he hath there the charge of; for a parson who hath cure of souls, and is non-resident, *non est dispensator, sed dissipator, non speculator sed spiculator*; and therefore no such thing as non-residence shall be ever presumed. 11 *Co.* 70. *b.*

4. Between *Goodale*, informer *tam pro se, &c.* upon the statute 21 *H.* 8. of non-residence, and *Butler*, parson of *Downeham* in *Norfolk*, resolved on special verdict, That the parson ought to reside on his living, *viz.* in the parsonage house, and not in any other, though such other be within the parish; for the statute means not only for serving the cure, and for hospitality, but also for the maintenance of the house, and habitation of the parson, and that not only for himself, but also for his successors, that they also might maintain hospitality there, *&c.* though it was agreed that lawful imprisonment, *without covin*, is a good excuse for non-residence, or if there be no parsonage house; (*but that also, I hold, must be understood,* **without covin**; *for if there be a fund to provide such an house, or there be an house, though never so poor an one, the neglect of the parson to apply the fund, or his pretence that it is not suitable to his rank, is even no legal excuse, however he may deceive his own conscience. As in the first case, he is cheating God and charity, that he may be more at leisure to serve the devil; and as to the last, that as he knew what the house was when he took his living, and always was at liberty to resign, he ought either to suit himself to it, or leave it to, perhaps, a better man, who will*); for *impotentia excusat legem*, and these cases are excepted out of the act by construction of law. *Note*; It was held in the exchequer, *Trin.* 39 *Eliz.* That sickness *sans* fraud is also a good excuse, so the patient remove, by advice of his physicians *bona fide*, for better air, and recovery of his health. 6 *Co.* 21. *b.*

5. A bill was brought for discovery of tithes by a lessee of a parson. The defendant pleads 13 *Eliz. cap.* 20. against non-residence, in bar. Agreed by lord chief baron *Gilbert*, Mr. baron *Price*, and Mr. baron *Page*, that the plea was good; and that no construction could be too liberal to make parsons reside, and take care of their parishes. *Gilb. Quilter* and *Mussendine*'s case.

6. References, 4 *Co.* 117. *b.* 118. *a.* *Mo.* 540, 448.

7. *Vide* rule, *Quando duo jura concurrant in una, &c.* *Impotentia excusat legem.*

313. *No distress can be taken for any services that are not put into certainty, nor can be reduced to any certainty.*

SEE rule, *Id certum est quod certum reddi potest.*

314. *Nomen non ſufficit, ſi res non ſit de jure, aut de facto.*

THE pope could not found or incorporate a college within this realm, nor aſſign, nor licence others to aſſign temporal livings to it; but this ought to be done by the king and no other. *Nomen non ſufficit, ſi res non ſit de jure, aut de facto.* 4 Co. 107. b. *Vide* 1 Ju. Eccl. *under tit.* The pope an uſurper throughout.

315. *No man can charge his heir but as part of himſelf.*

1. REference, ſee *Hob.* 131.
2. Rule, *Haeres eſt eadem perſona cum anteceſſore.*

316. *None ſhall take by deed but parties, unleſs in remainder.*

General.

1. ANY ſtranger to an indenture may take by way of remainder, but he cannot take a preſent eſtate in poſſeſſion if he be a ſtranger. *Co. Lit.* 231.

Particular caſes.

2. *A.* ſeiſed of lands in fee, covenants with *B.* in conſideration that *B.* marries his daughter, that from the time of ſuch marriage he will ſtand ſeiſed to the uſe of himſelf for life, and after to the uſe of *C.* and the heirs of his body begotten, and after to the uſe of *D.* and to the heirs of his body begotten, and afterwards to the uſe of *B.* and the ſaid daughter of the ſaid *A.* and to the heirs of their bodies begotten, there, after the ſaid marriage had, the ſaid *A.* ſhall be ſeiſed by the common law, to the uſe of himſelf for life, then to the uſe of *C.* in tail, then to the uſe of *D.* in tail, and after thoſe eſtates to the uſe of *B.* and his ſaid wife, daughter of the ſaid *A.* in tail, according to the limitation; and yet he had no conſideration for the ſaid *C.* and *D.* having the uſes in tail; for the marriage of *B.* is a private and ſeveral conſideration for them to have their eſtate-tail, but it is no conſideration to *C.* and *D.* who are ſtrangers; but though it be not, yet foraſmuch as the eſtate to *B.* and his wife is limited after the death of *A.* and after *C.* and *D.*'s death *ſans* iſſue, and not before, it follows, that *B.* and his wife ought to take in ſuch form, and not otherwiſe, and this is in remainder; and this remainder ought to be in them immediately after the marriage had; for *A.* hath covenanted, that from the time of the marriage he would ſtand ſeiſed to the uſes, *&c.* and therefore, for the neceſſity, the uſes ſhall veſt in *C.* and *D.* becauſe of the remainder to *B.* and his wife, to whoſe eſtate theirs was to precede: but if the limitations to *C.* and *D.* had been after the eſtate to *B.* and his wife, or if the covenant had been, that *A.* ſhould ſtand ſeiſed to the uſe of himſelf for life, and after to the uſe of *B.* and his wife in tail, and then to the uſe of *C.* in tail, and after to the uſe of *D.* in tail, there the remainder to *C.* and *D.* ſhould be void; for there was no conſideration to

 make

make them good; for the marriage between *B.* and his wife is only a consideration for the eſtate of *B.* and his wife; for the marriage only concerns and touches their ſingle perſons, which can be no conſideration to a ſtranger: but money might be a good conſideration for all the eſtates, whilſt the conſideration of marriage is, as hath been ſaid, ſingular to their perſons who are married, and to the father whoſe daughter is preferred in marriage, and is no conſideration to a ſtranger. *Plow. Com.* 307. *b.*

3. *Thomas* lord *Paget*, being ſeiſed of the manors of *B. L.* &c. *in Com. Stafford*, by deed indented 10 *Oct.* 20 *Eliz.* covenanted with *Farmer*, Eſq; and others, that in conſideration of diſcharging his funeral, payment of his debts and legacies, out of the profits of his lands, and for the advancement of his ſon, brother and others *de ſon ſanke*, he and his heirs ſhould ſtand ſeiſed of the ſaid manors, to the uſe of *Farmer*, &c. for life of lord *Paget*, and after his death to the uſe of *Ch. Paget* and others for 24 years, and after the expiration or end of that term, then to the uſe of *William Paget* his ſon in tail, with divers remainders over; after lord *Paget* was attaint of treaſon; adjudged that the term to *Ch.* was void; for that it wanted good conſideration; for that *Ch.* and the others were ſtrangers to the conſideration; but if he had made them executors, ſo that they had been chargeable to the payment of the debts and legacies, and ſo privies to the conſideration, then the conſideration had been good. But the doubt of the caſe was, tho' the term was void, yet foraſmuch as the uſe to *Will. Paget* was to be raiſed by covenant out of the eſtate of the covenantor, and not by tranſmutation of eſtate, if the uſe ſhall ariſe and veſt in *William* till the 24 years expired, by effluction of time? For in the ſame caſe it was ſaid by Sir *Roger Manwood*, lord chief baron, that if a man make a feoffment in fee, to the uſe of *A.* for life, and after to the uſe of *B.* for life, and after to the uſe of *C.* in fee, in this caſe if *A.* refuſe, *B.* ſhall take preſently; for the feoffor, by his feoffment, hath given all his eſtate out of him, and all the uſes are created out of it, as out of a root; and therefore ſo long as any of the uſes may take effect, the feoffor ſhall have no meddling with the land; but in caſe of a covenant to raiſe an uſe, there the conſideration, which is the cauſe that raiſeth each ſeveral uſe, is ſeveral, and all the uſes ariſe and grow out of the eſtate of the covenantor; and therefore if one refuſe, the next in remainder may not take preſently, but the covenantor ſhall retain, &c. It was adjudged in the principal caſe, that lord *Paget* himſelf had an eſtate for life; and it was alſo agreed that though the term was void *ab initio*, yet if the covenant had been, and after the end or expiration of the ſaid 24 years, that then he ſhould ſtand ſeiſed to the uſe of his ſon *ut ſupra*, that his ſon ſhould not have it till the years incurred; for though the term was void, yet the eſtate of the ſon, by expreſs limitation, did not commence till the 24 years expired; but foraſmuch as the words of the covenant were, (after the expiration or end of the ſaid term of 24 years) and the term imports in itſelf an eſtate and intereſt in the land; therefore the term being void, the eſtate of the ſon ſhall commence preſently; and thereupon *William Paget* had by the rule of the court an *amoveas manum*. 1 Co. 154.

4. References, 1 *Vent.* 380. *Cro. Eliz.* 10, 56, 905. *Salk.* 214. 2 *Lev.* 74. 3 *Lev.* 139. *Lutw.* 305. 2 *Inſt.* 673. 2 *Co.* 51. *Hob.* 313. *Dy.* 109, 126. *An.* 258. *Hut.* 88. *Car.* 76. *Poph.* 182. 3 *Keb.* 115. *Mod. Ca.* 115.

317. *None to be judge in his own cause.*

General.

1. THE king may not grant to a man to be judge in his own cause, or to be his own judge. *Da.* 75. *a.*

2. One may not sue in the chancery of *Chester* for a thing which in interest concerns the chancellor there; for that he may not be his own judge; therefore in this case he ought to sue in the chancery of *England*; for otherwise there should be a failure of right. *Ro. Abr.* 374.

Three things are to be help'd in conscience, fraud, accident and things of confidence. *Ro. Ab.* 374.

Particular.

3. In chancery between Sir *John Egerton* and the earl of *Derby*, chamberlain of *Chester*, and others, for a farm in that county, Resolved by the lord chancellor, chief justice of *England*, master of the rolls, *Dodderidge*, and *Winch*, justices, 1st, *That the chamberlain of* Chester, *being to be judge of equity, cannot decree any thing wherein himself is party; for he cannot be judge* in propria causa; *but where he is party, the suit shall be heard in chancery,* coram domino rege. 2dly, *If a defendant dwell out of the county palatine, he who hath cause to complain in equity, may also complain here in the chancery*; for in respect that proceedings in chancery do bind the person only, if the person be out of the jurisdiction, the chamberlain of *Chester* cannot relieve the party; and therefore *ne curia domini regis deficeret in justitia exhibenda*, the suit shall be here in chancery, else the subject should have good right and no remedy, which should be inconvenient; and this pursues the reason of the common law, *&c.* altho' an action will lie in *Wales*, yet because he who hath cause of action cannot have justice there, he shall sue in the king's bench; for where the particular courts cannot do justice to the parties, they shall sue in the king's general courts at *Westminster*, *&c.* in all cases where it appears to the court, that those who have liberty to take cognizance, do fail of right; as in matter of foreign plea, *&c.* the matter shall be determined in the general courts of *Westminster*. 3dly, The king cannot grant a commission to determine any matter of equity, but it ought to be determined in chancery, which hath had time out of mind jurisdiction of those matters, and that by the law, *&c.* On consideration of a certificate of lord *Dyer et al'* justices in queen *Elizabeth*'s time, concerning the jurisdiction of the county palatine of *Chester*, it was resolved, that for things transitory, though within the county palatine, the plaintiff may alledge them to be done in any place within *England*, and the defendant may not plead to the jurisdiction of the court, that they were done within the county palatine. 12 *Co.* 114. See *Dy.* 202, 716.

4. References, 12 *Co.* Earl *Derby*'s case. *Hard.* 502, 503. *Co. Lit.* 167. *Hob.* 107, 108. 2 *Vern.* 32, 33.

5. See rules, *Cujus est divisio, alterius est electio*, case 1. 2. *Chancery not to be ousted of its jurisdiction*, case 1. 2. *Iniquity bars equity*, case 4. *Jurare in propria causa*, *&c.*

318. *Non*

318. *Non valet impedimentum, quod de jure non ſortitur effectum.*

IT was adjudged, if a copyhold eſtate be forfeited to the lord, or eſcheat, or otherwiſe come into his hands, if the lord make a leaſe for years or for life, or other eſtate, by deed, or without, that this land may never after be granted by copy; for the cuſtom is deſtroyed, *&c.* So if the lord make a feoffment in fee of it *ſur* condition, (*according to* Co. Lit. 202. b.) and enter for the condition broken, yet it may never be granted by copy. But if the lord keep the lands in his own hands a long while, or leaſe them at will, he or his heirs may regrant at pleaſure; ſo if the interruption be tortious, as if the lord be diſſeiſed, and the diſſeiſor die ſeiſed, or the land be recovered againſt the lord by falſe verdict or erroneous judgment; in theſe caſes, till the lands are recovered, or the judgment reverſed, *&c.* by the lord of the manor, the lands were not demiſed or demiſable, yet after they are recontinued, they are grantable again by copy; for *non valet impedimentum, quod de jure non ſortitur effectum, &c.* but if the land ſo forfeited or eſcheated, before any new grant made be extended *ſur* ſtatute on recognizance acknowledged by the lord, or if the wife of the lord in a writ of dower had this land aſſigned to her, though theſe impediments are by acts in law, yet foraſmuch as they are lawful interruptions, the lands may never after be granted by copy. If a copyholder accept a leaſe for years of his lord, the copyhold is deſtroyed for ever, and may never more be granted, *&c.* 4 *Co.* 31. *a. b.*

319. *Nothing ſhall be a ground to direct a new trial to avoid a judgment at law, that would not be a ground for a bill of review to reverſe a decree.*

1. THE defendant's wife had pawned her huſband's plate to the plaintiff for 110*l.* the defendant in trover, for this recovered 115*l.* damages againſt the plaintiff, and had judgment. The bill was to be relieved againſt this judgment; for that the defendant was privy to the pawning, and had the 110*l.* and proofs being read, it appeared that the defendant had confeſſed ſo much, which if it had been proved at the trial, it was agreed that the defendant could not have recovered in trover; and there being no proof now, that the defendant at law could not, by reaſon of any accident, have his witneſſes at the trial, the court would not on any neglect of his grant a new trial; and it was inſiſted on as a rule, *That nothing ſhall be a ground to direct a new trial to avoid a judgment at law, that would not be a ground for a bill of review to reverſe a decree; and a confeſſion ſubſequent to a decree, is no ground for a bill of review, nor is the want of any evidence or matter which might have been uſed in the firſt cauſe, and of which the party had then knowledge, any ground for a bill of review*; and here is no proof but that the plaintiff might have had the witneſſes, that were examined here at the trial; and ſo this cauſe was diſmiſſed. 1 *Chan. Ca.* 43, 44.

2. References, 1 *Chan. Ca.* 2, 42. *Nelf.* 42, 63, 64. 2 *Vern. Cafes* 344, 382.

320. *Nullus debet agere actionem de dolo, ubi alia actio fubeft.*

1. WHERE one may have an ordinary remedy, as by action of debt, which is a formed action in the regifter, he fhall not have the extraordinary remedy as cafe, which is an action extraordinary, and not limited to any certain form in the regifter. 4 *Co.* 92. *b.*

2. *Vide* rule, *Ubi ceffat remedium ordinarium, &c.*

321. *Nullum iniquum eft in jure praefumendum.*

1. THerefore though the rule be, *That all the term is to be taken as one day in law*, yet the precife time when the deed was inrolled, and the like, are to be tried and proved in *Pais.* It is true, the inrolment, or other matter of record, fhall not be tried *per pais*; for the inrolment fhall never be drawn in queftion, but the time of it may; for *nullum iniquum eft in jure praefumendum*; *et ftabit praefumptio donec probetur in contrarium.* 4 *Co.* 70. *Hynde*'s cafe.

2. If an heretic convict would recant, he was to be received, and not punifhed; but if he relapfed, he was to be burnt without more ado: fo the law of God wills not the death of a finner, but rather that he fhould repent and be faved; therefore it would be contrary to reafon and the law of God, not to receive an offender upon his repentance, or to deprive him of the benefit of his repentance. *Nullum iniquum in lege praefumendum eft.* Hard. 64, 65.

3. References, *Stat.* 2 *H.* 5. *cap.* 7. 1 *Eliz. cap.* 1. 2 *H.* 4. *cap.* 15. 29 *Car.* 2. *cap.* 9. *Vide etiam* 3 *Inft.* 43. *Bro. Prefentment* 54. *Godb.* 33. *Doct. & Stud. lib.* 2. *cap.* 29. 12 *Co.* 56, 57. *Terms del ley* tit. *Mifcreant. Ridl. Review* 81. 1 *Ju. Eccl.* tit. *Excom'.* 2 *Vol.* tit. *Herefy or Mifcreancy.*

4. See rule, *Actus legis nulli facit injuriam.*

322. *Nullum tempus occurrit regi.*

General.

1. THE king's prerogative is, that no time fhall prejudice him, *nullum tempus occurrit regi*, in point of prefentation to a church. *Stat. De praerogativa regis*, 17 Car. 2.

2. Againft the king there fhall be no occupant; becaufe *nullum tempus occurrit regi*; and therefore no man fhall gain the king's lands by priority of entry. *Co. Lit.* 41. *b.*

3. On promotion of the incumbent to a bifhopric, the crown has a general right to the next avoidance, and is not reftrained to within the life of the prefentee. *Nullum tempus, &c. The King* againft *The Bifhop of Armagh and Dr. Whaley*, 1 Ju. Eccl. 25.

4. If

4. If the villain of the king purchaseth lands, and alieneth before the king (upon office found for him) doth enter, yet the king, after office found, shall have the land; *quia nullum tempus, &c. Aliter* of a common person, yet after office found the king shall not have the mean profits; because the title is by the seisure. *Co. Lit.* 118. *a.*

5. If the six months be incurred, yet the patron's clerk shall be received, if presented before the church be filled by lapse, and the patron may also present against the king's lapse; a lapse cannot be granted over, as the grant of the next lapse of such a church, neither before it fall nor after. If the lapse incur, and then the ordinary die, the king shall present, and not the ordinary's executor; for it is rather an administration than an interest. *Fitzh. Nat. Brev.* 34. (*G.*) 25 *E.* 3. 24. *Dy.* 87. is doubtful whether to the king or to the metropolitan, and I (says lord *Hobart*) hold it clear that if the patron present, and his clerk is instituted, and remains 18 months without induction, the king shall not present upon him by lapse, as he may do upon a direct patronage, accruing to him by guard of temporalties, or of his tenant's heirs after institution before induction. *Fitzh. Nat. Brev.* 34, 36. (*K.*) *For the king cannot have a lapse but where the ordinary might have had it before.* A lapse is an act and office of trust reposed by law in the ordinary, metropolitan, and lastly in the king, (who is *certum et stabilimentum justitiae*) the end of which trust is to provide the church of a rector, in default of the patron; and yet as for him and to his behoof; and therefore as he cannot transfer his trust to another; so cannot he devest the thing wherewith he is intrusted, to any other purpose, and therefore, though the king or bishop may suffer the church to stand void (which yet is *culpa*) yet *they cannot bind themselves, that they will not fill the church; for that were* injuria et malum in se; and therefore shall be judged in law in deceipt of the king; for *eadem mens praesumitur regis quae est juris, &c.* Now the ordinary, or he who is to present by lapse, is as it were *negotiorum gestor*, or a kind of attorney, made by law, to do that for the patron which it is supposed he would do for himself, if there were not some let; and therefore the collation by lapse is in right of the patron, and for his turn. 24 *E.* 3. 26. And he shall lay it as his possession for an assise of *darrein presentment.* 5 *H.* 7. 43. *Fitzh. Nat. Brev.* 31. (*F.*) *Hob.* 154. *Cro. Ca.* 356. 7 *Co.* 28. *Dy.* 36. 5 *Co. De jure regis Eccl.* 14. *b.* 21 *E.* 3. *Pal.* 311, 312.

6. At common law, if any had usurped upon the king, and his presentee admitted, instituted and inducted, (*for without induction the church had not been full against the king*) the king might have removed him by *quare impedit*, and been restored to his presentation; for therein he hath a prerogative, *quod nullum tempus occurrit regi*; but he could not present, for the plenarty barred him of that, neither could he remove him any way but by action; to the end the church might be more quiet in the mean time: neither did the king recover damages in his *quare impedit* at the common law, but the *Stat. W.* 2. *cap.* 5. hath altered the common law in the cases aforesaid, as namely *quod hoc, quod si pars rea accipiat de plenitudine Eccl. per suam propriam praesentationem, non propter illam plenitudinem remaneat loquela, dummodo breve infra tempus semestre impetretur, &c.* and also hath provided remedy in other cases, as by the said act appeareth. *And if the king doth present to a church, and his clerk is admitted and in-*

ſtituted, yet before induction the king may appeal and revoke his preſentation. But regularly no man can be put out of poſſeſſion of his advowſon, but by admiſſion and inſtitution, upon an uſurpation, by a preſentation to the church, *cum aliquis jus praeſentandi non habens praeſentaverit,* &c. *and not by the collation of the biſhop*; for if he collate without title, and his clerk is inducted, this ſhall not put the rightful patron out of poſſeſſion; for as lord *Coke*, lord *Hobart*, and other authorities of higheſt credit and reputation ſay, it ſhall be taken to be only proviſional, made for celebration of divine ſervice, until the patron do preſent; and therefore he is not driven to his *quare impedit* or aſſiſe of *darrein preſentment* in that caſe; but an uſurpation by collation ſhall take away the right of collation that is in another. An uſurpation upon a preſentation ſhall not only put out of poſſeſſion him who hath right of preſentation, but right of collation alſo; and ſo it is, that at this day the incumbent ſhall be removed in a *quare impedit* or aſſiſe of *darrein preſentment*, if there be not a plenarty of ſix months before the teſte of the writ; but then the incumbent muſt be named in the writ, or elſe he ſhall never be removed: yet at the common law, if the ordinary refuſed to admit and inſtitute the clerk of the patron, or when any diſturbed him to preſent, ſo as he could not prefer his clerk, he might have his *quare impedit* or aſſiſe of *darrein preſentment*, and if the church were not full, have a writ to the biſhop, to admit his clerk; but ſo odious was ſimony in the common law, that before the *Stat. W.* 2. he recovered no damages. At the common law, if, hanging the *quare impedit* againſt the ordinary for refuſing his clerk, and before the church were full, the patron brought a *quare impedit* againſt the biſhop, (and hanging the ſuit, the biſhop admit and inſtitute a clerk at the preſentation of another,) in this caſe if judgment be given for the patron againſt the biſhop, the patron ſhall have a writ to the biſhop, and remove the incumbent who came in *pendente lite* by uſurpation; for *pendente lite nihil innovetur*; and therefore at the common law, it was good policy to bring the *quare impedit* againſt the biſhop as ſpeedily as might be. And it is to be obſerved, that albeit the clerk, who comes in *pendente lite* by uſurpation, ſhall be removed, yet if the rightful patron, being a ſtranger to the writ, preſent *pendente lite*, and his clerk is admitted and inſtituted, he ſhall not be removed; for elſe, by the bringing ſuch *quare impedit* againſt the ordinary, the rightful patron might be defeated of his preſentation; and therefore (even after the *Stat. W.* 2.) amongſt other things, it was inquired *ex officio* if the church were full? Of whoſe preſentation, &c. And if the plaintiff ſhould have a writ to the biſhop, and his clerk admitted, as in moſt caſes he ought, yet may the right patron have his remedy by law. And as it was good policy to bring a *quare impedit* as ſoon as might be againſt the ordinary; ſo it is good policy, at this day, to name the biſhop in the *quare impedit*; *for then he ſhall not preſent by lapſe*, becauſe his name is in the writ. What then, after the time is devolved to the metropolitan, ſhall not he preſent by lapſe, becauſe he is not named in the writ? To this it is anſwered *clearly*, that he ſhall not, in that caſe, preſent by lapſe; *for he ſhall never preſent or collate by lapſe after ſix months, but when the immediate ordinary might have collated within the ſix months, and had ſurceaſed his time*; *and ſo it is if the time be devolved to the king*; for the firſt ſtep or beginning faileth, and in human things, *quod non habet principium, non habet finem.* Co. Lit. 344. b.

 Parti-

Particular cases.

Presentation, how favoured.

* 7. A private act of parliament was, which divides the parish into three, and this act enacts right of patronage and presentation shall belong to the dean and chapter of *D.* in such manner as the nomination or presentation of the old church did, *and not otherwise*; the old church was donative, yet the new church shall be presentative. See case before the house of lords, *Shirt* and *Carr*, 9 *Feb.* 1717.

How becomes void.

* 8. By cession or the incumbent's becoming a bishop, *&c.* see case *Archbishop of Armagh* and *Attorney General*, before the house of lords, 21 *April* 1730.

9. See before *General. Vide etiam Pal.* 345, 459, 476, 477.

Lawful patron, how favoured.

10. Institution and induction are meerly void against him. See *Archbishop of Armagh*'s case, *supra.*

* 11. Tho' generally till foreclosure, the mortgagor is to present, yet where there was an express covenant in the mortgage that the mortgagee shall present to fill up all the avoidance till discharged, it was decreed for the mortgagee. In this case fraud was pretended by the heir of the mortgagor, but it not appearing, and he having consented before the ordinary to the presentation of the mortgagee, and not bringing his bill for relief till after the six months elapsed; the decree was against him. See case *Gardiner* and *Cooke and others*, before the house of lords, 31 *Jan.* 1728.

12. Vide supra etiam 6 *Co.* 29. 2 *Cro.* 252, also Dr. *Lancaster*'s case, and Dr. *Birch*'s case.

Of the ordinary's right.

13. See before, and *Archbishop of Armagh*'s case before mentioned.

Of the king's right.

General.

14. Whether the king's right determines by his promotee's death? *Ibid.*

15. Whether where the king has but a temporary right, as that by promotion, whether the rule, *nullum tempus*, *&c.* will hold? *Ibid.*

16. Whether where the king, or a common person, has but a right to present for one turn only, and he suffers a presentation, and the incumbent to die in possession, his turn be gone? *Ibid. Vide etiam ante General,* Case 3.

Whether

Whether institution and induction only, without presentation, be a full plenarty against the king; and a dying of such incumbent be a good bar to the king's right.

17. In this case, the judgment of the king's bench in *Ireland* was affirmed, and that in the king's bench here reversed. And the principal points were, Whether the king had not lost his title, accrued by promotion of the late incumbent, on one who was presumed the clerk of the crown's being instituted and inducted only without any presentation by the crown or other in right thereof, and dying in possession? Or whether after such distance of time and several mesn incumbencies, the king may re-assume his title to the presentation? It was said, the reason of their lordships judgment was, that if they should not adjudge the mistaken institution and induction (though there was no actual presentation) a compleat incumbency, the executors of such incumbent, who had so held meerly by mistake upwards of 30 years, without any intention of wrong, might be accountable to the crown for all the time such mistaken incumbent enjoyed. *Archbishop of Armagh*'s case *supra.*

18. References, 7 *Co.* 28. *Dy.* 36. *Bro. Parl.* 6. *Cro. Ca.* 356. *Pal.* 302, 311, 312. 4 *Inst.* 356. *Ro. Abr.* 319. *Mod. Ca.* 1. 2. *Prohibition. Mod. Ca.* 1. 2. *Fitzh. Nat. Bre.* 37. (*H.*) *Da.* 33. *b. Co. Lit.* 180. *b.* 11 *Co.* 74. *b.* *Hob.* 152, 347.

19. See rule, *Lands are holden mediately or immediately of the crown.*

323. *Nullus recedat e curia cancellariae sine remedio.*

General.

1. THE *chancellor* said, *Nullus recedat, &c.* But *Fineux* said, *Si nullus recedat sine remedio, ergo nullus indiget esse confessus.* But the common law is ordained for many matters, and some, such as are not remediable at common law, are to be relieved in chancery: but some are remediable by neither, *&c.* *Vide Elf. Obf.* 47, 48. 4 *H.* 7. 4. *Doct. & Stud. lib.* 1. *cap.* 18. 2 *West's Prec.*

Exposition of the rule.

2. This rule is to be expounded, That the chancery giveth remedy for the common law matters, by granting the original writs, which are for the most part returnable into the common law courts: and for matters of conscience, by examining them in chancery itself; but this rule by no means extendeth itself to the law of conscience divine. *Elf. Obf.* 49. 2 *West's Prec.* 176. *b.*

3. See rule, *Ipsae etenim leges cupiunt ut jure regantur.*

324. *Officers may not examine the judicial acts of the court.*

1. IT was (*inter al'*) resolved in the countess of *Rutland*'s case, that a *ca. sa.* being awarded against her, by the court of common pleas, the sheriff, or his officers by his warrant, might, without any offence, execute it; for they ought not to dispute the authority of the court, but

to

to execute the writs to them directed, and hereto they are ſworn, &c. 6 *Co.* 54. *a.*

2. See rule, *Executio juris non habet injuriam.*

325. *Omne crimen ebrietas et incendit et detegit.*

1. A Drunkard, who by his own vicious act depriveth himſelf of his memory and underſtanding, ſhall have no benefit or privilege, as being *non compos mentis*, either to him or his heirs, &c. *Co. Lit.* 247. *a.* See 4 *Co. Beverley*'s caſe.

2. As for a drunkard who is *voluntarius daemon*, he hath, as hath been ſaid, no benefit or privilege thereby; but what hurt or ill ſoever he doth, his drunkenneſs aggravateth it. *Omne crimen ebrietas et incendit et detegit.* Ibid.

One may not ſtultify himſelf.

3. See rule, *Actus non facit reum niſi mens ſit rea.*

I have met with it thus ſaid of a drunkard, *That he is ſport for the devil, a laughter to the world, and a beaſt to himſelf, and that he falls ſo often in jeſt, that at laſt he falls for ever. And to a man of good ſenſe and ſound morals, both an epicure and a ſot are odious.*

326. *Omne magnum exemplum aliquid habet ex iniquo, quod publica utilitate compenſatur.*

1. THE law preſumeth violently that a lay-man cannot be abſolutely diſcharged of tithes; and therefore will not allow a preſumption of ſuch diſcharge; holding it more reaſonable that ſome one man ſhould ſuffer a miſchief to loſe ſuch a privilege, being ſo improbable, and of ſo dangerous a conſequence, than for his particular, to admit a ſpoil of the church, and a decay of religion, according to the rule, *Omne magnum exemplum*, &c. So though he ſhall be allowed his diſcharge by grant, when it appears, yet, when it appears not, *ſtabitur praeſumptioni*, &c. Hob. 297.

2. See rule, *Ex malis moribus bonae leges natae ſunt. Law will rather endure a particular miſchief*, &c.

327. *Omne majus continet in ſe minus.*

1. BY a pardon of murder, manſlaughter is pardoned. *Fi. Law Eng.* 21.

2. A perſon attaint is one convict and more. *Omne majus continet minus.* 4 Co. 46. a.

3. An attaint, ſuppoſing a verdict to have paſſed before two juſtices, whereas it paſſed before four, is good enough. *Fi. Law Eng.* 21.

4. A Recovery pleaded of three acres where it was of ſix, alſo good. *Ibid.*

5. A condition that I ſhall not infeoff *J. S.* is broken if I infeoff him and *J.D.* *Ibid.*

6. Where the cuſtom is that a man ſhall not deviſe for any higher eſtate than for life, though a deviſe be in fee, yet if the deviſee will claim but for life, the deviſe ſhall be good. 18 *E.* 3.

7. Where by cuſtom a copyholder may demiſe in fee, he may demiſe any leſſer eſtate without other preſcription. 4 *Co.* 23.

8. And where the cuſtom is to demiſe for life, he may demiſe to his wife *durante viduitate*; for it is a leſſer eſtate than the cuſtom allows. 4 *Co.* 30.

9. By *Stat.* 32 *H.* 8. which gives power to deviſe two parts of the land, a deviſe of all, is a good deviſe of the two parts, though the ſtatute of 34 & 35 of *Explanations* had never been. *Dy.* 150. *b.*

10. If one who is to make a payment, tender more than he ought to pay, it muſt needs be good; for *omne majus continet in ſe minus*; though the other ought to take no more than his due; *quando plus fit quam fieri debet, videtur etiam illud fieri quod faciendum eſt. Et in majore ſumma continetur minor.* 5 Co. 115. a.

328. *Omne quod utile aliquando neceſſarium.*

1. SEE rules, *Natura appetit perfectum. Neceſſitas facit illud licitum, quod, &c. Legum vincula irridet. Vincit legem. Neceſſity creates equity.*

2. See alſo *Pal.* 528.

329. *Omnes reges dicuntur clerici.*

1. *REſolved*, That proxies, in their original nature being duties payable for viſitation, were grantable to the king, and that he was capable of ſuch grant, eſpecially ſince ſuch duties have been converted to certain ſums of money, in the nature of penſions or annuities; for by the antient law of the realm, the king had power to viſit, reform and correct all abuſes and enormities in the church: and by the ſtatute made in *H.* 8.'s time, the crown was but remitted to its antient juriſdiction, which had been uſurped by the biſhop of *Rome.* 33 *E.* 3. *Fitzh. Aid del roy* 103. *Reges ſacro oleo uncti ſpiritualis juriſdictionis ſunt capaces.* And proxy is a profit of juriſdiction. 10 *H.* 7. 18. *Rex eſt mixta perſona cum ſacerdote.* Alſo the king ſhall have tithes by the common law, whereof no lay perſon was capable. 22 *Aſſ. pl.* 75. 21 *H.* 7. 1. The king himſelf may viſit his free chapels and hoſpitals. 8 *Aſſ. pl.* 29. *Nat. Brev.* 42. *a. Omnes reges dicuntur clerici. Cauſa ſpiritualis committi poteſt principi laico.* And whereas it hath been objected, that by means *del grandeur del roy, et de ſon train,* competent proxies cannot be exhibited to him; and conſequently they may not be granted to him; this objection vaniſheth, as the proxies, at the time of the grant, were reduced to certain reaſonable ſums of money. *Da.* 4. *a.* See 1 *Ju. Eccl.* 5 *to* 26. *as to the ſupremacy of the crown.*

2. So he is capable of mortuaries. 2 *Inſt.* 491.

3. Alſo he is capable of tithes. 5 *Co. De Ju. Regis Eccl.* 15. *a.*

4. So he may viſit eccleſiaſtical bodies. *Ibid.* See alſo 21 *E.* 3. See alſo *Ha. Anal.* 23, 24. *Da.* 4. *a. Gilb.* 181. 2 *Pe. Will.* 119. 2 *Ju. Eccl.* tit. *Charities, Appropriations, Donatives, Chapels.*

5. He may exempt from ordinary jurisdiction or visitation. *Da.* 72, 73. 5 *Co. De. Ju. Regis Eccl.* 9. *b.* 10. *a.* 14. *b.* 15. *a.*

6. He may appropriate sole. 7 *E.* 3. *Fitzh. Quare Impedit* 19. *Salk. Bishop of St. David's* case, and *Farest. same case.* 11 *H.* 4. 213. *b.* *Da.* 73. 5 *Co.* 51. *Ha. Anal.* 19.

7. Resignation to him is good, as to the supreme ordinary. *Dy.* 294. 5 *Co. De Ju. Regis Eccl.* 34. *Palm.* 477.

330. *Omne testamentum morte consummatum est.*

General.

1. *ULtima voluntas est legitima dispositio de eo quod quis post mortem fieri velit.* Swinb. 18. Orph. Leg. sect. 2.

2. The will hath relation to the testator's death, and not to the making; for till death he is master of his own will. 2 *Ju. Eccl.* 35.

Particular cases.

3. If a man deviseth his lands to one and to his heirs, and the devisee die, living the devisor, the devise is void; for the will was alterable at the pleasure of the devisor, and the heir cannot be a purchaser. 1 *Co.* 155. *b.*

4. Yet there is a *Donatio causa mortis*, as where a man lying in extremity, or being surprised with sickness, and not having an opportunity of making his will, lest he should die before he can make it, gives his goods, with his own hands, to his friends about him; this disposition, if he dies shall operate as a legacy : but if he recovers, the property reverts. *Prec. Chan.* 269.

5. And this *Donatio causa mortis* is in the nature of a legacy, waiting on the death of the testator, and is ambulatory and open till that time; and by a revocation of all former wills it is revoked; and a subsequent devise is to be taken in satisfaction of such donation. It is a gift *in praesenti* to take *in futuro, &c.* Prec. Chan. 300. 2 Mod. Ca. the case *Mitford* versus *Lord Herbert et al'.* And it is to be observed that these donations are not to be countenanced or favoured; therefore ought to be fully proved in all circumstances. *Prec. Chan.* 300.

331. *Omnia praesumuntur legitime facta, donec probetur in contrarium.*

1. WHEN one hath a deed in his hand, and it is pleaded to the court, it shall be rather intended that he cometh to the deed by lawful means, than by wrongful. *Omnia praesumuntur legitime facta, donec probetur in contrarium. Injuria non praesumitur.* Lit. sect. 377. Co. Lit. 232. b.

2. *Vide* rule, *Injuria non praesumitur.*

332. *Omnia*

332. *Omnia praeſumuntur ſolemniter eſſe acta.*

General.

1. THough every pariſh church is ſuppoſed preſentative, and that the incumbent ought to come in by admiſſion, *&c.* yet one may preſcribe that it was appropriate, *&c.* And the commencement of a thing before time of memory cannot be known, *&c.* 21 *E.* 4. 65. *a.* 11 *Co.* 10. *a.*

2. Whether appropriations are good or not, may not now, at this diſtance of time, be called in queſtion, but ſhall be intended good and to have all requiſites to its perfection. *Concurrentibus, &c.* 2 Co. 46. *Archbiſhop of Canterbury*'s caſe.

3. *Stat.* 35 *Eliz.* all manors, lands, *&c.* which at any time thentofore were the poſſeſſions of any abbey, *&c.* after 4 *Febru. anno* 27 *H.* 8. granted or conveyed by letters patent by the ſaid king to any, *&c.* were to be adjudged in the real and actual poſſeſſion of the ſaid king and his ſucceſſors, where the ſame were granted by him or them. In the purview of this ſtatute, four things are to be obſerved, *&c.* Vide 2 *Ju. Eccl.* 462, 463. Notwithſtanding any defect, *&c.* in any ſurrender, grant, *&c.* of the ſaid manors, lands, *&c.* to the late king *H.* 8. or any other matter or cauſe whatſoever, *&c.* ſo that the ſcope and purport of the ſtatute was to veſt in this king and his ſucceſſors, all manors, lands, *&c.* which the abbots, *&c.* had, notwithſtanding the defects aforeſaid. 11 *Co.* 11 *b.* 12. *a. b.* 13. *a.*

4. All appropriations, howſoever defective, were given to the king and his ſucceſſors, *&c.* by the true meaning of the laws of monaſteries, which meant to give all, as well in reputation as in truth. *Hob.* 148.

5. Tho' there was a defect in the appropriation, yet if the rectory was in reputation appropriate, and ſo hath been uſed, it is given to the king by the ſtatute 27 *H.* 8. or 32 *H.* 8. and therefore 19 *Eliz.* in the caſe of the dean of St. *Paul*'s, it was adjudged that a chantery or college in reputation, and not in law, was given to the king *E.* 6. by the ſtatute 1 *E.* 6. by theſe words, *all and all manner of chanteries, colleges,* &c. 11 Co. 13. a.

6. Old appropriations are to be preſumed to be well and lawfully made, *&c.* *Tri. per Pa.* 301, 392.

7. In things of ſuch antiquity, *Omnia praeſumuntur ſolemniter eſſe acta.* Tri. per Pa. 406. Pal. 427.

8. Tho' the appropriation was defective, or that the advowſon did not paſs by the grant, yet it ſhall be intended that there was a lawful grant in reſpect of the antient and continual poſſeſſion; *Omnia praeſumuntur, &c.* which might make the antient impropriation good; for *tempus eſt edax rerum,* and records, *&c.* either conſume, or are loſt, *&c.* 12 *Co.* 4, 5. *Hard.* 382.

Particular caſes.

9. The caſe was between *Lord St. John* and *The Dean and Chapter of Glouceſter,* for the parſonage impropriate of *Fenmark* in *Glamorganſhire,* becauſe he who appropriated was but tenant in tail, yet as it had continued as a church appropriate, it was decreed that this rectory in reputation was given to the king, by the ſtatute of *Monaſteries.* 11 *Co.* 13. *a.* The ſame of *Humbalton,* 11 *Co.* 13. *a.*

10. *Bullenham* was appropriate, but no vicarage endowed, yet as there had been one in reputation, *&c.* Refolved good. 11 *Co.* 13. *a.* 12 *Co.* 4.

11. One had gotten an appropriation, and brought a *quare impedit*, and the defendant pleaded an appropriation; there was no licence produced, yet the court would intend it. 1 *Mod.* 117.

12. The abbot of *S.* held the parfonage of *L.* to his own proper ufe, which as a parfonage appropriate came to the king, *H.* 8. by the diffolution of monafteries, *anno* 31 *H.* 8. who 37th of his reign granted in fee-farm, under which the plaintiff claims; the defendant got prefentation from the queen, and to deftroy the appropriation fhewed the original grant or inftrument of it, 22 *E.* 4. with a condition in it, that a vicarage be completely endowed, and alledged it never done; and fo the appropriation void; and indeed there was no inftrument or proof of any endowment; yet as it all along had been reputed and taken to be appropriate, and a vicar prefented, admitted, inftituted and inducted, as a vicar rightfully endowed, and paid his firft fruit and tenths; it was refolved *per tout le Cure*, it fhould be prefumed the vicarage, by reafon of the continuance, was lawfully endowed; *Omnia praefumuntur*, *&c.* and it would be a dangerous precedent to examine the original of the appropriations of parfonages, and the endowment of vicarages; for the origin of them in time will be loft. 12 *Co.* 4.

13. One had gotten a prefentation to the parfonage of *G.* and brought a *quare impedit*; the defendant pleaded an appropriation, there was no licence of appropriation produced; but becaufe it was antient, the court would intend it. 1 *Mod.* 117.

14. On iffue, if it was a vicarage endowed, or only a ftipendiary curacy? 1ft, All agreed if there was a vicarage erected and eftablifhed, tho' there be no endowment, the vicar may not claim any thing: (*viz.*) *Crew*, *Dodderidge*, *Jones* and *Whitlock.* 2dly, It was fhewn to be appropriate by licence of the pope in the time of *E.* 2. *Dodderidge*, not good, *Jones econtra*, and it would be dangerous to thefe antient impropriations, if the confent of the king were now to be fhewn; and at that time it was taken to be good by the affent without the king. *Dodderidge* denied that the pope, even then without the king, could with the ordinary and patron appropriate. *Crew* agreed with *Jones*, and in things of fuch antiquity *Omnia praefumuntur folemnitur effe acta*, *&c.* Palm. 426, 427.

15. References, 1 *Chan. Ca.* 11, 12, 202, 293. *Cro. Jac.* 515, 255. 2 *Ro.* 97. *S. C.* *Stat.* 31 *Eliz.* *Ley's Rep.* 14. *Stafford*'s cafe. *Co. Lit.* 6. *b.* 11. *b.* 12. *a. b.* *Hard.* 82. *Tri. per Pa.* 301, 406. *Co. Lit.* 301. *a. b.* 2 *Ju. Eccl.* 480, 483.

16. See rule, *In odium fpoliatoris omnia praefumuntur.*

333. *Omnia quae funt uxoris funt ipfius viri.*

1. SO fhe is difabled to contract with any *fans* confent of the hufband; neither may fhe difpofe of any perfonal matter, though in her own right. *Co. Lit.* 12. *a. b.*

2. See rule, *Feme covert under obedience of her hufband.*

3. References, 1 *Chan. Ca.* 169, 170, 266, 280, 308. *Doct. & Stud.* 25, 28, 38. *Gilb.* 100, 101, 102. 2 *Lev.* 107. 1 *Mod.* 105. 2 *Ch. Ca.* 96. *Gilb.* 233, 234, *&c.* *Nelf.* 387, 436. *Gilb.* 37, 89, 140.

Cro. Jac. 222, 332. *Yelv.* 136. *Hob.* 216. *Hut.* 17. *Nelſ.* 346. *Prec. Chan.* 19. 1 *Chan. Ca.* 232. 3 *Rep. Chan.* 90. 1 *Rep. Chan.* 380. 2 *Vent.* 362. 2 *Vern.* 391, 428, 569, 595, 764. *Prec. Chan.* 305.

334. *Omnis forma, per quam quaeque res in propriâ ſpecie conſtituitur, perfectio quaedam eſt.*

1. WHERE a thing is not warranted by law in its conſtitution, it is not the thing it ſhould be, and then it can bear no execution at all; for *jura naturae ſunt immutabilia,* which extends to particular matters and forms of every thing, *quae dant eſſe*; for if you change the eſſential form, it may be ſome other thing, but it is not now the ſame that it was. *Omnis forma, per quam quaeque res in propriâ ſpecie conſtituitur, perfectio quaedam eſt. Perfectum eſt cui nihil deeſt ſecundum ſuae perfectionis vel naturae modum.* Hob. 151.

2. See rules, *Perfectum eſt cui nihil deeſt, &c. Jura naturae ſunt immutabilia.*

335. *Omnium rerum, quarum eſt uſus, poteſt eſſe abuſus, virtute ſola excepta.*

BY antient canons and councils, *un home ne puiſſoit aver forſque un benefice,* and yet by experience it was found convenient that ſometimes, (*viz.*) *in caſes of neceſſity or utility of the church,* a man ſhould have the charge and fruits of ſeveral benefices: this diſtinction was invented and allowed, that though a man could have but one benefice *in titulo,* yet he might have another *in commenda,* (*viz.*) that another benefice might be commended, and committed to his cuſtody and care, till an able imcumbent ſhould be provided for it. *But after, great abuſes being found in the granting of theſe* commendas *by ordinaries*; for *Omnium rerum, quarum eſt uſus, poteſt eſſe abuſus, virtute ſola excepta*; another canon was made in the council of *Lions, anno domini* 1274, for reformation. *Dav.* 79. *a.*

336. *Once a mortgage and always a mortgage.*

1. *H.* Mortgaged lands, provided that he himſelf or his heirs male of his body might redeem, yet decreed that his aſſigns ſhould redeem. *Once a mortgage and always a mortgage.* 1 Vern. 33.

2. Mr. *H.* ſettled a jointure on the plaintiff his lady, before marriage, and that proving defective, according to the marriage agreement, made an additional jointure, and after made a mortgage to the defendant, *anno* 1673, for 1000*l.* with intereſt, of part of the lands in the additional jointure. In the mortgage there was a ſpecial clauſe for redemption, that if Mr. *H.* or the heirs of his body ſhould in *June* 1686 pay the 1000*l.* and 60*l. per annum* intereſt in the mean time, then he or his heirs male might enter. And Mr. *H.* covenanted, that none but he or the heirs male of his body ſhould be admitted to redeem; and covenanted to pay the 1000*l.* on ſuch a day in 1686 and 60*l. per annum* in the mean time, by half-yearly payments. Mr. *H.* dies *ſans* iſſue, the plaintiff brings her bill to redeem, ſhe

being

being the jointress *ut supra* of part; and so intitled to redeem the whole. The defendant insists the lands are irredeemable. And on rehearing decreed for the plaintiff, as it was on the first hearing. On the face of the mortgage there is no appearance that there should be no redemption, *&c.* *Once a mortgage and always a mortgage.* Equity against a man's agreement will let him in to redeem a mortgage. If a mortgage be made to a brother, and in case the mortgagor have no issue male, his brother shall have the lands, such an agreement made out in proof might well be decreed in equity, *&c.* Decreed interest for the 60 *l. per annum* being in arrears. 1 *Vern.* 190, *&c.*

3. References, 2 *Chan. Rep.* 141. 1 *Vern.* 7, 160, 210, 232, 269, 488, 138. 2 *Rep. Chan.* 58, 147, 159.

337. *One may not do an act to himself.*

1. A Man cannot present himself to a benefice, nor make himself an officer, nor sue himself. When one hath a right to lands, and the freehold is cast upon him by a latter title, he shall be remitted to his first title; because there is nobody against whom he might have an action, and he cannot sue himself. 13 *H.* 8. 22. *Lit.* 147. *b.* So one cannot summons himself. 8 *H.* 6. 29. So if the sheriff suffer a common recovery, it is error; for he could not summon himself. *Dy.* 188.

2. A man cannot be both judge and party in a suit; and therefore if a judge of the common pleas be made a justice of the king's bench, though it be but *hac vice*, it determineth his common pleas patent; for if he should be a judge of both benches at once, he should controul his own judgment; for if the common pleas err, it must be reversed in the king's bench. *Fi. Ley* 6. *a.*

3. See rule, *None to be judge in his own cause.*

338. *One not to be prejudiced by the act of a third person.*

1. SEE rule, *Volenti non fit injuria.* *Usury odious in law.*

2. References, *Da.* 67. *a.* *Yelv.* 47. 2 *Ju. Eccl.* 484. *Co. Lit.* 152. *b.*

339. *One may not stultify himself.*

The sorts of persons of non sane *mind.*

1. NON *compos mentis* are of four sorts. 1. *Idiota*, who from his infancy by perpetual infirmity is *non compos mentis.* 2. He who by sickness, grief, or other accident, wholly loseth his memory and understanding. 3. *A Lunatic*, who sometimes hath his understanding, and sometimes not, *aliquando gaudet lucidis intervallis*; and therefore he is called *non compos mentis*, so long as he hath not understanding. 4. *And lastly*, he who hath by his own vicious act deprived himself of his memory for a time, as a drunkard, which last sort hath no privilege or benefit to him or his heirs; he is *voluntarius daemon*, and what hurt or ill soever he doth, his drunkenness aggravates it. *Omne crimen ebrietas incendit et detegit.* Co. Lit. 246. b. 247. a. 4 Co. 124. b.

The difference between them, &c.

2. It hath been ſaid, That the great difference between an ideot *a nativitate*, and he who was of ſound memory, but became by the viſitation of God of *non ſane memorie*, is, that an ideot is known by his perpetual infirmity from his nativity; for he never had any ſenſe or underſtanding to contract with any man, *&c.* in actions brought againſt him, he is to appear in proper perſon, *&c.* otherwiſe it is of him who is become *non compos mentis*; for he ſhall appear by guardian, if he be under age, and by attorney, if of full age. 4 *Co.* 124.

As to their acts and their committees.

General.

3. Regularly ideots cannot ſtultify themſelves. 1 *Chan. Ca.* 113, 153. As to what acts committees may not do, it is to be obſerved they may not make leaſes. 1 *Chan. Ca.* 19. 1 *Vern.* 262. They cannot incumber. *Ibid.* They cannot build or improve the eſtate. *Ibid.* They may not alter the nature of the ward's eſtate, as to make perſonalty realty, or realty perſonalty. *Ibid.* and 2 *Vern.* 192, 414. The acts of lunatics are regularly void, tho' reaſonable and for the general good of his family. 1 *Ch. Ca.* 19, 113. 1 *Vern.* 155. *Gilb.* 101.

4. Upon the books have been four ſeveral opinions concerning the alienation, or other acts of a man that is *non compos mentis*, *&c.* for 1. Some are of opinion that he may avoid his own act by entry or plea. 2. Others are of opinion, that he may avoid it by writ, and not by plea. 3. Others that he may avoid it either by plea or by writ; and of this opinion is *Fitz.* in his *Nat. Brev.* and 4. *Lit.* is of opinion, that neither by plea, nor by writ, or otherwiſe, he himſelf ſhall avoid it, but his heir (in reſpect his anceſtor was *non compos mentis*) ſhall avoid it by entry, plea or writ; and herewith the greateſt authorities of our books agree: and ſo it was reſolved with *Litt.* in *Beverley*'s caſe, (4 *Co.* 126, *&c.*) where it is ſaid, it is a maxim of the common law, *that the party ſhall not diſable himſelf*; but this holdeth only in civil cauſes; for in criminal cauſes, as felony, *&c.* the act and wrong of a madman ſhall not be imputed unto him; for that in theſe caſes, *actus non facit reum niſi mens ſit rea*; and he is *amens, id eſt ſine mente*, without his mind or diſcretion; *et furioſus ſolo furore punitur.* Co. Lit. 247.

Whether may be avoided, and how may be avoided.

General.

5. The inquiſition hath retroſpect. 1 *Chan. Ca.* 113.

6. *Reſolved per tout le Cure*, That every deed, feoffment or grant made by any one *de non ſane memorie* is voidable, but not by himſelf; becauſe of the maxim in law, that no man in pleading ſhall, being of full age, in any plea to be pleaded by him, be received by the law to ſtultify and diſable his own perſon. 4 *Co.* 123. *b.*

Their Laches.

7. When, in what cafes and how laches fhall prejudice an ideot or *non compos mentis*, fome have taken a difference between a bar of his right and a bar of his entry; for in cafe of a bar of his right, his laches fhall not prejudice him, but in fuch fpecial cafe, if he be one of *non compos mentis*, he fhall fhew that he was fuch. As if a *non compos mentis* be diffeifed, and the diffeifor levy a fine, in this cafe at the common law, though the year and day pafs, yet he who was *non compos mentis* fhall not be bound by it, but may enter, as is proved by the ftatute *de modo levandi fines*, made *anno* 18 *E.* 1. which was but a declaration of the common law, (*viz.*) that a fine is fo high a bar and of fo great power, that of its own puiffant nature, it fhould foreclofe not only thofe who were parties and privies to the fine, and their heirs, but all the world befides, who were of full age, out of prifon, of found memory, and within the four feas, at the day of the fine levied; unlefs they put in their claim by their action, or by their entry in *Pais*, within a year and a day; from whence it appeareth that no laches fhall bar one of *non fane memorie* of his right. Alfo it appeareth by the ftatute 4 *H.* 7. 24. if a man levy a fine with proclamations, and at the time he, who hath right, is *non compos*, and after recovers his memory, here he is to purfue his action or entry in five years after he becomes of found mind, and in fuch cafe in pleading he is to fhew, that at the time of the fine levied he was *non compos*, and all the fpecial matter; but if he never recovered his right mind, there his heir may make his entry, or have his action when he pleafeth; for he is excepted out of the act, and not bound to any time, as is the party himfelf. 4 *Co.* 125. And the law is the fame of him who is beyond fea; and in fuch cafe the lord by efcheat fhall take advantage of *non fane memorie*, infancy, imprifonment, or being beyond fea, of his tenant. 4 *Co.* 125. But an ideot or *non compos mentis* by their laches may be barred of their entry as if they are diffeifed, and the diffeifor dies feifed, it tolls the entry: but after their deaths their heirs may enter, and take advantage of the infirmity of their anceftor. And his laches, which prejudiced himfelf, fhall not prejudice his heir of his entry. An ideot or *non compos mentis* wants difcretion and underftanding, and as it comes by the hand of God, God forbid, that the fame perfon's act fhould bind him whilft under fuch vifitation, &c. *Furiofus autem ftipulari non poteft, nec aliquid negotium agere, quia non intelligit quid agit. Non multum diftant a brutis qui ratione carent.* 4 Co. 125. b. 126. a.

Particular cafes.

8. Decreed that conveyances made to the defendant by *Elizabeth M.* of an equity of redemption, be fet afide; the bill being grounded on weaknefs and lunacy of *Elizabeth*, the plaintiff's coufin german, and whofe heir the plaintiff is, and the defendant's coufin german in the fame degree. There was no proof of lunacy, but fhe was weak of underftanding, fhe could read, and taught a child to read: two days after the deed fhe faid, fhe had made it to the end the defendant fhould have the land; yet becaufe the former communication of fuch grant was before, and no confideration in the deed, but fraud to be prepared and obtruded on *Elizabeth*, it was fet afide by lord chancellor. 2 *Chan. Ca.* 103.

* 9. A lunatic by her guardian applies to ſet aſide a voluntary conveyance made in prejudice of the heir at law, and in reſtraint of that power ſhe had over her eſtate before ſuch ſettlement. Not to be ſet aſide for the guardian or heir; but in caſe the lunatic recover her right mind, ſhe to be at liberty to bring a new bill, or ſeek other remedy. See caſe before the houſe of lords, *Barbara Standard, ſpinſter, a lunatic, by her guardian,* verſus *Meetkerke et al'*, 29 *Mar.* 1733.

May not be avoided.

General.

10. There are however ſome acts done by men of *non ſane memorie* which no body may avoid. 4 *Co.* 124. *a.*

Particular.

11. Therefore if ſuch levy a fine, ſuffer a recovery, acknowledge a ſtatute or recognizance, neither his heir nor executor ſhall avoid them; for theſe being matters of record ſhall be avoided by no bare averment of *non ſane memorie*, for the inconvenience which might follow: and indeed ſuch averment would be againſt the office and dignity of the judges, who ought not to take any cognizance of the fine or recognizance of one *non compos.* 4 Co. 124. a.

12. There are, it is to be obſerved, four ſorts of privies. 1. *Privy in blood*, as the heir. 2. *Repreſentation*, as the executor and adminiſtrator. 3. *Eſtate*, as of a gift in tail, the reverſion or remainder in fee. 4. *Tenure*, as lord by eſcheat. And two of theſe privies may diſable him who was *non compos*, and avoid his grants, *&c.* and theſe two are, 1. Privies in blood, and 2. Repreſentation. But privies in eſtate and privies in tenure cannot, and therefore if donee in tail, being *non compos mentis*, make a feoffment in fee, and die *ſans* iſſue, he in reverſion or remainder ſhall not enter, nor take any advantage of his inſanity of mind. The ſame law if there be lord by eſcheat, and his tenant, being *non compos mentis*, makes a feoffment in fee, and dies *ſans* heir, the lord ſhall not avoid it. 4 *Co.* 123, 124.

Not to be relieved even in equity.

13. It was alſo reſolved, that it being againſt an expreſs rule or maxim of the common law, that the party ſhould diſable himſelf, that he ſhould not have any relief for the ſame in equity; for that would be a ſubverſion of a principle or ground of law. 4 *Co.* 124.

Where the matter is of record.

14. All acts done by one *de non ſane memorie* in any court of record, whether concerning his lands or his goods, ſhall bind himſelf, and all others whatſoever for ever. All acts which he doth concerning his lands or goods in *Pais*, in ſome caſes, ſhall bind himſelf only for life, and in other caſes ſhall bind all for ever. 4 *Co.* 124, 125. *Tamen quaere as to relief in equity in the caſe of* Standard *and* Meetkerke, *ſupra.*

Marriage of perſons non compos.

15. If one marry a lunatic under committee of the court, he ſhall be committed, and the marriage is no *ſuperſedeas* of the commitment, though there were conſummation. *Prec. Chan.* 203.

16. One by contrivance gets and marries a lunatic, for which both the party, and others concerned therein were committed, and the writings were taken care of for the lunatic, and iſſue, if any ſhould be of the ſaid marriage. *Gilb.* 99. Vide *Stat.* 15 & 16 *Geo.* 2. *cap.* 30.

As to their tuition, and cuſtody of their fortunes.

General.

17. The king hath the cuſtody of an ideot or lunatic's lands, the latter to account not the former. *Ha. Anal.* 27. Vide *Stat. de Praerogativa.*

18. The care of them may not be to one, his executors, Adminiſtrators and aſſigns. 1 *Chan. Ca.* 19. 2 *Chan. Ca.* 70.

Particular.

19. The law hath provided, as hath been ſaid, for theſe a tutor, and hath made a proviſion for the preſervation both of their inheritances and goods. And ſo in the caſe of an ideot, where there is no expectation but that he ſhould remain all his days *ſans* diſcretion, and the law hath given the cuſtody of him and all that he hath to the king, who is bound of right by his laws, to defend his ſubjects and their fortunes, and ſo every ſubject is in his protection. An ideot can neither defend, nor govern himſelf, or order his fortune; and therefore it is that the king ought to have and govern him and them, as was the antient common law. *Bracton, fo.* 16. who writ 5 *E.* 1. whereupon followed the ſtatute *de praerogativa regis*, which was but a declaration of the common law, *quod rex habebit cuſtodiam terrarum fatuorum naturalium, &c. vue les parols*; upon which lord *Coke* obſerves, 1: That the king hath but the cuſtody of the lands, though for the life of the ideot, and he hath not the freehold in fee, but that reſts in the ideot; for the ſtatute ſaith, *Quod poſt mortem eorum reddat eam rectis haeredibus.* 2. Though the ſtatute ſaith *cuſtodiam terrarum*, yet the king ſhall have the cuſtody of their bodies as well as of their inheritances, goods and chattels, and of all ſuch eſtates as they have by purchaſe, as thoſe they have by deſcent by the common law. 3. He ought to be an ideot from his nativity, *a nativitate, ſcil. fatuus naturalis*, and not by accident or infirmity. 4. That no feoffment, gift, leaſe or releaſe, made by an ideot of his inheritance, but may be avoided even during his life; as appears by theſe words, *Ita quod nullatenus per eoſdem fatuos alienetur, nec quod eorum haeredes exhaeredentur*; and that by office, at the ſuit of the king; and this ſhall reveſt the land, *&c.* in the ideot, *&c.* for the ſtatute is, *quod poſt mortem eorum reddat eam rectis haeredibus*, which he could not do if he might not have it in the mean time; and therefore by the office ſuch conveyance is deſtroyed: and this in no wiſe infringeth on the maxim; for here the ideot in no plea pleadant diſableth or ſtultifieth himſelf; but all this is found upon office by the inquiſition of 12 men, at the ſuit of the crown, who are

are not concluded to ſay the truth. And ſuch office ſhall bear relation *a tempore nativitatis*, to avoid all meſn acts done by the ideot; but tho' the words of the act are general and emphatical, *nullatenus alienetur*; yet if he alien by fine or recovery, it ſhall bind him, as hath been ſaid. And after ſuch office found, all gifts made by him of his goods and chattels, and all obligations made by him, are utterly void, and if after ſuch office found, he be ſued upon an obligation or writing which he hath made, the king by his writ, ſo long as the office remains in force, reciting the office, ſhall command a *ſuperſedeas* to the juſtices where the ſuit is commenced; but the king ſhall not have the cuſtody of the land the ideot held by copy, *&c.* and yet the ideot's alienation of it ſhall be void after office found, *&c.* By the common law the king ſhall have as great protection of the goods and chattels of an ideot, as of his lands; and that as well the diſpoſal of them as the alienation of his lands is to be remedied and redreſſed by the king, *&c.* but if no office be found before the ideot's death, none may be found after, and without office the king is not intitled; the ſame law if one become *non compos mentis*, *&c.* But the king is not to take any part of the *non compos*'s eſtate himſelf, but to let it go to maintain him and his family; neither hath the king any intereſt in the perſon of a *non compos*, as he hath of an ideot; becauſe he may recover his memory; and therefore in the caſe of an ideot the law ſaith, *rex habebit cuſtodiam*; but in the caſe of a *non compos mentis*, *rex providebit*; and as to any alienation made by a *non compos mentis*, the words are the ſame as in the caſe of an ideot; *ita quod praedicta terra et tenementa infra praedictum tempus nullatenus alienentur*; and therefore after office found, the alienation, gift, *&c.* of a *non compos mentis* are in equal caſe with the alienation or gift of an ideot; and the words in the writ in the *Regiſter*, *Quia accepimus, quod* J. *de* B. *fatuus et idiota exiſtit*, *&c.* extend as well to a *non compos* as to a natural fool, as appears in the ſame writ, where it is ſaid, *diligenter inquiras ſi idem* J. *fatuus*, *&c.* ſo as it appears in judgment of law, *fatuus et idiota* includes as well *non compos*, as *fatuus a nativitate*; and therefore they are in equal caſe. 4 *Co.* 126. *b.* 127. *a. b.* In treſpaſs, *quare clauſum fregit*, and felled his trees, by *Francis* againſt *Holmes*, the defendant pleaded that it was by office found that *Francis* was a lunatic, *&c.* and ſeiſed in fee of the lands in which, *&c.* whereby the king ſeiſed his perſon and lands, and granted the cuſtody of both to the ſaid *Holmes*, *quamdiu* he ſhould be lunatic, to take the profits to his own proper uſe, and ſo juſtified, and prayed in aid of the king; but adjudged that he ſhould not have aid; for this grant was utterly void; for the king is bound to keep the lunatic, his wife, children and family, with the ſaid profits of his lands, without taking any thing to himſelf, but all to the uſe of the *non compos* and his family; to the intent to provide that he who wants reaſon ſhould not alien his lands, nor waſte his goods. And after the office found, the king hath only the proviſion, and not any cuſtody or poſſeſſion of the body or lands of a *non compos*, as he hath of an ideot. But if the king provide one to have care and charge, that he who is *non compos mentis* and his family be maintained, and that nothing be waſted; or if one of his own head take this upon him, he is but as bailiff of the *non compos mentis*, and ſhall account as ſuch to the *non compos*, or his executors or adminiſtrators, and ſuch may not fell trees but for neceſſary houſe-bote, plough-bote and cart-bote, and to repair an-

 tient

tient pales, and this but as bailiff, and what a bailiff may do, and no otherwise. 4 *Co.* 127. *b.* *&c.*

Nota; As to civil causes there have been different opinions, how far a man shall be allowed to stultify himself, for the avoiding of his own acts, as his conveyances, *&c.* see *Co. Lit.* 2. *b.* 246, 247. *and* 4 *Co.* 123, *&c.* *Register* 228. *Fitzh. Nat. Brev.* 202. *B. C.* *Orp. Leg.* 24, 25. *Hard.* 153. 1 *Chan. Ca.* 113, 153. 1 *Keb.* 133. 2 *Chan. Ca.* 103. 3 *Chan. Ca.* 107. 2 *Vern.* 414. 1 *Rep. Chan.* 40. 2 *Rep. Chan.* 221, *&c.* *Gilb.* 121.

20. See rule, *Actus non facit reum nisi mens sit rea.*

340. *One shall not take advantage of his own wrong or laches.*

General.

1. A Disseisor infeoffs his father in fee, who dies seised, the disseisee may enter notwithstanding the descent; for he shall be adjudged as to the disseisee, but as disseisor as being *particeps criminis.* Lit. 93.

2. If one be obliged to appear before the justices such a day, at which time he is in prison at the suit of the party, so as that he cannot come, the bond is saved; otherwise if he were in prison for felony or other misdemeanor; for there the fault was his own. 31 *H.* 6. *Fitzh. Bar.* 60.

3. Where an infant is plaintiff in an appeal, the parol shall not demur till his full age; for the defendant shall not have advantage *de son tort demesne.* 27 H. 8. and Bro. Covert 2.

4. If one in execution escape, and the gaoler retake him, he shall remain in execution for the party again, if the party so will; for the escape is *son tort demesne.* 13 H. 7. 1.

5. A feoffment, which is one's own act, by which a tort is done, shall not avail to bar the donor of his rent; for a man shall not take advantage of his own wrong. 3 *Co.* 30. *a.*

6. When a man deviseth lands to be sold by his executors, it is the same as if he had devised the same to the executors to be sold; and the reason is, because he deviseth the lands whereby the descent is broken, and in such case he is to sell as soon as he can; because the mesne profits taken before shall not be assets to pay debts; therefore if he was not compellable to sell as soon as possible, he should otherwise take advantage of his own laches; but if the devise be, that his executors shall sell, there they may sell at any time; for that they have but a bare power and no profit. *Co. Lit.* 236. *a.*

Rule.

* 7. All agreements are to be considered as executed, which are made on valuable considerations: and are to be considered as done or performed at the time when, according to the tenor thereof, they ought to have been done or performed, and are deemed to have the same consequences, in regard that the person, or any other claiming voluntarily under him, ought not to profit by his own laches or default, nor those, for whose benefit such contract was made, to suffer thereby. See the case before the house of lords, *Frederick* versus *Frederick*, 4 *May* 1731.

Particular to it.

* 8. The case was upon the *Stat.* 13 *Eliz. c.* 10. That colleges, deans and chapters, parsons, vicars and others shall not lease for more than 21 years, or three lives, and *Stat.* 14 *Eliz. c.* 11. That in cities, boroughs, towns corporate, or market-towns, they may lease for 40 years, but no longer; in this case the covenant was to renew for 99 years, and the house of lords decreed the dean and chapter to renew for 20 years, and to lease accordingly with all other covenants, except that to renew, and that at the covenanted fine and rent. See case before the house of lords, Dr. *Betsworth* and others of *Doctor's Commons*, against *The dean and chapter of St. Paul's*, 2 *May* 1728.

9 References, 1 *Chan. Ca.* 176, 278. 2 *Chan. Ca.* 27, 126, 207, 208, 2 *Ju. Eccl.* 483, 484.

341. *One is to be just before he is generous.*

1. THE plaintiff's bill was to have satisfaction of a debt, owing to him from *Anthony Dean*; who by his will had devised all his lands to the defendant *D.* and to the heirs of his body, with remainder over to another, and in another part of his will, reciting that he owed the defendant *P.* money on account, he therefore devised to him all his personal estate and made him executor, willing him to pay his debts; upon reading the will, though the clause, as to payment of debts, seemed to relate to the personal estate only, and though the lands were devised to the defendant in tail, with remainder over to another, and that it was objected that the tenant in tail could not be a trustee; yet decreed both real and personal estate to be sold for payment of debts of the testator. 1 *Vern.* 411.

2. The plaintiff's father being seised of a little messuage in *Marlborough* of 8 *l.* a year, and also possessed of a personal estate of the value of 25 *l.* made his will, and gave several Legacies; and to the plaintiff his eldest son 5 *l.* yearly for 40 years, if the plaintiff should so long live, and made *James* his second son executor and residuary legatee; and also devised to him the said messuage in tail, with several remainders over. *James* proved the will, entered on the real, and possessed the personal estate, and paid the plaintiff his annuity to the time of his the said *James's* death; and at his death he left an infant heir, and other children, and made his wife executrix, who proved the will, and after married the now defendant. The defendants pretend that *James* in his life fully administered the estate of the first testator, or however if he had wasted, he left no assets to answer; and therefore refused to pay the annuity; and insisted the real estate was not liable, not being subjected thereto by will, and *James* having by fine docked the intail, and borrowed 50 *l.* of the plaintiff, for securing whereof, as also 5 *l. per ann.* for three years, *James* conveyed the messuage, *&c.* in fee to one *P.* in trust for the plaintiff, redeemable at three years end on payment of 50 *l.* and interest, and the three 5 *l.* which were repaid, and plaintiff had reconveyed, and so had extinguished what, if any right he had, upon the real estate. *Per Cur':* The devisee of the land being also executor, the land shall be liable to the 5 *l.* according to the Case of *Clowdesley* and *Pelham*; and the rather because it was a provision for the heir who was disinherited;

and the devisee all his time, which was above 20 years, regularly had paid the same. And as to the pretence of being extinguished, it was nothing in equity; and therefore decreed the plaintiff his arrears and growing annuity for the time to come, &c. account of the profits of the real estate for that purpose, &c. 2 *Vern.* 143, 144.

3. The defendant's brother being seised of freehold and copyhold, and designing to marry the plaintiff if he had lived, by will drawn by the defendant, by the testator's direction, devised to his said brother all his houses and lands; and also gave to Mrs. *Susan A.* the plaintiff 200 *l.* to be paid by his executor in 3 years after the testator's death, and also a stone ring to her, and made his said brother executor, and the testator proposing three years to pay the legacies, the executor desired five. The personal estate falling short, the real was decreed to be bound, and that they were charged even on the face of the will: he need not have devised the lands to his brother, as he was his heir at law, unless he intended he should take them subject to legacies. And he is devisee and executor, and desired to see the will performed; and therefore this is a stronger case than *Cloudesley*'s, which was confirmed upon appeal to the lords. Note; this decree was also confirmed on review, and after affirmed before the lords. 2 *Vern.* 228, 229.

4. One owed his niece *A.* 100 *l.* by bond, and having two other nieces *B.* and *C.* made his will, and bequeathed 300 *l.* to his niece *A.* and 200 *l.* to his two other nieces, and after he borrows 100 *l.* more of his niece *A.* and died 200 *l.* indebted to her. To prove this 300 *l.* should go in satisfaction of the debt, Mr. *Vernon* insisted the rule in equity was, *That where a testator indebted gives his debtee a legacy greater than his debt, it shall go in satisfaction; for a Man shall be intended to be just before he is kind, otherwise where the legacy is less, for that is neither to be just nor kind, and so shall not be taken to be in satisfaction of any part.* *Cooper* Lord Chan. said *it might be as good equity, to construe him to be both just and kind, if he intended to be both.* That if any part of this 300 *l.* be applied to the payment of the debt, as to so much it is no gift; whereas a *legacy must be taken to be a gift or gratuity*, and there being assets, and some proofs of the testator's greater kindness to *A.* than his other nieces, his Lordship decreed her the whole 300 *l.* over and above her debt. *Salk.* 155.

5. Mr. *Fisher* was indebted in 50 *l.* to *Cranmer*, and left him a legacy of 500 *l.* and made him executor, and after his will made, borrowed 150 *l.* more of him, and died. *His honour of the rolls* decreed, that this legacy should be in satisfaction of both the debts, that contracted after the will, as well as that before. But Lord Chancellor *Harcourt* reversed the decree; because a *court of equity ought not to hinder a Man from disposing of his own as he pleases*; and when he saith he gives a legacy, we cannot contradict him, and say he pays a debt; and as to the debt contracted afterwards, he said there was no pretence to make this to be a payment of that. *If a legacy be less than the debt, it was never held to go in satisfaction; so if the thing given was of a different nature, as lands, it should not go in satisfaction of money; so if a legacy be upon Condition; for by the breach he may be a loser, whereas the will intended it for his benefit. Note*; in all these cases, the intention of the party ought to be the rule. *Salk.* 508.

6. References, 1 *Vern.* 14, 69, 261. 2 *Vern.* 64, 480, 481, 482. 1 *Chan. Ca.* 137. 2 *Ju. Eccl.* *Charity not to hurt another's right.*

342. *One*

342. *One not to have advantage of another's good bargain.*

General to, and rules.

1. WHERE an heir or truſtee buys in an incumbrance, he ſhall be allowed no more than he pays, unleſs he bought it to protect an incumbrance to which he himſelf is intitled; but where a ſtranger, who hath one incumbrance on an eſtate, buys in another to protect his own, he ſhall hold till he is paid all arrears and intereſt due, *&c.* And in this caſe, it being ſpecially circumſtanced, he was allowed, on account, the whole money due on the incumbrance he ſo bought in, though he paid leſs for it. 1 *Vern.* 49. Vide poſt *Particular caſes*, caſe 4.

Particular caſes.

2. Tenant in tail, remainder in fee, levies a fine and ſettles his eſtate on truſtees. 1ſt, To pay his eldeſt ſon 100*l. per annum*, and then to make a proviſion of 100*l.* for each of his younger children, to be raiſed and paid according to their ſeniority: and maintenance in the mean time. Lord chancellor decreed, that whereas at the time of the ſettlement the party was a widower, and had eight children, and declared he never intended to marry again, that in regard he afterwards married a ſecond wife, and had many children by her, that the children by the ſecond wife were equally intitled with the children by the firſt; and that whereas the deed directs the proviſion to be raiſed and paid according to their ſeniority, that in caſe of deficiency they ſhould be paid in average; that ſome of the younger children dying in the life of the father, their adminiſtrators ſhould not have any benefit of this proviſion [*caſe* 320.] but the ſame ſhould ceaſe; but in caſe any of the daughters had been married in the life of the father, and died, their huſbands, as their adminiſtrators, ſhould have had their portions; and no certain time being appointed for payment, but the ſame being left indifferent, it does not naturally attach till the death of the father; and whereas the eldeſt ſon had purchaſed in a ſtatute, which was an incumbrance on the eſtate, he ſhould be allowed no more than he paid. [See *Caſes* 48, 445, 465.] And that the eſtate muſt be looked upon as liable, in the firſt place, to ſatisfy this incumbrance, and then to raiſe 100*l. per annum* and arrears, and the ſurplus for raiſing the proviſion for younger children, but that their maintenance ſhall go on in the mean time. 1 *Vern.* 335, 336.

3. *A.* mortgages his lands to *B.* who ſells his intereſt to *C.* for leſs than really due, the heir ſhall not be allowed any benefit of this agreement between *B.* and *C.* but *C.* ſhall have the whole intereſt due on the mortgage. [See *Caſes* 445, 465.] But if one had purchaſed without notice of this incumbrance, he might poſſibly have had an equity to have redeemed the incumbrance for what was actually and really paid. [See *Caſe* 445.] 1 *Vern.* 336.

4. The plaintiff had made a mortgage to *J. S.* who finding it a ſlender ſecurity, the plaintiff's wife having a right to dower, aſſigned it to the defendant for 100*l.* though 150*l.* was due thereon; the plaintiff brought his bill to redeem, and wanted the advantage of the defendant's agreement with the mortgagee. *Per Curiam:* Where there are ſubſequent incumbrances

or creditors in the caſe, he who buys in a prior incumbrance, ſhall be allowed no more than he paid; but where the mortgagor himſelf (as here) or his heir comes to redeem, there is no reaſon that he ſhould have the benefit of another's good bargain; and ought therefore to pay what is really due on the mortgage, without reſpect to what the aſſignee paid. Decreed *accordant.* 1 *Vern.* 476. *Vide etiam* 464.

343. *Oportet quod certa res deducatur in judicium.*

1. UPON an avowry damages cannot be recovered for that which neither hath certainty, nor can be reduced to any certainty, *&c.* *Co. Lit.* 96. *a.*

2. Error of a judgment in an ejectment, becauſe the declaration was of a meſſuage and 40 acres of lands, meadow and paſture thereunto appurtaining, and it was not diſtinguiſhed how much there was in land, how much in meadow, and how much in paſture, wherefore the judgment was reverſed. *Cro. Ca.* 573.

3. References, 5 *Co.* 34. *b.* *&c.* *Cro. Eliz.* 836. *Ca.* 9. 837. *Ca.* 10. 11. 838. *Ca.* 12.

344. *Pacta privata juri publico derogare non poſſunt.*

1. IF lands are given to an alien and the heirs of his body, he hath an eſtate-tail, and yet ſuch eſtate after his death is not deſcendible to his iſſue. 9 *Co.* 141. *a.*

2. *A confirmation may not add a deſcendible quality to him who is diſabled to take by deſcent.* 9 Co. 141. b. As if lord and tenant be of a carve of land, and the tenant hath iſſue, and is attaint of felony, and the king pardon him, and after the lord confirm the eſtate of the tenant, and the tenant dies, the lord ſhall have the land even againſt his own confirmation; for the confirmation may not add to the eſtate of the tenant a diſcendible quality to him who was diſabled to take the land by deſcent. 9 *Co.* 141. *b.*

3. So in the caſe at bar, the confirmation of the earl to *Eliz.* could not add a deſcendible quality to the iſſue in tail, who was diſabled by the fine to take by deſcent; if the confirmation in the caſe at bar ſhould add to the eſtate of the wife ſuch a deſcendible quality, it in effect as to that purpoſe, ſhould repeal two acts of parliament, that is to ſay, That of 4 *H.* 7. and 32 *H.* 8. by which the eſtate-tail is barred *quoad* the iſſue, and the iſſue diſabled to claim the land by force of the ſaid eſtate-tail; *ſed pacta privata juri publico derogare non poſſunt*, and theſe ſtatutes are *jura publica*; for they are two of the principal pillars of the law. 9 *Co. Beaumont's* caſe, 138. *b.*

345. *Panis egentium vita pauperum, et qui defraudat eos vir sanguinis est.*

General.

1. HE that taketh away his neighbour's living slayeth him, *&c.* and whoso bringeth an offering of the goods of the poor, doth as one that killeth the son before the eyes of the father; he that sacrificeth of a thing wrongfully gotten, his offering is ridiculous; and the gifts of unjust men are not accepted. The most high is not pleased with the offerings of the wicked; neither is he pacified for sin, by the multitude of sacrifices: the bread of the needy is their life; he who defraudeth them thereof is a man of blood; but the spirit of those that fear the lord shall live; for their hope is in him that saveth them, *&c.* for the eyes of the lord are upon them that love him, he is their mighty protection, *&c.* See *Ecclesiasticus chap.* 34.

2. Trustees for a charity may improve for the benefit of the charity, but can do no act to prejudice it, in breach of the founder's rules. 2 *Vern.* 412. for *Panis egentium vita pauperum, et qui defraudat eos homo sanguinis est.* 8 Co. 131. Co. Lit. 342. a.

Rules.

3. *Panis egentium vita pauperum, &c.*

4. *Summa est ratio quae pro religione facit.* 2 Chan. Ca. 18. Jenk. 233. 1 Ro. Rep. 452.

5. Charity is not barred by length of time, or any statute of limitations. 2 *Vern.* 399.

6. What was once given to charity ought to be so applied, and what hath been imbeziled ought to be restored and made good. *Doct. & Stud. lib.* 2. *cap.* 55. 2 *Vern.* 389.

7. Charity must pursue the intent of the founder. 5 *Co.* 14. 8 *Co.* 131. 11 *Co.* 73. *Mod. Ca. Wright* and *Hobart*'s case. 2 *Ju. Eccl.* 157. *Dr. Ratcliff*'s case. See in the same title throughout.

8. Trustees for charity may improve, but not hurt the charity, *ut supra.*

9. If one will receive a charity with the yoke tied to it by the founder, he must bear it; for they cannot be severed. *Skin.* 491.

10. Yet a gift to charity must be for relief of necessity only, and not for ornament, or superfluity. *Du. Ch. Uses* 132.

11. And it must be according to and not against law. *Ibid.*

12. Neither may it do wrong to another's right. *Du. Cha. Uses* 140, 142. *Hern's Cha. Uses.*

Particular.

13. Where the revenues of a charity increase, and there is no appearance that the founder had any other matter than the good of that foundation in contemplation, such increase shall go and be applied in augmentation of the allowance to the master and fellows and the like in proportion; and if any surplus remain, to increase their number, *and nothing be*

converted by the truſtees, feoffees, deviſees, or other governors or managers, to their own uſe; for *Panis egentium vita pauperum, &c.* 8 Co. 130. b. *The caſe of* Thetford *ſchool.*

14. The biſhop, dean, maſter of an hoſpital, and the like, though they have the fee and right in them, cannot diſcontinue, neither can they, or any parſon, vicar, archdeacon, prebend, or any other having eccleſiaſtical living, though with the aſſent of their deans and chapters, patrons and ordinaries, or the conſent of any others, make any leaſe, gift, grant or conveyance, eſtate, charge or incumbrance, to bind his ſucceſſors, other than for the term of 21 years or three lives, and that in poſſeſſion, and whereupon the accuſtomed rent or more ſhall be reſerved. And theſe, *as my lord* Coke *wiſely ſays*, are excellent laws, and have been well expounded, for the maintenance of religion, and good of God's church; for otherwiſe, *ſaith his lordſhip*, it is to be feared holy church would loſe more than it would gain in theſe days; to which his lordſhip is pleaſed to add, *Panis pauperum, &c.* Co. Lit. 342. a.

15. How charity is favoured, ſee 2 *Ju. Eccl.* 158 *to* 205, *incluſive.*

346. *Par in parem imperium non habet.*

WATSON, late biſhop of *St. David*'s was taken up upon an *excom' cap.* and brought by *habeas corpus* in *B.R.* and pleaded to the writ, That he a lord of parliament, and moved to be bailed; but his motion was rejected. This prelate was ſued at *Lambeth* before the archbiſhop for ſimony and ſeveral other offences, and now he applied again for a prohibition, on ſuggeſtion that he was cited to *Lambeth*, and not to the arches, *&c.* but that application proving alſo fruitleſs, the court being clear for the archbiſhop's provincial power over all his biſhops, *&c.* the archbiſhop proceeded and deprived the biſhop; whereupon he appealed to the delegates, ſuggeſting that at law the archbiſhop alone could not deprive a biſhop; but this allegation being alſo rejected, he moved this court again for a prohibition, ſuggeſting, that all biſhops were barons, and *inter ſe pares, et quod par in parem imperium non habet*; and though a biſhop may be cenſured, yet he cannot be deprived by an archbiſhop; becauſe their temporalties, which are protected by the common law, are concerned; but it ought to be by convocation, (which the lord chief juſtice *Holt* called a new fancy of Sir *Bartholomew Shower*'s,) *or by the eccleſiaſtical commiſſion.* The lord chief juſtice and the reſt of the court held **clearly**, *that an archbiſhop had power over his ſuffragans, and might deprive. That biſhops are co-ordinate, or* pares, jure divino, *but not* jure humano: otherwiſe their inſtitutions would be to no end. *And as to their peerage, it was by reaſon of their barony*, &c. *That by the common law the archbiſhop had a metropolitical juriſdiction, and archbiſhops are over biſhops, as biſhops are over the other clergy*; that his power was diminiſhed, and uſurped upon by the pope, but reſtored to its extent by the ſtatute *H.* 8. *That by admitting him power to viſit, all is admitted*; *for he who may viſit, may deprive as well as cenſure*; *theſe being but ſeveral degrees of puniſhment*, &c. And the prohibition was denied, and the ſuggeſtion ordered by the court to be entered on record, that the court might enter their reaſons of denial, and ſo the biſhop was taken into cuſtody, and com-

committed to *Newgate.* See Dr. *Watſon*'s caſe, biſhop of *St. David's*, in *Salk.* alſo *Fareſt. S. C.* and 2 *Ju. Eccl. S. C. ſtill more at large.*

347. *Particeps criminis not to be relieved.*

1. THE defendant being *particeps criminis,* no decree ought to be for him. 1 *Chan. Ca.* 209. *Vide* 76.

2. See rules, *He who hath done iniquity ſhall not have equity. He who would have equity muſt do it. In odium ſpoliatoris, omnia praeſumuntur. That ſhall have the benefit, which hath or would have ſuſtained the loſs.*

348. *Patents and grants of the crown to be taken ſecundum intentionem regis, et non in deceptione regis.*

SEE rules, *Apices juris non ſunt jura. Maledicta expoſitio eſt quae corrumpit textum.*

349. *Pater eſt quem nuptiae demonſtrant.*

Baſtard.

1. A Baſtard is in law *nullius filius*; and therefore can be heir to no one. *Lit. ſect.* 188.

2. *Cui pater eſt populus, pater eſt ſibi nullus et omnis. Cui pater eſt populus, non habet ille patrem.* Co. Lit. 123. a. 213. b. 244. a.

3. If a villain hath a baſtard, and after marrieth the ſame woman, yet this baſtard is no villain, as it is a baſtard, and conſequently *quaſi nullius filius.* Co. Lit. 123. a.

4. And for the ſame reaſon, when the ſtatute 32 *H.* 8. of *Wills* ſpeaketh of children, baſtards are not within the ſaid ſtatute; and the baſtard of a woman is no child within that ſtatute, where the mother conveys lands to him. *Co. Lit.* 123. *b.*

5. It was found by verdict, that *Henry* the ſon of *Beatrice*, who was the wife of *R. R.* deceaſed, was born *per undecim dies poſt ultimum tempus legitimum mulieribus conſtitutum*; and adjudged, *quod dict' Henricus dici non debet filius praedicti Roberti ſecundum legem et conſuetudinem Angliae conſtitutam*; now *legitimum tempus*, in that caſe, by law, at the furtheſt is nine months, or forty weeks, but ſhe may be delivered before that time. *Co. Lit.* 123. *b.*

Mulier.

6. *Haeres*, or heir, is he who is *ex juſtis nuptiis procreatus. Haeres legitimus eſt, quem nuptiae demonſtrant, &c.* Co. Lit. 7. b. 237. b. 243. b.

7. See next rule, alſo *Heir favoured.*

350. *Pater et mater et puer ſunt una caro.*

1. PUERI *ſunt de ſanguine parentum, ſed pater et mater non ſunt de ſanguine puerorum*; and this is the cauſe that no lands might deſcend from the ſon to the father or mother, but ſhould rather eſcheat; and therefore

fore if father, uncle and son are, and the son die seised of lands in fee, the uncle shall be heir to the son, and not the father, and yet the father is nearest of blood; but if a lease be made to the son, the remainder to the next of his blood, the father shall in that case take the remainder as purchaser, for in *Littleton*'s judgment he is next of blood. *Lit. sect.* 3. *Co. Lit.* 11. *a.* 3. *Co.* 40. *a.*

2. As *Littleton* saith, it is a maxim in law, that inheritances may lineally descend but not ascend, as appears also by *Glanvil* who wrote in *H.* 2. time, *lib.* 7. *c.* 1. *fo.* 44. *b. Quaelibet haereditas naturaliter quidem ad haeredes haereditabiliter descendit, nunquam autem naturaliter ascendit.* And by *Bracton* also, who wrote in the time of *H.* 3. *lib.* 2. *c.* 29. *Descendit itaque jus quasi ponderosum, quod cadens deorsum recta linea vel transversali, et nunquam reascendit ea via, qua descendit, post mortem antecessorum.* And herewith also agreeth *Briton*, who wrote in *E.* 1. time, *c.* 119. *De successione.* And herein, *though the common law differeth from the civil law*, yet in this point, *as in all others*, the common law is founded upon the law of God, which is the *causa causarum*, as appears by the 27 *Chap. Num.* where the case in judgment before *Moses*, was that *Salphaad* having three daughters and several brothers died, to whom the inheritance should descend was the question? As to the daughters, they claimed *in jure propinquitatis*, as their birth-right, as they were next heirs to their father. The brothers claimed as heirs male, *jure honoris*, to aggrandize and continue the name of their ancestors. This cause seemed of great difficulty to *Moses*; and therefore holy writ informs us he consulted with God upon it, who said to him, *justam rem postulant filiae* Salphaad *: da eis possessionem inter cognatos patris sui, et ei in haereditatem succedant : ad filios autem Israel loqueris hæc : homo cum mortuus fuerit absque filio, ad filiam ejus transibit haereditas. Si filiam non habuerit, habebit successores fratres suos : quod si et fratres non fuerunt, dabitis hæreditatem fratribus patris ejus ; sin autem nec patruos habuerit, dabitur haereditas his, qui ei proximi sunt, eritque hoc filiis Israel sanctum lege perpetua, sicut praecepit dominus Moysi*, by which general law, which extends not only to the particular case then in question, but also to all other inheritances, persons and times, it is clear the father himself, and all other lineal ascent is excluded, &c. 3 *Co.* 40. *a. b. Vue tout le case.*

3. References, 30 *E.* 3. *lib. Ass. pl.* 47. *Dy.* 374. *a. b. Bro. Abr. Administrator* 47. *Stat.* 21 *H.* 8. *cap.* 5. 9 *Co.* 39. *Hob.* 83, 520. *Dy.* 151, 264, 310. *Fitzh. Abr.* tit. *Administrator. Etiam* tit. *Executor*, 1, 37, 51. *Cay's Abr. Stat.* tit. *Administrator, etiam Executor.*

4. See rule, *Children are de sanguine patris et matris, sed pater et mater non sunt de sanguine puerorum.*

351. *Pendente lite nihil innovetur.*

1. AT the common law, if hanging the *quare impedit* against the ordinary for refusing his clerk, and before the church were full, the patron brought a *quare impedit* against the bishop, and (hanging the suit) the bishop admit and institute a clerk at the presentation of another, in this case, if judgment be given for the patron against the bishop, the patron shall

have a writ to the bishop, and remove the incumbent who came in *pendente lite* by usurpation; for *pendente lite nihil innovetur, &c.* Co. Lit. 344. b.

2. See rules, *Nullum tempus occurrit regi. Quod non habet principium non, &c.*

352. *Pereat unus ne pereant omnes.*

SEE rule, *Interest reipublicae ne maleficia remaneant impunita.*

353. *Perfectum est, cui nihil deest secundum suae perfectionis vel naturae modum.*

1. REference, *Hob.* 151.

2. See rules, *Omnis forma, per quam quaeque res in propria specie constituitur, perfectio quaedam est. Jura naturae sunt immutabilia. Quod ab initio non valet, &c.*

354. *Periculosum est res novas et inusitatas inducere.*

1. WHatsoever is against the rule of law is inconvenient, and an argument *ab inconvenienti*, is strong to prove it against law; and new inventions, tho' of a learned judge, and that in his own profession, are full of inconveniences. *Periculosum est res novas et inusitatas inducere.* Co. Lit. 379. a.

2. See rules, *Equity cannot change things*, &c. *Rectifies mistakes*, &c. *Regards substance*, &c. *Will not aid new inventions*, &c. *Relieves against accidents*, &c. *Est boni judicis ampliare, &c. Law and equity both shall prevail*, &c. *Law favours justice and truth*, &c. *Requireth order and decency*, &c. *Will not suffer wrong.*

355. *Perpetuities odious in law and equity.*

What.

1. A Perpetuity is where, if all who have interest join, yet they cannot either pass or bar the estate. 1 *Chan. Ca.* 213.

General to.

2. Perpetuities may neither be in law nor equity. 1 *Chan. Ca.* 239.

Rules.

3. A limitation of one fee upon another upon a contingency to happen within a reasonable compass of time, is no perpetuity. See Duke of *Norfolk*'s case, where it is said, That future interests, springing trusts, or trusts executory, and remainders which are to arise upon contingencies, are quite out of the rule and reason of perpetuities, if they are not of remote consideration, but such as will soon wear out; and though there can be no remainder arise after a fee, yet there may a contingent fee out of the first fee, *&c. Prec. Chan.* 72, *&c.* 3 *Chan Ca.*

4. Where are ſeveral remainders for life, one after another, but all *in eſſe* at one and the ſame time, they are all good; becauſe they produce no inconvenience; all wearing out in a little time by an eaſy interpretation. 3 *Chan. Ca.* 29.

5. A conveyance made, which breaks no rule of law, introduces no viſible inconvenience, ſavours not of perpetuity, tends to no ill example, ſure may be good, though it be a conveyance only of a leaſe for years. 3 *Chan. Ca.* 51.

6. A deviſe of a term for years to one, his heirs, executors and aſſigns, for ever, but if he die before 21, leaving no iſſue, then to *J. D.* the firſt deviſee dying before 21. The remainder was held to be good, being within the compaſs of 21 years. *Prec. Chan.* 15. 1 *Pe. Will.* 1, *&c.*

7. Deviſe of a perſonalty to one in tail; remainder over; the remainder is void. *Prec. Chan.* 421. *Gilb.* 75.

8. To one, and if he go about to alien, then to a charity, this is alſo a void remainder; as tending to a perpetuity. 1 *Vern.* 226.

* 9. Limitations of a perſonalty, tending to a perpetuity, not good. See caſe *Ford* and *Ford*, before the houſe of lords, 3 *Feb.* 1730.

10. For a perpetuity is a thing odious in law, and deſtructive to the commonwealth; and therefore not to be countenanced in equity, *&c.* 1 *Vern.* 163, 164.

11. *Note Lectеur*, If a term be deviſed to one and to the heirs male of his body, his heirs ſhall not have it, but his executors; for a term for years, which is but a chattel, may not be intailed; and ſuch deviſee might alien the lands to whom he would. 1 *Co.* 87, *a. b.*

12. Where limitations to ſons ever take effect, and the eſtate becomes veſted, the remainder and limitation to the daughters becomes void; but if there never was any ſon (*as in the principal caſe*) the remainder is good; for the limitation muſt be conſtrued, if there be a ſon, then to him, if no ſon, but a daughter, then to her. *Salk.* 156.

Particular caſes.

13. The caſe in queſtion was, A deviſe to one and his aſſigns, and if he died without iſſue then living, that it ſhould remain to another, it is a void deviſe; and it is all one as the deviſe of a term to one and his heirs of his body, if he die without iſſue, that then it ſhall remain to another, which is meerly void; for ſuch an intail of a term is not allowable at law, for the miſchief which otherwiſe would enſue, if there ſhould be ſuch a perpetuity of a term. And though lord chief baron *Tanfield* doubted, eſpecially by reaſon of a judgment given before in the king's bench, *Hill.* 9 *Jac. Rot.* 889. betwixt *Rotherick* and *Chappel*, where *William Cary* poſſeſſed of a term for years, deviſed it to his wife for life, and afterwards that *John* his ſon ſhould have the occupation thereof as long as he had iſſue; and if he died *ſans* iſſue unmarried, that then *Joſeph* his younger ſon ſhould have the occupation of the ſame, as long as he had iſſue of his body, and if he died without iſſue unmarried, he deviſed one moiety to *Dorothy* his daughter; the other moiety to *Robert* and *William* his ſons; and made his feme his executrix, who aſſented to the legacies and died. *John* and *Joſeph* both died without iſſue unmarried; and after *Robert* and *William* enters upon the defendant, claiming the moiety, and lets to the plaintiff: upon

upon a ſpecial verdict, all this matter coming out, judgment was given for the plaintiffs to recover the moiety, which is all one caſe with the caſe in queſtion: but the defendant's counſel in the writ of error ſhewed a difference; for that there is a deviſe but of the occupation only; but here of the term itſelf. [*Nota diverſitatem.*] 2. It is a deviſe here of his eſtate and term, to him and his aſſigns, wherein is authority given *that he may aſſign.* 3. The limitation is there, if he die without iſſue unmarried, which is upon the matter, that if he die within the term; for if he be not married he cannot have iſſue; but in the caſe here, he might have iſſue, and yet if that iſſue ſhould die *ſans* iſſue in his life-time, it ſhould remain, which the law will neither expect nor ſuffer. *Cro. Jac. Child* and *Baylie*'s caſe, ſee the whole caſe. *Vide etiam* 3 *Chan. Ca.* 50. *which ſeems to deny the authority of this caſe, there being nothing in it which tends to a perpetuity, nothing inconvenient, nor any rule of law broken; but a reſolution* quia volumus; ideo quaere.

14. Limitation of the truſt of a term to baron and feme, and the longer liver of them, for life; and after to the eldeſt iſſue of them, none being then born, a good limitation. So the limitation to huſband and wife is but one limitation; and ſo it was admitted by counſel, it being not controverted; for though the truſt of a term according to the rule in *Goring* and *Bickerſtaff*'s caſe, *fo.* 4. may be limited to divers perſons that are in being, one after another; becauſe the ſame is transferrable, yet it cannot be good beyond the limitation to a third perſon, not in being. *Ergo* the limitation to the huſband and wife, and longeſt liver of them, was admitted to be but one limitation in this caſe. 1 *Chan. Ca.* 33, 34.

15. In ejectment, a ſpecial verdict was found, and the caſe was, *H.* poſſeſſed of a term for years, deviſed his land to *A.* and to the heirs of his body, and if *A.* die without iſſue, living *B.* then to *B.* *Northey*, who argued the caſe, ſaid, that the judges would allow a limitation in remainder, not only to a perſon *in eſſe*, but to the firſt ſon of ſuch perſon *in eſſe.* *Vide* 1 *Sid.* 451. 1 *Cro.* 230. 1 *Rol.* 602. And the court held that this was a good limitation to *B.* the contingency ariſing within the compaſs of a life; and denied *Child* and *Baylie*'s caſe. Mr. *Gould*, in arguing the caſe, ſaid, if one make a feoffment to the right heirs of *B.* that this was a good ſpringing uſe: *Sed tota curia contra eum in hcc*; becauſe it is by way of preſent limitation; *aliter* where it is future, as to the right heirs of *B.* after his death. *Salk.* 225.

16. A deviſe of a perſonalty to *J. H.* for life, and after to all ſuch iſſue as he ſhould have, jointly, and for want of ſuch, to *Nicholas Downes*, this was veſted intirely in *J. H.* as being an intail of a perſonalty. *Gilb.* 75. *Prec. Chan.* 421.

17. In this caſe it was held clearly and decreed, that a deviſe of a perſonal eſtate to one and his iſſue, or to one, and if he dies without iſſue, the remainder to another, that the deviſe over is void, and that the whole intereſt veſted in the firſt deviſee, ſo as to be liable to his debts. And *Vernon* ſaid, that the reaſon that a deviſe over of ſuch perſonal eſtate, upon a life only was good, was, becauſe in conſtruction of this court the firſt deviſee had but the uſe of it, and not the intire property. *Gilb.* 79.

18. Goods and a library were given to the defendant for life, and after to her daughter and her heirs for ever. The plaintiff married the daughter, and now as adminiſtrator of the daughter, his late wife, he ſeeks ſecurity for the goods or value at the defendant's death. Decreed *accordant*. 1 *Rep. Chan.* 111, *et etiam fo.* 130, 260. 2 *Vol.* 66. *Abr. Eq. Ca.* 1. *Max. Eq.*

19. A deviſe of a term for years to the mother for life; the remainder to the ſon and daughter, is an executory deviſe, and not a bare poſſibility; and may be aſſigned over notwithſtanding the authority of *Lampet*'s caſe, 10 *Co.* 46, *&c.* to the contrary, tho' ſuch remainder-man may die in the life-time of the particular deviſee; for it is contrary to good conſcience, and a caſe wherein this court will interpoſe and hinder any proceedings at law to defeat it. And ſo 'twas decreed accordingly twice in this court, between *Theobalds* and *Duffoy*, 2 *Mod. Ca.* 101, 102, 103, 104. But if an eſtate is granted to *A.* for life, and then a grant is to *B.* that he ſhall have and enjoy the profits for ſo many years as ſhall be to come and unexpired at the death of *A.* this is but a poſſibility; becauſe *A.* hath a greater eſtate, than for years, though never ſo long; therefore if leſſee for 1000 years grant for life, he hath granted all his eſtate, and cannot make any limitation over. 2 *Mod. Ca.* 102.

* 20. Deviſe of all the perſonal eſtate to *A.* who was a feme covert; but declared that it was his mind, That the intereſt and produce ſhould be for her uſe, ſeparate from her huſband, and after her deceaſe to her children till 21, and then the principal to them; but for want of ſuch iſſue, then he gave all his eſtate to the iſſue of *J. S.* and made the ſaid *A.* executrix and reſiduary legatee; ſhe being only intitled to the intereſt or produce for her life; the perſonal eſtate was not veſted in her, and the limitation over to the reſpondent upon the contingency of *A.*'s dying without iſſue, is a good limitation. And as for the words *reſiduary legatee*, they only mean for the purpoſe in the will. See caſe *Staines* and *Maddox*, before the houſe of lords, 18 *April* 1728.

* 21. One having an aſſignment of a mortgage for 1000 years, with a covenant from the aſſignor, that the mortgagor and his heirs ſhould in ſeven years make abſolute the term, makes his laſt will and teſtament, and therein reciting, that the mortgagor and his heirs and aſſigns were to convey the inheritance to the teſtator and his heirs, deviſes as an inheritance to three ſeveral perſons, for life one after another, with remainders to their firſt and other ſons reſpectively, with remainders over to two others; theſe remainders over are void; as too remote, and tending to a perpetuity. See caſe *Wilkins Brett* verſus *Sawbridge et al'*, before the houſe of lords 26 *March* 1736.

22. Sir *James Gray* being poſſeſſed of an annuity of 14*l. per annum*, for 99 years out of the exchequer, on his marriage covenants with *A.* and *B.* to pay this annuity to his wife, for her ſeparate uſe, and after the death of either of them, then to the ſurvivor for life, and after the death of both to the child or children to be begotten between them, and in default of ſuch child or children, then to his own executors or adminiſtrators, for the reſidue of the term. Sir *James* and his lady had iſſue one only ſon, who lived to be five years old, and then died. And after the death of Sir *James* and his lady, the plaintiff took out adminiſtration to the ſon, and brought this bill againſt the executors of Sir *James* and his lady, for

this annuity. It was insisted by Mr. *Vernon*, That the limitation to the executors and administrators of Sir *James* was void; being after a limitation to the child or children, which is the same as if it had been limited to the issue; and the settlement of a term on trustees, in trust to permit the father to receive the profits for as many years of the term as he should live, and after to permit the mother to receive the profits for so many years as she should live, and then in trust to permit the child or children, or issue, to receive the profits for the residue of the term, will bear no limitation over in default of issue, or children, in case there be any one in being, no more than such a limitation of the term itself, would be good; for this would be to revive and introduce all the inconveniences of a perpetuity, which has been so long exploded; and *the trust of a term must be limited in the same manner as the term itself will bear a limitation.* But the chancellor said, This being by way of covenant, no more passed out of him, than to serve the uses expressed, and it was not a disposition of the annuity itself, but only a covenant to pay the 14*l. per ann.* in such manner; and since it was never devested out of Sir *James*, he would not by this bill, on any pretence of equity, tear it out of him or his executors, and so dismissed the bill: though he did not at all dispute the case, if it had been a term, or the trust of a term, settled in such manner, that the remainder would not have been good; but here it was only a covenant to pay the 14*l.* and not the annuity itself, which was thought by some of the bar, to be an over nice distinction. But this decree, says our reporter, seems to be reasonable, because the administrator comes for a specific performance of the covenant, and that he cannot do, who was not originally in contemplation, or intended to be provided for by the covenant; but if the term had actually been vested in these uses, then the interest of the term being vested in the child and the heirs of his body, as it must be, if the settlement had been drawn according to the covenant, it must have gone to his administrator. *Gilb.* 97, 98.

23. References, 1 *Vern.* 35, 39, 65, 161, 162, 234, 257, 329, 462. 1 *Rol. Abr.* 612. *sect.* 3. 1 *Vern.* 304, 475, 479, 499, 328. *Cro. Jac.* 459, 461. 3 *Chan. Ca. per tout, et perticularment fo.* 7, 19, 20, 21, 22, 28, 31. 1 *Pe. Will.* 106. *Mod.* 115. 3 *Chan. Ca.* 42, 46, 48. *Nels.* 181, 280, *&c.* 398, *&c.* *Gilb.* 105. 8 *Co.* 94. *b.* *Ro. Abr. Devise* 612. 1 *Co.* 156. 10 *Co.* 87. *Cro. Jac.* 590. 3 *Lev.* 64. *Cro. Eliz.* 204. 1 *Chan. Ca.* 8, 129. 3 *Chan. Ca.* 35, 36. *Nels.* 116. 1 *Lev.* 256. *Gilb.* 128, 149. *Pal.* 333. 2 *Vern.* 38, 43, 59, 195, 668, 680. 2 *Rep. Chan.* 66, 153. 3 *Lev.* 401. *Sir W. Jo.* 15. *Cro. Eliz.* 576. 2 *Rep. Chan.* 230. *Sid.* 37, 191. 2 *Sid.* 21, 26. 2 *Saund.* 198, 384, 387. 1 *Lev.* 131. 2 *Lev.* 232. 3 *Lev.* 408, 431. 2 *Vern.* 286. 6 *Mod.* 191. 1 *Vern.* 145, 146, 147, 150. 2 *Vern.* 65, 241, 245, 661, 759. *Fitzh. Abr.* 238. *b.* *Bro. Abr.* 234. *b.* 235. *a.* (13.) *Fi. Ley* 45. *b.* 1 *Pe. Will.* 651, *&c.* *Dy.* 74. *Plow. Com.* 521. *Ow.* 33. *Lit. Bro. sect.* 334, 388. 1 *Ro. Abr.* 610. *Mar.* 106. 1 *Chan. Ca.* 129. *Cro. Ca.* 346. *Sty.* 251, 274. 1 *Leon.* 259.

356. *Per rationes pervenitur ad legitimam rationem.*

RAtio eſt radius divini luminis, and by reaſoning and debating of grave learned men, the darkneſs of ignorance is expelled : and by the light of legal reaſon, right is diſcerned, and thereupon judgment given according to law, which is the perfection of reaſon ; and is by *Littleton* called *legitima ratio*, whereunto no man can attain but by long ſtudy, often conferences, long experience, and continual obſervation, *&c*. *Co. Lit.* 232. *b.*

357. *Perſonal eſtate to go in eaſe of the real.*

General and Rules.

1. THE perſonal eſtate is the general fund to pay debts. *Gilb.* 129.

2. The perſonal eſtate to go in aid of the heir. 2 *Chan. Ca.* 59, 84. *Nelſ.* 342, 353. *Gilb.* 164.

3. And that though the lands are actually charged, yet the perſonal eſtate is to be applied in aid, unleſs there be an expreſs clauſe to except it. *Nelſ.* 342, 343, 351, *&c.* 414, 416. *Gilb.* 72, 73, 125.

4. *Lord Chancellor* declared, that the perſonal eſtate, in the hands of the executor, ſhall be employed in eaſe of the heir, by whatever means he became indebted as heir. 2 *Chan. Ca.* 5, 84, 271. 1 *Vern.* 436. *Salk.* 449. 1 *Chan. Ca.* 297. 2 *Vern.* 349. 1 *Chan. Ca.* 271, 297. 1 *Chan. Ca.* 121.

Particular.

5. The heir being ſued, and having paid a debt of his anceſtor by bond, decreed he ſhould be reimburſed as far as perſonal aſſets came to his hands. 1 *Chan. Ca.* 74, 80, 81.

6. References, 1 *Vern.* 36, 302. 2 *Vern.* 183. *Max. Eq.* 19, *&c.* 72, 73, 125, 164. *Nelſ.* 414, 342. *Prec. Chan.* 2, 3, 101, 183, 209. 1 *Rep. Chan.* 48. *Bac. Abr. Eq.* 295, 296. 2 *Rep. Chan.* 377. 3 *Rep. Chan.* 190, 206 *to* 214. *Salk.* 159. 2 *Mod. Ca.* 66, 67. 2 *Chan. Ca.* 109.

7. See the rule, *That ſhall make ſatisfaction which received the benefit.*

358. *Perſonal things (actions) die with the perſon.*

1. WHEN corporal damage is done to a man, as battery or the like, if either he beaten, or he who did the battery die, the action is gone. 12 *H.* 8. *Fi. Ley* 5. *b.*

2. Leſſee for years doth waſte, and dieth ; a writ of waſte lieth not againſt his executors or adminiſtrators. *Co. Lit.* 53. *b.*

3. The leſſor covenanted to pay quit-rents during the term, his executors ſhall not pay them ; for it is a perſonal covenant which dieth with the perſon. 1 *&* 2 *Ph. & Ma. Dy.* 114.

359. *Perſonal*

359. *Perſonal things cannot be done by another.*

1. SUITS of court cannot be done by another. 7 *H.* 4. 19.

2. One cannot excuſe himſelf of a contempt, in not ſerving the king's proceſs, *&c.* by attorney, but he ſhall do it in proper perſon. 22 *E.* 4. 34.

360. *Perſonal things cannot be granted over; as matters of pleaſure, eaſe, truſt and authority.*

Pleaſure.

1. AS licence to hunt in my park. 7 *H.* 4. 36. 12 *H.* 7. 15.

Eaſe.

2. As to go to church over my land. To come into my houſe to eat and drink with me, cannot be granted over. 7 *H.* 4. 36. *b.* 12 *H.* 7. 15.

3. So a way granted for life over my ground. 7 *H.* 4. 36. *b.*

Truſt.

4. Patent for life of an office of truſt, as to be chamberlain of the exchequer, ſquire of the body, *&c.* may not be aſſigned over, unleſs it be provided or eſpecially limited in the patent that he may ſo do; for otherwiſe he might perhaps grant it to one whom the king would not truſt, or who would be careleſs, *&c.* 11 *E.* 4. 1.

5. The keeper of a park, ſteward of a bailiwick, of huſbandry, *&c.* for life, may not be granted over, being offices requiring ſkill and diligence. 12 *Eliz.* 379. *Fi. Ley* 5. *b.*

Authority.

6. *A.* licenceth *B.* to do ſuch an act, *B.* may not grant this licence to another. *Bro. Licence* 25.

7. Upon a warrant of attorney made to one to deliver ſeiſin, he may not grant it over. 19 *H.* 8. 10.

361. *Perſpicua vera non ſunt probanda.*

MY lord *Coke* obſerves of judge *Littleton*, that he cited no authority, but when the caſe was rare or doubtful; for he knew well the rule; *Quod perſpicua vera non ſunt probanda.* And the like obſervation, his lordſhip takes notice, is made of juſtice *Fitzherbert* in his *Natura Brevium*, *Co. Lit.* 16. *b.* See rule, *Quod conſtat clare, &c.*

362. Plea

362. Plea shall be taken most strongly against him who pleadeth it.

The order of pleading.

1. IN good order of pleading, 1. A man must plead to the jurisdiction of the court. 2. To the person. And therein, 1. To the person of the plaintiff, and then, 2. The defendant. 3. To the count. 4. To the writ. 5. To the action, *&c.* and if the defendant misordereth any of these, he loseth the benefit of the former. *Co. Lit.* 303. *a.*

The correspondency.

2. The count must be conformable to the writ; the bar to the count, *&c.* *Co. Lit.* 303. *a.*

Declaration.

3. The count or declaration, *narratio*, ought to contain, 1. Certainty. 2. Verity, *&c. Certa debet esse intentio et narratio, et certum fundamentum, et certa res quae deducitur in judicium.* Co. Lit. 303. a.

Plea in abatement.

4. Plea in abatement of the writ, *breve*, ought to be certain also. *Co. Lit.* 303. *a.*

5. And it must be direct, and not by way of argument. *Ibid.*

Of pleading to the record.

6. Precedent was shewn, which was *Mich.* 5 *H.* 5 *Rot.* 484. An *audita querela* was brought in *B. R.* and because the record was not brought into court, so as the party might have execution, if the matter was found for him, the judgment was, That *querens nihil capiat per breve.* Cro. Eliz. 33.

7. In debt the defendant pleads outlawry to the plaintiff, the plaintiff saith *nul tiel record*; and the truth was, That at the time of the plea he was outlawed, but before the day assigned for the bringing in of the record, it was reversed: the court ordered a *respondeas ouster.* *Cro. Ja.* 484. *Dy.* 228. 10 *E.* 3. 22. 29 *E.* 3. 15. 29 *E.* 3. 27. 38 *E.* 3. 17. 44 *E.* 3. 23. 45 *E.* 3. 11. 50 *E.* 3. 15, 16. 6 *H.* 4. 3. 7 *H.* 4. 2. 11 *H.* 4. 39, 41. 14 *H.* 4. 32. 2 *H.* 6. 14. 3 *H.* 6. 15. 4 *H.* 6. 23. 7 *H.* 6. 18. 11 *H.* 6. 49. 12 *H.* 6. 3. 20 *H.* 6. 33. 32 *H.* 6. 27. 33 *H.* 6. 8. 36 *H.* 6. 2, 13. 5 *E.* 4. 3. 6 *E.* 4. 4. 9 *E.* 4. 2. 19 *E.* 4. 6, 9. 4 *H.* 7. 11. 9 *H.* 7. 2. 10 *H.* 7. 20, 24. 11 *H.* 7. 5, 8. 12 *H.* 7. 13. 13 *H.* 7. 14. 21 *H.* 7. 9. *Cro. Eliz.* 33, 340, 572, 707. *Keilw.* 96, 138, 180. *Dal.* 19, 33, 100. *Fitz. Abr.* 65. *a.* 66. *a.* *Bro. Abr.* 191. 2 *Vent.* 170. *Vaugh.* 92. *Co. Lit.* 303, *&c.* *Tow. Tables* 191, 197. *Lutw.* 163, 1272, 1282, 1514. *Sid.* 216. 3 *Lev.* 192. 3 *Mod.* 80. 5 *Mod.* 9. 6 *Mod.* 263. *Salk.* 510, 520, 565, 566. *Skin.* 518, 520. *Plo. Com.* 46. 103. 1 *Co.* 46. 5 *Co.* 9. *Gilb.* 213.

Avowry.

8. The avowant, becauſe he is to make title, ought to avow the ſeveral things granted to be antient fees to his office; elſe the averring one to be antient, implies the other is not ſo; *for a plea ſhall be taken moſt ſtrongly againſt him who pleadeth it.* Cro. Ca. 50.

9. See Rule, *Regula peccatis quae poenas irrogat aequas.*

363. *Plenum eſt cui nihil addi poteſt, ſecundum modum ſuae capacitatis.*

1. A Benefice is ſo intire and indiviſible, as it cannot be preſented or commended by parts, as the cure without the fruits, nor the fruits without the cure, nor the glebe to one, and the tithes to another, *&c. Hob.* 153. ſee alſo 151.

2. The acts of preſentation, inſtitution and induction, are all authorities given by law, and muſt be executed according to the form preſcribed by law, and may not be modified; for *actus legitimi non, &c.* for the law gives the church, not the patron and ordinary; who are but ceremonious miniſters, and are appointed their manner and form, which they may neither exceed nor abridge, *&c. Hob.* 153.

3. *Vide* rules, *Omnis forma, per quam quaeque res in propria ſpecie conſtituitur, perfectio quaedam eſt. Perfectum eſt cui nihil deeſt, &c. Jura naturae ſunt immutabilia. Quod ab initio non valet, &c.*

364. *Pluralities odious in law.*

SEE rules, *No conſtruction can be too liberal to make parſons reſide, &c. In aequali jure melior eſt conditio poſſidentis. Nemo poteſt habere duas, &c. Quando dua jura concurrunt in una, &c.*

365. *Plus peccat author quam actor.*

1. ONE is preſent at the death of another, whom he incited a third perſon to kill; by this he is principal, as well as he who actually committed the murder. 13 *H.* 7. 10. 21 *E.* 4. 71. *Stamf. lib.* 1. *cap.* 45.

2. *Vide* rules, *Plus exempla quam peccata nocent. Acceſſorium ſequitur principale.*

366. *Politiae legibus, non leges politiis adaptandae.*

IT is not in any man's power to create new natures in law according to new inventions, except they may ſtand with *jus commune*, which is *natura univerſa*; to which purpoſe, in matter of manners, *Tully* gives good advice, *contra naturam univerſam nihil contendamus; eâ tamen conſervatâ propriam ſequamur*; was it not ſo in the caſe of *Perpetuities? In the days of popery*, every man made new laws, for his proper patrimony, *according to his own ſuperſtitious purpoſes*; and they ſtood long in vulgar opinion, not without the aſſiſtance of learned men; but now *exploſa eſt ſententia*, being contrary to the laws; for *politiae legibus, non leges politiis adaptandae*. Hob. 154.

367. *Poſſeſſio fratris de feodo ſimplici facit ſororem eſſe haeredem.*

1. WHERE one is ſeiſed of lands in fee, having iſſue a ſon and a daughter by one *ventre*, and a ſon by another, and dies, and the eldeſt ſon enters, and dies *ſans* iſſue, the daughter ſhall have the land, and not the youngeſt ſon; yet he is heir to the father, but not to his brother; but if the eldeſt ſon doth not enter, but die before, then the younger brother may enter as heir to his father; but where the eldeſt ſon had entered, and had poſſeſſion, the ſiſter ſhall have the land; becauſe *poſſeſſio fratris de feodo ſimplici facit ſororem eſſe haeredem.* If there be two brothers by divers venters, and the eldeſt is ſeiſed of lands in fee, and dieth *ſans* iſſue, and his uncle entereth as heir to him, *as he well may*, who alſo dieth *ſans* iſſue, now the younger brother may have the lands as heir to the uncle; for that he is of the whole blood to him, though he is but of the half blood to his elder brother. *Lit. ſect.* 8.

2. But tenant in tail, albeit he hath a fee-ſimple expectant, is out of this rule; and therefore if lands be given to a man and his wife, and to the heirs of their two bodies; the remainder to the heirs of the huſband, and they have iſſue a ſon, and the wife dieth, and he taketh another wife, and hath iſſue a ſon, the father dieth, the eldeſt ſon entereth, and dieth *ſans* iſſue; the ſecond brother, though but half blood, ſhall inherit, becauſe the eldeſt ſon by his entry was not actually ſeiſed of the fee-ſimple, being expectant, but only on the eſtate-tail. *The younger brother is now in* per formam doni *by the Stat. of* W. 2. 1. *and according to the intention of the party who thus ſettled the eſtate*; et cujus eſt dare, &c. *and the rule is* poſſeſſio fratris, &c. and here the eldeſt ſon was not poſſeſſed of the fee-ſimple, but of the eſtate-tail: and where *Littleton* ſpeaketh only of lands, yet there ſhall be *poſſeſſio fratris* of an uſe, of a ſeigniory, a rent, an advowſon, and other hereditaments. *Co. Lit.* 14. *b.* 15. *a. b.*

3. References, *Ha. Hiſt. Law* 219 *to* 223. 3 *Co. Ratcliffe's* caſe, *per tout.*

4. See rule, *Propinquior excludit propinquum, &c.*

368. *Poſſeſſion he who hath, hath right againſt all, but him that hath the very right.*

1. REferences, 1 *Chan. Ca.* 25. *Jenk.* 118. 3 *Co.* 52. 5 *Co.* 69. *Hob.* 103, 199.

2. See rules, *That ſhall have the benefit, which hath or would have ſuſtained the loſs. Treſpaſs none to have, but he who hath actual poſſeſſion. Melior et tutior eſt conditio poſſidentis.*

369. *Poſ-*

369. *Possession of the termor possession of the reversioner.*

1. THE father being seised in fee makes a lease for years, the lessee enters, the father dies, leaving a son and daughter by one venter, and a son by another venter, the eldest son dieth during the term, before entry or receipt of the rent; the younger son of the half blood shall not inherit, but the sister; because the possession of the lessee for years is the possession of the eldest son, so as he is actually seised of the fee-simple; and consequently the sister of the whole blood is to be heir. *Co. Lit.* 15. *a. For the eldest brother could not enter upon the termor without wrong, neither could he receive the rent till the same was due, which accrued not in his life-time, by means of the act of God; the death of the eldest son interposing before the rent became due.*

2. So it is, if the eldest son be within age, and the guardian in socage enters; but if in the case above, the father makes a lease for life, or gift in tail, and dieth, and the eldest son dieth, living the tenant for life or tenant in tail, the younger brother of the half blood shall inherit; because the tenant for life or tenant in tail is seised of the freehold, and the eldest son had nothing but the reversion, expectant upon that freehold or estate-tail; therefore the youngest son inherits as heir to the father, who was last seised of the actual freehold, *&c. Vide plus Co. Lit.* 15. *a. b.*

3. If the father makes a lease for life, and hath issue two sons, and dieth, and the tenant for life dieth, and the youngest son intrude, and die seised, this descent shall not take away the entry of the eldest; but if the father had made a lease for years, it had been otherwise; for that the possession of the lessee for years maketh an actual freehold in the eldest son. *Co. Lit.* 243. *a.*

4. *Shellito* and seven others were indicted of forcible entry into a cottage and croft in the *West-riding* of *Yorkshire*, and that they *manu forti* entered upon the possession of *Anne Binnes*, farmer of *Richard Freiston*, and so disseised the said *Freiston*, *et sic disseisitum eum extraten'* till the day of the inquisition. *Yelverton* moved that the indictment was insufficient; it not being found that *Binnes* was amoved and expulsed, and this was the whole force of the matter; for the possession of the farmer or termor is the possession of the reversioner; and without ousting of the lessee, the freeholder could not be disseised; *quod fuit concessum per totam curiam*, and the indictment discharged. *Yelv.* 165.

5. But if the indictment had not expressed *Anne Binnes* to be farmer, but generally that the cottage, *&c.* was in her possession, then by *Williams*, justice, the indictment which found the disseisin only had been good; because no title was found in any other person but in him who was found to be disseised; but finding the woman to be farmer, this is an estate known and certain, and such farmer ought to be ejected, otherwise he who hath the freehold is not disseised. *Quod nota, per totam Curiam.* Yelv. 165.

370. *Pos-*

370. *Possibility cannot be upon possibility.*

1. REferences, 1 *Co.* 156. 10 *Co. Loveis*'s case. 3 *Chan. Ca.* 29.
2. See rules, *Contingency may not depend upon contingency. Perpetuities odious.*

371. *Praesumitur rex habere omnia jura in scrinio pectoris sui.*

THE king shall not be intended misconusant of the law; and therefore when he licenceth expresly to alien to an abbot, *&c.* which is in *Mortmain*, there need not be any *non obstante* of the statute of *Mortmain*; for it is apparent to be granted in *Mortmain*, and the king is the head of the law; and therefore *praesumitur habere omnia jura, &c.* Co. Lit. 99. a.

372. *Power or authority cannot be greater than that from whence it is derived.*

1. THE attorney of the disseisee cannot make claim off the land, if the disseisee himself durst have gone upon the land. *Litt. Continual Claim.*

2. The bailiff of a disseisor may not say that the plaintiff had nothing in the land; for the master himself should not have had that plea; for that he is not tenant of the freehold. 28 *Ass. pl.* 24.

3. References, 2 *E.* 4. 16. *Pal.* 112. 3 *Chan. Ca.* 126. 1 *Chan. Ca.* 242, 264.

373. *Principia probant, non probantur.*

1. EVERY proof ought to be by the highest and most supreme cause, and nothing may be higher and more supreme, than the principles and maxims of the law themselves; and therefore they are always to be allowed and admitted without argument or question of their authority; for this very reason, because they are too supremely high to admit of any proof. See 4 *Co.* 40. *a.*

2. No reason, says *Dr. & Stud.* need be assigned, why they were first assigned for maxims, *&c.* and they are not only to be holden for law themselves, but also all other cases similar to them, and that follow upon the same, necessarily are to be governed and decided by them. *Doct. & Stud. lib.* 1. *cap.* 15.

3. They cannot be questioned, says my lord *Coke. Co. Lit.* 11. *a.*

4. They suffer no contradiction, but are of the same strength with acts of parliament, when the judges, who have only that power, have determined which are maxims; *contra negantem principia non est disputandum.* Co. Lit. 343. a. But they are good and necessary to all. *Doct. & Stud. lib.* 1. *cap.* 12. Yet they may be changed, namely, by act of parliament. *Doct. & Stud. lib.* 1. *cap.* 8.

374. *Probibetur nequis faciat in ſuo, quod nocere poſſit alieno.*

VIDE rule, *Every one ought ſic uti ſuo, ut alienum non laedat.*

375. *Propinquior exludit propinquum, et propinquus remotum, et remotus remotiorem.*

1. IF there be father and ſon, and the father has a brother, who is uncle to the ſon, and the ſon purchaſeth fee, and dies *ſans* iſſue, living his father and uncle; the uncle ſhall have the land as heir to the ſon, and not the father, yet the father is neareſt of blood; becauſe of the maxim in law, That inheritances may lineally deſcend but not lineally aſcend; yet if the ſon in this caſe die without iſſue, and his uncle enter into the land, as heir to the ſon, as by law he ought, and then dieth without iſſue, living the father, the father ſhall have the land as heir to the uncle, and not as heir to his ſon; for that he cometh to the land by collateral deſcent, and not by lineal aſcent. *Lit. ſect.* 3.

2. *Prochein couſin collateral inheritera*, doth give a direction to the next couſin; and therefore the father's brother and his poſterity ſhall inherit before the grandfather's brother and his poſterity. *Et ſic de caeteris*; for *propinquior excludit propinquum, &c.* Co. Lit. 10. b.

3. It is a maxim in law, *That the next of the worthieſt blood ſhall ever inherit:* as the male and all deſcendible from him, before the female, and the female of the part of the father before the male or female of the part of the mother, *&c.* becauſe the female of the part of the father is of the worthieſt blood; and therefore among the males the eldeſt brother, and his poſterity, ſhall inherit lands in fee-ſimple as heir before any younger brother, or any deſcending from him, becauſe according to *Littleton* he is *pluis digne de ſank. Quod prius eſt dignius eſt, et qui prior eſt tempore potior eſt jure.* Co. Lit. 14. a.

4. The reaſons of the common law, as ſaith lord *Coke*, are notable. Every one who is heir to another, *aut eſt haeres jure proprietatis*, as the eldeſt ſon ſhall inherit ſole before all his brethren; *aut jure repraeſentationis*, as where the eldeſt ſon dies, living the father, his iſſue ſhall inherit before the younger ſon; for though the younger ſon *ſit magis propinquus*, yet *jure repraeſentationis*, the iſſue of the eldeſt ſon ſhall inherit; for he repreſents the perſon of his father. And as *Bracton* ſays, *jus proprietatis*, that which his father had by birth-right deſcends to him *jure propinquitatis, &c.* 3 Co. 40. b. 41. a.

5. See rule, *Poſſeſſio fratris, &c.*

376. *Proximus ſum egomet mihi.*

1. SO an executor hath preference before others; for that he cannot ſue himſelf. So an executor of an executor may retain (*for he is in privity to the firſt teſtator, though not ſo of an adminiſtrator*); but where there is a ſurviving executor, the executor of the deceaſed executor may

I not

not retain; for he is not executor of the firſt teſtator; and equity favours not retainers. *Prec. Chan.* 180. Yet,

2. If an executor ſue for the *reſiduum* where he hath a legacy in the will, he ſhall pay coſts. *Prec. Chan.* 92.

3. Relief amongſt executors. 8 *Co.* 136. *Plow. Com.* 184. *Co. Lit.* 264. *Tot.* 150, 158. *Cro. Ca.* 373. *Orph. Leg.* 71, 113. *Swinb. 5th part, fo.* 7. *4to Edition.* 5 *Co.* 29. *Nelſ.* 171, 410. 2 *Vern.* caſe 532. 1 *Chan. Ca.* 200. *Prec. Chan.* 83.

4. Whether truſtee for next of kin. *Prec. Chan.* 92, 94, 82, 324, 566. *Nelſ.* 177, 178, 351, 352. 1 *Vern.* 473. 2 *Vern.* 648. *Gilb.* 74, 75, 106, 184, 200, 208, 209. 1 *Pe. Will.* 7, 8, 9. 2 *Ju. Eccl.* 48, *Maſon* and *Hawkin*'s caſe, *etiam fo.* 50. *Selwin* and *Brown*'s caſe.

5. Whether debt extinguiſhed by the obligee making the obligor executor. *Co. Lit.* 264. *b.* 8 *Co.* 136. *Plow. Com.* 184, 185. *Salk.* 153, 154. *Tot.* 150. 1 *Vern.* caſe 532, and *Selwin* and *Brown*'s caſe *ſupra*, and caſes there cited.

377. *Purchaſer, without notice, not bound to diſcover to his own hurt.*

General to, and rules.

1. WHEN one is obliged to give notice to another, it is thus, when the matter lieth more in the knowledge of the one than the other, and he cannot come to that knowledge but by his means; but when one knows as well as the other, neither is bound to give notice. 3 *Chan. Ca.* 104.

2. Regularly a purchaſer without notice ſhall not diſcover any thing to hurt himſelf. 2 *Chan. Ca.* 73.

3. A purchaſer *ſans* notice may buy in any mortgage, ſtatute or other incumbrance, and if he can defend himſelf at law, equity will not go againſt him or hurt him; for equity will not diſarm a purchaſer: and this rule in chancery is in maintenance of the common law, where the maxims, which refer to deſcents, diſcontinuance, non-claims and collateral warranties, are only the wiſe arts and inventions of the law, to protect and quiet the poſſeſſion, and ſtrengthen the right of purchaſers, &c. *Prec. Chan.* 249, 250.

4. So lord chancellor *Talbot* declared, if a purchaſer without notice ſell to another with notice, this is good; for ſaid his lordſhip, as it could not be impeached in the vendor's hands, being a purchaſer without notice, tho' the vendee has notice after, yet ſuch notice ſhall not hurt him; [*and indeed to me it ſeems the ſame thing to the ſufferer, whether the purchaſer* ſans *notice keeps or ſells the eſtate,*] and his lordſhip further ſaid [*and as I apprehend with juſt diſtinction*] That where a purchaſer with notice, conveys to another without notice, the ſecond ſale is vicious, becauſe of the former conveyance being with notice, at *Lincoln's Inn Hall*, 7 *April* 1736. *So that this reſolution over-rules the opinion of lord keeper in the caſe in* Prec. Ch. 51, 52. *and ſurely with the greateſt equity; for according to lord keeper's opinion,* B. *ſhould be in a better condition than* A. *from whom he purchaſed, which is unequal and unequitable. And again, the injured party who might have recovered*

recovered against A. *the first purchaser, as being a purchaser with notice, is thereby defeated of this remedy, by the further tortious acts of one or more who had notice of his title : so that by such resolution a wrong-doer should be still further advantaged of his own further wrong, which it is not, as I apprehend, possible equity should endure; as that would be to make equity countenance fraud and oppression; whilst lord chancellor* Talbot's *opinion squares with the highest equity, namely, that* A. *who had notice, and all claiming under or deriving title from him, should be concluded by his notice, whether the others have notice or not; for in such case it must needs be right equity, that they be precisely in the case of* A. *by whom they claim, and not that they take benefit by his further wrong in passing away his estate,* &c.

Particular cases.

5. One purchaseth of a trustee with notice of the trust, in such case the purchaser is trustee to the first trust, though he paid a consideration; *quia participes criminis, consentientes et agentes pari poena plectentur. Dolus et fraus nemini patrocinetur.* Elf. Obf. 94. Nelf. 378, 379.

6. References, 1 *Chan. Ca.* 34, 36, 37, 247, 264, 267. *Nelf.* 103, 130, 137, 212, 166, 167, 409. 1 *Chan. Ca.* 264. 2 *Chan. Ca.* 205, 208. *Nelf.* 366, 367, 9. 2 *Chan. Ca.* 135, 136, 157. 3 *Rep. Chan.* 28, 29. 2 *Chan. Ca.* 47, 264. *Prec. Chan.* 431. 2 *Vent.* 360. *Gilb.* 111, 112, *&c. Prec. Chan.* 108, 109, 159.

7. See rules, *Nemo tenetur seipsum prodere. Law and equity shall prevail against equity only.*

378. *Quae incontinenti, vel certo fiunt in esse videntur.*

1. IF the disseisee release to the disseisor, it cannot be defeated by indenture of defeazance made afterwards; but at the time of the release of feoffment, *&c.* the same may be defeated by indenture of defeazance; for it is a maxim in law; *quae incontinenti fiunt in esse videntur.* Co. Lit. 236. b.

2. If a man sue me in a proper court, and his suit be utterly without ground of truth, and that known to him, I may have an action *sur le case* against him for the undue vexation and damages sustained, though the suit was lawful, and as such I cannot complain of it; or if you charge me with a crime, in a court no way capable, I may have this action: so if one sue me in the spiritual court for a meer temporal cause. But if a man be imprisoned upon a formal suit, and give bond to procure his enlargement, he shall not avoid it by duress; for that it was lawful, though untruly procured. But in these and the like cases, 1. The new action must not be brought before the first determined. 2. There must not only be a thing done amiss, but also damages either actually sustained or inevitable. 1. As if a man forge a bond in my name, I may not have the action till I am sued, *&c.* 2. But if it were a recognizance, or fine, I may have deceit presently before execution; for *quae incontinenti vel certo fiunt in esse videntur, &c.* Hob. 266, 267. *Vue tout le case, excellent matter.*

379. *Quaelibet conceſſio fortiſſime contra donatorem interpretanda eſt.*

1. IF in the premiſſes lands be letten, or a rent granted, the general intendment is, that an eſtate for life paſſeth; but if the *habendum* limit the ſame for years or at will, the *habendum* qualifies the general intendment of the premiſſes; and the reaſon of this is, that it is a maxim of law, that every man's grant ſhall be taken, by conſtruction of law, moſt forcibly againſt himſelf. *Quaelibet conceſſio fortiſſime contra donatorem interpretanda eſt*, which is to be underſtood that no wrong be thereby done; for it is another maxim in law, *Quod legis conſtructio non facit injuriam*; and therefore if tenant for life make a leaſe generally, this ſhall be taken, by conſtruction of law, an eſtate for the life of the leſſor; for if it ſhould be a leaſe for the life of the leſſee, it ſhould be a wrong to him in the reverſion; and ſo it is, if tenant in tail make a leaſe generally, the law ſhall conſtrue this to be ſuch a leaſe as he may lawfully make, and that is for the term of his own life; for if it ſhould be for the leſſee's life, it ſhould be a diſcontinuance; and conſequently the eſtate which ſhould paſs by conſtruction of law ſhould work a wrong. *Co. Lit.* 183. *a. b.* ſee 42. *a.*

2. So if two jointenants grant a rent of 10*s.* the grantee ſhall have a rent of 20*s.* out of the lands.

3. See rules, *Conſtructio legis non facit injuriam. Every man's deed or covenant to be taken moſt ſtrongly againſt himſelf.*

380. *Quaelibet haereditas naturaliter quidem ad haeredes haereditabiliter deſcendit, nunquam quidem naturaliter aſcendit.*

SEE rules, *Inheritances may lineally deſcend, but not aſcend. Pater, mater et puer ſunt una caro.*

381. *Quae non valeant ſingula, juncta juvant.*

* 1. THOUGH a long length of time intervene, yet where there is apparent fraud, equity will direct an open account, and this court will never lay down rules to confine themſelves in caſes of fraud. A deed of purchaſe, after a conſiderable length of time, was ſet aſide, there being circumſtances of fraud; ſo where undue advantage has been taken of young heirs. And the lord chancellor further declared, that where ſeveral groſs miſtakes appear, thro' the whole complexion of the cauſe, the court has taken them together, as evidence of the fraud, and that the party was impoſed upon in other inſtances; eſpecially where (as in the principal caſe) great parts of the account conſiſt in bills of coſts, ſuch miſtakes ſhall impeach the whole account; and here his lordſhip ſaid, the rule may be well applied, which has been ſo often uſed in other caſes, *Et quae non valeant ſingula, juncta juvant. Giffard* and *Vaux*'s caſe, before the lord chancellor, 27 *Feb.* 1739.

* 2. *Robert Bertley Freeman*, being between 22 and 23 years of age, came acquainted with one *Biſhop*, a jockey, and bought of him, in the ſpace of 12 months, no leſs than 13 horſes; the method of their dealing was not for more than one horſe at a time; but the plaintiff generally rid them hard, or it was at leaſt ſo pretended, and then growing tired of them, he uſed to ſell them back again to *Biſhop*, greatly under the value at which he bought them in; and he never, at any of theſe bargains, paid any money down, but had the horſes on credit, and not only ſo, but at the ſame time *Biſhop* lent him alſo ready money; and then the plaintiff gave notes for the price of the horſes and the ready money together; the horſes were all or moſt at very extravagant prices, ſometimes 42 and ſometimes 40 guineas each; yet it was ſworn in the cauſe, that theſe horſes were not, ſave two of them, ſold for more than their real value, and as to thoſe two, one of them was not ſold for above two guineas more than it was worth at a market price, and the other not for more than 3 *l.* above his real value. Whilſt theſe dealings were carrying on, the plaintiff's father was alive, and had a good eſtate, and the plaintiff lived with his ſaid father, and had no preſent fortune, but only was intitled to ſome remainder or other expectancy on his father's death; however the money amounting to 300 *l.* the plaintiff made the defendant a mortgage of ſuch intereſt as he had, whatever it was; but it was part of the agreement, that this mortgage ſhould be writ in a running hand, and that not by any attorney in the neighbourhood, or other perſon acquainted with the parties. The plaintiff's preſent bill is for relief againſt this mortgage on payment of what is *bona fide* due for the horſes at their true value, and the money actually lent. And his lordſhip was pleaſed to declare, the plaintiff was well intitled to ſuch relief; and his lordſhip ſaid, as to the objection, that the preſent was not a caſe within the ordinary rules of the court of relieving young heirs againſt hard agreements; for that here the plaintiff had an eſtate expectant on the death of his father; his lordſhip obſerved, that circumſtance would make no difference; for that the court in theſe caſes, doth not enter into inquiries of that ſort; what they regard is, *that the heir is ſuch an one as in his father's life-time had no proper ſubſiſtence but from his father, and where in ſuch caſes the court have found that advantages have been taken of the difficulties the young heir lay under, in moſt of theſe inſtances they have relieved.* In the preſent caſe, his lordſhip obſerved, at the time theſe dealings were carrying on, the plaintiff was no more than two or three and twenty years of age; and that the reaſon acknowledged by the defendant himſelf, for truſting the plaintiff was, for that his father had a good eſtate; that the plaintiff himſelf was ſo intitled to an expectancy as aforeſaid, and that he was a favourite with his mother. Beſides his lordſhip obſerved, that abſtracted from theſe circumſtances, the nature of the tranſaction ſpeaks a fraud; here is a young gentleman entering into bargains with the defendant for horſes: his lordſhip further obſerved, that it had been ſaid, equity will not ſet aſide every contract of this ſort, where a bargain is to give a little more for a horſe than he is worth; and true it is, that if this had been a contract for a ſingle horſe, though the price agreed for was more than he was worth, a court of equity would not interfere and reſcind the bargain. But what is the nature of the preſent dealing? Here are thirteen horſes bought in 12 months time; and moſt of them at very high prices, 42 guineas contracted

tracted for ſome of them, 40 for others, three of them are reſold to the defendant at much lower prices than they were bought in at. Tranſactions of this kind, is rather a trading in the way of horſes than any thing elſe; the defendant too has not dealt with the plaintiff in the common way of ſelling horſes, by taking ready money, but upon credit, and at the ſame time of theſe contracts for theſe horſes, money is taken care to be lent. This his lordſhip took notice was a common way of drawing young perſons in to ſupply their extravagances; and another circumſtance, giving ground for relief in this caſe, is, that here is a mortgage given for 300*l.* and at the time the mortgage was made, there is no proof that any account was ſtated; no particular proof is there of what ſums of money were really lent: and beſides his lordſhip further obſerved, that there was a circumſtance of an intended concealment; the mortgage was to be writ in a running hand, and not by any attorney in the neighbourhood, *&c.* and why was it to be writ in a running hand, *&c.* if a concealment was not deſigned? For theſe reaſons his lordſhip was of opinion, that the mortgage ſhould only ſtand as a ſecurity for what was really due on account of the money lent, and what was due for the horſes; and to aſcertain what was due for the horſes, the defendant was at liberty to bring his *quantum meruit.* Decreed *accordant.* *Freeman* and *Biſhop*'s caſe, before lord chancellor, 28 *April* 1740.

382. *Quae ſunt minoris culpae, ſunt majoris infamiae.*

General.

1. SUCH may not be witneſſes, or joined of a jury, who are infamous.

Particular caſes.

2. As one attainted of a falſe verdict or of conſpiracy at the ſuit of the king, or convicted of perjury, or of a *praemunire*, or of forgery, *ſur le Stat.* 5 *Eliz. cap.* 14. and not upon *Stat.* 1 *H.* 5. *cap.* 3. or convicted of felony, or by judgment loſt his ears or ſtood upon the pillory or tumbrel, . or been branded, or the like; whereby they became infamous for ſome offence. *Quae ſunt minoris culpae, ſunt majoris infamiae.* Co. Lit. 6. a.

3. If a champion in a writ of right become recreant, he thereby loſeth *liberam legem*, and becomes infamous, and cannot be a witneſs. *Co. Lit.* 6. *b.*

383. *Quando duo jura concurrunt in una perſona, aequum eſt ac ſi eſſent in diverſis.*

General.

1. THE ſtatute 21 *H.* 8. *Of Faculties*, was always conſtrued ſtrictly againſt non-reſidence and pluralities, as things very prejudicial to the ſervice of God, and the inſtruction of his people.

Particular caſes.

2. And therefore if a biſhop be tranſlated to an archbiſhoprick, or a baron created an earl, now he hath both dignities, as *quando duo jura concurrunt in una perſona, aequum eſt ac ſi eſſent in diverſis.* Yet within this act

act he may not have but as an archbishop or an earl; for though he has several dignities, yet he is but one and the same person, to whom the attendance and service is to be done: so if a baron be made a knight of the garter, or warden of the cinque ports, he shall have but three chaplains in all, *et sic de similibus*; *quod fuit concessum, quia difficile ut unus homo vicem duorum sustineat.* But it was argued and resolved in the principal case, that *Carmel* being retained by lady *Montagle*, before her coverture, might yet take a second living after her ladyship's marriage, within the letter and meaning of the said act; for without question his retainer was not determined or countermanded by the said marriage, though her husband was a lord and peer of parliament, and so might retain chaplains, &c. 4 *Co.* 118. *a.*

3. See rules, *No construction can be too liberal to make parsons reside. In aequali jure melior est conditio possidentis.*

384. *Quando aliquid probibetur ex directo, probibetur et per obliquum.*

FEoffment *sur* condition that the feoffee shall not alien to such an one, naming him, is good; therefore if the feoffee infeoff *J. N.* of intent and purpose that he infeoff the party prohibited, this is a breach of the condition. *Co. Lit.* 223. *But if the condition had been general, that he should not alien, such condition had been void*; *as against the rule,* **That perpetuities are odious, and against the general good.**

385. *Quando jus domini regis et subditi concurrunt, jus regis praeferri debet.*

1. IF a man hold lands of the king by knight service *in capite*, and other lands of other lords, and dieth, his heir within age, the king shall have the wardship of all the lands by his prerogative, &c. *Co. Lit.* 77. *a.*

2. And the king, by his prerogative, shall not only have such lands and tenements which (as hath been said) the heir of his tenant by knight service *in capite* holdeth of other, but such inheritances also as are not holden at all of any, as rent-charges, rent-seck, fairs, markets, warrens, annuities, and the like, &c. *Co. Lit.* 77. *b.* 78. *a.*

386. *Quando lex aliquid alicui concedit, concedere videtur et id, sine quo res ipsa esse non potest.*

1. IF lessee at will sow the land, and the lessor, after the corn sown, and before it is ripe and cut, put him out, the lessee shall have the corn and free entry, egress and regress to cut and carry away the corn; because he knew not at what time the lessor would enter upon him; *aliter* of tenant for years, for there the lessor or reversioner shall have the corn, for he knew when his term must end. *Lit. sect.* 68. For when the law doth give any thing to any man, it giveth also, impliedly, whatsoever is necessary for the taking and enjoying of the same. *Quando lex aliquid*

2 *alicui*

alicui concedit, &c. And the law in this caſe driveth him not to an action for the corn, but giveth him a ſpeedy remedy; to enter into the land, and to take and carry it away, yet the law driveth or compelleth him not to carry it away at once, or before it be ready: but the law giveth all that which is convenient, (*viz.*) free entry, egreſs, and regreſs, as much as is neceſſary; and if he be diſturbed of this way, he may have his action upon the caſe, and recover damages; for *where the law giveth any thing, it giveth alſo a remedy for the ſame.* Co. Lit. 56. a.

2. Treſpaſs upon demurrer, the caſe was, That one ſells lands and, afterwards the vendee, by reaſon thereof, claims a way over the plaintiff's land, there being no other convenient way adjoining; and whether this were a lawful claim, was the queſtion? and reſolved without argument, that the way remained, and that he might well juſtify the uſing thereof, becauſe it is a thing of neceſſity; for otherwiſe he could not have any profit of his lands: *et e converſo*, if a man hath four cloſes lying together, and ſells three of them, reſerving a middle cloſe, and hath not any way thereto, but through one of thoſe which he ſold, though he reſerved not any way, yet he ſhall have it as reſerved to him by law; and therefore it is not any extinguiſhment of the way by having both lands: wherefore it was adjudged accordingly for the plaintiff. *Cro. Ja.* 170.

3. References, *Co. Lit.* 56, 153. *a.* *Cro. Ja.* 189, 190. *Noy* 123.

4. See rule, *Boni judicis eſt lites dirimere*, &c.

387. *Quando plus fit quam fieri debet, videtur etiam illud fieri quod faciendum eſt.*

SEE the rule, *Omne majus continet in ſe minus. In majore ſumma continetur minor.*

388. *Qui ex damnato coitu naſcuntur inter liberos non computentur, &c.*

1. SIR *Barth. Shower* moved for a prohibition to the eccleſiaſtical court, to ſtay proceedings there againſt a man for marrying his ſiſter's baſtard daughter; but it was denied; for the court muſt judge what is God's law, being mentioned in an act of parliament, (*viz.*) 32 *H.* 8. and by God's law there, is meant the Levitical law, which prohibits marriage with a man's ſiſter's daughter. The children of a concubine among the *Hebrews* were not illegitimate. Baſtards are by particular conſtitutions and laws deprived of the privilege of children. *Qui ex damnato coitu naſcuntur inter liberos non computentur, &c.* yet the reaſon of the prohibition ſeems yet to remain, if there be any morality in the law, 'tis as morally unlawful to marry a baſtard iſſue as legitimate iſſue. It muſt be *ſanguinis naturalis*, and not *legalis*, or *civilis*, elſe a woman might marry her baſtard ſon, &c. *Comb.* 356.

2. References, *Brac. lib.* 2. *c.* 29. *lib.* 5. *c.* 19. *Glanv. lib.* 7. *c.* 1. *fo.* 44. *b.* *Brit. c.* 119. *Lit. ſect.* 3. 188. 401. *Co. Lit.* 7. 11, 123, 213, 237, 243, 244. 3 *Co.* 40. 5 *Co. De Jure Regis Eccl.* 9 *a.* *Vaugh. Harriſon*'s caſe, alſo *Hill*'s caſe. *Hal. Anal.* 42. *Mo.* 907. 4 *Co.* 29. 6 *Co.* 22.

 Fitz.

Fitz. Abr. tit. *Baſtard. Stat.* 20 *H.* 3. 1 *H.* 6. 3. 32 *H.* 8. *c.* 28. *Bro. Abr.* tit. *Baſtard, Tryal, Viſne. Skin.* 455. *Salk.* 548. *Raſt. Ent. Baſtardy, fo.* 104. *Stat.* 9 *H.* 6. *c.* 11. *Kitch.* 64. *Dr. & Stud. lib.* 2. *c.* 5. *Dy.* 369. *Da.* 51, &c. *Comb.* 360. *Can.* 106, 107, 108. 4 *Inſt.* 339. 2 *Ju. Eccl.* Caſe *Sampſon et Ux'.* verſus *Cooke.*

3. Rules, Children are *de ſanguine patris, &c. Pater eſt quem nuptiae demonſtrant. Pater et mater et puer ſunt una caro.*

389. *Quid ſit jus, et in quo conſiſtat injuria, legis eſt definire.*

RULE, Law will not ſuffer wrong.

390. *Qui non habet poteſtatem alienandi, habet neceſſitatem retinendi.*

SEE *Hob.* 336. 2 *Ro. Ab.* 722. *p.* 19. *S. C.*

391. *Quicquid ſolvitur, ſolvitur ſecundum modum ſolventis.*

General and rules.

1. *Quicquid ſolvitur, ſolvitur ſecundum modum ſolventis.* 1 Ch. Ca. 106. 2 Vern. 606.

2. But according to this rule, the party paying muſt then expreſs it upon what account he pays it; for a declaration of that ſort afterwards will not do it: neither will an entry in his book, that the payment was on ſuch particular account, ſerve the purpoſe; but it muſt be a declaration on the payment only, that can apply it. 1 *Ch. Ca.* 106.

3. The creditor may chuſe to which debt he will apply the payment. 2 *Ch. Ca.* 84.

4. But where the payment was on account of both debts, it ſhall be proportioned ratably. 2 *Ch. Ca.* 84.

5. And if the payment be general, then the application is in the party who receives. 2 *Vern.* 606, 607.

Particular caſes.

6. A man owes money on mortgage and ſimple contract to the ſame perſon, and pays ſome money without ſaying on what account, it ſhall be taken to be towards diſcharge of the mortgage; becauſe it is natural to ſuppoſe a man would rather chuſe to pay off the money for which he was to pay intereſt, than the other for which none was payable. 1 *Vern.* 24. *Quaere ſur ceſt caſe.*

7. *P.* became bound as ſecurity for *J. S.* to *R. S.* and *J. S.* owed a further debt on ſimple contract. *J. S.* and *R. S.* came to an account for all monies owing to *R. S.* and there being due to *R. S.* on the foot of the account

count 85 *l.* *J. S.* makes a bill of ſale towards ſatisfaction of the whole debt. Mr. Solicitor inſiſted, that it ſhould firſt go in diſcharge of the debt on ſimple contract; for the bill of ſale is mentioned to be ſecurity, and there is no proof it was to go in diſcharge of the bond, before that on ſimple contract; but as the account was taken together, it was to go in diſcharge of both in proportion, and ſo decreed. But Mr. Solicitor was ſtrong in his opinion againſt the decree. 1 *Vern.* 34, 35.

8. The defendant was indebted to the plaintiff on articles under hand and ſeal, as alſo on ſimple contract, on a running account, and made ſeveral payments of ſums in groſs, and entered them in his own books as paid on account of what was due on the articles. Lord Chancellor: Though the rule be, *Quicquid ſolvitur, ſolvitur ſecundum modum ſolutionis*; yet that is to be underſtood when at the time of payment he declares on what account he pays it. But if the payment be general, then the application is in the party who receives, and the entries in the defendant's books are not ſufficient to make the application. 2 *Vern.* 606, 607. See *the two next foregoing caſes, and quaere, tho' this, I conceive, is the more equitable reſolution, that where the payment is general, the application ſhould be in the receiver; for elſe the payer might defer the debt which carries intereſt, and ſo eaſe himſelf of that charge againſt both the intereſt and intention of the debtee; and beſides, this reſolution, according to my apprehenſion, ſquares with the rule, That every man's act is to be conſtrued moſt ſtrongly againſt the actor.*

9. A ſcrivener at requeſt put out 50 *l.* for the defendant, and took the plaintiff's bond, and three months after delivered it to the defendant; the plaintiff all along paid the intereſt to the ſcrivener. In about 5 years time the ſcrivener called in the principal, and the plaintiff paid him 30 *l.* of it, and the ſcrivener not having the bond, gave him a receipt for the 30 *l.* in part. This was a void payment; for the plaintiff ought to have ſeen the money indorſed, beſides the plaintiff knew whoſe money it was; the receipt being for the uſe of the defendant, and many precedents were cited to the purpoſe. 1 *Vern.* 150, 151. See 2 *Ch. Ca.* 226, 227. *Pre. Ch.* 209. *Nelſ.* 441. 1 *Ch. Ca.* 93, 94, 111. 2 *Ch. Ca.* 177, 178.

10. References, 1 *Vern.* 57, 122. *S. C.* *Nel.* 84, 85. *Pre. Cha.* 178. *Barn.* 83, 128, 189, 321, 322. *Nel.* 89, 90.

392. *Qui facit per alium facit per ſe.*

1. IF the maſter command his ſervant to go to the land, and there to make claim to avoid a deſcent, and the ſervant do all which he received in command, and which his maſter might do; there it is as ſufficient as if he had done it himſelf, for *qui per alium facit, per ſeipſum facere videtur.* Co. Lit. 258. a.

2. See rules, *Qui per alium facit, &c. Acceſſorium ſequitur principale. Nemo poteſt plus juris ad alium transferre, &c.* Treſpaſs none to have, but who hath actual poſſeſſion.

393. *Qui habet jurisdictionem absolvendi, habet jurisdictionem ligandi.*

1. BY common intendment a bishop hath ordinary jurisdiction of all ecclesiastical causes, within his diocese. *Da.* 44. *a.*

2. *Holt* lord chief justice held an archbishop had power over his suffragans, and might deprive: That bishops are co-ordinate, or *pares, jure divino*; but not *jure humano*, otherwise their institution would be to no end: and as to their peerage, it was by reason of their barony: That several abbots sat in the house of peers in former times, and it might as well be pretended they were exempted, and therefore could not be deprived: That by the common law the archbishop hath a metropolitical jurisdiction, and archbishops are over bishops, as bishops are over the other clergy: That his power was diminished and usurped upon by the pope, but is restored to its extent by the statute *H.* 8. That by allowing his power to visit, all is admitted; for he who may visit may deprive as well as censure; these being but several degrees of punishment. By 26 *H.* 8. and 1 *Eliz. c.* 1. the only power given to ecclesiastical courts was to visit, without one word of deprivation; yet they were always allowed a power to deprive. From the time of *H.* 2. until *H.* 8. there hardly is an instance of deprivation of a bishop; and it is true, that before 17 *Ca.* 1. *c.* 11. confirmed by 13 *Ca.* 2. which takes away the court of high commission, instituted by queen *Eliz.* the deprivations that are of bishops, are by the court of ecclesiastical commissions; but the reason thereof was only, as that was the easier and shorter way, but it cannot be questioned, but a bishop may be deprived for dilapidations. 2 *H.* 4. 3. *Godb.* 259. 3 *Bulst.* 158, 279. 1 *Ro.* 86. *Mo.* 917. And it is as plain, the law takes no notice of any other who can deprive him. If issue be, whether a parson be deprived or not? the court must write to the bishop; and if it be whether a bishop be deprived or not? they must write to the archbishop of *Canterbury*, &c. *Salk.* and *Farest. Watson*, bishop of *St. David's* case, who was deprived for simony and other crimes. 2 *Ju. Eccl.* 365, &c. the same case at full. See 12 *Co.* 60.

394. *Qui haeret in litera haeret in cortice.*

SEE rules, *Apices juris non sunt jura.* Equity will not aid new inventions, *&c.* Law hath always suppressed new and subtile inventions in derogation of the common law.

395. *Quilibet potest renunciare juri pro se introducto.*

SEE rule, *Alienatio licet prohibeatur, &c.*

2

396. *Qui per alium facit, per ſeipſum facere videtur.*

1. WHERE a corporation paſſes an intereſt, the common law will not ſuffer the members of the corporation to give their aſſent, by proctors or ſubſtitutes. *Da.* 47. *b.*

2. The major part of ſuch corporation muſt conſent to all acts to bind their corporation, by the rules both of common and canon law. *Dav.* 47. *b.* 48. *a.*

3. Treſpaſs for taking an hundred ſheep *apud Melton Mowbray in regia via ibidem*; the defendant to all beſides one, pleaded not guilty, and *quoad* that he pleaded, that the lord *Berkley* was ſeiſed of the manor of *Melton Mawbray* in *Melton M.* aforeſaid, and that he and all thoſe, *&c.* had uſed from time to time, whereof, *&c.* to have toll, *viz.* 2 *d.* for every 20 ſheep of any ſtranger, brought or driven *per et trans* the ſaid vill by any ſtranger; and if he were denied by any ſtranger driving them *per et trans* the ſaid vill, then they had uſed, time whereof, *&c.* to diſtrain for the ſaid toll one ſheep ſo driven; and alledgeth *in facto*, that 220 ſheep of the plaintiff's, being a ſtranger, and not inhabiting there, were driven by one *Ludfield per et trans* the ſaid vill, by the plaintiff's command, and becauſe he refuſed to pay this toll, he that one ſheep *cepit et abduxit*, and detained till the toll was paid. *Et hoc*, *&c.* On demurrer, *inter alia*, it was moved that this plea was not good for the manner of pleading; 1ſt, becauſe the cuſtom is alledged to be, That if the ſheep of any foreigner be driven through, a toll ſhall be paid; and if it be denied by any foreigner who drives them through, that a diſtreſs may be taken; and it is not averred, that he who drove them through was a foreigner, but only that the maſter was a foreigner. *Sed non allocatur*; for the driving of the ſervant is the driving of the maſter, and if he be a foreigner, that ſufficeth. *Cro. Eliz.* 710.

4. A dean may not confirm a grant, or affix the chapter ſeal by proctor; for he, being meerly a ſtranger to the chapter, is not capable of ſuch procuration; and therefore all that he hath done is void by the rules both of common and canon law. The rule of canon law is, *Abſens non poteſt demandare votum ſuum, niſi uni de capitulo.* Inſt. Jur. Can. lib. 1. cap. *Electionibus.* Another is, *Oportet quod procurator ſemper inſtitutus ſit de collegio*; and a third, *Votum dari non poteſt per literas*: and the rule of the common law is agreeable to the canon law in this point; for in the high court of parliament the barons may give their votes by procuracy or proxy, but their proctor muſt be a baron, and a member of the ſame houſe; for a ſtranger is not capable of ſuch proxy. *Da.* 47. *a. b.*

5. The 11 *H.* 4. *fo.* 84. upon a compoſition for tithes, a parſon granted an annuity to the abbot of *Battel*, which grant was confirmed by the biſhop, dean and chapter, being patrons; and it appeared, by the deed of confirmation, that the dean was abſent, and did not put his ſeal to it, but the chaunter was his commiſſary, and put the ſeal for him; and there it was held, that though the dean might have a preſident or commiſſary, for the exerciſe of his ſpiritual juriſdiction, yet ſuch commiſſary may not charge the poſſeſſions of the church. *Da.* 47. *b.*

6 Cuſtom hath eſtabliſhed and ſo fixed the eſtate of the copyholder, that by the ſeverance of the inheritance from the copyhold of the manor, does not deſtroy it; for as the lord himſelf could not ouſt the copyholder, no more may any other claiming under him do it; for *nemo poteſt plus juris ad alium transferre, quam ipſe habet. Et quod per me non poſſum nec per alium.* 4 Co. 24. a.

7. References, 2 *Mod. Ca.* 195, 198. *Co. Lit.* 258. *a.*

8. Rules, *Nemo poteſt plus juris ad alium transferre, quam ipſe habet. Treſpaſs none to have, but he who hath actual poſſeſſion. Qui facit per alium facit per ſe. Acceſſorium ſequitur principale. Plea ſhall be taken moſt ſtrongly againſt him who pleadeth it. Every man's deed or covenant to be taken moſt ſtrongly againſt himſelf,* &c.

397. *Qui prior eſt tempore, potior eſt jure.*

1. BY the ſtatute of *Faculties* it is, that every counteſs, being a widow, may have two chaplains, whereof every one may purchaſe licence or diſpenſation; then when ſhe hath retained two, the ſtatute is executed, for ſhe may not have more than two capable of diſpenſations; and the retainer of a third may not deveſt the capacity of diſpenſation which was veſted in the firſt two by their retainer; and though a counteſs might have as many chaplains as ſhe would at common law, yet ſhe may not have more than two capable of diſpenſation by the ſtatute; and reaſon demands that he who has ſerved longeſt ſhould be firſt preferred, *Et qui prior eſt tempore, potior eſt jure.* 4 Co. 89. b. 90. a.

2. All the court agreed, that though an earl or baron, by the ſtatute, may have but two chaplains, capable of pluralities or two benefices; yet he may retain as many chaplains as he pleaſeth; but the firſt two are only the ſtatutable chaplains to have the privilege by the retainer, which ſhall not be taken from them ſo long as they remain chaplains, nor any ſubſequent retainer prevent them. *Cro. Eliz.* 839. *Qui prior eſt tempore potior eſt jure.* And a retainer is good without patent, by bare parol. *Mo.* 277. *Quaere ſur le caſe* Whitcombe *and* Hickford, *en le Common Pleas de'l Exchequer, anno* 35 *or* 36 Eliz.

3. References, *Co. Lit.* 14. *a. Prec. Chan.* 159.

4. Rule, *Propinquior excludit propinquum, &c.*

398. *Qui ſemel malus ſemper praeſumitur eſſe malus in eodem genere.*

1. ACTION for words, ſaying of a merchant, *he came a broken merchant from* Hamborough, held actionable; and not like the caſe where one ſaid of a merchant, *That he was a poor man within theſe ſeven years*; or of a workman, *That he was a weak workman, and had but little ſkill within theſe few years,* where action lieth not; for that he may be a rich man, or a good workman at the time of the ſpeaking; and there they do not charge him with any crime, and by intendment it may have a good conſtruction; but here he chargeth him with having been

once broken, *Et qui ſemel malus ſemper praeſumitur eſſe malus in eodem genere*, or at leaſt may have an inclination thereto, *&c. Cro. Ca.* 317, 318.

2. References, 4 *Co. Action de Slander. Jo.* 321. *Hut.* 125.

3. Rule, *Quae ſunt minoris culpae, ſunt majoris infamiae.*

399. *Qui ſentit commodum, ſentire debet et onus.*

1. IF an eſtate be made by indenture to one for life; remainder to another in fee, *ſur* condition, *&c.* if the tenant for life hath ſealed and die, and he in remainder enter, he is bound to perform all the conditions compriſed in the indenture, as the tenant for life ought to have done in his lifetime, and yet he in the remainder never ſealed any part of the indenture; but the caſe is, for that in as much as he entered and agreed to have the lands by force of the indenture, he is bound to perform the conditions within the ſame indenture, if he will have the land, *&c. Lit. ſect.* 374.

2. *Aver le terre, &c.* here is implied an antient maxim of the law, *viz. Qui ſentit commodum, &c. et tranſit terra cum onere.* Co. Lit. 231. a.

3. Though he in remainder be no party to the deed, yet when he entereth, and agreeth to have the land, by force of the indenture he is bound to perform the conditions contained in the indenture, *&c. Co. Lit.* 230. *b.* 231. *a.*

4. If *A.* by deed indented between him and *B.* letteth lands to *B.* for life; remainder to *C.* in fee, reſerving a rent; tenant for life dieth, he in remainder entereth into the land; he ſhall be bound to pay the rent, for the cauſe and reaſon yielded before by *Littleton. Co. Lit.* 231. *a.*

5. In the king's bench between the dean and chapter of *Windſor* and *Hyde*, the caſe was this; A man leaſed an houſe by indenture for years, the leſſee for him and his heirs covenants and grants with the leſſor, to repair the houſe at all times neceſſary; the leſſee aſſigns to *Hyde*, who ſuffers it to run to decay; the leſſor brings his action of covenant againſt the aſſignee; and it was adjudged by lord chief juſtice *Popham* and all the court, that covenant lay, though the leſſee had not covenanted for his aſſigns; for a covenant which extends to the ſupport of the matter demiſed, is *quodam modo* appurtenant to it, and ſhall run with it, and in reſpect that the leſſee had taken upon him to bear the charges of repairs, the yearly rent reſerved was the leſs, which turned to the benefit of the aſſignee, *Et qui ſentit commodum, &c.* 5 Co. 24. a. b.

6. The ſole queſtion of difficulty was, Whether an action lieth againſt the aſſignee for covenant broken, he being not named in the covenant? And *Tanfield* for the plaintiff in error, moved it lay not; for covenant lies not againſt the executor of covenantor, not being named, as 48 *E.* 3. 2. and *Dy.* 114. *a multo fortori* it lieth not againſt the aſſignee, not being named; as old *Nat. Brev.* 102. is; but if it be covenanted for him and his aſſigns, it is otherwiſe; as 25 *H.* 8. *Bro. Cov.* 32. wherefore, *&c.* But *Popham, Clinch* and *Fenner*, (*abſente Gaudy*) held clearly, that an action of covenant lies againſt an aſſignee in this caſe, though not named; for a covenant, which runs and reſts with the lands, lies for or againſt the aſſignees, at the common law; *quia tranſit terra cum onere*, though the aſſignee be not named in the

the covenant, and covenant lies againſt an executor in every caſe, though not named, unleſs it be ſuch a covenant, as is to be performed by the perſon of the teſtator, which they cannot perform: wherefore the judgment was affirmed. *Cro. Eliz.* 552, 553.

7. Leſſee for years covenants to repair the houſes during the term; this ſhall bind all others, as a thing which is appurtenant and runs with the land, into whoſeſoever hands, *&c.* as well thoſe who come in by act of law, as by act of the party; for it is all one in regard to the leſſor; and if the law ſhould be otherwiſe he might be injured; and reaſon requires that they, who take benefit of ſuch covenants as the leſſor made with the leſſee, on the other hand ſhould be bound by ſuch covenants as the leſſee made with the leſſor. 5 *Co.* 17. *b.*

8. References, 5 *Co.* 16. 7 *Co.* 39. *b.* *Cro. Eliz.* 552, 553. 2 *Inſt.* 489. *Cro. Ca.* 221, 222. *Cro. Ja.* 125. *Cro. Eliz.* 383. *Lutw.* 363, 1368. 4 *E.* 3. 3. *Dal.* 4, 47, 83, 101. 1 *Ro. Abr.* 521, 522, 915. 2 *Ro. Abr.* 743, 744. 2 *Inſt.* 298. *Lit. Bro.* 16. *b.* *Godb.* 70. *Thel.* 34. *Mo.* 179. *Bel.* 16. *b.* *Hob.* 176. 3 *Cro.* 361. 4 *Co.* 27. *Poph.* 38. 1 *Ro.* 576. *Dy.* 262. *Comb.* 185, 186.

400. *Qui ſentit onus ſentire debet et commodum.*

1. MAking of one to be parſon, is making him owner of the poſſeſſions of the parſonage. And he who is made abbot hath therewith the poſſeſſions of the abbey; for the ſpiritual office draws with it a right to have the poſſeſſions belonging to the office. So the making a body ſpiritual to be perpetual parſon, is not preciſely a grant of the glebe and tithes; but yet as ſuch body is parſon they may intermeddle with the glebe and tithes, as things annexed to the office of parſon. *Plow. Co.* 500. *a. b.*

2. Reference, *Salk.* 302.

3. Rule, See *laſt rule.*

401. *Qui poteſt et debet vetare jubet.*

1. THE plaintiff having a leaſe of certain mills for 12 years, which was near expired; the leſſor, upon his marriage, makes a ſettlement of them, to the uſe of himſelf for life, then to the firſt and other ſons of the marriage in tail male, remainder to his own right heirs. Afterwards the plaintiff takes a new leaſe of theſe mills from the original leſſor for 30 years, and lays out 2800 *l.* in new building and improving them; the defendant was the eldeſt ſon of the leſſor, and during the time the plaintiff was making the improvements, went to his father and told him he had no power to make any ſuch leaſe; that after his, the father's death, the eſtate would be his, the ſon's, but never acquainted the plaintiff with that, nor of the ſettlement made on his father's marriage; but on the contrary writ to the plaintiff to take care to keep one of his mills, in particular, in repair: then the father dies, and the ſon recovers in ejectment againſt the leſſee, who thereupon brought this bill to be quieted in the poſſeſſion, during the reſidue of the leaſe, for that the defendant was fully acquainted with the circumſtances of the leaſe, and knew his father had no power to make it, and yet never forbid or cautioned the plaintiff from going on with the repairs,

pairs, but on the contrary, ſtood by, and encouraged him in the proceedings therein; and ſo the plaintiff had a decree to hold during the reſidue of his term; for though the defendant was not privy to the making this leaſe, but that was only the fraud of the father, yet he being to have the eſtate after his father's death, and taking notice thereof to his father, and that he had no power to make ſuch a leaſe, and yet ſuffering the plaintiff to go on in the repairs of the premiſſes, with a deſign to reap the whole benefit thereof when his father was dead, was ſuch a fraud and practice in him, as ought to be diſcountenanced in this court; for *qui tacet conſentire videtur*; *et qui poteſt et debet vetare jubet.* And it was decreed that the plaintiff ſhould enjoy during the reſidue of his leaſe. *Gilb.* 85.

2. Reference, 2 *Lev.* 152.

3. Rules, *Wherever there is ſuppreſſio veri, &c. Particeps criminis not to be relieved, and the other rules there referred to.*

402. *Qui tacet conſentire videtur.*

1. REferences, 2 *Lev.* 152. *Gilb.* 85.

2. Rules, *Wherever there is ſuppreſſio veri, &c. Qui poteſt et debet vetare jubet.*

403. *Quod ab initio non valet, tractu temporis non convaleſcet.*

1. IF an infant or feme covert make their will, and publiſh it, and after die, of full age or ſole, yet the will is void. *Fi. Ley* 4. *b.*

2. If the huſband make a feoffment in fee to the uſe of *A.* for his life, and after to the uſe of his wife for her jointure, this is not within the act of 27 *H.* 8. of jointures, though *A.* die, living the huſband; for in this and other like caſes, as they were out of the act at firſt, as being uncertain, whether the eſtate of the wife ſhould commence and take effect immediately upon the death of the huſband, as it ought by the act, no ſubſequent act may make them within the act; for *quod ab initio non valet, tractu temporis non convaleſcet*; *et quae malo ſunt inchoata principio vix eſt ut bono peragantur exitu*, and therefore in all thoſe caſes, though the wife do attain to them and actually enter, and take the profits, yet ſhe ſhall have dower in the reſt; for if the ſaid act does not bar her, the common law does not conclude her, in ſuch caſe, of her dower, &c. 4 *Co.* 2. *b.*

3. By lord chancellor *Jefferies*, as the bargain was unrighteous at firſt, nothing happening after could make it better. 1 *Vern.* 167, &c. ſee *The caſe.*

4. References, 5 *Co.* 3. *a.* 8 *Co.* 135. 5 *Co.* 23. *b.* 4 *Co.* 90. 11 *Co.* *Dy.* 246. *b.* 312. *Cro. Eliz.* 585, 839. *Mo.* 145, 277, 678. *Ro. Abr.* 239. *Dal.* 48. *b.* *Fi. Ley* 4. *b.* *Da.* 32. *a.* 1 *Mod.* 200.

5. Rules, *Haeres eſt eadem perſona cum anteceſſore. Actus legitimi non recipiunt modum*, caſe 3. *In aequali jure melior eſt conditio poſſidentis.*

404. *Quod constat clare non debet verificari.*

1. IN a *quod permittat*, if it appear to the court, that the nusance is to the damage of the plaintiff, he need not shew it specially. 9 *Co.* 33.
2. See rule, *Perspicua vera non sunt probanda.*

405. *Quod contra legem fit, pro infecto habetur.*

1. REferences, *Co. Lit.* 200. 3 *Co.* 74. 4 *Co.* 31.
2. Rules, *Non valet impedimentum, quod de jure non sortitur effectum. Quod ab initio non valet, &c.*

406. *Quod est ex jure, id est justum, quod ab injuria proficitur injustum, &c.*

SEE rule, *Law will not suffer wrong.*

407. *Quod necessitas cogit defendit.*

I conceive I cannot, more to the benefit of those for whom these sheets are more immediately intended, illustrate this rule, than by travelling into the military laws and courts for matter to this end; and therefore without further ceremony I shall proceed.

Martial law,

What, and general to.

1. IN truth and reality this is not properly a law, but something indulged rather than even allowed as a law. The necessity of government, order and discipline in an army, is that only which can give these laws any countenance; *quod enim necessitas cogit defendit.*

To whom to extend.

Only to the army in time of war.

2. This indulged law was only to extend to members of the army, or those of the opposit army, but were never intended to be executed or exercised upon others; for others, not listed under the army, had no colour of reason to be bound by military constitutions, applicable only to the army, whereof they were not parts, but they were to be ordered and governed according to the laws to which they were subject, though it were in time of war.

In time of peace.

3. And the exercise of this law, whereby any person should lose his life, or member or liberty, may not be permitted in time of peace, when the king's courts are open for all persons to receive justice, according to the laws of the land. And this in substance is declared in the petition of

I right,

right, 3 *Car.* 1. whereby ſuch commiſſions and martial laws were repealed, and declared to be contrary to law; and like to this was that famous caſe of *Edmund* earl of *Kent*, who being taken at *Pomfret* 15 *E.* 2. the king and divers lords proceeded to give ſentence of death upon him, as in a kind of a military court, by a ſummary proceeding, which judgment was afterwards, 1 *E.* 3. reverſed in parliament; the reaſon whereof ſee in lord *Hale's Hiſt. Law* 40. For martial law, which is the rather indulged, as hath been ſaid, than allowed, and that only in caſe of neceſſity, in time of open war, is in no ſort to be admitted in time of peace, when the ordinary courts of juſtice are open. *Ha. Hiſt. Law* 39, 40, 41. *Neither concern they any but the ſoldiery.*

Their courts.

Where holden, and before whom.

4. The martial law or military court is held before the conſtable and marſhal antiently, as the *judices ordinarii*, or otherwiſe before the king's commiſſioners of that juriſdiction, as *judices delegati.*

The matter of their juriſdiction.

General.

5. Is declared and limited by the *Stat.* 8 *R.* 2. *cap.* 5. and 13 *R.* 2. *cap.* 2. and that not only by theſe ſtatutes, but ſtill more by the common law, is their juriſdiction declared and limited as follows.

Particular to.

I. *Negatively.* II. *Affirmatively.*

I. *Negatively*, They are not to meddle with any thing determinable at common law; and therefore as damages, and the quantity and determination thereof is of that cognizance, the court of the conſtable and marſhal cannot, even in ſuch ſuits as are proper for their cognizance, give damages againſt the party convicted before them, but at moſt order reparation in point of honour, as *mendacium ſibi ipſi imponere*; neither can they, as to point of reparation in honour, hold plea of any ſuch words or things wherein the party is relievable *by the courts of the common law.*

II. *Affirmatively*, Their juriſdiction extends to, 1. Matters of arms, and 2. Matters of war. 1. *Matters of arms* (*or heraldry*) the conſtable or marſhal had cognizance thereof, *viz.* touching the right of coat-armour, bearings, creſts, ſupporters, penons, *&c.* and alſo touching the right of precedency, in caſes where either acts of parliament, or the king's patent (he being the fountain of honour) have not already determined the matter; for in ſuch caſes they have no power to alter it; and though theſe things were antiently allowed and indulged to the cognizance of the conſtable and marſhal, as having ſome relation to military affairs; yet they were ſo reſtrained, that they were only to determine the right, and give reparation to the party injured in point of honour, but not to repair him in damages, as hath been mentioned. See *Ha. Hiſt. Law* 36, 37, 38. 2. *Matters of war*, and here the conſtable and marſhal had a double power, 1. A miniſterial.

ſterial. 2. A judicial one. 1. *Miniſterial power*, as they were two great ordinary officers, antiently in the king's army. 1. *The conſtable*, being in effect the king's general. 2. The marſhal was employed in martialling the king's army, and keeping the liſt of the officers and ſoldiers therein; *and his certificate* was the trial of thoſe whoſe attendance was requiſite. Vide *Lit. ſect.* 102. 2. *Judicial*, again the conſtable had alſo a judicial power, or a court wherein ſeveral matters were determinable, as 1. *Appeals* of death or murder committed beyond ſeas, according to the courſe of the civil law. 2. *The rights of priſoners* taken in war. 3. *The offences and miſcarriages of ſoldiers*, contrary to the rules and orders of the army, for always preparatory to an actual war, the kings of this realm, by advice of the conſtable and marſhal, were uſed to compoſe a book of rules and orders, for the due order and diſcipline of their officers and ſoldiers, together with certain penalties on the offenders; and this was called martial law: we have an extract in the black book of the admiralty, and elſewhere, ſeveral exemplars of ſuch military laws, eſpecially that 9 *R.* 2. compoſed by the king, with the advice of the duke of *Lancaſter* and others. *Ha. Hiſt. Law* 38, 39.

Derived from the crown.

7. The juriſdiction exerciſed in theſe courts (*and indeed in all other courts governed by the civil or common law*) are derived from the crown of *England.* And the laſt devolution is to the king by way of appeal. *Ha. Hiſt. Law* 43.

How they proceed.

8. In this military court, whether, 1. of honour, or 2. court martial, the civil law has been uſed and allowed in ſuch things as belong to their juriſdiction, as the rule or direction of their proceedings and deciſions, ſo far as they are not contrariant to or contradicted by the laws of the kingdom, and thoſe cuſtoms and uſages which have obtained in *England*, which even *in matters of honour* are in ſome points derogatory to the civil law; but this court has been long diſuſed upon great reaſon. But though in theſe courts the civil law has been *under ſuch reſtrictions, as aforeſaid, allowed*, yet herein, the common law of *England* has retained thoſe *ſigna ſuperioritatis*, and the preference and ſuperintendancy in relation to thoſe courts, and theſe are but *leges ſub graviori lege*, for the honour of the king and the common law: and ſo it is alſo, that the common law, and the judges at law have the expoſition of all ſuch ſtatutes or acts of parliament as concern the extent of the juriſdiction, or thoſe matters depending before thoſe courts, &c. *Ha. Hiſt. Law.* 41, 42, 43.

408. *Quod non habet principium, non habet finem.*

1. IT is good policy to name the biſhop in a *quare impedit*, becauſe in ſuch caſe he ſhall not preſent by lapſe; and as he ſhall not, ſo ſhall not the metropolitan, *for he ſhall never preſent or collate by lapſe after the ſix months, but when the immediate ordinary might have collated by lapſe within the ſix months, and had ſurceaſed his time: and ſo it is if the time be devolved*

to the king, for the first step or beginning faileth; and in human things, *quod non habet principium, non habet finem.* Co. Lit. 334. b. 345. a.

2. Rules, *Nullum tempus occurrit regi.* *Pendente lite nihil innovetur.*

409. *Quod per me non possum, nec per alium.*

RESOLVED, That custom hath so established and fixed the estate of the copyholder, that by the severance of the inheritance from the copyhold of the manor, the copyhold is not destroyed; for that the lord cannot oust the copyholder nor any other claiming under him, *nemo potest plus ad alium transferre, quam ipse habet*; *et quod per me non possum, nec per alium.* 4 Co. 24. b.

410. *Quod prius est dignius est.*

1. IF there be three brethren, and the second purchaseth lands in fee-simple, and dieth *sans* issue, the eldest brother shall have the land by descent and not the younger, &c. So of the younger purchasing and dying in like manner; for the eldest is most worthy of blood, &c. *Lit. sect.* 5.

2. It is a maxim in the law, That *the next of the worthiest blood shall ever inherit*, as the male and all descendant from him before the female, and the female of the part of the father before the male or female of the part of the mother, &c. because the female of the part of the father is of the worthiest blood; and therefore among the males, the eldest brother and his posterity shall inherit lands in fee-simple, as heir, before any younger brother, or any descending from him; because, as *Littleton* saith, he is *plus digne de sanke. Quod prius est dignius est, et qui prior est tempore potior est jure. Si quis plures filios habuerit, jus proprietatis primo descendit ad primogenitum, eo quod inventus est primo in rerum natura*, &c. Co. Lit. 14. a.

3. Rule, *Propinquior excludit propinquum*, &c.

411. *Quod quisquis norit, in hoc se exerceat.*

1. IT was resolved by Sir *Edward Anderson* lord chief justice, and all the justices of the common pleas, That the verdict found in the case at bar was well found. They held that all pleas, as well of the crown as common pleas, *viz.* actions real, personal and mixt, and upon all issues joined, whether between the king and the party, or between party and party, the jurors might find the special matter, which is pertinent and tends only to the issue joined; and they doubting in point of law, may well pray the advice of the court; and that by the common law, which hath ordained, that matters in fact should be tried by the jurors, and matters in law by the judges: and as *ad quaestionem facti non respondent judices, ita ad quaestionem juris non respondent juratores*, but their office is to find *veritatem facti*, and to refer the discussion of the law to the judges; and therefore their finding is called *veridictum, quasi dictum veritatis*, the saying the truth; and the censure of the judges is called *judicium, quasi juris dictum, ipsa viva vox juris*, the saying of the law. *And the wisdom of the law was to refer things to persons who were cognizant of, and expert in*

in them, according to the antient rule, quod quiſquis norit, in hoc ſe exerceat; and therefore the law will neither compel the jury, *who have not knowledge in the law,* to take upon them the cognizance of points of law, whether in the caſes concerning life, member, inheritance, freeholds, goods or chattels, but to leave them to the conſideration of the judges: neither are the juſtices of aſſiſe, nor any other judges, whether in pleas of the crown or common pleas, to put points of law upon the jurors, but they are to have the truth of the caſe, or matter of fact found for them, and upon conference and conſideration to judge according to law in ſuch caſes, *&c.* 9 *Co.* 13. *a.*

2. Matters in law ſhall not be put in iſſue to be tried *per pais*; for the rule is, *quod quiſquis norit, in hoc ſe exerceat*; and therefore *ſicut ad quaeſtionem facti non reſpondent judices, ita ad quaeſtionem juris non reſpondent juratores:* and if the jury take upon them the knowledge of the law, and find the ſpecial matter, but miſtake their law, the judges ought to give judgment upon the ſpecial matter according to law, without any regard had to the concluſion of the jury, who ought not to have taken upon them judgment of law. 11 *Co.* 10. *b.* and herewith accord *Plow. Com. Amy Townſend*'s caſe. 5 *H.* 7. *Carew*'s caſe. 9 *H.* 6. 38. 13 *H.* 7. 22, *&c.* and Lord *Berkley*'s caſe, *Plow. Com.* 230.

3. References, 12 *Co.* 67. 9 *Co.* 13. *Co. Lit.* 125.

4. Rule, *Sicut ad quaeſtionem juris non reſpondent jur', &c.*

412. *Quod ſemel placuit in electionibus, amplius diſplicere non poteſt.*

1. ONE grants, by deed, a rent-charge to another, and the rent is behind; the grantee may have a writ of annuity or diſtreſs at his election, but he may not have both; for if he bring annuity the land is diſcharged; and if he diſtrain, and the tenant bring his replevin, as he may, and the grantee avers in a court of record, then the perſon is diſcharged. *Co. Lit.* 146. *a.*

2. References, 2 *Chan. Ca.* 24, 87, 200. 1 *Vern.* 103, 105, 298, 471. 2 *Rep. Chan.* 2, 9, 21. *Gilb.* 183. *Barn.* 39, 278, 391.

3. Rules, *Every man's deed or covenant to be taken moſt ſtrongly againſt himſelf. In things of election, he who is to make it, is to ſhew that he hath made it.*

413. *Quod tacite intelligitur deeſſe non videtur.*

1. THE judges in all ſucceſſions of ages have allowed copyholds to be eſtabliſhed, and ſure by cuſtom, and to be deſcendible as other eſtates are. 4 *Co.* 22. *a.* *Co. Lit.* 63. *a.*

2. And it was reſolved, That when cuſtom hath created ſuch inheritances, and that the lands ſhall be deſcendible, then the law directs the deſcent according to the rules and maxims of the common law, as incidents; *quia quod tacite intelligitur deeſſe non videtur.* As 5 *E.* 4. 7. When uſes had gained the reputation of inheritances deſcendible, the common law directed their deſcent; as that there ſhould be *poſſeſſio fratris* of

an uſe, as well as of an inheritance at law. But it was reſolved, that ſuch cuſtomary inheritances ſhould not, by law, have any other collateral qualities, which do not concern deſcent, as other inheritances at law have; for as *ſans* cuſtom ſuch eſtates are not deſcendible, ſo, without cuſtom, they may not have any collateral quality incident to inheritances at law; for they are but inheritances *ſecundum quid, viz.* to be deſcendible by cuſtom, to their heirs, and not to be determined by their deaths, nor ſubject to the will of the lord, like other eſtates at will; yet they are not inheritances *ſimpliciter*, to have all other collateral qualities, but only ſuch as cuſtom hath allowed, *&c.* 4 *Co.* 22. *a. b.*

414. *Quoties in verbis nulla eſt ambiguitas, ibi nulla expoſitio contra verba expreſſa fienda eſt.*

RENT granted out of the manor of *D.* and if the rent is behind, that the grantee ſhall diſtrain for the rent in the manor of *S.* this is but a penalty in the manor of *S. &c.* *Co. Lit.* 147.

415. *Ratio eſt anima legis.*

1. AMONG all the gifts God gave to man, reaſon is the nobleſt, for thereby man not only excelleth beaſts, but is made in dignity like to the angels, diſcerning truth from falſhood, and good from evil; and therefore reaſon is the power of the ſoul that diſcerneth between good and evil, and between good and better, comparing the one with the other; the which alſo ſheweth virtue loveth good and flieth vice. And reaſon is called righteous and good; as it is conformable to the will of God, which is the firſt thing and firſt rule that all things muſt be ruled by, *&c. Doct. & Stud. lib.* 1. *cap.* 14. This law of reaſon may not be changed or put away, *cap.* 2. and is the firſt ground of the law of *England. cap.* 5.

2. Rules, *Conſtructions to be with equity and moderation. Therefore to moderate the rigour of the law. Lex plus laudatur quando ratione probatur. Ratio eſt radius divini luminis.*

416. *Ratio eſt radius divini luminis.*

1. *QUIA per rationes pervenitur ad legitimam rationem*, ſays *Littleton*, *ſect.* 377. for *ratio eſt radius divini luminis*, and by reaſoning and debating *of grave learned men* the darkneſs of ignorance is expelled; and by the light of legal reaſon the right is diſcerned, and thereupon judgment given according to law, which is the perfection of reaſon. This is by *Littleton* called *legitima ratio*, whereunto no man can attain but by long ſtudy, often conference, long experience, and continual obſervation. And certain it is, ſays lord *Coke*, that in matters of difficulty, the more ſeriouſly they are debated and argued, the more truly they are reſolved, and thereby new inventions juſtly avoided. *Co. Lit.* 232.

2. Rules, *Equity cannot change things, nor make them act contrary to their eſſential natures and properties. Has a power upon circumſtances, to relieve,* &c. *Looks upon that as done which ought to be done. Is to execute the intention*

tention of the parties. Rectifies mistakes, and supplies defects. Regards substance, not ceremony. To prevent multiplicity of suits. Will never decree a suit where it may decree a remedy. Will not relieve where no fraud or covin. Will not aid new inventions, &c. *Relieves against accidents. Against fraud. Where the matter lieth in compensation. Against one's own act,* &c.

Law and equity both shall prevail against equity only. Driveth no man to shew what he doth not know. Favours justice, &c. *Life, liberty and dower. The public quiet. Hath always suppressed new and subtile inventions in derogation of the common law. Is the perfection of reason. Prefers the public good. Regards the intent. Requireth order and decency. Respecteth the excellency of some persons, Time. Tendereth the weakness and imperfection of men. Will rather endure a particular mischief,* &c. *Will not suffer wrong.*

Lex necessitatis est lex temporis. Nihil facit frustra. Non cogit ad impossibilia. Spectat naturae ordinem.

Liberty the greatest jewel. Ratio legis est anima legis. Summa charitas est facere justitiam, &c. Summa ratio est quae pro religione facit. Summum jus summa est injuria.

417. *Ratio legis est anima legis.*

1. THE outward words of the law are not the law, but the inward sense and meaning thereof; for our law, as all others, hath two parts, flesh and soul, the letter resembleth the flesh, and the intent and reason the soul; *Nam ratio legis est anima legis.* 2 West's Prec. 176. a. b.

2. See *Two last rules, and the rules referred to there.*

418. *Recovery in one action, a good bar to another of equal or more base nature, but not to one of more high nature.*

THE rule of law is, *That recovery or bar in one action is good in another action of either an equal or inferior nature, but not in actions of higher nature.* As a recovery or bar in one assise is good in another. 44 *E.* 3. 45. 9 *H.* 7. 13, *&c.* But not in a *Mortdancestor.* 5 *Ass. pl.* 1. Neither is a recovery or bar in a *Mordancestor* a good bar in a writ of right. *Fitzh. Nat. Brev.* 5, 50. *Ass. pl.* 15. 11 *E.* 3. *Entre* 56, *&c.* 4 *Co.* 43.

419. *Refert a quo fiat perquisitum.*

1. REference, *Co. Lit.* 12. *a.*

2. Rule, *He to inherit must be of the blood of the first purchaser.*

420. *Reges (sacro oleo uncti) spiritualis jurisdictionis sunt capaces.*

The royal supremacy.

General to.

1. THE king's immediate, personal, originary, inherent power which he doth or may execute *authoritate regiâ supremâ ecclesiasticâ*, as king and sovereign governor of the church of *England*, is one of those flowers, *quae faciunt coronam*, which makes the royal crown and diadem in force and virtue; whilst the power given to the archbishop or dean and chapter, by the statute of *Dispensations* and *Faculties*, is but *authoritatem ordinariam, limitatam et delegatam.* Hob. 143.

What the king may do in virtue thereof.

2. The king may constitute appropriations, unite churches, erect ecclesiastical benefices, or dignities, dispence with irregularities, exempt from ecclesiastical jurisdiction, and the execution of their sentences; he can suspend the effect of their sentences, even in causes criminal. *Ha. Anal.* 19.

3. He hath both ecclesiastical and temporal jurisdiction. 5 *Co. De Ju. Regis Eccl.* 28.

4. He may dispence with the ecclesiastical laws. *Hob.* 140. *Colt* and *Glover*'s case. *Palm.* 470. *Mo.* 755. 1 *Ju. Eccl.* tit. *The King supreme.*

5. The king of *England*, who is, and always was of right, the fountain of all justice and jurisdiction in all causes, whether ecclesiastical or civil within his dominions, though he allows prelates to exercise jurisdiction, yet he hath the superintendancy of their proceedings, and the power of directing when, and how they shall proceed, and of restraint and correction if they do not proceed duly, as is evident from the writs of several natures directed to bishops, *&c.* whereby he commands them, *&c.* *Da.* 51. *b.* 52. *a.*

6. References, *Stat.* 25 *E.* 3. 16 *R.* 2. 2. 25 *H.* 8. 1 *E.* 6. 1 *Eliz.* 1. *Cro. Eliz.* 599. *Da.* 4. 1 *Ju. Eccl.* tit. *King supreme head of the church.*

7. Rule, *Omnes reges dicuntur clerici.*

421. *Regula peccatis quae paenas irrogat aequas.*

THIS was an action of trespass for taking away two steers. To which the defendant pleaded, That *William Morgan* was seised of the manor of *Brecon* in his demesne as of fee, and that he and all those, *&c.* had time, *&c.* a court leet, or view of frankpledge three times a year, *viz.* on *Monday* next after the close of *Easter*, on *Monday* next after the feast of *St. Michael*, and on *Monday* next after *St. Hilary*. That in this manor there was a custom, that every tenant of every freehold tenement within the said manor, used and ought to appear personally, without any notice or summons, once in every year, at one of the said three courts of view of frankpledge, so to be held; and if he did not appear at the two other courts, then he was to pay the steward for the use of the lord of the manor an essoign penny for each of the said two courts for his default; and that every such tenant not appearing at either of the said three courts

courts, was to be amerced by the ſteward for his default 7*s.* for each of the ſaid three courts; and that every tenant, being lawfully ſummoned to appear, and inquire and preſent upon oath all ſuch matters as ought to be inquired into and preſented, and therein making default, was to be amerced by the ſteward for his contempt at 7*s.* and that the bailiff of the ſaid manor, by warrant of the ſteward, ſhould levy theſe amerciaments by diſtreſs and ſale of the goods and chattels of the defaulters. And the defendant further ſays, that *John Edwards* the plaintiff, then and for three years before was tenant, *&c.* and that there was a court held on *Monday* next after the cloſe of *Eaſter*, *&c.* and that the plaintiff was lawfully ſummoned to appear, and to be put upon the jury, *&c.* and that he did not appear, for which he was amerced by the ſteward at 7*s.* and ſo on the ſecond and third court, *&c.* for which he was amerced in another 7*s.* and another 7*s.* and for not paying thoſe ſeveral amerciaments, the ſteward directed his writ to the four perſons named, and which was delivered to them, by virtue whereof they took the ſaid two ſteers, in the declaration mentioned, as a diſtreſs and levied on the ſaid ſteers the ſaid ſeveral ſums, amounting to 1*l.* 8*s.* to the uſe of the ſaid *William Morgan*, *&c.* and had ſold the ſame, *&c.* and paid the ſaid 1*l.* 8*s.* to the ſaid *William Morgan*, and were ready and offered to pay the overplus to the plaintiff, which he refuſed to receive, which is the ſame tranſgreſſion of which the plaintiff complains. The plaintiff replies *De injuria ſua propria*, whereto the defendant demurs. The queſtion in this caſe is, Whether the cuſtom be good? And we are of opinion that this cuſtom is not good, for many reaſons. 1. Becauſe this cuſtom is not affeered. By *Stat. Magna Charta*, *cap.* 14. it is directed expreſly, that *nulla praedictarum miſericordiarum ponetur niſi per ſacramentum proborum et legalium hominum de vicineto*; and 27 *H.* 8. *cap.* 26. all laws and ſtatutes in *England* are to run in *Wales*; and ſo if this cuſtom be againſt *Magna Charta*, it is as much aboliſhed in *Wales* as it is in *England.* The ſtatute of *Magna Charta* was intended to take away all fines and amercements at the will and pleaſure of the lord and his ſteward, and alſo all exceſſive fines and amercements, if they were never ſo certain: for before this charter of liberties, the lords uſed to ſet ſuch exceſſive and grievous amerciaments on their tenants, that under pretence of ſuch amerciaments they uſed to ſeiſe the whole profits of the tenement which they had granted; to hinder which oppreſſion, *Magna Charta* appoints, that every amerciament ſhould be affeered. This has been ſo underſtood, that though a court may award that the party ſhall be amerced, yet the quantity of the amerciament is to be ſettled by the affeerers; becauſe they do affeer, or bring in the quantity of the amerciament. In a court baron where the ſuitors are judges, the homage may preſent the defaults on ſmall treſpaſſes within the manor, but the amerciament muſt be afterwards particularly affeered by the affeerers. *Hob.* 129. and *Kitchin* 153. ſays, That the office of the homage and that of the affeerers are not to be confounded; the homage are to preſent the little offences, and treſpaſſes within the manor, as *Kitchin* ſays; but the affeerers are in nature of truſtees, to ſettle the quantity of the amerciament. Indeed *Hob.* goes ſo far as to ſay, That the homage may ſet a ſum upon the offence, but then the affeerers are ſo to mitigate it, that the quantity of the amerciament is totally to be ſettled by the affeerers; and ſo in the courts above, where amerciaments were ordered either againſt

plaintiff

plaintiff or defendant, they were carried down to the coroner to be ſettled and affeered. In a court leet, which was a court of record, if an amerciament impoſed was affeered even by the jury, and not by ſworn affeerers appointed for that purpoſe, it was a void amerciament, and the lord of the leet could not maintain his action for it. 3 *Lev.* 206. It is very reaſonable there ſhould be ſuch an affeerment; for in this very caſe it is very poſſible the tenant might not have been ſummoned, and that this might come to the knowledge of the affeerers, and that would be an excuſe for this default. Objection, This is an amerciament in nature of a fine, and a fine may be ſet by a court without any affeerment. Anſwer, It is true, a fine may be ſet without affeerment; becauſe it is out of the ſtatute of *Magna Charta*; for the ſtatute of *Magna Charta* doth not comprehend the caſes where a court of juſtice may impriſon, and where a fine is ſet by way of mercy, as a ranſom and purgation of the offence; for the ſtatute was deſigned in mercy to offenders, and not to hinder them from mercy; and ſo did not extend to offences that might be puniſhed by impriſonment. So in all breaches of the peace, the court may ſet a fine, and ſo for all contempts; becauſe the court may impriſon. So a ſteward of a court leet may impoſe a reaſonable fine, for a diſturbance committed *in facie curiae*, which is *Grieſley*'s caſe, 8 *Co.* 39. And ſo he may if a ſuitor will not be ſworn of the homage, becauſe he may impriſon in thoſe caſes, as is expreſly reſolved in *Fitzh. Abr.* tit. *Leet*, *N.* 4. *Dalt. Sher.* 400. And when ſuch a fine is impoſed, it becomes a debt to the lord, for which an action of debt lieth. *Cro. Eliz.* 581. No body can ſay, that a default for not appearing in a court leet, is ſuch a default, upon which a ſteward may impriſon the party; and ſo he cannot ſet a fine as a ranſom from impriſonment; but it is ſaid that this may be good by cuſtom: now as to that, it is in the very teeth of *Magna Charta*; for it is a cuſtom to amerce without affeerment, and this ſtatute was made to abrogate and aboliſh ſuch cuſtoms. 2. Another reaſon againſt this cuſtom is, that the amerciament is too exceſſive, it is not *ſalvo contenemento*: now if the amerciament was ſo great as to ſweep away the whole profits of the freehold of the offender, it was too great; as if he were a ſock-man, and it extended to take away the beaſts of his plough; if he were a military man, and it extended to take away his arms; if he was a merchant, and it extended to take away his merchandize; if he were a villain, if it took away his cart or wainage; all theſe amerciaments were too grievous and againſt ſtatute of *Magna Charta*, which ſays, *Liber homo non amercietur pro parvo delicto; niſi ſecundum modum illius delicti; et pro magno delicto ſecundum magnitudinem delicti, ſalvo ſibi contenemento ſuo, et mercator eodem modo ſalva merchandiza ſua; et villanus ulterius quam noſtri eodem modo amercietur, ſalvo wainagio ſuo; ſi inciderit in miſericordiam noſtram.* And this makes an eſſential difference between a fine and an amerciament; for an amerciament is to be ſet, that he may ſuſtain his ſtation as feudatory to his lord; but the caſe of a fine has no relation thereunto; for where the offender is impriſoned, he cannot ſuſtain that Station; this caſe is among the *minora delicta*, and as ſuch, there ſhould be only an amerciament, and that reaſonable; but according to the cuſtom, it may happen, that the amerciament may ſweep away the whole profit of the tenement; for a man who has but a rod of land, or tenement of 5 *s.* a year, muſt be obliged to pay 1 *l.* 8 *s.* for his default.

Lord

Lord *Coke* in 2 *Just. fo.* 28. expounds the words of the *Stat.* in ſuch a manner, *that the amerciament muſt not deſtroy the livelihood of the offender*; but ſuch amerciaments as theſe in antient times would certainly have been thought very exorbitant before the quantity of the money was ſo very much increaſed; and even at this day, the fine would ſwallow the annual profit of a ſmall tenement. 3. Another reaſon againſt the amerciament here is, that it admits of no eſſoign to excuſe the default. Now there are ſeveral eſſoigns that excuſe even an appearance at the king's courts upon demand, as the eſſoign *de malo lecti*, *de malo veniendi*, *de ſervitio regis*, *&c.* But if a man were ſummoned at this court, and were taken ill the day before the leet, or ſent for into the king's ſervice, it was to be no excuſe, but immediately the amerciament was to run upon him, which is againſt reaſon, as theſe eſſoigns excuſe theſe defaults: but by this cuſtom he is to be amerced even where the law excuſes his non-appearance. 4. It is not *ſecundum modum delicti*; becauſe the non-attendance of a poor man or day labourer is a leſs fault, than of a rich man that has his time to command; and the ſtatute was made on purpoſe to proportion puniſhments to the default: but this cuſtom runs alike upon all defaults, ſmall and great. This is contrary to that known rule, *i. e. Regula peccatis quae paenas irrogat aequas.* Objection, though this cannot be maintained as an amerciament, yet it might begin by tenure, and the lord might ſettle what ſum he pleaſed, on the making default at his leet, and ſuch ſum ought not to be reckoned exceſſive, and ſubject to affeerment, becauſe it was ſettled in the original ſettlement of the tenure. Anſwer, 1. This is pleaded as an amerciament for a default, and not as a ſum due by tenure; *and we muſt take it as it was pleaded*, and not by any imagination out of the plea. 2. *If it were due by tenure, it muſt be laid upon the lands and tenement in certain*, and not perſonally upon the tenant, becauſe upon the contingency it will be a ſum iſſuing out of the land. 3. This would never grow into a cuſtom; becauſe upon an alienation of part of the land, or any diviſion of the ſame upon deſcent, the ſum muſt be devided, and could not be the ſame intire and uniform ſum. This was the opinion of the court, delivered by lord chief baron *Gilbert*. *Gilb.* 209, 210, 211, 212, 213.

422. *Remainder can depend upon no eſtate but what begineth at the ſame time that the remainder doth.*

1. IF a man make a leaſe to another for term of life, and after of his meer motion he confirmeth his eſtate for term of his life to remain after his death to another, and to his heirs; in this caſe the remainder is void in law and conſcience; *for by the law there can no remainder depend upon any eſtate, but that the ſame eſtate beginneth at the ſame time that the remainder doth.* And in this caſe the eſtate began before, and the confirmation enlargeth not his eſtate, nor gave him a new eſtate. *Doct. & Stud. lib.* 2. *c.* 20.

2. But if a leaſe be made to a man for term of another's life, and after the leſſor, only of his meer motion, confirmeth the land to the leſſee for term of his own life, the remainder over in fee, this is a good remainder in law and conſcience. *Doct. & Stud. lib.* 2. *c.* 20.

3. References, *Co. Lit.* 21, 54, 264, 298, 299, 353, 378. *Palm.* 50.

423. *Remedies to be reciprocal.*

1. A MAN being feifed in fee makes an abfolute conveyance to the defendant, but by another deed of the fame date, the lands were made redeemable on payment of 1000 *l.* and intereft at any time during the life of the grantor, and in cafe he fhould not redeem in his life-time, then he covenants that the fame fhould never be redeemed: the grantor dies without redeeming. The heir exhibits his bill to be let in to redeem. It appeared in the proof, that the mortgagor had a kindnefs for the mortgagee, and that this was by way of fettlement. Decreed by lord chancellor *Nottingham*, an account and redemption, but reverfed by lord keeper, and the original bill difmiffed. 1 *Vern.* 7, 8. [*See fame report,* Cade's *cafe,* 212, *and* 217.

2. The lord keeper in this cafe faid, that he was fully fatisfied that it was not originally a mortgage, but an abfolute purchafe, but believes *Sabine* might complain he had fold his eftate too cheap, and that thereupon ferjeant *Barrel* might declare, that if he would pay his money within a year, and 100 *l.* for his pains, that he might have his eftate again; and cited *Sir Anthony Cage's* cafe of a claufe to repurchafe, which made fo much ftir in *Weftminfter Hall*; and faid where there was a claufe or provifion to repurchafe, that the time limited ought to be precifely obferved. And as to the ferjeant's agreement, it was but reafonable for his trouble; and for that the eftate was more valuable, as having gone through a lawyer's hands who underftood the title; and that might be a means to incourage purchafers, and difmiffed the bill. 1 *Vern.* 268.

3. References, 1 *Ch. Ca.* 1, 2, 48, 86, 87, 202, 209, 302. 1 *Rep. Ch.* 122, 123. 2 *Rep. Ch.* 58, 159, 247. 1 *Vern.* 192, 215.

4. Rule, *Quando lex aliquid alicui concedit, &c.*

424. *Remoto impedimento emergit actio.*

1. BETWEEN *William Paget*, Efq; plaintiff and *Edward Cary* and *Elizabeth* his wife defendants *in wafte.* It was refolved in *C. B.* That if tenant for life be, remainder for life, remainder in fee, if tenant for life do wafte in the trees, and after he in remainder for life die, yet the action is maintainable for the wafte done in the life of him in remainder for life, for it was to the difinherifon of him in remainder in fee, and now the impediment (which was the mefne eftate for life) is tolled; *et remoto impedimento emergit actio*; and as it was there faid, fo it was adjudged. *Anno* 9 *Eliz. Reginæ.* 5 *Co.* 76. *b.*

2. And the law is the fame, if he in remainder for life, after the wafte, furrender to him in reverfion or remainder in fee. And whereas it was objected, that at the time of the wafte, it could not be faid to the damage of him in remainder in fee, becaufe of the mefne eftate for life. To this it was anfwered and refolved, that when the trees are fevered they are the property of, and belong to him in remainder in fee; and fo it is where fome of the books have faid, that he in remainder or reverfion in fee, fhould not have wafte, they muft be underftood, during the continuance of the

the meſne remainder; and where it is ſaid in other of the books, that an action of waſte lieth, they muſt be taken to mean, after the death of him in remainder for life. *Quia cum aliquid impeditur propter unum, eo remoto, tollitur impedimentum*; and ſo all the books are well reconciled. 5 *Co.* 76. *b.* 77 *a.*

3. *Boothe* brought waſte againſt *Skevington*, and declared that *Sir William Boothe* demiſed for life to *Enſor*, who aſſigned to *Skevington*; the defendant pleaded an aſſignment to *Elizabeth Cave*, before which no waſte was; the plaintiff replied, and ſhewed the *Stat.* 11 *H.* 6. *c.* 5. and that the grant to *Cave* was to the intent, that they ſhould not know againſt whom to bring their action, and averred that he took the profits. The defendant rejoined that *Cave* granted to *A.* who demiſed to the defendant at will, without that, *&c.* whereupon the plaintiff demurred in law, and in this caſe three points were reſolved. 1. That though the words of the act are, that where tenant for life or years have demiſed or granted away their eſtate, with intent that they in reverſion, *ſcil.* their leſſors, their heirs or aſſigns, ſhould not know their names, and yet the firſt tenant continues the occupation of the lands, and commits waſte, *&c.* it is ordained and eſtabliſhed, that he in reverſion ſhall maintain waſte againſt ſuch tenants for life or years, and there is proviſion for the firſt tenants; yet it was reſolved, that every aſſignee from the firſt leſſee, whether mediate or immediate, is within the act; *for it was made to prevent and ſuppreſs fraud and deceit; and therefore muſt be taken beneficially.* 2. It was reſolved, that he in remainder is within the ſaid act, as well as he in reverſion; *for that he is in equal miſchief*, and yet both the preamble and body of the act ſpeak only of him in reverſion. 3. It was reſolved, that the intent aforeſaid was not traverſable in the preſent caſe, but the taking the profits, which is a thing notorious, and whereof the country might have cognizance; and the taking the profits implies the intent. *Vide* 4 *H.* 7. 9. alſo 4 *E.* 4. 29. and many other books which agree herewith. 5 *Co.* 77. *a. b.*

4. References, 11 *E.* 3. *Receit*, 118. 4 *E.* 3. 18. *Cole's Ca.* 33 *E.* 3. *Waſt.* 114. 5 *E.* 3. 3. 10 *E.* 4. 9. *Regr.* 74. *b. and the note there, fo.* 75. *Co. Lit.* 53. *b.* 54. *a.* 220. 4 *Co.* 62. 11 *Co.* 48, 81. *Dy.* 90. 1 *Cro.* 243. 2 *Cro.* 688. *Mo.* 18.

425. *Repellitur a ſacramento infamis.*

PRopter delictum, As if the juror be attainted or convicted of treaſon or felony, or for any offence to life or member, or in attaint for a falſe verdict, or for perjury as a witneſs, or in a conſpiracy at the ſuit of the king, or in any ſuit, (either for the king, or for any ſubject) be adjudged to the pillory, tumbrel, or the like, or to be branded, or to be ſtigmatized, or to have any other corporal puniſhment, whereby he becometh infamous; for it is a maxim at law, *repellitur a ſacramento infamis.* Theſe and the like are principal cauſes of challenge. So it is if a man be outlawed in treſpaſs, debt, or any other action; for he is *exlex*; and therefore is not *legalis homo.* And old books have ſaid, that if he be excommunicated, he could not be of a jury. *Co. Lit.* 158. *a.*

426. *Reputatio eſt vulgaris opinio, ubi non eſt veritas.*

What.

1. NOTE, *Lecteur*, The rule is, *Quod reputatio eſt vulgaris opinio, ubi non eſt veritas.* 4 Co. 107. b.

The ſorts.

2. *Et vulgaris opinio eſt duplex, ſcil. opinio vulgaris orta inter graves et diſcretos, et quae vultum veritatis habet; et opinio tantum orta inter leves et vulgares homines abſque ſpecie veritatis.* 4 Co. 107. b.

Particular caſes.

Of colleges, chauntries, &c. *where given to the king.*

3. It was reſolved, That colleges or chauntries in reputation, though they wanted ſufficient foundation and incorporation in law, yet were given to the king by the act 1 *E.* 6. for it was the intent of the makers of the act to toll all ſuperſtition out of the minds of men, *&c.* and ſuperſtition was as well maintained in reputative chauntries, as in others; and yet it was not within the letter of the act; for in judgment of law it was not a college or chauntry; for *reputatio eſt vulgaris opinio, ubi non eſt veritas.* 4 Co. 106. b. Dy. 368. a. b.

Where not given to the king.

4. But where there is a college or chauntry only in vulgar reputation, *ſans* any commencement or countenance of lawful foundation, or erected by ſuch means which could not poſſibly be a lawful foundation, there ſuch college or chauntry is not given to the king by this act, *&c.* 4 *Co.* 107. *b.*

427. *Rerum ordo confunditur, ſi unicuique juriſdictio non ſervetur.*

1. AS the body of man, ſays lord *Coke*, is beſt ordered when every particular member exerciſeth its proper duty; ſo it is of the commonwealth, it is beſt governed when every ſeveral court of juſtice executeth its proper juriſdiction, *&c.* If one court ſhould uſurp or incroach upon another, it would introduce incertainty, ſubvert juſtice, and bring all things in the end to confuſion; *rerum ordo confunditur, ſi unicuique juriſdictio non ſervetur.* Proem to 4 Inſt.

2. This kingdom hath been beſt governed in peace, and quiet preſerved, when both temporal and eccleſiaſtical courts and judges have kept themſelves within their proper juriſdictions, without incroaching or uſurping one upon another; and where ſuch incroachments and uſurpations have been made, they have been the ſeeds of great trouble and inconvenience, *&c.* 4 *Inſt.* 321.

3. For

3. *For the dismal effects of church encroachments*, &c. see 1 Ju. Eccl. the course thereof, *&c.* 2 Ju. Eccl. 15, 266, 349. *See also* 1 Ju. Eccl. *tit.* How ecclesiastical courts restrained, *&c.*

428. *Res est misera, ubi jus est vagum.*

BY lord chief justice *Holt*, the house of lords have no jurisdiction over an original cause mixt with matter of fact. 1. Because that the supreme court is the dernier resort; as well as that it is beneath the dignity of so supreme a judicature to try a matter of fact: wherefore error in fact in *C. B.* must, of necessity, be redressed before the judges of this court. 2. If the parliament should take cognizance of original causes, the subject would lose his appeal, *so much indulged by common law in all cases.* Causes come not to parliament till they have tried all other judicatures: for this reason, within these four years, judgment being given against the earl of *M. in Scac'*; he brought error in parliament; and the question was, Whether by 31 *Eliz.* the exchequer-chamber should not interpose? And the writ was abated, and it was held that the exchequer-chamber should interpose. And his lordship said further, no precedent, in the principal case, hath been shewn to warrant the determining inheritances originally *per legem parliamenti.* If it be so determinable, it must be by act of parliament, but there is no such act; or by custom; but there is no such custom; but if inheritances were determinable in parliament, without their having jurisdiction, they would have uncontroulable power; *et res est misera, ubi jus est vagum.* Salk. case *Rex et Regina* versus *Knollys.*

429. *Res inter alios acta alteri nocere non debet.*

1. *RES inter alios acta alteri nocere non debet, et factum unius alteri nocere non debet*, are true rules with this exception, unless an inconvenience should follow; for *lex citius tolerare vult privatum damnum, quam publicum malum*; and an argument *ab inconvenienti* is forcible in law. *Co. Lit.* 152. *b.*

2. Rules, *One may not be prejudiced by the act of a third person. Law will rather suffer a mischief, than an inconvenience. Volenti non fit injuria.*

430. *Res judicata pro veritate habetur.*

1. WHEN a matter hath received the sanction of a judgment or decree on its side, the presumption is, that it is right; for *res judicata pro veritate habetur*; as when our judges or courts of law acknowledged the pope head and grand sovereign from whom all ecclesiastical persons had their power. And *Therning* in particular called him *Apostle*; so that his ecclesiastical acts were allowed lawful; so upon clearing the king's supremacy, when the clouds of ignorance were dispersed, the consequence of his authority was as clearly declared, *&c. Hob.* 147.

2. References, *Co. Lit.* 39. *a.* 236. *b.* 103. *a.* 4 *Co.* 70.

431. *Restrictions of redemptions of mortgages discountenanced in equity.*

1. H. Mortgaged lands, provided that he himself, or the heirs male of his body, might redeem. Yet decreed that the assignee should redeem. *Once a mortgage and always a mortgage.* 1 Vern. case 31. *Vide* case 6.

2. References, 1 *Vern.* 7, 190, *&c.* 214, *&c.* 394, *&c.* 2 *Rep. Chan.* 147.

3. Rules, *Remedies to be reciprocal. Once a mortgage and always a mortgage.*

432. *Rex est caput et salus reipublicae.*

IN some cases a *non compos mentis* may commit high treason; for the king is *caput et salus reipublicae, et a capite bona valetudo transit in omnes*; and therefore the persons of the kings are so sacred, that none may offer them violence, but he is *reus criminis laesae majestatis: et pereat unus ne pereant omnes*; but *non compos mentis* may not commit petit treason. 4 *Co.* 124. *b.*

433. *Rex est mixta persona cum sacerdote.*

REsolved that proxies, being in their original nature duties payable for visitation, were grantable to the king, and he capable of such grants, especially since they have been converted into certain sums of money in the nature of a pension or annuity; for by the antient law of *England* the king hath power to visit, reform and correct all abuses and enormities in the church; and by the statute *H.* 8. the crown was but remitted and restored to its antient jurisdiction which had been usurped by the bishop of *Rome. Reges sacro oleo uncti spiritualis jurisdictionis sunt capaces.* And proxy is a profit of jurisdiction; *rex est mixta persona cum sacerdote*; also he may have tithes by the common law, which is a matter of which no lay person was capable; he may visit his free chapels and hospitals. *Omnes reges dicuntur cleri*; and *causa spiritualis committi potest principi laico.* Da. 4. a.

434. *Rex est monarcha et imperator in regno suo.*

1. *REGES absoluti habent imperium, et dici possunt imperatores; et rex angliae est monarcha et imperator in regno suo. Rex angliae est absolutus monarcha; et absolutum habet imperium. Rex plenitudine potestatis* might create a county palatine with *jura regalia*, which consist of these two things or principal points. 1. Royal jurisdiction. 2. Royal seignory, *&c. Da. le case del countie palatine, &c.* The king is head of the commonwealth immediately under God; and by his taking the crown, all attainders of his person are purged, without any reversal; he cannot be a minor; in him is no imperfection, negligence, laches or folly; he can do no wrong; it is his prerogative to make war and peace; to coin and give

 foreign

foreign coin its value, by his royal proclamation without parliament; he is the fountain of honour; all jurisdiction is from him; he is supreme ordinary, supreme patron, head of the church, and his prelates but his ministers; he is guardian of ideots, *&c.* he has all mines of gold and silver; he calls, continues and dissolves parliaments; he is supposed present in all his courts; all lands are holden of him; all franchizes are derived from him; all escheats and forfeitures of all lands and franchizes belong to him; also all deodands, treasure trove of gold and silver, estrays, waifs, and goods and chattels of all felons and fugitives; he hath also all royal fish, white swans not marked which have gained their natural liberty; he is not to be supposed ignorant or misconusant of the law; he is not bound by acts of parliament, unless either expresly named, or the cause of religion, charity or the public good be concerned; in a word he hath a prerogative in all things that are not injurious to the subject; yet this plenitude of power comes all from the law; for,

2. The law is to the king, as the king is to the law; *lex regi quod rex legi.* As the king upholdeth and maintaineth the laws, privileges and rights of the land, so the law keepeth men in subjection and obedience to the king, and thereby giveth glory and safety to the king, with peace and dignity to the kingdom. *Mason's Reasons Monarch. 8vo. p.* 126.

3. *Bract.* also, *Rex sub nullo nisi tantum sub deo et lege.* Acts of justice the king may not, nay he cannot put off, as says lord *Hobart*, *Cessa regnare, si non vis judicare.* The king is never supposed in law to be ill affected, but abused and deceived; for *eadem praesumitur mens regis, quae est juris, &c.* Hob. 155.

4. *Rex quod injustum est facere non potest.* Jenk. 325, margin. Co. Lit. 19. a. Doct. & Stud. lib. 1. cap. 8. for he governs by law. *Co. Lit.* 232.

5. *Rex non potest fallere, nec falli.* Jenk. 48. 4 Co. *Bozoun*'s case. 12 Co. 3. Co. Lit. 98. b. 99. a.

6. *He can do no wrong*; for he is the fountain of justice and common right, and God's vicegerent. 11 *Co.* 72. *a. Bracton* hath it, *Nihil aliud potest rex in terris, cum sit dei minister et vicarius, quam quod de jure potest; et paulo post: itaque potestas juris sua est, non injuriae; et (observe bien) cum sit autor juris, non debet inde injuriarum nasci occasio, unde jura nascuntur.* 11 Co. 74. a. For *law is the perfection of reason, a ray of the divine mind, and cannot be the author of wrong,* &c.

435. *Rex est persona mixta, medicus regni, pater patriae, et sponsus regni.*

1. References, 11 *Co. Magdalen College's case. Da.* 4. *a. Ha. Hist. Law.*

2. Rules, *Omnes reges dicuntur clerici. Rex est mixta persona cum sacerdote. Summa est ratio, quae pro religione facit. Charitas est facere justitiam. Rex est monarcha et imperator in regno suo.*

436. *Rex non debet judicare sed secundum legem.*

THE king submits himself to the law; for *Bracton* saith, *quod non debet judicare sed secundum legem*; and his prerogative is so excellent, that he cannot take a part with any thing, but by matter of record, neither can he draw the right or possession of any one in question upon a bare surmise, but by office or other matter of record; for *a record always carries credit with it.* Poph. 26.

437. *Rex non debet esse sub homine, sed sub deo et lege.*

1. REferences, 12 *Co.* 65. *Bract.* 7.

2. Rules, *Rex est monarcha, &c. Rex est mixta persona, &c.*

438. *Rex non potest fallere, nec falli.*

General.

1. HE is not to be supposed misconusant of the law. *Co. Lit.* 99. *a.*

Particular cases.

2. And therefore when he licenceth expresly to alien to an abbot, *&c.* which is in *Mortmain*, he need not make any *non obstante* of the statute of *Mortmain*; for it is apparent to be granted in *Mortmain*, and the king is the head of the law; and therefore *praesumitur rex habere omnia jura in scrinio pectoris sui*, for the maintenance of his grant to be good according to the law, *&c.* *Co. Lit.* 99. *a.*

3. Though the queen's grant was *ex gratia speciali, certa scientia, et mero motu*; yet this shall not extend the queen's grant against her intention and meaning expressed therein; nor by any strained construction make any thing to pass against the apt and proper signification, or the main, common and usual sense of the words of her grant. 4 *Co.* 35.

4. Though the king or ordinary may suffer a church in lapse to stand void (which yet is *culpa*) however they cannot bind themselves that they will not fill the church; for that were *injuria et malum in se*; and therefore shall be judged in law, as deceit of the king; for *eadem mens praesumitur regis, quae est juris, &c.* Hob. 154.

5. References, 3 *Co.* 1. 4 *Co. Bozoun*'s case. 12 *Co.* 3 *Co. Lit.* 98. *b.* 99. *a.* *Jenk.* 48.

6. Rules, *King can do no wrong. Neither grant, take,* &c. *but by matter of record. Is the fountain of justice. May not be supposed ignorant of the law. Rex est monarcha, &c. Non debet judicare sed secundum legem. And the next rule.*

439. *Rex quod injuſtum facere non poteſt.*

General.

1. THE king can do no wrong by his prerogative. 13 *E.* 4. 8.

2. The king may diſſeiſe no man, nor no man him, nor pull any reverſion or remainder out of him. *Doct. & Stud. lib.* 1. *cap.* 8.

Particular caſes.

To the king's grant.

3. The king's grants are to be conſtrued beneficially for his honour and relief of the ſubject, and not ſtrictly to the ſubverſion of ſuch grants.

To bar others.

4. Before the ſtatute *de donis*, if lands had been given to the king and to the heirs of his body, he could not, before iſſue had, have aliened in fee, but only to have barred his iſſue, as any common perſon might have done, but not to have barred the reverſion; for that ſhould have been a wrong in the caſe of a ſubject, and the king's prerogative cannot alter his caſe, nor make it greater than the donor gave unto him: and it is a maxim in law, *that the king can do no wrong.* Co. Lit. 19. b.

In matters of truſt, &c.

As preſentation by lapſe, &c.

5. A lapſe is an act and office of truſt repoſed by law in the ordinary, metropolitan, and laſtly in the king, who is *certum et ſtabilimentum juſtitiae*; the end of which truſt is to provide the church of a rector in default of the patron; and yet as for him and to his behoof; and therefore as he cannot transfer his truſt to another, ſo cannot he deveſt the thing wherewith he is truſted to any other purpoſe; and therefore, as hath been ſaid, though the king or biſhop may ſuffer the church to ſtand void, yet they may not bind themſelves not to fill it, as that were *injuria et malum in ſe*, and therefore to be adjudged in deceit of the king; for *eadem mens praeſumitur regis, &c.* and if the ordinary, metropolitan or king himſelf, have not collated or preſented by lapſe, the patron may preſent, and the king or metropolitan can no where preſent but where the ordinary might; and even where lapſe accrues to him or to any other to preſent by lapſe, he is but as it were *negotiorum geſtor*, or a kind of attorney, made by law, to do that for the patron, which it is ſuppoſed he would do himſelf, if there were not ſome let; and therefore the collation by lapſe, is in right of the patron, and for his turn, and he ſhall lay it as his poſſeſſion in an aſſiſe of *darreign preſentment, &c.* Hob. 154.

6. Rules, *King can do no wrong. Rex eſt mixta perſona, &c. Non poteſt judicare, &c. Fallere nec falli.*

I 440. Rights

440. *Rights never die.*

What, and general to.

1. DE *recto, rectum*, is a proper and significant word for the right which any hath; and wrong or injury is in *French* aptly called *Tort* becaufe it is wrefted or crooked, being contrary to right and ftreight, *&c. Co. Lit.* 158. *a.*

2. *Jus*, or right, in general fignification, includeth not only a right for which a writ of right lieth, but alfo any title or claim, for which no action is given by law, but only an entry. *Co. Lit.* 265. *a.* 345. *a. b.*

Yet may merge.

3. Eftates in lands are properly merged or confounded when the leffer eftate meets with the greater in the fame perfon, and in the fame right; as *terminus et feodum non poffunt conftare fimul in unâ eademque perfonâ.* Da. 4. b. 5. a.

To the writs of right.

Wherefore fo called, the forts and nature, &c.

4. *Brief de droit, breve de recto*, are of two forts. 1. A writ of right mentioned by *Lit. fect.* 234. which is the higheft of all other real writs whatfoever, and hath the greateft refpect, *&c.* and the moft affured and final judgment; and therefore it is called a writ of *right right*, and in the old books *droit droit*, and this writ *eft darrein remedie de touts recoveries enter touts orders des pleas*, and the jury in this writ is called *magna affifa*, or *magna jurata.* 2. Writs of right in their nature, as the *rationabili parte*, and *ne injufte vexes.* Co. Lit. 158. b.

Never die.

General.

5. *Un droit ne poit pas morier; dormit aliquando jus, moritur nunquam*; for of fuch an high eftimation is right in the eye of the law, as that it preferveth it from death and deftruction; trodden down it may be, but never trodden out; for where it hath been faid, that a releafe of right doth in fome cafes enure by way of extinguifhment, it is to be underftood either as *Littleton* doth *fect.* 478. in refpect of him who makes the releafe, or in refpect that by conftruction of law, it enureth not only to him to whom it is made, but to others alfo who are ftrangers to the releafe. *Co. Lit.* 279. *Da.* 4. *b.* 5. *a.*

Particular.

6. As if there be lord and tenant, and the tenant make a leafe for life, the remainder in fee, if the lord releafe to the tenant for life, the rent is wholly extinguifhed, and he in remainder fhall take benefit thereof; even fo when the heir of the diffeifor is diffeifed, and the diffeifor makes a leafe for life, the remainder in fee, if the firft diffeifee releafe to the tenant for life, this is faid to enure by way of extinguifhment; for that it fhall enure to him in the remainder who is a ftranger to the releafe, and yet in truth the right is not extinct, but doth follow the poffeffion, *viz.* the tenant for life

life hath it during his time, and he in remainder to him and his heirs, and the right of inheritance is in him in remainder; for *a right to land cannot die, or be extinct in deed*; and therefore, if after the death of the tenant for life, the heir of the disseisor bring a writ of right against him in the remainder, and he join the mise upon the meer right, it shall be found for him; because in judgment of law he hath, by the said release, the right of the first disseisee. *Co. Lit.* 279. *b.* *Da.* 4. *b.* 5. *a.*

441. *Rights or titles to lands or tenements of inheritance or freehold, may not be barred by collateral satisfaction, but by release or confirmation, or other act which tantamounts.*

Rule.

1. THE rule of the common law is, that a right or title, which any one hath to any lands or tenements of any estate of inheritance or freehold, may not be barred by the acceptance of any sort of collateral satisfaction or recompence. 4 *Co,* 1. *a.*

Particular cases.

2. As if *A.* disseise *B.* tenant for life, or in fee, of the manor of *Dale*, and after give him the manor of *Sale*, to him and his heirs, in full satisfaction of all his rights, and actions that he hath in or on account of the said manor of *Dale*, which *B.* accepts; yet he may enter into the manor of *Dale*, or recover the same in any real action; *for a right or title of freehold, or inheritance, may not be barred by any collateral satisfaction, but by release or by confirmation, or other act which tantamounts*; and therefore it is commonly said in our books, *That accord with satisfaction is a good plea in personal actions, where damages are only to be recovered; but not in actions real.* And this was the reason that no collateral satisfaction or recompence made a woman in satisfaction of her dower, was any bar thereto at law. 4 *Co.* 1. *b.*

3. So if a man in consideration of marriage after to be had with *A.* made an estate of certain lands to her for life, in full satisfaction of all dower, which after marriage might accrew to her in any of his lands, and after they intermarried, yet this was no bar at law to dower, for two reasons. 1. Because she had no title at the time, but it accrewed afterwards. 2. Because no collateral satisfaction might bar a right or title to an inheritance or freehold, but now the law is altered by the *Stat.* 27 *H.* 8. to which the clause concerning jointures was added. 4 *Co.* 1. *b.* 2. *a.*

4. Covenant for not repairing from such a time to such a time. The defendant pleaded an agreement, that the plaintiff should retain 5 *l.* he owed the defendant for satisfaction of the said want of repairs. The plaintiff demured. Objection, A parol agreement or accord is pleaded in discharge of a matter by deed. *Cur':* good; because only for a matter executory, and it is but a temporary bar, and not a perpetual bar of the covenant. *Noy* 110. 6 *Co.* 43.

5. References, 3 *Co.* 64. *b.* *Perk.* 407. 13 *H.* 7. 13, 20. *Stat.* 27 *H.* 8. 6 *Co.* 43. 9 *Co.* 79, 47. *Cro. Ja.* 99.

442. *Right where double, it ſhall be preſumed he took in that right which was moſt favourable, or beneficial to him.*

1. IF land, and rent out of the ſame land, come to the ſame perſon of like eſtate, and like ſurety of title, the rent is extinct. *Dr. & Stud. Lib.* 1. *c.* 9.

2. Alſo if lands deſcend to him who hath right to the ſame lands before, he ſhall be remitted to his better right. *Dr. & Stud. Lib.* 1. *c.* 9.

3. Alſo if two titles be concurrent together, the eldeſt ſhall be preferred. *Dr. & Stud. Lib.* 1. *c.* 9.

4. Diſſeiſſor leaſeth the lands to the diſſeiſſee for years, or at will, who enters; the law ſaith, he is in of his antient and better eſtate. *Lit.*

5. References, *Co. Lit.* 278. *b.* 279. *a.* 283. *Bac. Uſe of the law* 71.

443. *Rogationes, quaeſtiones, et poſitiones debent eſſe ſimplices.*

MUltiplex indiſtinctum parit confuſionem, et rogationes, quaeſtiones, et poſitiones debent eſſe ſimplices. Hob. 143.

444. *Sale of lands directed, and none ordered to ſell, he muſt do it who had the eſtate.*

1. IF one will that his lands ſhall be ſold, and ſhew not by whom, his executors ſhall ſell; for they have the greateſt confidence put in them; having the diſpoſition of the money for which it is ſold. *Elſ. Obſ.* 93.

2. One having feoffees upon truſt, wills that his executors ſhould ſell his lands, and dies, if that executor makes an executor, the executor of the executor cannot ſell; becauſe the firſt executor had that power, as an authority ſeveral from his executorſhip: and though the firſt had refuſed to act, yet he might have ſold the land. And if he had willed that the chief juſtice ſhould ſell his land, though he reſigned his office, and another chief juſtice was placed therein, yet the firſt ſhould ſell the land; and if the will were that *J. S.* ſhould ſell the land, if he die his heir cannot ſell it, becauſe the truſt is determined. *Elſ. Obſ.* 95.

3. References, 5 *H.* 7. 12. *b. per Hyde, Fenwick* and *Finneux.* 1 *Lev.* 304. *Nelſ.* 416. *Prec. Chan.* 185. 1 *Chan. Ca.* 177, 178, 179, 180, 211, 262. *Nelſ.* 167, 170, 262. *Prec. Chan.* 123. *Dy.* 371. *Co. Lit.* 112. *b. &c.* *Dy.* 271. *Hard.* 204.

4. Rule, *Intention being clear, all means, without which that cannot be attained, muſt be ſupplied by a court of juſtice.*

445. *Salus*

445. *Salus populi eſt ſuprema lex.*

General.

1. A Cuſtom may be prejudicial to a particular intereſt, and yet be reaſonable, where it is for the good of the commonwealth in general. *Da.* 32, 33. *Dy.* 36, 60. 8 *E.* 4. 18. 21 *E.* 4. 28.

Particular caſes.

2. As a cuſtom to make bulwarks upon another's land, for the defence of the realm. *Dy.* 60.

3. And to raſe houſes *in publico incendio.* Dy. 36.

4. So of turning the plough upon the head-land of another, in favour of huſbandry, or to dry nets upon the lands of another, in favour of fiſhing, and maintenance of navigation. 8 *E.* 4. 18. 21 *E.* 4. 28.

5. But a cuſtom which is contrary to the public good, *which is the ſcope and general end of all laws,* (*Salus populi ſuprema lex,*) or injurious and prejudicial to the multitude, and advantageous only to a particular perſon, is contrary to the *law of reaſon, which is the moſt poſitive of all laws*; and therefore could not have a reaſonable or lawful beginning, but was void *ab initio*, and no preſcription of time could make it good; and therefore many cuſtoms, which have been adjudged void in our books, as being unreaſonable, againſt common right, or meerly againſt law, if their nature and quality are conſidered, will be found injurious to the multitude, and prejudicial to the commonwealth, and to have their beginning, for the moſt part, by oppreſſion and extortion *des ſeigniors et grand homes.* All cuſtoms ought to be certain; for *incerta pro nullis habentur*; and *conſuetudo ex certa cauſa rationabili uſitata privat communem legem.* The three eſſential qualities of a good cuſtom are, 1. Certainty. 2. Reaſonableneſs, and 3. Uſage or Continuance. *Da.* 32. *b.* 33. *a.*

6. Reference, *Jenk.* 166.

7. Rule, *Law will rather ſuffer a miſchief than an inconvenience.*

446. *Semper praeſumitur pro legitimatione puerorum.*

A Man leaveth his wife *enſient* with child; iſſue ſhall not be taken that ſhe was not *enſient* by her huſband on the day of his death; for *filiatio non poteſt probari*, but the iſſue muſt be, whether ſhe was *enſient* the day of his death. *Co. Lit.* 126. *a.*

447. *Senſus verborum ex cauſa dicendi accipiendus eſt.*

Rules.

1. *SEnſus verborum eſt duplex, ſcil. mitis et aſper, et verba ſemper accipienda ſunt in mitiori ſenſu.* 4 Co. 13. a. 17. b.

2. *Sermo relatus ad perſonam intelligi debet de conditione perſonae.* 4 Co. 16. a.

3. Actions for words not to be countenanced. 4 *Co.* 18. *a.*

4. In caſe of ſlander for words, the ſenſe of the words is to be taken: and that appears from the cauſe and occaſion of ſpeaking of them; for

ſenſus verborum ex cauſa dicendi accipiendus eſt; et ſermones ſemper accipiendi ſunt ſecundum ſubjectam materiam. 4 Co. 13. b. 14. a.

5. When the words cannot poſſibly be true, they cannot be actionable. 4 *Co.* 16. *a.*

6. Words tending to a man's diſinheriſon are actionable, unleſs he claims himſelf as heir, *&c.* 4 *Co.* 17. *a.*

7. So of ſlandering one's title.

8. References, 1 *Ro. Ab.* 37. (45.) 38. (5. 10.) *Hut.* 104. 4 *Co.* 105. *Cro. Ca.* 192, 436, 437, 480, 469. *Cro. Jac.* 240, 241, 473, 514, 642, 674. *Jo.* 395.

9. Rules, *Verba ſemper accipienda ſunt in mitiori ſenſu. Sermones ſemper accipiendi ſunt ſecundum ſubjectam materiam, et conditionem perſonarum of whom they are ſpoken.*

448. *Sermones ſemper accipiendi ſunt ſecundum ſubjectam materiam, et conditionem perſonarum of whom they are ſpoken.*

RULES, *Senſus verborum ex cauſa dicendi accipiendus eſt. Verba ſemper accipienda ſunt in mitiori ſenſu.*

449. *Sicut ad quaeſtionem facti non reſpondent judices, ita ad quaeſtionem juris non reſpondent juratores.*

General.

1. MAtter in law ſhall not be put in iſſue to be tried *per pais*; for the rule is, *quod quiſquis norit, in hoc ſe exerceat*, and therefore *ſicut ad quaeſtionem facti non reſpondent judices, &c.* and if the jurors take upon them the knowledge of the law, and will find the ſpecial matter, and miſtake the law, the judges of the law ſhall give judgment upon the ſpecial matter, according to the law, without any regard to the concluſion of the jurors, who ought not to take upon them the judgment of law. 11 *Co.* 10. *b.*

Particular.

To the judges.

2. The judges and ſages of the law, for their authority, wiſdom, learning, experience, *&c.* are to be honoured, reverenced and believed. *Lord Coke's Epiſtle to the Reader, 4th Report.*

3. Judges in *England* are expoſitors of the *Iriſh* law. 1 *Vern.* 405, 406.

Of what bound to take notice.

4. As they are to obſerve the rules above, under rule *ſenſus verborum, &c.* ſo they are alſo to pay a regard to, and take notice of the ſenſe of the words in the places, where, *&c. Pal.* 102. And alſo they are to take notice of the king's title; for the court and judges are of the king's council, but then his title muſt be inconteſtably clear againſt both plaintiff and defendant. *Hob.* 163, 164.

To the jury.

Who exempted from.

5. References, 28 *E.* 1. 9. 13 *E.* 1. 38. *Co. Lit.* 156, 157, 158, 172. *Hard.* 389.

6. Rules, *Clerici non ponantur in officio.*

What crimes disable one to be a juror.

7. References, *Stat. W.* 2. *cap.* 38. *Art. super Chart.* 9. *Co. Lit.* 6. *a. b.* 158. *a. b. Tri. per Pais.*

Who may be jurors, and who not, and their properties.

8. Reference, *Co. Lit.* 155, 156, 157, 172.

Of what they are to determine.

The fact.

9. See before *General.*

10. General References, *Co. Lit.* 125. 9 *Co.* 13. *a.* 12 *Co.* 67. *Plow. Com.* 230. *Tri. per Pais.*

11. Rule, *Quod quisquis norit, in hoc se exerceat.*

450. *Simplicitas est legibus amica, et nimia subtilitas in jure reprobatur.*

General.

1. EVERY estoppel ought to be reciprocal, certain, and a precise affirmation of that which maketh the estoppel, and not to be spoken impersonally. *Co. Lit.* 352. *b.*

Rules.

2. As if it be said, *ut dicitur*; *quia impersonalitas non concludit, nec ligat*; *impersonalis dicitur, quia sine persona*; neither doth a recital conclude, because it is no direct affirmation. *Co. Lit.* 352. *Vide* 103.

3. Rules, *Equity will not aid new inventions*, &c. *Law favours justice*, &c. *Prefers the public good*, &c. *Requireth order and decency*, &c. *Will rather endure a particular mischief*, &c. *Will rather suffer things against the principles of law*, &c. *Will not suffer wrong. Will admit no proof against what the law presumeth. Hath always suppressed new and subtile inventions in derogation of the common law.*

451. *Si mulier nobilis nupserit ignobili, desinit esse nobilis.*

1. THERE is a difference between a woman who is noble by descent, and one only noble by marriage; for if a woman, who is noble by descent, marry one under the degree of nobility, yet she remaineth noble still; but if she only gained it by marriage, she loseth it if she marry under the degree of nobility, and so is the rule, *si mulier nobilis, &c.*

to be underſtood. But if a ducheſs by marriage, marrieth a baron of the realm, ſhe remaineth a ducheſs, and loſeth not her name, becauſe her huſband is noble; *et ſic de caeteris.* Co. Lit.

2. References, 2 *H.* 6. 11. 14 *H.* 6. 18. 22 *H.* 6. 52. *Bro. Abr.* 6 *Co.* 53. 4 *Co.* 118.

452. *Solum rex hoc non poteſt facere, quod non poteſt injuſte agere.*

1. REferences, *Co. Lit.* 19. *b.* 1 *Co.* 44. 6 *Co.* 55.
2. Rule, *The king can do no wrong.*

453. *Solus deus haeredem facere poteſt, non homo.*

1. *HAeres*, in the legal underſtanding of the common law, implieth that he is *ex juſtis nuptiis*; for *haeres legitimus eſt, quem nuptiae demonſtrant*, and is he to whom lands, tenements or hereditaments, by the act of God, and right of blood do deſcend, of ſome eſtate of inheritance; for *ſolus deus haeredem facere poteſt, non homo. Dicuntur autem haereditas et haeres ab haerendo, quod eſt arcte inſidendo; nam qui haeres eſt, haeret, vel dicitur ab haerendo quia haereditas ſibi haeret; licet nonnulli haeredem dictum velint quod haeres fuit, hoc eſt dominus terrarum, &c. quae ad eum perveniunt.* A monſter, &c. may not be an heir. *Co. Lit.* 7. *b.* 8. *a.*

2. References, *Co. Lit.* 22. *b.* 237. *Prec. Chan.* 3. *Gilb.* 129.

454. *Spiritual office draws with it a right to have the poſſeſſions belonging to the office.*

SEE rule, *Qui ſentit onus ſentire debet et commodum.*

455. *Stabit praeſumptio donec probetur in contrarium.*

Preſumptions of law favoured.

General.

1. PReſcription and antiquity of time fortifieth all eſtates, and ſuppoſeth the beſt beginning the law can give them. *Hob.* 297.

2. There are preſumptions of law ſo violent, as though they are falſe, a man ſhall not be received to aver againſt them. *Hob.* 297.

3. A law grounded on preſumption, if the preſumption be untrue, it is not to be holden in conſcience; for *ſtabitur praeſumptio donec probetur in contrarium.* 1 Chan. Ca. 201.

The ſorts.

4. There are three ſorts of preſumptions. 1. Violent. 2. Probable, and 3. Light, &c. *Co. Lit.* 6. *b.*

Parti-

Particular cases.

5. A deed is inrolled in such a term; it shall be intended in law, that the deed was inrolled the first day of the term; for the term, as to many purposes, is but one day in law. Yet as the plaintiff had, in the particular case, by his demurrer confessed the inrolment to be after; the presumption is vanished and became of no force; for *stabit praesumptio donec probetur in contrarium.* 4 Co. 71.

6. True it is, that *records import in themselves verity*, and conclude all people to deny any thing apparent in the record, *&c. Vide* 37 *H.* 6. *fo.* 21. *b. Plow. Com.* 7. *Dy.* 242. But an averment which stands with the record, and which does not impeach any thing within the record, the law allows, as against a fine upon a release, to say that the cognizee had nothing at the time of the fine levied. So against letters patent of the king under the great seal shewed in court, regularly none may deny them, but *non concessit per praedictas literas patentes* is a good plea; and so in the case next foregoing, though the inrolment, or other matter of record, shall not be tried *per pais*; for that the inrolment might not be brought in question, yet the time of it may, *&c.* 4 *Co.* 71. *b.*

7. So if profession be denied, it shall be tried by the court christian, but if the time of the profession be in issue it shall be tried *per pais*, as is held 9 *H.* 7. 2. 4 *Co.* 71.

8. In a *praecipe* the tenant pleaded himself villain to *T. S.* and that he hath nothing but his villainage; the demandant had no reply, though it were false, but his writ must needs abate, till *Stat.* 37 *E.* 3. admitted the counter-plea. *Mansel*'s case. See *Hob.* 297.

9. So in replevin, if upon an avowry the tenant disclaims, he shall have judgment, though it be false; for the law believes the parties will not do themselves wrong in so high a degree. *Hob.* 297.

10. So the law presumeth violently, that a layman cannot be absolutely discharged of tithes; and therefore it will not allow a prescription of such discharge; (*but this* in favorem ecclesiae, *least laymen should spoil the church*) holding it more reasonable, that some one man should suffer a mischief to lose such a privilege, being so improbable, and of so dangerous consequence, than, for his particular, to admit a spoil of the church and a decay of religion, according to the rule, *Omne magnum exemplum aliquid habet ex iniquo, quod publica utilitate compensatur.* So though you shall be allowed your discharge, when it appeareth; yet when it appeareth not, *stabitur praesumptioni, donec probetur in contrarium.* Hob. 297.

11. References, *Co. Lit.* 74. 2 *Co.* 48. *a. Hob.* 44. *Palm.* 118, 119. *Cro. Jac.* 57, 58. *Cro. Eliz.* 578, 579.

12. Rules, *All the term in law but one day. Law will admit no proof against that which the law presumeth. Nullum iniquum est in jure praesumendum. Omnia praesumuntur solemniter esse acta.*

456. *Statutes made againſt fraud, are to be conſtrued liberally, and expounded beneficially to ſuppreſs fraud, &c.*

RULES, *Dona clandeſtina ſunt ſemper ſuſpicioſa. Rex eſt mixta perſona cum ſacerdote.*

457. *Statutes penal to be conſtrued ſtrictly.*

RULES, *Ad ea quae frequentius accidunt jura adaptantur. Rex eſt mixta perſona cum ſacerdote.*

458. *Statutes, the preamble of is to be taken for truth; and it cannot be ſuppoſed that ſtatutes made by authority of the whole realm will recite a thing againſt truth.*

1. IT cannot be thought that ſtatutes made by authority of the whole realm, king, lords and commons, will recite a thing againſt the truth. *Doct. & Stud. lib.* 2. *cap.* 55. *fo.* 165. *b.*

2. The rehearſal or preamble of a ſtatute is to be taken for truth; for it cannot be thought, that a ſtatute made by the authority of the whole realm, as well of the king, as of the lords ſpiritual and temporal, and of all the commons, will recite a thing againſt the truth. *Co. Lit.* 19. *b.*

459. *Statutes to be conſtrued according to natural equity.*

RULES, *Aequum et bonum eſt lex legum. Dona clandeſtina ſunt ſemper ſuſpicioſa.* Ca. 1.

460. *Statutes to be conſtrued in equity.*

1. *Affirmatives in ſtatutes that introduce new laws do imply a negative of all that is not in the purview.* Hob. 298.

2. *A court of equity is not to alter the law.* Statutes are binding in equity as well as at law, and if a judgment be good at law by a ſtatute it cannot be ſet aſide in equity. 2 *Vern.* 697.

3. References, 1 *Chan. Ca.* 71, 72. *Fi. Ley* 6. *b.* 15. *a.* *Co. Lit.* 382. 4 *Co.* 22.

4. Rules, *Equity proper interpreter of ſtatutes. Conſtructions to be ſecundum aequalitatem rationis.*

461. *Statutes are to be construed that the innocent may not be damnified.*

1. REference, *Co. Lit.* 11. *b.* 381, 24, 79, 290, 365, 280, 336, 42, 183.

2. Rule, *Constructions to be according to equity.*

462. *Summa charitas est facere justitiam singulis, et omni tempore quando necesse fuerit.*

General.

1. THE law will never presume that any one will do a thing either against religion or any religious duty. 11 *Co.* 70. *b.*

Particular.

2. So a parson shall be intended by the law resident upon his benefice for the cure of the souls he hath there; for a parson with cure of souls, who is non-resident, *non est dispensator sed dissipator, non speculator, sed spiculator.* 11 Co. 70. b.

3. So in the case at bar, the law will never make constructions against the support of religion, advancement of learning, and maintenance of the poor, *&c.* 11 *Co.* 70. *b. Vue tout le case.*

4. Rules, *Rex est mixta persona cum sacerdote. It is the office of temporal judges to advance laws made for religion according to their end, though the words be short and imperfect.*

463. *Summa ratio est quae pro religione facit.*

1. THE statute 1 *Eliz.* proves that acts, which restrain ecclesiastical persons from wasting their possessions, which were given to maintain the service of God, bind the king, unless special provision be made to the contrary by the same act. *Et summa ratio est quae pro religione facit.* 5 Co. 14 b.

2. References, 11 *Co.* 70. *Hob.* 295. *Jenk.* 162, 166, 233. 2 *Ch. Ca.* 18. *Salk.* 294. *The Bishop of St. David*'s case.

3. Rules, *Favendum est ecclesiae, quam personae. Rex est mixta persona cum sacerdote. It is the office of the judges to advance laws,* &c.

464. *Summum jus summa est injuria.*

1. *LAWS are compared to grapes, which being too much pressed yield an hard and unwholesome wine.* Ira viri non operatur justitiam dei.

2. According to *Aristotle*, strict or precise law, or *summum jus*, is so called, because that if it have no allay in it to qualify the harshness and severity of it, it is unpleasant and sower in taste, and repugnant in equity. And *Budaeus* saith, that amongst the civilians it is the same as a very hard law, exact and full of rigour, and almost unjust; and this strict or precise

law is ſet by thoſe who write of law oppoſite to equity; and this law, by ſome lawyers, is termed alſo *ſubtile jus*, a ſubtil law, by others *ſummum jus*, or law in the higheſt degree, or moſt exact; and it is ſo to be taken when men regard more the letter than the law itſelf. *Oldendorpius* divideth this *ſummum-jus* into proper and improper. 1. Proper is an undoubted and infallible rule of honeſty, which may generally, without exception, be put in execution in any commonwealth, whether originally grounded upon the law of nature or upon the law of nations: but here is no reſpect had to any circumſtances, but that belongeth to equity, or the court of conſcience. Now becauſe preciſe law, as it is a fixt rule, and cannot conſider circumſtances, is, though very wrongfully, called wrong in the higheſt degree, *ſummum jus ſumma eſt injuria*; yet it is the juſteſt reaſon that may be, nay it is the perfection of reaſon, and hath no fault in itſelf, but the error is in the minds of men prone to evil, and not judging aright of the circumſtances of the fact, wherein law and right ſtandeth. 2. Improper, when by an over rigorous and hard interpretation it is drawn to inconvenient kind of facts, or by colour is forced to fruſtrate the good meaning of the law. 2 *Weſt's Prec.* 173. *b.* 174. *a. b.*

3. *Summum jus* often regardeth the very words and letter of the common law, for remedy whereof the parties grieved pray aid of chancery to bridle the extremity, and reduce ſuch rigour to equity and conſcience. 2 *Weſt's Prec.* 173. *b.* *Hob.* 145.

465. *Simony odious in law.*

1. THE law abhors ſimony, ſo that before the ſtatute *W.* 2. *cap.* 5. the plaintiff in a *quare impedit* recovered no damages for the loſs of his preſentation; and this is the reaſon that guardian in ſocage ſhall not preſent; becauſe he can take nothing for it, and ſo cannot account for it; and by the law he can meddle with nothing he cannot account for. *Co. Lit.* 18. *a.* 344. *b.* 6 *Co.* 51. *a. b.* 52. *b.*

2. If an incumbent were guilty of ſimony in obtaining a benefice, he was made incapable of that benefice for ever, by the words of the ſtatute 31 *Eliz.* which are largely to be expounded. *Hob.* 75.

3. And ſuch incumbent as cometh in by reaſon of any corrupt agreement, is ſo abſolutely diſabled for ever to be preſented to that church, that the king cannot by lapſe preſent him thereunto. *Co. Lit.* 20. *a.* *Plow. Com.* 502.

4. If pariſhioners pay tithes to him who came in by ſimony, it is at their peril. *Hob.* 168.

5. Statutes of ſimony extend not only to benefices with cure, but alſo to dignities, prebends and all other eccleſiaſtical livings. *Co. Lit.* 120.

6. References, 4 *Co.* 49. 3 *Inſt.* 204. *Salk.* 294. *Watſon, Biſhop of St. David's* caſe. See *Can.* 40. *Salk.* 322. 5 *Co.* *De Ju. Regis Eccl.* 9. *a.* *Co. Lit.* 344. *b.* *Hob.* 75. *Co. Lit.* 120. *Plow. Com.* 502. *Hob.* 165, *&c.* 6 *Co.* 51, 52. 2 *Vent.* 39, 213.

466. *Talis interpretatio ſemper fienda eſt, ut evitetur abſurdum et inconveniens, et ne judicium ſit illuſorium.*

1. REferences, 1 *Co.* 14. *Sir William Pelham*'s caſe. *Mo.* 423. 2 *Leon.* 60. *Co. Lit.* 362. *a.* 18 *E.* 3. 4. 16. 4 *Co.* 48. *Andrew Ognel*'s caſe.

2. Rules, *Conſtructio legis non facit injuriam. Law favours juſtice,* &c. *Is the perfection of reaſon. Requireth order and decency,* &c. *Will not ſuffer wrong.*

467. *Talis non eſt eadem; for nullum ſimile eſt idem.*

TALIS indentura, qualis as in the count is alledged, is no direct anſwer to the indenture mentioned in the declaration; for *talis indentura non eſt eadem indentura*; for *nullum ſimile eſt idem.* 4 Co. 18. b.

468. *Tempus eſt edax rerum.*

1. IN the caſe of a charter of feoffment, if all the witneſſes to the deed be dead, as no man can keep his witneſſes alive, and time weareth out all men, then violent preſumption, which ſtands for a proof, is continual and quiet poſſeſſion; for *ex diuturnitate temporis omnia praeſumuntur ſolemniter eſſe acta.* Co. Lit. 6. b.

2. References, 12 *Co.* 4, 5. *Palm.* 426, 427. *Hard.* 382. 1 *Mod.* 117.

3. Rule, *Omnia praeſumuntur ſolemnitur eſſe acta.* Ca. 8.

469. *Term for years regularly cannot be intailed, though it may be made to wait upon an inheritance that is intailed.*

General to, and rules.

1. THO' a term cannot be intailed, yet it may wait on an inheritance which is intailed, and when it is thus limited, it is not properly an intail within the ſtatute *de donis*, but governable partly by equity, and partly by law. 3 *Chan. Ca.* 3, 4, 5, 7, *&c.* 23.

2. And the truſt of a term to attend the inheritance muſt be to the ſame uſes with the inheritance. 3 *Chan. Ca.* 4, 10, 11, 23, 24.

3. And ſuch a truſt is but a creature of equity, and may be barred *ſans* fine or recovery. 3 *Chan. Ca.* 3. 6.

4. Yet where a term attends on the inheritance, it may be barred by recovery. 3 *Chan. Ca.* 16.

5. Rule, *Perpetuities odious in law and equity.*

470. *Terminus et feodum non possunt constare simul in unâ eademque personâ.*

What merger is.

1. ESTATES in lands are properly merged when the lesser estate meets with the greater in the same person, and right; as *terminus et feodum non possunt constare simul, &c.* for a term is finite, and a fee-simple infinite; and the finite, of necessity, must be swallowed and lost in the infinite; but this is confounding and not extinguishing. *Da.* 4. *b.*

Particular cases.

2. For if the particular tenant grant or surrender his estate to him in reversion, the particular estate is not extinct, though it be merged; for if the particular tenant had charged the land with a rent, or other incumbrance, the estate remains in *esse* as to that. *Dav.* 4. *b.*

3. And true it is, that estates in land, and right to lands, are things of the substance, that they cannot be extinct, or *interire penitus*, and so it is that *Littleton* saith, that if the Disseissee, when his entry is tolled, release to the tertenant, all his right, that it shall enure by way of extinguishment, for the right which he had passed to the tenant by his release: and it should be inconvenient that such antient right should be utterly extinct; for *rights never die.* *Da.* 4. *b.* 5. *a.*

4. Yet things that are issuing out of lands, as a seigniory, rent-charge, *&c.* are liable to extinguishment to all intents. *Plow. Com.* 419 *a.* *Lit.* 112. *b.* So real actions also and conditions, are subject to extinguishment. And this is *quasi* by unity of possession, as in all cases of remitter, he who hath right of action for the lands, having the possession of the lands, there is none against whom he may bring his action; and therefore the action is extinct for ever. And, on the same reason, a condition which gives title of re-entry into land is extinct by purchase of all or part of the land, 8 *H.* 7. 8. *b.* 33 *H.* 8. *Bro. Extinguishment* 49. So a warranty is extinguished by re-feoffment, or descent of the lands to the same person who hath the warranty. So of unity of possession in some, though not in other cases, *&c.* *Da.* 4. *b.* 5. *a. b.*

5. Rule, *Lesser estate mergeth in the greater.*

471. *Testamenta cum duo inter se pugnantia reperiuntur, ultimum ratum est.*

SEE rule, *Ultima voluntas testatoris perimplenda est secundum veram intentionem suam.*

472. *That shall have the benefit, which hath or would have sustained the loss.*

1. A Mortgage in fee is forfeited, the mortgagee dies, and the mortgagor comes to redeem; equity will decree the money to be paid to the executor or administrator of the mortgagee, the mortgagee being dead. 1 *Ch. Ca.* 283. So the mortgage land shall be decreed to the executor or administrator, and not to the heir. 1 *Vern.* 412. And the heir of the mortgagee shall be compelled to convey to the executor or administrator. 2 *Ch. Ca.* 50, 51.

2. But where one purchased of a mortgagee under an apprehension that he had an absolute estate, the mortgagor coming to redeem, the money was decreed to the heir; and not to the executor. 1 *Vern.* 271. For as in the first case the personal estate bore the loss; it being intended only a security for money: so in the latter case, the real estate bore the loss; it being an absolute purchase. *Francis's Max. Eq.* 21. 3 *Rep. Ch.* 222.

3. That in the case of a mortgage in fee, and the mortgagee dying before payment, the money should be paid to the executor or administrator, and not to the heir, was an unsettled point; for where there was neither bond nor covenant for payment, nor any defect of assets to pay debts, and the condition was to pay the heirs of the mortgagee, or to the heirs or executors, *&c.* the court many times doubted, and sometimes decreed the mortgage money to the heir. *Vide* 1 *Rep. Ch.* 183. 2 *Rep. Ch.* 155, 242. 1 *Ch. Ca.* 88. 1 *Vern.* 170. But all these doubts are now ousted, and the money, in all cases, is to be paid to the executor or administrator. *Vide* 1 *Ch. Ca.* 283. 2 *Ch. Ca.* 50, 51, 220. 2 *Vern.* 348, 351. *Vide etiam* 1 *Vernon* 412. *Max. Eq.* 21.

4. The *East India* company sued their factor for an account of 12000 *l.* in gold, which he carried thither from hence. He, on his account, demanded (according to the usual custom) allowance for so much paid for customs to the king of *India.* It was insisted, that he never paid the custom there, for the gold; so whether he, or the principal merchant should have the custom, was the question? On reference, two merchants certified, That, by the course of merchants, the factor should retain the benefit of the non-payment of the customs; for that if the principal freight, by his non-payment of the customs, had been lost, he must have answered for it to the employer, and so run the hazard of it wholly. And in this case, the factor, by the law of *India,* had it been discovered, that he had made such concealment, and not entered into the custom-books, would have lost his life as a felon. Two other merchants certified, That the employer was to have the benefit of the non-payment of the customs. And, upon these certificates, it was decreed, That the factor should have the benefit of these customs; for it was a duty to be paid, and the employer could make no title to it, against him who was in possession; and *he who hath possession hath right against all but him that hath the very right.* 1 Ch. Ca. 25. And yet as the margent observes, *a factor is only in nature of a trustee for his principal.* See 2 *Vern.* 638.

5. The

5. The factor hath ſtolen the cuſtom of divers goods, whereof the bill ſought an account and diſcovery, whether he paid the ſaid cuſtoms or not? The defendant in his anſwer inſiſted, he was not bound to anſwer that part of the bill; for that the plaintiff, who was the employer, was not intitled to thoſe cuſtoms, nor any advantage, whether they were paid or not. Exceptions being taken to this anſwer, the maſter certified it ſufficient. And, on exceptions to the report, it came now before the court, and the caſe *Smith* and *Oxenden fo.* 25. was cited: but on the plaintiff's ſide it was inſiſted, that this caſe was not like that; for that was of cuſtom ſtolen from a foreign king, and this was of cuſtom ſtolen from our own king, and that it would be of evil conſequence, and an encouragement to evil factors, if the court ſhould give an opinion for them in a matter of fraud, as this was. And whereas it was inſiſted by the defendant's counſel, that it was the courſe of merchants, that factors ſhould have the benefit of cuſtoms themſelves, and not the principals, becauſe the penalty would fall on the factor if diſcovered, it was declared that could not be called a cuſtom, being grounded upon fraud; and therefore the court ordered, that the defendant ſhould anſwer whether he paid the cuſtom or not. 1 *Ch. Ca.* 30. *Quaere, Whether this caſe doth not bear hard upon the rule,* Nemo tenetur ſeipſum prodere; *as well as for that the wrong done is, in truth, to the revenue of the crown, and not to the plaintiff; who, by this bill is ſeeking advantage of another's wrong, and that of a fraud too committed againſt the crown.*

6. The defendant had employed the plaintiff as his factor beyond ſea, and brought an action at law againſt the plaintiff, and had judgment, *quod computet.* The plaintiff brought his bill here for an allowance, upon account of what he had ſaved in not paying the cuſtoms of the goods (which could not be allowed before the auditor, as was ſaid) and an allowance was accordingly decreed him againſt the defendant, the employer. 1 *Ch. Ca.* 76. *It is obſerved in the margin, That this caſe is founded upon the general rule above, where he is not* particeps criminis; *for then it is otherwiſe; for no man ſhall take benefit of his own wrong.*

7. References, 1 *Ch. Ca.* 98. 2 *Ch. Ca.* 49, 152, 156, 187. 1 *Vern.* 1, 188, 341, 436, 415. 2 *Ch. Ca.* 115. 2 *Ventr.* 359. *Salk.* 154. 1 *Vern.* 403, 435. *S. C.* 2 *Rep. Ch.* 377. 1 *Vern.* 133. 2 *Ch. Ca.* 36. *S. C.* 1 *Vern.* 297. 6 *Mod.* 162. 2 *Vern.* 638.

473. *That ſhall make ſatisfaction which received the benefit.*

1. IF it be a duty or charge in equity, the perſonal eſtate ſhall be firſt applied. 2 *Ch. Ca.* 84.

2. If the real eſtate be charged with the legacies, yet the perſonal eſtate ſhall be firſt applied. 1 *Ch. Ca.* 297.

3. But where the anceſtor purchaſed the equity of redemption which deſcended to his heir, the mortgage was not ſatisfied out of the perſonal eſtate. 1 *Vern.* 37. *Salk.* 449. For by the purchaſe of the equity of redemption, the perſonal eſtate was not increaſed but diminiſhed; and this was formerly decreed otherwiſe; that in caſe there was no covenant in the mort-

mortgage deed for payment of the mortgage money and intereſt, the adminiſtrator was not obliged to diſcharge the ſame. 1 *Rep. Ch.* 275. Here the money came out of the perſonal eſtate, and it cannot be equity, that the perſonal eſtate ſhould be further charged with the redemption; as that would be to convert the perſonal eſtate, to the manifeſt hurt of thoſe intitled thereunto, into a real eſtate, for the benefit of the heir. Debts ſhall (but legacies ſhall not) be paid out of the perſonal eſtate, though it be thereby diminiſhed to the prejudice of a widow, who claims her thirds by cuſtom. 2 *Ch. Ca.* 84, 85. 1 *Vern.* 36. *S. C.*

4. If the perſonal eſtate be not expreſly deviſed to the executor, it then remains in his hands as executor; and conſequently to go in eaſe of the real eſtate. As where a man conveys his lands to truſtees to pay his debts, and made his wife his executrix, but did not expreſly give her the perſonal eſtate, it was decreed to be applied in eaſe of the real. 1 *Ch. Ca.* 297. *And yet this was in caſe of a wife, who is intitled to more favour than other executors commonly are, as I conceive appears from the caſe, where a huſband deviſed all his books to another, except ten books, ſuch as his wife ſhould chuſe, as plays, romances, ſermons, but not law books, where it was agreed this was not a deviſe of the books to her, but an exception out of the deviſe of his library or ſtudy, and that it was not to be thought the teſtator intended to bar his wife of the benefit of the executorſhip, by ſo inconſiderable a deviſe.* Pre. Ch. 231. See alſo 263, 264.

5. The heir being ſued, and having paid a debt of his anceſtor by bond, the executor was decreed to reimburſe him. 1 *Ch. Ca.* 74. Lord chancellor declared the perſonal eſtate in the hands of the executor ſhall be employed in eaſe of the heir, by what ever means, he became indebted as heir. 2 *Ch. Ca.* 5. 1 *Ch. Ca.* 271. Though there be no covenant in the deed for payment. 1 *Vern.* 436. *Salk.* 449. for the perſonal eſtate received the benefit by the contract; and therefore ſhall make ſatisfaction. *Max. Eq.* 19.

6. But though in the caſe of an heir, debts affecting the real eſtate ſhall be paid out of the perſonal aſſets, yet not ſo in the caſe of a deviſee, 1 *Ch. Ca.* 271. but after, that difference was diſallowed in the caſe *Pockley* and *Pockley*, where lord chancellor declared, that not only the heir, in caſe he be charged with the debts of his anceſtor, but alſo the deviſee of the land ſhall be diſburthened of the debts lying upon the lands, by the perſonal eſtate in the hands of either executor, or adminiſtrator 2 *Ch. Ca.* 84. 1 *Vern.* 36. *S. C.* where it is reported to be ſaid by lord chancellor, That not only he, who is *haeres factus*, ſhould pray in aid of the perſonal eſtate in eaſe of the real, but even an ordinary deviſee ſhould have the like benefit: for the rule is, **That ſhall make ſatisfaction which received the benefit,** *and that was the perſonal eſtate which was increaſed by the money borrowed on the mortgage; therefore, according to this rule, and good equity, the perſonal eſtate ought to make ſatisfaction.*

7. The heir of the mortgagor ſhall have the perſonal eſtate firſt applied to pay off the mortgage; and that though there were no covenant for payment in the mortgage deed; and that though the perſonal eſtate was deviſed away; becauſe it is a debt. *Pre. Ch.* 61.

8. And so it was that the heir being sued, and having paid a debt due from his ancestor on bond, the executor was decreed to reimburse him, as far as personal assets come to his hands would extend. 1 *Ch. Ca.* 74.

9. And therefore the heir, though liable to pay his ancestor's debts, and cannot otherwise be discharged therefrom, is to have aid over, and to be reimbursed out of the personal estate, and out of the land directed by the ancestor to be sold to pay debts, so far as both will extend. 1 *Rep. Ch.* 155, 156, 157.

10. The testator held the lands subject to a rent, which he let run; though his person was not liable at law, to payment, yet decreed the executor, and not the present tertenant should pay the arrears, as far as assets, &c. because by non-payment the personal estate was increased. 1 *Ch. Ca.* 121.

* 11. Although a real estate be made liable to debts, yet it shall only come in aid of the personal estate, and the personal estate shall be first applied. See case before the house of lords, *Nokes* and *Derby*, 12 *April* 1727.

* 12. So also the personal estate was decreed to be first applied to discharge the mortgage (after debts, legacies and funerals discharged) in ease of the real estate. See case *Braine et ux'* versus *Woolaston et al.* before the house of lords, 24 *Feb.* 1728.

* 13. So where one conveyed all his lands *in trust* for the payment of debts and legacies, and then by his will devised all his personal estate to his wife; yet the personal estate was directed to come in aid of the real estate. See the case *French* and *Christopher*, before the house of lords, *Feb.* 1707.

* 14. Yet, in this case, the personal estate was not allowed, to be applied to discharge a real lien on the real estate, laid by the ancestor. See case *Evelyn* and *Evelyn*, before the house of lords, 8 *May* 1733. *Note, as I presume, this case was circumstanced with honest creditors, whose demands only affected the personalty; therefore their lordships most equitably denied the heir this benefit, in favour of such creditors, where, should their fund be exhausted in satisfying such superior debts, they must, in equity, stand in the place of such superior creditors, for so much as their own fund has been diminished by such improper application; and therefore, to prevent circuity of actions or multiplicity of suits, their lordships denied the benefit to the heir in the first instance.* Tamen quaere.

15. References, *Max. Eq.* 19, &c. 1 *Ch. Ca.* 80, 81, 98. *Pre. Ch.* 423, 477. *Gilb.* 106, 107. 1 *Ch. Ca.* 223. *Nels.* 220, 230, 476. *Gilb.* 57, 69. *Pre. Ch.* 494, 511. *Gilb.* 151. 2 *Vent.* 349, 366, 367. 1 *Vern.* 204, 324. 2 *Vern.* 416, 439, 424, 508. *Eq. Abr.* 268, 269. *Gilb.* 72, 73, 74.

16. Rule. *See last rule. Personal estate to go in aid of the real.*

474. *That which is the open and publick treaty and agreement on marriage, shall not be lessened or infringed by any private agreement.*

1. ON a treaty of marriage between the plaintiff and her husband, her father would not consent, because the intended husband was indebted 200 *l.* to *B.* on bond, wherein he and his mother were bound. To

remove this difficulty, the mother and her younger ſon gave a new bond to *B.* and the former bond was cancelled: but the huſband after gave the brother a counter-bond, and actually paid the intereſt during his life; and it was in proof, that the widow the plaintiff, being in love, contrived this way to ſatisfy her father, that the marriage might take place; but now being ſued by the brother on the counter-bond, as adminiſtrator to her huſband, ſhe brought the preſent bill to be relieved. Lord chancellor: This is a plain fraud and contrivance by which the father was drawn in; and declared if the huſband had been plaintiff, he ſhould have been relieved; and therefore decreed the bond to be delivered up. 1 *Vern.* 348.

2. A marriage was in treaty between *Gale* and the ſiſter of *Edward Pitman*; the woman not having as great a portion as *Gale* inſiſted on, prevailed with her brother to let her have 160*l.* to make up her portion, and gave her brother a bond for it, and thereupon the marriage was had; and the huſband, who knew nothing of this bond, died *ſans* iſſue, and then the wife died, and made the plaintiff her executor; and *Pitman* the brother dies alſo, and makes the defendant his executor, who put the bond in ſuit againſt the plaintiff to recover back the 160*l.* and thereupon the plaintiff brings his bill for relief. For the defendant it was inſiſted, that though it might be a fraud as to the huſband, or any iſſue of his, who were to have the benefit of the marriage agreement; yet the huſband being dead, and there being no iſſue, the bond ſhould be good againſt the wife herſelf, and by conſequence againſt the executor, there being no creditors in the caſe, nor deficiency of aſſets. Lord chancellor: You admit the huſband might have been relieved; *that which was once a fraud will be always ſo*; and the accident of the wife's ſurviving the huſband will not better the caſe. Decreed the bond to be delivered up. 1 *Vern.* 475. *Quaere*, If the condition of the bond had been, that in caſe the woman ſurvived the huſband, that ſhe ſhould pay it, whether ſhe would have been relieved. *Note*; It was proved in the cauſe, that after the death of the huſband the wife agreed to pay the money, and actually did pay part. *Sed non allocatur.* 1 *Vern.* 475.

3. The plaintiff on marriage with the defendant's daughter, whoſe portion was 1200*l.* was obliged by the father to give a bond, in order to get his conſent for 200*l.* if the plaintiff's wife died *ſans* iſſue, or the iſſue died before 18 or marriage; the wife died without iſſue; and the bill was for relief againſt the bond; the portion being given by the plaintiff's wife's aunt, and the father giving her nothing. *Cur'*: It is in the nature of a brocage-bond, and to be delivered up to be cancelled, and the defendant to refund intereſt paid, but without coſts. 2 *Vern.* 588.

4. References, 1 *Vern.* 240, *&c.* 2 *Vern.* 500, 527. *and Lord Mohun's* caſe. 2 *Mod. Ca.* 3, 4, 98. 1 *Chan. Ca.* 243. 2 *Mod. Ca.* 106, *&c.* 131, *&c.* 160, *&c.* 1 *Rep. Chan.* 87. 3 *Rep. Chan.* 31. *Prec. Chan.* 165, 267, 522. *Gilb.* 148. *Show. Parl. Ca.* 76. See alſo *Fraud, &c.*

475. *That which was once a fraud will always be ſo.*

RULES, *Quod ab initio non valet*, &c. *Alſo the laſt rule*, caſe 2.

476. *The next of the worthieſt blood ſhall ever inherit.*

RULE, *Propinquior excludit propinquum, &c.*

477. *Things to be done by him who hath moſt skill.*

OBligation *ſur* condition that the obligee ſhall bring to the obligor's ſhop (being a taylor) ſo much cloth, which is to be cut out, and the obligor is to make the obligee a gown of it; here the obligor muſt cut the ſame out, as well as make it. So if a merchant agree with the king's collectors that his merchandize ſhall be weighed at the king's beam, and the king to have his duty as it riſeth, the collectors muſt weigh it. 9 *E.* 4. 4. 4 *E.* 6. 15. 4 *Eliz.* 230. *Lit.* 22. 11 *E.* 4. 36.

478. *Things ſhall not be void which poſſibly may be good.*

1. LANDS given to a man and the wife of another, and the heirs of their two bodies, is a preſent tail executed; for the poſſibility that they may marry. 15 *H.* 7. 10. 1 *Co.* 113. *Chudeley*'s caſe.

2. A meſnalty is given in tail, reſerving rent, and good; for the tenancy may eſcheat to the donee, and then he ſhall diſtrain for all the arrearages. 1 *H.* 4. 1.

3. A man hath iſſue a daughter, and leaveth his wife *privement enſient*, the wife may detain the charters from the daughter; for the poſſibility that the child the wife goes with may be a ſon. 41 *E.* 3. 11.

479. *Traditio loqui facit chartam.*

IN ejectione firmae between *Clayton* and *Preſenham*, the caſe was, Indentures of demiſe were bearing date 16 *May*, *anno* 25 *Eliz.* but were delivered at four o'clock on the 20th of *June*, *anno* 25 *ſupradict.* and when this leaſe ſhould have its commencement, whether from the day of the date or the delivery, was the queſtion? Reſolved by *Wray* chief juſtice, Sir *Thomas Gaudy et tout le court*, that *from henceforth*, ſhould be accounted from the day of the delivery of the indentures, and not from the date; for *from henceforth*, is tantamount to ſay from the making, *ou del' temps del deliverie des indentures*, or *a confectione praeſentium*; for the leaſe hath its commencement and efficacy by the delivery, and the words *from henceforth*, or any other words of the indenture, are not of force or avail till the delivery; *quia traditio loqui facit chartam.* 5 Co. 1. a.

480. *Tranſit terra cum onere.*

General to, and rules.

1. WHEN the covenant extends to a thing in being, parcel of the demiſe, the thing to be done by force of the covenant, is *quodammodo* annexed and appurtenant to the thing demiſed, and ſhall go with the land, and bind the aſſignee, though not named or bound by expreſs

prefs words; but when the covenant extends to a matter not in being at the time, it cannot be appurtenant or annexed to fuch matter, not having effence at the time. 5 *Co.* 16. *a. b.*

2. It was refolved, in the principal cafe, (*being the cafe of* Spencer et ux', *which follows*) that if the leffee had covenanted for him and his affigns, that they fhould make a new well on any part of the demifed premiffes; that as it was to be done upon the lands demifed, that it fhould bind the affignee; for though the covenant goes to matter to be newly done, yet it is to be done upon the thing demifed, and the affignee is to take the benefit; and therefore it fhall bind the affignee by the exprefs words; but though the covenant be for him and his affigns, yet if the thing to be done, be meerly collateral to the land, and no ways concerns the thing demifed the affignee fhall not be charged. 5 *Co.* 16. *b.*

3. It was alfo refolved, that if a man demife fheep, or a ftock of cattle, or any other perfonal goods, for a term, and the leffee covenants for him and his affigns, at the end of the time or term, to deliver other cattle or goods, as good as thofe demifed were, or fuch a price for them, and the leffee affigns over, this covenant fhall not bind the affignee; for it is but a perfonal contract, and wants fuch privity as is between leffor and leffee and his affigns of the land, in refpect of the reverfion; but in cafe of goods perfonal, there is no privity, nor any reverfion, but meerly a matter in action, and that only in the perfonalty, which can bind none but the covenantor, his executors or adminiftrators who reprefent him. The law is the fame if one demife an houfe and lands for years, with a ftock or fum of money, rendering rent; and the leffee covenant for himfelf, his executors, adminiftrators and affigns, to deliver the fame at the end of the term, the affignee fhall not be charged with this covenant, for though it be true, that the rent referved was increafed on account of the ftock, or in refpect of the fum of money, yet the rent did not iffue out of the ftock or money, but out of the lands only; and therefore as to the ftock or money, the covenant is perfonal, and binds the covenantor, his executors and adminiftrators, but not his affigns; for it is not certain that the ftock or money came to the hands of the affignee; for it might be otherwife wafted, or made away by the leffee; and therefore the law could not determine, at the time of the leafe made, fuch leafe to bind the affignee. 5 *Co.* 16. *b.* 17. *a.* *Quod ab initio non valet, &c.*

4. If the leffee *pur ans* covenant to repair the houfes during the term, this covenant fhall bind all others, as a thing appurtenant and running with the land, into whofefoever hands the term comes, as well thofe who come in by act of law, as by act of the party; for it is the fame thing in refpect to the leffor, and if the law were not fo, great prejudice might enfue to him. *And reafon demands, that thofe, who take advantage of fuch covenant which the leffor made with the leffee, fhould be bound with the covenants the leffee made with the leffor.* 5 Co. 17. b.

Particular cafes.

5. *Spencer* and his wife brought covenant againft *Clarke*, and the cafe was, *Spencer et ux'* by indenture demifed an houfe and lands (the right of the wife) to *S.* for 21 years, and by this indenture *S.* covenanted for him, his executors and adminiftrators with the plaintiff, that he, his

2 execu-

executors, adminiſtrators or aſſigns, ſhould build a brick wall upon part of the lands demiſed, &c. *S.* aſſigned over the term to *J.* and *J.* to the defendant. For the not building the brick wall upon part of the lands demiſed, the plaintiffs brought their action of covenant againſt the defendant as aſſignee; and, after many arguments at the bar, the caſe was ſtrongly argued and debated at the bench: and reſolved, *int' al'*, by Sir *Chriſtopher Wray* lord chief juſtice, Sir *Thomas Gaudy*, *et tout le court*, that when the covenant extends to a thing *in eſſe*, *parcel of the demiſe*, the thing to be done by virtue of the covenant, is *quodammodo* annexed and appurtenant to the thing demiſed, and ſhall run with the land, and bind the aſſignee, though he be not bound by expreſs words; but when the covenant extends to a thing not in being, or that hath not eſſence at the time of the demiſe made, it cannot be appurtenant or annexed to ſuch thing not *in eſſe*; as if a man covenants to repair the houſe to him demiſed during the term, this is part of the contract, and extends to ſupport the thing demiſed; and therefore is *quodammodo* annexed and appurtenant to the houſe, and therefore ſhall bind the aſſignee, though he is not expreſly bound by the covenant; but in the caſe at bar, the covenant concerned a matter not in being at the time of the demiſe made, but new, and to be done afterwards; and therefore, though it ſhall bind the covenantor, his executors or adminiſtrators, it ſhall not bind the aſſignee; for the law will not annex the covenant to a matter not in being. 5 *Co.* 16. *a. b.*

6. If the leſſee covenant for him and his aſſigns, to build an houſe on the lands of the leſſor, not parcel of the demiſe, or to pay a collateral ſum to the leſſor, or to a ſtranger, theſe ſhall not bind the aſſignee, becauſe it is meerly collateral, and in no ſort toucheth or concerneth the thing demiſed, or that is aſſigned over; and therefore the aſſignee of the thing demiſed, cannot be charged with it, no more than any other meer ſtranger. 5 *Co.* 16. *b.*

7. In *B. R.* between *The Dean and Chapter of Windſor* and *Hide*, the caſe was, One leaſed an houſe by indenture for years; the leſſee covenanted and granted for him and his executors with the leſſor, to repair the houſe at all times neceſſary: the leſſee aſſigns to *Hide*, who ſuffers the houſe to run out of repair, whereupon the leſſor brings covenant againſt the aſſignee. And it was adjudged by lord chief juſtice *Popham*, *et tout le court*, that the action lay, though the leſſee had not covenanted for his aſſigns; for covenants which extend to the ſupport of the thing demiſed, is *quodammodo* appurtenant to it, and ſhall run with it; and in regard the leſſee had obliged himſelf to bear the charges of the repairs, the annual rent was certainly the leſs, which trenched or turned to the benefit of the aſſignee; *et qui ſentit commodum ſentire debet et onus.* If one grant to another eſtovers to repair his houſe, this is appurtenant to his houſe. *Fitz. Nat. Brev.* 181. 28 *H.* 8. 28. If leſſee covenant to diſcharge the leſſor *de omnibus oneribus ordinariis et extraordinariis*, and to repair the houſe, an action lieth againſt the aſſignee. 5 *Co.* 24. *a. b.*

8. In 42 *E.* 3. *fo.* 3. the caſe was, Grandfather, father and two ſons, the grandfather was ſeiſed of the manor of *D.* whereof a chapel was parcel. A prior, with conſent of his convent, by deed, covenanted for him and his ſucceſſors with the grandfather and his heirs, that he and his convent ſhould weekly chaunt in his ſaid chapel, for the lord of

the ſaid manor, and his ſervants, *&c.* The grandfather infeoffed one in fee, who gave it to the younger ſon and his wife in tail. It was adjudged tenant in tail, as tertenant, (for the eldeſt brother was heir) ſhould have covenant againſt the prior; for the covenant is to do an act which is annexed to the chapel which is within the manor, and ſo annexed to the manor, as hath been mentioned. *Finchden* ſaid, he had ſeen a judgment where two coparceners made partition of lands; and one covenanted with the other to acquit of a ſuit due; and he to whom, *&c.* aliened, and the ſuit was in arrear, and the feoffee brought covenant againſt the parcener to acquit him of the ſuit, and the writ was maintainable, notwithſtanding his being a ſtranger to the covenant, becauſe that the acquittal ran with the land. [*Co. Lit.* 385. *a.*] But if ſuch covenant had been to ſing divine ſervice in the chapel of another, there the aſſignee ſhould not have had covenant; for that the covenant, in ſuch caſe, could not be annexed to the chapel; becauſe the chapel did not belong to the covenantee; as is adjudged in 2 *H.* 4. *fo.* 6. but there it is agreed, that if the covenant had been with the lord of the manor of *D.* and his heirs, *lords of the manor of* D. *and inhabitants in it*, the covenant ſhould be annexed to the manor, and there the tertenant ſhould have the action of covenant without privity of blood. *Vide* 29 *E.* 3. 48. *and* 30 *E.* 3. 14. 5 *Co.* 17. *b.* 18. *a.*

9. *Covenant:* whereas by indenture bearing date, *&c.* between the executor and teſtator of the defendant, *teſtatum exiſtit*, that the executor demiſed ſuch a meſſuage or tenement with a garden adjoining to the plaintiff's houſe, to the teſtator for 21 years; and the teſtator covenanted for himſelf, his executors and aſſigns, that he would not erect any buildings in the ſaid garden, to the prejudice of the plaintiff's lights. The plaintiff alledges that ſuch aſſignee of the teſtator, againſt the ſaid covenant, had erected to ſuch prejudice, *&c.* for which, *&c.* the defendant pleads that the leſſee aſſigned to *J. S.* who entered, and paid his rent to the plaintiff, and he accepted ſuch aſſignee for his tenant; and therefore demanded judgment *ſi actio*; whereupon it was demurred, and inſiſted for the defendant, that the privity of contract was determined; the leſſor having accepted the rent of the aſſignee, *&c.* But all the court conceived, that inaſmuch as it is an expreſs covenant, that he ſhall not build, it ſhall bind him and his executors, and no aſſignment or acceptance of the rent by the hands of the aſſignee ſhall take from him the advantage of ſuing him or his executors upon an expreſs covenant, no more than if the leſſee had obliged himſelf by obligation to pay his rent, *&c.* *Judgment pro quer'.* Cro. Ca. 188, 189.

10. Covenant againſt the defendant as aſſignee of *Dalton*, for that *Dalton* had covenanted for himſelf, his executors and adminiſtrators, to leave 15 acres every year for paſture *abſque cultura*, and that he granted to the defendant, and that the defendant *non reliquit* 15 *acras ad paſturam*, but ſuch a day and year ploughed up all. Demurred, becauſe aſſignee not named, *&c.* But all the court held, that this covenant is to be performed by the aſſignee, though not named; becauſe it is for the benefit of the eſtate, according to the nature of the ſoil. But to do a collateral covenant, as to build *de novo*, or ſuch like, ſhall not bind him, unleſs named; wherefore it was adjudged for the plaintiff. *Cro. Jac.* 125.

11. *Debt*, and declares that he let certain lands to *Agar* for 21 years, rendering annually at the *Temple Church*, *London*, 30*l.* at *Michaelmas* and the *Annunciation*, *&c. et si contingat*, that the said rent should be behind and not paid at the day, *&c.* that then the said *Agar*, his executors and assigns should forfeit *nomine poenae* 3 *s.* and 4 *d.* for every day which should incur after such default, until the said rent and arrears should be paid. That after 28 *Feb.* 37 *Eliz.* *Agar* granted to the defendant, and that after the grant, *Mich.* 33 *Eliz.* the rent was in arrear, and not paid for 576 days, and that at another rent-day it was in arrear 12 days; wherefore he had forfeited, *&c.* whereupon he demanded 300 *l.* 16 *s.* 8 *d.* The defendant pleaded *nil debet*; which was found against him; and it was now moved in arrest of judgment, that an action lay not against the assignee; for this penalty is founded meerly upon the contract, which is in privity between the lessor and lessee, and runs not with the land. But *Gaudy* and *Clench* held that it well lay; for the land is charged therewith, and the assignee, for his own time, shall be chargeable. But *Fenner* held *contra*, for the penalty is *quasi* collateral. And it was also moved, that he was not intitled to the penalty, unless the rent was demanded, no more than he should be to the forfeiture of a lease for non-payment. *Gaudy*: It is not alike; *for the condition which goes in defeasance of an estate shall be taken strictly*, but the penalty is in nature of the rent, and as he shall have the rent itself without demand, so he shall have the penalty. And to that opinion *Clench* agreed, *Popham absente*; wherefore it was adjourned. *Cro. Eliz.* 383.

12. References, 4 *E.* 3. 3. *Dal.* 4. 47, 83, 101. 10 *E.* 3. 9. 24 *E.* 3. 30. 2 *Inst.* 489, 298. *Co. Lit.* 23, 385. *Cro. Eliz.* 552, 553. *T. Jo.* 144. *Nat. Brev.* 146. *Dy.* 257. *Lit. Bro.* 16. *b.* *Bel.* 16. *b.* *Godb.* 70. *The.* 34. *Mo.* 179. *Co. Lit.* 210. *a.* 215. *b.* 384. *b.* 385. *a.* 5 *Co.* 97. *b.* *Plow. Com.* 286. *Dy.* 45, 152. *Mo.* 44, 419, 855. 2 *Ro. Ab.* 743, 744. *Leon.* 3. *Lutw.* 1367. 1 *Cro.* 188, 222. 2 *Cro.* 125, 523. 1 *Saund.* 239, 240. *Cro. Ca.* 23, 24, 221, 222. *Lutw.* 369. 1 *Ro. Abr.* 521, 522, 915. 2 *Ro. Abr.* 743. *Hob.* 23. *Poph.* 38. 1 *Ro.* 576. *Dy.* 264. *Yelv.* 222. *Comb.* 185, 186.

13. Rules, *Qui sentit* { *Commodum* / *onus* } { *sentire debet et* { *onus.* / *Commodum.* *That shall make satisfaction which received the benefit. That shall have the benefit, which hath or would have sustained the loss. Equality is equity. Equity will do no wrong*, &c. *Law will not suffer wrong.*

481. *Trespass none to have, but he who hath actual possession.*

What it is, and from whence derived, &c.

1. TRespass, *transgressio, derivatur a transgrediendo*; because it passeth over that which is right.

2. *Transgressio autem est cum modus non servatur, nec mensura: debet enim quilibet in suo facto modum habere et mensuram. Nota*; in the highest and lowest offences, there are no accessaries, but all are principals. As in riots, routs, forcible entries, and other transgressions, *vi et armis*, which

are

are the loweſt offences. And ſo in the higheſt offence, which is *crimen laeſae majeſtatis*, there are no acceſſaries. But in felony there are acceſſaries both before and after. *Co Lit.* 57. *a. b.*

Where and for what it lieth, &c.

General.

3. *None ſhall have treſpaſs, but he who is in the actual poſſeſſion.* Quod fuit conceſſum per curiam. Hob. 224.

Particular caſes.

4. The lord cannot at his pleaſure put out his lawful copyholder, without ſome cauſe of forfeiture, and if he do the copyholder may have treſpaſs; for albeit he is *tenens ad voluntatem domini*, yet it is *ſecundum conſuetudinem manerii*. And *Brit.* ſpeaking of theſe kind of tenants, ſaith they are privileged, that none of them may be ouſted of their tenements, neither may their ſervices be increaſed, or changed, to make more or other ſervices. And herewith agreeth Sir *Rob. Danby*, chief juſtice of the court of common pleas, *Mich.* 7 *E.* 4. 19. and Sir *Thomas Brian* his ſucceſſor, *Mich.* 21 *E.* 4. 80. (*viz.*) That the copyholder, doing his cuſtoms and ſervices, if put out by his lord, ſhall have an action of treſpaſs againſt him. *Co. Lit.* 60. *b.* 61. *a.*

482. *Truſt is a creature of equity, and to be governed and diſpoſed by the rules of equity.*

1. LORD chancellor: *Truſt is a creature of chancery, and not within the* Stat. W. 2. de donis, *&c.* and though if tenant in tail of a truſt cannot bar the remainder by fine, yet if he make a feoffment, or bargain and ſale, he may bar his iſſue. 2 *Ch. Ca.* 64.

2. *Truſt is a creature of equity, and diſpoſable by the rules there.* And on queſtion, where tenant in tail bargained and ſold his eſtate, ſeeing he had power over it, though there was no fine or recovery, whether equity would decree againſt the heir? To which lord chancellor anſwered, he would not ſuperſede fines and recoveries, but where it was a truſt and equitable intereſt, *&c.* 2 *Vent.* 350.

3. References, *Salk.* 154, 159, 160. *Skin.* 78, 232. 1 *Vern.* 67, 104, 181. 2 *Vern.* 428, 463, 619, 626, 644, 647.

483. *Truſt of a term governed by the ſame rules in equity, as the limitation of a legal eſtate is at law.*

1. AT law they could not, but by *Stat.* 21 *H.* 8. *c.* 15. it was enacted, That a termor might falſify a recovery, as tenant of the freehold might do, by the courſe of the common law, where he was neither privy nor party to the ſame; and that notwithſtanding any ſuch recovery, he ſhould hold and enjoy his term according to his leaſe, againſt the recoverer, his heirs and aſſigns, *&c.* 2 *Mod. Ca.* 102, 103.

I 2. On

2. On review to reverse a decree made by the late lord chancellor, several errors were assigned, the principal one insisted on, was, that the limitation of the term over was void. Lord keeper, upon pronouncing the decree, said, when he assisted the chancellor with two more judges, his opinion was against it, and that though he could find no reason to alter his opinion, yet the cause came before him with prejudice, unless they could, by new matter, or new reason convince him: and made a proposal for a trial at law, but the defendant's counsel declined it, and said their title was better here than at law; and insisted much upon the trust of a term different from the limitation of a term. The plaintiff's counsel relied much on the cases, *Child* and *Bailey*, and *Burges* and *Burges*. 2 *Cro.* 456. *Pol.* 40. The lord keeper saw no reason to alter his opinion, and said on the former hearing, the lord chancellor declared, *That the trust of a term was to be governed by the same rules as the limitation or devise of a term at law was*; and therefore thought the defendant's counsel pressed him unreasonably, who insisted on the equity of the case, and would make a difference between the limitation of a trust of a term, and the limitation or devise of a term itself; said, **a perpetuity is a thing odious in law, and destructive to the commonwealth, and therefore not to be countenanced in equity**, &c. *If a man settles a term to another and his heirs, it shall go to the executors*, &c. *and the rule of law must be observed.* Decree reversed. 1 *Vern.* 163, 164.

3. *Bullock*, for a marriage to be had between *Henry* his son and *Bridget* the daughter of *Knight*, being possessed of a lease of one thousand years, articled to settle those lands in consideration thereof to the use and in trust for himself 'till the marriage, and after to the use of himself for life, and after his death to *Henry* for life, and then to the use of *Bridget* for her life, and after their deaths, to the use of the issue of their two bodies to be begotten, according to the descent of lands so intailed. The marriage being had, the lease was assigned to those uses, then, the father being dead, *Henry* the husband, granted his interest over and died. *Bridget* survived and died; the defendant administered to *Bridget*. The assignee sued for the benefit of the trust. And the dispute on plea and demurrer was, to which the benefit of the trust belonged? There was no issue living, but the plaintiff made title also as administrator to the issue. Sir *John King* for the plaintiff objected, that the trust of a term limited to a feme covert, was disposable by the husband, and did bind the wife for the trust; *for the trust of a term shall be of the same nature as the term is.* Lord keeper: I should not doubt, if a feme have the trust of a term for years, and marrieth, but to decree it to the alienee of the husband; (*sed quaere* if to the alienee, but it seems it must be to execute the decree to the husband, and then the husband may alien; but the lord keeper said as before) *where a term is settled for the maintenance and jointure of the wife, the husband shall never bind the wife by his alienation.* 2. It was debated, whether the trust limited to the issue were here in nature of a limitation, or by way of purchase, so as the issue born had then an interest vested in him? for the wife's administrator could have no title. It was pressed to be a limitation, not a purchase, the rather for these words, *in course of descent.* Lord keeper: *An use to the husband and wife, and after to their issue, they then having none, is all one as if limited*

4 Q

mited to them, and to the heirs of their bodies; and the iſſue takes nothing as a purchaſer. 3. Yet then it was objected by Sir *John King*, that the huſband may alien his part. But (ſays the reporter) It was not to my intention fully enough preſſed, that here the articles were made before the marriage; and conſequently they took by divided moieties. The lord keeper ruled the plea good. 1 *Ch. Ca.* 265, 266.

4. 1 *Vern.* 164. 3 *Ch. Ca.* 3, 4, 6, 10, 11, 16, 20, 21, 23, 24. 1 *Ch. Ca.* 8, 287. *Pre. Ch.* 50, 253. 3 *Ch. Ca.* 28, 44, 48. *Gilb.* 238. *Nelſ.* 258, 341. 2 *Ch. Ca.* 182, 186. *Gilb.* 24, 119, 120.

484. *Truſtees for a charity may improve for the benefit of the charity, but can do no act to prejudice it.*

General.

1. TRuſtees *for a charity may improve for the benefit of the charity, but cannot prejudice it.* 2 Vern. 412.

Particular.

2. If lands or goods are given to one by will, or a remainder limited to one by deed, to perform a charitable uſe, if the deviſee will refuſe the legacy, or the grantee waive his remainder by fraud or covin, they are compellable to take the land and to perform the uſe. *Du. Ch. Uſes* 139.

3. And in caſe of miſbehaviour, or miſapplication, by the truſtees of a charity, chancery will oblige them to aſſign. 2 *Ju. Eccl.* 177, 178.

485. *Truſt is either expreſſed or implied.*

General.

1. EVERY truſt is either expreſſed or implied.

The difference and what each are.

2. An expreſſed truſt, is when it is either expreſſed. 1. By parol. 2. Or in writing.

3. An implied truſt, is when a man makes a gift without any conſideration, or in conſideration of nature, or blood only, *&c.* 3 *Co.* 81. *b.*

4. Rule, *Equity requires that ſuch gifts as defeat others be made upon as high and good conſideration as the things to be defeated by them are of.*

486. *Trust of a term may be limited to divers persons who are in being, one after another; because the same is transferrable: Yet it cannot be good beyond two limitations to a third person not in being.*

1. A TERM is limited to husband and wife, and the longest liver of them for life, and after to the eldest issue of them, none being then born; a good limitation: So the limitation to husband and wife, is but one limitation; for though the trust of a term according to the rule in *Goring* and *Bickerstaff*'s case, *fo.* 4. may be limited to diverse persons that are in being, one after another; because the same is transferrable, yet it cannot be good beyond two limitations to a third person not in being; *ergo* the limitation to husband and wife, and the longest liver of them, was admitted to be but one limitation. 1 *Chan. Ca.* 33, 34.

2. References, 1 *Chan. Ca.* 4, 8, 213, 230, 239.

3. Rule, *Perpetuities odious in law. Trust of a term governed by the same rules*, &c. *Trust is a creature of equity*, &c.

487. *Trust of a term limited must be in the same manner as the term itself would bear a limitation.*

RULES, *Perpetuities odious, &c.* case 21. *Term for years regularly cannot be intailed, though it may be made to wait on an inheritance which is intailed.*

488. *Trusts survive.*

1. LANDS are devised to executors to sell, and one of them dies; it is regularly true, that being but a bare authority, the survivor cannot sell. But if a man deviseth his lands to *A.* for term of life, and that after his decease his lands shall be sold by his executors generally, and maketh three or four executors, and during the life of *A.* one of the executors dies, and then *A.* dieth, the other two or three executors may sell, because the land could not be sold before, and the plural number of his executors remain; but if they had been named by their names, as by *J. S. J. N. J. D.* and *G.* his executors then, in that case, the survivor could not sell the same; because the words of the testator could not be satisfied; a special verdict was found, that *A.* was seised of certain lands in fee, and devised the same in tail, and if the donee died without issue, that his said lands should be sold by his sons-in-law; he in truth having five sons-in-law; one of the sons-in-law died in the life of the donee, and after the donee died without issue, and then four of the sons-in-law sold the said land; and adjudged the sale good; because they were named generally his sons-in-law, and the lands could not be sold by them all. And the words of the will, in a benign interpretation, are satisfied in the plural number, tho' they had but a bare authority; but if they had been particularly named it had been otherwise. But if a man devise lands to his executors to be sold,

ſold, and maketh two executors, and one dieth, yet the ſurvivor may ſell the lands; becauſe the eſtate to the truſt ſhall ſurvive, &c. *Co. Lit.* 112. *b.* 113. *a.*

2. A man ſeiſed of divers manors, lands and tenements, in fee of ſocage tenure, by his laſt will and teſtament in writing, deviſed all the ſaid manors, &c. to his ſiſter and her heirs for ever, (except out of this general grant, my manor of *R.* which I do appoint to pay my debts,) and makes two executors by name, and dies, and one executor dies alſo, and the other takes upon him the burthen of the execution of the will, and ſells the ſaid manor of *R.* for 300*l.* for the purpoſe aforeſaid, in fee, and by the opinion of the court he might well ſo do; for, by reaſon and circumſtances, it was the intention of the teſtator, and not to leave it to revert to his heir, but to truſt his executors with the ſale of it, for the ſpeedy payment of his debts. *Dy.* 271. *b.*

3. Upon a bill *in ſcac'*, the caſe was this, The father of the defendant *Rowel*, gave inſtructions for his will to be put into writing, that his meſſuages and lands ſhould be ſold by *Howe* and another, for payment of his debts and legacies, and made other executors, and died without making any other publication of his will. One of the truſtees for the ſale of the houſes and land, died before any ſale made, and now the ſurvivor and the heir were compelled to ſell; becauſe the lands were tied with a truſt which ſurvived in equity. *Hard.* 204.

4. References, *Co. Lit.* 236. *a. b.* 1 *Chan. Ca.* 177, 178, 179, 180, 211, 262. *Elſ. Obſ.* 93, 95. *Nel.* 167, 170, 262, 416. 1 *Lev.* 304. *Prec. Chan.* 123, 185. *Barn.* 47, 303, 425.

489. *Tithes favoured in law.*

Stat. 31 H. 8. *Of Monaſteries.*

The alteration it hath made in this doctrine.

1. THE ſtatute of 31 *H.* 8. *Of Monaſteries*, hath made two main changes in the learning of tithes. 1. That it hath, by force of the clauſe of the diſcharge, continued certain diſcharges which were before that ſtatute. 1. By bill. 2. Compoſition, and 3. Order. And conveyed them over to the king and lay perſons, which elſe would have vaniſhed and diſſolved with the ſpiritual bodies themſelves whereto they were annexed. 2. The next is that it hath created and made one new diſcharge, which was not at common law, *i. e.* The unity of the poſſeſſion of the parſonage and the lands titheable in one hand. *Hob.* 297, 298. *Vue le liver ſur unity of poſſeſſion. Vide etiam Yelv.* 31, 32. *Vide poſt.* caſe 4.

General to.

2. The law, *in favorem eccleſiae*, preſumes violently that a lay-man cannot be abſolutely diſcharged of tithes; and therefore will not allow a preſcription of ſuch diſcharge; holding it more reaſonable that ſome one man ſhould ſuffer a miſchief to loſe ſuch a privilege, being ſo improbable and of ſo dangerous conſequence, than, for his particular, to admit a ſpoil of the church; and decay of religion, according to the rule, *Omne magnum exemplum aliquid habet ex iniquo quod publica utilitate compenſatur*; ſo

 though

though you ſhall be allowed your diſcharge by grant, when it appears, yet when it appears not, *ſtabitur praeſumptioni*, *&c.* Hob. 297.

3. Yet a ſpiritual perſon may preſcribe, for him and his copyhold tenants, *in non decimando.* Yelv. 2. Cro. Eliz. 206, 475, 511.

4. In a prohibition, the ſuggeſtion to ſtay the ſuit in the ſpiritual court for tithes was, That the abbot of *Vale Royal* in *Cheſhire* was ſeiſed of the parſonage of *W.* and of the *Grange of Darnal*, whereof the tithes were demanded by the now parſon of *W.* and that the ſaid abbot and his predeceſſors, time whereof, *&c.* were ſeiſed of the ſaid parſonage of *W.* and of the ſaid *Grange of D.* in their demeſne as, *&c.* in right of their abbey, and *ratione inde* ſhewed the unity of poſſeſſion in diſcharge of tithes upon the ſaid *Stat.* 31 *H.* 8. To which the defendant pleaded, that the ſaid abbey was founded 5 *E.* 1. (which is within time of memory) and ſhews and confeſſeth the unity of poſſeſſion of the parſonage and of the *Grange*, after the time of the foundation. And upon the motion of *Coke*, attorney general, (*per totam curiam*) The plea in bar is good, and need not traverſe the preſcription; for the ſhewing the foundation of the ſaid abbey to be after the time of memory is a ſufficient confeſſing and avoiding. *Yelv.* 31, 32.

5. An abbot diſcharged of tithes *quamdiu in manibus propriis*, made a gift in tail, and 31 *H.* 8. the abbey was diſſolved, the donee ſhall not be diſcharged: Yet whenever the land returns, *either before or after the ſtatute*, the king and his patentees, *&c. ſhall hold diſcharged*; for that the land was diſcharged at the time of the diſſolution, *quoad* the abbot. *Hob.* 302. *And by the ſtatute ſuch lands diſcharged, were given to the crown and its ſucceſſors and patentees,* &c. *in ſuch full and ample manner as the ſame were held by the ſaid abbots and their predeceſſors, and as the ſame would have been held by them and their ſucceſſors, had the ſaid diſſolution not been, and had the reverter been to ſuch abbots,* &c. *So that theſe diſcharges are favoured in law,* **under the ſtatute of Diſſolutions,** &c. **though in the hands of lay perſons,** *as much as if the ſame had remained, or as any now are diſcharged in the hands of eccleſiaſtical perſons: And tithes in the hands of lay perſons are now a lay fee.* Stat. 32 H. 8. Fitzh. Nat. Brev. 49. Cro. Ca. 201. *And* Fitzherbert *in his* Nat. Brev. *holdeth that long before theſe days, even before the ſtatute* 18 E. 3. cap. 7. *right of tithes were determinable in the temporal courts, at the election of the party.* 5 Co. De Ju. Regis Eccl. 16. a. *And before the council of* Lateran *there were no pariſhes nor pariſh prieſts to claim them.* Hob. 296. Poph. 156. *And thus ſtands the law, the bulwark of liberty, as to the learning of tithes, notwithſtanding the dream of champion* Ridley, *and other advocates on the other ſide of the queſtion, of a* jure divino *right to tithes; and particularly of turves, timber, minerals,* &c. *ſee* Ridley's View of the Civil and Eccleſiaſtical Law, fo. 314, *&c.* 320, *&c.* 330, *&c. &c. &c. Yet I freely confeſs, with my lord* Coke, *that unity within the ſaid act* 31 H. 8. *ought to have the four qualities mentioned by his lordſhip in his* 11 Rep. fo. 14. *Though I muſt inſiſt, if the unity be rightful, equal, perpetual and free, that though an abbot could not, where his abbey was founded within time of memory, preſcribe to be diſcharged of tithes* omnino, *as is* 11 Co. 15. a. *Yet the crown and their patentees,* &c. *may claim to hold diſcharged, where the abbot,* &c. *held ſo diſcharged,*

though they only so held quamdiu in manibus propriis. *And there are many things by our laws, says my lord* Hale, *in his* History of the Law, fo. 32. *which are privileged and totally exempted from tithes, though perhaps by the canon law (which is* quasi *no law to us where we have not received it) are tithable, namely, timber, oar, coals and many more, without a special custom (which custom is common law) subjecting them thereunto; and if the right be founded in custom or common law, then I must refer the* jure divino *right to the learned civilian above and other advocates of might on his side of the argument, who no doubt of it, were they allowed to be judges, jurors and parties too, would soon root up this learning, together with that of* Modus's, *and all other disagreeable to them out of our books and records.*

* 6. Tithes of a malt-mill is only personal; for it is not a natural increase; being only a profit arising from the invention of a machine and the labour of man and horse; and if only personal, there can only be tithes of the neat profits, deducting all charges; and personal tithes can be only due by custom, and not of *common right.* See case *Chamberlain* and *Plimpton*, before the house of lords, 20 *Feb.* 1706.

Note, *That common right is the same as to say at common law.*

* 7. Bill was by the rector of *S.* for tithes of beasts fed upon such a common; the defendant by answer insisted, that the common extended into several parishes, and that the custom was that every farmer should pay tithes to the rector where he lived, and that he lived in another parish, and paid tithes to the rector there; but there being proof, that the cattle were driven upon that part of the common which lieth in *S.* there was a decree for the rector of *S.* but reversed by the house of lords; because the custom was good; there being no inclosure. See case before the house of lords, *Michelburgh* and *Crispe*, *Jan.* 1710.

* 8. Custom was for the vicar to have all tithes of peas and beans, set, drilled or sowed in rows in garden-like manner, after a new improvement was found out to use the plough instead of the spade, yet such beans and peas shall pay tithes. See case before the house of lords, *Austin* and *Nichols*, 23 *Jan.* 1717. Note; *These are matters renovant and of yearly increase*, &c.

* 9. Lands exempted from, *&c.* (being inclosed) shall not be made liable to tithes, by the general words of an act of parliament for inclosing. See case *Pratt*, *Arm'*, *contra*, *Hopkins*, before the house of lords, 2 *May* 1730.

* 10. Yet exemptions are not favoured. See case before the house of lords, *Honourable Henry Berckley*, *Esq*; and *Fox*, also * *Griffith* and *Lewis*'s case, *June* 1737.

11. References, 2 *Co.* *Bishop of Winton*'s case, 2 *Co.* 48, 49. *Cro. Ca.* 393, 403, 404, 423. *Hob.* 10, 11, 92, 250. *Yelv.* 86, 87.

12. Rule, *Consuetudo semel reprobata non potest amplius induci.*

490. *Vana est potentia quae nunquam venit in actum.*

1. A Remainder ought to vest in estate during the particular estate, and ought to take effect in possession when the particular estate endeth; for *Vana est illa potentia quae nunquam venit in actum.* 2 Co. 51. a.

2. Rule, *Remainder can depend upon no estate but what beginneth at the same time that the remainder doth.*

491. *Ubi cessat remedium ordinarium, ibi decurritur ad extraordinarium, et nunquam decurritur ad extraordinarium ubi valet ordinarium.*

1. *JOHN SLADE* brought case against *Humphrey Morley,* and declared, that being possessed of a close, *&c.* for several years, then and yet to come, the plaintiff such a day sowed the same with wheat and rye, which such a day was growing in blades; the defendant such a day, in consideration of the plaintiff's selling the defendant said wheat and rye, (tithes excepted) assumed and promised to pay the plaintiff 16*l.* at *Midsummer* then coming, and for non-payment was the action; on *non assumpsit* pleaded, and special verdict, against the action divers objections were made by *Dodderidge,* of counsel with the defendant, that the plaintiff might have ordinary remedy, by action of debt, which is a formed action in the register, and therefore he ought not to have case, which is an extraordinary action, and not tied to any certain form in the register; for *ubi cessat remedium ordinarium, ibi decurritur ad extraordinarium, &c.* but it was (*inter al'*) resolved by all the judges of *England,* that the action well lay; and that the plaintiff should have judgment; for though debt lay upon the contract, yet the plaintiff might have debt or case at his election; in respect of the infinite precedents, *&c.* and also for that *every contract executory imports an assumpsit in itself*; for when one agrees to pay money or to deliver such thing, hereby he assumes and promiseth to pay or deliver it; and therefore when one sells goods to another, and agrees to deliver them at a future day, and the other, in consideration thereof, agrees to pay so much money at such a day: In these cases both parties may have debt or case upon the *assumpsit*; for the mutual executory agreement of both parties imports as well a reciprocal action upon the case as debt; and again, here the party was not only to recover damages for the essential loss, but also for the intire debt, so that the recovery or bar in this action should be a good bar in debt brought upon the same contract. So *vice versa,* a recovery or bar in debt is a good bar in case upon the same *assumpsit*: And in some cases it should be mischievous, if debt only, and not case, should be brought, *&c.* And *case is as well a formed action, and contained in the register, as debt is,* &c. and so it was concluded, *that in all cases where the register hath*

hath two writs for one and the ſame caſe, it is at the election of the party to take which he will, &c. 4 Co. 92. b. *Slade*'s caſe.

2. Reference, *Hard.* 63.

492. *Ubi eadem ratio, ibi idem jus.*

1. *SI deux homes ſont un treſpaſs a une auter, &c.* here is to be underſtood when divers do a treſpaſs, the ſame is joint or ſeveral, at the will of him to whom the wrong is done; yet if he releaſe to one of them, all are diſcharged; becauſe *his own deed ſhall be taken moſt ſtrongly againſt himſelf*; but otherwiſe it is in the caſe of an appeal of death, *&c.* and if two men are jointly and ſeverally bounden in an obligation, if the obligee releaſe to one of them, both are diſcharged; and ſeeing the treſpaſſers are parties and privies in wrong, the one ſhall not plead a releaſe to the other without ſhewing it, albeit the deed appertaineth to the other. If an action of debt on an obligation be brought againſt an heir, he may plead in bar a releaſe made by the obligee to the executor; but albeit the deed belong to another, yet muſt he ſhew it forth; for both of them are privy to the teſtator; *ubi eadem ratio, ibi idem jus.* Co. Lit. 232. a.

2. References, *Co. Lit.* 191. *Hard. Duke of York* and *Sir John Maſſam*'s caſe.

493. *Ubi factum nullum, ibi fortia nulla.*

1. IT was reſolved *per totam curiam,* That if principal and acceſſory be, and the principal is pardoned, or hath his clergy, the acceſſory may not be arraigned; for the maxim is, *ubi factum nullum, ibi fortia nulla; et ubi non eſt principalis, non poteſt eſſe acceſſorius*; then before it appears that there is a principal, one may not be charged as acceſſory, and none may be ſaid principal before he is ſo proved, and adjudged by law, and that ought to be by judgment or verdict or confeſſion, or by outlawry; for it is not enough, that *in rei veritate* there was a principal, unleſs this appear by judgment in law; and this is the reaſon, that when the principal is pardoned, or takes his clergy before judgment, that the acceſſory ſhall never be arraigned; for it doth not appear, by judgment of law, that he was principal, *&c.* though the acceptance of the pardon and praying of clergy is an argument, yet there is no judgment of law, that he is guilty; but if the principal, after attainder, be pardoned, or hath his clergy allowed, there the acceſſory ſhall be arraigned; and that becauſe it appeareth judicially that the other was principal. 4 *Co.* 43. *b.*

2. Rule, *Ubi non eſt principalis non datur acceſſorius.*

449. *Ubi non eſt condendi authoritas, ibi non eſt parendi neceſſitas.*

1. AFTER *the biſhop of* Rome *had arrogated to, and taken upon himſelf to be ſpiritual prince or monarch of the whole world, he attempted to give laws to all mankind, as a mark of this his ſovereignty; but knowing very well, that* ubi non eſt condendi authoritas, ibi non eſt parendi neceſſitas, **he like the other ſubtile one,** *went cunningly to work, and did not at firſt offer laws to all people, but only cauſed certain rules to be collected for the government* **of his own creatures and willing ſlaves,** *the clergy only, which he called* decreta, *and not laws or ſtatutes, but theſe decrees being received though by the* Weſtern *church only, for the* Eaſtern *church never received any of his rules, canons or decrees,* **or other like trumpery,** *then he ſet about, and not before, drawing alſo the laity by degrees to obedience to his ordinances, and to this end, he firſt propounded certain rules or ordinances for abſtinence, or faſting days to be obſerved by the laity as well as the clergy, which on their firſt appearance and inſtitution, were called by the gentler name of* rogationes, rogations, (*from whence, it ſeems, came the weeks of abſtinence next before pentecoſt, to be called* rogation week) *and when this uſurper, this man of ſin in high place, found the laity, of their abundant zeal, received and obſerved theſe rogations or ordinances of abſtinence, then he proceeded further, and made further reſcripts and orders by the name of decretals to bind all the laity of every degree, in matters concerning their civil and temporal eſtates, which however were not univerſally received, but only in his own territories; but many of them were totally rejected, nay ſet at naught, contemned, deſpiſed and ridiculed as well as their author, eſpecially in* England *and* France; *and though it muſt be allowed that ſeveral eccleſiaſtical canons have been received and uſed here, yet it ought to be remembered, and particularly by the men of holy church, that ſuch canons ſo received and uſed here, have received their force only from their acceptance and uſe, and not from any power the pope or church had to impoſe laws on theſe realms; for they neither have nor ever had any authoritative force in themſelves, but all that ever the church or churchmen did here, more than they had the royal ſanction and aſſent of the people for, were meer incroachments, as far as they were the acts of the biſhop of* Rome, *and they were acts of treaſon and rebellion, as they were the acts of our own clergy; as all the books antient and modern declare, though the contrary notions have, againſt all colour, been avowed and practiced, to the diſinheriſon of the crown and people, to the diſparagement of the common law and our antient conſtitution itſelf, by thoſe glaring church lights, St.* Anſelm, *St.* Thomas a Beckett, *and ſome other ſaints of the ſame order of latter ages; but theſe holy fathers and their works being moſtly defunct, and retired to their deſerved oblivion, may they ever reſt there.*

2. References, *Da. le ca. de commenda. Ha. Hiſt. Law* 27 *to* 34, 70, 71, 72. 1 *Ju. Eccl.* 61.

495. *Ubi non eſt lex, ibi non eſt tranſgreſſio.*

1. THE purpoſe or intent of a man, without action, is not puniſhable by the law; and *ubi non eſt lex, ibi non eſt tranſgreſſio, quoad mundum.* 4 Co. 16. b.

2. Rules, *Intention, without act, not to be puniſhed. Verba ſemper accipienda ſunt in mitiore ſenſu.*

496. *Ubi non eſt principalis, non* { *poteſt eſſe* / *datur* } *acceſſorius.*

1. *JOHN GOFFE*, brother and heir of *Richard Goffe*, brought an appeal of murder of the ſaid *Richard*, againſt *Bibithe* as principal, and againſt *Hoel David* as acceſſory before, and againſt *David ap Thomas* as acceſſory after. The principal pleaded *non cul'*, but by *niſi prius* in the county of *Monmouth* he was found guilty of manſlaughter, and not of murder, and had his clergy. And upon this matter, 1ſt, It was reſolved *per Popham* chief juſtice, *et per totam curiam*, in the king's bench, that *Hoel David* was diſcharged; becauſe there could not be an acceſſory before the fact in the caſe of manſlaughter; for manſlaughter ought to follow on ſudden quarrel or fray; for if it be premeditate, or of forethought, it is murder. 2dly, It was reſolved that though the principal was convicted by verdict, yet as he had his clergy before judgment, ſo that it did not judicially appear, *ſcil.* by judgment of law, who was principal, and therefore for the cauſe alledged in *Syer*'s caſe, [*mentioned before, under* Rule *Ubi factum nullum, ibi fortia nulla*] it was awarded that both the acceſſories, as well he before as he after, ſhould be diſcharged. The ſame law, if the principal, upon arraignment, had confeſſed the felony, and before judgment obtained a pardon, or had his clergy allowed him; for there the acceſſory is diſcharged. 4 *Co.* 43. *b.* 44. *a.*

2. One *Stephens* and *Alice* his daughter were indicted at the ſeſſions of the peace in the county of *Cambridge*, before the juſtices of peace there; becauſe the ſaid *Alice* feloniouſly ſtole a rake and fork of the value of 3 *s.* and a rope of the value 1 *s.* 6 *d.* and that *Stephens* the father knowing thereof received and comforted the ſaid *Alice*, and ſo was acceſſory, and thereupon they were arraigned, and pleaded not guilty: And by means of one *Spicer*, the under ſheriff, who returned two of his ſervants to be of the jury (as appeared by affidavit of ſome of the jurors) they were found guilty, and *Alice* the principal, becauſe the goods were under value, according to the ſtatute, was awarded to be burnt in the hand, and that ſhe ſhould forfeit all her lands and tenements, goods and chattels: And againſt the ſaid *Stephens* judgment was given (becauſe he had prayed his book, and was returned *legit ut clericus*) that he ſhould be burnt in the hand; and ſo it was done immediately to them both; and that he ſhould forfeit all his lands and tenements, goods and chattels; and preſently the under ſheriff ſeiſed the lands and alſo the goods and chattels of the ſaid *Stephens* being of the value of 500*l.* and returned into the exchequer, that he ſeiſed his goods only to the value of 3 *s.* (as it was informed at the bar); and upon this

 judgment,

judgment, *Stephens* brought a writ of error: And *Grimſton* being of counſel with the plaintiff, aſſigned error in judgment, and *Berkley* and myſelf being only in court, upon reading of the record, held it to be manifeſt error; for the principal not being attainted, but diſcharged by burning in the hand only, according to the ſtatute; the acceſſory ought to have been diſcharged without any burning in the hand, and without being put to his book; for he ought not to be condemned but where the principal is attainted, and not where he is only convicted, and had his clergy; and ſo is the common experience and practice. Alſo the judgment is erroneouſly given; becauſe it is, that he ſhall forfeit his lands and tenements, after ſuch conviction and clergy allowed; wherefore the judgment was reverſed: And the clerk of the crown was directed to draw an information upon this miſdemeanor of *Spicer*, for the procuring of the ſaid *Stephens* in ſuch an undue manner to be convicted. *Cro. Ca.* 566, 567.

3. References, 2 *E.* 3. 27. 22 *E.* 3. *Tit. Coron.* 260. 7 *H.* 4. 1. *and* 7. *Fitzh. Coron.* 53. 9 *Co.* 114. *Lord Sanchar*'s caſe. *Stat.* 2 *E.* 6. *cap.* 24.

4. Rule, *Ubi factum nullum, ibi fortia nulla, &c.*

497. *Verba accipienda ſunt cum effectu.*

1. TEſtament, *teſtatio mentis,* is favourably to be expounded according to the meaning of the teſtator. *In contractibus benigna, in teſtamentis benignior, in reſtitutionibus benigniſſima interpretatio facienda eſt. And in wills the latter doth controul the firſt; for voluntas teſtatoris eſt ambulatoria uſque ad mortem.* But though it be the laſt will that countermands the firſt, yet the firſt grant is of the greateſt force; and in one will where there are divers deviſes of one thing, the laſt deviſe taketh place, *cum duo inter ſe repugnantia reperiuntur in teſtamento, ultimum ratum eſt.* Co. Lit. 112. a. b.

2. References, 39 *H.* 6. 18. 3 *Co.* 23. 4 *Co.* 48. *Co. Lit.* 183. *b. Plow. Com.* 197. *b.* 213. *a. Cro. Ca.* 293. *Sir W. Jo.* 195. 3 *Cro.* 330, 359, 382, 526, 679, 742. 1 *Sid.* 153, 379. 2 *Sid.* 26, 149, 151. 1 *Lev.* 304. 2 *Lev.* 15. *Plow. Com.* 344. *Dal.* 3. 68. *Salk.* 237. 1 *Show.* 350. 2 *Show.* 63. *Hut.* 32. *Sty.* 301, 307. *Show. Pa. Ca.* 195. *Raym.* 335. *Pol.* 37, 403. *Comb.* 195. 1 *Leon.* 251, 254. 2 *Leon.* 120. 3 *Leon.* 19, 130. 4 *Leon.* 73. *Owen* 35. *Hob.* 65. 2 *Mod.* 9, 292. 1 *Vern.* 250. *Eq. Abr.* 199, 207.

498. *Verba currentis monetae tempus ſolutionis deſignant.*

What current money.

1. REſolved, though at the time of the contract and obligation made in the principal caſe, pure money of gold or ſilver, was current in the place where the payment was aſſigned, yet mixt money being eſtabliſhed before the day of payment, it might be well tendred in diſcharge of the obligation, and the obligee is bound to accept it: and if he refuſe it, and ſtay 'till the money be again changed, the obligor is not bound to pay him in other money of greater value; it's enough he be always

always ready to pay the mixt money, *&c.* according to the price it was current at the time of the tender. *Da.* 26. *b.* 27. *a.*

Time of payment and place.

2. Future time is intended by the words *current money*; for things paſt are not current; therefore all have agreed in this rule, *verba currentis monetae tempus ſolutionis deſignant*; and to this purpoſe are many caſes cited in our books. 6 and 7 *E.* 6. *Dy.* 81. *b.* After the fall of money 5 *E.* 6. debt was brought againſt the executors of a leſſee *pur ans* for two years rent in arrear, ending at *Mich.* 2 *E.* 6. at which time the ſhilling, which at the time of the action brought was cried down to 6 *d.* was current at 12 *d.* The defendant pleaded tender at the day *in peciis monetae Angliae vocat'* ſhillings, *et que cheſcun ſhilling al temps del' tender fuit ſolubilis pro* 12 *d.* but that the plaintiff, nor any for him, were ready to receive them, *&c.* and concludes that he is ſtill ready to pay the arrearages *in dictis peciis, &c. ſecundum ratam, &c.* the plaintiff took the money *ſans* coſts or damages. And to the ſame effect is the caſe of *Pollardes* adjudged 29 *E.* 1. reported by *Dy.* 7 *E.* 6. *fo.* 82. *b.* in debt on an obligation for 24 *l.* at two ſeveral days. The defendant pleaded, that at the day, *&c. currebat quaedam moneta quae vocabatur Pollardes loco ſterlingi, &c.* and that he the firſt day of payment had tendred a moiety of the ſaid debt in the ſaid money called *Pollardes*, which the plaintiff refuſed, and that he is ſtill ready, *&c.* and offered it in court; which not being denied by the plaintiff, *ideo conceſſum eſt*, that he ſhould recover a moiety in *Pollardes*, and the other in pure ſterling. *Vide* 9 *E.* 4. 49. *a.* A notable caſe upon the change of money, where it is ſaid that if a man in an action of debt demand 40 *l.* it ſhall be underſtood of money that is current at the time the writ purchaſed. And there a caſe of *E.* 1. is put direct in point. Debt is brought *ſur fait* of 30 quarters of barley, price 20 *l.* It was found for the plaintiff, and the jury were charged to inquire of the price at the time of payment; and it was ſaid that at the time of payment, it was 32 *s. per* quarter, but at the time the deed made it was but at 30 *s.* and the plaintiff recovered 18 *l.* for the corn, according to the price it bore at the time of payment. To this purpoſe *Linwood* hath a notable gloſs upon the conſtitutions of *Simon Mepham, lib.* 3. *de teſtamentis, cap. item quia.* For where the conſtitution is ſuch, *pro publicatione teſtamenti pauperis, cujus inventorium bonorum non excedit centum ſolidos ſterlingorum, nihil penitus exigatur*, he makes this gloſs, *hic ſolidus ſumitur pro duodecim denariis Anglicanis, &c. ſed quaero, inquit ille, numquid circa hos centum ſolidos debet conſiderari valor in monetâ jam currente, vel valor ſterlingorum qui currebant tempore ſtatuti?* And there he reſolveth, *quod ubi diſpoſitio ſurgit ex ſtatuto, ut hic, licet moneta ſit diminuta in valore, tamen debet conſiderari reſpectu monetae novae currentis, et non reſpectu antiquae; nam mutatâ monetâ mutari videtur ſtatutum, ut ſcilicet intelligatur de nova, et non de veteri. Vide* regiſter *fo.* 50. *a.* and 54. *b.* where the king ſent his writ to be certified of the value of the church, the words of which writ are, *ſecundum taxationem decimæ jam currentis.* Anno 31 *E.* 3. *Fitzh. Anuitie* 28. An annuity was granted to *J. S.* 'till he was promoted by the grantor to a ſufficient benefice. *J. S.* brought his writ

writ of annuity against the grantor, who pleaded his tender of a sufficient benefice to the plaintiff, and the issue is there taken upon the value of the benefice at the time of the tender. It was said, that although, in contracts these words, *currentis monetae*, shall refer to the time of payment, yet in last wills they shall refer *ad temps conditi testamenti*, for the bequest is in the present tense, Item, *I give and bequeath*, &c. therefore legacies shall be paid in such coin as was current at the time the will was made, or according to the rate of it. It was also said, That if a man hath 100 *l.* pure silver, in marriage with his wife, and after they are divorced *causa praecontractus*; for which cause the wife shall have her portion back: or if a man recover by erroneous judgment 100 *l.* in debt, and hath execution in pure silver, and after the judgment is reversed, so that he shall be restored to all that he had lost, though base money be established in the mean time, yet restitution shall be in such money as was current at the time of the marriage, and at the time of the recovery: but these last cases were not resolved. And as to the circumstances of the place, it was resolved, That though the contract was in *London*, yet *Dublin* being the place appointed for the payment, it is of necessity, that the obligor might make his tender in mixt money, at the time of payment; for all other money was then decried, and this only established; so that had the obligee refused this money, he had committed a contempt for which he might have been punished; also *the judges of the law are not obliged to take notice of any other money than what is current by proclamation.* And therefore *Prisot* said, 34 *H.* 6. *fo.* 12. *a. Nous ne somus apprize de* 6 *l.* Flemish, *come somus de cent nobles.* And therefore *in all contracts between merchants, consuetudo et statuta loci, in quem est destinata solutio, respicienda sunt. Budelius, de re nummaria, lib.* 2. *cap.* 21. And therefore it was said, upon judgment of debt given in *England*, *sur testatum*, that the defendant *ne ad riens en England*, but that he had goods and lands in *Ireland*, and execution is awarded to the justices or deputy of *Ireland* to levy the debt there, which writ is found in the *Reg. Brev. Judicialium*, *fo.* 43. *b.* The sum in such case shall be levied according to the rate of *Irish* money, and not of *English* money, and that in such coin as shall be there current at the time of execution made; and according to this resolution, many other cases upon the same point were afterwards ruled and adjudged in the several courts of record in *Dublin. Da.* 26. *b.* 27. *a. b.* 28. *a.*

3. Rules, *Quicquid solvitur solvitur secundum modum solventis. Moneta est justum medium et mensura rerum commutabilium.*

499. *Verba aequivoca et in dubio posita, intelliguntur digniori et potentiori sensu.*

1. GRegory brought error against *Blachfield*, and the case was, That *B.* brought a plaint in the court of *Ludlow*, which is a court of record, against *C. tam pro domina regina quam per seipso*, upon the *Stat.* 4 & 5 *Ph.* & *Ma. cap.* 5. (which see in *Rast. Draperie* 135.) which prohibits any to weave woollen cloth or kersies, unless he had been an apprentice, or exercised the trade, &c. for seven years, on the penalty of for-

 feiture

feiture of ſuch cloth or its value, *the penalty to be recovered by action, bill, plaint or information, in any court of record*, in which no eſſoign, protection, *&c.* and three errors were aſſigned. 1. That the ſaid branch of the act was abrogated and taken away by *Stat.* 5 *Eliz. cap.* 4. *ſed non allocatur*; for *inſpecto ſtatuto*, both might well ſtand together, and it was ſaid, *that a latter ſtatute in the affirmative did not toll a former act*, et eo potius, *if the former be particular, and the laſt general.* 2. That by the *Stat.* 18 *Eliz. cap.* 5. he ought to have ſued either by original or information: And ſo it was adjudged *Hill.* 30 *Eliz.* in this court, where the defendant was ſued by bill *ſur le ſtat.* 23 *H.* 6. *de Viſcount*, and adjudged it lay not. 3. That though *Ludlow* be a court of record, yet it is not ſuch an one as is intended by the ſtatute for three reaſons. 1. The courts intended by the ſtatute *propter excellentiam*, are the four courts of record at *Weſtminſter*, which are the general courts of record, and therefore in common parlance it ſhall be ſo intended; as eſcuage is either certain or uncertain; the latter is *ſervitium militare*, the former *ſervitium ſocae*, *quia quemadmodum certitudo ſcutagii facit ſocagium, ita incertitudo facit ſervitium militare.* And *Littleton* ſaith, if a man ſpeak generally of eſcuage, it ſhall be intended (*ſecundum excellentiam*) in common ſpeech, of the more worthy ſervice, *&c.* and 10 *E.* 4. 11. *b.* if it be ſpoken of proof generally, though there are ſeveral proofs in law, yet it ſhall be underſtood of the higheſt, which is by jury, *Perk.* 790. and 20 *H.* 6. 17. if it be general ſpoken of the feaſt of St. *Michael*, if there are two ſuch feaſts, it ſhall be intended of the moſt worthy and notorious. And 37 *H.* 6. 29. 21 *H.* 6. 8. and 13 *H.* 4. 4. If it be ſpoke of *J. S.* generally, it ſhall be intended of the father, or of the eldeſt ſon; for they are the moſt worthy. And with the caſe at bar agrees in effect *Mich.* 6 *&* 7 *Eliz. fo.* 236. where any court of the queen of record ſhall be underſtood one of the moſt eminent and excellent courts at *Weſtminſter.* 2. If the act ſhould be taken according to the letter, *ſcil.* in any court of record, then courts of *Oyer* and *Terminer*, gaol-delivery, ſewers, the ſheriff's torn, leet, pye-powders, and others, ſhould be within the act; for theſe and many more are courts of record; then the matter being left to the conſtruction of law, the rule is, *Quod verba aequivoca et in dubio poſita, intelliguntur in digniori et potentiori ſenſu.* 3. The uſage in all ſuch popular actions or informations hath been, that though the informer *tam pro domina regina quam pro ſeipſo* exhibited the information, yet if the defendant pleaded a ſpecial plea, the queen's attorney ſhould reply only; and it was intended by the makers of the act, that the ſuit ſhould be in ſuch court where the queen's attorney might attend for the advantage of the queen which ſhe is ſuppoſed to take by ſuch ſuit, and that muſt be in the four courts of record at *Weſtminſter*, and for theſe two laſt errors the judgment was reverſed. 6 *Co.* 19. *b.* 20. *a.*

500. *Verba relata hoc maxime operantur per referentiam, ut in esse videntur.*

AS if the father infeoff the son, to have and to hold to him and his heirs; and the son re-infeoff the father as fully as the father infeoffed him; the father hath a fee-simple, *quia verba relata hoc maxime operantur per referentiam, ut in esse videntur.* Co. Lit. 9. b.

501. *Verba chartarum fortius accipiuntur contrà proferentem.*

1. REferences, 4 *H.* 7. 7. *b.* 5 *H.* 7. 33. 6 *Co.* 57, *&c.* 9 *Co.* 58, 59. *Cro. Ca.* 510. 1 *Ro.* 88.

2. Rules, *Every man's deed is to be taken most strongly against himself. Constructio legis non facit injuriam.*

502. *Verba semper accipienda sunt in mitiori sensu.*

In cases of the king himself.

In the king's grants or patents.

1. THE king's grants or charters, made for the erection of pious and charitable uses, shall always be taken in the most benign and beneficial sense. 10 *Co.* 28. *a.*

In acts of parliament.

Where the king is bound tho' not named.

2. See rule, *Rex est mixta persona cum sacerdote.*

In actions for words.

Where spoke of private persons.

3. Action *sur le case* for words, *Sir* Thomas Holt *struck his cook on the head with a cleaver, and cleaved his head, the one part lay on the one shoulder and the other part on the other.* Not guilty pleaded; moved in arrest of judgment, words not actionable, not being averred the cook was killed, but *argumentative*; the court of that opinion; for the slander ought to be direct, against which there may not be any intendment; but here, notwithstanding such wording, the party may be yet alive, and it is then but trespass; therefore it was adjudged for the defendant. *Cro. Jac.* 184.

4. If one woman sue another for calling her *quean*, a prohibition lieth; for that it is not well known what is meant by the word, and it is but a word of heat and anger. *Rol. Abr. Prohibition* 296. *case* 14.

5. If a man sue another for calling him *son of a whore, and his mother was a bitch*, for which he sueth in the ecclesiastical court, a prohibition lieth;

eth; for they are but words of anger. *Ro. Abr. Prohibition, caſe* 15. *ſee alſo caſe* 17 *and* 19. *and alſo* 1 *Ro. Rep. where ſpoken of eccleſiaſtical clerks.*

6. A prohibition was moved for by Mr. ſerjeant *Wright*, now Mr. juſtice *Wright*, to the ſpiritual court of *Norwich*, in a ſuit pending there for defamation; *you are an old rogue and a thief, and I will prove you ſo, and an old whoring rogue, and a baſtard-getting old rogue*; he agreed the latter words were of ſpiritual cognizance; but as the firſt were temporal, a prohibition lay for the whole, for which purpoſe he cited, 2 *Inſt.* 493. Rule to ſhew cauſe. *Eaſter* term following, ſerjeant *Eyre* coming to ſhew cauſe, argued theſe words were not of temporal nature ſufficient to ground a prohibition; but the court, holding the contrary, made the rule abſolute. 2 *Ju. Eccl.* 215.

7. If a parſon call A. *a drunkard*, whereupon *A.* anſwereth *thou lieſt*, if the parſon ſue *A.* in the eccleſiaſtical court for giving him the lye, a prohibition lieth; for that the cauſe was not ſpiritual, but depended upon a precedent temporal matter. *Ro. Abr.* 295. *caſe* 5.

8. If a man call a miniſter *knave*, ſerjeant *Roll* ſays he may be ſued for it in the eccleſiaſtical court, and no prohibition granted. *Prohibition* 295. *caſe* 8. *tamen quaere de hoc Jur* 1 *Vent.* 2. *ou une prohibition fuit grant en tiel caſe.*

9. If *J. B.* ſay to *J. D.* it is reported *J. N.* did or doth keep in his houſe a man or boy to bugger, whereto *J. D.* anſwereth, the vile villain would have done as much to me. If *J. N.* ſue *J. D.* averring himſelf to be a miniſter, a prohibition lieth; becauſe it is no ſpiritual defamation, and is felony by ſtatute. *Mich.* 8 *Car. B. R. Higgon* and *Coppinger*, *intratur Hill.* 8 *Car. Ro.* 129. *Ro. Abr. Prohibition* 2. *fo.* 297. *caſe* 20.

10. One libels in the court chriſtian againſt another, for ſaying of him *thou art fitter for the pillory than for a preacher*, and that he ſpoke the words in time of divine ſervice; and hereupon ſentence is given, that he ſhould recant the words, *&c.* if the defendant ſhew to the temporal court, that he ſpoke them of a certain releaſe, *&c.* ſaying that the plaintiff had forged the ſaid releaſe, and that on that account the words were ſpoken, ſo that he might have had an action at law for the words, in ſuch caſe, though the words may maintain a ſuit in the eccleſiaſtical court, being ſpoken in ſervice-time, yet for that ſentence is given that he ſhould revoke the words, which is for all, a prohibition ſhall go for the whole. *Rol. Abr.* 316. *caſe* 7.

11. *Prohibition*, becauſe *Parlor*, the plaintiff in the prohibition, was convened before the high commiſſioners, for ſaying to *Butler*, a parſon, *that he was fitter to ſtand on the pillory than preach in the pulpit, and that he had taken two orders already, that he wanted but taking the third, which was to have his ears cut off*; *Parlor* juſtified, becauſe the parſon had forged an acquittance, and ſhewed it in certain; the commiſſioners would not allow of this juſtification, but cenſured him to aſk pardon; whereupon he brought prohibition, and well; for the high commiſſioners had nothing to do with the cauſe, unleſs it was in time of divine ſervice. *Mo. fo.* 460. *caſe* 639.

12. Dr. *Parſons* libelled againſt *Coxeter*, for ſaying of him, *he had no ſenſe, was a dunce, and a blockhead, and he wondered the biſhop would lay his hands upon ſuch a fellow, and that he deſerved to have his gown*

 pulled

pulled over his ears; a prohibition was granted; for a parfon is not punifhable in the fpiritual court, for being a knave or a blockhead, more than another man; and whereas it was urged, that a parfon might be deprived for want of learning; the chief juftice faid, if that be the cafe he may bring his action at law; for that was a temporal damage. So prohibition granted. *Salk.* 692. *Vide etiam* 1 *Vent.* 2.

13. A prohibition went to the court chriftian, to ftay a fuit there for calling a parfon, *fool, afs and goofe*, for they are but words of heat, and do not touch him in his profeffion. 2 *Lev.* 49.

14. A clergyman being bailiff of a manor, oppreffeth the tenants, whereupon one of them fays to him, *you are a knave and fitter to wear a white cloak than a black one*, a prohibition fhall go to ftay the fuit in the court chriftian. *Rol. Abr.* 295. *cafe* 6.

15. The parties being both clergymen, the plaintiff libelled againft the defendant in the court chriftian for faying, *you are an old rogue, and a rafcal, and a contemptible fellow, defpifed and hated by every body*; and likewife for faying of him at another time, *you are a lyer*. Moved by Mr. *Filmer* for a prohibition; notwithftanding the firft fet of words were faid to be fpoken againft the plaintiff in his profeffion or function. Rule to fhew caufe.

Where fpoken by men of a profeffion in fuch their profeffion, and where not, the difference, as judges, counfel, &c.

16. One is accufed, before juftices of the peace, to be the father of a baftard, and a juftice in the examination faid, *it is his baftard*, and for fo faying, is fued in the court chriftian; a prohibition fhall go; for that the words were fpoken in his office. *Ro. Prohibition, fo.* 303. *cafe* 1.

17. But *aliter* had the juftice fpoken them at another time after the examination. *Ibid. Tamen quaere, fince it feems to me the matter might be well juftified from the proof on the examination, and the order finding him the father, and ordering him to provide for it, as the father of fuch baftard.* See 2 Ro. Prec. Chan. 87. Cro. Jac. 625.

18. Sir *Thomas Hughes* of *Gray's Inn* applied by *Henden* ferjeant, for a prohibition; the cafe was, he being of counfel with the defendant in cafe for thefe words, *the plaintiff hath murdered three children*; on not guilty pleaded, *Hughes*, to extenuate the damages for his client, preffed the fact to make the matter probable; and becaufe it was in his profeffion, and pertinent to his client's caufe, though it was not directly to the iffue, a prohibition was granted. *Hob.* 328. *Vide* 2 *Rol.* 59, 293. *Mo.* 915. *Godb.* 215. *Reg.* 49, 51. *Fi. Ley* 142. *Dy.* 79. 2 *Sid.* 152. 6 *Mod.* 26, 287.

19. In the cafe of fcandal, *&c.* in a bill or anfwer, it is now a commendable practice to charge the counfel with cofts. 1 *Chan. Ca.* 71. *Margin.*

Where fpoken of men of the law.

Judges.

20. *Skinner*, a merchant of *London*, faid of *Manwood*, lord chief baron, *that he was a corrupt judge*; and adjudged that the words were actionable.

Vide 4 E. 6. *Action sur le case* 112. 4 *Co.* 16. *a.* See also judge *Hutton*'s case. See also judge *Croke*'s case. *Marsh. Rep. Ca.* 119.

Masters in chancery.

21. The plaintiff *Othelwal* was a master in chancery, and as such a matter was referred to him by the lord keeper, between the defendant *Holman* and one *Gotts*, and the plaintiff made his report, which was decreed; and the defendant being served with the writ of execution of the decree, and the money demanded of him, the defendant being discontented, said he would not pay the money, but prevent it if he could; for that he knew the old course, that the plaintiff and *Gotts* were sharers, thereby falsly and maliciously slandering and charging the plaintiff with corruption, and agreeing to take part of the money; and to the further scandal of the plaintiff, the defendant had preferred a petition to the lord keeper, whereby he falsly charged the plaintiff with divers wrongs and injustices done him in the said report. And for this scandal the defendant was committed to the *Fleet*, fined 1000 marks, and ordered to acknowledge his offence, and make his submission in the court of chancery. *Mich.* 3 *Car. in the Star-Chamber.* See *Rush. Col.*

22. The plaintiff, Sir *Euble Thelwal*, being a master in chancery, the defendant being dissatisfied at several reports made by the said master, contrived a libel in nature of a petition, containing that the said master had made a false report in his cause against one *Hughes & al'*, and that he was not an indifferent person in the cause; and to this petition annexed a schedule of exceptions, containing that the said master had made two false reports against him, that he was become his prosecutor by indirect means, *&c.* and caused the said petition to be delivered to his honour of the rolls, desiring the reference to be transferred. And by another writing delivered to the master himself, he falsly charged him with ordering things not referred, making of false reports in two causes without warrant, cause or colour, and that he was become a party against him; and therefore required him to meddle no further in his business; for which he was committed, fined 200*l.* and ordered to acknowledge his fault at the chancery bar, at the great sessions for the county of *Denbigh*, and the decree to be then read. *Mich.* 6 *Car. in Star-Chamber.* See *Rush. Col.*

Counsel.

23. Whereas the plaintiff was of the *Middle Temple* for divers years, and called to the bar, and gave counsel to divers the king's subjects, and practiced the law, and had married the daughter of *J. S.* that the defendant having communication with the said *J. S.* concerning the plaintiff and the marriage of his daughter, said of the plaintiff *he is a dunce, and will get little by the law,* to which words the said *J. S.* answering, that others had a better opinion of him, he replied, *he was never but accounted a dunce in the* Middle Temple. Defendant pleaded not guilty, but found against him, and damages to 100 marks, *&c.* *Cro. Ca.* 382, 383. *Vide* 1 *Rol. Abr.* 55. (5.)

Attornies.

24. Said of a sworn attorney, *he was a corrupt man, and known to deal corruptly*; being before speaking of the manner of his dealing in his profes-

ſion. It was reſolved, theſe words, *ex cauſa dicendi,* import that he dealt corruptly in his profeſſion; and therefore it was ſaid, *quod ſermo relatus ad perſonam intelligi debet de conditione perſonae,* and the plaintiff had judgment for two reaſons. 1. Becauſe it is ſcandal in his oath. 2. The words ſcandalize him in the duty of his profeſſion by which he got his living. 4 *Co.* 16. *a.*

25. Action for theſe words of an attorney, *Thou art a knave, and ſtirreſt up ſuits betwixt parties; and ſtirreſt up ſuits betwixt ſuch parties to their undoing; and it is great pity ſuch perſons ſhould go unhanged.* Adjudged the action lies. *Cro. Ca.* 229.

Actions de ſcandalis magnatum, ou de les haut homes del' realm.

The ſtatutes relating to this learning, which are.

26. *Stat. W.* 1. *cap.* 33. made 25 *April,* 3 *E.* 1. *anno domini* 1275. 2 *R.* 2. *cap.* 5. and 12 *R.* 2. *cap.* 9. 1 & 2 *Ph.* & *Ma.* 3. and 1 *El.* 6. both which laſt are expired.

The purport.

27. By the ſtatute *W.* 1. a teller of tidings whereof diſcord or ſlander may grow between the king and his people, or the great men of the realm, ſhall be taken and put in priſon, till he hath found and brought into the king's court him that ſhewed him the tale.

28. And by the ſtatute 2 *R.* 2. *cap.* 5. tellers of falſe news and falſe meſſengers, [*or liers*] of prelates, dukes, earls, barons, and other nobles, alſo of the chancellor, treaſurer, clerk of the privy ſeal, ſteward of the houſe, juſtices of the one bench or of the other, *and of other great officers of the realm,* &c.

29. And by the ſtatute 12 *R.* 2. *cap.* 9. if he cannot find the author, he is to be puniſhed by the advice of the king's counſel.

Who haut home within the intent of the ſtatutes.

30. Viſcounts are within the ſtatute of *Scandalis Magnatum,* though there firſt creation was not till 18 *H.* 6. *Palm.* 565.

31. *Alſo I conceive that peereſſes in their own right, are intitled to the benefit of theſe ſtatutes, and not only ſo, but alſo the wives and widows of peers; as the term* home *takes in and comprehends both ſexes, and as I conceive, theſe are as tender in point of honour, as any of the others expreſly named in the ſame ſtatutes.* Tamen quaere.

32. This remedy lies for the barons of the exchequer, though the ſtatute be for the judges of the one bench and the other. *Palm.* 565.

33. But the king is not included therein. *Dy.* 155.

How to be conſtrued.

34. Theſe ſtatutes are to be underſtood of ſuch ſlanders as touch the nobles, and great officers named therein; and muſt not be underſtood of the king; for he is an exempt perſon, and not implied in theſe words, *les haut homes, ou grand homes ou nobles.* Dy. 155.

Where-

Wherefore qui tam.

35. As it is ſaid in the ſtatute, that great peril, miſchief and deſtruction might enſue to all the realm, *&c.* and that it concerned the king, who is head of the realm; for theſe reaſons ſuch actions *de ſcandalis magnatum* have been brought upon the ſaid ſtatute, *tam pro domino rege quam pro ſeipſo.* 4 Co. 13. a.

Wherefore to be taken notice of, and how by the judges.

36. The ſtatutes of ſcandal of *les haut homes de l' realm*, are to be taken notice of by the judges *ex officio*, as theſe ſtatutes concern the king; foraſmuch as they are of the prelates, nobles and great officers of his crown, *&c.* 4 *Co.* 13. *a.*

Particular caſes.

Of prelates.

37. *Action de ſcandalis magnatum* brought by the plaintiff, the biſhop of *Norwich*, for theſe falſe and ſcandalous words ſpoken of him, *You have writ a letter to me, which I have to ſhew, which is againſt the word of God, againſt the queen's authority, and to the maintenance of ſuperſtition; and that I will ſtand to prove againſt you:* He confeſſed the words at the trial, to be ſpoken by him. And damages were found to 500 marks, which were awarded, and 8*l.* for coſts. *Cro. Eliz.* 1, 2.

38. The defendant for publiſhing a ſcandalous libel againſt the plaintiff, (*Thornbroughe*) being a reverend and learned biſhop, was committed to the *Fleet*, fined 100*l.* and ordered to make an humble acknowledgment and ſubmiſſion to the plaintiff, at *Worceſter* aſſiſes, the judges ſitting, and the decree to be then and there read. *Biſhop of Worceſter* verſus *Bowyer, in the Star-Chamber,* Paſch. 5 Car. *See* Ruſh. Col.

39. The defendant framed and wrote a witleſs and malicious libellous letter, directed to Mr. *Brookes* a proctor at *York*, and *Squire*, a clerk in the office of conſiſtory there, or to either of them, wherein was contained, *That the biſhop is ſo ſtrong, that if bribery will be taken, you muſt lie all along, becauſe the biſhop ſhits warrants at every door,* meaning thereby the biſhop of *Cheſter*; and ſent that letter to them at *York*, by one *Markland*, and *M.* delivered to *Leigh* who broke it open; and for this the defendant was committed, fined 500 *l.* adjudged to ſtand in the pillory at *Wiggan, Lancaſter* aſſiſes, and at *Cheſter*, with a paper on his head, inſcribed with words declaring the nature of his offence, and in each place publickly and penitentially to acknowledge his offence and ſcandal of the biſhop, in ſuch manner as it ſhould be penned and delivered unto him. *Attorney General* verſus *Reignolds, in the Star-Chamber, Paſch.* 9 *Car.* See *Ruſh. Col.* See alſo *Scandal ſpoken of the archbiſhop of* Canterbury, *the term of Hil. in the ſame court and year, in* Ruſh. Col.

Of temporal, or hereditary peers.

40. *Henry* lord *Cromwel* brought an action *de ſcandalis magnatum* againſt *Edmund Denny*, vicar of *Northingham* in the county of *Norfolk*, *tam pro domino rege quam pro ſeipſo*; and declared upon the ſtatute

2 *R.* 2. *cap.* 5. That if any ſhould contrive *aliqua falſa nova, horribilia et falſa nuncia, de praelatis, ducibus, comitibus, et aliis proceribus, et magnatibus regni*, &c. whereby debate might ariſe between the lords and commons, whereby peril, miſchief and deſtruction might enſue to all the realm, &c. *et quicunque contra fecerit* ſhould incur the pains of the ſtatute *W.* 1. *cap.* 33. [*that he lie in priſon till he produce the author*] and the defendant was charged that he ſaid to the plaintiff, then a baron of the realm, *It is no marvel that you like not of me*; *for you like of thoſe that maintain ſedition againſt the queen's proceedings.* The defendant juſtifies the words; whereupon the plaintiff demurred, and the bar was held inſufficient. And term *Trin.* 23 *Eliz.* in arreſt of judgment it was moved for the defendant, that the declaration was inſufficient, the act being miſrecited; the words being *ſi aſcun controver: aſcun faux novelles, et horribles et faux meſſoignes*, which word (*meſſoignes*) he, who tranſlated the ſtatutes at large into *Engliſh*, had tranſlated (*meſſages*) which occaſioned him, who drew the declaration in the caſe at bar, to inſert the word (*nuncia*) where it ſhould have been *mendacia.* 2. The ſaid act ſays, *et quicunque le fra incurgera*, &c. the plaintiff in his declaration ſaith, *et quicunque contra fecerit*, which *tantamounts* to ſay *que ceſtuy que ne fra.* But to this it was objected, that the ſaid act was a private act, and concerned only the prelates, nobles, and certain great officers, whereof the court were not, *ex officio*, to take notice; and therefore the court were to take the act as the party had alledged it. But it was reſolved by *Wray* chief juſtice, Sir *Thomas Gaudy*, and all the court, *That it was ſuch an act whereof the court ſhould take notice, et eo magis*, becauſe *per un meane* it concerned the king himſelf. 1. Inaſmuch as it concerned the prelates, nobles, and great officers, which are of the king's council, and of eminent quality, and ſerve him in high and honourable offices which they hold under his majeſty; and by his royal authority have the adminiſtration of juſtice to his ſubjects; by which it appears, *that ſlander of them principally concerns the king himſelf in his royal government.* 2. As the ſtatute ſays, that peril, miſchief and deſtruction might enſue to all the realm, &c. *it concerns the king, for he is head of the realm:* and theſe are the cauſes that always ſuch actions, as have been brought upon the ſtatute *de ſcandalis magnatum*, have been brought *tam pro domino rege quam pro ſeipſo.* And of *all ſtatutes which concern the king, the judges are bound to take notice.* Alſo it was reſolved, if the act were private, and the court to take it as alleged, then it were againſt law and reaſon, and therefore void; for thoſe who had not offended might be puniſhed, which were *condemnare inſontem et dimittere reum*; whereupon judgment was given againſt the plaintiff, *quod nil capiat per billam.* And after the plaintiff brought a new action, and amended the inſufficiencies of his count; and then the court was moved, that the ſaid words were not actionable; becauſe it might well be that the plaintiff conceived a liking to ſome who maintained ſedition againſt the queen's proceedings, and yet not know that they maintained ſedition; neither do the words import that he knew they maintained ſedition. And it was ſaid, *quod ſenſus verborum eſt duplex, ſcil. mitis et aſper, et verba ſemper accipienda ſunt in mitiori ſenſu*; to which it was ſaid, that *ſedition is a public matter*; *et dicitur ſeditio quaſi ſeorſum itio magni populi, quando itur ad manus*, &c. That ſedition, (being ſo public and violent) it was ſaid, that by common

 intend-

intendment the plaintiff had notice of it: It was not to be likened or resembled to felony or murder, which might be clandeſtine and done in ſecret. But to this the judges gave no opinion; for they ſaid, that upon argument and conſideration, they might alter their preſent opinions, which might be hurtful to the party; and therefore they told the counſel for the defendant, to be well adviſed, and to plead or demur at their peril: So they pleaded a ſpecial juſtification, (well knowing that the other matter would be ſaved to them); and the effect of the juſtification was, that the defendant was vicar of *N.* which was a benefice with cure, and that the plaintiff procured *J. T.* and *J. G.* to preach ſeverally in the ſaid church of *N.* who in their ſermons inveighed againſt the book of common prayer, eſtabliſhed by the queen and parliament, *anno primo* of her reign, and affirmed it to be ſuperſtitious and impious, *&c.* upon which the plaintiff and defendant diſcourſing in the church of thoſe ſermons, the ſaid vicar knowing they had not licences nor were authoriſed to preach, when they were going and ready to preach, before their ſeveral ſermons, inhibited them; but they, by encouragement of the plaintiff, proceeded: And the plaintiff ſaid to the defendant, *thou art a falſe varlet, and I like not of thee*; whereto the vicar ſaid, *it is no marvel that you like not of me, for you like theſe, (innuendo praedict'* J. T. *et* J. G.) *that maintain ſedition, (innuendo ſeditioſam illam doctrinam) againſt the queen's proceedings*, and ſo juſtified: And it was moved by plaintiff's counſel, that the bar was inſufficient, for two cauſes. 1. That the matter of juſtification was inſufficient; becauſe ſedition could not be committed by words, but by public and violent action. 2. If the juſtification were ſufficient, then upon the ſaid dialogue between the plaintiff and the defendant, the defendant were not guilty: But it was ſaid that ſuch a juſtification, dialoguewiſe, had never been before ſeen; but if the truth of the caſe was ſo, he ought to have pleaded *non culpabilis*, and giventhe ſpecial matter in evidence: But if he will juſtify, he ought to juſtify the words in the ſame ſenſe as they import upon the matter alledged in the declaration: As if a man bring caſe for calling the plaintiff a murderer, and the defendant will ſay, that he was talking with the plaintiff of unlawful hunting, and the plaintiff confeſſed that he killed ſeveral hares with a certain engine; whereto the defendant anſwered and ſaid thou art a murderer, (*innuendo* the killing the ſaid hares) this is no juſtification; for he does not juſtify the ſenſe of the words which the count purports; and therefore he ought to plead *non cul.* But as to this it was anſwered by the defendant's counſel, and reſolved by all the court, that the juſtification was good; *for in caſe of ſlander for words, the ſenſe of the words are to be taken*, and the ſenſe appears by the cauſe and occaſion of ſpeaking of them; for *ſenſus verborum ex cauſa dicendi accipiendus eſt. Et ſermones ſemper accipiendi ſunt ſecundum ſubjectam materiam*; and then in the preſent caſe the counſel for the defendant had well done to ſhew the ſpecial matter, by which the ſenſe of this word (*ſedition*) appeared, upon the coherence of all the words, that the defendant's intention, was the ſeditious doctrine againſt the queen's proceedings on the ſaid act of parliament, *anno primo*, whereby the book of common prayer was eſtabliſhed, and that he did not mean any ſuch public or violent ſedition as had been deſcribed, and as *ex vi termini per ſe* the word itſelf imports. And it was ſaid, *God forbid*, that any one's words

 ſhould

ſhould, by ſuch ſtrict and grammatical conſtruction, be taken by parcels againſt the manifeſt intention of the party, upon conſideration of all the words which import the true cauſe and occaſion, and which manifeſt the true ſenſe of them: *quia quae ad unum finem loquuta ſunt, non debent ad alium detorqueri*; and therefore in the ſaid caſe of murder, the court held the juſtification good, and that the defendant ſhould not be put to the general iſſue, when he confeſſes and juſtifies the words, and, by ſpecial matter ſhews they were not actionable: and though he varies from the plaintiff in the ſenſe and quality of the words, yet *that* can be no cauſe to drive him to the general iſſue: as in maintenance, the plaintiff charges the defendant with unlawful maintenance, the defendant may juſtify by reaſon of a lawful maintenance, and need not plead the general iſſue: whereupon the plaintiff replied and ſaid, *quod praedict' Edwardus Denny dixit et propalavit praedicta verba, &c. de injuria ſua propria, abſque tali cauſa*; and hereupon iſſue was joined, *et poſtea partes concordaverunt.* 4 *Co.* 12. *b.* 13. *a. b.* 14. *a.* In this caſe, *our very learned author and right reverend judge*, adviſes his readers to take notice of an excellent point of learning, in actions of ſlander. *Namely*, 1. His lordſhip's advice is to obſerve the occaſion, and cauſe of ſpeaking of the words, and how to plead in excuſe of the defendant. 2. When the matter in fact will clearly ſerve for the client, and you hold that the plaintiff has in law no cauſe of action, yet take a great care that you hazard not the matter upon demurrer, (in which, upon the pleading and otherwiſe, perhaps may ariſe more than you were aware of); but firſt take advantage of the matter of fact, and leave the matters in law, which always ariſe upon the matters in fact *ad ultimum*, and never demur in law at firſt; when after trial of matters in fact, matters in law (as in this caſe was) ſhall be ſaved to you. 4 *Co.* 14. *a.*

41. *Scandalum magnatum*, for that the defendant ſpoke theſe words, *My lord*, (praefat' comit' innuendo) *is a baſe earl, and paultry lord, and keepeth none but rogues and raſcals like himſelf.* Found guilty, and moved in arreſt of judgment, that the words were not actionable; for that they touch him not in his life, nor any matter of his loyalty, nor import him in any main point of his dignity; but are only words of ſpleen concerning his keeping of ſervants; which is not material. And to that opinion *Yelverton* and *Fleming* ſeemed to incline; but *Williams* and *Crook* to the contrary; becauſe they touched him in his honour and dignity; and to term him *baſe lord*, and *paultry earl*, is matter to raiſe contempt betwixt him and the people, or the king's indignation againſt him. *And ſuch general words, in caſe of nobility, will maintain an action, although it will not in the caſe of a common perſon*; wherefore they held that the action lay. *Fleming abſente, adjournatur.* Afterwards the defendant died, and thereupon the bill abated. *Cro. Ja.* 196.

42. The defendant *Pettinger* ſaid of the *earl of* Kingſton *the plaintiff, he is a baſe lord a t—— in his teeth*; *he is but a cur, and a baſe lord, and of no account*; he was committed, fined 200 *l.* adjudged to pay 2000 *l.* to the plaintiff, at *Nottingham* aſſiſes to be publickly whipped, and before enlargement, to find ſureties for his good behaviour. *Kingſton Comes* verſus *Pettinger*, in the *Star-Chamber. Mich.* 10. *Ca.* See *Ruſhw. Coll.* See alſo *Lord Northumberland's Ca. Hill.* 9 *Ca. in Ruſhw. Coll.*

43. General

43. General references, 30 *Aff. pl.* 19. *Kel.* 26. *Cro. Ja.* 18, 90, 625. 1 *Ro.* 217. *Ro. Abr. Prohibition, Ca.* 17, 19. 4 *Co.* 20. 1 *Co.* 111. *Salk.* 207, 552, 692. *Ro. Ab.* (*N.*) 4, 11, 13. *fo.* 303. *Ca.* 2. *Hob.* 328. 2 *Ro.* 59, 82, 293. *Mo.* 915. *Godb.* 215. *Reg.* 49, 51. *Fi. Ley* 142. 2 *Sid.* 152. 6 *Mod.* 26, 287. *Dy.* 79. 1 *Vent.* 2. *Ro. Ab. Prohibition, Ca.* 6, 7, 20, 22. 2 *Lev.* 45.

44. Rules, *Senfus verborum ex caufa dicendi accipiendus eft. Sermones femper accipiendi funt fecundum fubjectam materiam. Sicut ad quaeftionem facti non refpondent judices, ita ad quaeftionem juris non refpondent juratores.*

503. *Verdict at law a bar to equity.*

General.

1. AFTER a recovery or verdict at law, refolved on demurer, that the party fhall not be put to anfwer. 1 *Vern* 176, 177.

Particular cafes.

2. The plaintiff recovered in trefpafs by verdict, and fhewed in the king's bench, that the chancellor had awarded an injunction againft him, (and now pending the injunction) he prayed his judgment, and had it, but no damages for his vexation in chancery by the injunction. *Elfm. Obf.* 72, 73.

3. In trefpafs the defendant was found guilty by verdict, and the plaintiff fhewed in *C. B.* that the defendant had fued a *fubpoena* in chancery, and obtained an injunction to ftay his proceedings at law, by means whereof the plaintiff had fpent 10 marks, and now the injunction was diffolved, and the defendant difmiffed to common law, where he prayed his cofts to be increafed, becaufe of this vexation. And *Brian* chief juftice awarded, that the plaintiff fhould recover three pounds for his cofts, befides his damages in *C. B.* *Elf. Obf.* 73. *Quaere as to the cofts in chancery.*

4. A bill was brought to be relieved againft a recovery at law, on an *indebitatus affumpfit* for goods fold and delivered. The bill furmifed it was for goods fold the plaintiff as he was mafter of the buck-hounds, and that the lace and linen were for the king's fervants, and that it was the king's and not the plaintiff's debt, and that what he acted was in his office, and not as a private perfon. And that the defendant was only to expect his money from the king, and that the plaintiff was only to pay it if he received the money from the king. The defendant pleaded his verdict and judgment, and that the plaintiff infifted on the fame matter at law, where it was ruled againft him, and that his writ of error being near fpent, he now brought this bill for delay. And demurred for that the matter was cognizable at law, and the bill contained no equity: yet the court over-ruled the plea, and ordered the defendant to anfwer the bill. 2 *Vern.* 146.

5. References, 22 *E.* 4. 37. *b.* *Damages* 138, *and judgment* 86. 21 *E.* 4. 78. *b.* *Confc.* 22. & *b.* *Cofts. Stat.* 4 *H.* 4. *Hard.* 23, 120, &c. 2 *Vern.* 146.

6. Rules, *Equity not to relieve where remedy may be had at law. Has a power upon circumftances,* &c. *Is part of the law of the land. Is to moderate the rigour of the law. May carry the debt beyond the penalty,*

nalty, &c. *Rectifies mistakes*, &c. *Prevents multiplicity of suits*, &c. *To relieve where no relief at law. Will redress or prevent wrongs*, &c. *Relieves against accidents. To relieve against frauds. Where the matter lieth in compensation. To relieve against one's own act*, &c.

504. *Vigilantibus et non dormientibus jura subveniunt.*

1. IF the king's officers have neglected their duty, as to find an office for him, as was the principal case, *&c.* it is no reason that the negligence of his officers, nay perhaps their compact and combination with the adverse party, should defeat the king. *Vigilantibus et non dormientibus jura subveniunt*, is a rule for the subject, but *nullum tempus occurrit regi*, is the king's plea. *Hob.* 347.

2. References, 5 *E.* 3. 222. 4 *Co.* 10. *b.*

3. Rule, *Law favours justice and truth*, &c.

505. *Vir militans deo, non implicetur secularibus negotiis.*

General.

1. BY *Stat.* 21 *H.* 8. *c.* 13. Spiritual persons are prohibited civil acts. As keeping of tan-houses, brew-houses, *&c.* save as in the statute, also to traffick in cattle, corn, lead, tin, hides, leather, tallow, fish, wool, wood, or any manner of victual, or merchandize, save as in the said act. Also to farm any manor, lands, tenements, or other hereditaments for life, years, or at will, save as in the said act. Under the penalties in the statute. *Vide* 27 *H.* 8. *fo.* 21, 22. Also serj. *Ewer*'s readings upon the two first branches of this act in *Gray's Inn Hall, Lent, anno* 1637.

2. *Una ecclesia unius rectoris*, as one wife to one husband; that the parson should not farm, graze, *&c.* nor mingle himself with secular affairs, that might withdraw his mind, *&c.* *Hob.* 157.

Particular cases.

3. *Scot* brought debt against *Laws*, Clerk, *sur le Statute* 21 H. 8. And the writ was *quod reddat nobis et* Johanni Scott, *qui tam pro nobis quam pro seipso sequitur*, 110 *l. quas nobis et praefat'* Johanni *debet*, *&c.* And declared, for taking to farm six acres of land, and holding the same six months, *per quod actio*, *&c.* for 60 *l.* And for holding other lands for five month, *per quod actio*, *&c.* for 50 *l.* The defendant pleaded, *quod ipse non debet praefato* Johanni *qui tam*, *&c. praedict'* 110 l. *nec aliquam inde denar'*, *in formâ qua*, *&c.* Whereupon issue being joined, the jury found the defendant owed 30 *l.* and for the rest *quod non debet: Henden*, in arrest of judgment, took two exceptions. 1. The verdict expressed not for which farm, nor for which of the months, the 30 *l.* was due; but this exception was not regarded by the court; because the demand and issue were for 110 *l.* in general, though it had been more formal to have distinguished it better. 2. That the defendant had not answered the writ and declaration; for the plea ought to have been as the demand is,

quod ipſe non debet dicto domino regi et praefato Johanni *qui tam, &c.* which the court regarded, and the rather, becauſe the ſtatute of *Jeofailes* excepts penal ſtatutes. *Hob.* 327, 328.

Dr. Ridley, *in his* View of the Civil and Eccleſiaſtical Law, *ſpeaking of clerks of holy church, and delivering himſelf from the law of holy church, ſays, if any ſuch are hunters or hawkers, if they oftentimes uſe and ſport themſelves therein; if biſhops, they are to be ſuſpended from the communion three months; if miniſters or prieſts, two months only; but if a deacon, he is to be ſuſpended from his office,* fo. 114. *And according to the ſame gentleman in the ſame place, if a clerk oftentimes ſtrikes other men, and being admoniſhed to forbear ſuch kind of violence, does nevertheleſs continue in his follies he is to be depoſed. And our own canons forbid miniſters of the church eſtabliſhed, being tavern haunters and players at unlawful games, as for that purpoſe are mentioned in the canons. And our ſtatute laws have denied their exerciſing themſelves in, or mingling themſelves with, ſecular concerns; to the end they might be totally given up and devoted to the ſervice of God and his church.*

4. References, 2 *Keb.* 693. 1 *Vent.* 105. 1 *Lev.* 303. *Dy.* 28. *b.* 358. *a.* 1 *Vent.* 273. *Co. Lit.* 70. *b.* *Ridley's View, &c.* 110, 111, 114, *&c.* 2 *Ju. Eccl.* ſub tit. *Where clerk criminoſus, and wherefore one may be deprived.*

5. Rule, *Clerici non ponantur in officio.*

506. *Ultima voluntas teſtatoris eſt perimplenda ſecundum veram intentionem ſuam.*

What it is, and when it takes effect.

1. *TEſtamentum, id eſt teſtatio mentis,* which is made *nullo praeſentis metu periculi, ſed cogitatione mortalitatis. Omne teſtamentum morte conſummatum eſt.* Co. Lit. 322. b.

General to.

2. *Ultima voluntas teſtatoris eſt perimplenda ſecundum veram intentionem ſuam; et reipublicae intereſt ſuprema hominum teſtamenta rata haberi,* and ſo it is that a man may have a fee-ſimple by deviſe without the word *heirs,* though not ſo by deed; and that becauſe the will of the deviſor, expreſſed by his teſtament, ſhall be performed according to the intent of the deviſor. *Co. Lit.* 232. *b.*

3. And the law will manage and marſhal the words in a will according to the intent, which here was to repreſerve contingent eſtates, in places after the contingencies; for if it ſo ſhould ſtand, in conſtruction of law it cannot preſerve them; therefore clearly ſhall be conſtrued before them. 2 *Chan. Ca.* 11. *Vue le caſe.*

4. Divers teſtaments, for *voluntas teſtatoris eſt ambulatoria uſque ad mortem,* and the latter will countermands the firſt. And it is truly ſaid, that the firſt grant, and the laſt will, is of the greateſt force. *Co. Lit.* 112. *b.*

5. Divers deviſes, *&c.* is to be underſtood as well of deviſes of chattels real or perſonal, as of freehold and inheritance. *Co. Lit.* 112. *b.*

6. Where there are feveral devifes of the fame things in the fame will, the laft taketh place. *Cum duo inter fe pugnantia reperiuntur in teflamento, ultimum ratum eft.* Co. Lit. 112. b.

7. *Sed legum fervanda fides, fuprema voluntas*
Quod mandat fierique jubet, parere neceffe eft.
Termes de l'Ley, *tit.* Devife.

8. Devife to be conftrued according to the intent of the teftator. 3 *Leon.* 55. 2 *An.* 123, 124.

9. In all cafes a court of equity muft confider what was the real intent of the teftator; and they cannot declare a truft according to their own fancy, nor according to what the teftator fhould have willed; for then they make the will, and not the teftator; but they may, according to the real intent of the teftator, declare a truft, upon fuch wills, although it be not contained in the will itfelf; which is thefe three cafes. 1. In cafe of fraud upon a legatee. 2. Where the words imply a truft for the relations, as in the cafe of a fpecific devife to the executors, and no difpofition of the *refiduum.* 3. In the cafe of the legatees promifing the teftator to ftand as a truftee for another. *Gilb.* 209.

Particular cafes.

10. A devife was to the defendant's father, whofe fon and heir the defendant was, of 20*l. per annum*, out of a rectory, with a claufe of diftrefs for non-payment; the glebe belonging to the rectory was but 40*s. per annum*, and the tithe not being fubject at law to diftrefs; and fo no fufficient remedy at law for the rent; thereupon the plaintiff brought his bill to have the whole rectory liable to the rent; and the defendant was decreed to pay it. On the defendant's part it was infifted, that this court ought not to extend a remedy beyond what the devifor appointed, and the plaintiff muft take fuch remedy as by law he might. To which the plaintiff's counfel replied, that the devifor gave the annuity out of the whole rectory, and intended the tithes as well as the glebe fhould be liable to it, and that in cafe of a rent feck, where the grantee had no feifin, this court had frequently given relief, by decree here. But the defendant's counfel infifted, that that was not like this cafe, becaufe in that cafe there was no remedy at law at all. Decreed the whole rectory liable, and the defendant to pay arrears and cofts. 1 *Chan. Ca.* 79, 80. *Yet obferve it is there noted to have been otherwife held fince.*

11. *Fofter* devifed to the plaintiff, Item, *I give to my coufin* Thomas Martin, *clerk, late minifter of* Houghton *in* Northamptonfhire, *and living thereabouts, and order* 40l. *to be paid him, to be difpofed of for certain ufes, which I fhall, in a private note, acquaint him with,* and gave him no note or direction how to difpofe of it, but died, leaving the defendant his executor; and whether the plaintiff fhould have the 40*l.* was the queftion? And his honour of the rolls decreed the plaintiff the 40*l.* for that the teftator did not intend it fhould come to his executors, but had, by his will, given it away from them; therefore ordered the defendant to pay the 40*l.* to the plaintiff. 1 *Chan. Ca.* 178. See 1 *Vern.* 255, 462.

12. The

12. The will was begun, and ſeveral legacies given to the next of kin, and likewiſe to the executors, and then at the beginning of the next ſentence, the will ſtopt, and was left unfiniſhed. Lord *King:* The teſtator having given legacies to the executors it is moſt likely he would have given away the reſidue from them; and therefore decreed the undiſpoſed reſidue to be diſtributed according to the ſtatute. *Gilb.* 184.

13. References, *Co. Lit.* 112. *b.* *Termes del Ley*, tit. *Teſtament*, *etiam Deviſe.* 1 *Chan. Ca.* 178, 309. 2 *Chan. Ca.* 11, 155. *Poph.* 131, 132. *Nelſ.* 27, 159, 160, 351, 403, 433. *Gilb.* 11, *&c.* 118, 119, 133, 136, 209. *Plow. Com.* 523. *a. b.* *Nelſ.* 312, 313. 1 *Vern.* 37, 38, 470. *Barn.* 14, 160, 253. *Prec. Chan.* 62, 92, 94, 231, 269, 300, 324. *Gilb.* 74, 75, 126. 2 *Vern.* 648. *Prec. Chan.* 566. 2 *Ju. Eccl.* 48. Caſe 6. 50. Caſe 9.

14. Rules, *Equity favours younger children. Is to execute the intent of the parties. In teſtamentis ratio tacita non debet conſiderari, ſed verba ſolum ſpectari debent. Multa poſſunt movere mentem teſtatoris, quae nos latent; ideo per divinationem mentis durum eſt recedere, &c.*

507. *Unumquodque eodem modo, quo colligatum eſt, diſſolvitur.*

1. AN obligation or other matter in writing may not be diſcharged by parol. 19 *E.* 4. 1. *b.*

2. An annuity by preſcription, *rien arrear* is a good plea; for preſcription is matter in deed; but in annuity by deed it is not a good plea without ſhewing an acquittance. 5 *H.* 7. 33.

3. When a man avoids the king's title by as high a matter of record as the king claimeth, he may have it by way of plea, without being put to his petition; though the king be intitled by double matter of record; as where a man is attainted of treaſon by parliament, and his lands are found on office, whereby the king ſeiſeth; the party may alledge reſtitution by parliament, and a repeal of the former act. 4 *H.* 7. 7. *b.*

4. In preſentable caſes reſignation may be to the king as ſupreme ordinary, and is as good, to every purpoſe, as to the biſhop; and that even though the clerk were collated by the biſhop or ordinary. *Dy.* 294. 5 *Co. De Ju. Regis Eccl.* 34. *b.* *Palm.* 474. But in the caſe of an impropriation, reſignation muſt be to the impropriator and not to the ordinary, for he hath nothing to do therewith. *Da.* 20. *Fitzh. Abr. Excommengment* 9. 1 *Mod.* 12, 260, 261. 2 *Mod.* 257. *S. C.* *Hob.* 186. *Cro. Jac.* 517, 518. 1 *Show.* 252. *Da.* 72, 73. *Skin.* 464, 519. 3 *Mod.* 295. 2 *Ju. Eccl.* 473, 477, 480, *&c.*

5. All the court held that this, being a donative, began only by the foundation and erection of the donor, and he hath the ſole viſitation and correction, and the ordinary nothing to do therewith. And as he, *the clerk*, comes in by him, *the donor*, ſo he, *the clerk*, may reſtore it to him, *the donor*; for *unumquodque eodem modo, quo colligatum eſt, diſſolvitur.* And though the preſentee, when he is in, hath the freehold, yet he may reveſt it by his reſignation, *ſans auter ceremonie.* And the ordinary hath nothing

 to

to do therein; for admiſſion and inſtitution are not requiſite in caſe of a donative. *Cro. Jac.* 63. *Yelv.* 60. and *Mo.* 765. *S. C.*

508. *Una perſona non poteſt ſupplere vicem duarum.*

General.

1. THE ſtatute of *Faculties* is always conſtrued ſtrictly againſt non-reſidence and pluralities, as matters ſtrongly hurtful to the ſervice of God, and the inſtruction of his people. 4 *Co.* 118.

Particular caſes.

2. And therefore if a biſhop be tranſlated to an archbiſhoprick, or a baron created an earl, where he hath both dignities; as is commonly ſaid, *quando duo jura concurrunt in una perſona, aequum eſt ac ſi eſſent in diverſis*; but yet within this act he is but one and the ſame perſon to whom the attendance and ſervice ſhall be done. So if the patron be made a knight of the garter, or warden of the cinque ports, he ſhall have but three chaplains in all; *et ſic de ſimilibus*; *quod fuit conceſſum*; *quia difficile eſt ut unus homo vicem duorum ſuſtineat.* 4 Co. 118. a.

3. References, 4 *Co.* 46. *a.* 1 *Ju. Eccl.* tit. *Faculties, the odiouſneſs, &c.* 2 *Ju. Eccl. The King* and *The Biſhop of Cheſter.*

4. Rules, *Quando duo jura concurrunt, &c. No conſtruction can be too liberal to make parſons reſide,* &c. *In aequali jure, &c. Nemo poteſt habere duas, &c. and references under theſe ſeveral rules.*

509. *Volenti non fit injuria.*

1. LORD, meſne, and tenant; the king is lord, and the meſne holdeth of him *in capite*, and the tenant of him in ſocage; if the tenant obtain a releaſe from the meſne, or forejudge him, now he holds *in capite*; for *volenti non fit injuria*; and it ſhould be injurious to the king, if he ſhould loſe his tenure *in capite*, by the act of the tenant, and have in lieu of it only a tenure in ſocage. *Dav.* 67. *a.*

2. *In ejectione firmae* between *Thompſon* plaintiff and *Trafford* defendant, the caſe was, *Magdalen College, Oxon,* 20 *December* 8 *Eliz.* let a meſſuage in *Southwark*, to which no land appertained, to *Standiſh* for 20 years, from the feaſt of St. *Michael* next enſuing, rendring the antient rent, and 25 *October* 21 *Eliz.* they let the ſame meſſuage to the ſame *Standiſh* for 20 years, from the feaſt of St. *Michael* then next enſuing, rendring alſo the antient rent, and 31 *Auguſt* 30 *Eliz.* the preſident and ſcholars made a new leaſe of the ſaid meſſuage to Sir *George Carew*, for 20 years from the making, rendring the antient rent, which leaſe was conveyed by meſne aſſignments to the plaintiff, upon which the action was brought againſt the ſaid *Trafford*, who had *Standiſh*'s intereſt by meſne aſſignments. *Popham* ſaid, that *ipſo facto*, upon the laſt leaſe made and accepted by *Standiſh*, the firſt leaſe was determined and gone; for this laſt contract diſſolves the firſt, when the one and the other cannot ſtand together, and they cannot here; becauſe they intermix one with the other; and ſo was the opinion in the common bench about 1 *Eliz.* in the caſe of the abbey of *Barking*. And here *Standiſh*, before *Michaelmas* next after the ſecond leaſe made to

 him,

him, could not grant over his firſt term to be good to the grantee; for if this ſhould be, the ſecond leaſe ſhould not be good to *Standiſh*, but for the remnant of the years after the firſt term finiſhed, which cannot be becauſe it ſtandeth in the power of the grantor, with the aſſent and acceptance of the grantee, to make the ſecond grant good for the whole term, to wit, from *Michaelmas*; and this cannot be but by a determination in law of the firſt term immediately, which is made by his own acceptance, and therefore a prejudice to none but himſelf, *et volenti non fit injuria*, and the firſt term cannot have its continuance till *Michaelmas*, but is gone preſently by the acceptance of the ſecond leaſe in the whole; for the firſt contract which was intire cannot be ſo diſſolved in part, but in the whole, as to that which the party hath; and therefore the firſt term (as the caſe is here) is gone in the whole, to which *Clench* and *Gaudy* agreed; and if ſo, then this laſt leaſe to *Standiſh* was but as a leaſe made to begin at a time to come, which is made good by the ſtatute of 14 *Eliz.* if it do not exceed the time of 40 years from the making of the leaſe; for the purpoſe of this act was, that colleges and the like ſhall not make grants in reverſion, tho' for a year; becauſe by ſuch grants in reverſion they ſhall be excluded to have their rent of the particular tenants for the time, &c. *Poph.* 8, 9.

3. If an impropriator preſent to his church, and his clerk is inſtituted and inducted, hereby he hath diſappropriated it, and made it preſentable ever after; for, as *Manwood* ſaid, *volenti non fit injuria*, but it is preſentation, with inſtitution and induction, which makes it preſentable; for then he is ſaid to come in by the ordinary's means. *Plow. Com.* 501. *a.*

4. References, 11 *H.* 6. 18. *b.* 3. 44 *E.* 3. 33. *b.* 44 *Aſſ.* 37. *Fitzh. Nat. Brev.* 35. (*F.*) 1 *Rol. Abr.* 240. 2 *Rol. Abr.* 338. 1 *Danv.* 112.

510. *Voluntas donatoris in charta doni ſui manifeſte expreſſa obſervetur.*

IF lands are given to *B.* and his heirs, to have and to hold to *B.* and his heirs, if *B.* have heirs of his body; and if he die without heirs of his body, that it ſhall revert to the donor; this is an eſtate-tail, and the reverſion is in the donor; for *voluntas donatoris in charta doni ſui manifeſte expreſſa obſervetur.* Co. Lit. 21. a.

511. *Voluntas teſtatoris ambulatoria eſt uſque ad mortem.*

1. REferences, *Co. Lit.* 112. *a. b.* 4 *Co.* 60. *Hob.* 349. 2 *Ju. Eccl.* 35. *Burk* and *Morgan*'s caſe.

2. Rule, *Ultima voluntas teſtatoris eſt perimplenda ſecundum veram intentionem ſuam.*

512. *Voluntate et poteſtate repugnantibus*, *all is void.*

CRO. *Eliz.* 719, 720.

513. *Uſury odious in law.*

General to, and rules.

1. IF in truth the contract be uſurious againſt the ſtatute, no colour or ſhadow of words will ſerve, but the party may ſhew it, and ſhall not be concluded or eſtopped by any deed, or other matter whatſoever; for the ſtatute gives an averment in ſuch caſe. 5 *Co.* 69. *b.*

2. And *Popham* chief juſtice ſaid, if *A.* comes to *B.* to borrow 100 *l.* who agrees to lend it, if he will give him for the loan of it for a year 120 *l.* if the ſon of *A.* be then alive; this is uſury within the ſtatute; for if ſuch uſury ſhould be out of the ſtatute; by reaſon of the incertainty of the life, the ſtatute ſhould be of little effect; and for the ſame reaſon that he might add one life, he might add more; and ſo it ſeemed a mathematical line which *eſt diviſibilis in ſemper diviſibilia.* 5 Co. 69. b. 70. a.

3. Juſtice *Dodderidge* took theſe differences, in caſe of caſual uſury. 1. If I lend 100*l.* to have 120*l.* at the year's end upon a caſualty; if the caſualty goes to the intereſt only, and not to the principal, it is uſury; for the party is ſure to have the principal again, come what will; but if both principal and intereſt are in hazard, it is not uſury. 2. Though I ſecure both principal and intereſt, if it be at the will of the party who is to pay it, it is no uſury, as if I lend to one 100 *l.* for two years, to pay for the loan thereof 30 *l.* and if he pay the principal at the year's end, he ſhall pay nothing for intereſt, this is not uſury; for the party hath his election, and may pay it at the firſt year's end, and ſo diſcharge himſelf. *Cro. Jac.* 508, 509.

4. Lord keeper declared it ſhould be the rule, That a mortgagee of a mortgage forfeited, ſhould have intereſt of his intereſt, and ſhould be only accountable for what profit he ſhould receive, and not for what he might have received, unleſs there were fraud. And *Note*, That it was the rule, That the mortgagee aſſigning, the aſſignee ſhould have intereſt for the intereſt then due; and never was contradicted but in *Porter* and *Hobart*'s caſe, in the time of the lord *Shaftsbury.* 1 Chan. Ca. 258.

Particular caſes.

5. *J. S.* lent 100 *l.* for a year and took 5 *l.* intereſt at the end of ſix months, and *Popham* and *Gaudy* held it not uſury; as not being above 10*l.* for 100*l.* as if it had been only lent for ſix months; but *Fenner* and *Yelverton contra*, for when 100*l.* is lent for a year, the ſtatute intends the profits and increaſe not to be received till the end of the year, and if 5*l.* be received at the end of ſix months, he to whom the 100*l.* is lent, hath but the uſe of 95*l.* for the whole year; *and the ſtatute is to be taken ſtrictly againſt the offender*, *and largely in puniſhment of uſury:* and therefore if 100 *l.* is lent for a year, and he who lends it takes 10*l.* at two days,

days, it is usury. And here when *J. S.* took the 5 *l.* it is to be presumed, he would lend that, and take interest of it within the year, which is more than the statute allows; for the most profit of 100 *l.* ought to be, *by no means*, more than 10 *l. per annum.* And judgment was given by all the judges in *England* against the plaintiff. *Yelv.* 30, 31. *Cro. Ja.* 25. *S. C.*

6. *In debt*, for 120 *l. Warnes* was indebted to *Alder* in 100 *l.* upon an usurious contract; and *Alder* was indebted over to *Ellis* the plaintiff in 100 *l.* good debt, for which just debt *Warnes* and *Alder* were bound to the plaintiff. In debt upon this obligation, *Warnes* pleaded the usury between him and *Alder*, in order to avoid the bond; *Ellis* the plaintiff replied, that *Alder*, before the bond was indebted to him in 100 *l.* just and true debt, for the payment whereof *Warnes* and *Alder* were bound to him in the bond now in suit; and that he had no notice in any sort of the usury between *Warnes* and *Alder:* whereupon *Warnes* demurred; and it was adjudged by *Gaudy*, *Yelverton*, and *Williams*, for the plaintiff; for it is no usury in the plaintiff, and therefore shall not prejudice him; *for though the statute is to be taken strongly for the suppressing usury, yet it ought to be* between *the parties, who use corruption, and not to punish the innocent*, as the plaintiff here is; for it could be no shift in him, having a due debt precedent; but if no such debt had been due to the plaintiff before, then clearly it had been usury in the plaintiff; there being no lawful cause for giving the bond, but only to countenance the usury between *Warnes* and *Alder*. And *Yelverton* justice said, if this plea should be good for the defendant, every man might be defrauded of his just debt; for commonly the creditor demands surety: and by this case, if the bar should be allowed, then by corruption between the debtor and surety, whereto the creditor is a mere stranger, he might lose his debt, which should be mischievous. *Yelv.* 47. *Cro. Ja.* 33. *S. C.*

7. It was well and wisely said, that God gave riches to supply others needs; and that therefore he is a thief and a murderer, who doth not apply his store to the end God proposed: but alass the covetous man cannot thus employ God's goodness to him; because his heart is set upon his riches, which when he either loseth, or miscarrieth in any his expectations of gain, his heart sickens, sinks, and dies within him: so that had, they bind him; not had, they torture him: these are the miserable circumstances of every one greedy of filthy lucre, which never faileth to take away the very life of the owners, by anctious cares fretting the mind, and emaciating the body, wasting the very bones and marrow, with continual pains and labour after worldly dross; which often, after all his fatigues, to the ruin both of body and mind, take to themselves wings and fly away; and indeed should they stay longer with him, he is still miserable and wretched, being thus inveloped and twisted together with his wealth. Such an one is rather a slave to his hoards than a master of them, even in the midst of his false enjoyments, false both as they are void of all solid satisfaction, even whilst possessed, and uncertain in their stay; he is saddled, bridled, and ridden, by the world and it's emptiness; like the proud horse, he is not only ridden, managed, and taught subjection, but lashed and spur-galled by his rider; he enlargeth his desire as hell, and as death which cannot be satisfied; whereas in the matters of the last and most important conse-

 quence

quence to him, his affections are more than moderated; being quite thruft out of door by the impetuofity of the other; whilft on the other hand, the good man, whofe confidence is in the fountain of all good, has a treafure laid up fure and permanent, which the malice of neither bad men nor worfe beings can difpoil him of; but wretched, bad, and foolifh as the avaritious man is, there's another, namely the ufurer, ftill more fo; he not only is covetous, and fo hath all the anxious cares of mind and fatigues of body with the other, who, perhaps, abating his infatiable thirft after them, is honeft in the means of obtaining his gain, and his unrighteoufnefs refts in his immoderate defires, and in his want of a heart to ufe them as he ought when obtained. Whereas the ufurer or extortioner goes into the vileft methods to become rich: he grinds the face of the poor, makes the neceffities of the indigent and wretched, which ought to move his compaffion, the means of advancing his oppreffive ends. He lends, but not to the Lord, gain is his god, and profit his almighty, he liveth upon the fweat of the poor, he drinketh up their blood, and fucketh in greedily their very marrow; he fubfifts, nay grows corpulent upon the induftry and needs and at the coft of thofe, who, by the laws both of God and nature, have an indefeazable right to his relief without any his cruel confiderations, which govern all his actions. This man ftands compared to the hare, that at one and the fame time litters, gives fuck, and is with young. So the ufurer's money is bringing forth, nourifhing, and breeding profit all at once: nay the ufurer may be properly faid to make that breed, gender and increafe, which by nature is barren and unapt; for the ufury money begets and produceth money: whereupon the philofopher faid truly, that the ufurer maketh fomething out of nothing: his gain is night and day purfuing its deftructive journey, and refteth not even on the Lord's day, fo that he's always at work, in defiance of all command, defpifing what the cafuifts hold, that ufury is a fin againft nature, as the ufurer hath fhut up all bowels of compaffion to the wants of his brother, that he neither loveth the author of goodnefs, whom he hath not feen, nor his brother whom he hath: fo far is this man of fin from loving his poor brother for God's fake, or his own, that he has no brother in his own confideration, but hath faid, with the fool in the pfalmift, there is no God, whilft the good man readily and chearfully alloweth, that ufury and extortion are hateful to both God and man: and that the moft moderate gain growing from loan, is at beft but a *conceffum propter durities cordis.*

514. *Utile per inutile non vitiatur.*

1. A WIFE, *uxor*, is a good name of purchafe, without a chriftian name: and fo it is if a chriftian name be added and miftaken, as *Eme* for *Emelyn*; for *utile per inutile non vitiatur.* Co. Lit. 3. a.

2. References, *Co. Lit.* 227. *a.* *Cro. Ca.* 48. *Hob.* 171. *Du. Ch. Ufes* 177.

515. *Ut Poena ad paucos, metus ad omnes perveniat.*

RULE, *Actus non facit reum, nisi mens sit rea.*

516. *Uxor non est sui juris, sed sub potestate viri.*

1. THE wife is *sub potestate viri*, and disabled to contract without his consent, and *omnia, quae sunt uxoris, sunt ipsius viri: non habet uxor potestatem sui, sed vir, &c.* Co. Lit. 112. a.

2. Rule, *Feme covert under obedience of her husband*, &c.

517. *What is done, by way of judgment, in a different manner than the law allows, is against law.*

THE old law is that, which past ages have approved, and that by which justice is to be administred, and *whatsoever is done, by way of judgment, in a different manner than the law allows, is against that law.* Show Parl. Ca. 122.

518. *What one cannot transfer, he cannot compel by articles.*

1. *WHAT a man cannot transfer, he cannot oblige by articles: and if he cannot grant, he cannot by articles bind.* 1 Ch. Ca. 210, 211.

2. *He, who may transfer, may covenant, that his trustees shall do it.* 1 Ch. Ca. 211, 212.

519. *When a man shall do an act, he must, by the law, at his peril, see that that he doth be lawful.*

RULES, *Ignorantia facti excusat. Ignorantia juris non excusat. Executio juris non habet injuriam.*

520. *When the common and statute law concur, the common law shall be preferred.*

1. IT was unanimously agreed by Sir *Edmund Anderson*, and his companions, justices of the common pleas, That when *H.* by deed indented bargained and sold to *Lyb* and his heirs, and before inrolment levied a fine to *Lyb* and to his heirs, and after the deed is inrolled within the six months, the cognizee shall be in by the fine, and not by the indenture inrolled; for when the fee-simple is passed, by the fine, to the cognizee and his heirs, the inrolment after may not devest it, and turn that estate out of him, which was absolutely established in him by fine; for

for then whereas he was in before in the *per*, he ſhould be now in *in le poſt*: alſo *when the common law and ſtatute law concur, the common law ſhall be preferred*. 'Tis true the inrolment ſhall have relation to the delivery of the deed, but that is for the avoiding of meſne eſtates, or charges made by the bargainor, to any ſtranger after delivery of the deed and before inrolment: but not to deveſt any eſtate lawfully ſettled, in the mean time, in the bargainee himſelf. And the *Stat.* 27 *H.* 8. *c.* 16. of inrolments, ſpeaks by bargain and ſale only; and here it is not by bargain and ſale only, but the eſtate originally paſſed by the fine. 4 *Co.* 71. *a.*

2. References, *Co. Lit.* 49. *a.*

521. *Where ever there is ſuppreſſio veri, or ſuggeſtio falſi, the releaſe, &c. ſhall be void.*

General.

1. WHO is partaker with a thief, hateth his own ſoul; he heareth curſing, and bewrayeth it not. *Prov.* 29. and 24.

2. The defendant by a trick got a deed into his hands, and burnt or cancelled it. *Per cur'*: Where writings are ſuppreſſed, *omnia praeſumuntur*. 1 Ch. Ca. 293.

Particular caſes.

Suggeſtio falſi.

3. He who has right, tells the purchaſer the vendor has a good eſtate, though he knew to the contrary at the time, yet the purchaſe eſtabliſhed. 2 *Ch. Ca.* 108, 128. *Nelſ.* 287.

4. A man being ſeiſed, in right of his wife, in an inn of 69 *l. per annum*, is drawn in to ſell it, having a mortgage upon it before the deſcent for 80 *l.* My lord *Keeper* was of opinion, that though the purchaſe was not a fair bargain, yet it was not ſuch fraud as to ſet it aſide. *Pre. Ch.* 206.

5. Three daughters being equally intitled as coheirs, the huſband of one fearing to be in law, and being made to believe he ſhould pay coſts, releaſed his ſhare to the other ſiſters, who were to bear the charges of the ſuit. His ſhare amounted to 1000 *l.* this releaſe was ſet aſide, and *Luxford*'s caſe cited, that *a miſapprehenſion of the party ſhall avoid his releaſe*. 1 Vern. 32.

6. An aſſignment of an intereſt in a leaſe of the value of 200 *l. per annum*, in conſideration of 200 *l.* under falſe pretences, was ſet aſide, as obtained by fraud. 2 *Mod. Ca.* 83, 84, 85.

Suppreſſio veri.

7. Sir *Edward Duke* deviſed 2000 *l.* to his daughter; but if ſhe ſhould marry one *Bacon*, it ſhould be void. She was married to *Bacon* before her father's death, and ſhe took advice, which was that her legacy was void: her brother paid her 800 *l.* and ſhe releaſed her legacy. A bill was to have this releaſe ſet aſide; ſuggeſting that her brother told her that ſhe was raſed out of her father's will: and that he ſuppreſſed it, and did not prove it till af-

ter

ter the releafe. Lord chancellor: It is the conftant rule, *wherever there is* fuppreffio veri, *or* fuggeftio falfi, *the releafe fhall be void.* But it appearing, the father himfelf had revoked this devife, the chancellor decreed againft the plaintiff. But where a legacy is upon condition that a woman marry with the confent of *J. S.* though fhe marry without, it doth not avoid the legacy; for it is only *in terrorem*; but the father here did what was equitable on his daughter's difobedience. 1 *Vern.* 19, 20.

8. The landlord of an inn, being the means of cattle being put into the ground belonging to the inn, fhall not diftrain them for rent. *Prec. Ch.* 7. 2 *Vern.* 129.

9. A mortgagee having accepted of feveral bonds for intereft, by contrivance with the mortgagor, on the mortgagor's treaty of marriage, tells the woman's father (on his inquiring what was due) of only the principal mortgage money. Redemption decreed on payment thereof only. *Prec. Chan.* 132.

* 10. *A.* makes an abfolute conveyance to *B.* for 1500*l.* *B.* executes a defeazance upon payment of 1500*l.* in 16 years. *B.* upon his marriage fettles this, as an abfolute eftate, upon the wife and iffue of that marriage; there being proof that *A.* made the conveyance to enable *B.* to get a fortune, though the defign was really upon another lady, and not the lady *B.* actually married; yet decreed *A.* was bound as *particeps criminis.* See cafe before the houfe of lords, *Webber* and *Farmer*, 21 *Jan.* 1718. *Note*; That the wife's father had notice of the defeazance before the fettlement made, notwithftanding which, the decree of the court of chancery was affirmed, by eight lords to feven lords; *Cowper* and *Harcourt* againft the decree, and lord *Parker* for it. * See cafe *Lord Forbes* and *Denniftone*, 22 *Feb.* 1722, and 6 *March* 1724, and * *Walker* and *Glafcoine*, 6 *March* 1726, and *White* and *Leighbourne*, 5 *Feb.* and 12 *Nov.* 1722.

11. References, 1 *Chan. Ca.* 293. 2 *Chan. Ca.* 128. 3 *Chan. Ca.* 120. *Nelf.* 287. 1 *Vern.* 453.

12. Rules, *Equity to relieve againft fraud. Fraus eft celare fraudem. He who hath done iniquity fhall not have equity. Qui poteft et debet vetare jubet. In odium fpoliatoris omnia praefumuntur.*

522. *Wherefoever words of a deed, or of the parties without deed, may have a double intendment, and the one ftandeth with law and right, and the other is wrongful and againft law; the intendment that ftandeth with law fhall be taken.*

1. A. Tenant in fee made a leafe of lands to *B. to have and to hold* to *B.* for term of life, without mentioning for whofe life it fhall be; it fhall be deemed for the term of the life of the leffee; for it fhall be taken moft ftrongly againft the leffor; and an eftate for one's own life is higher than for the life of another. But if tenant in tail make fuch a leafe, it fhall be taken for the life of the leffor, for two reafons. 1. *When the conftruction of any thing is left to the law, the law, which abhorreth injury and wrong, will never fo conftrue it, as it fhall work a wrong*: And in this

case, *of the leaſe by tenant in tail*, if by conſtruction it ſhould be for the life of the leſſee, then ſhould the eſtate-tail be diſcontinued, and a new reverſion gained by wrong: But if it be conſtrued for the life of tenant in tail, then no wrong is wrought. And it is a general rule, *That whereſoever the words of a deed, or of the parties without deed, may have a double intendment, and the one ſtandeth with law and right, and the other is wrongful and againſt law, the intendment that ſtandeth with law ſhall be taken.* 2. The *law more reſpecteth a leſſer eſtate by right, than a larger eſtate by wrong*; as if a tenant for life in remainder diſſeiſe tenant for life, now he hath a fee-ſimple; but if tenant for life die, now is the wrongful eſtate in fee, by judgment in law, changed to a rightful eſtate for life. If a man retain a ſervant generally, without expreſſing any time, the law ſhall conſtrue it to be for one year; for that retainer is according to law. *Vide* 23 *E.* 3. *cap.* 21, *&c.* *Co. Lit.* 42. *a. b.*

2. It hath been adjudged, that where tenant in tail made a leaſe to another for term of life generally, and after releaſed to the leſſee and his heirs, albeit between the tenant in tail and him a fee-ſimple paſſed; yet after the death of the leſſor, the entry of the iſſue in tail was lawful; which could not be if it had been a leaſe for the life of the leſſor; for then by the releaſe it had been a diſcontinuance executed. *Co. Lit.* 42. *a. b.*

3. Rule, *Every man's deed to be taken moſt ſtrongly againſt himſelf. Verba chartarum fortius accipiuntur, &c. Conſtructio legis non facit injuriam.*

523. *Where the foundation faileth all faileth.*

A Church is appropriate to a ſpiritual corporation; now if the corporation be diſſolved, the church is diſappropriate. 3 *E.* 3. 74, *and* 49 *E.* 3. 8.

524. *Where the law giveth any thing, it alſo giveth a remedy for the ſame.*

RULES, *Quando lex aliquid alicui concedit, &c. Boni judicis eſt lites dirimere, &c. Eſt boni judicis ampliare juriſdictionem.*

525. *Where there is no purchaſer or creditor in the caſe, but both parties concerned are volunteers, equity will not hurt or prevent either of them from enjoying the advantage which he hath at law.*

1. REferences, 1 *Pe. Will.* 45.

2. Rules, *Aequitas ſequitur legem. Alligari non debuit, quod probatum non relevat. Iniquity bars equity. He who hath done iniquity ſhall not have equity.*

526. *Will, the last revokes all former.*

General.

1. WILLS *are ambulatory and always changeable.* Hob. 349. And revocations are favoured for the benefit of the heir. 2 *Mod.* 71, 77. Yet the revocation of a will is not to be intended, no more than the disherison of the heir; but must be by express words. *Idem* 73. Yet a will may be revoked by a subsequent one, though such subsequent will be void in itself, it is good as a revocation. 2 *Ju. Eccl.* 82. *Vide postea* ca. 7. 14. 17. Yet privacy in making a will, or loose words to hide the testator's intent, or to keep the family quiet, &c. are not to be regarded, much less to be taken to amount to a revocation. 3 *Chan. Ca.* 81, 82, 87, 88, 117, 127.

2. So a will may be revoked either *pro toto,* as 1 *Vern.* 23. 2 *Vern.* 742. or only *pro tanto,* as 1 *Vern.* 23, 30, 141, 182, 329, 342. 2 *Ju. Eccl.* 83, case 4.

3. And *as a will is to be construed as one intire act,* though the heir is to be favoured when the case is doubtful; yet if the devisor devise to one and then by the same will devise to another the same estate, this is not to be taken as a revocation, but they are jointenants; which shews that the will is to be construed as one intire clause, and not as different; and by this means contradictions will be avoided in the construction thereof. 2 *Mod. Ca.* 77.

4. The revocation of a will is a matter meerly temporal, and discharges the court christian to have any thing to do with it; it is in no sort dependant of the will; for those things are called dependant which go in affirmance, and not what disannuls or disaffirms, as the revocation doth. And though the court christian hath power of the will, and of what is demanded thereby, yet in its original nature, the will itself was temporal. And *things which go in abridgment and restraint of the common law, shall be taken strictly, and are not to be favoured in construction.* So that the revocation being a thing meerly collateral to the will remains at common law, as to the proof, as is 1 *R.* 3. *Yelv.* 92, 93. 9 *Co.* 37, 38.

5. And since the statute of *Frauds,* wills for lands, as they must be made, so they must be revoked, with the solemnities required by that statute. *Vue le Stat.*

6. So before the statute, a man designing to revoke his will, was to do it *in praesenti*; and as one ought to be of good and *sane memorie* at the disposing, so he ought to be of as good and *sane memorie* when he revokes it; and as he ought to make his will by his own directions, and not by questions, so ought he to revoke it of himself, and not by questions. *Cro. Jac.* 497.

* 7. Mr. *Attorney General* cited a case, where a man had formerly published a will, and afterwards executed another; but the second not being duly executed, and published within the statute of *Frauds*; Lord chancellor *Cowper,* as Mr. attorney said, but as some others of the bar, lord *Macclesfield,* set up the former will. Before lord chancellor *King,* 22 *June* 1731. Vide *Gilb.* 130, 131.

* 8. He who will claim a benefit by part of a will, must abide by the whole will. At the rolls, 4 *July* 1737.

Particular cases.

9. If a feme sole make a will, and take husband, this is a countermand, and that for two reasons. 1. The making of a will is but the inception of it, and it takes no effect till the death of the devisor; for *Omne testamentum morte consummatum est. Et voluntas est ambulatoria usque ad extremum vitae exitum.* Then it should be against the nature of a will to be so absolute, that it being made by one of sound mind, may not be countermanded; and therefore this taking of an husband, in the case at bar, being her own proper act, shall amount to a countermand in law. But when a man of sound memory makes his will, and after becomes of *non sane memorie* by the visitation of God, (as almost every one is before his death) God forbid that this act of God should in law amount to a revocation of his will which he made when he was of sound mind. 2. It should be mischievous to women, that after their intermarriage they might not, for no cause whatsoever, countermand their wills. 3. As the law will not allow of any custom that a feme covert might make a devise, for the presumption that the law hath, that it might be made by coertion of the husband, as is adjudged in 3 *E.* 3. So if it should be in the power of the wife, after marriage, to revoke her will, the law will not suffer it to continue after marriage; because that, by coertion, the husband might cause her against her will, to revoke or continue it. 4 *Co.* 61. *a.*

10. *Cooke*, 24 *Eliz.* devised his lands to his sister in fee; and 12 years after let the same lands by indenture to the same sister for sixty years, to commence after his death, and delivered the deed to a stranger to the use of his sister, but the stranger did not deliver it over, till after the death of the devisor, and the sister never agreed thereto, but claimed by the devise. *Tanfield* argued for the plaintiff, that it was a good countermand, for it is the same person, *&c.* All the court held, that it was a good revocation of the whole estate; for both those estates cannot stand in her to begin at one time, whereby his intent appeared to be altered, and to give to her a lesser estate. But by all the justices, besides *Walmesley*, if such a lease had been made to a stranger, it had been no revocation for the term. But *Walmesley* held, that in regard it is an intire devise, it is a revocation for all: But the devise of a manor, and after a lease, or a devise of part thereof to another, is no revocation for the residue; for they are several and may be severed; but in the principal case they all agreed, that it is a revocation; for the estates cannot stand together; but if it had been made unto her to begin presently or futurely in his life-time, that had not been any revocation; for it might have determined in his life-time, and have well stood with his will; wherefore it was adjudged for the plaintiff. *Cro. Ja.* 49.

11. *Ejectione firmae* upon a special verdict, the case was, That *John Rogers* was seised of this land in fee, holden in socage, and devised by his will in writing to his wife for life; the remainder in fee, *&c.* And afterwards leased by writing the said lands for two years, to begin after his death, Whether that was a countermand of the will was the question? *Henden* serjeant moved, that it was not any countermand but only for two years; and cited one *Marshal's* case in this court, *Mich.* 2 *Jac.* to be adjudged accordingly. But *Hutton* and *Winche*, being only in court, conceived it to be doubtful, in regard the lease is made to take effect at the same time when

when the will takes its effect; but if he had made the leafe for years to commence prefently, which well might have determined in his life, it had not been a countermand, therefore they required him to fearch the precedents by him cited, and to fhew them in court, and then they would deliver their refolutions *poft. Quaere. Adjournatur.* Cro. Jac. 690, 691.

12. Lands are devifed to one in fee, and after mortgaged to the fame perfon, this is a revocation *in toto*; but if the mortgage be to a ftranger, then it is only a revocation *quoad* the mortgage. *Prec. Chan.* 514.

13. Trefpafs upon a fpecial verdict, the cafe was, One by his will devifed his lands to *J.* his youngeft fon, and his heirs, and afterwards married; and by another will in writing, devifed his lands to his wife for life, paying annually to *J.* his youngeft fon and his heirs fuch a rent. *Anderfon* and *Glanvile* held this no revocation, but that both may ftand, and though they be by feveral writings, unlefs it be manifeftly contrary to the firft will, or that there be an exprefs revocation therein; but they ought to ftand together if they may, as made by and in one and the fame writing: and here his intention appears, that he had not any purpofe to alter it, as to his fon, but only to provide for his wife, whom he had efpoufed after the firft will; and by appointing the rent to his fon it appears, that his intent was that the reverfion fhould be to his fon. *Cro. Eliz.* 721, 722.

14. One makes his will, and thereby devifeth certain lands, and this will is attefted by three witneffes according to the ftatute of *Frauds*; after he makes another will, which revokes all former wills, but the laft is not duly executed; the laft being no will, and void, will not amount to a revocation of the former. *Prec. Ch.* 459. See 3 *Rep. Ch.* 150, 155. *Gilb.* 18, 136. *Hard.* 374.

15. *Wilkinfon* makes his will, and his brother executor, and devifed to his executor all his eftate real and perfonal. Four years after he marries, and by a codicil makes his wife executrix. It appeared in proof, that he had no real eftate whatfoever. Lord chancellor faid, that the perfonal eftate was only intended the brother as executor; and thereupon decreed for the widow executrix. 1 *Vern.* 23.

* 16. A man by will devifeth all his houfes in *Mompelier Row* to his wife, and after makes a codicil, and thereby devifeth one of his houfes in *Mompelier Row* to his wife; this is not a revocation of the devife by the will; for the codicil doth not vacate the will, as a fubfequent will would; therefore it is only a tautology, a giving over again a part of what he had before given her. At the rolls 4 *July* 1737, before his honour.

17. A devife was of lands to *A.* and after a devife of the fame lands to *B.* who was a papift; fo both devifes were void; for though the laft is void as a will, yet it is good as a revocation. 2 *Ju. Eccl.* 37.

18. References, *Prec. Chan.* 459. *Hard.* 374, 375. 2 *Vern.* 293, 742. 3 *Rep. Chan.* 155. 1 *Chan. Ca.* 193. 2 *Vern.* 209, 241, 496, 680, 720, 742, 498, 598, 625, 722. *Barn.* 91, 311, 386. *Cro. Car.* 51, 52. 3 *Lev.* 108. 3 *Mod.* 204, 206, 217, 218, 260. *Salk.* 158, 592, 593. 1 *Vern.* 106. 2 *Vern.* 680, 742. *Skin.* 72. *Cro. Jac.* 115, 497, 690, 691. *Orph. Leg.* 254, 255. *Stat. Frauds and Perjuries.* *Prec. Chan.* 32, 33, 183, 354. *Gilb.* 130, 131. 2 *Vern.* 246.

A TABLE OF Principal Matters.

A TABLE of PRINCIPAL MATTERS.

Con-

A TABLE of PRINCIPAL MATTERS.

Error.

Eſtate-tail.

Exception.

A TABLE of PRINCIPAL MATTERS.

See *Baron and Feme.*

Pos-

A TABLE of PRINCIPAL MATTERS.

Legacies.

Liberty.

A TABLE of PRINCIPAL MATTERS.

He

Statutes

F I N I S.

www.ingramcontent.com/pod-product-compliance
Lightning Source LLC
LaVergne TN
LVHW062140200926
848484LV00007B/1835